THE FOREIGN MISSIONS CONVENTION
AT WASHINGTON

1925

THE FOREIGN MISSIONS CONVENTION of the U.S. and Canada, AT WASHINGTON 1925

ADDRESSES DELIVERED AT THE
FOREIGN MISSIONS CONVENTION OF
THE UNITED STATES AND CANADA
HELD AT WASHINGTON, D. C.,
JANUARY 28 TO FEBRUARY 2, 1925

EDITED BY
FENNELL P. TURNER
AND
FRANK KNIGHT SANDERS

NEW YORK
FOREIGN MISSIONS CONFERENCE
OF NORTH AMERICA
FLEMING H. REVELL COMPANY
NEW YORK AND CHICAGO

FOREWORD

The 1925 Foreign Missions Convention of the United States and Canada, held at Washington, D. C., January 28 to February 2, inclusive, has passed into history. It was the latest and not least impressive of a series of noteworthy foreign missionary gatherings during the last half century, each registering progress in the difficult art of expressing the increasing conviction of Christian men and women that in practical service the bonds that unite are stronger than the forces that would separate.

Cooperation in Christian Missions calls for two kinds of assemblies: those which come together to discuss a common program and policy and those which are distinctively inspirational. Each is equally important. The former affords opportunity for the interchange of opinion and for the adoption of measures essential to the formulation of plans to enlist the energies of great constituencies. The latter contributes to an increase in intelligent loyalty to the cause of missions through the inspirational messages of experienced and recognized leaders. The former must necessarily be limited in size; the latter permits bringing together great numbers.

Of the former class are the regular annual sessions of the Foreign Missions Conference of North America, the agency through which the foreign Boards of Canada and of the United States act together in dealing with the current problems of foreign missions. These annual sessions, which are attended by officially appointed delegates, afford a distinctive example of the way in which earnest men and women of markedly different opinions and views on many details of church and missionary administration may reveal a true unity of spirit and purpose to act together in developing a common constructive program. The Conference reviews, year by year, the progress of missions as furthered by our North American churches and carefully considers plans for normal enlargement. The value of these annual gatherings in promoting cooperation and a world-wide approach to the problems of the missionary enterprise of today cannot well be overstated. This value is increased by the fact that similar organizations, also holding annual gatherings and representing the Protestant churches of vast areas, are found in other parts of the world, both in Europe and in the Orient. These are the Conference of Missionary Societies of Great Britain and Ireland, the Deutscher Evangelischer Missionsbund in Germany, Societe des Missions Evangeliques de Paris, the Norwegian, Danish and Swedish Councils, the National Christian Council of India, Burma and Ceylon, and the National Christian Councils of China and of Japan. Binding all these and other national missionary organizations into a truly representative

v

fellowship is the International Missionary Council. The stated meetings of the International Missionary Council and of its standing committee afford the opportunity for discussion of missionary problems by representatives of different nations. In size these meetings are small enough to provide for thorough discussions. These discussions are carried on by men and women whose knowledge of the missionary work and whose administrative responsibilities give weight to the conclusions reached.

To the other type of assemblies, represented in the past by various missionary gatherings, such as the memorable one of 1900 in New York City, preceded by others at intervals as far back as 1854, belongs the recent Convention at Washington. While this gathering made provision in its program on three afternoons for discussions in simultaneous conferences upon a wide variety of themes, its purpose was inspirational, as indicated by the following statement, printed in the first announcement issued by the Committee of Arrangements:

"The primary purpose of the Convention is for the information and the inspiration of the churches of Canada and the United States. It will be an educational, not a deliberative or legislative, assembly. It will not deal with questions and problems of administration on the mission field. Its messages will be designed to enlarge the interest and deepen the conviction of the Christian people at the home base as to their foreign mission responsibilities and obligations."

Testimonies concerning the wide range and impressiveness of the Convention program are emphatic and many. From first to last a singularly deep conviction seemed to dominate the vast assembly, representing the churches of North America, as it faced an outlook over the world and into the problems of missions, hitherto unequalled in completeness, range and power.

Whatever success may have attended the Convention was due to both the careful preparation and to the devout spirit of prayer that dominated the committees which worked in its behalf and the mission Boards which were behind it. For two years it had been under consideration. On January 11, 1923, the Foreign Missions Conference took action requesting the International Missionary Council to consider the advisability of holding a world missionary conference within the next two or three years. Another resolution was adopted directing its standing committee (the Committee of Reference and Counsel) to consider the advisability of holding an international conference for North America, if the way did not seem clear for a World Conference. In July of that same year the International Missionary Council concluded that the time had not arrived for another great world missionary gathering like that of Edinburgh in 1910. The Foreign Missions Conference of North America, at its annual session in January, 1924, expressed its definite approval of the proposal to hold in North America an international convention in 1925. It authorized the Committee of Reference and Counsel to organize a Committee of Arrangements to be responsible for the development of the plan and program; it voted that the Convention should be a delegated body, representing the churches through the mission Boards; and it approved the suggestion that measures be taken to give the program a "strong international outlook and message."

At the meeting of the Committee of Reference and Counsel, February 20, 1924, the following Committee of Arrangements was appointed: Rev. James L. Barton, D.D., LL.D.; Miss Helen B. Calder; Rev. William I. Chamberlain, Ph.D., D.D.; Rev. Stephen J. Corey, LL.D.; Rev. George Drach, D.D.; Rev. James Endicott, D.D.; Miss Mabelle Rae McVeigh; Mrs. Thomas Nicholson; Rev. Frank Mason North, D.D., LL.D.; Rev. Eugene H. Rawlings, D.D.; Rev. Joseph C. Robbins, D.D.; Mrs. Charles K. Roys; Rev. William P. Schell, D.D.; Rev. Egbert W. Smith, D.D.; Mrs. Hume R. Steele; John W. Wood, D.C.L.

The Committee organized as follows: Dr. Barton, chairman; Dr. Robbins, vice-chairman; Mr. Alfred E. Marling, treasurer; and Mr. Fennell P. Turner, secretary. On this Committee rested the responsibility for the Convention. During the period from February, 1924 to January, 1925, it held eleven regular meetings in addition to many sub-committee meetings. On special occasions it invited into the deliberations of the Committee leaders in educational and mission work who were not officially related either to the Committee of Arrangements or to missionary administration.

There were held also special consultations with leaders and experts, going patiently over every aspect of the varied program. Not only were secretaries of the mission Boards thus consulted, but leaders in other activities—especially men and women who have recently visited and studied first hand the work of missions in the field. No pains were spared in order that the meetings at Washington should adequately express the purposes of the Foreign Missions Conference. The outcome of all these labors was the Convention program, covering over three hundred separate appointments which were, almost without exception, carried out as planned (See pages 411-427).

Much of the credit is due to the exceedingly efficient service of the organization which was formed for the handling of the Convention at Washington. The personnel of this organization will be found on page 430.

The statistics of the Convention, as presented by the registrar, Mr. Leslie B. Moss, were as follows: Eighty-five mission organizations and eleven missionary training schools were represented in the gathering, making ninety-six bodies in all, with 3,419 registered delegates. In addition, 1,150 tickets were taken by the Washington churches and used by different people, so that probably over eight thousand Washington people attended one or more sessions of the Convention.

The presence of important delegates of the historic churches of Europe and of the rising churches of Asia and South America, representatives of different countries and national organizations, was a notable feature of the Convention, as their participation contributed a very helpful element to the program of the main sessions as of the simultaneous conferences. Formal welcome was given to these foreign representatives at one of the sessions of the Convention.

In the minds of those who were permitted to share in this Convention there is a profound sense of gratitude to God that it reached such heights of understanding and devotion. It stood upon a high plane of international and interracial thinking; it faced unflinchingly the problem of reaching the men and women everywhere with the saving gospel; it embodied in itself the spirit of cooperation, without which the world can never know that the Son of God has been sent for its redemption; it experienced blessed hours of devotional and spiritual fellowship. At every session declarations of loyalty to Jesus Christ were put forth and repeated; and throughout, as the Convention sang and prayed and sought the way together, there was engendered a spirit of mutual confidence and a common purpose to keep the unity of the spirit in the bonds of eternal love, while all renewed their consecration to Him whose we are and whom we serve.

FENNELL P. TURNER, *Secretary.*

CONTENTS

CONTENTS

CONTENTS

THE OPENING ADDRESS

THE REVEREND JAMES L. BARTON, D.D., LL.D., BOSTON, MASS.

Chairman of the Committee of Arrangements

This Convention is both interdenominational and international. It is held under the auspices of the Foreign Missions Conference of North America, as representing the foreign mission Boards and sending Societies of Canada and of the United States, and it rejoices in the participation of similar Societies in England, and on the continent of Europe. In times past the reproach has been levelled against Christendom, with some justification, that in the Church of Jesus Christ there have been many and bitter divisions and controversies through which the body of our blessed Lord has been dismembered and its physical and spiritual resources wasted. It is therefore a significant fact that in the realm of foreign missions the Church of Christ with exalted idealism has entered upon practical measures of fraternal cooperation such as have never been experienced in any other field of Christian activity. When the Protestant churches of various denominations entered upon the seemingly impossible task of imparting to the hundreds of millions of the non-Christian world a saving knowledge of the gospel of Jesus Christ, they were so overcome by an overwhelming sense of inadequacy and responsibility that they began to submerge sectarian differences and to unite alike upon the eternal verities of their common faith and upon a common program of activity.

For thirty-two consecutive years the foreign mission Boards of North America have assembled by official delegates at their annual conference to consider and put into operation methods of practical cooperation in all forms of missionary endeavor in the foreign mission fields. Some one hundred Boards, Societies and organizations are now united in the Foreign Missions Conference of North America, which, through its standing committee, the Committee of Reference and Counsel, acts in an increasing number of categories in the interest of all. This Committee, through its seventeen organized sub-committees, puts into practical operation the decisions of the Conferences. As a result of such cooperative measures, vast improvements have been made in the scientific handling of missionary operations on the field, and in the bettering of conditions of missionary service, and important union enterprises have been developed and are maintained. Significant progress has been made in the unification of missionary interests both at home and abroad, so that every type of ability or form of resource is becoming available for practical use in the steady advancement of the Kingdom of God in mission lands. The Boards participating in the Foreign Missions Conference and in this Convention receive annually from their respective constituencies and disburse in the support of their work more than forty millions of dollars. They sustain and direct in the foreign field over eighteen thousand American missionaries.

There are assembled at this great Convention the delegates from nearly one hundred missionary organizations in North America, including with a few exceptions, all the Protestant ecclesiastical bodies on the American continent. These organizations are represented by their executive officers, by the members of their missionary Boards and by their sustaining constituencies.

There are organizations similar to our Foreign Missions Conference, in Great Britain, on the Continent of Europe, in Australasia, in South Africa, and on the great mission areas. These organizations, representing in the same comprehensive way the churches of each nation and area, demonstrate in a fresh and convincing way the welding power of a mighty task undertaken under the imperative of a divine command. They have not only united in order to carry forward with efficiency the missionary enterprise in their own districts, but they have all united in the creation and support of an International Missionary Council which represents the Protestant foreign missionary interests of the whole world.

This Convention does not represent a novel idea. It is the immediate successor of the historic Edinburgh Missionary Conference of 1910, which in turn follows the Ecumenical Missionary Conference held in New York City in 1900. But that conference was antedated by others—by one in London in 1888, preceded by a similar one in Mildmay Park, London, in 1878, which was preceded by one in Liverpool in 1860, antedated by two in 1854, one meeting in New York and one in London as conferences in the interests of the great foreign missionary enterprise shared in by representatives of many Christian communions. Thus for no less than seventy years the different denominations most deeply interested in the foreign missionary work of the church have been putting the differences which separated them into the background and have been emphasizing those fundamental elements of Christian belief and practice on which they were willing to unite for the achievement of their great common task.

The times are propitious for the assembling of this great body to consider together the application of the principles laid down by Jesus Christ to meet world conditions. Economic, social, political, national, international and religious revolutions have swept over the world since the conference at Edinburgh. "The whole creation groaneth and travaileth in pain together." Many panaceas are being offered for healing the world's sorrows and alleviating its pains. Many of these have their proper place in any scheme of progress. But we are here assembled under the overwhelming conviction that not by education or culture or civilization or treaties or disarmament, however helpful these may be, can the world be redeemed. The only way is by implanting in the hearts of men and in the hearts of nations the seeds of the kingdom of our Lord Jesus Christ. There must be created in the souls of men of every nation and kindred, and translated into their life, the will for self-surrender, for peace, for personal sacrifice, for unhesitating loyalty to Jesus Christ. There must be an understanding recognition that God "hath made of one blood all nations of men." Only by the practical application of what Jesus Christ calls "my gospel" to this sin-sick and passion-torn world can the world be saved.

In devout reliance upon the God of missions and believing that we serve under his divine commission, we are assembled in this Convention to submit ourselves and the causes we represent to that unerring guidance that shall lead us into all truth.

ADDRESS
PRESIDENT CALVIN COOLIDGE

It is a pleasure to receive and welcome here the members of this international conference in the interest of Christian missionary work throughout the world. One of the most Christian things I have observed about organized Christianity is the missionary spirit which pervades it. It was this spirit which from the beginning gave to the gospel of Christ its power over the hearts of men. For it is of the essence of Christian ethics and spirituality that those who have once felt their full inspiration are thereafter enlisted in carrying these blessings to all who need them.

Whoever will study that wonderful story of the spread of Christianity throughout the Roman world in the early centuries of our era, must get from it a deep conviction of the service which was rendered. In a time when old pagan systems were breaking down, when civilization was falling into decadence and unspeakable corruption, the Christian faith came with its new and better conception of life. It revealed a real justice and a real mercy. It brought promise of immortality, a vision of man as the possessor of a soul that should not perish. To a world in which the vast majority were born to lives of hopelessness and misery, it brought realization of a new destiny. The basis of this new concept was brotherhood. Its essence was an unselfishness which, flowering into the wonderful missionary movement of those early centuries, sought to carry the new dispensation to all mankind.

Those early Christians, living so near to the time of the apostolic mission, were animated by a zeal and a simple faith which, if they could be revived in all their early power, would bring to our world a great blessing. We have come upon a time which men often compare to the later generations of Roman history. Just as, in that older time, there was need for the spirit of Christianity in the world, so now there is need for a revival of faith, for a dedication to the works which that revived faith would show to us as the need of the race, and for a renewal of the spirit of brotherhood at all times and in all places.

The Christian nations have become, in an intensely practical as well as a highly spiritual sense, charged with a great trust for civilization. Whatever misgivings we may sometimes feel about their administration of the trust, we cannot doubt, as we survey the world, that it has been imposed upon them. They are the custodians of a faith which, despite momentary lapses and some perversions, has on the whole been a continuing inspiration to human betterment. Wherever it has gone, there the light of a better understanding has shone; there the works of charity, of benev-

4

olence, of mutual helpfulness, have prospered. Intolerance has been lessened. Education has been summoned as an ally in the struggle against ignorance and bigotry. Science in a thousand realms, the mechanic arts in all their varied departments, have been laid under contribution to improve the estate of men.

For Christianity, let it be impressed, is a highly practical, as well as a profoundly spiritual, mode of life. It loses nothing of its spiritual quality because of its practical helpfulness; but it touches all its practical workings with the spirit and purpose of lofty aspiration. Our confidence in it is justified by our knowledge of its accomplishments. Wherever it has been carried and made a force in the affairs of men, it has wrought for their good. But we must recognize also that it has added greatly to the complexity of human life and problems. Its encouragement to education, to knowledge, to scientific advancement, has created new forces in the world. The spirit of our organized, industrialized, machine-made and inter-related world has touched men wherever they live, and profoundly affected their modes of life and thought. It has aroused in them new yearnings and new aspirations. It has truly converted this planet into a brotherhood of races and nationalities, interdependent in a thousand ways, tending more and more to develop a common culture, a common thought and purpose toward the great business of living. The problems which in this new order of life present themselves, will not be solved except through a greater and constantly greater projection of the spirit of neighborship and cooperation, which is the true basis of the Christian code. As Christian nations have assumed the responsibility for bringing this new and higher civilization in touch with all peoples, so they must recognize their responsibility to press on and on in their task of enlightenment, education, spiritualization, Christianizing. There can be no hesitancy, no cessation of effort. Not only must they go forward with this great task, but they must be sure that they go with the right purposes. They must carry help and real service.

Let us look this part of our problem fairly in the face, and see if we can find what is demanded. Not everything that the men of Christian countries have carried to the other peoples of the world, has been good and helpful to those who have received it. Our civilization is yet far from perfect. Its aims are liable to much distortion, when it comes in contact with peoples not yet equipped through generations of race experience to absorb, to understand, to appreciate it. One of the greatest things that a missionary movement could do for the less favored communities, would be to assure that all who go out from the Christian to the non-Christian communities, should carry with them the spirit, the aims, the purposes, of true Christianity. We know that they have not always done this. We know that the missionary movements have repeatedly been hampered, and at times frustrated, because some calling themselves Christians, and assuming to represent Christian civilization, have been actuated by un-Christian motives. Those who have been willing to carry the vices of our civilization among the weaker peoples and into the darker places, have often been more successful than those who have sought to implant the virtues.

The Christian churches and governments have no greater responsibility than to make sure that the best, and not the worst, of which Christian society is capable, shall be given to the other peoples. To accomplish this is the dominating purpose of a true missionary movement. It is one of the most important, most absolutely necessary movements in the world today. We shall ourselves be the gainers, both spiritually and materially, by our efforts in behalf of those whom we shall thus help. The early Christians fairly burned with missionary zeal. Our missionary efforts will be the more effective, just in proportion as we shall render them in the same spirit of brotherhood and charity which marked the earliest Christian efforts.

Such a service as you aspire to do for mankind, can be rendered only under the inspiration of a broad and genuine liberalism. It must rest on toleration. It must realize the spirit of brotherhood. And the foundation of all missionary effort abroad must be toleration and brotherhood at home. The most effective missionary work will be that which seeks to impress itself rather through example in living rightly than through the teaching of precept and creed. The works of charity and benevolence, of education and enlightenment, will best lay the foundation upon which to rear the permanent structure of a spiritual life. Our liberalism needs to be generous enough to recognize that missionary effort will often build better on foundations already laid, than by attempting to substitute a complete new structure of morality, of life, and of ethics. Indeed, those who shall go out from among us, carrying the missionary message into the twilight places of the world, will there find much that is worthy to be brought back to enrich our ideals and improve our life. They will learn many lessons of industry, of humility, of reverence for parents, of respect for constituted authority, which may quite conceivably become adornments to our own social fabric. If those who bear our message abroad shall realize and accept the lessons that may be learned from the humbler and simpler peoples, they will be the more successful in planting the spiritual truths of Christianity. Beyond that, they will be able to bring back much that will serve us well. We have not all the wisdom that has been diffused among the sons of men. But we have been greatly favored and have much wherewith to aid those less richly endowed. A becoming modesty, a discriminating sense of our real opportunities and responsibilities, are altogether to be desired as helps in the great work we wish to do. The missionary effort of the nation cannot rise higher than its source. If we expect it to be successful in this field, we must provide the correct influences for it at home.

THE GOSPEL FOR THE WHOLE WORLD

THE COMPELLING CHARACTER OF THIS MESSAGE

BISHOP EDWIN D. MOUZON, D.D., NASHVILLE, TENNESSEE

The great missionary enterprise moves forward by the command and under the authority of our Lord and Savior, Jesus Christ. Back behind His command is His authority. After His resurrection from the dead He said to His disciples, "All authority hath been given unto Me in heaven and on earth. Go ye therefore and make disciples of all the nations." His authority is the authority of His divine personality. His authority is the self-evidencing authority of His message. His authority is the compelling authority of His cross. His authority is the authority of the risen and reigning Lord. The compulsion of the missionary enterprise, then, is the compulsion of the Divine Christ.

I mean something more than that we must carry the message, because He has commanded us to carry it. I mean to say that upon those of us who have heard His voice and whose hearts have been opened to His influence, His divine personality lays its compelling power; and we must needs carry it, because He compels us to acknowledge Him as the Master of our thinking and the Lord of our lives. The earliest disciples did not believe in Him as Christ because He had first announced the fact that He was Divine. The power of His personality was brought to bear upon them, until little by little and more and more they were compelled, almost in spite of themselves, to cry out, "Thou art the Christ, the son of the living God; my Lord and my God." If today we do not have this message to give to the world, and if we do not know Jesus Christ as Lord and Master, there is upon us no compulsion and there can be upon us no compulsion.

Jesus Christ, the son of God, our Lord and our Savior, this is He that we bring to the world in a message of salvation, and never was the world in greater need of that message than today, never was the world more hungry for that message than today. I say, then, that the compulsion of the Gospel is the divine compulsion that has been laid upon us by the personality of Jesus Christ. About him we sing with the saints of all ages:

> "Thou art the King of Glory, O Christ,
> Thou art the everlasting Son of the Father."

No lesser Christ than this is sufficient for the needs of the world today. The call of all the nations is for the Christ of the New Testament, the Christ of Christian history, the Christ of living personal experience.

Again the compulsion of the missionary enterprise is the compulsion of the self-evidencing message that Jesus Christ has brought into the world. It is altogether commonplace—we have heard it always and we read it in all books—to say that Jesus Christ is the greatest ethical teacher that the world has ever seen. But in these recent months, having again made a careful study of the teachings of Jesus, it has been borne in upon me that there has never been any teaching in all the world like the teaching of Jesus. The intellectual superiority of the teachings of Jesus— mark you, I am saying "the intellectual superiority of the teaching of Jesus"—over all ethical teachers that have ever lived, over all teachers of sociology that have ever lived, is the outstanding consideration in our thinking today.

The fact is, the Christian world is now as never before brought face to face with the question whether or not we are going to be Christians, whether or not we are willing to be Christians, whether or not we dare to follow Jesus. Dare we be Christians? Dare we cease to compromise? For let it be confessed that throughout all these years we have compromised. The nation has compromised; the church has compromised; we ministers have compromised; individual Christians have compromised. But now the compulsion of the message of Jesus is upon us, as he tells a distraught world anew that God is the Father of all men, that all men are brothers, that there is no value like the value of the soul, that the law of the cross must prevail everywhere, that the principle of self-sacrificing service is the only principle that is going to save the world. We have come to see that the teachings of Jesus must apply, not merely to the individual, and not merely to the home and to the school, but to all economic conditions whatsoever, and to all interracial relations whether in America or in Africa, or in Japan, or elsewhere; and that the principles of Jesus must be made to apply in all international relationships. One finds out that when our greatest sociologists, having made a scientific study of human conditions, state their principles and say, "only thus and thus can the world or society be saved," they have simply restated in modern and scientific form the marvelous things that Jesus said in Galilee and in Judea in the long ago.

But as you know, we have been much more concerned about being theologians than about being Christians. The one supreme "heresy" that the Church confronts today is the heresy that has to do with the building of the Kingdom of God in human society. We must, therefore, ask ourselves, if we dare be Christians, if we dare follow Jesus Christ, if we dare make our religion a practical thing, having to do with all the affairs of life in this world. As modern Christians we are convinced that only this way lies the salvation of human society.

Again, the compulsion of Jesus, the compulsion of the missionary message, is the compulsion of the Cross.

"In the Cross of Christ I glory,
Towering o'er the wrecks of time,
All the light of sacred story,
Gathers round its head sublime."

"The Son of Man came, not to be ministered unto, but to minister and to give his life a ransom for many." So said Jesus, and in order that the law of the cross and that the truth of his atoning sacrifice might forever be in the very center of our thinking, he instituted the sacrament of the Lord's Supper,—"This bread is my body, broken for the world." "This wine is my blood, shed for humanity."

"If you pluck the Cross out of the New Testament, you have plucked out its heart. If you take the Cross out of our message, you have taken out the Christ message. It would be far better to keep the Cross central in our thinking, although it might be in the crudest and rudest and even in a very uncouth theology, than to give to men the latest refinements in theological thinking and lose the significance of the Cross where Jesus died.

This is what the world is hungering for. Christianity is the religion of redemption. The deepest human need is the need of redemption. As one seems to hear the cry that goes up from human hearts all over the world, it is this cry, "Help! help! help!" Thank God, He has laid help upon One that is mighty. The hand of the Redeemer, the pierced, blood-stained hand of the Redeemer, is reached down to the men who are crying "help," to render the only help that will heal the hurt of the world and bring redemption to a sin-cursed race.

The story is told of a missionary in India how one said to him, "Stop telling that story of the cross. We have many religions here, and we have many stories here, but we have no such story as the story of the cross. Stop telling that story. If you keep on, people will cease to follow us and will all go to following Jesus." What I say to you, gathered together here today from many lands and many ecclesiasticisms, is this: Tell the story of the Cross unceasingly; and as you tell it men will turn away from their false gods and will go to following Jesus. Heine dreamed that he was at the supper of the gods. Heavenly wine was brought and they all drank and lived at ease. Then, in the midst of the feast, the door opened and a pale form came in, staggering under the weight of a great cross, which he flung down upon the table. Then the faces of the gods turned pale and, one by one, they vanished away. Which is a parable. As Jesus Christ and his Cross come into this world the faces of false gods everywhere turn pale and vanish out of sight.

"All hail the power of Jesus' name!
Let angels prostrate fall."

Once more, the compulsion of our message is the compulsion of the risen and reigning Lord. It is the compulsion of him who says: "I am he that liveth, and was dead; and, behold, I am alive forevermore." The resurrection of Jesus Christ is a two-fold fact. It is a fact of history and it is a fact of experience. The fact of the empty sepulcher and the recovered and victorious faith of the disciples—there is the fact of history. But throughout all the centuries we have had the fact of experience. The saints of God, the men who have followed Jesus, have come to know him not merely as a marvellous character written about in an ancient book, but have come to know him as one with whom they have fellowship, one whom they meet not merely in the sanctity of their closet, nor in the holy places of the temple of worship, but one whom they meet as they sit by the side of the broken-hearted, as they minister to the dying, and as they go out where men toil and suffer and wonder and fall and die. They have met the living Christ there; and unless you and I have some personal knowledge of Him who lived and died and is alive forevermore, there will be no compelling power in our message and there will be no particular reason why we should carry what we may choose to call "the gospel" to the uttermost parts of the earth.

Are we ready, then, to be Christians? Are we ready to make the surrender, the absolute, the complete, the eternal surrender that is necessary, if the great task remaining to be done is done? Are we ready to attempt the romantic enterprise? Pardon me for telling an old story. You remember the story of Douglas and the heart of Bruce, how Bruce had longed that he himself might win the holy sepulcher, but had died without doing so, and how he charged Douglas that, if he ever made the pilgrimage to the Holy Land, he should carry Bruce's heart in a casket of silver and deposit it at the sepulcher of his Lord. So it came about, by and by, that Douglas was on his way to the Holy Land, when he encountered a band of Saracens who challenged him to mortal combat. As he got ready for the fray he unloosed the casket from about his neck and threw it into the midst of the band of Saracens, crying after it, "Go, heart of Bruce, and where thou leadest Black Douglas will follow thee, or die." Here, then, this day, in the presence of God, one and all, let us say: "Lead on, O Son of God, and where thou leadest, we will follow thee or die."

THE CONTINUOUS PROMISE OF OUR LORD

MISS JEAN KENYON MACKENZIE, FORMERLY OF AFRICA

I was listening with a very great interest to the speaker who preceded me and thinking how surely in Christ's plan for us the promise has followed the commission, and that before He sent us forth with the commission upon us, He assured us of His great power, and that it was the power through which this work was to be done. I seemed to see on a moonlit path in Africa, with a machine, the engine for a saw-mill, resting upon the path. Mr. Fred Hope, who was taking the machinery into that forest country, was sleeping beside the engine with a friend of his, the moon lying over all. A group of people were walking by. People walk at night in our country, who can do so, to escape the sunlight on the highways that the white man has put through the African forests.

Mr. Hope says that he heard a little controversy on the far side of the path where the engine had been placed. The women and the men, who were carrying loads on their backs, spoke together. They were speaking in fear of that strange thing so unknown to them, so potential in its unknown power. There was in that caravan a person of the tribe of God. She was dubiously asserting her power to pass this monster. She said it was a thing of the people of the tribe of God, and could do her, who was a person of the tribe of God, no harm. So she agreed that she would pass it with due caution; and that if she arrived safely beyond where it was, then her friends might dare to do as she had done, and might pass it too. In the moonlight her brown body slipped by the passive engine, and no damage was incurred. One by one each member of the caravan followed after and went on rejoicing, doubtless to tell in many villages how one may pass the strange and fearsome creature of the saw-mill, provided he is a person of the tribe of God, or walking in the company of such.

Now, I do not regard that attitude—a belief that it is not going to do us any harm—as the ideal attitude toward the power of Christ in this world. Rather is it true that here upon the pathway of this world is the great power of Christ as he promised it to us, not to be slipped past quietly in the night, but abundantly available to those of us who will put our hands upon it for the making of a new clearing, for the making of a new town, for the making of a new order.

I remember how mightily I have seen the power of God at work in the world and I want to declare, first of all, what we all may know, that it comes to us most fully in our weakness. We have a saying in Africa, "The little stream does not fear the forest." It does not, because the forest is its element. And God has made for us too a native element, which is the power of God at work in this world. All of us have been at some time in a close room crowded with people, noisy with the clamor of voices. Going into the open, we have felt our very being expand with the freshened vital air we breathed. Some such experience we missionaries have had when first we went out into the work and found that Christ was there before us in all His power. How we expanded, how we felt, at last, as though we were in our native element. The power of Christ at work in the world gives such a setting for the human soul.

No one will deny that the best of us are very weak. We realize this weakness when we attempt to do the work of Christ. Yet how wonderfully we have found that Christ keeps His promise about His power, and that it is made perfect in weakness.

This declaration we must never forget. The power of God is made perfect in our weakness,—as if our weakness were a little boat and the power of God were the cargo,—as if our weakness were a slack sail and the power of God were the wind; as if our weakness were an empty purse and the power of God were the gold piece,—well, we know whose would be the superscription on the money.

But, not only in power is our Lord to be with us, but in personal companionship. It is the most lonely people who are to be most conscious of that personal companionship. I am thinking of such people all over the world. We all know how much happier any kind of a task becomes, if someone does it with us, but many a task has to be undertaken alone. I think now especially of student volunteers, of young people turning over within their own hearts, in their own families, in their own college circles, the lonely way in which they seem to be starting out, and wishing very much that they had some one who was such a companion, that they could sincerely discuss the secret things of the heart.

Jesus said to Nathaniel, "I saw you under the fig tree." When and where was that fig tree? No one has ever told its story of that secret companionship, of the presence of Christ with Nathaniel in some lonely hour when Christ himself was present, though Nathaniel himself was unaware of his nearness. What a precious thought for puzzled young people that truly in decisions, truly in dreams, even perhaps truly in resentments against the world as it is, Christ can be present, though unseen.

I am thinking also of people who are called upon to make pecuniary sacrifices for His sake. Many a one has put his hand into his pocket and has drawn out what was there, not lightly, and has laid it aside for God's work in the world. I want to remind them that Christ is present with them in that effort. You remember the widow who put her two mites into the treasury. Jesus was there to see that high resolve and to bless it, though I suppose she was unconscious of His presence. Many here are going to go back home to make severe financial sacrifices, but it is a glorious fact that in every stage of that sacrifice our Lord is present. I once saw a youth in Africa give away a pair of green trousers. One sees many astonishing things in Africa, whether they are curious animals, or women with their bodies painted red, but I never was more surprised than when that youth on Sunday when the great collection baskets were passed, put in his pair of green trousers. It was the extreme of sacrifice.

I am likewise thinking today of ministers on the night before they make their plea for their budgets and when they have made their final collections. I think of Board treasurers, men and women who carry the great financial burdens of God's work in the world and who feel themselves lonely indeed among such cares. They go to conventions; they address meetings; they seem to be surrounded by people who eagerly listen to what they have to say; but when the last gong is sounded and the last convention door is shut and the family itself is asleep in their beds, there is a window lit and a man above a desk and he is watching in the third watch. But One there is who says, "Blessed is he," and that is our Lord Jesus.

Sleeping at night in trains, knocking about in steamers, going hither and yon upon the things of our Lord's kingdom in this world, the Lord's messengers do not go alone. Casting up your accounts at the last and putting in your two mites at the last, encouraging a congregation to rise to the emergency that lies before it,—these efforts are not without witness,—our Lord is with such even to the end.

Let me turn from these lonely efforts to think about the church invisible in the world. There is a kind of disreputable herald that goes before the great caravan of God's people. He is always shouting, "It can't be done." I speak to the young and to the old alike. When you wake to the sound of the trumpet that says "It can't be done," rise to your feet, for the Kingdom of God is at hand. After that disreputable herald there comes another and he says, "All power," and that is the herald of our Lord.

After them come the great company of the redeemed who voice their acclaim. Some of them look rather disreputable. If Mr. Couve, who is here from Africa, and my fellow-missionaries from Africa could trail our crowds of converts into this assembly today, they would not be as impressive as if Dr. J. C. R. Ewing were to come in with his Indian people; but one and all, we follow the man who says, "All power," for that is our Lord.

I was spending the night in an African village. Because I had a headache, my tent was turned away from the village. I was putting all the affairs of the village out of mind, it might be, because in those villages, when one of the tribe of God sleeps there, all the people come to speak about all the things of God as practiced in the village life, and especially about the keeping of the ten commandments. So I said to the head man, "It is going to be a moonlight night. I wish you would not drum for the neighbors to dance." On many and many a moonlight night the drum has been beaten and the neighbors have danced during the night and I have slept, but on this night I begged them not to make a noise. He said he would not, and I went to bed.

The moon rose rather late and with it there arose a great clamor of drums, a clapping and shouting and all the music of a dance in the village. Presently going out into the moonlight, I looked for the great company that should be dancing there, and there was none, not a soul, yet I heard a sound of drumming in the back yard of the village. When I went back of the huts, I found a man at a drum who looked at me. There were three little girls who had been dancing. They stopped. In the moonlight all these brown faces were looking at me kindly and attentively to hear what the white woman would be saying. I said, "Where are the dancers and the drummers?" "I am the drummer," he said, "and these are the dancers." "And is that all?" "Yes," he said, "that is all." And that was all. No neighbors, no company, only the members of a household at play in the moonlight. I had just imagined the uproar.

When I look at this great company I see that this is not that kind of gathering. If I should say to our presiding officer, "Where are the neighbors?" He would say, "Why, here they are." At least one hundred Boards are represented here, people of all sorts who are followers of our Lord. The drummer at the drum and the one who causes us to come together in one common cause under one roof, is our Lord. Having come from our villages to unite as neighbors, and lovers of Christ, let us do so and rejoice. He is present with us, even to the end of this convention, and of the efforts of our denominations, and of the goings forth of ships with missionaries, until that day shall come when, one and all, to the sound of a common drum we shall gather at His good pleasure and at His good place, and in His good way.

THE PRESENT WORLD SITUATION

THE SITUATION IN THE FAR EAST
BISHOP HERBERT WELCH, D.D., LL.D., TOKYO

In the thirty minutes allotted to me, I have been asked to speak of the present world situation with special reference to the Far East. One might as well be asked to take all the air in this large auditorium and condense it into a quart jar. The thing can be done, but it demands enormous pressure and perhaps certain low temperatures which I may not be able to command.

Asia is the continent of contrasts and of superlatives. In Asia the highest mountains of the globe, off the coast of Asia the deepest seas. The single continent of Asia contains about three-tenths of the land surface of our planet, and the population not only surpasses that of any other one continent, but even that of all the other continents put together; for more than half of the human race dwells in Asia. Perhaps this is not to be wondered at when one remembers that, so far as our knowledge goes, human life had its origin on the continent of Asia, and that civilizations of an advanced order had an early development. From Asia in ancient times came practical inventions, science, philosophy, true contributions to the resources of the world. From Asia, more significantly, have come all the great religions of the race, and on the soil of Asia was born of Mary our Lord and Saviour, Jesus Christ.

It is not strange, as it seems to me, that in our day the eyes of the world are turning again to Asia with peculiar interest. Gen. Jan Smuts of South Africa, worthy to rank, I judge, with many a man in more eminent position as a world statesman, has indeed declared that the scene has shifted away from Europe to the Pacific basin and the Far East, and that the world problems of the next fifty years or more are the problems of the Pacific. When one considers the vast populations, the enormous possibilities, whether in peace or in war, of those hundreds of millions, the wealth that is still undeveloped and the markets that are still uncaptured, it is not strange, I say, that the thought of the world should be turning to Asia with peculiar interest.

If Asia be regarded, especially eastern Asia and southern Asia, from the purely missionary standpoint, the outlook is by no means discouraging. The best available statistics show that in the last twenty-two years the number of Christian communicants in India, where Christianity has advanced, so far as numbers are

16

concerned, far beyond any other Asiatic country, has been multiplied by more than two.

The number of Christian communicants in Japan and China has been multiplied by more than three. In Korea—little Korea, that Benjamin among the peoples, that Holy Land of Eastern Asia, where twenty years ago the number of Christian adherents was still very small—the multiplication in the last twenty-two years has been by more than a dozen to produce the present Christian church.

Yet, after that is said, how insignificant the number of professed Christians in the Far East—not more than two per cent of the population in any one of these lands, a "contemptible little army," it might seem, setting out to capture the strongholds of heathendom. However, I am very glad to be able to report in this survey that the influence of Christianity is vastly extended beyond the boundaries of the Christian church itself, and in this land and in that, it may be found permeating the thoughts and the activities of almost the entire population.

Let me draw my illustrations for this from Japan, and remind you that the temperance movement in Japan, that daring movement which has ventured to take for its slogan nothing less than "Prohibition for Japan," is led by Japanese and American Christians. The social purity movement of Japan, which is seeking to blot out the commercialized and legalized vice that is the disgrace of the Sunrise Kingdom everywhere, is led by Christian men and Christian women. The labor movement, which is raising the standards of life and unifying those forces which are gaining increasing influence in the Empire, is led by a Christian man, Mr. Suzuki. The movement for international peace, which is causing Japan to stretch out friendly hands to all the rest of the world, is molded on Christian ideals.

A very high authority in Japan, not himself a Christian, has recently declared without qualification that the popular conceptions of liberty and humanity throughout that Empire have been influenced directly or indirectly by the teaching of Jesus Christ.

Even the old ethnic faiths are being touched, if not positively transformed, by the power of Jesus Christ. I do not mean simply that Japanese Buddhism, for example, is organizing Young Men's Buddhist Associations, that it is planting Sunday-schools by the thousand, up and down the country, whose methods and whose very songs are taken from our Christian Sunday-schools; but that the thinking of Buddhism is being permeated by the thoughts which came first from our Lord and Saviour. Doubtless some of you have read that Japanese drama entitled "The Priest and His Disciples," written by a Buddhist, from a Buddhist standpoint throughout; a book in which any Christian may find great spiritual profit, yes, which is thoroughly Buddhist, except for the fact that its loveliest thoughts are Christian and not Buddhist at all!

Jesus Christ is coming to His own in the Far East in a larger degree than the number of listed Christians would indicate. The attitude of the populace, the attitude of governments toward Christian institutions is changing. A generation ago our missionaries had to go out and pay children to come in to their schools or to gather in the waifs from the streets in order that classes might be full. Today we are turning away not hundreds, but thousands, every year, from the schools which have no room to receive those who desire to place themselves under Christian educational influences. May I say that the Government of Japan, in Japan and Korea,—that Government which sometimes has been reputed to be determined to stamp Christianity out of the Japanese Empire, is subsidizing many of our Christian schools in order that they may be brought to a higher degree of efficiency.

On the other hand, one finds in the Far East an opposition to Christianity which, while not altogether new, has some recent and disagreeable developments. Take, for instance, the movement among the Chinese students of higher schools, not merely anti-religious in general but anti-Christian in particular, an opposition belligerent and determined, led by members of the faculties of universities, and based upon the belief that Christianity is opposed to modern science, from which they hope for great things for their growing republic, and that Christianity means militarism and capitalism, which systems they do not desire to have fastened upon their own land. Now, this recent opposition, I think one may say, is only a new development of an attitude of fear and suspicion regarding the West which has obtained in the East for more than one generation.

China found years ago that these foreigners, admitted and welcomed, were endeavoring to exploit her wealth, to control her trade, to mix in her politics, to interfere in her purely domestic concerns, until the name "foreign devils" seemed all too fit from the Chinese point of view. More than that, as the Oriental peoples have been watching the progress of the white races (under the dubious leadership of the Kaiser, there was talk here of the "yellow peril"), there has developed some talk in the Far East of the "white peril." A certain newspaper in the Orient not long ago uttered such bitter words as these: "The so-called Anglo-Saxon domination of the world is being steadily carried into effect. All the sweet juice of the world is about to be sucked by them. Will God make them really happy?"

What is the occasion for such suspicion and fear? May I remind you of what Mr. Basil Mathews recently set forth in very picturesque form—that in the year 1450 or thereabouts, the white races were confined practically to Central and Western Europe, hemmed in on the east and on the south by men of other races and other faiths; and that then in the latter part of the fifteenth century came two great discoveries—the discovery of America by Columbus, and the discovery of the route to India around the Cape of Good Hope—two discoveries that set the white race free on a career of world expansion.

You will remember how America, and the Pacific Islands, and Australia, and continental Asia (Siberia and India) and Africa have gradually, through these four centuries, come under the political, if not the complete financial and social, control of the dominating white race. Then you will also remember that in the last decade of the nineteenth century, just four hundred years after Columbus had sailed the Western seas, came the Russo-Japanese war, whose historical significance has scarcely been appreciated to this day—a war that put a stop to the aggressive career of the white race.

The red man had been pushed back, and the black man and the brown man had been pushed back, and encroachments upon the rights of the yellow man were steadily proceeding. Foreign concessions and foreign courts and foreign post-offices and extra-territoriality, where it had not been almost by force repudiated— all sorts of aggressions in the seizure of ports and of foreign rights were crowding back the yellow man, until Japan, as the champion of the Far East, stood out and fought to a standstill great Russia, the first European race, in modern times at least, to be conquered by an Oriental people.

More than one-half of Asia had come under the control of European races, and the significance of this halt to which the white race was brought bears very directly upon our missionary as well as our political problems.

The President of the United States said with absolute accuracy this afternoon that not all of the things sent to other countries from this dear land of ours had been for their blessing. When one remembers the rum that went with our Bibles, and the arms that we have exported for our profit for the use of contending factions, and the vulgar films and the narcotics which we have sent to the Orient; when one remembers how much of Western civilization of the purely materialistic type has been almost forced upon the Far East without the moral and spiritual dynamic which should enable those old civilizations to rejuvenate themselves and to use wisely the new powers put into their hands, he may indeed believe that Western contacts have not been an unmixed blessing!

What we see before our eyes in the Far East today, if we are to name some of the outstanding and obvious changes, is this: A partial Westernization in athletic sports, in architecture, in dress, in food, in music, in medicine, in practical and in pure science, in law, in social customs, in education, and in political institutions.

By the spread of the English language and its literature the West has been steadily infiltrating into those stranded and staid civilizations of Eastern Asia. The natural result is ferment— material progress, intellectual and social awakening, a new outlook for womanhood, the foisting of all the evils and the horrors of our Western industrialism on a people ill prepared to bear them, and a state of unrest and turmoil, behind which it seems to me is a great spiritual hunger.

One of the outstanding facts of the Far East is the progress of democracy; for if you have been thinking what democracy has been winning through these decades, you must remember not simply Germany, Russia, shall we say, Turkey perhaps, Persia and the rest of them—you must remember also China, with its Republic in form not yet fifteen years old, but with a people resolute to make representative government a fact in its great national history. You must remember Korea, where five or six years ago the "Independence" movement produced a new people, alert, ambitious, in touch with the currents of world life, eager for the best the world has to offer.

And you must remember Japan, sometimes called "the last of the world's great autocracies," never deserving that title, but coming slowly to be one of the world's democracies. The labor movement, the woman movement, the student movement, the increasing freedom of press and speech and assembly, the demand for universal manhood suffrage, the tendency toward a party government with cabinets responsible directly through the representatives of the people to the people themselves—all speak of the growing influence of democratic ideals in the Empire of Japan.

Still another of the outstanding facts is the growing national and race consciousness of these Eastern peoples. This touches very directly our missionary problem. It was not an iconoclast, but a balanced and sagacious Chinese leader, who said a little time ago that foreign missions had been a big, capable, kind nurse to the Chinese Church but that *foreign missions must now come under the Christian Church which they had nurtured.* Our interest is not simply in the application of this feeling to missionary affairs, but also in wider circles.

I cannot forbear to make very definite the thing that I am trying to say by applying it to the immigration question. Not that I am going to discuss the immigration question in the United States as a whole (it is a highly complicated and difficult problem, with its economic and its social factors); not that I am going to lay down any platform, such as I think might be projected, which might give a basis at once American and scientific and Christian on which an immigration policy might be based; much less am I speaking for the Far East to touch upon the question of inter-marriage and the amalgamation of races; much less am I to ask for any open gate, which all the thinking people of our country, I doubt not, oppose. We believe unanimously, I take it, for the present at least, in the close restriction of immigration, until we can do better justice to those whom we have already admitted to residence within our borders.

But I am bound to say that this immigration question, touching not simply the admission of aliens but the treatment of aliens after they are admitted, has a very direct connection with the progress of Christianity in the Orient. The Conference on Disarmament held in this city some four years ago cleared the sky of the clouds of suspicion that had been hanging low. It produced a new sense of safety, a new sense of confidence in the intentions of the United States of America in particular; and when the marvelous relief was poured out by this nation after the great earthquake of September, 1923, the hearts of the Japanese people were moved in gratitude to an extent that was positively pathetic. But the feeling of confidence and of affection, based upon these two historic incidents, has very largely been destroyed by the Japanese Exclusion clause of the "Immigration Act of 1924" passed by our Congress last spring. I do not mean to exaggerate the situation. Its effects have not been wholly evil. It has produced in Japan a movement toward religious fellowship, which has found expression in certain gatherings of Christians with the Shintoists and the Buddhists, not with any purpose (as the press reported), of amalgamating those three religions into one, but simply that the representatives of all the faiths of Japan might act together in certain social and political objectives. That movement is to be praised. My friend, Bishop Harris, used to say that most of the good people in Japan were Buddhists, a thing which, I take it, was literally true; and fellowship with every man everywhere who stands for righteousness and for truth, for holiness, is the privilege as well as the obligation of the Christian. However, I do not want to see any such movement toward religious fellowship based upon an anti-foreign sentiment.

We have had a new movement toward self-support, and that in itself is wholesome, that the Japanese church should take upon its shoulders more of the burden of its own support and of its own extension; but I do not want to see churches become self-supporting with a feeling of resentment and alienation from the churches of Great Britain and America.

There has been a new movement toward friendship with China and Russia. Have you noted that the treaty recently signed between Japan and Russia, by which Japan exchanges certain economic advantages for the political profits that may come to Russia, was signed in Peking? Have you noted that first Russia, and then Japan, is changing the rank of its representative at Peking to that of ambassador? Have you noted that Russia has relinquished in China its right of extra-territoriality, treating the Chinese as though they were its equals rather than its inferiors? Have you noted that the man coming nearest apparently to supreme power in China at this moment is Chang Tso-lin, the Manchurian war lord, who for years has been reputed to be the close friend of Japan; and that Sun Yat-sen, coming from the south to join in the consultations in the capital city of the north, is the man who has been the leader of friendly sentiment for the Soviet government?

Now, the movement for friendship between China and Japan is one that I would gladly foster, but I do not want to see that friendship based upon an antagonism to the Anglo-Saxon world.

We have a new movement for racial solidarity, a quickened race consciousness, not only in the yellow but in the brown peoples of Asia as well. Rabindranath Tagore has been this last summer lecturing in China and Japan on the arrogancies of the white race, and summoning the colored peoples of Asia to resist this aggressive and would-be dominating race of the world.

I want to see a new fellowship between men of different colors, but I want to see included in such a fellowship, the white race itself. If there can be but one new fellowship, it ought to be a fellowship between the two strongest races, numerically and otherwise, that the world holds—the white race with about half the world's population, and the yellow race with about one-third of the world's population.

Do you remember the lines written by Edwin Markham, the great poet of democracy?

"He drew a circle that shut me out,
    Heretic, alien, a thing to flout;
But love and I had the wit to win
    We drew a circle that took him in."

Christianity is always on the side of the larger circle, inclusive and not exclusive; and we, the favored peoples of the West and of the white race, are the ones who should be drawing the larger circle of a common interest and a common fellowship that would go to fulfill the words of our Lord and make all men one!

The missionary problem of the Far East is to be met most of all not by new methods of missionary administration but by sheer friendliness, by a new assertion (as the President said this afternoon) of the fundamental doctrine of human brotherhood, a brotherhood which is absolutely real and not merely theological, a brotherhood which is absolutely inclusive of men of all colors.

The West has given charity to the East. Will it give brotherhood? The challenge of the East to the West lies more than anywhere else at that point—will you give us brotherhood, a brotherhood on which your politicians shall ˌbase their legislation, a brotherhood which your leaders shall carry out in social affairs as well as in the life of the Christian church?

> "Come, clear the way, then, clear the way,
>   Blind creeds and kings have had their day;
> Break the dead branches from the path,
>   Our hope is in the aftermath.
> Our hope is in heroic men
>   Star-led to build the world again.
> To this event the ages ran,
>   Make way for brotherhood, make way for man."

THE NEW LEADERSHIP OF TURKEY

THE REVEREND FRED F. GOODSELL, D.D., CONSTANTINOPLE

Pity, prejudice and confusion of mind are words which characterize most Western people, as they think of the Near East today. This is not a new difficulty. In the Near East we always face a conspiracy of misinformation. It reminds me of a homely story. A certain generous man had a donkey which he was accustomed to loan occasionally to those who wanted it. One morning a friend came and asked him if he might use the donkey. For some reason the man did not want to comply that day and so said, "No, I can't loan it to you today." But the borrower was insistent. He said, "I must have that donkey, I have something very important to do." "Well, you can't have it." The borrower was still more insistent and finally the owner said, "No, I tell you the donkey isn't here. I have loaned him to some one else." Just at that instant the donkey burst out of the stable and announced his presence as only a donkey can. "Now I can take him, can't I?" "No. Are you going to believe that beast rather than me?"

Cyrus Hamlin, something over fifty years ago, said that when he listened to an address on the Near East or took up a newspaper article with reference to the Near East, he felt like praying the good Lord to endow him with an adequate sense of unbelief. I know that there are many perplexed people in this convention, perplexed when they consider how the cause of Christ may be promoted today in the Near East. I have talked with some of them. I have listened to their questions. All I can bring you at this time is a personal word of humble testimony, after living and working for seventeen years in the Near East.

I am convinced that the Near East has entered upon a new era. The last two years have witnessed developments of creative significance. Few individuals in the Western world have even begun to take account of the changes that are taking place. Every segment of life in every land from Abyssinia to Jugo-Slavia, and from Afghanistan to Albania and Morocco, is feeling the thrills of rebirth. Governments and peoples, particularly the student class, are plastic for good or for evil as they have not been for centuries. The fires of nationalism, fanned to high flame by the Great War, are melting the traditions and destroying the landmarks of the ages in every land.

On the surface, this great upheaval seems to be a political movement, and some of its Western interpreters are inclined to say that it is simply a protest against Western political domination. I don't deny that there is an element of protest in it, but I see there something far deeper and far more significant. This turmoil is a hungering and a thirsting for life. This restlessness is an ill-guided search for a regenerating power, something that will lift and satisfy. It is a muffled cry for social justice, and social justice on an international scale is something which has begun to inspire the imagination of misled multitudes throughout the East.

Recent events and present tendencies in the Republic of Turkey are raising that country to a place of leadership. The rebirth of Turkey is fact, not fancy. I am thinking of a friend of mine who bade me goodby four weeks ago on the quay at Constantinople. He is a professor of law in the University of Stamboul, a trusted friend and adviser. He said to me, "Don't forget to tell your friends in America that there is a new country here."

I am thinking also of a notable utterance of Professor John Dewey of Columbia University, who recently visited the Near East. What measured words he uses! He seems to be convinced after close observation that we should attribute to Turkey a genuine change of spirit and aim, and he adds this remark, "The ultimate ground for confidence is in the fact that the Turks have that intangible something we call character. They have virility, sobriety of outlook, and sincerity of purpose." The rebirth of Turkey is a fact; it is no idle fancy. The year 1922, or rather its Moslem equivalent, 1338, may prove to be the 1776 of Near Eastern civilization. Let me assure you that at the back of the diplomatic triumph of the representatives of Turkey at Lausanne, lay the iron resolution and the untold sacrifices of a reborn Turkish nation.

I stood four months ago in the little hall in a school in an interior town of Asia Minor. There in that hall the present leaders of Turkey, and some of their friends gathered to swear to each other in the spirit of Patrick Henry, "Give me liberty or give me death." Have we Americans no sympathy with them?

Western diplomats at Lausanne had great difficulty in realizing that they were dealing with a new Turkey, a reborn nation. As a matter of fact, military movements had been of far less significance than social tendencies. This has become increasingly evident since then. The Sultan has been deposed; the Caliph himself has been deported. The church has been separated from the state. A republican form of government has been established. Complete national sovereignty has been achieved. With unprecedented rapidity the Republic of Turkey has been relaying the foundations of a vigorous national life.

Let me be more specific. While the two great events which justify the assertion that there is a new Turkey are the establishment of the Republic and the complete separation of church and state, estimate, if you can, the significance of these evidences of social change, some of them trifling, some of them tremendous, some of them wholesome, some of them harmful. Freedom to travel is a fact. I wish I could say ease of travel was likewise a fact, but you would be surprised, perhaps, to learn that you can travel today from Constantinople to Angora in a sleeping car as comfortably as you can travel from Washington to New York. Censorship on periodicals and books has been removed. This is true even though, as in some other countries, complete freedom of the press and of speech is still a storm center. The traditional Moslem law regarding the use of liquor has been set aside. Unfortunately, intemperance is increasing very rapidly throughout the country.

Many of the most striking changes center about the position of women. Modern women in Turkey have discarded the veil. Recently by government order the heavy curtains separating the men's apartments from the women's apartments in the street cars were removed. The University of Stamboul has opened its doors to women.

Polygamy now is bad form and there is a strong movement to outlaw it. Men and women mingle freely in such organizations as teachers' associations and in other public gatherings.

Changes like these make those who knew Turkey ten years and even five years ago rub their eyes to see whether they are in a dream. And the end is not yet. Shortly before I left Constantinople the editor of an outstanding Turkish fortnightly journal came to me with a request. He asked me to translate a statement of the principles which govern him in the administration of his paper and which are really a part of his convictions. He prints the statement frequently in his magazine in French and in Turkish, and he wanted to put it into English. I know that my editor friend means what he says. I know that he has great influence through his books and articles as he champions those principles. I know that his ruling passion is to banish war from human society. I cannot read the entire statement but I wish to read six brief items which he makes in that statement of principles:

"Of all forms of liberty, that of the liberty of conscience is the most essential and the most sacred. A man who is not free to choose and to declare his belief loses half his soul.

"It is a capital error to believe that the misfortune of one nation constitutes the good fortune of another nation. The interdependence of peoples is inviolable. An injustice done to a single one is a menace to all.

"War is no means for the solution of international questions. Every aggressive war is wicked.

"The real greatness of a country does not inhere in its density of the population nor in the fertility of its soil nor in the extent of its territory, nor in the military power of its government, but in the social value of its citizens.

"One of the chief reasons why the Orient is more backward than the Occident is the position of woman.

"There is only one civilization and that is the inheritance of the great human family."

One cannot come into contact with a Turkish editor of the influence of this man who champions such principles without realizing that changes are going on in the thought life of Turkey today.

If I were asked to point out the most significant, the most challenging fact in the new Turkey as I see it today, my mind would run back to a series of interviews which I had with the minister of education at Angora not very long ago. We were dealing with the subject of religious education in mission schools. I know now why Turkey expelled the Caliph; I know now why they separated the church and the state. As I went out from his presence, I realized that he and his associates had come to the reasoned conclusion that religion as an organized, constructive, social force in human society has failed throughout the world. It was not simply that Christianity or Judaism failed in his estimation, but religion, including Islam—religion, as such, had failed. Therefore it ought to be excluded from public life and from the consideration of the statesmen.

As I went out to think over somewhat in detail what he had said to me so frankly, so honestly, and indeed in such a friendly way, as an American, I seemed to see him pointing at great Christian Russia and saying, "Your religion is worthless. You yourselves have discarded it." I seemed to see him pointing at Christian Europe and saying, "Your religion is worthless. Look at your hostile and deceitful and unfriendly secret diplomacy and your heavy armies." I seemed to see him pointing at Christian America and saying, "Your charity is fine; your passion for freedom is glorious; your strength is unmeasured; but I do not see that religion plays much part in your life. Look at your public scandals; look at the way you treat the negroes; look at your industrial injustices."

He knew all about these things. The lives of the so-called Christian nations of the world are an open book to the non-Christian world today. The thing that most of them, including Turkey, are reading is that the Christian nations of the world do not take the teaching of Christ seriously. From this and from her own experience, Turkey has drawn the conclusion: "We can expect no help from religion, from any religion, in the rebuilding of our national life." This is truly a tragic crisis.

What are we going to do about it? I know what we ought to do about it. The real tragedy of the situation lies in the fact that the leaders of Turkey realize that they must get into contact with some regenerative power. They are turning to education, to economics, to social enterprises. In this seeking they are turning to America for help. They admire America in so many ways. A member of the Grand National Assembly said to me recently, "As we shift our national life from a military to an economic basis, we need your help. We used to ask Englishmen to come and help us strengthen our navy. We used to ask Germans to come and help us rebuild our army. We want you Americans now to come as social experts and help us to build a new society."

Will we co-operate? Are we big enough in heart and soul to be fair and friendly with the new Turkey? Are we deeply enough in earnest to purge our own national life of its inconsistencies? Are we single-minded enough to pursue our missionary purpose so patiently, so humbly, and so intelligently that even the most prejudiced in that misunderstood land may understand? Are we Christ-like enough to give ourselves as well as our money?

If we are, let us instruct those who go out to represent us in the world of Islam to exclude ecclesiasticism in all its forms from their missionary activity and to make Christ supreme. If we are, let us find a way to ratify that treaty of amity and commerce with Turkey. I would that every American citizen here this evening might write soon to his Senators and stress the moral necessity of ratifying it at once, without acrimonious debate. If we are, let us find a way to join the nations of the world in giving Turkey a new place in the family of nations, and challenge her to make good.

To the Americans I would say: The United States cannot fill her great trust in the Near East by charity alone, colossal though it may be. The United States, and at the heart of the country, the Christian churches, born again according to the Spirit by self-giving service and genuine aggressive, international good will, must prove to the peoples of the Near East, and especially to Turkey, that in Christ alone can abundant life be found.

THE SITUATION AT HOME
BISHOP CHARLES H. BRENT, D.D., BUFFALO, NEW YORK

It would appear to me that I can make my best contribution to this convention and this subject by confining myself to a study of the character of the Christianity which is being, not professed, but lived in so-called Christian nations. I shall assume that the United States of which I am a citizen, is a fair sample. May I begin by expressing to you the joy that I experience in standing in the presence of such a multitude of people whom I know to be Christian at heart and probably more Christian in character than I myself. It is told, and I believe with truth of a great American sculptor, that prior to his last, or one of his last, great works of art he had occasion to make a special study of the gospel. At the conclusion he said, "Now that I have come to know this Christ, anything I have is His, and where He is I want to be." He became a true follower of the living Christ. Today, if we are to realize the hope of an evangelized world and of the Orient brought to the Lord Jesus Christ, then the so-called Christian nations, including the United States of America, have to be really converted to Jesus Christ. There is no other solution of the missionary problem.

We are in our day searching for leaders, clamoring for them; and when we get our leaders, we are very apt to criticize them, if we do not crucify them. But the great need of the world is not for leaders, it is for followers. When He whom we call Master walked in the midst of men, His chief invitation was, "Follow me." He talked little about leadership, but this curious thing happened—those who became the truest and most loyal followers by this very fact became the most powerful leaders.

It was as one would expect it to be. If we scrutinized the life of Jesus Christ, we would realize that He is not an end in Himself and never so professed. He, too, was a follower who came, not to do His own will, but the will of Him who sent Him, and by virtue of the fact that He became lost, that He was always lost in the will of the Father, He was the greatest leader that the world has ever seen.

Today, whether it be in little communities, in the nation or in the world at large, what we need is men and women who are so completely followers that they have lost their self-consciousness in the larger consciousness of a noble cause, of the church, of God Himself, so that all their vitality is preserved, not for self-aggrandizement, not for the lust of acquisition, but for service of the highest and deepest kind. Today the only thing that is going to save Christianity or Christian civilization is a higher type of Christianity, a conversion to the living Christ, so that His way will become our way, His thoughts our thoughts, His will our will.

We are here, this vast throng of people, to further the greatest enterprise on earth. All other enterprises are of no avail without it. Taken alone they are but a great mass that has no meaning and no cohesion. Until some unifying force comes into the intricacies of society and trade, of national and international life, there cannot be that which God has purposed for the human race, and which my predecessor so clearly enunciated—a brotherhood binding man to man and nation to nation.

It is the function of the West to minister to the East. Why? Because we have a privilege that they yet do not possess; we have the Evangel. We have tried it. In a measure it possesses us. We have reached a certain stage in missions, where there must be an advance in the Christianity of the church and of the nations, if there is to be an advance in China and Japan and India.

In the early days of missionary enterprise, the oceans divided the continents. Today the waves of the sea unite the shores they separate. In the old days a heavy curtain hung between the East and the West, and when we sent out our missionaries who were our very best, names that are written in the annals of fame, those to whom they were sent took for granted that they were sample Christians. Inasmuch as they did not know how the part of the world from which these men came was living, they assumed that it was living the gospel which was being preached by its representatives. They saw only a very high type of Christian in the mission field, men and women of heroic mold, true to the precepts of Jesus Christ, who would endure anything rather than relinquish their faith.

Now the times are changed; the veil is torn down. Yonder Orient knows only too well how the Christian churches and the people in those churches are living, and how in so many instances and in such wide areas of life they are betraying the gospel that is being proclaimed to the yellow and brown and black races. What we expect in the mission field, we must do ourselves. Is it not so, that we are disappointed if the records that come from so-called foreign fields do not show a high type of Christian being produced; and do we not rejoice when instances are brought to us of how this man or this woman has broken away from the heathen customs, perhaps has been ostracized by those of their own blood in homes where they have hitherto lived in peace and quietness? Do we not inscribe on the roll of the martyrs those who have stood true till death? This is what we send our missionaries out to do, to equip people with such a knowledge of God, to introduce them into such fellowship with Jesus Christ that they will be able to stand against all temptations, move out of their old environment, and if need be, lay down their lives for the gospel's sake.

Have we any business to expect such things unless we ourselves are doing them? Is our Christian society (I am speaking now of all the so-called Christian nations) so completely

devoid of heathen elements that we can trust ourselves to accept its conventions without challenge and so move in the midst
of the great populations which compose the Christian countries
as to make it indistinguishable who are Christians and accept
the Lord Jesus Christ as their leader and who are the pagans
and the heathens? That is the situation in the United States of
America in the year of our Lord, 1925. There is no one compact body of persons whose bearing and character declare them
to be Christians.

In the first place, we demand of those who become Christians that they put away their heathen gods and then that they
put God as revealed in our Lord Jesus Christ before all else.
There is a mystical side to religion, the binding of the individual
human soul to the living God in Jesus Christ. We, of the
Western world, can hardly appreciate just what this means to
the Oriental who is contemplative, who loves to dwell upon the
mysterious, who has eyes to see the invisible and the immortal,
as perhaps we have not. Our gospel of today, at least, is a
gospel of activity and of doing, but if this Western civilization
of ours is to be saved for the fine service it can render to the
whole world, it will have to become more meditative, more
ready to learn the meaning of worship, more empowered to use
silence, until God once more burns His power and His life into
our human life, so that we can turn our practical affairs into
means of exhibiting the Christian truth.

The second step for us to take who desire to help foreign
missions, as they are called (the term is wrong; we are all so
closely knit together now there is nothing foreign), is to endeavor to apply at whatever cost the principles and truths by
which Jesus Christ lives, first to society, as we know it, and as
we move in it; then to industry; then to politics; and then to
the relations between nations. No more can we think of one-
day-a-week religion, when we will be pious for a brief space, and
quite regardless of religion and of its deepest and most refined
principles during the rest of the week.

The home is the great shrine of religion, but it stands today
in need of a considerable amount of regeneration. I am within
hailing distance of old age. I have one great fear lest I should
consider that the freedom which I demanded for myself when
I was young was so complete a thing that now that I have got
to old age or am approaching it, I must see to it that the young
folk only come within my definition of freedom and that they
be denied the freedom that I demanded for myself when I was
young.

We talk about the revolt of youth today in this country
and in Europe. We bemoan, as very probably our parents bemoaned over us, the new ways of youth and their lack of

obedience. We may be right, in some instances without doubt we are right; but let us remember that if we are to win the youth of to-day, we must with Christian sympathy in the home discover what their idea of freedom is and guide them and help them sympathetically, instead of constantly carping.

Again, is the license of youth to-day wholly due to the rebellious character of the children of the new generation? We talk of their lawlessness—how can the daughter or the son of a bootlegging father be anything but lawless? A short time since a young girl of sixteen said to her father, "I don't see why I can't drive your car." "Because," said he, "the law of this State forbids it. You are not of age, and I am a law-abiding citizen." "Oh, are you?" she said, "Then what about those cases of liquor that are constantly coming into the house?" A large part of the lawlessness and the evil-doing of the youth of our land is directly traceable to the home and to the lack of any Christian principles being definitely applied to all departments of life on the part of the parents.

Then again, what shall I say about industry and the economic world as we know it to-day? Can we say it is Christian? Do we wonder that the Orient is rather alarmed that our ideas of economics should be passed on to them? It is a gratifying fact that today in the various industries in this country, there are something like eight hundred distinct codes of ethics. That is a move forward, but I maintain that until and unless the truths and principles by which Jesus Christ lived are applied intelligently and definitely to every department of life, industry, and economics as well as to the domestic affairs of the home, we are failing in what the Master of Life, Jesus Christ, expects of us.

I once said not long ago to a prominent citizen of the State of New York, that the next step for the churches to take was to endeavor to apply the teachings of the Sermon on the Mount to practical affairs, and especially to industry. "Well," he said, "If you do that, you will declare war." Possibly this is so, but it would be a holy war.

As to politics, what shall I say about politics in this city? There is no phase of life in our nation, and so far as my observation goes, in all other nations, the nations of Europe, that is so much in need of religion, as politics. So far as I can see, it has no code of ethics. We rejoice in the separation of church and state, but it is a separation, and not a divorce. There was a time (and this exists in some countries still), when the church and politics were entangled in a very embarrassing embrace, but they broke away. They were separated, yet not divorced; each has its own sphere, but neither can stand without the aid of the other. They should be mutual servants, and not, as in many cases they seem to be, enemies. I thank God that in this country we have a separation between church and state, and I also thank God that there is no divorce. So far as religion is concerned, the moment you take religion out of politics, then you have begun to destroy the state. I am of the mind that every citizen who believes that in a democracy he has a living share in the legislation of his country, should watch legislation and use that powerful influence which is his to register what he thinks in Christian terms by telegrams and letters to Congressmen and Senators on any question of moment.

Do not think for one minute that these telegrams and letters are put into the waste paper basket with little or no notice. Far from it. They are scrutinized with care. If the citizens of our country would register their Christian judgment on public questions in this way, we would have a higher type of legislation, and we would not have some of the legislation that is enacted.

Now I come to what, to me, is the great opportunity of Christians and the greatest opportunity of this nation of ours. What is the relation of nation to nation today throughout the world? What does international intercourse mean? I have just come from the League of Nations, where, by appointment of our own Government, I sat as a plenipotentiary in an International Conference for the creation of a treaty or the amendment, rather, of a treaty, dealing with an extremely intricate and difficult problem—a moral question, a question that has to do with commerce, a question that has to do with health. Some forty nations were there represented. I am not going to discuss the procedure of the Conference. It was stormy at times but a calm has descended upon it.

I will simply say this—that the international treaty for which that conference stands is one of the chief means of binding the nations of the world together in mutual understanding and cooperation when there is any great question to be discussed that all the nations have in common.

An international treaty is quite distinct from the kind of treaty which is agreed upon by two nations. For instance, this country has a large number of individual arbitration treaties with other countries. They are admirable as far as they go. But distinguish between the scope and the value of such individual treaties and a mutual compact between all the nations of the world. More and more must we who believe in the establishment of good will between nations stand for international treaties.

There are three distinguished—the most distinguished that the world has yet known—expressions of this type of treaty at the present time before mankind. One of them, the Covenant of the League of Nations, has been too much discredited in this country by prejudice and by ignorance. At a largely-attended meeting last week, I had not had opportunity to discover the mind of the people present. I asked how many had ever read the Covenant. Perhaps ten persons held up their hands. I said, "If there are those of you who did not hold up your hands who have taken an antagonistic position toward the League, I would ask you by what right you have done it? If you are going to be an enemy of a thing, be sure that you know the character of that of which you are an enemy. You have no business to oppose the League unless you at least have read the Covenant."

I am not appealing tonight for adherence to the League. I am only saying that here is a distinguished instance of an attempt of the nations of the world to gather together in good-will, to live at peace. The Covenant may be poorly drawn, or it may be well drawn, but it is a glorious endeavor, and the world has never seen anything like it before, it is taking the Christian ideal, if you read the first words of the Covenant, and trying to put it into practical form on an extensive scale.

Then there is the World Court. I speak of these things, my friends, because they are Christian in their aim and in their possibilities. The Christian Church and individual Christians can no longer dally about this matter of war. It is time for the Christian Church to declare just exactly under what conditions, if any, what we ordinarily call murder can become a glorious virtue. The Christian Church has got to say in no uncertain voice whether it accepts war as an evil necessity and will support war when it arises, or whether it believes that it is a barbarous atrocity, that there is a substitute for it, and that we must discover and use that substitute. The time has come when this decision must be made and when in no uncertain terms the Church of God must speak. I say for myself, and I say it in the name of Christ, I am against war, I hate war and I think it is an atrocious barbarity and must be dethroned from the position which it has usurped.

Let me be perfectly clear so that no one will misunderstand me. Never while I live will I allow one whisper against the glory of that body of youth, the best of our land and of other lands, who thrilled by an ideal which they saw clearly, responded (as I did) to the call of country and went forth. I happened to survive, but many of them laid down their lives and their names are written forever in the annals of our national fame. But, just as a day came in the history of religion when God laid His hand on the arm that was uplifted to offer human sacrifice and said, "No more of this, there is a better way," so now God has laid His hand upon the Christian nations and has

said, "No more of this, there is a better way." All our hatred
of war, all our abuse of war will be of little avail unless we get
war's substitute.

What is war? It is the abuse of force and not the use of
force. It is guile and deceit added to force. I stand for the
use of force under righteousness and law. The idea of a police
force suggests the legitimate use of force, but here is what we
do in connection with disputes between nations. We say that
we will decide who is right and who is wrong by asking Chief
Justice War to decide.

We have no certainty that force will ever take its side, or
will always take its side, with the right, avoiding the wrong;
indeed, it is conceivable that more often it will choose the wrong
than the right. At any rate, that happens. Now are the greatest problems that come before mankind to be settled in this
way, when we would not think of so settling a dispute between
two neighbors? One might just as well appeal to the trial by
fire as to appeal to such an arbiter. So, what must we do? We
must do what our President is trying to lead us to do, and
which, when a certain stubborn group in our Senate come to
their senses, we will be able to do. I speak as an American
citizen who has won his citizenship. I want to see the constitution of our country obeyed; I want to see the Senate of
the United States *advise* the President in matters pertaining
to foreign affairs, but I refuse to be silent, when any clique or
group, whatever they may call themselves, in the Senate block
the way to the will of the people. I am speaking not only as
a citizen; I am speaking as a Christian.

Now, I know all of the weaknesses of the Court. I have
studied its statute, which is the creation of one of our very best
minds and one of our foremost statesmen, Elihu Root. At least,
he had a larger share in it than any one else. In that Court I
see in embryonic form a Supreme Court of the World, which,
when any question of dispute arises between nations, will be
able to give judgment, and its judgment will be accepted as
quietly and as simply as when our own Supreme Court gives
judgment, as it has done in eighty-seven cases between two
States that have had disputes. There is no other course. We
must insist that our nation take its place in good faith and in
good will by the side of all other nations in this attempt, and,
please God, it will be a successful attempt, forever to turn out
of the Supreme Court of the World Chief Justice War, and put
in its stead Chief Justice Law.

There is still another great international treaty before the
world for consideration. It has in it a note that is full of interest and which every Christian and every citizen should study. I
refer to what is called the Geneva Protocol. I am giving these

instances of an attempt of the nations of the world to express good will toward one another, and to outlaw war. In that Protocol, war is placed exactly where it ought to be placed. It is made an outlaw; and, as was said in Geneva at the time the Protocol was born, "he is the aggressor who will not arbitrate or bring his cause to a Court of Justice."

I have spoken out of the fullness of my heart and out of something that is akin to a passion. I see but two things to live for: one of them is the unity of the church of God; the other is the good will among the nations that will forever banish war. More than ever the mission field demands that there should be unity of the church in the homeland. That cannot come in a moment; but at any rate, we can think unity, we can pray unity, and to a large extent, we can practice unity.

I was sectarian enough once to be shocked when some one who did not belong to our own branch or part of the Christian Church came in to fellowship with us, and we happened to think that he did belong, and afterwards discovered that he did not. But let us start in a new and better way. Let us always look on a Christian as a brother and be ready to give him, even if he does not belong to our own special group, our fullest Christian confidence. I believe it is with that spirit, more than by any formal meetings or endeavors, that we will cultivate the spirit of Christianity, and in the end the unity of the Church of God.

The Kingdom of Heaven is at hand! All these things to which I have made reference have to do with the coming in of the Kingdom. But are you and I thinking only in terms of this world? Are we merely trying to build up something that will make the world of tomorrow better for our children, happier, more prosperous, more spiritual? If so, there is something wrong in our Christianity.

At a meeting of Copec*, as it is called in England, within the last year, a distinguished German, a theologian, went away inspired by all that he had taken part in, but puzzled. He said, "Here are a group of Christians who have been together for two whole weeks, and yet the second coming of Christ has never even been mentioned." (Laughter.) Don't laugh. Remember that Germans today who have really suffered, are men who now are not looking (and this also is true of some of the great sufferers of other nations in Europe) for anything in this world in the way of comfort and joy, but they are looking beyond into the Kingdom as it is just on the other side of that divide which you and I before many years at longest, will cross.

---

*The Conference on Christian Politics, Economics, and Citizenship, held in Birmingham, England, April 5-12, 1924.

The Church has lost too much of other-worldliness. How Christ shall come and when none of us can say, but if He does not come in some dramatic way and wind up the universe as the literalists may believe, He will surely come to everybody in this auditorium before a century passes, and then what? Why, then we shall move out into that great Kingdom for which we are here on earth to prepare, and to gather material, wherewith to build it.

It is not that we are going to get something from that Kingdom when we enter; it is rather, that the Kingdom is waiting for us to come with our arms full of sheaves as good reapers, and that, therefore, our horizon must not be confined to this world, but a new and a higher type of other-worldliness must descend upon us. Then, I think, there will be a higher type of faith in our midst. There is not only unity between East and West, but also between here and beyond.

Faith today is very often nothing more than very wise calculation, but the kind of faith that God has for His Church on earth is of a higher sort. It will open our eyes so that we will be able to see—as we cannot now see—where the key lies and what is its shape that will unlock the doors that form barriers between races and nations and peoples. A Church full of faith that works for the beyond and not merely for time is the Church which God will endow with His blessing and with His power of sight and wisdom, as well as with His strength and vitality, of which today the Church is scant.

The good Lord is with us, and I know that He has seen my desire at any rate to help you, His children, my brethren, and that He will forgive what I may have said amiss and that He will bless what I have said in accordance with His will.

CHRIST: THE SOLUTION OF THE PROBLEMS OF THE WORLD

HIS MESSAGE TO THE INDIVIDUAL
THE REVEREND JOHN B. MC LAURIN, INDIA

It is my very great privilege this day to speak to you of what Christ means to the individual; and I do this the more gladly because we have found in missionary work that the transformation of the individual in Jesus Christ is not only the basis, but also is the vindication of all that we are doing through Him, and that He is doing through us, throughout the world today.

It is the basis of all that we are doing, absolutely fundamental to all our work. We have seen many ambitious schemes collapse and we have seen many noble enterprises fail. They had organization behind them; they had wealth behind them; they had consecrated service behind them; but they came and they grew and they passed, because they were not surely founded on that one rock, Jesus Christ.

There are cities in India today where, in the sixteenth century—so we are told by travelers who went through the Mogul Empire—there were great churches. The largest building in the royal city of Agra was a Christian church, and the chimes in the tower of the church could be heard to the farthest confines of that great city. If you go there today you will find that not one stone is standing upon another of that church. There are no Christian chimes which can be heard for more that a few blocks, much less to the confines of that city. Founded upon diplomacy, founded upon cleverness, those stately edifices were—yes, but something was lacking, something which brought them under the condemnation of that uncompromising text, "Every tree which is not planted of my Heavenly Father shall be uprooted."

It is indeed fitting that we should turn our attention to what Jesus Christ will do for the individual and to His message for the individual, because it has been found over and over again, sometimes at the cost of much life and treasure, that there is no other permanent foundation.

The new life in Jesus Christ in the heart of a man ransomed, redeemed, saved and transformed; there you have the basis, there you have the living stones with which you can go on and build the city of God throughout this world. Not only is it absolutely foundational to all our work, but it is the vindication of all that we are doing. The educated Hindu of today (and I presume the thinking Chinese and Japanese as well), cannot believe that there is a power in Christ which will solve the problems of sin, of impurity, of self-seeking in the social group and in the nation, if that power is not able to solve those problems in the heart of the individual man.

Today the thinking Indian (and I presume, the thinking men of every country of Asia), is looking for a salvation for his beloved land. A new spirit of patriotism is abroad. In those Eastern lands you can feel it rising about you like the incoming tide; and the genius and heart of that new spirit is simply this: Where can we find some power which can lift our beloved nation and country out of those chains and out of that darkness which now bind and imprison her and place her shoulder to shoulder with any other nation on the face of the world; so that she may go forward and fulfill her national destiny? They are asking this question today, and in asking the question they are judging our Savior and our holy faith by what it can do down among the scavengers, among the outcasts, among the middle classes, the artisans, the farmers as well as among the Brahmans of India.

If we can show truly that this transforming power exists, that in Jesus Christ life is made new and victorious; if we can show that in the individual heart sin and all that is low and mean can be stamped out and conquered forever, then the old gods will pass, and they will look more and more to the Savior who has saved this one and that one as the One who is to be welcomed with open doors into their land.

This principle is the vindication of all our work, because it is always true that the individual and not any social group is the common denominator of the race. It is not because we have a sense of obligation to others of our family or to others of our race that we have this divine obligation to all the world; but the heart that has truly experienced, as we have heard stated so eloquently from this platform, the transforming power of Jesus Christ, that through Him has won the victory, that heart leaps forth to give that message to the farthest bounds of the human race, because it has found for itself the secret of victory over sin.

It is such a heart that knows Christ, that knows there is no difference, "for all have sinned and come short of the glory of God, being justified freely by His grace through the redemption that is in Christ Jesus." It is because I am a man and as a man I have a man's temptations and a man's possibilities, the temptation conquered in Jesus Christ and the possibilities developed, that I know that Jesus Christ has a similar message for my fellowman, no matter where he lives, to the farthest bounds of this world.

In order that I may make these points clear this day, I am going to bring to your notice, two instances which have come under my personal observation. I will draw one of these from the lowest level of Hindoo society, and one from the very highest levels of that society. The first individual of whom I am thinking belonged among the scavengers of India. I can not say the "scavenger caste" because you know that below the caste system are the untouchables, one-fifth of the population of India. You probably know something of the conditions under which they live. Still, below these there is another group of slaves, the scavengers, even more wretched, their religion even more of a devil worship, their social life more of a human pig sty. Such are the conditions of grinding poverty under which those poor people live, the nature of the work that they must do, which they share with the swine and the dogs of an Indian village, that such conditions would smother any human soul in a week, and crush out of it all possibility of rising superior to such circumstances and of laying hold of the living God.

The one I have in mind was a woman, a small, fair, frail creature, in a certain town of South India. Among her other duties she came daily to sweep out the mission house. She attended the prayer services held in the house and in the town, and duly the regular teaching of the life of Christ, the words of eternal life and the deeds of healing began to have their effect. One day, she announced that she would follow Christ, that she had accepted Him as her Savior and her Master. The missionaries were frightened. They knew the conditions under which that woman lived. They knew that beyond the village there was the outcast settlement about which a certain text in the Hindoo scriptures writes, "They shall be outside the habitations of man and their wealth shall be dogs and donkeys." They knew that beyond these untouchables, and untouchable by the untouchables themselves, was the little group of scavengers, four huts, one occupied by the man whom I cannot call the husband of four women, one of whom at his desire and his command lived with him, the other three living with their families in the other three small huts awaiting their turn. He came up on the mission house verandah one day to talk over her salary. The missionary was not very sympathetic for the simple reason that he knew she would never see anything of the salary herself. I remember him as he stood there, a powerfully-built man, the dirt on him in flakes, his matted hair roped with dirt. As I looked into his face, I saw stamped there pure bestiality as I have never seen it before or since. It came like a blow in the face that any one made in the image of the living God, could possibly sink so low, as I looked into his eyes and saw the swine, and the fox and the snake leering out at me in a sort of degraded self-confidence.

He commenced to talk. We carried on a conversation for a while. He was sent home unsatisfied. He took a five-foot staff, beat the woman until she fell unconscious on the floor. She was carried out by her own children, some water from the nearest ditch was thrown on her, and the next one took her place. She lived her life under these unspeakable conditions, carrying on the work she had to do, day by day, going through that village as a scavenger.

So, when she announced her intention to follow Christ there was a missionary council. What could be done? Could she be sent back to her own parents? Certainly not. They knew no other manner of life. They would at once send her back again to this beast. Could she be kept near the mission house? Certainly not. How could we kidnap her, as it were? Besides, she did not care to come. She seemed to have an idea that she should go back and fight her fight and win her victory where she lived. She was never allowed to join the Christian church, but she went back to her home, after making her decision, and announced it there. Impossible and incredible as it may seem, there under that cloud of lust and cruelty and bestiality, day by day, she showed forth the true white witness of a Christian life. As she came to Christian prayers on Sunday the men sitting on the right of the church and the women on the left, this little fair creature would be sitting up in the front row and at the mention of the name of Jesus Christ, you could fairly see her face shine with hope, and joy and love, and the patience of Jesus Christ.

How could she do it? I doubt whether one of us would have lasted a week under her trials without the inner power of the heart which she had found, the power of Christ which can take one from the very mire, can transform and cleanse, can strengthen and glorify and can place as a light in the darkness, walking like the few in Sardis, in white garments. It is a miracle. There is no other explanation for it.

The other instance of which I wish to speak as I said, is one from the very highest, or one of the very highest, grades of Hindu life, a Neyogi, one of the highest sub-castes of the Brahmans. Their life was very different. The largest house on the village street—a village of about twenty thousand inhabitants—had a deep cool verandah, floored with mud it is true, but at the same time deep and cool, and within could be seen the courtyard and the rooms on each side. There this boy lived with his elder brother and his mother.

He was a graduate of Madras University in Arts and in Law. You could go into their house, and if they would allow you to go into the kitchen or their dining room, you could eat your dinner off the floor, spotlessly clean—the brasses, the pots, and the pans shining, until you could see your face in them. They were the lords of several hundred acres of land, the center of the social life of the whole village, "Proud were they of their name and race," and that pride was not altogether without justification. Culture, refinement and education had been traditional in that family for generations and perhaps for centuries.

Ananda Rao went down to Madras, and came back with his legal degree and with his arts degree. His heart was burning as he looked forward to a successful legal career, and there was in his heart too a great passion for India. He longed to find the Divine Power, to have the message which should lift India out of the weakness and degradation which makes the young Indian today grind his teeth, as he contemplates Western nations. He was eager for some power which should strike the shackles of caste and idolatry from India's wrists and which would place her in the light of true freedom.

As he looked about him and took stock of his native village, his task resolved itself in his mind into two problems—the problem of purity and the problem of service. Where would he find the one who could cleanse his heart, who could give him the secret of victory over sin, and where should he find the one in whom he would find his ideal of service for others?

He walked restlessly down the streets of that town, he went into this place of worship and that, and read many books. One day he met the pastor of a little group of Christians in the outcast hamlet. They became friends, and the friendship deepened. Then the young pastor very wisely gave him a copy of the four Gospels. Ananda Rao went home and sat on his little string cot, reading it by the light of his tin lamp on the wooden stand. You and I know what he read. He read about the leper by the roadside and how with his eyes on the eyes of Christ, he came nearer and nearer until he went to the feet of Christ with that cry, "Lord, if Thou wilt, Thou canst make me clean"; and, how Christ touched and cleansed the leper with the words, "I will, be thou clean." Out of that sacred page there came a hand, a wounded hand, and it touched the heart of that boy, so that he rose to his feet and said, "I have found the power and I have found the Savior." He threw down his old books, went out and got hold of the hand of our Christian preacher and said, "I am with you; I have found it. I am with you for Christ forever."

It was hard to give up his inheritance and to meet with the execration of his townsmen. His elder brother cursed him and spat in his face, and his mother came with disheveled hair and torn garments and threw herself at his feet and wept. Aye, but he knew what Jesus Christ meant when He said, "He that loveth father or mother more than me is not worthy of me," and with many another he knew what Christ meant, when he said, "He that would come after me let him deny himself and take up his cross daily and follow me." The proud Brahman did forsake all, going to the seminary he became a Christian preacher, and found his ideal in purity of heart and in loving service with Jesus Christ to the point of suffering and sacrifice with Him.

Jesus Christ, what does He do for the individual? He saves them and he saves them to the fullness of the Christian life, for there is "no other Name given under heaven amongst men whereby we must be saved."

HIS MESSAGE TO SOCIETY

MISS MABEL K. HOWELL, NASHVILLE, TENNESSEE

While we have been listening to the one who has just spoken, our hearts have rejoiced that in the great message that Jesus Christ gave to the world there is that which will transform and redeem all the individuals whom God has made out of all the nations. We have never known in all its fullness the wonderful story of the twice-born men of all the peoples of the earth. We can but rejoice this morning that our Christ gave to the world a message and a gospel that is adequate to save the individual.

But I am here this morning to call your attention to the other side of the gospel message. I am here to tell you that society must be saved, that the social order must be redeemed, that the group mind, the group will and the group conscience must be brought into harmony with and be vitalized by the principles and teachings of Jesus Christ. This in no way controverts the belief that the message of Christ was spoken to the individual, but assumes that we would not be presenting the whole gospel of Jesus Christ were we not to claim for Him the power to redeem all the associated life of men.

Do we need another religion to save the social order? There are men today, leaders in the thought life of the world, who would make us think that the gospel of Jesus Christ was not sufficient for the salvation of the associated life of men, and that the world awaits a great new teacher, a great new social philosopher, who shall speak the word which will redeem the life that we try to live together as peoples, as races, as nations throughout the world. Are we, this morning, prepared to say as a great missionary conference that because Jesus Christ has not had His chance to redeem the world in all of these interrelationships, His message is not adequate for the redemption of the world? Or are we ready to say with Charles A. Ellwood in one of his recent books entitled "Religion and Social Reconstruction," that Jesus laid a foundation in religion and ethics that is as solid and as stable as the foundation that was laid by Copernicus in astronomy and by Darwin in biology.

If I understand why we are here this morning, it is to face together whether or no, we, as a great body of missionaries, as a great body of Christian leaders of all the churches of the United States and Canada, are ready to proclaim a great new crusade to bring all the relationship of this world of ours into captivity to the principles and the teachings of our Lord Jesus Christ.

1. Jesus knew that His message had in it the power to *redeem society*. He knew that in the word that He spoke, which became the watchword on his lips, the Kingdom of God, was to be found the principle which would redeem mankind. Jesus knew the value of that word. In that expression, the Kingdom of God, He answered, as you and I well know, the two great fundamental cries of the heart of humanity, those cries that were voiced by Philip when he said, "Show us the Father and it sufficeth us." And by that young lawyer who came and said, "Who is my brother?" In that wonderful enunciation of the Kingdom with its sonship to the Father based upon regeneration, and its brotherhood based upon a common fatherhood, are the principles, ideals and teachings which, if applied, will redeem the associated life of men today.

Jesus knew He was bringing into the world a teaching which ultimately would revolutionize the social order; and yet He also knew that individuals had to be won as a basis for that social order. So He gave his time, thought, labor, and prayer to the winning of a considerable body of sons who would serve as a basis for the social order that would be redeemed under the great thought of the brotherhood of man. But as we turn from Jesus and come down through the ages, we realize that,

2. *The aggressive and missionary leadership of the world throughout the ages has realized that in the message of Jesus was that which would save the associated life of men.*

The early Christians knew it. They were conscious that they were being called upon to be the stewards of a revolutionary doctrine that if applied would destroy the great Roman Empire. Those men put into practice the principle of brotherhood. They brought together into their organization the Jew and the Gentile; the rich and the poor; the master and the slave; the ruler and the tax collector; binding all together by the tie of Christian brotherhood.

We know today that the teachings of those early men, like Peter and James, dealt with these great problems of the interrelationship of men. We know too, that these great Christian leaders gave their lives in martyrdom, not so much because they, as individual men, were the followers of Jesus Christ, but because the Roman rulers knew that in the doctrine they professed, in the Master to whom they were loyal, were to be found the principles and the teachings which would ultimately overthrow the Roman Empire. Their very death as martyrs is a proof of the social mission of those early Christian fathers.

As we come down into early missionary endeavor in all the missionary fields of the world, we find that the men and women who were sent out from the churches of the United States and Canada and from other nations to speak the word to the nations beyond, in no sense separated in their thinking the great message of Christ to the individual from His message to the new social order in which they found themselves. This assertion needs no proof before this body. Several years ago, Mr. Robert E. Speer described forcefully the social conscience, and the social activity of that early group of missionaries. It is a marvelous story of improved agricultural methods, of the manufacture of cotton cloth and silk, of the introduction of steam engines, in short, of the bringing to the economic life of the peoples of the world that which would make it possible for them from the economic standpoint to live the Christian life.*

But what of our later missionaries—the missionaries who are working as our representatives in all the mission fields of the world today, what do they say? There is a new consciousness on the part of the missionaries today that they must interpret the full gospel of Jesus Christ, that they must give to the peoples that they are teaching the brotherhood side of the gospel of Jesus as well as the sonship side of his wonderful message. As one goes about among missionaries it is evident that they are consciously feeling that they must, in some way, bring to the thought and conscience of the peoples to whom they are ministering the fact that in Jesus and in His teachings is the power to redeem the life that they live together politically and industrially, as well as the life that they live as individual sons of the Lord Jesus.

There is a new technique in the missionary body. It comes from the great social work of the West. But after all the thing that characterizes the missionary on the mission field today, as I see him at work, is a great social passion to see even whole

*See paper by Dr. Robert E. Speer, "The Social Ideals of the Founders of Modern Missions"—28th Foreign Missions Conference Report, 1921.

communities redeemed by the power of Jesus. It has seemed to me, as I have stood at the side of some of these men and women on the mission field, that they were looking out over their villages, as in Korea, or over their cities and rural communities, as in China, with the heart of Jesus when he said, "Jerusalem, Jerusalem, how would I have gathered thy children together even as a fowl gathereth her brood under her wing, but ye would not." There is a realization in the missionary body that if they truly present the full message of Jesus it will, because of its principles, redeem that community life and bring it into touch, sympathy, and alignment with the great cause and purpose of Jesus Christ.

One of the most inspiring sights on the mission field today is the way in which the social passion has taken hold of the native Christian churches. In all of these lands, where the Christians are coming into self-consciousness and organizing their associations, as they have done in China in their China Christian Council, you come face to face with a program for the redemption of society. I have sat in conferences in China and heard them discuss how they could apply the principle of Christian brotherhood to the new industrial order that is emerging; how they could apply the principle of the worth of the human personality to the condition of womanhood in China; how they could reach out into all the difficult and un-Christian phases of their society and bring to bear upon it the wonderful principles that are to be found in our gospel of Jesus Christ. And so today, it seems to me, that the native church in the mission fields has caught a vision of the fullness of our gospel such as probably none of the churches that sent the missionaries forth had at the time it sent them forth.

3. *Public opinion in the world today is demanding that the church of Jesus Christ release the principles and teachings of Jesus and apply them to the social order.* We can not say that too forcefully. The church of Jesus Christ has a stewardship of those principles that in the opinion of mankind today will save the world in all of these relationships of life. It is needless to elaborate upon this. The great social reformers of the world today are saying it from their platforms. They have tried the transformation of the social order without the spiritual part of Jesus' message and they know it does not work. They know it is superficial, they know it will not stand and it will not abide, but they are beginning to realize that in the Christian gospel of divine sonship through regeneration and of brotherhood through common sonship is to be found the principle that will ultimately redeem mankind. The leaders in the social science world today are saying that our gospel is the perfect social religion, that it has in it every element that is needed for the

salvation of the social life that we live together. What is the trouble, men and women of this convention? We have not applied it. Today we are thwarting the carrying of the message to the uttermost ends of the earth, because our great inter-relationships in America and England and among the nations do not represent the great social principles and teachings of our Lord Jesus Christ.

4. *The Church is ready.* The Church is convinced; the church wants to go forward in this great new crusade; she wants leadership. Time does not permit the development of this theme.

5. *The youth of the world today is ready.* The students of our colleges and churches, as we met them at Indianapolis, were saying, "We want as missionary volunteers to put into effect a crusade to bring to pass the 'Jesus way of life' in all the world." Yes—the Church is ready and the young life that is to be the foundation of the missionary leadership of the world for the next generation is ready.

6. *Are we ready?* Will there go forth from this great Conference representing the very heart of the missionary spirit of the churches of Christ of America and Canada, leadership in the application of the teachings of Jesus to all the inter-related life of men? Are we here this morning to start that crusade? God wills it.

HIS MESSAGE TO NATIONS AND RACES

MR. JOSEPH H. OLDHAM, M.A., LONDON
Secretary, The International Missionary Council

When I was asked to speak on this topic the first question which suggested itself to my mind was whether Christ had a message to nations and races. In a deep and true sense, as Mr. McLaurin has reminded us, Christ's message is addressed primarily to the individual. I know no way in which we can get a better world except through the conversion of individual men and women. I know no way in which the Kingdom of God can come except as individual men and women by an individual act of repentance turn from their false ideas and their selfish ways and by an individual act of faith receive the new life which is the gift of God in Jesus Christ.

And yet I think it will be apparent to all of us that it was indispensable that such a topic as this should have a place on the program of this Conference, if we reflect on the extraordinary transformation which has taken place in the world since the missionary movement began. Since the day when William Carey more than a century ago preached his great sermon, since many of the great Boards that are represented in this Conference were born, we have witnessed the invention of the locomotive steam engine, of the steamship, of the automobile, of the airship and the airplane, of telegraphy, of the telephone, of wireless telegraphy. Accompanying these inventions, and, to a large extent, due to them, we have seen more fundamental changes take place in the structure of society. We have witnessed the growth of the industrial revolution with a social order based largely upon capital and the growing power of organized labor.

We have witnessed the extension through the world of representative institutions with the power passing into the hands of the people. We have seen coming into existence in the West and now beginning to come into existence in Asia and Africa the powerful engine of popular education. We have seen the growth of the press with its enormous influence. We have seen the rise of the modern, highly-organized bureaucratic state. We have seen the increasing growth of international commerce and international finance, so that every part of the world in which we live has become economically dependent upon every other part.

I have been very much interested in the last few months in missionary conditions in East Africa, which as you know, was visited last year by the Phelps-Stokes Commission under Dr. Thomas Jesse Jones. What is the keyword in regard to all the colonies in East Africa? The keyword to the situation there at the moment is cotton. Why is that the keyword? It is because the mills of Lancashire cannot get from other sources a sufficient supply of raw cotton to keep them going. Therefore, they have to develop new sources of supply. That is but one illustration out of a hundred of the way in which the fortunes of the different peoples of the world have become economically linked together.

What I wish to suggest to you is that all these new continents of human life and human activity which have come into existence during the past century are just as much a part of the world to which the Christian witness has to be borne as the physical continents of Asia and Africa where the gospel has to be preached. That was the truth that Bishop Brent so powerfully and impressively put before us last night. It is not my purpose to enlarge upon that theme but to deal only with one aspect of it, viz., that those individuals in the world to whom we have to carry our gospel exist as members of nations and races, and that that fact, that sense of solidarity that they have with those of their own nation and their own race, is something which may color the whole texture of their minds.

I do not myself believe that there is anything in racial differences which need separate men from one another, or interfere with spiritual fellowship and unity; but when these racial differences are associated, as in fact they are associated as we find them in the world today, with different civilizations, with different political systems, and with different economic systems, then you may have in that fact of national solidarity, or racial solidarity, something which determines the attitude of men to those who belong to a different nation or race than themselves. Consequently, this sense of nationality, or the sense of race, may come to constitute an insuperable barrier between minds and minds, so that men are unwilling to receive a message from those to whom they are nationally or racially opposed.

A hundred years ago those who were interested in the missionary cause were praying that the doors might be open. China was a closed land. Today, physically, the world is open to the preaching of the gospel; but a very serious fact still remains to be faced in that, while the doors are physically open, there may grow up in men's minds that which closes them to the preaching of the gospel.

It may be of no advantage to us to be physically present in the continents, where we desire to preach the gospel. We may be living in a world of illusion in thinking that we are necessarily preaching the gospel to people's minds, because we have missionaries located in these different centers, if there grows up through national and racial prejudice a consciousness which closes their minds.

Bishop Brent reminded us last night that the cause of international good-will was a fundamental humanness. That is profoundly true. It is also a fundamental missionary interest. What then has Christ to say to us in a situation like this, a situation that touches the missionary cause at its very heart? I have time to speak this morning of only two adjustments, two personal changes which, if we will allow our Lord Jesus Christ to reign over our hearts and lives, will give Him the opportunity of transforming the situation in which we find ourselves today.

In the first place, if we will allow our minds to be converted, if, as St. Paul says, we allow ourselves to be transformed by the renewing of our minds under the influence of the mind of Jesus Christ, we shall be delivered from the danger to which we are constantly subject of *losing sight of the individual in the nation or the race.*

In the Christian scheme of things a man is intended to live in human relations as a person with persons. The whole tendency of modern life, with its increasing complexity and organization, tends to make us forget this fundamental human and Christian truth. Life during this past century has become immeasurably more complex. We deal with corporations, with organizations and federations of employers, with organizations of labor, and even with nation over against nation and race against race. There is no more fundamental need of our modern life, than that of humanizing the relations of men with one another. That is profoundly true of races. The tendency all the time is to lose sight of the individual Indian in an abstraction which we call India, of the individual Japanese with his human need and his human aspirations in an abstraction called Japan, of the individual negro in an abstraction called the negro race.

What we have to do if we wish to be Christian, or truly human, is to rediscover the individual in all his unique and appealing individuality, to see him as Christ saw him, as an interesting human being, as one who has human needs. The only power that is going to enable us to do that adequately is religious faith. In a naturalistic view of the world the individual has no such value. Life is plentiful, human life just as plant life. It is plentiful and it is cheap; and the only real reason, if we think it out, why the individual has a value, the kind of value that is attributed to him in the Christian view of things. is because there once lived on this earth a carpenter who took upon himself our human nature and conferred upon it an immeasurable dignity; because every individual, no matter what race he belongs to, is an object of God's care and God's love, and therefore must be an object of interest and care and love to those who know and understand God's purpose; because that individual, no matter how humble his circumstances, how backward his race, is an individual for whom Christ died.

It is this Christian view of things that is going to enable us to bring to civilization, to this world situation what it sorely needs, the rehumanizing of the relations of men with one another through the discovery of the individual. That in itself will not provide a solution of our racial problems, but it will set to work in the world a new creative force, without which no solution of these problems will be possible at all. In the light of this Christian and human way of looking at life we get at the only solution that matters of the problem of equality. The only equality that is worth talking about is the equality of men as human beings, and the fact that a great deal of this discussion which is so common in our day, as to whether races are equal is, in the Christian view of things, quite beside the point.

It is no more relevant to the difference in humanity than to differences in the members of a family. There are all kinds of differences of gift and capacity in a family, but the members know that they are equal as members of one family. The real meaning of equality is quite irrespective of differences of gift and capacity in the different races. Men are equal as human beings; and as we get this Christian outlook upon our fellowmen, and see them in their human need and their human potentialities, as those who have been born to grow up into sons of God, we establish a genuine equality within which all differences find their proper place.

Just think what an emancipation it would be in the world in which we are living, if we could break free from the prison house into which we shut ourselves by our hates and our prejudices and our fears and could go out to breathe the ampler and freer air of a world in which nothing human is alien to us and in which we live in human relations with our fellowmen as persons with persons.

St. Paul tells us that the end of the whole creative process, what the world is waiting anxiously for, is the manifestation of the sons of God. I believe that the sons of God are those who, like the great Son of God Himself, live on earth with their fellowmen of every class and of every race in the relation of human friendliness and helpfulness and love. Now that is what Christ will do for the world, if we allow Him to reign over our hearts and minds and convert them, and so to transform our outlook upon life.

The other change that He will bring about in us is this. *He will emancipate us from the error of supposing that differences between people are necessarily causes for antagonism.* That idea is extraordinarily deeply implanted in the mind of our time. We have got to root it out.

If one keeps his eyes open to what is written in the press or in our fiction, to what he finds written even in works of science, he will find this utterly ungrounded assumption that because men are different they are necessarily opposed to one another.

I was reading recently the work of a scientist in which several hundred pages were devoted to the careful and exact measurement of a human skull. While throughout these hundreds of pages the book proceeded with these mathematical calculations, on the last page I came across an astonishing statement. After describing the great powers of the Yellow Race this writer allowed himself to use a sentence to this effect: "With this race (the Yellow Race) so richly endowed the dominant White Race must engage in the greatest conflict in all its history."

What right had he to such a conclusion as that? There is no more reason, because the skulls of these two races differ in their measurements that they should engage in a suicidal conflict than that I should strike my friend suddenly in the face, because I observe that he has dark eyes, while mine are light.

Differences do not need to divide. They may enrich. They may be complementary as in the case of sexes. There is no more reason why races should fight because they are different, than that husbands and wives should always be quarreling because they are different. St. Paul taught us a great truth, when he said that what constitutes a body is that it is made up of different parts. If it were all hands or all eyes, it would not be the body. The conception of human society that Christ would help us to reach is one in which the parts are seen to be complementary one to another.

I am proud of my Scottish ancestry; I am proud of the contribution that Scotland has made to the world, but I believe the world would be a less rich place, if it were composed entirely of Scotchmen. America has something to give to the world that Scotland does not have. I believe that China and India have something to give to the world that Scotland lacks. The trouble is not with the fact that men are different. The trouble is entirely with this false idea, so deeply implanted in men's minds. It is extraordinarily widespread, and our task is to root it out and to plant in its place that truer conception of human society which Jesus Christ has enabled us to reach.

That is to say, our task is to root out of men's minds this thought of people separated from one another, incapable of mutually understanding one another, of people necessarily opposed to one another, because of their differences. We must assist the mind of our time to be captured by the much truer picture of a bewildered and groping humanity, a humanity born to a high destiny, called to sonship of God, but held in fetters and chains by poverty, by disease, by ignorance and by sin, and waiting for its deliverance. If we could plant in men's minds this truer picture of the meaning of this strange and tragic scene of human life, we should learn to think of all our fellowmen as potential comrades in the great fight against these enemies of human life, disease, and poverty, and ignorance, and sin, as potential allies in the common search of humanity for truth and beauty and goodness, and as companions in that long, upward march toward the City of God.

Now, that is the difference that Christ will bring to us, if we allow His outlook upon life to dominate our thoughts. That is the great and high task to which we are called. The meaning of this Convention is that by the grace of God we should go away committed, dedicated to Him to change the mind of our time, to root out of men's minds these false ideas which dominate them and to plant in their minds those truer ideas of human relationship which we have received from our Lord Jesus Christ.

The future of civilization itself depends upon whether we can achieve that task, or whether we can make the mind of our time more humane, more Christian, richer in its conceptions of human relationships, and the power to do that comes from the fact that we have seen the truth and the glory of God in the face of Jesus Christ, Our Lord.

THE AIM AND MOTIVE OF FOREIGN MISSIONS
THE REVEREND E. STANLEY JONES, D.D., INDIA

There is a good deal of misunderstanding as to what constitutes the aim and motive of foreign missions; and there was never a time when we needed more to clarify the issue. We are told that we are "international meddlers," that we are creed-mongers to the East, that we are the religious aspect of imperialism, that we are the forerunners of capitalism, that we represent a great hunger to see an ecclesiasticism prevail around the world. There was never a better time to face the problem and to face it squarely; and, under the closest scrutiny to tell what we are after, what we are trying to produce, just what we are trying to give.

There are two places where we can battle this thing through. One is in the quiet study, where we brood over human motives and human ends to find out where we should emerge. The other place is in the thick of the battle, in the struggle of interests where ideas and civilizations meet. I have come to my own personal conclusion in the thick of the battle. I have been brought to certain ends and aims and motives by the sheer exigencies of the battle itself.

When I first went to India I was trying to hold a very long line, one that reached clear from Genesis to Revelation and on to Western civilization and the Christian church. I was bobbing up and down the line, fighting behind Moses and Abraham and Jesus and Paul and Western civilization and the Christian church. There was no well-defined issue. The non-Christian invariably pitched the battle at Moses or at Western civilization. He always seemed to get away from the central thing.

Then I saw that I could shorten my line, that I could refuse to know anything before the non-Christian world save Jesus Christ and Him crucified, to take my stand there and make Him the sum total of the aim and the motive of my message. Then it seemed that the way was cleared, that missionaries were not sent to make converts into pale copies of the West, but were there to respect anything that was fine in their civilization, contributing to their struggle upward after God. We were there not to wipe out that struggle, but to give them a person—that person, Christ. We were to ask them to interpret Him through their own national genius and history and to express Him in a living, first-hand and real way.

Then the issue began to clear in my mind. May I say that up to that time we missionaries in India seemed to have been up against a stone wall. Christian missions seemed to have come up to a certain plane of the thinking of the educated mind without penetration. We were making great progress among the outcasts, but we were scarcely making any progress among the educated classes; but when we clarified the issue and made this the one issue, there was a new burst of power. We found ourselves in the midst of a revival of interest in Jesus as a person far beyond the border of the Christian church, captivating the mind and thought of the East. Men said, "Is this the issue?" They had seen standing amid the shadows of Western civilization a Person. That Person greatly attracted them, but they thought they would have to take both, if they took either, if they took Christ, they would have to take Western civilization also.

But when the revelation dawned upon the minds of the East, as it is dawning more and more, that they can have Christ with as little or as much of Western civilization as they desire, there came a new outbreak of spiritual power and interest in Jesus Christ that far surpasses anything of which we had dreamed or thought.

Some time ago, in thinking over this matter, I tried to compare what the different religious systems tried to produce, what the aim and end of the whole progress has been. Here was Greece; Greece said, "Be moderate; know thyself"; Confucianism says, "Be superior, correct thyself"; Buddhism says, "Be disillusioned, annihilate thyself"; Hinduism says, "Be separated, merge thyself"; Mohammedanism says, "Be submissive, bend thyself"; Shintoism says, "Be loyal, suppress thyself"; Judaism says, "Be holy, conform thyself"; Modern materialism says, "Be industrious, enjoy thyself"; Modern dilettantism says, "Be broad, cultivate thyself"; Christianity says, "Be Christlike, give thyself." Now, if the end in view of Christian missions is to produce Christlike character that it may give itself as Jesus gave Himself, I suggest that we have no reason to apologize in the slightest degree for that end and motive, since there is nothing higher for God or man than to be Christlike.

The end of Christian missions then is not to propagate Western civilization around the world nor to project an ecclesiasticism throughout the world, but we are in a land frankly and without apology, openly and without the slightest hesitation to say that we think it is worth while to make men like Jesus Christ.

We think, first of all, that this is a worthy end for our own lives. We ourselves would like to be like Him. We too would like to catch His spirit, His thought, His mind, His purpose, and His power. We too, would like to give ourselves after the manner in which He gave Himself. If the end of Christianity is to produce men who will catch the Spirit of Jesus Christ and will give themselves as He gave Himself, I see no slightest reason in the world why we should hesitate for one single moment to make that the end and motive of our lives and of Christian missionary endeavor. For in Him I see the summing up of human life.

Jesus is not a way of life. He is life itself. He came not to bring a set of truths to set alongside of other truths. Jesus came to be truth itself. In him I see truth looking out at me from sad eyes and touching me with redemptive hands, loving me with a warm, loving heart. Jesus came not to bring a religion, as Dean Inge says, "to set alongside of other religions"; Jesus came to be a religion itself. If we go deep enough into religion, we must stand face to face with Jesus, who is religion itself in its final expression.

We have no apology whatever in regard to this as the aim and motive and end of our missionary life. Jesus sums up the finest of the East and the finest of the West, and supplies a supreme motive for Christian missions.

Greece said there were three things that caught her attention in worship, the good, the beautiful and the true. That sums up the finest thinking of the West. The East, brooding over these same problems, has come to the conclusion that there are three other ways out, namely the gyan marg, the bhakti marg and the karm marg. The gyan marg is the way of knowledge. The bhakti marg is the way of devotion. The karm marg is the way of action or works. But Jesus said, standing midway between East and West, "I am the way, the truth and the life." I am the way—that is, the good. I am the truth, that is, the true. I am the life—that is, the beautiful. He is what the Greeks unconsciously desired.

Turning to the East he says, I am the way—that is the karm marg—a way of life, a method of acting. I am the truth— that is the gyan marg, the way of knowledge. I am the life— that is the bhakti marg or the way of devotion. He is what India has unconsciously desired. Jesus then stands midway between East and West and fulfils every thing that life strives for, and East and West will one day find in Him what they need.

I was talking one day to a group of men. A lawyer rose in the crowd and said, "Mr. Jones, is that what you are after? Do you want to give us Christ and Christ alone?" I said "My brother, I have got nothing else to give. That is what I want to give." Then he said, "I do not see how we Indians can object. I thought you had come here to wipe out our whole past and all our culture. If your aim is to give us Christ, to let us take Him and interpret Him through our own genius and life, I do not see how we Indians can oppose." I said, "My brother, we have no other motive whatever."

When we put our finger upon that one single motive and let Jesus touch men with his own vital presence and power, there comes a new vitality into the whole work of evangelization, for Jesus appeals to the soul as light appeals to the eye, as truth fits the conscience, as beauty speaks to the aesthetic nature. Christ and the soul were made for one another; and round the whole world, if we can bring a soul into contact with Jesus Christ, we will find that it sees in Him not a way of life but life itself, not a truth but truth itself, the one thing that life craves.

I was in a group with some prominent men one day. I turned to them and said, "My brothers (they were all non-Christians), here are 60,000,000 outcasts. We want to raise them, to lift them higher."

I didn't talk as though India was foreign to me, for, frankly, India is no longer foreign to me. I was born here in America. I love her rocks and rills, her woods and templed hills, but India has become my home, India's people are my people, her problems are my problems, her future is my future. I would like to wear her sins upon my heart, if I could lift her to my Savior. I said to these men, "Brothers, what are we going to do with these 60,000,000 outcasts? They are a millstone around our national neck, and we can never be strong until we lift them." A non-Christian arose and said, "Sir, it will take a Christ to lift them." I said, "Yes, my brother, a Christ to lift them and to lift me and you and to lift the rest of us. I see no other way." That non-Christian brother, standing amid his problems and searching for some redemptive force put his finger upon Christ as the one way out.

Nine years ago Dr. John R. Mott was speaking in Victoria Hall in Madras. In the midst of his address, he used the name of Christ. The audience hissed him. Nine years later we were in that same hall for six nights with one topic: Jesus Christ and Him crucified. The crowd increased, until on the last night people were standing around the windows and doors and everywhere. That last night I did something I had never dared to do before. I asked men publicly, openly and frankly to give themselves to Jesus Christ. Generally the best we had been able to do, hitherto, was to take a man away privately for such testimony in order to shield him and shelter him from the storm that would break upon him; but, that night, I said "Brothers, I have nothing to cover; will you frankly and openly give yourselves to Jesus Christ? Will those who do so come and take these front seats?" If one had come, I should have been grateful. If five had come, I should have been overwhelmed. But that night between 100 and 150 came from among those leading men, and took their stands frankly and openly as followers of Jesus Christ in the very hall, where nine years before the name of Christ had been hissed.

It was not the difference in the speakers, for every thing was in favor of the first speaker, but in the meantime a new revelation has dawned upon the mind of India, that Christ belongs to her need and to her future as much as He belongs to the West. That new revelation is bringing us face to face with one of the most wonderful facts that the Christian church has ever faced, namely, that Christianity is breaking out far beyond the borders of the Christian Church. The question that we must face in this Convention is this: is the Christian Church going to be big enough and great enough and Christlike enough to be the medium through which Christianity will express itself before the non-Christian world? If so, there must be a finer and more utter abandon to Jesus Christ than there has ever been in the past, less of the supercilious, less of racial patronage, less of that bending over the East and saying, "I come to do you good," and more of the catching of the spirit of service that animated Jesus, and of the feeling of real brotherhood that throbbed in His every act.

The leading social thinker of India said to me, before I left India, "Mr. Jones, Western civilization was never at a lower ebb in our estimation, but your missionaries never stood higher. You come not to exploit us but to serve us." This man put his finger upon the touchstone of the future. If one goes to serve, if he goes in the spirit of Jesus Christ, the whole East is wide open, there will be a universal response to that touch of service. One who goes with the thought of patronage finds the East closed to him.

A friend of mine was talking to a Brahman gentleman, who said, "I do not like the Christ of your creeds and the Christ of your churches." This friend with swift intuition replied," If you do not like the Christ of our creeds and the Christ of our churches, how would you like the Christ of the Indian road?" The Brahman gentleman thought a moment—the Christ of the Indian road, can we picture him, with long flowing garments alongside the road with the crowd about him, touching blind eyes, and letting the light stream in, his hands upon the heads of unclean lepers, sending them back to healing and to health, announcing the good tidings of a new kingdom to stricken humanity, and telling of the coming brotherhood that is to be, dying upon a wayside cross for men, and rising again? Such a Christ would be one with the Christ of the Galilean road. We must take our Christ to be naturalized upon the Indian road, and upon Chinese pathways and upon the highways of Japan, letting every nation find in Him the true expression of its own national outreaching of heart and see in Him what they have craved and longed for through the weary centuries.

I was talking to Mr. Gandhi one day. I said to him, "Mahatma Gandhi, I am very anxious to see Christianity naturalized in India, not something identified with foreign people and with foreign governments, but a part of the national life of India, contributing its power to India's uplift. What would you suggest that we do, in order to make that possible?" He thought a moment and then replied: "If you are going to do that I would suggest to you four things: First, that all you Christians, missionaries and all, must begin to live more like Christ." I knew that he was not speaking alone. Through his eyes three hundred and twenty million people were looking, and through his voice those millions were speaking. The leading non-Christian of the world there looked me in the face and said, "If you would come to us, you must come in the spirit of Jesus Christ, and if you come in His spirit we cannot resist you." I do not know of any greater or more compelling challenge that should send us to our knees in humble search after a finer, deeper, more Christlike living than that simple phrase, "Be more like Jesus Christ."

"Secondly," he said, "I would suggest that you must practice your religion without adulterating it or toning it down." Now, I was amazed at that remark. I would have thought that any getting together might mean compromise and toning down in order that we should meet the non-Christian world half way. But let me say this: I do not believe that the non-Christian world wants a toned-down Christ. I do not believe that the non-Christian world wants the heart of the gospel taken away. The non-Christian world has discovered its high challenge, its amazing appeal, its mighty call, and it says to us, "Do not adulterate these or tone them down; take Christianity in its rugged simplicity and in its high demands and live out its life; then we cannot resist you."

Are we doing this? Some one has justly declared that we are inoculating the world with a mild form of Christianity so that it is practically becoming immune to the real thing. Why should we offer the East a mild form of Christianity? I am not interested in giving India a mild form of Christianity. I would wish her to take Christ just as He is in His mighty, saving, overwhelming power to change human nature and to make men new. I would offer the real thing, expressed in utter abandon to Jesus.

"Thirdly," he said to me, "I would suggest to you that you put your emphasis upon love, for love is a central thing in Christianity." Note that the Mahatma did not mean love as a sentiment but love as a working force. If God is love, then the highest power is love; the highest power of omnipotence was revealed at Calvary, and the one way out of our world's difficulties is just to catch the spirit of love that Jesus Christ exhibited and to embody it in race relationships, in international relationships, in every single relationship of life.

"Fourthly," he said, " I would suggest to you that you study the non-Christian religions more sympathetically to find out the good that is in them, in order to have a more sympathetic approach to their peoples." He was quite right. We should be unafraid of truth found anywhere because Christ is the fulfillment of that truth. It is sure to be a signpost that points toward Jesus who is truth itself.

Put your finger again upon those four suggestions of the Mahatma: Live more like Jesus Christ; practice Christianity without adulterating it or toning it down; put your emphasis upon love; be unafraid of truth anywhere. The leading non-Christian of the world says to us, "If you will come to us in this spirit and in this way we cannot resist you." As a Christian, that challenges me; it sends me to my knees to search for a finer, bigger and greater life. May this missionary Convention mean, to every one of us, a deeper searching of motive and of life. We cannot go to the Orient and glibly say, "We give you Christ"; we must rather say, "We give you Christ expressed through our lives. We give you Christ, not merely described in a book, but written in looks and outlook and in the very temper of our lives." We find the East helpful as a teacher. Many of us are better men because we have been in contact with its gentle heart; but it is our honest conviction that the one thing that India and the whole East needs is just what we have our finger upon this morning, namely, Christ Himself.

A leading non-Christian said to me, one day, "Can you put your finger, Mr. Jones, upon something that you have in your religion that we do not have in ours?" I said, "Shall I tell you in a word?" He said, "If you can." I said, "I can. You have no Christ." That is the heartbreaking and pathetic lack of the non-Christian world. Its peoples have no Christ. I see no one anywhere around the world who is getting along well without Christ. I see no hope for any one around the world except along this one way of Jesus Christ. I make no apology, then, for being a Christian missionary, since the making known of Jesus Christ is the supreme and controlling motive of the missionary's life.

I was, one day, in a great meeting of non-Christians. The judge of a native state was the chairman of the meeting. When I got through my appeal, he said this, "You have heard tonight what it is to be a Christian. If to be a Christian is to be like Christ, then I hope you will all be Christians in your lives, though I am not one myself. I see nothing better than for you to be Christians, if to be a Christian is to make you like Jesus Christ." Then he turned and in a very gracious but very compelling manner said, "May I say one word to you who are Christians here? If you Christians had always lived more like Jesus Christ, if you would live and talk and act like Him and have His outlook on life, this process of conversion would go on much more rapidly."

If this Convention will mark a new era of emphasis upon Jesus Christ, not an emasculated Jesus, but one able to do all things that human nature needs to have done, a Christ that is sufficient and compelling; and if out of this convention will go a new Christocentric emphasis in this whole missionary propaganda, then I believe there will be a new burst of spiritual power around the world. I believe that obstacles that have looked like stone walls will suddenly reveal open doors, for Christ, the risen and triumphant Lord, can enter through doors that have been closed. He can find His way into the crannies of human life and can meet men face to face in a new and living way.

I was talking to the leading philosopher of India, a man deeply read in the philosophy of East and West. I said to him, "Professor, I want you to tell me what you think of Christ." I knew that his criticism would be keen, for he was a very keen-minded man. I steeled myself for the shock of his criticism. He said, "Mr. Jones, we had high ideas of God before Jesus came, but Jesus is the highest expression of God that we have ever seen; he is conquering us by the sheer force of his own personality even against our wills."

O majestic Christ, thou who art walking across the nations, and bidding for the heart of the world, give us something of Thy touch, Thy presence and Thy power.

I listened to another address by a leading lawyer of Calcutta. The man stood there in Eastern garb, in the simplicity that the East so dearly loves; and addressed the audience on this topic, "The Inescapable Christ." He said, "We have not been able to escape Him. He confronts us. There was a time when our hearts were bitter and sore against Him, but we have not been able to escape Him. He is melting our hearts by the sheer force of His own Person."

May I speak out of the seventeen years' experience that I have spent in India in evangelistic work among these leading men. I see no other way out. There are scars on every word that I am saying just now. I see no other way out for East or West than the way that Jesus offers, namely, Himself. I see no other hope for human character save to be made like Jesus Christ. I see no other way out of the world-troubled situation than the way that Jesus would point. I see no other way except Jesus, who Himself is the Way, the Truth and the Life.

A Hindu professor in South India once said to me, "My study of modern history has shown me that there is a moral pivot in the world. The best life of the East and the West is more and more revolving around that moral pivot. That moral pivot is the person and life of Jesus. Around that center the best life of the East and the West is revolving. If we have slipped off a bit into denominationalism and denominational propaganda merely, if we have felt that our business was to create a kind of supremacy of the white race through Christianity, if we have got off the center a bit and have gone off into other interests, then this conference should bring us back to that center. Let us work out from that center to our problems. He must be real to us. We cannot talk about Christ in the East, we have got to take Him; we can't talk about God, we must bring Him.

A leading man, a thinker of India, said to me, "My brother, what do you think of Jesus?" He said, "Mr. Jones, there is nobody else who is seriously bidding for the heart of the world except Jesus Christ. There is nobody else on the field." Really there is no one else seriously bidding for the heart of the world except Jesus Christ. The missionary enterprise has many critics; but no real rival; there are other great religious founders, but none with such an aim, namely, to make this world a Christlike world, giving itself for the sake of all others, as Jesus Christ gave Himself for the sake of us all. If the motive and aim of Christian missions is to produce this sort of Christlike character, I have no apology for being a missionary.

INTERCESSION: THE TRANSFORMING POWER OF CHRIST

PRESIDENT W. DOUGLAS MACKENZIE, D.D., HARTFORD, CONNECTICUT

We have been holding high fellowship this morning. We have been dealing with the highest relations of the human spirit. We have been trying to understand a little of those relationships both towards God and between man and man. We have allowed ourselves to place no limits upon our conception of that human spirit. We have accompanied with it, as it appears among primitive men in the jungle. We have held fellowship with the cultured Eastern saint in his lonely search for God. We have accompanied with our brother the missionary of Christ, whether like His Master He is speaking to the individual or toiling with the multitude. We have thought of the church of Christ lavishing itself upon humanity and finding itself again, like our Lord Himself, confronted with the fierce forces that are resident in this heart of man, making havoc of his earthly life, and darkening the future.

We have allowed no limits to the range of our great task or to our conception of the power of God over this human nature of ours. We have watched Him as he came in the person of His Son, Jesus Christ, to the individual seeking to enter into fellowship with the lowliest and lifted him to the loftiest of human experiences. We have stood with the toiler among the masses both at home and abroad, as he tried to deal with the great and tragic divisions that exist even within the national lives of men, class against class, interest clashing with interest; and we have once more tried to see the living God in Jesus Christ entering into that strife with his own sorrow and his ancient love, to make peace.

We have watched Him once more dealing with nations and with governments of the world, and we have remembered Him, who is called in the last book of the New Testament, "the ruler of the kings of the earth," and our hearts have been lifted with that strange pride and exaltation known only in all history to the Christian spirit, when we have said to ourselves, "He is our King; and the Lord God Almighty, the source of all being, is speaking in Him to all the kings of the earth, to the governments of all the nations of the world."

And we have been holding fellowship with the missionary, the man, the woman, whom we have sent out from these shores all over the world, (18,000 of them from North America alone), all entering into the fellowship of human hearts, and all of them living in the fellowship of the living God in Jesus Christ.

I have been asking myself, sitting here, What is the tremendous power that is resident in that Name of Jesus Christ? What is the secret of this strange, unmeasured influence, which He is exercising over all men? The teacher? Yes. The prophet? Yes. The friend? Yes. The healer of diseases? Yes, all these and more than all these. For our source of power lies in the fact that in Jesus Christ God has entered into the fullest, the most complete fellowship with man of which we can conceive. It is the act of God in Christ that redeems the world. Behind that name of Christ there is always that mystery of God. When Gandhi, and Indian professors, and learned men say, "He is our Master," somehow through the word "He" their spirit is feeling up toward the mystery that is beyond and hidden, to find in Jesus Christ the living God that speaks in Him.

And when we remember that the great and secret power of the gospel of Christ lies in the fact of God's fellowship with man in Him, we ask ourselves the next natural question, How has that fellowship been manifested? Where is it in the story of Jesus Christ that the fellowship of God with human nature comes to its climax? Where is it that at last we find the fountains of eternal power over the souls of men opened and the waters of life flowing over the deserts? Where is it? The answer is obvious, for we know that there is carried over the world a certain symbol that gives the answer. We know, though we Protestants carry no crucifix upon our persons, we know that in our imaginings and in our words there goes everywhere, with every kind of missionary, into every corner of the world, that word, that picture, that symbol, that revelation of God which we call the Cross of Jesus Christ.

To worshippers at the stately altars of the East, in presence of the crescent and the cruel scimitar of the Mohammedan, before the dull imaginations of primitive tribes, 18,000 missionaries today, representing these churches of North America, are presenting this cross of Jesus Christ.

He died on a cross and in His death God entered into the deepest conceivable fellowship with the human spirit, that spirit even in its sin, in its blindness and weakness. There He entered into all the darkness, all the crime, all the horror, all the shame of human nature and of human history. He came indeed, that He might serve. And the world likes to think of Christ as the servant of humanity. But He served even unto a death that He called "ransom for many." In that fellowship of God with the human spirit we find the secret of the transforming power of Jesus Christ. No Oriental philosopher surely ever forgets when he speaks his admiration for Christ the Teacher, the Master, the Leader, the Inspirer of men, that Christ was crucified, that the world did Him to death, that God, His Father, allowed Him, the Prince of Glory on that wondrous Cross, to die.

What is that fellowship of God with humanity on the Cross which has changed the very name of God for us all and changed the very name of man for God? There are a hundred and one theories, are there not, of what the Cross did, of what the theologians call the "atonement"? Somehow or other, when I read any one, even the poorest, of these, I always find there is some truth there; and when I read the best and the greatest, I lay down the book and say, "Still, still, there is more in the Cross of Christ than the greatest has ever seen; something there in that communion of the eternal with the temporal, of the infinite with the finite, of the holy with the sinful, of God and man, in the mingled horror and glory of that death,—something there which will always elude and surpass our utmost theories of what the Cross means."

We have to think of it largely in pictures, if ever our theories are to become food for the soul. Let me just name three such pictures, to make the divine power of the Cross vivid for us today. The first is from our Christian lyrist when he surveys the wondrous Cross. "See," he says, "See from his head, his hands, his feet." What is it that he bids us see? It is not just physical life-blood, but the life-blood of the soul. It is "sorrow and love flow mingling down." Whose sorrow, whose love? The sorrow of God, the love of God, before the eyes of men—flowing, mingled in the red life-blood of Jesus Christ.

> "Did e'er such love and sorrow meet,
> Or thorns compose so rich a crown?"

There is the redeeming power of the eternal God.

Then another picture. One of the ancient families of Scotland has a strange device, a crest that I often have brooded over, for it is the crest of my mother's clan. In the center of it there is a red, red heart, life-blood showing in that heart. Above it there is a glorious, glittering crown of majesty; below it is a scroll, and on the scroll is the word, "Forward." On each end of the scroll there is a wing, and the two wings seem to be carrying that crest FORWARD, the red heart and the glittering crown between them. That has been to me for many, many years, a picture of what happened when God entered into that intimate fellowship with man on Calvary. The red blood revealed and proved for ever the sorrow and love of God; and through that sorrow and love came his power, his crown rights over the human spirit; and the wings of the Divine Spirit are carrying that message right around the world, "forward" into light. "Your God," it says to every man, "the One Being that made us all, the living God is the God of the red heart and the conquering crown. Forward into the eternal life." That is the atonement.

Another picture is from a very recent and tremendous event in which many of you shared. For I stood, last Saturday morning, and watched that awe-striking transaction of God in the great eclipse. When the weird light broke upon the buildings and streets around me, my soul seemed to shudder with affright, in sympathy even with the animal world. And as I gazed at the sun, suddenly, when that moment of supreme darkness swept over me, and the dark, obliterating moon was centered on the sun, the corona broke out—the corona that is always there, the colors that have been there since the sun began its history, which I had never seen before. But it needed the dark, black, centered mass of the moon to come between me and the glory of the sun that I might see the corona of the sun.

And methinks something like that was what happened when Peter, and James, and John, and Mary the mother of Jesus, and others saw Him die on the Cross. It was all black, and all despair. The night had fallen upon their souls, and no light seemed to be possible again for their eyes, no hope for their shattered hearts.

A few days later and more clearly a few weeks later they learned to see in the new world. And now when they gazed back upon that Cross as they had seen it through their streaming eyes and with breaking hearts,—when they saw it now, their souls saw it in a great vision of joy. They looked upon the blackness, and it seemed that that which had obliterated God revealed him. Behold around the Cross of Jesus Christ the corona of God!

So for us, and for every missionary, and for every hearer of the gospel throughout the world, there is always this story of Jesus, who died,—having lived, having taught, having mastered human life as a human being, and then died, crucified. Wherever the story is told, somehow or other the eyes of human beings see the glory, the majesty of the sorrow of the Eternal God coming home, home to their own hearts; the eternal love of the everlasting Creator and God, lifting, lifting each individual and all men and all their fellowships into the light of His holiness and His love.

We now come to pray; pray we must. Let us do it at the foot of the Cross that has become a throne, at the foot of the throne of God who revealed His sorrow for us, His love for us, for human beings there, supremely, tragically, triumphantly, and made that darkness and that story the pivot of the history of the world. Let us pray!

O Thou Living God, Eternal Father, in whom our very being is grounded, in whom every living man in the world today has his existence, before whom the darkest and the best are present as living children of Thine eternal love, we pray to Thee, Thou hearer and answerer of prayer, Thou creator of the spirit that must speak with Thee, Thou awakener of the desires that must rise to Thee.

We beseech Thee to look down upon this Convention. Pour, this morning, Thine own spirit upon all our hearts, that spirit of sorrow and of love, of personal penitence and personal confidence, of personal humility and yet of personal and ambitious devotion.

Do Thou look down upon all who represent Thee through our churches in the far lands. Grant unto them the spirit of Jesus Christ in a very real, in a very actual, in a very powerful manner. Grant them to realize that their words are the channels of the life of God; that their own lives are the manifestation of the sorrow and the love of God; that their manner of ministry must be a continuous revelation of the meaning of Calvary, and the presence of the throne of Christ.

Do Thou draw them into deeper fellowship with Thyself that they may be thus manifestations of Thee, O holy and loving God, to the hearts of all men among whom they labor.

We pray that Thou wilt comfort them in their distractions and perplexity; that Thou, O Christ, who hast faced crowds that hated Thee and derided Thee, that Thou wilt be with them when crowds deride them and when they face eyes that are shot with hate. We pray that Thou wilt be with them in the joy of delivering Thy message, that it may come pure and straight from the fellowship of God with man in Jesus Christ, His present fellowship with that man, that woman, who speaks the word to others. We pray that Thou wilt be with them in their own secret and inner life, giving them the joy and the reality of that divine fellowship.

O God, who didst so love the world, who hast not withheld the greatest of all conceivable deeds of love from man, do Thou look down in Thy mercy upon the nations of the world, upon all the distractions and class hatreds within Christendom. O God, let them not forget that the centuries have fled, and that Christ's name has been stamped upon their names. Behold we confess with shame and sorrow the divisions and the hatreds, which mar the name of Christendom.

O Lord, forgive; cleanse the heart of Christendom, that we may be ashamed that the dominion of Christ has not been fully accepted even among ourselves.

We pray Thee, O Father and Lord of all mankind, to look down upon the nations of the world Thou has created, all the races. In the mystery of Thy purpose they have been divided by color, and by residence, and by all the environing experiences of their nativity. We pray that Thou wilt overcome all the bitterness and strife which spring from these differences and separations, O Thou Son of God, who lovest every color Thou hast made, who seest through it to the heart that makes us all one, who didst shed Thy blood for the blood that is in the heart of all humanity. Do Thou draw the races to an understanding of their relations in Thy presence, in Thy name, that they may know how to live with one another in the distinctions of earth, and in the unities of heaven.

We pray Thee, Lord, to look down upon all preachers and teachers of Thy truth at home and abroad, giving to them the end and the motive that comes from Thy heart. O Thou God and Father of our Lord Jesus Christ, grant unto them not to be ashamed at any time of the Gospel which is the power of God, the power that is able to save human nature in every individual instance of it, and in all masses of it, even to the end of the world.

Heavenly Father, beyond all our dreaming and asking, beyond all our vision and faith, do Thou continue to act. For we know not what to ask for our world, but we feel the presence now of a spirit wiser, greater, than ours, that with divine groanings which cannot be uttered, pleads with Thee, Thy very heart, O God, speaking of Thyself in our hearts.

Answer these prayers; fulfill these purposes; reveal these glories, establish these kingships over the hearts of men. All this we ask in the Name of Him who is our Lord, and the Lord of all men, our Savior, and the Savior of all the generations, even Jesus Christ, Son of Man and Son of God.

THE PROCLAMATION OF THE GOSPEL

THE GOSPEL IN A GREAT ORIENTAL CITY
THE REVEREND WILLIAM AXLING, D.D., TOKYO

The dreamy, tranquil Tokyo of fiction and fancy is gone. In its place there is a city of two and one-half million people. It is a city that holds its head high, as the proud capital of Japan's empire of 4,000 sea-girt islands and the metropolis of the Orient. Japan is a fast moving nation, and Tokyo is the pace-setter. In the far-flung fields of culture, commerce, industry and politics Tokyo sets the ideals which sway men's minds and manners all over the Empire. The life of Tokyo colors the life of the entire nation.

Here have come to the birth all those movements that have created modern Japan and have made her mighty. More than this, Tokyo stands at the cross-roads of the nations. Here meet the surging tides of life that sweep in from the Occident and from the Orient. Here are focussed all those creative as well as destructive forces which flourish in the cities of both the Eastern and the Western world. Here the good out of these two civilizations is at its best and the bad at its worst.

Into this teeming, throbbing city, with its ancient scenes and setting, its modern movements and life, the gospel of Jesus Christ has come as a challenging dynamic force. It followed the age-long course of first coming to grips with individuals, here one, there one, until pivotal personalities, transformed by its power and incarnating its ideals and its spirit, were gradually planted all up and down this cosmopolitan center's crowded life. These twice-born personalities project their potent selves upon their environment, and lo! the age-long miracle repeats itself.

Kobayashi, captain of industry and king in the dentifrice industry, is a typical example. He became a Christian, adventuring with Christian ideals in Tokyo's industrial and commercial life. His business was transformed from a mad race after gold to a far-flung arm of opportunity to serve. In his factory there are hours not only for work, but for prayer and for play. Fair hours, a living wage, profit-sharing, educational and recreational privileges made his concern a pioneer in applying the Jesus way of life to Japan's new industrial age.

In his relation with the customer and the public Kobayashi's master motive is not to get but to give. He looks upon his business as a God-opened channel through which to benefit the other man. Onward he goes blazing a shining trail for Christ right through the heart of Japan's industrial world.

Other industrial concerns have come under the spell of the same Christ and the same ideals. The Mikimoto Pearl Concern, far famed for its cultural pearls, is pioneering in the same high Christlike fashion. The Fuji Spinning Company and the Kanegafuchi Spinning Concern, two of the largest industrial organizations in the Orient, though not entirely under Christian management, have thrown open the doors of their manifold plants to a straight-from-the-shoulder presentation of the gospel to their hundreds of thousands of employees. Gradually the leaven is spreading and all along its path is bringing lives and commercial concerns under its power and blazoning new ideals and new standards across Japan's industrial sky.

It works, the gospel works, it works wonders in this work-a-day world of Tokyo. Converts from one of the Fuji Spinning Company's factories have multiplied, so that on their own initiative they have launched a church organization, manned by their own men, supported by their own means, and are aggressively attacking the task of evangelizing their factory-fellows and their neighborhood.

Some two hundred churches, scattered like beacon lights across Tokyo's seething sea of life, are carrying forward the preaching and teaching program of the Christian faith. All of these are manned by Japanese pastors, many of whom, in culture and character, in brains and faith, are the peers of their colleagues in the Western world. Many of their churches are self-governing, self-supporting and self-propagating. Among them the spirit of cooperation is strong. Repeatedly, they line up as a solid phalanx, advance with a united front and carry on city-wide evangelistic campaigns and public service efforts. Some twenty Christian schools are annually throwing 8,000 of Tokyo's finest sons and fairest daughters into the Christian mould and planting them as potent personalities all up and down the Empire.

Institutions and organizations like the Tokyo Misaki Tabernacle, the Christian Center of the Woman's Christian Temperance Union, Mr. Kagawa's Christian Settlement, the Salvation Army and others, less ambitious but not less effective in their field, with seven-days-a-week programs planned to reach the last man, woman and child, are digging in and laying siege to whole communities and using the method of mass attack.

The Young Men's and Young Women's Christian Associations, the Waseda Brotherhood and other groups are in the campaigns for special classes, pushing the battleline into the city's great student centers and into the fields where Tokyo's young men and women flock.

The gospel in Tokyo finds the child heart wide open. Approximately two hundred and fifty Sunday-schools are turning the children Christward. When the world's Sunday School Convention met in Tokyo, a few years ago, 25,000 of Tokyo's children turned back the thundering traffic and sang their triumphant way through the city's most crowded thoroughfares. Not only Tokyo, but far and wide Japan, wide-eyed and wondering, stopped and listened to that joyous, irrepressible song. Those of understanding hearts realized that the gospel of Christ had laid hold of the very heart strings of the capital and of the land.

In September, 1923, when twenty-seven square miles of this fair city were turned into earthquake-wracked and fire-swept debris, the Christian forces made a forward run with the flag of Christ and planted it right in the citadel of Tokyo's child world. The city authorities saw the children, 200,000 strong, sitting among the ashes and the ruins, sad and dejected beyond their young years. Fearful of the effect of this on their plastic mental and spiritual life, they sought for a way to broadcast hope and cheer across that wreckage and to turn the children's hearts again to music and to song. But where could hope and joy be found in such a dark and tragic hour? Where, except in the hope-giving and song-inspiring gospel? Only the triumphant, radiant, singing Christ could answer that high challenge. Instinctively, they turned to Him. And ere many weeks had passed, the educational authorities of that great Oriental city flung open the doors for expert tellers of Bible stories and masters of Christian song to team up and go from primary school to primary school, giving the Christian message in song and story in every one of Tokyo's hundreds of schools of this grade.

Strange though it sounds, even this is not the end of the story. A group of Christian Japanese laymen, sensing this strategic opportunity, have launched a supporters' organization, and purpose to put this unique work on a permanent and continuous basis. Osaka with its 1,500,000 people had pioneered in this field with Christian laymen as promoters. Thus it happens that in Japan's two largest cities the gospel has found a triumphant entry into the public primary schools. This forward march of the gospel into the heart of a nation's child world probably cannot be paralleled in any age or in any other land. Certainly it cannot be paralleled on the pages of the history of missions in foreign lands.

The gospel in Tokyo has fired the souls of her native sons with a passion to broadcast its story. Kagawa, the apostle to the poor, Kanamori, the Moody of Japan, Kimura, Japan's Billy Sunday, Colonel Yamamuro, the Japanese General Booth, Bishop

Uzaki of the United Methodist Church of Japan, Pastor Uemura, editor and educator, Dr. Kosaki, dean of Japan's pastors, Uchimura, the Christian mystic, and a great host of others are carrying the gospel like a flame of fire all up and down this city's thronging ways.

There is no area in Tokyo's life where this conquering gospel has not won its victories. In the courts of culture it has its devotees. Christian professors are conspicuous leaders on the faculties of the Imperial and Waseda Universities. Other institutions and professional schools have an outstanding group of Christians on their teaching staff. Many of these Christian professors are national figures, exerting a potent Christian influence far beyond the confines of the nation's capital.

In all of these institutions there are great groups of Christian students bringing the impact of the gospel to bear upon Tokyo's vast student host, an army 100,000 strong. These Christian students are the flower of the nation's youth today, and will be its leaders tomorrow.

In the political world are Christian men who are mighty; Matsumoto, Tagawa, Ozawa are but a few of Tokyo's political leaders who sit in Parliament, who make the Empire's laws, and from this high source bring the impact of Christian ideals to bear upon the city's and the nation's life.

The city of Tokyo has in recent years launched an unbelievable number of welfare institutions as a part of its municipal program. And it is a notorious fact that the army of welfare workers connected with these centers is led and honeycombed with men and women who were chosen because they had learned from Jesus the genius of service and have caught from Him its inward spirit.

The gospel has also captured the pen of men who loom large in the world of letters. Three of the city's leading daily papers are wholly or in part under Christian control. Christian ideas and ideals have permeated the capital's literature. Of late years Mr. Kagawa's Christian novels "Across the Death Line" and "Piercing the Sun" have been the best sellers at Tokyo's innumerable book stalls. Translations of such books as the Fosdick series and Papini's Life of Christ have had an unprecedented sale.

The gospel has focussed its white light on moral standards and sanctions that wreck character and undermine society. These standards and sanctions had gone on unchallenged and unquestioned across the years until the gospel came to Tokyo. Under its white light these practices hoary with age stand challenged and ashamed and the fight to outlaw them is on.

The gospel in Tokyo has passed on to the dying ethnic faiths a new lease of life. Its impact upon them is causing them to dream new dreams, to think in new terms and to speak a new language. Buddhism and Shintoism are throbbing with new ideas, new ideals, a new program, and a new life, all of which are borrowings from the gospel.

The gospel in Tokyo has come to grips with the most challenging and baffling task of our time—the adjustment of race prejudice and of racial pride. It is blasting the color line and laying the foundation for a world brotherhood, rooted in God and centered in Jesus Christ.

Following the enactment of America's exclusion law a small group of Christian men in Tokyo attempted to start a movement to oust American missions and missionaries. In response the Japanese Christians arose in a body in protest. They declared that in the Christian brotherhood there should be no color, nor race, nor national distinctions. They insisted that Christians of all lands are brothers in a great world brotherhood and colleagues in a great world task, and the movement died before it was born.

I shall never forget standing a few days after the earthquake and the fire in the door of our gutted Tabernacle in Tokyo with a prayer in my heart and a question mark stalking through my brain. The whole situation seemed appalling. I was wondering what to do and where to begin. Suddenly there appeared a non-Christian Japanese physician, trained in the best schools of the Japanese empire, and in the best schools of Europe, standing at the very head of his profession, and offered his services. With his help we turned the entire gallery of our auditorium into an emergency hospital, built an operating room and opened a free dispensary. In January he gave himself to Christ. He came to us in September with a desire to serve, but in January, when he had crowned Christ as his King, the passion to serve literally flamed and flashed in his heart. He went in and out among the refugees like a flaming torch. I became greatly concerned about him. Again and again, I called him aside and warned him that the pace which he was setting for himself was too stiff. He never argued the matter. He always answered me with a smile. He seemed to say, "You have not yet sounded the depths of my soul." Then he was back and at it again.

In March he broke. We found that his nerves were shattered and that the fever was running through his veins and arteries like a forest fire. In May before I left for America I had to lay him away. After the funeral service I went back to our emergency hospital, the operating room and our free dispensary and looked over the record; I found that this man with the help of two nurses, in six brief months of time, had handled with his own hands and taken into his own heart over 22,000 calls and cases. Many of these were major operations.

Six months, and the chapter of his life had closed! But oh, what a chapter! He lived more in those six months than many of us will live in sixty years. Was it worth while? Is it worth while to link a heroic spirit like that up to Jesus Christ and to send him out like a flaming torch into the heart of some great need or of some great opportunity? And do you suppose, as I worked with this colleague of mine across those tragic months, that I could be conscious of or for one brief second remember that he belonged to the yellow race and I to the white? Never! Never! When I felt the beat of his heart, it was the heart of a brother. A brother who shamed me and challenged me by his fine heroism, his great passion of soul and his flaming spirit of sacrifice and service.

Thus in every field the gospel in Tokyo is not only a challenging but a conquering force. It is winning its way into every phase of the city's life. In its wake men are transformed, institutions come under the spell of Jesus' way of life, and society starts off toward a new and ever upward-moving goal. Japan's capital in its quiet sober moments is conscious that a renewing, uplifting force has been flung into its midst. Many discerning spirits have caught the vision and walk in the presence and under the power of the compelling, conquering Christ.

WINNING A PROVINCE

THE REVEREND WATTS O. PYE, SHANSI, CHINA

We have been hearing during the last few years that there is great unrest in China. It is the unrest which comes from progress. The people want something better. In spite of the political chaos which now exists in China, the country is making sound progress commercially, industrially, and intellectually. Under cover of political disturbances which appear on the surface, a national consciousness is taking definite shape, giving rise to a strong undercurrent of new thought that is making itself felt more and more every day.

This progressive spirit is deeply permeating the Christian movement of China. There is an increasing admiration of Jesus on the part of the more educated classes of the country. There is also an increasing appreciation of the practical value of Christianity. It is what Christianity does rather than what it says, that has won the confidence of the Chinese people. There is, too, an increasing sense of responsibility within the Chinese church itself for maintaining its own work.

To show how this is working out, in practical experience in the Christian centers of China, I am to review briefly the development in one of these centers.

It is in the city of Fenchow, located in northwestern China, a field which includes a portion of west-central Shansi and northern Shensi.

When Dr. Watson and I took up again in 1907 the work which had been largely destroyed by the Boxers in 1900, we knew little of what the nature of this field might be or of what it contained, and we had practically no Chinese leadership. The first step then was, on the one hand, making a careful survey of the field as a whole; and, on the other, the training of a band of preachers, teachers and doctors who might inaugurate the work. This survey was intended to show the resources of the country, the occupations of the people, the lines of communication and where the centers of population might be, in order that we might know a little more intelligently where the centers of Christian work should be opened in order to bring about the Christian occupation of the entire field.

Our available maps at the outset of this enterprise showed over this area of some forty thousand square miles only twenty-eight cities, towns and villages definitely identified and located; but as a result of our surveys carried on through these years in district after district, we are now able to identify something over eight thousand cities, towns and villages in the same area.

Our policy in the occupation of the field was to open centers of Christian effort from twenty to forty miles apart, that is to say, one day's journey by mule-back, our only means of travel in the mountainous regions. In the opening of these centers themselves certain principles were used. In the first place, we determined, so far as possible, to see that the centers were opened only with Chinese leadership, the foreign missionary keeping in the background. We did this in order that, on the one hand, the people themselves might not come to feel that the Christian movement was a foreign movement, or one connected with foreigners. On the other hand, we felt that it would give to the Chinese leader his proper place, we foreigners supporting him with sympathy, interest, loving inspiration and help at every step of the way.

In the second place, we definitely aimed to reach in the beginning the more influential classes of people in the community, because through these the community would be opened to the Christian movement in the future. The way this worked out, we soon came to see, gave us immediately the opportunity of reaching the entire population of the district. I have myself spoken, day after day, to multitudes, ranging from hundreds to even thousands, speaking sometimes three and four times in a single day, the people having been gathered through the influence of some influential man of the place.

In the third place, we tried to follow, as far as possible, the Chinese customs of the place in which we were at work. For instance, all through that area of China, it is a regular Chinese custom that whenever a business man brings into the community a new business enterprise, such as a shop, he must call upon the other business men of the town to explain the new business which he desires to introduce. We make use of this custom. We plan to open a place of business in a new community. Therefore, we call upon the Government officials, upon the public institutions, upon the school teachers, upon the gentry, upon the business men, up and down the streets, presenting to them the cards of the church, explaining what we have come for, what Christianity stands for, and telling them that on such a street we have opened a chapel, inviting them to drop in for a visit.

Now, Chinese custom also requires that such a man called upon must make a return call. In the commercial world this is merely an advertising scheme. Any business man may be certain that at least once in his career, if never thereafter, every influential man in the community will visit his place of business and see with his own eyes what he is doing.

It works the same way with us. We make our call and pass on. In a little while the one on whom we called takes his card and goes down the street to the place of which we have told him. He is met at the door by two men who are there for the purpose. He is ushered in. He has a little visit with our preacher. Once again and this time too from the lips of one of his own fellow countrymen, he hears a clear, concise explanation of what the Christian movement is, and what the Christian church intends doing in that community. This means that by the time any man has done what, according to Chinese custom, simple etiquette requires him to do, he has listened to two explanations of what the Christian faith is, not enough to convert him—that seldom happens—but enough to enlighten his ignorance. It has been enough generally to overcome any suspicion or any opposition which otherwise such an one might have, and which might linger in the community for years to hinder the progress of the work. The whole movement is forced into the open; every one knows what it stands for and what it intends to do.

Now, from the beginning down to the establishment of the church center, all of this work has been done by the Chinese leader himself. Some of these faithful men, living such consecrated, devoted, self-sacrificing lives as would put the rest of us to shame, are the men who today are responsible for carrying forward this movement. The foreign missionary stands in relation to him, somewhat as John the Baptist did to Jesus, when he said, "I must decrease, but He must increase."

For the development and the nurture of the Christian community which has in this way been established, we have been working along certain definite lines of policy, which are making especially prominent the work of our Chinese collaborators.

We are trying in the first place to place upon the members of the church themselves the responsibility for the winning of new people. "Every Christian a missionary" is our motto; and many of the rank and file of our church membership are today themselves bringing in during the year from one to five, even twenty, thirty, and forty new people into the Christian life. The responsibility of the preacher is to train, instruct and prepare for church membership those whom his people thus bring within the range of his influence.

In the second place, with the church at the center developing, and with new strength and new energy exerting itself within the church, we are seeking to lead each one to reach out into the district round about for the gathering of little village groups. I said a moment ago that these centers were located some twenty to forty miles apart. That means that each church has a field of its own from twenty to forty miles square in which may be located anywhere from one dozen to one hundred other towns and villages. The pastor at the center has the oversight of little village groups as they begin to develop in the surrounding district. This larger parish is but the old circuit-rider system brought down to date.

In the next place, the religious education program calls for the training through short courses of a lay leader in each of these village groups, the man thus trained goes back to his village and to his former occupation, but to become the leader of the little Christian group developing in his town. Through institutes held at different times during the year means are provided for the training and inspiration of these lay leaders.

In the fourth place, we are making the church the community center, not alone for spiritual teaching, but also for community service, for sanitation, for public health, and popular education programs. Our people are agriculturalists. For the Province of Shansi the average farm is less than four and one-half acres, and the average income from that farm for each family is only $34 for the year. This means that we must help our people to new standards of living, if they are to be in a position to meet the legitimate expenses of their church and of their school and community work.

Working in these ways, whereas in 1907, there were no organized churches or church centers in the field, due to the destructiveness of the Boxer year, we today have some two hundred church centers developing; whereas there were no Christian leaders, we today have an earnest, consecrated, devoted band of something over two hundred and fifty; whereas the Christian constituency in 1907 was but one hundred twenty-seven, today it is nearing the 15,000 mark. In these ways we are seeking to do our part in meeting the most pressing task of the church in China, namely, to show that the faith which it holds is truly an interpretation of hard facts for daily needs. We are seeking to make the church itself stand in the community as the embodiment of the spirit of the Servant who sought to serve every need.

THE EVANGELISTIC METHODS IN HONAN

THE REVEREND JONATHAN GOFORTH, D.D., CHINA

Thirty-seven years ago I went to China, firmly believing that the Lord Jesus Christ could and would win the Chinese to himself. In the early years I preached in a district containing two or three million of people. I sowed beside all waters, on village streets, at market towns, and at fairs and theatres. At times I met with serious opposition when clods, etc., were hurled, but on the whole I have been well treated by the people I sought to help. I preached the gospel depending upon the Holy Spirit to make it all powerful. At the story of God's love in Christ Jesus I have seen people convicted and converted the first time they listened. Once two of the evangelists said to us, "We have watched the effect of your preaching on the unsaved crowds for more than a month, and every time we notice that one or more are under conviction; tell us the secret." I replied, "If there was not that result I would be alarmed lest I had grieved the Spirit of God." Some of our best evangelists were raised up and tested under fire in those early days. I always had the conviction that the Lord of the harvest had more concern in getting his harvest reaped than I could have. It was my part to pray for and his to send the reapers. I was always on the look-out for the men he called to reap. I did not delay until I saw that they were perfect before I invited them to come and help reap. During my thirty-seven years in China the Lord has used me to introduce about thirty men into the work of an evangelist.

Of necessity there are times when the missionary must be at his home center. There, as far as possible, Mrs. Goforth and I kept open house for the Chinese. When thirty years ago, my wife and I went to open the city of Changteh-fu we resolved that every one, even a beggar, must have liberty to approach us, if he wanted to hear the gospel. This sometimes kept us busy, for one day we showed over one thousand men through the house and hundreds of women besides. Every group listened to the gospel message for a time, before they were shown through the house. Some may think that this makes the missionary cheap, but we have proven that it makes him effective. We have never felt a call to work solely for any one class, but when the opportunity came we concentrated all effort to save that class. For example, under the old system of education, at times there would be four or five thousand students coming up for examinations who were in the city for a month. The evangelists kept the preaching going on at the front, while all through the day I would be handling the students in my study. With a globe and maps and astronomical charts we would explain to these students the fixed stars, and by that time they were so awed and humbled that you might say what you liked about God the Father and his Son the almighty Saviour. I have given as many as fourteen talks to students in a single day. It made friends all over the districts so that I was welcomed in almost every scholar's home. In one of our districts the inspector for boys' schools is an elder in our church and in the same district the inspector of girls' schools is also an elder in our church. There are many other scholars in that county in the church, so that the educational work of the district is under the control of Christian men.

Another kind of work which we carried on after 1900, was the opening of new centers throughout our field. My wife joined me in this and we took our children along. We would rent a compound and stay at least a month at a center. This had the decided advantage in that it reached the women as well as the men. A man may hear the word of God and believe, but his heathen wife or mother can make it hot for him at home. In this way we opened many centers of light. Now we have proved it so often that we have a conviction that we could go into any unevangelized center in North China, with an earnest band of male and female workers, and within a month have the beginning of a church for Jesus Christ. The doors are open and the fields are white unto harvest. These dear people could be saved, if we had a sufficient number of Spirit-filled harvesters to reap the fields. We could carry the gospel to all the Chinese in this generation, if we were only energized and impelled by the spirit of Jesus.

Still another kind of work which we have seen to be very effective is the evangelistic band. We spent five months last winter with one of these bands going from outstation to outstation in Honan. Our tent would seat about five hundred, but so many men and women came that often the sides had to be taken down to enable all to hear. We held four meetings a day, the first commencing at seven a. m. and the fourth closing around ten p. m. I gave on an average more than two addresses a day. Much of my time was spent in personal dealing with the chief men of each center. The local church leaders always brought these men to me hoping that they would be converted to God. To give some idea how the gospel is the power of God unto salvation let me run over the results at a few of the centers visited. At one place in four days, seventy-three men and women gave in their names as enquirers, among them being the three leading men of the district. At the next center we spent three days and the mayor of the town and about sixty others turned to God. During four days at the next market town one hundred and three names were taken down. Right after that in three days seventy names were received, two of them being teachers in the government school. Then at a large pottery town in four days one hundred and twenty-four gave in their names. In that town one of the biggest kiln owners is out and out for Jesus. At the next place in four days eighty-seven turned from idols. It was now time to go home for the annual mission meeting. Just then several converted scholars from a district where there was no local church, came and asked that our band go to them for a few days. We replied that there was no time, for the whole five months' itinerary had been planned ahead. "We notice," said they, "that you have nothing on from the second to the sixth of our new year month." "Yes, that is true," we replied, "but your Chinese people so completely give themselves to feasting and gambling, especially in the early part of the new year that our going would be in vain." "Come," said they, "and we will secure the crowd." We arrived at that center in a snow storm, scraped and swept the snow off the threshing floor and put up the tent, and in four days, ninety turned to the Lord. Right after that, in four days at another outstation, one hundred and one names were received. The elder at that center is headmaster of one of the largest government schools in the county and the parents all know that he stands four-square for Jesus Christ. When our band was at that center dozens of the boys turned to the Lord. Thus we might multiply instances of gospel triumph for five months of last winter.

MOVEMENTS TOWARD CHRIST IN INDIA
PROF. JOHN JESUDASON CORNELIUS, LUCKNOW, INDIA

A few months ago there was a world conference of the Methodist Episcopal Church in Springfield. There were delegates from all parts of the world; among them were a few of us from India. We were asked to wear our turbans while there. As we went from our hotels to the auditorium and from the auditorium back again we created not a little excitement in that quiet city. One day as we were on our way to the auditorium, a school having just closed, a number of little boys streamed forth into the street. whose attention was suddenly arrested by our peculiar head-dress, the like of which they had never seen before. A group of them followed us, block after block. Their curiosity, aroused by our turbans, became still greater, when they became conscious that we were speaking a language which they did not understand. When we noticed their interest, one of our group turned round and said, "Boys, what is it you want?" You should have seen their faces! One little fellow immediately brightened up, and turning to his comrades, said, "Oh boy! It speaks!"

We are standing today at the threshold of the greatest period in the history of missions; I say it is the greatest, because India speaks, and in no unmistakable terms, to the nations of the world. In what way is she speaking? What, indeed, is her message? Why is it that a single figure, slender and slim, whom some have called the pocket edition of a full-grown man. that great individual known as Gandhi, is having the largest following today that any one man has ever had in human history during his own life time? What has made him the most compelling personality of the day? Why is it that so much is being said and written about his greatness and his influence? Is it not because that day, which missions have long looked for, has come, namely, the day for India to interpret Christianity to the world? A century or more ago, the good Christians of Western lands sent out to foreign countries their beloved sons and daughters. These forsook the comforts of their homes, left their loved ones behind, and in the face of overwhelming obstacles, made their way into these great non-Christian lands carrying the gospel of Christ. Those who returned to their homes from India brought back the message, that the people of India possessed a soul, that they had as their heritage a spiritual genius, that when the right time came India would interpret the teachings and principles of Christ as no nation has yet been able to do. I am standing before you bearing testimony and thanking God that that day has come, and that we are at its very threshold. Is not Gandhi's most uncompromising attempt to live Christ's way of life a challenge to the relentless application of His principles by the West?

My subject for this evening is: Movements toward Christ in India. What are these movements? The first one is the movement of politics toward Christ. I am not satisfied with the way I have worded it, but it carries best my meaning. In the West the history of the church is full of the stories of the struggle of the state to separate itself from the church and of its final separation. Now the life of the church is different from that of the state. The activites of the church are supposed to be peculiar to herself, and that of the state, peculiar to herself. Organized Christianity thus became more and more an organization to evangelize peoples, but not to socialize societies. This differentiation of functions and the tremendous emphasis on organization are choking the spirit of the gospel, and we are failing, therefore, in the conscious control of human and social evolution. Form remains while substance is fast vanishing. Ministers preach because it is Sunday, people go to church because it is Sunday. Is it not tragic to think that the teachings of Christ, without permeating the very life of our society in all its activities, has become rather a religion of the Sabbath day? Christianity is becoming more and more a matter of form.

During the time of the war the question, "Has Christianity failed?" was frequently asked in the Orient, as it was in the Occident. I am glad to say that though India is non-Christian, she said as often as the question was raised: "It is not Christianity that failed, but it is Western materialism that failed. The West has chosen mammon rather than God." Can Christianity fail? Thank God it never can fail. If there is anything that fails, it is politics.

We find today the greatest movement the world has ever known, the movement of non-violence on a large scale, a movement based upon the ethical principles of Christ. That movement has found congenial soil in the land which is clearly and unquestionably the home of religions, and it is within that hospitable atmosphere that it has taken root. It is now teaching the people of the world that belief in, and the practice of, such principles as, "might is right," "survival of the fittest," reduce human beings to the level of beasts. It is soul force and not brute force, which raises men to the heights of gods; in spirit is the real source of strength.

I have heard over and over again that the gospel of Gandhi, that of non-violence, is the gospel of the weak. Is it really so? Is physical force then the gospel of the strong? Let us see for a moment what the product of physical force, the world war, cost mankind. Historians tell us that it is the greatest war ever fought. It was the greatest demonstration of the power of organization; never in human history was science applied so effectively for the destruction of humanity as in that great war. What did it mean after all? Please listen to the story. The human cost was as follows: 10,000,000 dead soldiers, 3,000,000 dead but unidentified, 13,000,000 dead civilians, that is, 26,000,-000 total dead; 20,000,000 wounded, 3,000,000 prisoners, 5,000,-000 widows, 10,000,000 refugees. At the time of war, when the Lusitania was sunk, there were some 1,000 souls lost. America was greatly indignant when that happened, but to equal this 26,000,000 dead would require the sinking of a Lusitania every day for seventy years.

Such, indeed, has been the cost of this great war, in human life. What about the cost in money? The total cost has been estimated at 332,000,000,000 dollars. We can form no idea of what so many billions mean. Let me put it in another way. The total cost of war equals $20,000 for every hour since the birth of Christ.

Is this all? What about the moral cost of war? The moral loss is inestimable. Have we not seen the tremendous increase of fear and suspicion, of bitterness and hatred, of licentiousness and lawlessness, of disbelief and moral unrest, of poverty and misery? Do we not see that physical force means nothing but destruction? Shall we then speak of this brute force as the gospel of the strong? Not long ago, there was a conference of the leading scientists of the world in Philadelphia, some 300 of these wonder workers—men who are harnessing nature to serve human needs. At one meeting, a professor, who is known as the father of poisonous gas, made the statement that now he is attempting to produce a gas, which, when spread, would put a whole nation to sleep for twenty-four hours. The world war is over, but we are still thinking in its terms. When I think of all the advances we are making in scientific knowledge without an equal advance in morals, my heart sinks within me, and I feel sad at the thought that humanity is still marching forward toward its own destruction. As long as our advances are purely along economic and scientific lines and not along moral lines, we can be sure that we are heading the wrong way.

Therefore, I say that Gandhi's movement in India is certainly the first movement of its kind showing not only that the Sermon on the Mount can be practiced by any individual, but that its application should be carried into politics, and into all international relationships. We are, therefore, glad that India, true to her spiritual heritage has taken the first step in that direction. Mr. Gandhi, in reply to an address given to him after his release from prison, said: "For me humanitarian service is religion and I draw no distinction between such religion and politics. Indeed, I cannot conceive a life of full service apart from politics. I am endeavouring to prove by my experiments that politics without a religious background is a dangerous pastime, resulting in nothing but harm to individuals and

nations indulging in them; but I see that my attempt to introduce religion as here defined into politics has frightened some
of my best friends and co-workers. While these friends fear
my attempt to treat politics in terms of religion, another group
would have me restrict myself to what they imagine is social
service. I believe the time is fast coming, when politicians will
cease to fear the religion of humanity, and humanitarians will
find entrance into political life indispensable for full service."
We have certainly fought shy of religion entering politics. Can
we think of anything greater than what Mahatma Gandhi is
experimenting on—the introduction of religion into politics?
Every activity in which humanity is engaged must be the religion of man. This, then I say, is the movement of politics toward religion. There is no time to deal with this question more
fully.

The next movement I wish to call your attention to, is the
movement in mind toward Christ. The Bishop of Madras spoke
of the great movement in thought of the educated classes toward Christ's way of life, as "the mass movement in mind."
Unfortunately Christianity came to us from the West, and became identified with the lives of men who came to India singing:

> "Ship me somewheres east of Suez,
> Where the best is like the worst,
> And there ain't no ten commandments,
> And a man can raise a thirst."

They both sang and lived that kind of life. Therefore
India was not as hospitable to Christianity as she might have
been. We are, however, witnessing a new appreciation of
Christ's teaching which has resulted in a critical attempt to dissociate and disentangle Christianity from Western civilization.
I do not wish to spend more time on this point, important as
it is, since it was very well presented to you this morning. In
passing I should like to mention that at the political congress
which was held a year ago last December, the president, who
happened to be a Hindu gentleman, made use of some seventy
quotations from the Bible, in his presidential address. Does
not this show a greater appreciation of the ethical teachings
of Christ?

The third movement toward Christ is the movement of untouchables. You have already heard that there are something
like sixty millions of people who are considered "untouchables."
It is the message of the gospel that really uplifts them and
emancipates them from their social bondage. We thank God
that Christ came into this world not to be ministered unto but
to minister to those who needed His ministry. These poor
people wedded to filth and degradation needed Christ first; and
it is they whom Christianity first reached. We have seen some

wonderful sights in connection with this great mass movement of untouchables towards Christ. In a recent report based upon the census reports for the last thirty years, these facts were given: In the Church Missionary Society Missions the number of baptized persons increased between 1900 and 1923 in the Punjab from 6,000 to 30,000; in Western India from 3,000 to 10,500; in the Telugu section from 13,000 to 53,000. In the Church Missionary Society Missions in India, during the last twenty-three years, there has been a growth from 130,000 to 265,000. Under the Wesleyan Mission in Hyderabad, the Christian movement in sixteen years grew from 7,000 to 33,000, while in the next eight years, the number, including adherents, passed 50,000. These figures, huge as they are, sink into insignificance, when the mass movement in North India is considered. There the Methodist, the American Presbyterian and other Missions are truly overcome by the tremendous tasks of attending and properly instructing these great masses. For four years, from 1915 to 1919, the Methodist Episcopal Church baptized on an average 31,000 people a year. The average increase in the last thirty years has been at the rate of 2,000 per week. It is a great task to get people to come to Christ in such great numbers, but the greater task is to properly care for them and give them the instruction they need. We do not have forces adequate to cope with this situation; and this fact alone is enough of a challenge for greater zeal. It is not the number baptized that counts, but it is getting them to live the Christ way of life, which is of paramount importance.

What gratifies me most is the fact that the social gospel of Christ, which has begun to uplift these untouchables, has also aroused a new consciousness in the higher classes. Mahatma Gandhi himself has made the vow that one of his life purposes would be to efface untouchability from India. To that end he has adopted a girl from an untouchable family; he has not only done that, but has infused into the hearts of the higher caste people a determination such as India had never known before, bent on wiping out this blot from Hindu social life.

Christian missions have undoubtedly prepared the way for the mobilizing of thought power in India. During the last hundred years the missionaries have fought all debasing social evils without fear and without ceasing; they have founded schools and colleges in the various sections of the country; and today we are reaping the results. It may be that the missionaries have not received their full share of credit, but let us all thank God that the work has been done, and that the people have now begun to shoulder the responsibility of fighting social evils.

Friends, has this movement toward Christ in India any meaning to you? Has it a message for the people of the West? If there is a movement toward Christ, as I have tried to point out, then does it not come to you as a great challenge? Let me not give the impression that India is ready to be baptized; no, not by a long way. While there is a movement toward Christ, while India is turning her face towards Christ hanging upon the Cross, yet, she is incessantly asking the question: "Is Christianity practicable? Have the West proved to us that it can be practised?" For two thousand years the West has prided herself on the possession of Christianity, but to what extent has she lived the principles of Christ in her social life, and in her international relationships? Never has there been a time in human history so critical and so challenging. At no time was Western civilization so much discredited in the Orient, as today. The West and the East have become closely intertwined through commercial and territorial expansion. Such expansion has really made the practice of Christ's principles almost impossible. Has not the time come for the West to appraise its own civilization, to rethink and reëvaluate its elements? Has the expansion of the West been on the principle of selfish exploitation of the weaker peoples, or has it been on the other—regarding contributive principle? Is there more race hatred and bitterness in America? Is there selfishness so great as to stand in the way of America's making her contribution to the greatest effort ever made to help human families live in peace? Is American civilization tending to crowd out religion? Is it really incapacitating Americans for religion? Is America making scientific and economic advances ends in themselves? Is material progress making Americans forget the necessity of moral progress, without which society will go to pieces? Answer these questions frankly and then ask yourself the question: Is there need for a movement toward Christ in America?

Last night Bishop Welch referred to the Asiatic movement in the Orient, saying that Mr. Tagore had sounded the call in Japan and in China for a compact of the yellow, brown, and black men. Why has this call come? What has given rise to this Asiatic consciousness? Have not the Western races mercilessly and unscrupulously exploited the weaker peoples of the world? Has not the West wilfully forced opium upon an unwilling people, driving them to a life of degradation and debauchery just to fill its own coffers with blood money? Have not the Western races, driving away weaker races, robbed their natural resources, and in many cases even their lands? When such things have been done in the name of civilization, is it any wonder that the peoples of the Orient, after suffering for many decades unspeakable misery and humiliation, are now working for an Asiatic compact to rid themselves of such debasing domination? The weaker races of the world have been nailed to the cross by the nails of poverty and filth, illiteracy and superstition, suffering and sorrow. The Western races must not forget that they are responsible to a great extent for such conditions which have been brought about by Western expansion for selfish purposes, and that they are under a tremendous moral obligation to those weaker peoples.

Once the East had great confidence in the West but, alas! now she is mentally armed against the West. Is this not a grave situation? If the East has so armed herself, because of the behaviour of the West, then the only thing that the West can do is to help her to disarm herself mentally. Such disarmament can only be brought about by arousing in the peoples of the East confidence in the integrity of the Western nations. To this end, I make the plea that while there is a movement toward Christ in the Orient, a similar movement should be set afoot toward Christ in the Occident. This can only be brought about if the people, I mean the Christians of America, will band themselves together, and say, "We are through with the mere preaching of the gospel; we are from now on going to see that Christianity is applied or practised in our personal lives, in the lives of groups, in the lives of nations and in all international relations, irrespective of what it costs." When that is done you may rest assured that the Orient will go more than half way to join hands with the West to bring about this democracy of God.

I thank you for giving me this opportunity of bringing to you this message; it is my prayer that God should bless you even more abundantly to carry on this good work, so that some day it will be your privilege to see the non-Christian nations of the world joining the Christian nations to crown Jesus Christ Lord of all.

EVANGELISM IN THE NATIVE CHURCH

BISHOP BRENTON THOBURN BADLEY, INDIA

Evangelism is perhaps the greatest word in our work in India. The people of that land are more interested in religion than in anything else, and the fruitfulness of Christian Missions in India may be judged by the fact that while in the past ten years the population of that land has increased by one and two-tenths per cent, the Christian community has grown 33 per cent. In the Punjab during the same period the Christian community increased 92 per cent, while the highest increase of any other religious community was only seven per cent. The Methodist Episcopal Church during the past twenty years has baptized 600,000 people in India.

A great necessity at the present time is for the utmost co-operation between the missionary and the indigenous workers in the task of evangelism. There is a very real danger in the missionary becoming so absorbed in administrative work and in the general work of our great institutions as to leave very few men with any time for direct evangelistic work. It would be a serious mistake to suppose that the work in India can be satisfactorily carried out if the missionaries cease to be preachers of the Word and turn their main attention to finance and educational affairs. Not only is the cooperation of missionaries essential in this work, but also their example, so that our Indian brethren may clearly see that the highest importance is attached to the actual ministry of the Word. Recent years have shown a real tendency towards emphasizing organization and education and finance at the expense of evangelistic work on the part of the missionary body. The best results can only be achieved when the missionary cooperates in the fullest way with all the evangelistic undertakings of the Church.

It is also of the utmost importance that the missionary should have the fullest and most sympathetic touch with national ideals and movements on the foreign fields today. The temper of the people of Asia, in particular, is such that unless a man is able and willing to show his interest in all the rightful aspirations of the people for the development of their national life, he can hardly expect to have any influence in appealing to these people through his message. This also means that the training of our Indian preachers should be more practical, with a more direct thought of the growing national life of the people, and that there should be less of Western elaborations in all our plans for training preachers. Movements in these directions are clearly in evidence, but many forward steps are yet to be taken.

The use of lay workers in connection with evangelistic work is of supreme importance. The method by which Mohammedanism uses its ordinary membership to propagate its teachings, is one that should be taken more to heart by the church in her approach to this question. In the Mass Movement, considerable use has been made of a class in North India called *Chaudhris,* or village head-men of certain low caste people. In many instances such men, without any ordination and with only little teaching regarding Christianity, have gone out among their people and prepared hundreds of them for baptism. The task of evangelists, who come into a situation such as this, is very different from what it would be, had the field not been prepared. Not only is this a good method for spreading the work but it is the best possible way for the development of Christian character.

It is of the utmost consequence that the evangelist, whether missionary or Indian, should give the message through his life as well as his teachings. India, in particular, is insisting today that we live up to the level of the teachings that we seek to introduce. The wonderful hold of Sadhu Sundar Singh upon the people of India is due not only to his preaching in simplicity and power the message of the Christian gospel but to his living the Christian life in all humility, self-sacrifice, love and devotion. No foreigner can expect to preach successfully on the Beatitudes or the Sermon on the Mount unless he can himself exemplify the virtues that Christ has so highly commended. The East is demanding today not only that we preach the gospel but that we live it.

For the evangelistic worker it is necessary to remember that not sermonizing but witnessing for Christ is the real need of our times. India says, "Tell us your Christian experience." So far as the Bible is concerned, multitudes of them can read it and the number is very rapidly increasing, but when it comes to incarnating this Evangel, any people to whom the Christian gospel is first taken have need of great help. There can be no true passion for evangelism which does not come from a glowing heart, and it is quite conceivable that we have gone far in the matter of training men to prepare sermons and give expositions of Bible texts, when we have done little to cause them to maintain the spiritual glow within.

For any church, whether on the foreign mission field or at the home base that is undertaking to preach the gospel, it is of fundamental importance to remember that the task is vain unless there be adequate spiritual power for it. A Hindu once spoke to a Christian preacher in India at the end of a sermon and said that he had read the New Testament and had noted that the men who carried the Evangel were men of amazing power, and then asked this preacher whether he had received what they had found in the Acts of the Apostles. The Hindu was thinking, of course, of the second chapter of Acts and of the pentecostal power, and his question was not only proper but a most searching one. Is it not too frequently necessary for evangelistic workers in all parts of the world to ask themselves this question after they have preached? Any Hindu can tell the difference between a Peter before Pentecost and one after Pentecost, and unless there be that power in the life of the preacher, there are very meager results for him. Christ still says to His disciples, "Go . . . but tarry."

I have stood in India on a plain where 3,000 laymen of the Chamar (tanners and leather dressers) caste, met for three days to consider the one question as to whether their entire community should adopt Christianity. They represented 30,000 people in that region, and after three days' discussion they agreed that they would all be baptized. When, however, they came to ask for baptism it was found impossible to shepherd so vast a multitude all at once and the Church was unable to give them what they asked. I have known of some districts in India where 10,000 names of people from the depressed classes were on the waiting lists for baptism year after year. These are but instances of the embarrassment that Christian missions have faced in India during recent years, and indicate that the task of evangelism is not merely to proclaim the gospel until people are willing to accept the message, but to care for the multitudes who are ready to accept Christ and to give them the spiritual shepherding through the years that alone can make it possible to develop these vast communities into true Christian congregations. In India it is generally true that only a small part of the work has been completed when families have been baptized. Evangelism is the one continuous task of the whole Church.

THE GOSPEL AMONG PRIMITIVE PEOPLES
THE REVEREND HENRY C. MC DOWELL, OF ANGOLA, AFRICA

I have the good fortune to represent the great interior region of West Central Africa, where conditions are still primitive, where people are still very interested in the simple gospel and where the impact of so-called European civilization is just being felt. In the past five years I have done some pioneering in an untouched region in the Southern part of Angola, Portuguese West Africa. During my travels in that part of the country, entering some regions where the people did not even know the term "Jesus Christ," I have been able to introduce (and I use that term advisedly, because it has been merely introducing) many, many thousands of people to it. I count it a great privilege to stand before an audience of people and say to them, "I have the pleasure of introducing Jesus Christ, the Lord of all" and truly it is a wonderful privilege. I remember one time especially, when I was far down in the southern part of the colony in a region where the people build their villages differently than the Ovimbundu where we live. Our villages are not very large; very often, not more than fifteen hundred people live in a village, but down in the lower parts of the Ganguela region there are some villages with as many as six thousand people.

While touring in that country I sent heralds ahead to the paramount king of the region announcing my coming. I happened to be the first foreigner to go into that country since a Portuguese captain had passed through, some thirty-five years ago, when the country was subjugated by the Portuguese. They proclaimed a great holiday. I was not acquainted with the customs of that particular tribe and did not know how they received their guests; so I was considerably disturbed when, about three miles out from the village, I was met by several hundred people. My carriers were a good way behind me; I was riding a bicycle perhaps thirty or forty minutes ahead of them. When I met this grand number of people I stopped and greeted them. They greeted me, and then one man proceeded to take my bicycle. Two others lifted me up bodily and put me in a hammock that was made of banana leaves. I had no blanket under me, and since it was a cold morning, those banana leaves were not very comfortable. The cavalcade started off down the road singing songs and having a great time. I took it as easily as I possibly could under the circumstances. When I reached the village, I found that the king had decreed that nobody was to leave the village that morning. All the women stayed away from their fields. No men went to the woods to hunt. Everybody was at the village. I was quite at a loss as to how best to greet that great multitude of people and make myself heard. We have no amplifiers in Africa, and I would not have been seen or heard standing amidst the crowd. I, therefore, climbed up into the fork of a tree and began to introduce that great body of people to Jesus Christ our Saviour. I look back upon that experience as one of the richest of my life. As soon as I had finished, the king told me that he had sent word to all of the headmen of the villages round about so that they were expecting me to visit them. Their villages were anywhere from two to five miles distant. On that same day I spoke in eight of those villages. I can conservatively estimate at sixteen thousand the number of people to whom I spoke on that single day. I was received as the guest of the king.

However, it has been my task and pleasure, to merely introduce the people to Jesus Christ. We must depend upon the natives that are being trained to better acquaint the people with Jesus Christ. I am glad that in Africa we have no difficulty at all in having a missionary church. The church is naturally missionary. It is missionary from the beginning and every Christian is an evangelist. It is very often quite embarrassing to the missionaries, because the native Christians don't always understand these delimitations of territory and a great many other points of polity. They just go out to make Christians of their fellows; and too often, we with our organizations seem to run greatly behind.

At our boarding school in Southwest Africa, we have a custom that everybody on the place is expected to do some definite piece of evangelistic work at least once a week. The young people of the boarding school take Sunday afternoon as the time when they can best render that service. On Saturday evening at our prayer meetings, we find out just where the various groups are going, so that too many groups will not go to the same locality. One Saturday evening one of our young Christians stood up before the people and gave them a charge. I was greatly interested by his remarks. He began to say, "Now, fellows, as we go to our people back in the villages, let's go sympathetically; let's realize that they are still blood of our blood and flesh of our flesh." Then, he added this illustration: "You know that as boys all of us have herded cattle. When we let the cattle out of the pen early in the morning, sometimes, when we have just taken one or two sticks off of the fence, three or four of the cattle will stick out their heads and can get no further; then you have to beat them on the nose to get them back so that you can remove some other sticks and then all of them can pass. This door of opportunity has just been opened a little bit and many of us merely have our heads through and as the main body of this thing is still left behind we have got to get that in too. All of us have got to go along together. You never have seen a cow whose head could travel any faster than the tail, so that all of us have got to move as a body."

This desire is one of the things over which we rejoice greatly. Another matter over which we rejoice about our people down there in Southwest Africa is the fact that they are anxious to help others too, not only those of their tribe. One of the bravest acts I think I ever performed in my life was on the first Sunday in March, 1924. I stood before our young group of Christians and preached to them a missionary sermon. I told them about people in other parts of the world who did not know the Lord Jesus, and who were suffering perhaps more than they were. I did not know just how my message was going to be taken. I thought they ought to know such facts, that their horizon ought to be broadened. That day, before I had finished my dinner, our living-room was crowded with people. When I came out, they said to me, "Teacher, we have been greatly touched by your message this morning. We want to do something about it. It hurts us to feel that there are other people who are suffering the way that you indicate."

"All right," I said, "I will be glad to have you do something. What do you suggest?" "We have been talking it over. This is the time of the year when we haven't very much to give, but we have decided that if you can give any sort of employment to us here during the coming week, we will come and work a whole week. Whatever we earn during that week, we will contribute next Sunday for foreign missions to help other people not so fortunate as ourselves in the knowledge of the Lord Jesus."

I was greatly surprised. I had not expected any such result. I had to invent many jobs on the place so as to have something for them to do to encourage them. Not only the native Christians, but also many others came. In the villages around they got some others who were interested. On the following Sunday morning, when we took an offering to help others in other parts of the world, I was greatly interested to find that not a single one of the envelopes that we had passed out as the pay envelopes on the previous Saturday afternoon, had been broken. Many of them were inscribed, "For the sake of the Lord Jesus" and "For the sake of spreading the Gospel." "For the sake of carrying the God News." Some envelopes carried a verse of Scripture, but all had deposited those envelopes just as they were. That offering came to $30. I have had considerable experience with that $30 since then. We sent part of it to the Woman's Board of Missions of the Interior, and they sent it back to us. They didn't know how to accept it, but the people in Africa are anxious to help others in other parts of the world, and it is just a sample of what might be done.

In my work among the primitive peoples of Africa I have been greatly interested to note their reactions on a great many things. There are many matters, of course, of which they have never heard before. Many thoughts are quite new, hence, to note their reactions is most interesting. I am going to state two experiences that I have had to show how my own spiritual life has been deepened by some of these reactions and how they have really led me into deeper paths in more ways than one. We had considerable trouble, during the opening days of our work there, in getting a concession of land from the Portuguese government. One evening about eight o'clock a message came from the administrator of that district, the Portuguese local Governor, who had his seat of authority about sixty-five miles away, to be at his office the next morning at nine o'clock to discuss some matters pertaining to our concession of land.

My only means of transportation was a bicycle. There was not a very good road through that region. Those sixty-five miles didn't look very near. I dropped the suggestion to some of the fellows that they would do well to pray for me. The next morning, when I came out of our house about three o'clock, I was surprised beyond measure to find about a dozen fellows standing outside of our door. They said that they thought perhaps I would be coming out about that time and so they came to escort me to the main path, about three-quarters of a mile away, because I would have to cross a stream where there was not a very good bridge and they were going to take my bicycle.

When we got to that main path, before I knew it, they formed a circle around me. They joined hands and then one of them spoke and said, "Teacher, we wish that we could go for you, but we can't. We have decided that the only thing that we can do is to pray you there." I told them that I thought myself that would be about the only way I would get there. Then the most beautiful prayer I have ever heard in my life was offered. One fellow began to pray and he prayed that the Lord would really give me strong legs, and that my bicycle would not break down, and that as I came to the different streams I would find that there were bridges there that had not been washed away. Then he said, "As our teacher reaches that arid region, it will be just about time the sun comes up. As the sun comes up and takes the dew off the grass and off the flowers and off the trees, somehow or other, Lord, have that get into the throat of our teacher, so that he won't be thirsty when he passes through the arid region." As I listened to that wonderful prayer and jumped on my bicycle that morning, and started on my journey, why you can see I had a wonderful prayer band behind me. That trip came out all right, but the simplicity of that prayer, the straightforwardness of it, I have not been able to get over to this day.

At another time I had an experience that caused me to have great regard for my people. That was when an old man in a village about four miles from us who had been attending our services quite regularly and who a few Sundays before had told me that he wanted to confess, sent word over one morning about four o'clock for me to come at once to him for he was dying. As soon as I could get ready I went. When I reached the village the old man told me to get the better mat and place it on the bed that was there, that he was soon going to pass away. I began to make those preparations and then he said to me, "Call in some of the people here who can sing some of the songs, because I want to have a few about me as I pass over." I called in some and I asked "What songs shall we sing for you?" Then with a smile he stretched out his hands and told me. At his wish we began to sing a rendition of "Father, I stretch my hands to Thee, no other help I know." To this day that experience has been the symbol to me of Ethiopia stretching forth her hands unto God. We talk about the time when Ethiopia is going to stretch forth her hands unto God. Friends, I have seen young Ethiopia, old Ethiopia, dying Ethiopia, stretching forth her hands unto God. Too often, instead of that hand being placed into the hand of God and poor Africa led sympathetically to a better life and to a higher life, it has been placed in charge of the slave driver and Africa's children have been scattered to the ends of the earth; or it has been placed in the hand of the exploiter and Africa has been bled white. Poor Ethiopia is still stretching forth her hand unto God. God grant that we shall answer that call and give the blessing to poor Africa of which she stands in sore need.

Would to God that I could plead here tonight! I feel quite seriously over this thing. We American Negroes have a tremendous love for Africa. We want to help Africa so that she shall be able to make her contribution to the Christ that is to be; but, friends, just let me say this one word. I thoroughly believe that the real task, the real test of the motive of the Christian nations is going to be faced and is going to be worked out in Africa. Poor Africa stands there helpless with her hands tied behind her. Anything that is done for Africa must be done from sources outside of her. We have said to Africa, "You are not to think for yourself, you are not to work out your problems for yourself, we take you as a mandate." What are we going to do with those mandates? God grant that we may really see the great task that we have in the redemption of Africa.

Recall the great law of sacrifice and suffering. I thoroughly believe that if the law of suffering and sacrifice holds true, God must have some high destiny for Africa. Has she not a price? She has passed through great suffering and still the dawn does not seem to be near.

I am glad that in my five years in Africa I have had occasion to get a real faith in at least one thing. I have found out that God can be trusted. When I say that, I have delivered my message. Off in primitive Africa, time and again, when we have not been able to do anything but call upon God, I have found that He can be trusted. Back yonder in Chattanooga, Tennessee, when I was the pastor of the church there, before I went to Africa as a missionary (it was before I was married and my mother was living with me) this challenge came to me straight from the shoulder and I tried to face it in the same way. One night my mother and I knelt down beside her chair and we prayed over this matter. We talked it over. When I went to my room that night there was very little sleeping that I was able to do. The next morning I went down to my study at the church, and wearily sat down at my desk. Haphazardly I opened my Bible and in a moment my eyes were fastened upon those wonderful words of promise to Israel "Fear Not, for I have redeemed thee. When thou passest through the waters I will be with thee, and through the rivers they shall not overflow thee; thou shalt walk through the fires and shalt not be burned, neither shall they kindle upon thee, for I am Jehovah, thy God, the Holy One of Israel."

This came back to me at one time during the early part
of the dry season when they burn the bush in Africa. I was
making a journey. My wife and my little boy were along in
a hammock. We had about a dozen carriers along with us. In
the distance we saw smoke. We paid little attention to it.
Our route led down into a valley. As we mounted the other
side, the natives gathered around me saying, "Teacher, we are
surrounded by fire. What are we going to do?" In just a
moment the small buck and the rabbits and other small animals
were running by us, almost over us. I looked around, and took
in the situation and I said to my wife, "I guess the only thing
we can do now is to look to the Lord." Yet, of course, I did
what I could to save my wife and baby. Every man took pieces
of brush and we began to beat down the fire on both sides,
while those with the hammock followed closely behind. In a
few moments we were outside the danger zone and the natives
began to tease one another about it. It became a great joke as
soon as it was over. I told the fellows that I didn't see how
they could take it as such a great joke. "After you have passed
through trouble," they said, "the next best thing to do is to forget it." I have found that was pretty good sense, too. But
it was not much fun to me as I looked into the faces of those
men who had walked through that fire with my wife and baby
and I thought again, "Thou shalt walk through the fire and shalt
not be burned."

Friends, God grant that we may see the fields in Africa
white unto this harvest, and that from the Convention forces
may be released so that we missionaries in the heart of Africa
shall no longer have to continually say to the throngs of people,
"I am sorry, we have not the room," but may we soon be able
to say, "Africa, shine, for thy light is come, and the glory of
the Lord is risen upon thee. Whereas thou hast been forsaken
and hated so that no man passed through thee, I will make thee
an eternal excellency, a joy to many generations."

THE GOSPEL AMONG PRIMITIVE PEOPLES
THE REVEREND CHARLES E. HURLBURT, AFRICA

A maritime steamer had stopped for a few hours at Djibuti
at the east end of the Gulf of Aden. As a few of us walked
about the quaint old scattering town, we found one of the
greatest missionary statesmen that any age has ever produced,
sitting on a little stool, drawing the picture of one of the quaint
old mosques of that little town. For Bishop Tucker was an
artist as well as a missionary statesman. As we talked a little
later, I asked him the question, "How is it that you have been

able to do so great a work as has been done in the tribe that murdered Hannington, lying on the east of the Nile to the north of Lake Victoria."

The substance of that story was this, "I turned aside to other places for men sent out by the Home Committee and waited until I found a warm-hearted Irishman. I sent him into that tribe. That one man by the power of the gospel of Christ has transformed it in a very short life service. That tribe, the lowest according to anthropological estimates of any of the tribes in either the Nile or the Congo Basin, has become one of the most productive, one of the most peaceful and one of the most nearly Christian of any of the tribes of Central Equatorial Africa."

When Roosevelt came out to visit East Africa he came to our headquarters station in what is now Kenya Colony. After asking a few questions and looking about the station a bit he said to me, "I want to see your finished product." I said, "What do you mean?" He said, "I want to see your Christian men and Christian women; I want to see a Christian home."

He went to two or three of these homes and found, instead of the little grass huts that he had been in the habit of seeing during his hunting trips, houses where the men themselves had built fireplaces, real homes with doors and shutters. Even the missionaries had no glass windows, so of course, these houses had none, but they had chimneys and were clean and the food that he examined was clean. He then inquired what they were doing and what they were earning.

When I gave to him the facts, still true, that one-fourth of the baptized Christians were giving their entire time to preaching the gospel to their fellows; and that their homes and their lives were truly transformed so that men who had been indifferent to the rights and privileges of women were learning as the first experience of their Christian life to carry the wood and the water and to do the deeds of kindly service for their wives, he said, "I like your finished product. It is the right sort of thing."

A year ago there died by accident, away up in the Masai Reserve in Kenya Colony, a young giant in body, in mind and in spirit. We shall lament him for many a day, for he was the first native out of the twenty-four tribes in Central Africa in which we, as a mission, are working, who has, almost unaided, translated the whole New Testament into the language of his tribe. He was a handsome man, a man of gentlemanliness, and of Christian power, whose life was transformed by the gospel of the grace of God in Christ Jesus.

Six years ago, a tribe away up on the west of Lake Albert, on the high hills of that country, degraded by corrupted Baal-worship, one of those tribes with a very difficult language, mixed with the three great groups of Africa, that seemed to government officers and to ourselves to be almost impossible to reach, said that it had no word for us and wished no word from us. Within three months the word has come to us that that very tribe wants a Christian teacher in every chief's village.

About forty of those most sorrowful of human creatures, lepers, gathered about our mission station in far Northeast Belgian Congo, two or three years ago, thinking they might get some help. I said to them one night as they gathered together, "If you will stay here, we will provide homes for you, we will give you gardens. You may remain here permanently, and we will do what we can to help you." In the morning all were gone. They were afraid of being confined or segregated. A letter received a week ago from the nurse in charge of the Leper Home said, "We have more lepers than we can take care of. Several have gone back because quarters were so crowded. Some who have all their fingers are cooking for those who have none, and they are helping one another. Do pray for a doctor, and do pray that we may treble and quadruple the quarters for the many lepers wholly untouched and unreached."

But of what value is it to us who are gathered here in the capital of Christian America tonight to assure ourselves again that the gospel of the grace of God has transforming power to change a nation, to change a home, to change the individual life, to transform a tribe of people? Every man who is born from above knew that before we gathered here; and our gathering would have been in vain if, it only reassured us that omnipotence is omnipotent, that omniscience is omniscient and that God's grace has transforming power, if we do not give that knowledge to Africa.

Shortly after that visit with Bishop Tucker, I took a journey of six hundred miles in what was then German East Africa, and camped for a few nights on the very place where Livingstone, more than a generation before, had pitched his tent on his way from Lake Tanganyika to the Indian Ocean. I realized that in that six hundred miles of journey, I had not found a Protestant mission nor a Protestant missionary, and that since Livingstone died a whole generation had passed into eternity utterly unwarned, though the entire Christian world knew that Africa's door was wide open.

What value will it be to us if we consider China, and India, Japan, andAfrica, and the whole wide world tonight and fail to tell them what our fathers knew and what we knew when we learned to know God, that "the Gospel of Christ has power to transform human life?" Two great facts need to be faced. One is that there are still hundreds of tribes in Africa that have never heard the gospel of Christ. Another is that both we and

our fathers have sinned in the belief that men and women of
inferior education might reasonably be sent to the great Dark
Continent as missionaries.

There are today not only some hundreds of tribes where
the language has never been reduced to writing, but there are
at least scores of tribes where men and women of limited ability
are seeking to translate the Bible into the language of the people.
There is scarcely a mission anywhere in Africa that is able to
staff adequately the schools that are training thousands of
young men who are preparing, and should be better preparing,
to be teachers and preachers and the leaders of their own people
into the reality of this transformed life.

The second great fact we need to face is what the greatest missionary statesman of his age said, "It is God who said,
'Out of darkness light shall flame,' who hath kindled a flame in
my heart to make me a world's beacon of the knowledge of the
glory of God in the face of Jesus Christ."

Until we, who attend missionary conferences, realize that
God has given us light in order that we may be "world's bea-
cons" and that it is our obligation not simply to know the
transforming power of the gospel, but also to make that fact
known to every kindred and tribe and tongue, and until we send
our sons and our daughters and our very best, and carry this
message of redeeming grace, we have failed and our knowledge
is in vain.

CHRISTIAN EDUCATION IN THE MISSION FIELD

THE SIGNIFICANCE OF CHRISTIAN EDUCATION IN THE EVANGELIZING PROCESS

PRESIDENT JAMES M. HENRY, D.D., CANTON, CHINA

Where there is no vision the people perish. The churches and Christian communities that have been weak and backward in their development are those which among other failings have been weak and backward in the matter of education. Who can fully evaluate the work of Christianity's intellectual leaders, Paul, Athanasius, Augustine, Erasmus, Luther, and all the others past and present? Who can estimate the contribution of Christian education and of educated Christians to the world of government, of art, of literature, to the onward sweep of the Kingdom in that part of our world which is the seat of what we call Christian civilization, to the revealing of ever higher and more compelling ideals of conduct and aspiration? Without the highest training of the intellect and the soundest scholarship under the guidance of His spirit, how shall the more excellent way be commended, the truth illumined, the life quickened, and Christ Himself lifted up even in our own Christian lands, where every phase of life is saturated in one way or another with Christianity?

Today in Christendom itself strange new forces are being felt, old values are changing, new emphases are being made, much of life is in a kind of blind revolt against established custom and the habits of the past. What some call the creative urge, an insistence upon the right of individual self-expression and development, is setting itself up as a kind of new god demanding universal worship. On every side we hear fears expressed, we see apprehension for the future of our youth, and we look to our educated Christian leadership for guidance. But we believe that God's spirit of wisdom will speak to the mind of the church and show it the next step, that in Christian education lies the solution to many of the most pressing problems of the day.

Far away from our shores and below our horizons a new world outside of Christ is fast emerging. In the Near East, in India, in China, in the Antipodes, a mightier transformation than the world has yet seen is in actual process. And here again who can evaluate the part which Christian teaching and Christian education have already had in the breaking up of the old and in the inspiration and preparation for the new? Who can say what

98

Christian education in the Near East, in India and in the Far East has already meant? The social and political development of the Balkan States and of Turkey, the emancipation of the womanhood of those lands, has been profoundly influenced by Robert College and the Woman's College of Constantinople. The graduates and students from the great university at Beirut, coming as they have from Syria, Greece and Armenia, and latterly in increasing numbers from Egypt as well, from the Sudan, from Persia and Mesopotamia, with last year a remarkable accession from the hitherto almost unreachable sect of Shiites, one of the strictest and most fanatic of the Moslem sects, are having and will increasingly have an almost unbelievable influence in the remaking of these varied communities and nations.

In the new life throbbing throughout India, of which we have already so movingly heard, the influence of Christian leadership is being strengthened and more effectively felt at Lahore, Lucknow, Madras, Madura, Vellore, Jaffna and at the other centers which train the students thronging educational halls in Christian idealism and lift up Jesus Christ before them.

And in China, where if any one class of the population rather than another has been potent in developing a national spirit, in fostering and promoting progress and national ideals, it has been the student, the educated class, name after name comes to mind, products of Christian education and of a Christian environment. T. T. Lew, Chang Po-ling, C. T. Wang, C. C. Wang, W. W. Yen, David Yui, even Dr. Sun Yat-sen himself. How different these might have been had it not been for Christian education! The traveler with any insight at all, who goes from Peking in the north to Canton in the south and sees the work of the Christian colleges and universities in that coming master nation of the Orient, sees the marvelous, undreamed-of opportunities that are there for Christian conquest and for the advancement of His Kingdom, that kingdom of righteousness and peace and joy in the Holy Ghost.

The so-called general work of evangelism on the mission field is a wonderful thing. It is carried on by personal work, in chapels and churches, through Christian literature, through the divine work of healing in Christian hospitals. In so far as it deals with those whose characters are already formed it is a sort of salvaging, the making over of old material, the altering and adapting of old machinery; and it is but a further proof of the wisdom of God and His power that this can be done, a further proof of the magic of the divine alchemy that elements already fixed can through His spirit be changed into the gold and precious stones of His Kingdom, that men can really be reborn. It makes the true heart burn to hear of it, to observe it, to be privileged to take part in it. But to have as your parish the tender souls of the youth of any land, not the chaos of adult confusion, the welter of warring passions, burning prejudices, and selfish habits, but the sweet plastic precious clay of God's kingdom, to have them under your guidance in the most impressionable period of life, when they still trail their clouds of glory, are still attended by the vision splendid, are still of the stuff itself of which Christ said the Kingdom of God is made, full of faith, vibrant with idealism, is one of the most moving experiences of life. It is an experience which makes one so privileged cry out as Isaiah of old, "I am a man of unclean lips" and to long to be touched with the fire from God's own altar that in His strength and His wisdom so matchless an opportunity can be met.

Will you look through my eyes at the scene of one such opportunity? It is our own campus at Canton Christian College. I speak of this spot because I know it, but with minor local variations, the same exhibit may be seen at any other of the great Christian campuses in God's countries overseas, in Beirut, in Constantinople, in Peking, at the Doshisha, in Judson College, Burma, in Lucknow and Lahore. A thousand students are there, ninety per cent of whom come from non-Christian homes. A thousand students are living in dormitories side by side with teachers, American and Chinese, whose great desire is to share what Jesus Christ has given them. A thousand students, influenced not merely by Bible classes, the chapel services, the Sunday services, the Boy Scout or athletic activities, the Student Christian Association work, full though the campus life is of every form of Christian social service, but by the rich Christian tradition of the campus, by its living spirit of service, by the quiet influence of the strong Christian character and the true Christian devotion of a Christian staff and by the steady but unobtrusive solicitude of their fellow students, who having known Him whom to know is life eternal, are eager to share that knowledge and that life with their fellow students. What a sacrament you would have experienced could you have seen the culminating service on Sunday of the annual "harvest" week last Spring, when ninety-one students, twenty-three workmen and six women servants publicly took their stand for Christ. There, a few weeks hence, the same story will be repeated. What a fresh baptism of the Holy Ghost, what a quickening of faith, what an ache of longing would be yours, could you stand before this great body in some public assembly as, fired perhaps with some patriotic message, their very souls are revealed and you realize that before you under your very hand, is the future of a great people! And when you learn that eighty-five per cent of those who stay two years or more in this environment pledge their allegiance to the King of Kings you gain some idea of the matchless, incomparable significance of Christian education for pure evangelism.

And when you see buildings on that campus given by Chinese in Java, or the Federated Malay States, when someone tells you that its chief Chinese executive officer has just raised over $80,000 from the Chinese in South America for its work, and when you have pointed out to you Chinese boys from South Africa, from Australia, from Europe, from Canada and from the United States, whose parents have entrusted them body and soul to this Christian institution for their education, you see the streams of Christian influence and power pouring out in unsuspected ways and reaching regions and communities and individuals otherwise utterly inaccessible. And again when you see the women students, the flower of the nation's womanhood, and reflect on the influence of the Christian home, especially of the homes which these Christian students, women and men, are going to make, you begin to realize the unique, the complete, the blessed significance of Christian education for evangelism.

The gospel evangel for the world is awaiting the enriching and creative contributions yet to be made from these Oriental lands. Over India, we were told last night, the day of Christ has begun to dawn. But He is the Christ of China, the Christ of the Andes, the Christ of Africa, the same yesterday, today and forever, and yet ever new and ever giving a fresh revelation of God! But how can He be thus uplifted save as the Indian mind, the Chinese mind, the Latin mind, the African mind, become consecrated, inspired, illumined by His spirit? The leaven which can leaven the whole lump, whether it be Islam as such, or the Indian civilization with its unique religious texture or the civilization of the Far East, of China and Japan, with its sturdy substructure of Confucian ethics, is the leaven of Christian education, and the real hope of the winning of all this to Christ is the nurturing and training and inspiring of its youth, its coming leadership under thoroughly Christian auspices. God has opened such doors today as men never dreamed to exist. Have His people, His church, the faith and the will to enter these open doors?

The educational commission which visited China three years ago, after months of the most careful survey and expert study, made as its considered conviction the statement that "Christian principles may yet become the controlling force in Chinese life. If Christian education fails, the growing stream of non-Christian education and of anti-Christian influence will submerge the Christian movement and reduce it to a place of minor importance." What is true of China is true of other lands: of India, the Near East, Africa, South America. The coming leadership of the coming world! Christian principles, the controlling force! Has the

Kingdom of God ever been more nearly within our grasp? Have the hills of that far country ever been so near to our horizon? May He, our Master and our King, who took the little children in his arms and blessed them and said, "Of such is the Kingdom of Heaven," may He, as He sees the opportunity for Christian education and the controlling of Christian leadership throughout the world, open our eyes, that we may see with Him and may in Him and through Him consecrate every purpose, every resource of our lives and of the church to bringing in the Kingdom through His spirit and in His way.

THE SCHOOL AS AN AGENCY IN THE BUILDING OF CHARACTER

MISS IDA BELLE LEWIS, PH. D., CHINA

Jesus said, "Let the little children come unto me." He is the only great religious teacher who set the child in the midst. Go where you will, where Jesus has not been known, and you will find the children neglected. They die. They are allowed to grow up in ignorance, but the school has always followed the banner of Jesus Christ. He brings light and life more abundant to the children of mankind.

Furthermore, it is the children who come to him. Doctor Athearn made a study of 6,194 persons, joining the church in one year in forty-three states. They were Methodists, Baptists, Congregationalists, Presbyterians and Disciples. The median age of these church members was fourteen years, four months and twenty-two days. The median age for the Methodist Church was eleven years, nine months, four days; for the Congregational Church was fifteen years, ten months, fourteen days. The children come to Jesus. Those older usually do not. Early youth makes the life choice. If any race is to be won to Jesus Christ, the children must be won to him.

Childhood is the habit-forming time. William James says that by the time an individual is twenty years of age his personal habits are, for the most part, fixed. The stimulus-response bonds are fixed; behavior under the ordinary routine of life has been determined. The miracle of Christ's power is that he does change men, sometimes after they are grown; but such cases are miracles, and are not the rule. The rule is this: The habits of Christian behavior: kindliness, truth telling, service, prayer, . . . must be planted deep in the growing child, if he is to become Christlike.

In Christian lands these life decisions and the formation of habits are influenced by four dominant factors: the home, the church, the school and the social order. All these powerful factors uplift Jesus and his teachings. The home is especially strong. Mr. A. R. Pierson of Chicago asked one hundred boys why they attended Sunday-school. Out of seventy-two answers forty-one said they came because of the rule of the home. How many of the people in this room today are active Christians because of the leadership and inspiration of fathers and mothers who made a Christian home?

Contrast this with the struggle of the young girl who came to a Christian school in China and learned a new way of life. Her father had seventeen wives. She was the daughter of the thirteenth. She hated the home and all it stood for. In Christ's teaching she found the rule for the purity of the home she sought. At first she dared not tell the people there that she had determined to follow Christ. But her great secret could not be kept. It was revealed in her whole attitude toward those with whom she lived.

One day the fifteenth wife called on the principal of the school. You will remember that this pupil was the daughter of the thirteenth. Said she, "What makes Edna so different, since she came to you? Before, she used to be hateful and mean to all of us who are younger than her mother, and proud and distant to those who are older. Now she seems to love us all. She teaches songs to all the little children and tells us women stories. What has made the change?" The principal answered, "Edna has let Jesus come into her life as Lord and Master. She obeys Him first. He has commanded us to love each other." "Then," said the little concubine, "if that is what being a Christian means, I should like to become one, too."

The Christian school makes a miniature Christian social order in which the children live. It frequently reaches out and touches the home into new ideals. Drop the Christian school, leave the church to work alone with the problems of home and social order, and the task will be well-nigh impossible. We must keep the Christian school and we must keep the school Christian.

This is done only when everything in the school is permeated by the spirit of Christ. Too often there has been a tendency to give the Bible in memory hunks, trusting that the mere mechanical swallowing will produce the needed nourishment. It is not strange that this has brought indigestion and distaste for this food upon which strength of soul depends. The Bible must be taught, but it must be made a delight as well as a necessity. The Oriental child may understand it better than we do. Quick as thought they see the story pictures and their meaning. Dramatization and illustration follow naturally. Let us bring the children to Jesus through the Bible and they will love him.

But the curriculum, be it ever so theological and psychological, can never make a school Christian. The teacher is the interpretation of Christ to the little children who watch her day after day and year upon year. Is she kindly? Is she gentle? Is she just? Is she always loving? These are the questions to which they will have an answer. There is no judge more astute than a child. When a teacher has been weighed in the balances and not found wanting, the children receive her into their heart shrine. She never takes the place of the mother, for that place is always sacred to one alone, be she ever so ignorant and unwise. But the place of a Christian teacher is holy, when the children make her their confidant, their guide and their ideal. Her example is irresistible in the formation of character.

The teacher also makes the atmosphere of a Christian school. There can be no deep-seated hatreds and jealousies between the pupils, if true Christianity is taught. Games, gardening, love for birds, beasts and fish, happy cooperation in schoolhouse sanitation may bring keen appreciation for the finer things of life.

It was the day before a great fete in a village school in China. The children decided to take a holiday and clean up. Some washed the benches, others scrubbed the floor; a committee bought fresh oiled paper and fixed the windows. A group of the wee ones went out and pulled the weeds from between the bricks in the court, and the pride of every pupil in "our school" overwhelmed the pride in new garments. They had found the joy of working together.

Perhaps the greatest element in the building of character is the habit of service. Christian schools have developed this to a large degree. From Hwa Nan one hundred and thirty-five school girls go out every Sunday to carry the message of truth to the surrounding villages. Fukien Christian University, Gamewell School and Yenching in Peking, Ginling at Nanking and many other schools dedicate Sunday to evangelistic service in their immediate vicinities.

One day, eleven years ago, I stood on our upper veranda and looked off across the Tientsin plain. There were twenty villages within sight that had never heard of the Gospel. When the challenge was given to the highschool girls, the six seniors declared their purpose of going, if I would go with them. So we started off to the nearest village, eight minutes' walk away. Although we were so near, the women of that village had never before seen a white person. They saw us coming along the paths and gathered in a knot at the village edge. "Come and see the sight," they called to their neighbors. "Come and see the sight," but when we came near, they were frightened and shouted, "Here come the big feet." Then they rushed into their houses and closed the doors. But women, the world over, are curious, and when we passed, they opened the doors a crack and peered through. Then it was that the student girls reached them. "Come to the end of the village street," they invited, 'we are going to sing a song and tell a story." The first week fifty women dared to come. The school girls chose a wise story, Ruth and her mother-in-law. The obedience of Ruth touched the hearts of those toothless Chinese women. "Yes," they nodded, "that is a good doctrine. We believe that daughters-in-law ought to obey."

The next Sunday a hundred women came; the third week one hundred and fifty, the fourth week two hundred, and the fifth week two hundred and fifty. The schoolgirls loved it. Said one of them who wore a dainty silk dress, "I didn't know our people lived like that in the villages. I think we ought to know it. At first, I didn't want them to touch me, but now I understand them, and I really love old Grandmother Wang," and often the dainty educated girl slipped along the village path to have a cup of tea and pass the time of day in the mud hut of dear old Grandmother Wang.

But the Christian schools serve not only in the evangelistic field, but also in the educational field. A very large proportion of the schools support at least one charity school nearby. The boys of Hwei Wen, Tientsin, are poor and have no money, but the mission mule died and the stable was empty. This the boys cleaned out and fixed up with old benches. They advertised a free school, and fifty youngsters arrived. The boys could not afford a teacher, so they divided up the free time of their own school day. Number One, who has a nine o'clock free period, taught arithmetic; Number Two, who was free at ten o'clock taught reading; Number Three came at eleven and played games with the children; Number Four taught history from eleven-thirty until twelve-fifteen. Thus the day was divided, and the school flourished. The school boys have carried on this work for three years. The government schools have taken up the idea; and the question, "Have your students a charity school" almost always brings a flush of pride and eager stories of service to the children who live near.

Thousands of students carry the daily vacation Bible schools to the villages of China in the summer time. In many industrial centers, students are helping the factory workers. In rural districts, agricultural students instruct the farmers. Christian students cooperate with the government schools in the popular education movement. They unite in health campaigns. They are helping others, it is true, but they are also forming ideals and habits of service that will become an integral part of their own lives. If character is to be built, we must have the Christian school. The school must be Christian. Then truly

"Our sons will be like saplings, grown tall in their youth,
Our daughters like corner pillars, carved as in a palace."

CHRISTIAN EDUCATION AND CHRISTIAN LEADERSHIP

DEAN J. D. MACRAE, SHANTUNG, CHINA

I speak with some conviction on this subject, after ten years spent as an evangelistic missionary among the villages of North China, an experience which taught me that what the Orient needs is not so much improved methods and better policies, although it does need these, as men and women of dynamic personality, the secret of whose influence is to be the life of the spirit. We need a Chang Po-ling, David Yui, C. Y. Cheng, C. T. Wang, T. T. Lew, Feng Yü-shiang and many more such, multiplied indefinitely and at once. These men and women would be the first to admit that what they are they owe largely to Jesus Christ and to Christian education. Five years in university education has only served to deepen my own impression of the paramount importance of Christian education in the Orient today.

1. *In the Sphere of Personal Religion:* In the sphere of personal religion, the Orient is calling out for reality. It needs men and women who have had an inner, personal experience of Jesus Christ, in what China speaks of as the "innermost heart," a living faith. We are apt to rest content when we see growing up on the soil of China a replica of the church in which we have been born and nurtured. The real question is whether or not the religion of Jesus Christ has been rooted there.

A short time ago a student who is now in London in postgraduate work, spoke in a moment of confidence of his own personal experience. He had been brought up in a home where he was subject to the cruelty of an opium-using father. His little sister had been sold into captivity; his mother had been almost beaten to death; he himself had finally come to a position where he found his richest possession in his personal experience of Jesus Christ, and so he said, "What China needs is more Jesusism."

There are scarcely any fixed stars in the firmament of the religious thinking of young China today. When Dewey or Bertrand Russell visit the East, there is produced, at once, a whole crop of young philosophers of this school or that, and these persist only until there comes some other influential visitor, and then a new movement is set on foot. A "New Tide" has been sweeping over China and has brought with it literary revolution, social upheaval, moral chaos, and bewilderment in the sphere of religion. What we need today is the leadership of men and women who have had a real religious experience.

I take off my hat to the first Chinese Christians, the men and women who were born out of the testing times of the Boxer days and of other times like them. What we need for our new day in the Orient is a race of men and women who, with sound education, the best personal culture, discipline, character, personality and qualities of leadership, will combine a personal religious experience as real as those men had "of whom the world was not worthy."

2. *In Home, Social and Industrial Relationships*: We may smile at the old type of Chinese home, but it was a great contribution out of China's past. It had about it a kind of moral sanction which has contributed more than all else, perhaps, to maintain the moral life of China upon a high level. There were some things which the Wang family would not and could not do. But the large family is giving place to the small. The stationary family is being broken up into more mobile ones. The marriage relationship in China tends to become less permanent. Earlier marriage is giving away to later marriage. Everything is changing in home relationships.

In industry the Orient is making tremendous strides. Think what that means! For instance, China, industrialized and without Christ—I ask you, can you contemplate that with equanimity? Yet that is the change which is taking place very rapidly. My mind goes back to a match factory in the heart of China where there are employed perhaps three thousand people, for the most part women and children, at work under conditions which, from the point of view of physical health and moral health too, are the very worst possible. They are at their posts for ten, twelve, fifteen hours a day, driven by a boss whose sole aim is to turn out matches and more matches. Then when their hour of work is over, they go stumbling out into the street or into quarters which have been prepared for their existence between work and work.

Now the significant fact is that upon these vital questions not even Christian thought has quite crystallized itself as yet. There are organizations like the Young Women's Christian Association which have been pioneers in the field of industrial reform. There are a host of missionaries over in the Orient who would fain do something to help in the confusion as to family conditions. Perhaps they have achieved most of all by the Christian homes with which they have dotted the Orient. But, it is clear that what the East is calling for today is for men and women who know the social psychology and the social traditions of their own people. There is a clarion call for men and women of this type to lead— to do constructive work in helping to solve these great problems. Hence the demand for Christian education; to delay here is fatal.

3. *Citizenship:* One reads with a sigh the reports of civil war and of political chaos in China. What are we doing to change such conditions? Stable government waits on general knowledge, discipline, character, personality. In this sphere Chris-

tianity has always shown itself to be creative, and nowhere more than in the Orient. The few Christian leaders of today exercise an influence out of all proportion to their numbers.

That latent moral sentiment, admired by all keen observers, which is widespread among a people like the Chinese, stands in need of leadership which will call it forth into courageous action, on behalf of the well-being of a great nation hard beset by her own internal foes. China once moved with decision to suppress opium; with disinterested leaders such as she is now producing, only greatly increased in numbers, she will not fail to deal it a death blow again and set her own house in order.

In commercial life the old ideals of honesty and loyalty which have stood the test of centuries and have gained respect for the Chinese merchant wherever he has touched the life of the West— these priceless ideals, through the coming of the Western contract system, and somewhat superficial imitation of what is least worthy in modern business practice, are losing their influence. It is the leadership of Christian business men which must restore these old and sound Chinese principles to the place which they must occupy in the commerce of the nation, that she may rise even higher and far surpass her glorious past in the scale of commercial integrity. Common honesty and reliable character are the supreme requisites for genuine progress on the road to national wealth. We have given to the Orient the externals, the mere "clothes" of our Western civilization. Shall we keep back the better gifts of the soul which make men and make them noble?

4. *Nation and Nation:* There is deep distrust and suspicion around about the Pacific on the other side. The history of the impact of the West upon the East, in the past, does not make some of the questions which arise more easy of answer.

Who are to be the people in China, or in India, or in Japan who, in spite of daily happenings to the contrary, will be able to keep their minds firmly fixed upon the good intent and the better spirit of Christian people in the West? Who are those who will have the courage to discount the discourtesy between nation and nation—the mistaken policies which emerge almost every day, and resolutely fix the mind and heart of the peoples of the East upon the real desire in the West for carrying out the principle of brotherhood? I take it the answer is to be found in such a document as the manifesto issued by the Church of Christ in China a year or two ago, "The Message of the Church." It was a message from the very heart of the Church of China, through the mind of some of her choice young leaders, the product of Christian education; a group of men who have caught the vision of China for Christ and Christ for the world. Christian education alone can answer these questions.

5. *The Church of Christ:* The Church in the West has had a large part in building up branches of the Church out in the East, in China, in India and in Japan. We have passed through, one may say, three stages. We had, first, the period when the missionary did the work and was in control; we then had the stage where the missionary was in charge, with his Chinese fellow workers as associates. As I see it, we have now entered upon the stage where it is to be the Chinese leader, the Indian leader or the Japanese leader with his missionary fellow workers as associates. Note the difference in the order.

Thus it is clear that the demand today is for Christian education, in order to produce the kind of leadership which is required for that growing and developing church. We must never permit our attachment to any kind of work, however close it may lie to the heart of the church at home, not even, may I say, the great and glorious task of getting the Gospel preached, to come into competition with the demand for Christian education of the highest quality. For I wish to assert, and that most emphatically, that Christian education is in itself closely linked with the work of evangelism. The two cannot be separated. One is essential to the success of the other.

May I ask secretaries and members of Mission Boards when faced with budgets and possible deficits not to take the evangelist, with his enthusiasm for the preaching to the people on the street, in the market place, or in the chapel—the magnificent figure that he is—and put him in competition with the teacher who, through the slow, difficult processes of the school is seeking both to sow the seed and to cultivate the plant. It is a mistake to assume that the work of the teacher and that of the evangelist are in competition. Christian education, as we know it in the Orient today, is one of the greatest evangelistic forces in the world. I am prepared to say further, that Christian education is evangelism, pure and simple, and, therefore, it deserves your solid support and sympathy. See to it that you do not fail to facilitate the training of the leader, because the process is costly, difficult, and slow, and will produce results for the future rather for today.

6. *Education:* There is growing up in China, as in Japan, a government system of education, led by a group of younger men, who are forward-looking in the very best sense of the term. It is being improved in method and technique day by day. Alongside that, and in close association with it, comes the demand for Christian education, which must be characterized by the highest quality, from the point of view of science and education itself. Will you help young China, and young India, and young Japan through their Christian forces, to build up such a system of education?

It is ours, as we are engaged in Christian education, for instance, to establish a tradition as to the practice of medicine in those lands. It is ours to impress upon medical students who are to be leaders, the fact that the profession of medicine is an avenue for service, to be rendered in the spirit of Him who "came not to be ministered unto, but to minister." That such a tradition is being created is proved by an incident like this. In March of 1921, there swept down from the North, outside the great wall of China, a terrible epidemic. So far has medicine advanced, that it is possible now by the skilful use of all forces to combat such an epidemic. So the medical men were called on. Among the group was one young Chinese doctor. He gave himself with complete abandon and enthusiam to the work of fighting the epidemic. In the end he was taken down with it himself. Just before he died he passed on in writing a message to his own family. I cannot recall the whole message, but it contained one or two sentences like this, "I have no complaint. I die for my people." Can that be beaten on this side of the Pacific?

It is the privilege of those engaged in education to create a tradition as to the work of the teacher among the young, in the East, a conception to which China, in particular, has already made a contribution out of the past.

I sometimes look with longing to the old village dominie, with his long gown and little pill box cap. He was a man of simple life, and often of quite blameless character; a man who was a real influence in his own community. Everybody went to him for advice; his students retained toward him an affection, a respect and a loyalty which remained throughout their years. But he is passing, and who is to create the standard for the teacher of the new day, if it is not men and women who have been trained through Christian education and the Christian schools? Who will present the idea of what is meant by genuine social betterment, if it is not men and women who have caught the spirit of Christ? The Christian pastor, too, who propagates his faith among the people not only by teaching but also by preaching, is a new type in the social life of China. It will take constructive thinking, it will take positive work by many a young leader to make clear to the society of China and the East what his proper function is to be.

7. *The Challenge:* I will throw out the challenge to you along two lines: *Firstly*: The Church in the West must realize that the responsibility for carrying on Christian education in the East, for the present at least, is hers. There are many types of education which can pay their way; but the education of which we have been speaking will draw its human material, for the most part, from humble homes, and it will ask men and women to enter vocations where there is little remuneration, where the standards are not set by silver dollars. And so you must be satisfied, while

China and India and Japan experiment in Christian education, to do your part largely in the form of helping to pay the bills. You must devise large and generous things for Christian education in the East, and *secondly,* you must cease to look upon education in the East as a replica of that which you know in the West, for clearly, thought, and truth, and science must take new and different shape in the minds of China and India and Japan, and the whole East. So you must be satisfied to give the privilege of self-expression to those peoples in working out *their* systems of Christian education.

I camped a short time ago, on Tai Mountain, in company with a group of students. A short distance away was the resting place of Confucius, the great Chinese sage. In the rear rose the mountain with its procession going up daily, a procession of pilgrims extending back into the centuries. Among those young men, clean, straight and Christian, one saw the hope of the new day. As surely as morning by morning the sun rose over the shoulder of Tai Shan and cast its light over that great plain, the scene of human activity, spread out before us. It is because Christ is the Light that I, at least, count it the greatest privilege of my life to have a part in Christian education in the East today.

CHRISTIAN EDUCATION AND CHRISTIAN WOMANHOOD

DEAN HELEN K. HUNT, RANGOON, BURMA

The work which must be shouldered by the Christian people of the world is growing so heavy and so complicated, that we cannot consent to limit the workers to any country or any class. Every country and every class must labor together, if so heavy a load is to be moved, and the world is to go forward. We have long recognized our responsibility for the depressed classes and rejoiced in their developing powers, which promise great things for the future. We must have the help of the women, too. The Christian women of the West have done more than can be measured. What may we not hope for, when the women of the East have equal training and vision!

Are the educated Christian men of the Orient not to have wives whose background of reading and thinking will enable them to understand and sympathize with their husbands' hopes and plans for their country? Too often we have seen men eager to throw themselves into some form of unselfish service, with small salary and little recognition, only to be thwarted by wives who were not willing to share in such a gift of life. Why should these women be ready to give what they value most when they have caught no glimpse of the vision which lures their husbands?

We know how strong national and race consciousness is growing in both East and West. Hardly a village in British India has escaped the irritation of the political agitator, and as a result of constantly increasing pressure and demand, more and more power is being given into the hands of the people. Democracy is always their slogan, but the very conception of a government for all the people, regardless of wealth or class, is as yet incomprehensible to the masses. Democracy is not fostered by a Hinduism which justifies and defends the continuance of the privileged Brahman and the hopeless untouchable; it can not be a real part of a Mohammedanism which preaches a Holy War; and it must be foreign to Buddhism for no Buddhist can help another, but must work out his own happiness and prosperity. Democracy, with its whole social program, is a heritage of Christianity.

We shall never stop the terrible epidemics so common in the Orient until quarantine is enforced. That will be an impossibility just so long as the women of the towns and villages refuse to submit to it; and there is no hope of persuading them to accept it until at least some of them know enough of science to understand the reason for it.

In every department of public and private health the women hold the balance of power, and all men's efforts to better laws will prove fruitless as long as the women quietly but persistently refuse to obey them. These prejudices, due to a lack of understanding must be broken down by women and by women of their own race. Time after time a Western woman's careful explanation is met with courtesy and an unchanged attitude. But watch a woman of that country tell a story, or perhaps quote a proverb which does not seem to us to even apply to the case, and her listener's attitude changes as if by magic. It requires minds that understand, as well as hearts that feel, to win and direct the cooperation of women with men toward such movements as the lessening of infant mortality, the segregation of lepers, the proper care of the insane, pure food regulations and the other myriad lines of improvement that touch the home so intimately.

We cannot expect children in the lower schools to grasp the biggest and hardest problems that we are all thinking about these days the world around—the clash of class with class, race and race, East and West, peace and war. But a Christian college in the Orient is a laboratory in which these elements are daily being tested. In the college where I teach there are somwhat more than three hundred men and women students. They represent the following races: Burmese, Karen, Anglo-Indian, several nationalities of Indians, and pure Chinese. The faculty includes representatives of all these races, plus British and Americans. Month by month we see these young people, most of whom have not personally known these other races before, working together and watching each other. It is not necessary to include courses on internationalism in the curriculum. No student can avoid practical experiments. I have heard many conversations among those college girls, indicating minds and hearts waking up to subjects bigger than gossip; and they intend to have something to say about the working out of these questions in their own country.

The by-products of our Christian education are often far greater than we realize. One day a Burman Buddhist girl came to me and confided to me her day-dream. Her father is one of only three Burmans entrusted with the supervision of a whole district. She was one of the first two Burman Buddhist girls to ever receive a bachelor's degree. She said, "It seems to me I ought to be able to do something. You know my father travels all through his district and at every town and village he stops and calls together the officials there and they go into such questions as the public finances, public health, prevalence of crime and such things. I would like to travel with him, and then when he summons the officials to meet him, he could call the women to meet me somewhere. And if he summoned them they would come! Then I would like to talk to the women about the care of the children and food for children and how to take care of sick children."

Where did she get that idea? Certainly not from Buddhism. I said, "Have you said anything at home about this?" "Yes, I told my mother." "What did she say?" "Well, she said she thought I must be crazy." I then said, "Did you say anything to your father?" "I told him. He didn't say anything for a while and then he said he believed it would be a very good thing."

This summer I have had letters from her, telling about the greatly increased activity of the country women of the district there, who are being aroused to violent opposition to the government by a group of the priests. She, a Buddhist girl, accused these priests of both ignorance and malevolence, but we have women suffrage in Burma and the priests want to get these women. How could those ignorant country women find the inconsistencies in the men's harangues?

She ended with a wail, "I wish I were not the only woman in this whole district who had ever studied logic."

It is the trained women of the Orient upon whom we must depend to teach the girls who are crowding our preparatory schools, and who but Christian college women can built these schools into what we dream for them? Where can you find a more alluring quest? To do for the Orient what our great women educators have done for us, is a task which will call forth all that is best in Oriental womanhood.

And to whom but Christian college women in the East can we appeal for pioneers? The world still has frontiers, physical frontiers as well as those of mind and spirit. Among primitive races, only women who know the thoughts of women can draw their minds and hearts. Some will say that it is useless to talk of pioneer work for women now in the East, that the bonds of custom and convention and habit and public opinion are so strong that for many centuries yet it will be impossible for the Oriental women to break through and enter such new and unaccustomed spheres. But the pioneer, whether he is a man or woman, is always a surprise. He never does the expected. Already Pandita Ramabai and our fine group of Oriental women physicians have shown what may come, and even now the East is travelling too fast to measure her own rate of progress. Our pioneers are sure to appear, but shall we ask them to undertake such great tasks without the best of thought and training?

The women of the Orient have courage and keenness. They are just beginning to look out beyond their own families, and desire to know and have a part in the activities of the world as as well as their nations, a number too large for our knowledge and too powerful for our imagination. But must they make all the blunders that we have made and waste all of time and life that we have lost? Shall we not share with them all we have won by painful effort, and then go forth together in Christ's name, working for all the human family?

UNION AND COOPERATION IN EDUCATION IN INDIA

THE REVEREND J. ROY STROCK, MASULIPATAM, INDIA

Union and cooperation have been thought of in India, particularly along the lines of colleges, theological seminaries and teacher-training institutions. Advantages derived through such cooperation are, among others, the following:

(1) These forms of education are comparatively expensive and the needs of the missions are varied and pressing. Hence the necessity of avoiding wasteful competition.

(2) The need of today is for fewer but more efficient institutions. Quality is essential at present or the years of missionary education are numbered. Efficiency on the educational side and effectiveness on the missionary side can be achieved only by means of the concentration of our resources and our men.

(3) The bringing together into one college of the strongest missionary and Indian Christian teachers and also practically all of the Christian students of an area will provide conditions most favorable for an effective presentation of Christ and for the influencing of character.

(4) The college will give convincing testimony to the essential oneness of all Christians in Christ. The moral effect of this upon the Indian public will be great.

(5) No mission can of itself have the influence on the government and on the University that a union college will have. It is certain that the only way for Christian educationalists to have influence in regard to higher education in India today is by maintaining efficient colleges. The influence that the Madras Christian College has had on the University of Madras for many decades shows clearly what a really efficient Christian College can accomplish.

(6) Instead of becoming a gradually diminishing factor in the life of India through the spread of national education, Christianity, by means of first-rate and centrally located colleges, will become a positive, determining force—a growingly important influence.

In India—and I refer especially to South India—we have two types of union institutions. One type is represented by the Women's Christian College, Madras, and the Vellore Medical College for women. These institutions have been established and are maintained by various missions cooperating on a basis of equal contributions and equal representation. Other institutions of the same type are the Bangalore Theological Seminary and the Teachers' College for Women in Madras.

The other type of union institution is represented by the Madras Christian College in the city of Madras. This college was founded many years ago by the United Free Church of Scotland, with the promise of assistance in respect of maintenance from the Church of Scotland. Gradually, however, through the course of the years, other missions have been joining with these in the support of the institution, so that at the present time, although the United Free Church of Scotland is the predominant mission, seven missions are actually having a share in the support and conduct of the college. Another institution of this type is one which is just now being founded, namely, the Teachers' College for male graduates in Madura. In this case several missions will cooperate in the maintenance of a college established by the mission of the American Board.

At a meeting of the Andhra Christian Council, in December, 1923, the Council came to the conclusion that it is absolutely essential for the missions to have a strong Christian college in the Telugu or Andhra country. It decided, in view of the inability of most of the missions working in that part of the country to enter into a scheme depending upon equal contributions from all, to urge the American Lutherans to undertake the establishment of the college and to propose a basis of cooperation for other missions to have a share in the work. This invitation of the Andhra Christian Council was considered by the United Lutheran Church at its convention in Chicago, in October, 1924, and was accepted.

Funds are now being raised for the establishing of the Andhra Christian College. The two Christian colleges now in existence in the Telugu country, namely, the Lutheran Junior College at Guntur and Noble College at Masulipatam, will discontinue their college class and will function as Christian high schools from the date of the opening of the new college. It is obvious that this college will be similar to the Madras Christian College.

It is the idea of the Andhra Christian Council that this new college should have as its first care in every respect the youth of our Christian Church in India. It will, however, admit as many Hindus and Mohammedans as conditions may make it practicable or advisable to admit to its privileges, and thus it will be not only a training ground for Christian leaders but also an evangelizing force. In order that the Christian influence of the institution may be as strong as possible, the number of students will be limited.

In order that those who have gathered at this conference may realize the spirit in which the missionaries are now attempting to solve some of the large problems which are coming before them, I shall quote a passage from the official report of Noble College for the past year. This report was written by a missionary of the Church of England who is now acting as principal of that college:

"What was the Church Missionary Society doing to help? The Church Missionary Society sorely hindered by accumulations of deficits during the war, has promised $17,000 towards capital expenditure and two missionaries on the staff. It has promised the "good will" of the Noble College, after eighty years of progressive work. It has the humility to see that if more powerful shoulders can bear a heavier burden of finance for the sake of a finer college, it should cooperate and let the more powerful mission take the lead. Selfish worrying as to who is the greatest should have no place in the cooperative glory of noble educational and Christian work. 'All in one' is the root of our strength. The prospects for a more glorious Andhra Christian College are as bright as we could hope for."

CHRISTIAN EDUCATION IN RELATION TO GOVERNMENT DEVELOPMENTS

MR. JOSEPH H. OLDHAM, M.A., LONDON, ENGLAND

I doubt whether in the whole history of Christianity there has been anything more striking than the contribution which Christian schools in Asia and in Africa have made to the development of the peoples of these continents. In Japan, in China, in India and in the Turkish Empire their contribution has been remarkable. Up to the present, ninety per cent of the education given to the African race by the West has been given to them through Christian schools.

The fundamental fact however with which we have to reckon is that conditions are changing out of all recognition. During the Great War there arrived one day at Simla, the summer capital of the Government of India, two representatives of one of the hill tribes. They had heard, they said, that the King-Emperor was having trouble with his enemies, and their chief had sent them down with two rifles and a bag of gunpowder as a contribution to the struggle. The attitude of some Boards to the new conditions which are emerging is perhaps not very different from the understanding possessed by this chieftain in the Himalayan mountains of the conditions of modern warfare.

Everywhere, throughout the countries of Asia and Africa, Governments are entering the field of education. The State is assuming the responsibility for education. The missionary schools have been pioneers, but it may be that in a relatively short time they will be put out of the business. This is not inevitable, but it is certainly a possibility. Even if they are not put entirely out of the business, they may be put out to a great extent. Mr. T. Z. Koo said to me not long ago that what he feared in China was not that the Christian schools would be left without pupils, since the task of education was so gigantic that for a long time to come there would be pupils for every school, but that Christian schools might have only those pupils who were not able enough or ambitious enough to go elsewhere. When I was in Lahore, twenty-five years ago, there were four colleges there—a government college, a Mohammedan college, a Hindu college and the Forman Christian college; and of these the Forman College got the pick of the students. It is quite possible that this situation may be reversed, and that Christian schools may have to take the leavings from the others.

The missionary task is always to be in the central stream of the world's life.

If we are to seize the present opportunity four conditions must be fulfilled:

In the first place we must act together. The determining voice in education is always that of Government. If we have twenty or thirty different policies Government will go its own way. Whatever we may think, Government will inevitably treat private effort as a unity.

Secondly, we must have a clearly thought-out philosophy of education in our own minds. We must believe that it is a sound thing from the national point of view that in the national system of education there should be a place for private effort. It leaves room for experiment. We have high educational authority for believing that this is sound policy. We must also have strong convictions that religion is an essential element in sound education. I have a profound belief in the efficiency of truth, and if the educational convictions to which I have referred represent the truth we may hope that if we stand for them firmly, reasonably and temperately, we shall achieve success.

Thirdly, we must make our schools national. No Government likes to see education in the hands of aliens. If we are to retain our schools we must at all costs make them as national as we can. This means giving as large as possible a share in their control to the people of the country. It means also that we must take the lead in bringing into our curriculum the best that there is in the past of the nations among which our schools are working. This is what Mr. Fraser is setting himself to do in the work to which he has gone in Achimota, on the Gold Coast of West Africa.

Fourthly, if we are to maintain our position we must make our schools good, better than any other institution. The challenge is one that we must not be afraid to meet. The aim of sound education is the formation of character, and our business as Christian missionaries is also the formation of character. We ought not to shrink from the test that boys and girls educated in a Christian school bear the marks of the Christian training they have received in strong and trustworthy character. If we achieve that kind of result there is good reason to hope that even a non-Christian Government will not put an end to schools which are serving the nation in this way.

THE PERIOD OF INTERCESSION

THE REVEREND ROBERT FORGAN, D.D., EDINBURGH, SCOTLAND

Before we unite in our common intercession at this time let us listen for a few moments to the voice of Jesus Himself as He taught the multitudes and set Himself also to educate His chosen disciples. From the substance and quality and method of the Master Teacher, missionaries and ministers and all Christ's fellow-workers may learn the secret of all true teaching.

"And Jesus returned in the power of the Spirit into Galilee: and there went out a fame of Him through all the region round about. And He taught in their synagogues, being glorified of all.

"And Jesus went about all the cities and villages, teaching in their synagogues, and preaching the gospel of the Kingdom, and healing every sickness and every disease among the people. But when He saw the multitudes, He was moved with compassion on them, because they fainted, and were scattered abroad, as sheep having no shepherd.

"Then saith He unto His disciples, The harvest truly is plenteous, but the labourers are few;

"Pray ye therefore the Lord of the harvest, that He will send forth laborers into His harvest.

"Say not ye, There are yet four months, and then cometh harvest? Behold, I say unto you, Lift up your eyes and look on the fields; for they are white already to harvest.

"And he that reapeth receiveth wages, and gathereth fruit unto life eternal; that both he that soweth and he that reapeth may rejoice together.

"And herein is that saying true, One soweth, and another reapeth. I sent you to reap that whereon ye bestowed no labor; other men labored, and ye are entered into their labors.

"And seeing the multitudes, He went up into a mountain; and when He was set, His disciples came unto Him;

"And He opened His mouth, and taught them, saying,

"Blessed are the poor in spirit, for theirs is the kingdom of heaven.

"Blessed are they that mourn, for they shall be comforted.

"Blessed are the meek, for they shall inherit the earth.

"Blessed are they which do hunger and thirst after righteousness, for they shall be filled.

"Blessed are the merciful, for they shall obtain mercy.

"Blessed are the pure in heart, for they shall see God.

"Blessed are the peacemakers, for they shall be called the children of God.

"Blessed are they which are persecuted for righteousness' sake, for theirs is the kingdom of heaven.

"Blessed are ye, when men shall revile you, and persecute you, and shall say all manner of evil against you falsely, for My sake.

"Rejoice, and be exceeding glad, for great is your reward in heaven: for so persecuted they the prophets which were before you.

"Ye are the salt of the earth, but if the salt have lost his savor, wherewith shall it be salted? It is thenceforth good for nothing, but to be cast out, and to be trodden under foot of men.

"Ye are the light of the world. A city that is set on a hill cannot be hid.

"Neither do men light a candle, and put it under a bushel, but on a candlestick; and it giveth light unto all that are in the house.

"Let your light so shine before men, that they may see your good works, and glorify your Father which is in heaven."

We have been listening this morning to a most interesting and helpful discussion upon Christian education. All expert educators in these days attach supreme value to what they call "atmosphere" in their colleges and schools. By that word they describe what they desire to be the moral and spiritual tone which should prevail among teachers and pupils. Unless the right spirit pervades an educational institution, the highest and best results cannot be obtained. It is all-important, therefore, that in seeking to impart a Christian education in our different mission fields, our educational missionaries should give careful attention to securing a high and pure spiritual atmosphere in which to carry on their work. Our risen Lord realized the need of teaching, when He gave His last command to His apostles, "Go ye therefore and teach all nations." Literally the word used here in the original Greek means "make disciples" or "learners" of all the nations. The nations had much to learn then, as they have much still to learn today. They required to be taught, and our Lord went on to explain both what was to be the substance of the apostles' teaching and what was to be the spirit in which they were to fulfil their commission. "Teaching them"—and here the Greek word is quite different; it is the technical term for "imparting instruction"—the former word "teaching the nations" meant "making disciples" that they might learn. But now we have the definite word which signifies technical instruction, "Teaching them to observe all things whatsoever I have commanded you; and, lo, I am with you alway." So their teaching was to be carried on by the apostles and Christ's followers through all the coming generations in His presence. "Lo, I am with you." He Himself was to be there, unseen yet near, in every school the apostles set up, as He is present in every school His missionaries set up today. And the substance of the teaching was to be "all things whatsoever He has commanded"; and He also told his apostles how they themselves were to learn the things they were to teach. The spirit of truth was to come upon them, and that spirit was to lead them into all the truth. And that Spirit, receiving the things of Christ, still reveals them to His followers that they in turn may go and teach them to the world.

Our theme today lies very near to the center of world evangelization. We call it education, Christian education in the mission fields, and we have been considering various aspects of that theme this morning. The importance of religious education has received fresh attention in the home lands of late years, as well as in the mission fields; and if we put a sufficiently deep meaning into the word, it is not too much to say that, broadly, Christianity has for its supreme aim the education of mankind. A liberal education is a Christian education. Teach men to know, and with the knowledge give them understanding. Teach men, above all, to know God as Jesus Christ reveals Him, and you have solved the riddle of the universe, the problems of our generation and of each new generation that will arise; for in so educating men you have freed them from the darkness of ignorance, from the tyranny of the unworthy and the base, and have lifted them to the level of the sons of God.

The aim of all true education is the making of character. So all our wisest modern educators are agreed. And it is certainly true that the aim of all Christian education, whether at home or abroad, is the making of Christian character. In particular, in the mission field our missionaries have come to realize that education is not a mere adjunct or auxiliary in the task of world evangelization, but one of their principal agents, one of the best of their evangelizing instruments. There should be no sharp line of demarcation between educational and evangelistic missions. Rightly understood, the two are one.

So now, after all we have heard this morning, we do well, do we not, to draw near into the presence of God, to make united intercession for the progress and prosperity of all earnest endeavor, by means of education, to enlighten the minds, to purify the hearts and to elevate the character of the children of men.

Let us bow before God and in silence pray for teachers and their pupils in all Christian lands:—

O, God, our Father, do Thou so inspire and guide all parents and all other responsible educators that they shall recognize the education of the youth of this generation as at once the noblest and the gravest task committed to their charge. Set before all teachers, we beseech Thee, the true ideal, and grant them the vision and the faith, the patience, the firmness, the love and the understanding, which will fit them for the worthy fulfillment of their task.

Let us further remember before God all universities, colleges and schools of learning in which any of us here have a special interest, whether in our different home lands or in the mission fields which are best known to us:—

O God, the Fountain of knowledge and Source of all wisdom, we entreat Thee that in all these halls of learning which we have now named in our hearts, the search for truth may be undertaken, not only with diligence and perseverance but with humility and reverence; that the teachers and students may find Thee as they study the work of Thy hands in nature and in history. O Lord God, we pray that in science, in art and in literature Thou wilt control the thoughts of men and reveal Thy glory, and suffer no pride of discovery or joy of achievement to hinder men from recognizing that the fear of the Lord is the beginning of wisdom, and that in Jesus Christ, Thy Son, dwelleth all fulness of knowledge, both for the life that now is and for that which is to come.

And shall we now give thanks to Almighty God for all He has already accomplished through the agency of Christian missions in the opening of blind eyes, and in dispelling the darkness from the minds of men and nations by the rising of the sun of righteousness, by the revelation of Jesus Christ who proclaimed Himself here upon earth to be the Light of the world, the Light and the Life of men?

Let us recall with gratitude the progress made among primitive peoples, as in darkest Africa and the islands of the sea; and also among peoples who have inherited an ancient civilization which needs the light of Christ to lift it to a higher level:—

O God, the Father of all men, of every race and every color and every tongue, we pray that whatever of good exists in the life and character of the peoples who, as yet, have not received the full and gracious revelation of Thyself in Jesus Christ, may form for those peoples a stepping stone and may be used by Thee to raise them to the fulness of the knowledge of Thy salvation and of all that that means for their life here and hereafter.

For all institutions devoted to the training and preparation of educational missionaries we make our common intercession, that those thus trained and equipped may go forth in the Spirit of the Master to prepare and train men and women in the far lands who, in their turn, shall become the leaders of their own peoples.

O God, our Father, we bless Thee for all we ourselves have learned, for all that we have been taught by the gracious operation of Thy Spirit in our hearts, for all that we have learned by the lessons of Christian living in our Christian lands up to this present time. We pray that Thou wilt enlarge our hearts' desires that we may bear before Thee the burden of the needs of this world and of all our fellow men, that they may share those sacred privileges which we have enjoyed and be brought to a knowledge of the truth as the truth is in Jesus.

Most gracious God, let Thy blessing abound toward us in this great convention; and in all the various gatherings in which we assemble ourselves together may the Spirit of all truth work mightily among us that in due time we may return to our different tasks with a fresh inspiration and a fresh consecration of ourselves and of all we hold nearest and dearest to that great service of the Kingdom of God upon the earth to which Thou has called Thy Church.

These things we pray for in the name that is above every name, the all-prevailing name of our Lord and Saviour, Jesus Christ. Amen.

CHRIST REVEALED THROUGH DEEDS OF MERCY AND LOVE

MEDICAL MISSIONS

T. DWIGHT SLOAN, M.D., PEKING, CHINA

Some fifteen years ago, before I had gone out as a medical missionary, I was asked why I had decided to take up this work. These three reasons flashed into my mind.

First, because I believe it is the best professional strategy. Dr. Osler has stated that the aim of modern medicine is to create an environment in which health, and not disease, will be the normal thing. Vital statistics in America and in Europe will show that we have progressed far in the achievement of that ideal, yet I knew that the strongholds, not only of the common contagious diseases, but of leprosy, small pox, cholera, plague, and many other great scourges as well as the most un- favorable sanitary conditions, were not to be found in this country, but in the so-called mission countries. I wanted to get in where the line was farthest-flung, and where I believed I could make the greatest contribution to the professed aim of modern medicine.

Second, because it is the truest patriotism. I knew that with increasing trade relationships and better communications we were more and more threatened with diseases brought in from the Orient. We had been reminded of this very forcefully just at that time, as we have been only within the last few months again reminded, by an outbreak of bubonic plague in California, this last time, in its pneumonic form; and we have not only paid the toll in the lives of our citizens, but we have expended millions of dollars in stamping it out.

I said to myself that it would be a more patriotic thing to attack such diseases at their source and to help to clean them up than to wait till they had actually attacked us. Moreover, I was even then thoroughly convinced that it was a real patri- otic service to promote friendly relationships with other peoples by a spirit of helpfulness. I could think of no finer instance of this spirit than the service of the medical missionary.

Third, because it affords the opportunity to put the Chris- tian stamp on the ethics of the coming medical profession of these countries. I was thinking of China especially, because it was to that country that I intended to go.

Each one of these reasons has proven true, far more true than in my moments of greatest enthusiasm I had been able

123

to imagine; but experience on the field has taught me an added reason for this work, namely, it has put within the hands of the Christian church on the field a most effective means of reaching men for Christ. The Christian hospitals speak a message which is understood by Christian and non-Christian alike. This was strikingly illustrated several years ago in Nanking, China, when it seemed probable that the University hospital would have to be given up. The University Medical School had amalgamated with the school of the Shantung Christian University in another city. Many believed that this would force the closing of the hospital in Nanking. There was much discussion concerning it. Pastor Swen, who was in charge of one of the Presbyterian churches in the city, came to the superintendent of the hospital, much alarmed by the rumors which he had heard. "Why," he said, "if you close the hospital, we had just as well close our churches, too. We simply must have the hospital." This was, of course, an extreme way of stating the case; still, Pastor Swen knew that the community needed the practical expression of Christianity at work for men which the hospital afforded. He felt that to lose the medical work would seriously handicap all Christian effort.

That the non-Christian community held the hospital in high esteem will be seen from the statements of the Vice-President of the Chinese Red Cross Society. When civil war was threatening with Nanking as the prospective storm center, he requested the superintendent of the University hospital to become the honorary head of the Red Cross organization which was to care for the wounded. The superintendent asked his visitor which of the local hospitals under Chinese management could be counted upon to share in the work. "Not one," he replied, "we propose to use only the mission hospital." The Nanking hospital was not closed and remains today an increasingly outstanding witness of a living Christian faith in that community.

Similar testimony to the esteem in which mission hospitals are held could be obtained from every section of the mission field. Here in America we take these institutions largely as a matter of course. Not so in non-Christian lands. Here we often forget the Christ whose influence inspired the enterprise. We may even set up a charitable institution, flaunting perhaps an anti-Christian front, while at the same time capitalizing the stimulus, example, and sympathy of those made charitable through the direct or indirect influence of the Christian message. Out yonder, however, these Christian institutions are recognized by all as the embodiment of the spirit of the Christian message. How important it is, then, that they worthily represent the cause!

This at once suggests the type of men and the character of the plants that are required for this work. When we think of the type of men, our minds instantly revert to some of those great pioneers who blazed the way for medical missions; Drs. Parker, Lockhart and Kerr in China, Drs. Thomas and Scudder in India, Dr. Hepburn in Japan, David Livingstone in Africa, and many other noble souls of like motive. Women as well as men have played a most important part in this work. Dr. Clara Swain, pioneer woman physician in India, heads a long list of noble names of women who share with the pioneers already mentioned the honor of opening the way. With scant equipment these leaders accomplished seemingly impossible tasks. How eagerly we cherish the heritage they have left us! But what shall we say of the type of men required at the present time? It is true that in the past medical missionaries have been very generously judged by what they had, and not according to what they lacked. We have, however, now arrived at a time when, if we are to maintain the commanding influence of medical missions, we must provide a personnel thoroughly abreast of the latest developments in modern medicine, and furnished with a physicial equipment in which standard medical work may be done. Training that was acceptable even ten or twenty years ago will not suffice for today's requirements. A plant and equipment that were formerly considered good may fail utterly to meet the present demands.

Many of the citizens of non-Christian countries have already become familiar through travel and study abroad with the best hospitals in Europe and America. They are in a position to know whether mission institutions are efficient or not, and to criticize their shortcomings. Nine years ago at a meeting of the Foreign Missions Conference of North America, where an extensive report of field investigations was presented, and where resolutions were adopted looking forward to improving medical mission work, there was unanimous agreement to the principle that there must be a decided advance in the methods hitherto employed. Among the statements quoted were the following: Dr. Venable of China, one of the ex-presidents of the China Medical Missionary Association said, "I do not wish to disparage the medical mission work of the past, but I believe the time has come for making radical and sweeping changes in our work in the direction of consolidation and concentration. We have spread out too thin." Dr. Norton of Korea added, "The time has come when we can no longer get along with the scanty outfit and the slipshod methods of ten years ago. I think every hospital should be outfitted to do the most careful and scientific work." Dr. King of Banza, Congo, was quoted as saying, "A doctor goes through years of long, hard preparation and then on the field finds his hands tied through lack of hospital equipment."

Nine years ago they were saying these things, and yet only this week one of the medical secretaries of a large mission Board said to me that it seemed to him as if his Board in its medical policy was standing still. It simply must not be allowed to stand still. Not to advance medically is to recede, for the procession is marching forward. We must face squarely at this point our objective. Is our aim to be quantity or quality production? Should we aim to treat the greatest possible number of sufferers, or should we aim to treat only so many as we can handle creditably and in accordance with the best medical traditions? In the past the former view has perhaps been the dominant one. We are now shifting to the latter.

It is manifest on a moment's reflection that we can after all treat only the merest fraction of the sick of the non-Christian world. The entire output of all the schools of medicine and of nursing in the United States and in Canada, if it could be made available, would not suffice for China's need alone. All, therefore, that the few who can respond to this need can do is to furnish an example and by training a few leaders of a future medical profession, to lay the foundation on which an indigenous modern medical system may be developed.

Our present duty seems to be two-fold: First, to send out men and women who measure up to the best standards of professional training and ability, who also possess, together with this training and ability, the requisite spiritual qualities. Second, to provide in each case a physical plant and equipment such as are required for doing creditable work. If we do these, it will undoubtedly mean that we will take the next step, which is a corollary to these two: namely, we will abandon some of the isolated poorly-manned and badly-equipped centers of medical work, which cannot within a comparatively short time be brought up to a minimum standard.

This does not mean that there is no place for the itinerant type of pioneer in missionary work, since manifestly there is still demand in some remote regions for this type of physician, but it does mean that a sounder policy would be to strengthen and improve existing centers of medical work, rather than to continue the process of expansion at the sacrifice of efficiency in the centers that have already been established. It will also mean union and cooperation with other societies in certain special centers, where a number of societies are at work. This would permit specialization on the part of the doctors in those hospitals, which tends to efficiency.

Moreover, this program will require a far more thorough-going cooperation in medical education of the various societies in order that adequate provision may be made in a few selected centers for the careful training of physicians and nurses. Yesterday in the Conference that was held on medical work three themes were considered: First, the "Contribution of Medical Missions"; second, "The Present Policy of Medical Missions"; third, "The Most Urgent Needs of Medical Missions." From each of these angles the discussion invariably focussed on medical education as the pivotal point in the program. It must be so. I am profoundly interested in maintaining a high standard of scientific efficiency in these schools and hospitals. I am even more concerned that along with professional excellence shall go the Christian ideal.

A good beginning has been made at the Shantung Christian University Medical School in Tsinan-fu, at the Hunan-Yale Medical College in Changsha, Hunan, at the Severance Medical College in Seoul, Korea, and in other centers too numerous to mention. It would be difficult to over-estimate the influence of these schools.

In addition to all this, the program will compel a well-planned campaign of popular education in health matters in order to create a strong supporting public sentiment. A striking example of what can be done in health education is afforded by the very excellent work of Dr. W. W. Peter and his associates in China. By means of arresting exhibits, lectures, and demonstrations, and by creating a considerable body of health literature, they are attracting the attention and securing the interest of large numbers of people in health matters. In this case, however, as in every phase of the program, which we are proposing, we would insist that the quality rather than the quantity of the work done is to be emphasized.

Another very effective means for improving the quality of medical mission work is the recognition on the part of the Mission Boards of the necessity for periodic post-graduate courses for medical workers. Occasionally, satisfactory courses may be offered by some institution within the bounds of the country in which the missionary resides, as, for instance, at the Peking Union Medical College in China. More often, however, provision for post-graduate studies must be made during furlough. Some Boards very wisely provide more frequent furloughs for medical workers than they do for those less likely to suffer from the overcrowding and isolation of missionary life. No one feels that so much as the physician.

Already the missionary body is demanding improved standards for hospitals. In China, for example, the China Medical Missionary Association, following the example of the American College of Surgeons, appointed a committee to formulate certain minimum requirements by which the acceptability of a hospital could be judged. The standards proposed, modest as they are, will, when accepted, probably place a majority of the mission hospitals in a non-approved list. They will not, however, remain long in the unacceptable class, if we, who are here representing the home base as well as the workers over there, do our duty.

The requirements proposed by the Committee relate to the keeping of satisfactory records, the provision of reasonable laboratory facilities, and the securing of a plant, staff, and equipment capable of rendering efficient service to the patients. The technical details do not concern us here. When these standards are put into effect, it will be evident to all that the missionaries themselves recognize that a new era in medical work is already upon us. Surely we will not fail them in their endeavor to maintain this work at such a high standard of efficiency that it will continue to be a mainstay to the cause. Anything short of the best will not suffice.

What, then may we expect men and institutions of the type that I have been endeavoring to portray, to accomplish? In the light of experience, the following facts seem established: (1) They create an atmosphere favorable to all forms of Christian work; (2) They form the groundwork and furnish the example on which an indigenous medical profession strongly influenced by Christian standards is to be built up; (3) They conserve the health and working efficiency of the entire missionary body; (4) They promote public health education; and (5) They reach many untouched by other Christian agencies.

In the hospital with which I am at present connected, a woman had undergone a dangerous and difficult surgical operation and was convalescing. One morning, just after her dressing had been finished, she said, "I want to be a Christian. Before I came here, I did not understand much about Christianity. I did not imagine before that there was such kindness in all the world as has been shown me by all the doctors and the nurses who have attended me in this hospital. I want to be baptized." I tell you, it is worth while to follow the Great Physician, as we thus minister to the physical and the spiritual needs of men. I can think of no work which furnishes so much of the real joy of living as this.

WOMEN AND CHILDREN IN INDUSTRY IN THE FAR EAST

MISS MARGARET E. BURTON, NEW YORK

Several of us in this room are wearing hair nets. I wonder how many of us, as we put them on, were conscious of the fact that in all probability the fingers of Chinese women and little girls made those nets. Comparatively few of the women who still use hair nets realize that the great center of the hair net industry is in the city of Chefoo, China. And probably even a smaller number of those who have discarded nets for bobbed locks are aware that they have thereby contributed to the unemployment of hundreds of women in that far-away city of north China. Yet only a short time ago a letter from a friend in Chefoo contained this sentence: "I don't know what will happen to us, if you women in America don't stop cutting your hair. We are all losing our jobs. There were 18,000 women and girls in the hair net factories here two years and a half ago, and now there are only a few over 2,000."

Modern industry has come to the East, and has suddenly precipitated upon ancient civilizations all the bewildering problems which have arisen in the Occident during a hundred years of experience with modern machinery. Nations which have for centuries been sustained by agriculture and handicrafts are suddenly called upon to meet the problems which arise with the substitution of great factories for hand industries; the substitution of the impersonal relation of corporation employers to employees for the side-by-side cooperation of master and apprentice in the little shop; the questions arising from the emigration of thousands of workers from the rural community to the industrial centers, the congestion of population in cities, and the far-reaching changes in family and social life brought about by the employment of women in factories.

Whether or not we regret the industrialization of the East, it has come, and it has come to stay. There is no possibility of stemming the irresistible tide of modern civilization of which it is a part. There is no question that it will be a factor of tremendous importance in the future life of the East. But there is still question what kind of a factor it will become. One of my Chinese friends has summed up the situation in words which refer to China, but might also be applied to other countries of the Orient. "Whether the development of our national resources will be a blessing to mankind, or a curse to humanity in the future, will greatly depend upon the attitude of mind of thinking people. Shall modern industry serve a few people at the expense of thousands of human beings?"

You will notice that my friend does not say, "Whether the development of our national resources will be a blessing to China or a curse to China." She does not even say, "Whether they will be a blessing to Asia or a curse to Asia." She says, "Whether they will be a blessing to mankind or a curse to humanity." The spirit and conditions which govern modern industry in any part of the world today will inevitably either bless or curse men and women in every part of the world. For our scientific discoveries and inventions have, as Maude Royden has put it, created "the kind of a world in which no one can prosper without helping others to prosper, and no one can suffer without causing others to suffer."

It is a far cry from Wilkes-barre, Pa., to Tokyo, Japan. But when, a few months ago, the girls in a silk mill there petitioned for higher wages, their employer said that to grant their request would mean the failure of his business. When pressed for an explanation, he gave competition with the silk mills of Tokyo as the reason for his answer.

This summer, I described to some women of the South the conditions I had seen in cotton mills in Shanghai. When I had finished a woman who has been working for better labor laws in Georgia told me that when she had gone to a cotton mill owner of Atlanta to ask him to support an eight-hour day, he had blazed out at her, telling her that if she knew what he was up against in competition with Shanghai mills, she would not talk to him of an eight-hour day. Paul's long-ago words are true of a world today. If one member suffers, all suffer; if one is honored, all rejoice. Because we are citizens of a world, and because the conditions under which industry in the Orient develops will affect every part of the world, we cannot but be profoundly concerned about them.

And then too, because we are Christians. He, whose Name we bear, came that men might have life and might have it abundantly. May I share with you two pictures of industrial conditions as I saw them in China, and ask you to judge for yourself what opportunity there is, under such conditions, for abundant life— physically, mentally, socially or spiritually.   ,

It is almost exactly three years ago today that I went from the cold, raw winter air of a Shanghai January into the almost intolerable humidity of a silk filature. I can close my eyes and see it again—a long, narrow room, down the length of which stretched two rows of tables, on one side of which sat Chinese women, on the opposite side of which stood little Chinese girls. In front of each woman and of each child was an open kettle of steaming water—the whole room was so full of steam that those of us who had on glasses had to take them off to see. The women were unwinding the silk from the cocoons floating in the water, and the children were keeping a fresh supply soft in the caldrons, stirring them constantly lest they become waterstained. I watched one mite for a long time. She did not keep her cocoons moving gently in the water—she stirred them so hard that my arm ached in sympathy with hers. I measured where her head came on me. It was just to my waist. I asked how old she was. The women opposite her said that she was seven, Chinese count, which means that she was six, or even five, as we measure age.

We asked the owner about wages and hours and age limits. He said the women and children came at five in the morning and worked until seven in the evening. The women received 20 cents and the children 10 cents a day. Ten cents for fourteen hours work, *standing!* We asked him what his age limit for the employment of children was. He said he had none, but that if they were too young they were not much use. The report of the Municipal Commission appointed last year to study child labor in Shanghai shows that this situation is true for practically all Shanghai's industries. "The commencement age" the report says "varies with the nature of the employment, but it can be asserted that, generally speaking, the child begins its work in the mill or factory *as soon as it is of any economic value to the employers.*"

What hope have these little girls of a abundant life, even of physical life? A recent article in the China Medical Journal calls attention to the high percentage of tuberculosis and other pulmonary diseases among the women and especially the children who work in the hot and humid atmosphere of silk filature or cotton mill. Paul Hutchinson, in his book "China's Real Revolution," tells of the effort of a group of Christians to bring a little cheer into the lives of these little silk mill girls, by giving them a Christmas party. "One hundred and twenty of them came," he says— one hundred and twenty morsels of dismal humanity—the tips of their fingers white from constant dipping into the hot water in which the cocoons are handled. These children, ranging from six to twelve years of age, were curious to see what was in store for them. But the best efforts of the most accomplished recreational leaders of the city could do nothing to arouse them. They had been utterly beaten down by the monotony of the factory. Their young strength had been mortgaged, even before they were born." And with the most reverent recognition of the power of the Christian spirit, it must nevertheless be admitted that the utmost efforts of the most earnest and consecrated Christians can never succeed in bringing abundant life to men or women or little children who live and work and have their being under such conditions as these.

Let me give you one other picture of a cold January night, three years ago, when, at four in the morning, I went from a quiet, dark street into the glare and heat and din of the night shift of a cotton mill going full blast. My memories of the hour spent in that mill are of almost unbearable heat, air filled with cotton fluff showing white against the black Chinese heads, and of exhausted workers, too weary even to look up at the most unusual spectacle of three foreign women going through their mill between four and five in the morning. Especially, I remember a little huddled heap, a little girl perhaps eight years old, sound asleep between two rows of whizzing and wholly unprotected machines.

One of the friends who was with me that night sent me after I had left China, a laconic little clipping from a Shanghai newspaper. It read: "An inquest was held yesterday by Magistrate Li and Mr. Jacob on a child employed in the Anglo-Chinese Cotton Mill, who met her death in tragic circumstances. She was drawn into the machinery from underneath a handrail by her feet while asleep at four o'clock in the morning." My friend had written on the margin, "You remember the weary little bodies we saw that morning."

The article in the China Medical Journal to which I have already referred reports, "We find the children in factories have the highest accident mortality. In seeking the cause for this, we are reminded of what has already been said, that it is among the young and inexperienced that accidents are most frequent and severe." "The young and inexperienced!" The article reports an injury to a factory worker of *five years old.* Such youth, such inexperience, has no place in factories at all. But in the cotton mills of China at this moment, hundreds of little boys and girls are working on a twelve-hour shift, one week on a day shift, the next on a night shift. They are working at unprotected machines, and when, especially on the night shifts, the utter exhaustion of sleep-denied childhood brings relaxed vigilance, it is not surprising that tragedies occur.

What are we going to do about it? There would be no use in bringing you these harrowing pictures of what I myself saw of modern industrialism in the Orient, unless there is something we can do. Of many things, which might be said, may I briefly make four suggestions:

First of all, because we have made the world so small and closeknit a neighborhood, anything that we can do to help to bring a Christian way of life in industry in this country, will help to make things better in the East. Bishop Brent reminded us that our own industrial life is far from what it should be—it is full of wrongs which we must right—and the righting of them will have its immediate effect in far-away countries.

A letter from a woman who has spent the last few years in Japan gives a vivid picture of her visit to a glass factory there. "An unlighted shed, pitch black except for the blinding flare from gas ovens—scores of little ten to fourteen-year-old girls and boys, darting from oven to cooler, to annealing oven, blowing the fiery mass of molten glass into bottle shape—numbed, stupefied, expressionless little gnomes, feeding a fiery monster. No color in the little thin faces, no response to my smiles, no interest in anything outside the task that was set for them; for nine hours to plod in this blackness, choked by the fumes from the seething glass, eye brows and eyelashes singed—at the end of the long day to receive from fifteen to thirty cents—a pittance less than the cost of the coarse rice that the little tired body needs to keep going." And she added, "I was sick at heart—but more depressed still to have the owner tell me that he had visited over 100 glass factories in America and had studied our methods." Just what he had learned from those factories, which of his methods he had patterned from them, I do not know, but I do know that Oriental employers are studying industrial conditions here and are being greatly influenced by them.

A friend who has been pouring her life into China during the last few years in an effort to help create a public opinion that will do away with the child labor which I have described, says that no one who has not been there can realize the disastrous effect in China of learning that America had declared its national child labor law unconstitutional. Again and again I have heard her say "Nothing will mean more for the cause of the child laborers of China than to have the states of America ratify the child labor amendment to the Constitution." If one member suffers, all suffer. Yes, but it is also true that if one is honored, all rejoice. For we are all members one of another.

Another way in which we can help is to set ourselves steadfastly against the investment of money from Christian countries in industries where such conditions as those I have described exist. When I was in China, my attention was called to an article which appeared in a trade journal. There was nothing secret, or confidential, in this report—anyone who would might read it. Let me give you a part of it.

"The profits of the ———————— factory again surpassed $1,000,000. For the past two years it has been running night and day with scarcely any intermission. The number of hands employed is 2,500 and the following is the wage table per day:

Men	15 to 25 cents
Women	10 to 15 cents
Boys (about 15 years)	10 to 15 cents
Girls (about 15 years)	5 to 10 cents
Small boys (about 10 years)	5 to 10 cents
Small girls (about 10 years)	3½ to 5 cents

"The working hours are from 5:30 A. M. to 5:30 P. M. and from 5:30 P. M. to 5:30 A. M. No meals are supplied by the factory. It will be seen that the company is in an exceptionally favorable position, with an abundant and *absurdly cheap labor supply to draw on, and no vexatious factory laws to observe;* it is not surprising that their annual profits have exceeded their total capital on at least three occasions."

Whatever the nationality of this company may have been, the unashamed acknowledgment of such conditions as are here described, reveals a situation to which every nation which is in any way participating in the industrial development of China has a relation. Citizens of Christian nations must do nothing which would help to increase or perpetuate such conditions. They must rather help China to avoid the tragic mistakes of the West.

In the third place, this situation demands a goodly number of missionaries who are equipped both by thorough training and experience to be helpful cooperators with the people of the Far East in dealing with these complex and difficult problems. The Christian churches of the East have already manifested their profound concern. You will remember, for example, that the Church of China in its first national conference adopted three labor standards, one pertaining to child labor, one to one day's rest in seven, the third to the protection of workers. And the National Christian Council of China has appointed a Commission on the Church and Industry which is carrying on a most vigorous and intelligent campaign of education.

At a conference held in England last Spring, on the preparation of missionaries, attended by delegates from practically all mission fields, I was interested to find this statement: "One memorandum after another referred to the spread of an industrialism which reproduced in more aggravated form, and without essential safeguards, conditions which are imperilling society in the West." . . . "The resulting situations," the report goes on to say, "bear at every point upon such questions as the type of missionary who will be welcomed, the attitude he should take, the work he must be prepared to do."

Only as we have missionaries, thoroughly prepared by definite training and special experience to deal with these perplexing problems, can we give the most effective cooperation to the Christian churches of the East in their courageous and determined facing of this situation.

Just one thing more. It is a commonplace to say that much of the most effective education and influence comes through demonstration and example. We must make sure that all enterprises for which our Mission agencies are responsible are above criticism. Are the builders who erect our mission buildings given one day's rest in seven? Are they working for reasonable hours and under safe conditions? Are all of our Bible women and village pastors and village teachers receiving an adequate living wage? If we can answer, without embarrassment, all such questions as these, then we are in a position to join all our forces with the Christians of the Orient to help hasten that day when His Kingdom shall come, and His will be done *on earth*—as it is in heaven.

SIXTEEN YEARS' CAMPAIGNING FOR CHRIST IN JAPAN

THE REVEREND TOYOHIKO KAGAWA, TOKYO

It was just fifteen years ago, on a cold evening, the night before Christmas in 1908, I entered the slums of Kobe to live. Then I was twenty-two years old and a student in the theological seminary. I rented a small house which had altogether only five

mats (a mat is three feet to six feet wide) one room with two
mats and the other with three.

The man who led me to the slums was twenty-four years old,
two years older than I. He was a drunkard, a murderer and an
ex-convict just out of prison. He had found me a house where
a man had been killed so that nobody liked to live in it, thinking
that it was haunted. This man had set fire to a house in order to
rob it with the result that more than two hundred neighboring
houses were burned down. He was caught and had been in prison
full nine years. He had learned his alphabet for the first time in
prison from his New Testament. After getting out of the prison
he came straight to me and declared that he wanted to be a Christian minister.

I was then suffering from tuberculosis and thought that I
would not live very long. Therefore, I desired to do some good
thing before I died, and I prayed my Lord that He would give me
strength to help the needy in the slums. That first night I had
no light, no fire and no shoji in my room. I went to bed early,
praying to God that He might give His light, His fire, and His
protection even in that terrible slum district.

Early the next morning—it was Christmas—I had to welcome
a guest. I had only seven dollars and fifteen cents for my own
support for a month. The rent of the house was only three and a
half cents a day. Had I been alone I could easily have lived for
that money, because, in the slums of Kobe, over 11,000 people live
on less than two dollars and a half a month today. My Christmas
present was an old man who had a habit of drinking strong liquor
and hated to work. One of the chief gamblers accompanied him
to my house and told me that he ought to live with me. It was
pretty hard to live on only seven dollars and a half for two persons,
but I had no other way than to let him live with me. The next
day, another man came and on the following day I had to add
one more. There were now four big fellows to support with only
seven dollars and a half. At first, when I had only two men to
care for, I cut off my second meal and shared the available food
with them, but when two more were added, I could scarcely get
hard rice enough for two meals. I had to put more water in my
rice. For many weeks we had only thin rice and later rice soup
"okai" but we were contented even with this soup as we sat together without any table or any napkins, taking our food like barbarians. The meaning of the Lord's Prayer—"Give us this day
our daily bread"—for the first time dawned in my life.

The first year of my sojourn (1909) I had to bury fourteen
corpses, because the people there had no money to bury their
dead. I took alcohol or hot water and washed the dead bodies
before putting them into a coffin, but usually I took them to the

crematory. It was quite a trying experience at first, but the Lord blessed me and I was willing to do His work. The second year I had to bury nineteen more. Aside from this work, I had to look after the sick people, who had no place to lie down, as most of them came to me from lodging houses. At one time I had sixteen patients in my small room. The policeman did not like this arrangement, but I could not help it, because nobody else cared for them.

My pulpit was at the street corners. After preaching there, I usually invited all who would to come to my small five-mats room to a service. At times, I had over seventeen people there. Dr. H. W. Myers helped me not a little in my slum work. I went down early on Sunday morning to baptise those whom I had led to Christ. There were about fifty converts in four years and eight months. Three of them were murderers, many were ex-convicts, some of them secret prostitutes.

There were half a dozen most promising young working-men. I liked them and helped them, with others, teaching early in the morning at five o'clock and also early in the evening. The class, even though composed of both sexes, was very small, not more than four at one time. Yet one of them is now my wife, and another has become my successor in the slum work of Kobe. He is the chief of the city employment bureau, and preaches at night for us in the slum district. His name is Mr. Masaru Takeuchi, and his unselfish devotion to the cause of Jesus Christ is worthy of mention.

While I was studying at Princeton University (1915-1917) Mr. Takeuchi with a group of young men organized a self-supporting church. They practiced religious communism; they pooled all their savings, taking what was required for the help of the poor and needy, and dividing the remainder equally among themselves. After I went back to Kobe in 1917, I found the church more prosperous than before.

Small-pox was raging in the slums of the city at that time. Seventeen were taken at one time on the ninth of May, 1917. I felt that it would be wise to organize a free clinic and a free dispensary, to help the poor people in their need. I asked Dr. C. Majima, a graduate of a medical college, and his sister-in-law, to help me. We started settlement work in a district of Kobe where in a small area over 6,500 outcasts lived. Some laborers invited me to organize a labor union for them, so I helped, not in a Bolshevistic spirit but in the Name of the Carpenter of Nazareth, in the organization of a Federation of Labor in West Japan. I supported these men in calling strikes. Three times I was taken to court and fined.

I was asked to contribute to newspapers and magazines. My books began to be read pretty well, so I continued to write. I taught in three schools at the same time to get money to help the poor people around me. I preached day and night at any time whenever I could find the time and place. I usually got up at four o'clock every Thursday morning to preach to the people at the docks. In the evening I preached at the street corners. There were many converts. The story runs in a similar way to that of Mr. Harold Begby in "Twice Born Men," or of Hadley in "Down in Water Street."

Sometimes I was greatly discou·aged upon finding that many of my Sunday-school girls had beer. sold to the brothel houses, or that some of my boys had become pickpockets, influenced by the chief of gamblers. The results so.netimes seemed meagre, considering the energies which I spent upon my work. Still the public gradually began to give attention to what I was trying to do, and I found my friends quite willing to help me.

The labor movement was quite successful, but the road was not smooth. I had to fight on through many misunderstandings and persecutions from the authorities. I wanted Japan to be more democratic in politics and in industry. I expressed freely what I thought was right in order to improve the conditions in Japan, applying Christian principles. Many times, I was called to appear before the court and was put in prison for sixteen days in connection with a general strike in Kobe city in 1920. I was glad to be there. For a long time I had not had a good rest. I was able to make a special study of the Gospel of Mark. When I was set free I turned my attention to the desperately poor tenant farmers. I organized a Tenant Farmers' Union. There were over 5,600,000 peasant families, nearly half of them being without a single lot to cultivate. The annual income of a family was not more than $200. They paid an average rental of 55 per cent of the whole product of a farm, sometimes 75 per cent. Now the Union has power to better these conditions. There are 600 branches and some 50,000 family members.

A novel which I wrote when I was nineteen years old, attracted a publisher's attention, so I added about one-third more and published it with the title "Across the Death Line," in Japanese—"Shisen wo keete." It gained a large circulation, so with the income of the book I started a labor school in Osaka, the Manchester of the Orient, and a campaign to organize the miners in the coal field of North Kiushiu. With some of that money we have also sent a missionary to evangelize the "aborigines," the "head hunters" of Formosa. I organized two cooperative consumers unions, one in Osaka and one in Kobe. I preached or lectured on trade unions almost every night, somewhere in the big cities and whenever I was asked, I gave lectures from four to five days successively. The Lord was so merciful to me that we had many converts at those meetings.

After the earthquake I organized a relief organization in Tokyo. It afforded an opportunity to preach. I preached 124 nights continuously and the Lord gave nearly 5,700 converts in and around Tokyo. I told these that if they wished to follow in the steps of Jesus Christ, they could sign their names and addresses on the cards.

I am now looking forward to doing more evangelistic work among the laboring classes in Japan. There are thousands of farmers in the Japanese villages, 4,500,000 factory laborers, 2,500,000 fishermen, 400,000 sailors and 300,000 miners. Among these multitudes the Christian gospel has not made progress. If God permits me, I shall be His servant to them in Japan. I am willing to renounce all else if my countrymen may be saved for Christ. I want to be one of the disciples of our Lord, who is worthy to be called a Christian, who is ready to bear the Cross for His sake.

SHOULD MISSIONS CARRY ON SOCIAL WORK?
THE REVEREND ALDEN H. CLARK, INDIA

It seems almost unnecessary to ask ourselves this question. Yet perhaps it may not be amiss to put our answers together in some clear-cut way. Surely we need not ask the question "why" in regard to such emergency social service as is rendered in times of famine, plague and flood. Probably no one would question that these are a natural and inevitable part of our missionary task. Here are six brief answers to the general question why we should follow the regular lines of social service.

1. In the first place, we should do so because it would be a reversal of mission policy begun and followed by the pioneer missionaries not to go forward in social work. From the first missionary who ever left America until today, a great majority of the missionary force have engaged in some form of social work and their services along these lines have met with the success that cannot be interpreted otherwise than a proof of the blessing of God.

Gordon Hall, arriving in Bombay in 1813, found crowding the streets of the city a throng of little children who had no schools; and before he and his associates had been in the land for five years, they had gathered some 550 of these little children into their schools. Soon was started the process of preparing school books for them which went on under missionary supervision for generations, until the Government became aroused to this need. When Gordon Hall was making a tour in rural India, he found himself in a place of pilgrimage which was undergoing the ravages of an epidemic of cholera. Naturally he threw himself into the work of relief. Always in such touring work he carried with him a case of medicines. These he gave to the stricken people, and when at last medicine and strength were exhausted, he himself was attacked by the dread disease and died, a witness to the fact that from the very beginning missionaries not only preached but practiced the Gospel.

I think of that great missionary, Samuel Fairbank (1822-1898), who established himself in a center of village life in India. He used to walk about among the villages, stopping in the fields to talk to the farmers about their crops, bringing them suggestions about improved seed, starting a model farm himself, opening schools for their children, acting as umpire in cases of dispute. He was followed by his like-minded sons. For over sixty years they have been living in the district until every one looks to the bungalow of the missionary as to the home of their best friend. Although Indians love law-suits, no law-suit has ever gone to the courts from the village of Vadala because the people have trusted the missionary, and he has solved their problems with such wisdom and such kindly good-will that they have accepted his decisions. No wonder that in such a district as this Christianity has progressed more rapidly and more significantly than in any other part of Western India, sending out to all parts of that language area a stream of Christian workers and reaching all classes of the people.

New methods of social work we may bring in with the new experience of the West and the new industrial needs of the East; but in so doing, we are simply carrying to its logical next step the work of our predecessors. The question is not *why* we should do such work; it is rather *why* should we *not*.

2. We should emphasize social work because of an acute and growing need for which the West is primarily responsible. It is Western industrial civilization which is bringing its newest and most difficult problems to the East. Where a few years ago the Oriental people were predominantly rural and the vast majority of the cloth was woven on country looms, we are now facing the great movement toward factory production with all that that means of disorganization of the old and need of reorganization of the new. It is not at all to be wondered at that Gandhi, seeing the evil results of the present industrial movement, should speak of all industrial civilization as diabolic. Yet we know well that the movement cannot be arrested as he would have it. It is bound to go on and increase. It is, therefore, peculiarly incumbent upon us of the industrial West to help the East solve this primarily Western problem which we have thrust upon them.

3. We should emphasize social work because we have been accumulating in the West experience in such work which can be

of the greatest value in the East. I do not mean to say that the Eastern problem is identical with that of the West or that we can transfer without alteration the methods of Western social work; but I do mean that experience is abundantly showing that the problems are so nearly alike that we can carry a surprisingly large share of the best experience of modern social work in our own country into the Orient, adapting the details and conserving the principles. We have, therefore, the two great elements of a compelling appeal, a great need, and a peculiar ability to meet that need.

4. We should emphasize social work because our Western young people are filled with the social passion, and many among them who have this passion want to express it in service in the Orient. If, in our missionary work, we are to conserve this fine enthusiasm and the growing body of experience of our young people, we must do so by emphasizing the social work which they believe to be the crying need of the hour. "What I have given unto you" is and must be a fundamental principle of service. Our coming generation most emphatically has a social gift to give.

5. We should enter such service with increasing confidence and joy because it is growingly clear that it was Christ's way of service. We are coming to see as we never saw before how great an emphasis he placed on the Kingdom of God, that is, on a redeemed social group. As we read the story of his life, we realize that again and again he emphasized deed ahead of word. "Go and tell John the things which ye have seen and heard," he said; and in that hour he not only preached, but he healed and ministered to the varied needs of the people who came to him. It was as though he sent word to John the Baptist, "Here, in one who gives himself to homely service to the common needs of humble people, you must find the Messiah."

6. An emphasis on social work gives us a unique approach to the growing body of non-Christian men of good-will in the Orient. In such service as this they and we can work in a common task. The suspicion is still very strong among Orientals that we missionaries come from some ulterior and unworthy motive. They often think of us as mere propagandists, caring for nothing but the adding of numbers to our lists of converts. But if we work side by side with them in attempting to solve the great modern social problems to which they are becoming increasingly alive, we shall be making clear the real spirit and motive of our work and shall open the way for them to understand the compelling attractiveness of Him who gave Himself to such ministries to his fellowmen.

These, then, are some of the answers which might be given to the question "Why?" It is not as a supplement to our great task that we enter social work; it is as a vital, throbbing expression of it. May we so effectively labor in this field that Jesus will have his rightful influence in the efforts of the Orient to meet its social problems.

THE CONTRIBUTION OF CHRISTIANITY TO THE WOMANHOOD OF THE ORIENT

PRESIDENT MARY E. WOOLLEY, LITT.D., LL.D., SOUTH HADLEY, MASSACHUSETTS

My subject must be narrowed, practically, to China, since five months spent there gave me more right to speak about that country than two weeks in Japan and no first-hand knowledge of India. The influence of Christianity upon the women of China may be considered from several angles, and the first is the educational angle. Education, in the modern sense, is the gift of the Christian West to the women of China. It began with the Christian missionary, before the middle of the last century, when the opening of the five treaty ports to foreigners made possible the English missionary school at Ningpo in 1844, soon followed by American schools, eleven in the treaty ports between 1847 and 1860, one in Peking and one at Tientsin in 1864, and the pioneer school in Central China at Kiukiang in 1873.

These schools marked the beginning of an era, since, although the girls of Old China, in the more privileged and progressive families, had some share in instruction under private tutors in the home, being taught penmanship, painting, poetry, music, and committing to memory many of the classics, as well as being trained in ethics and etiquette, this was quite exceptional, the great mass of girls receiving no education, not even learning to read or write. Truly it was a humble beginning, for the little girls in these schools, almost without exceptiton were the very poor, fed and clothed as well as taught, but the confidence in the potentialities of Chinese womanhood shown by Christian teachers has been more than justified. One has only to visit the Christian colleges for women, like Yenching, affiliated with the University of Peking, or Ginling in Nanking, to be convinced that the seed sown seventy-five years ago has borne fruit a hundredfold.

What has Christianity contributed to the womanhood of China through education? It is impossible in these few moments to do more than touch upon some of the conspicuous features in the preparation for service. Beginning at the foundation, much has been accomplished by physical education not only for the Chinese woman herself, but also for the general welfare, through her increased capacity for service. As I speak, recollections of Chinese scenes are almost as vivid to me as this audience. For example,

I seem to see a great drill ground on the outskirts of Hangchow, on a brilliant November day, with thousands of Chinese spectators, intent for hours on the athletic exercises of the annual "meet," in which girls from Christian and Government schools had as important parts as the boys and performed them—at least from the point of view of one feminine spectator—quite as well. Another picture is of an autumn morning in Central China on the Yangtse and of a class of girls with all the freedom and abandon of our American students, running through the charming garden of the Rulison School at Kiukiang and into the gymnasium for their "setting-up" exercises before beginning the day's work.

Most significant, perhaps, was the impression made by the young women teachers of physical education in government schools of typical Chinese cities like Wuchang, teachers trained in the Young Women's Christian Association School of Physical Education in Shanghai, now affiliated with Ginling College, significant because government schools, with their insistence upon physical education, would admit Christians to their staff in this subject, if in no other.

In no field of education for service has the contribution of Christianity been more marked than in the training of teachers. China's extremity has been in a peculiar sense Christianity's opportunity. In a country where the last census indicated that of the 70,000,000 children of lower primary school age, less than 5,000,000 had an opportunity for such education, no argument is necessary to prove the importance of the education of women along this line. Ginling College, in a recent letter, traces the development of its work in education from theory alone to theory and practice combined, with special emphasis on the training of teachers for the middle schools and including such courses as music, physical education, biology, social problems, English, Chinese and Chinese history and religion. If it is true that "The education of its citizens is the safeguard of a republic," the contribution which Christianity has made to Chinese women in this line alone justifies the cost.

It is not strange that among China's outstanding women are her physicians. Medical care and health efforts have long been a crying need and the call to Christian service in this line is an imperative one. I can think of no more direct way of converting those who are skeptical as to the value of Christian missions, than by taking them to see the Chinese women physicians—and their hospitals.

My experience in speaking of what education has done for the women of the West, has taught me that it is expedient to allude to preparation for the home. Women are likely to take that for granted, knowing the homes of educated women, and realizing that they speak for themselves. That is true, also, of the Christian Chinese home. In a way, it offers the most eloquent testimony of the contribution of Christianity to the women of the Far East.

No one familiar with China needs to be reminded that the country is in the early stages of a great industrial transformation. In some typical cities like Wuchang, the industry of the Middle Ages and that of the twentieth century exist side by side. Already there is opportunity for women in social service, an opportunity to which the alert, earnest Oriental is fully alive. Increasingly, the changing industrial conditions, the rise of the factory, the employment of women and children, the partial substitution of Western types of manufacture for the home crafts, with all the social problems involved, are leading to new vocations or avocations for Chinese women. The ideal of service and the preparation for it, in the face of these social and industrial problems, rightly called "as difficult and complex as they are grave and pressing," are a part of the contribution which Christianity has made.

The political and social as well as educational ideals of the New China, place women on an equality with men, the result, at least in large measure, of Christian teaching. In this day of a troubled political China, a prediction may not be out of place. The hope for the New China lies largely in her leaders. If they are self-seeking, disloyal, treacherous, with low ideals—a long and difficult way stretches before the new civilization. If they are patriots in the true sense of that word, loyal, trustworthy, idealistic, the new political East may have much to give to the family of nations. When that day comes to China, her women as well as her men, will have a part in shaping her future, a part for which they have been prepared by the education that in its most complete development, has been the gift of the Christian West.

The greatest contribution of Christianity to the womanhood of the Orient, has been the knowledge and appropriation of the spirit of Jesus. In the meeting with the women of Japan, in Tokyo and Kyoto and Kobe; in the more intimate knowledge of the women of China,—in Peking and Shanghai, and the characteristic Chinese cities of the interior; in the friendships with the Indian girls from Ceylon and Madras and Lahore—wherever one has known the women of the Far East, there has remained the impression of dignity and charm. To them, in this age of transition, in the days when the inrush of the new saps at the foundations of the old, Christianity is a stabilizing as well as the progressive force, affording a sense of freedom without a loss of dignity, an equality with men based on the best that each has to give, a Christian standard of the home, ideals for life and the strength to press toward their attainment. The supreme contribution of Christianity to the womanhood of the Orient, in all relationships of life, is the knowledge of Jesus' way.

THE POWER OF CHRIST REVEALED IN PERSONAL LIFE

PROFESSOR RUFUS M. JONES, LL.D., HAVERFORD, PENNSYLVANIA

There was a man driving through a country town in the State of Maine along what seemed to be a road that went endlessly uphill. He stopped a native farmer and asked him whether there was any end to this hill. Said he, "I have been riding for more than two hours continuously up this hill." The old farmer said, "Hill? Why, stranger, there ain't no hill here. You have lost off your hind wheels." Somewhat so the hills of difficulty which now confront the world are due, not so much to the contours of external nature as to the breakdown of something in ourselves, loss of spiritual power, feebleness of faith and vision, failure to make our contacts with eternal realities.

As we toil at our tasks, we are very much like children trying to put together a jigsaw puzzle when some of the pieces are lost. They are in the baby's crib, maybe, and in trying to make the puzzle go together there is nothing but failure possible. Some of our pieces are lost. They are the very foundation pieces with which we ought to be building our world; and we shall never succeed until we learn how to reconstruct ourselves. We must find new spiritual forces, a new driving power, a new dynamic.

Men built Babylon out of their own Babylonish hearts. They built the kind of world they wanted. They built the kind of Babylon that suited their lives, and we have been building a kind of world which we wanted, the kind of world which fitted our lives. We have been building out of fear and hate and suspicion and rivalry and jealousy and selfishness and greed and materialistic aims. Now we must learn how to build our world out of faith and hope and love. We must make the great discovery that our universe at bottom is a spiritual universe with inexhaustible spiritual forces, and we must learn to see that the mightiest thing on earth is a person who has learned how to let the life of God, the power of Christ, flow through him.

Emerson once said, "If you hold a straw parallel to the Gulf Stream, the Gulf Stream will flow through it." The most significant thing about St. Paul was his discovery that he could make his life an organ of the spirit and power of Jesus Christ. That was the Aegean Gospel, the Gospel that St. Paul preached and demonstrated in the great cities around the shores of the Aegean Sea, the Gospel which St. John, in one of the cities on that same sea, preached and demonstrated in the Fourth Gospel and the First Epistle, the Gospel that, though He is no more visible, Jesus Christ is life and spirit and can pour His life through men and can work effectively through receptive and responsive souls.

St. Paul's great word is *dynamos,* "power," and he learned how to be the transmitter of that power. "It is no longer I that live; Christ lives in me." "I bear in my body the marks of the Lord Jesus." "We are more than conquerers through Him that loved us." "I can do all things through Christ who puts his energy in me." "We are builded together for an habitation of God through the Spirit." To which we add St. John's great saying, which he flung out against all the forces of the Roman empire: "That which is born of God overcomes the world."

All the great advances in mechanical science have been made by the discovery of new ways of letting the immense energies of the universe break through and operate. The dynamo makes no electricity; it is a contrivance which lets electricity break through and do its work. The magnetic needle creates no magnetism. It merely lets vaster energies operate. That is what the broadcaster and the transmitter of the telephone and the coherer of the wireless does. They all let energies break through and manifest themselves.

We used to think of gasoline as a dangerous explosive, but we have invented a carburetor that lets the gasoline explode in minute quantities, very rapidly; and presto, it makes our Ford go and raises our aeroplane! As soon as we learn how to invent a contrivance for it, we shall also be able to liberate the boundless atomic energies of matter, and then every teaspoonful of water will give us 175,000 horsepower, and every copper penny you carry in your pocket will have energy enough to drive a freight train two and one-half times around the globe. I hope you will be able to make some use of those pennies!

Some years ago, some of students at West Point took an old cannon and wound ten miles of copper wire about it and then charged it with a dynamo. That turned the old cannon into a magnet. When you brought a cannon ball up anywhere near the cannon it leaped up and hung under it. When a man came up and backed up against the cannon and became charged you could stick spikes all over him, and they stuck to him till he was all covered with them. Anybody who got anywhere near the man was charged through him.

Twice every day the invisible energies of the moon lift a great plateau of the ocean several feet above the level of the surrounding water, and, as the earth revolves, that great plateau of water bursts up in our shores and up into our creeks and inlets and makes our tide, an irresistible energy if we only knew how to utilize it. Well, energies of a greater sort break through human life. The real business of being a Christian is discovering how to be a transmitter of spiritual energies.

> Like tides on the crescent sea beach
>   When the moon is new and thin;
> Into our hearts high yearnings come,
>   Welling and surging in;
> Come from that mystic ocean
>   Whose rim no foot has trod.
>
> Some call it "yearning,"
> But others call it God.

These spiritual energies are no more mysterious than any other energies are. Energy is ultimate. We can never get in behind energy. The great thing is the discovery of how to transmit and utilize energy, and the early Church is as great a demonstration of spiritual energy as the trolley car is a demonstration of electricity, or Niagara Falls a demonstration of gravitation.

In a talk with one of my students, he said, "I am going to make my life a miracle." I can see him still—his radiant face, his inspired look—and that young man is making his life a miracle. He is letting the spiritual energies of Jesus Christ work through his personality. It is not in spectacular ways that we want to be revealers of spiritual energy. It is not in startling and abnormal fashion that we want to work this great miracle of spiritual power. We have had a demonstration here this evening of precisely what it means. It is in the normal, simple, every-day way of daily life that the greatest miracles are wrought. The stupendous forces are not thunder and earthquake but tiny rootlets and the capillary oozing of water, the small continuous every-day forces. The stupendous things that move the world and transform life are revelations of faith and hope and of a love that knows no frontier.

"They who wait for God shall renew their strength, they shall mount up with wings as eagles, they shall run and not be weary, they shall walk and not faint." I hope you will notice the climax. It is not climbing Mount Everest and seeking for north and south poles that are, after all, important things in the universe. It is learning how to walk among men in the every-day affairs of life and be a revealer of the divine life in a love that never lets go, that never fails, that believeth all things and hopeth all things and endureth all things and is never provoked and thinks no evil. The simple inter-relationship of spiritual life of man with man is what transforms the world.

God invaded Africa through Livingstone. God invaded Europe through St. Paul. God invaded England through George Fox and John Wesley. God is waiting to invade the countries we represent here today through us. He is invading Japan through the man who preceded me. He wants to invade our country that we love so much, in whose capital we meet tonight, and the invasion will be an invasion of spiritual energy through personal lives.

One of my great mystic friends of the fourteenth century said, "I would fain be to the eternal God what a man's hand is to a man," the organ through which he does his work in the world. "The Christian's life is the book in which God is now writing His new testament," is the saying of another great mystic of the seventeenth century. It is through lives like ours that the New Testament of today is being written by the spirit of God.

"You are the body of Jesus Christ," St. Paul said, "You are the body of Jesus Christ and each one a particular member of it." We look in vain for that body of Jesus Christ in some holy sepulchre of the East. The greatest discovery St. Paul made was that Christ is making His new body out of us, out of men. We are the body through which He reveals himself in the world today.

There was a little drummer boy in Napoleon's army, a little boy who had caught the spirit of the Emperor, who had the same daring and the same courage. One day he had received a bullet wound. In the hospital the surgeon was probing for the bullet. He bent over the little drummer boy and said, "Do I hurt you?" The boy answered back, "Never mind whether you hurt me or not, go on probing for the bullet. If you probe deep enough into me, you will find the Emperor."

We want personal lives that are so close to Christ and so filled with His spirit that if you probe deep enough into one of them you will find the Christ living there.

> "Leave me not, God, until—nay until when?
> Not till I am with Thee, one heart, one mind;
> Not till Thy life is light in me, and then
> Leaving is left behind."

THE CHURCH IN THE MISSION FIELD

THE CHURCH IN LATIN AMERICA

THE REVEREND J. H. MCLEAN, D.D., CHILE

My theme lacks what the photographers term "sharp definition." Nevertheless, if you remember as I do with gratitude the masterly presentation of Christ's onward march throughout the earth, how his servants from Great Britain, Canada and the United States have been the messengers of his everlasting gospel to Europe, Asia, Africa and the islands of the sea, please remember that Latin America is the rest of the earth. And if Christ with his bleeding hand has traced upon your heart a chart of humanity, Latin America is on that map. Between the Rio Grande and the Straits of Magellan, there dwell seventy million souls for whom Christ died. Unlike India, Latin America has no untouchables. Neither has Latin America any unmentionables although Latin America has been so infrequently mentioned at this gathering.

We here are very close to the headquarters of the Pan-American Union. Not far from where we sit there are the chancelleries of nineteen South American Republics. These states are our neighbors. Is it not true that such a gathering as this calls for the highest display of good-will and international candor? Even if the walls have ears, let them hear some expression of loving-kindness from those who are met in the name of our Lord Jesus Christ, who alone can save the people from their sins and enrich all nations with His own abundant life. When He, who has all authority, instructed His disciples to preach the gospel to every creature, who has authority to exclude from the scope of His redemption our brethren who have just been described?

Latin-American peoples have always been in some respects, far in advance of their contemporaries. The Latin-American nations gave to the League of Nations its first president, and have no reason to be ashamed of their contribution. The Latin-American nations repeatedly have submitted their disputes over territory to courts of arbitration, and are firmly convinced that this is not only the best mode of settlement, but one inspired by Christ Himself. Almost 100 years ago, they confessed, regarding their spiritual problems, what has repeatedly been admitted and bemoaned upon this platform, viz., that conventional religion and daily living, both private and collective, needed to be made Christian. Just such appeals as we have heard from this platform evoke the response of men and women who believed it Christlike to serve wherever their fellowmen yearned for Christ. Paul has planted, Apollos has watered, God has given the increase, and we have the native church of Latin America. Let us devoutly thank the Lord of Harvest that this church exists and functions in that country. We are not dealing with an objective, but with an entity, with another confirmation of the claim that faith in the Son of God is adaptable to all nations, and that His life is essential to their highest interests.

What unsung heroisms lie behind this achievement! There is the same fascinating record of fearless witnessing, of patient loving, of continuance in well doing; and the divine element in the evangel, coupled with the divine dynamic in the messengers, has wrought its marvel in the human product, so that all over Latin America the seed has taken rootage in new soil and modified by racial tinge and social environment, has brought forth fruit after its kind.

Our natural Christian organizations are not state churches under official patronage, but groups of disciples upholding the best traditions of New Testament Christianity. Let me speak in general terms, so as not to burden you with statistics, of "the first hundred thousand," that expeditionary army that will make possible, we believe, the final triumph of our adorable Lord in Latin America. All honor to these comrades of the Cross! They were and are the brave and true and the loyal. Booker Washington once observed that it is much easier to be a descendant than an ancestor. They are the pioneers of the new day in Latin America. It is estimated that there are seventy-two thousand of them in Brazil alone; and we must remember that, back of the professing church in Latin America, there lies a circle of men who, like Nicodemus, are waiting for the shades of night to fall, or who express their admiration before they surrender their hearts.

There are enrolled in the Church in Brazil some of her most eminent citizens, and her scroll of honor would take too long to describe in such a gathering as this. But let us not forget that Brazil has offered hospitality to Christ in greater measure than any country in Latin America. And of Argentina and Uruguay let it be said that their prestige among the nations of the Atlantic seaboard is due to their ready acceptance of the ambassadors of Christ, to their willingness to sit in council and the courage of their faith in trying the program of Jesus. If you should visit the capitals of these countries, or even any of their remote hamlets, you would have reason to rejoice that there the fruit of the spirit is the same as in North America. And so, the total of all of those who have received the word with gladness and have endeavored to live it out simply, humbly and sacrificially through Central America and Mexico is "the first hundred thousand." And as the men who took part in that memorable campaign and formed the nucleus of a victorious host now relate to their children's children that this was the day of their opportunity and of their high distinction, so some of us will thank the Lord forever that we were permitted to share in the trials and the labors of this first epoch in Latin America's evangelization.

There are servants of our Lord Jesus Christ in those lands whom you ought to be proud to call brethren, for Jesus Himself is not ashamed of them—the saints, the martyrs, the men and the women who have hazarded their lives for the gospel's sake and who have been the most delightful brethren in daily fellowship and toil. One of them, as he lay a-dying, summarized for you and for me, in words as admirable as any from Carey or Livingstone, the task before us and the resources behind us when he said, "Sin, how terrible; grace, how wonderful; time, how short; the gospel of Christ, how glorious."

In those lands almost three thousand of their choicest sons and daughters have enlisted in the service of Christ as pastors, teachers, evangelists, nurses and as members of the staffs in the Young Men's and Young Women's Christian Associations. Just imagine this vast concourse on the ground floor of this auditorium as the contribution of the first two generations in service to our Lord Jesus Christ! They are scattered over a vast territory; but, bring them together and we should be convinced that Jesus Christ sees of the travail of his soul and is satisfied in Latin America.

Now, a word or two concerning the type of church that is found there and its tendencies and ideals. It is a church of evangelistic fervor, kindled with the vision of conquest and aglow with the throes of brotherhood, a church of passionate devotion to the welfare of mankind; a church in which sacrificial giving is the rule and not the exception; a church of commendable ambition to deserve and achieve self-government and self-extension, to embody the ethic of our Lord Jesus Christ in the daily lives of its members and in the communions which they have organized. This church has little patience with the rivalries of denominationalism or with the controversies of theologians and dogmatists. They consider them not merely fruitless, but highly detrimental to Christianity. They have emphasized the essentials, and have deprecated every effort to promote minor issues, honestly striving to fulfil the supreme function of a living church on this earth—to evangelize the non-Christian population, to foster self-support by maximum giving and to follow a scheme for permanent expansion.

This church has an appeal to its brethren in this land. Let me act as advocate for the remaining moments, presenting it to their mother church and to their sister churches. They would have you remember that new occasions teach new duties, that we have entered upon another stage of development in Latin America, that today the balance of contribution has been transferred from North America and Europe to Mexico, Central and South America, and that today they wish to see some measure of adjustment between their brethren here and themselves on the field. There is no lack of appreciation, of genuine thanksgiving, for they have oftentimes charged me, whenever I stood before a congregation in this land, to express in the kindliest terms their sincere gratitude to their Christian brethren in North America who had sent them the gospel, for in so doing they say, "You have conferred upon us an inestimable benefit, far beyond comparison with anything that any land has ever done for these republics of ours."

There is in them no spirit of rebellion, merely of friendly cooperation. Hitherto the missionaries who have been sent to Latin America have been chosen as most Latin-American brides are selected,—by foreordination. Two couples, representing the older generation, meet in solemn conversation in the front salon and, before the session is ended, the destiny of two members of the rising generation has been determined. We may smile at that method in matrimony, but I trust we may grow indignant with that method in missionary administration. The time has come when our brethren to the south of us, who have given every evidence of worthy partnership ask reasonably for a larger participation in the choice of those who are to serve them, in the disposition of forces, and in the expenditure of funds. We ought to be magnanimous enough to grant them every responsibility which is properly placed on Christian brethren.

These republics have produced from among their own sons and daughters great emancipators, statesmen, educators and reformers; and these men and women, touched by the spirit of our Lord Jesus Christ, awakened to the possibilities of human life through Christian witness and daily living in the land where they were born, and whose people they understand,—these people, I firmly believe, will, in the days to come, be the men and women in the vanguard of the Christian movement.

The slogan of our missionary enterprise has been "leadership." That is a word of sinister connotations in Latin America, where there are at present five undisputed leaders of their fellowmen but whom we call "dictators." We have spoken of brotherhood and partnership, but let me leave with you as the watchword for our effort, for the next decade, the word "comradeship." There abide leadership, partnership, and comradeship, these three, but the greatest of these, palpitating with the love of Christ and a signal honor to His trusted servants, is comradeship, divine comradeship on earth.

THE CHURCH IN INDIA

THE REVEREND BHASKAR PANDURANG HIVALE, BOMBAY, INDIA

When talking recently with an American evangelist in India, he referred to the Indian Christian Church as a "poor, pale and dependent thing." I have Indian Christian friends who regret the continuation of this foreign institution in my country. Some non-Christians have argued its uselessness by saying that organized Christianity failed when the Great War confronted humanity a few years ago. The ministers of the churches, both in the allied world and in Germany, claimed that God was on their respective sides and prayed for complete victory. There are many abler members of my profession to defend this course of action, but I want to say that I am not afraid of the word 'foreign.' If we study the history of nations, I think we get a pretty good idea of the way in which civilizations are built. Your Western civilization did not start from nothing. I believe one can find therein traces of the Babylonian, the Assyrian, the Hindu, the Egyptian, the Greek and the Roman civilizations. The problem in India, therefore, is not how to throw away everything foreign and keep everything Indian. No, we are going to keep the best that the Indian genius has produced, and yet take the best that your Western civilization is offering to us. We have, as a matter of fact, already adopted a Western system of education. Our legislatures are functioning as efficiently or otherwise, as they are in other parts of the world! The real solution is bound to come through a right sort of union of the two cultures—Oriental and Occidental.

No doubt, the church in India is poor and dependent on foreign help. India is one of the most poverty-stricken countries in the world. Several million people in my country are so unfortunate as not to have two square meals a day. The churches share the poverty of the country.

I have been in America for some years and have watched the methods of raising money in your churches. You raise large sums. And yet how much more is spent for chewing gum than for Christian work in the mission field! The money that is given by you comes from consecrated business men and women. I believe our well-to-do people in India will more and more catch the vision of stewardship and support the churches. But the difficulty at the present time is, since the visit of Dr. John R. Mott and Dr. Sherwood Eddy, in 1911, that many students, who have the ability to make a good deal of money, are responding to a call of sacrifice and consecration and are giving their entire selves to direct Christian service! In my undergraduate days, when I came to a definite conclusion that the best way to spend my little life was to give it for Christ in the service of my motherland, I looked round about me to find the best avenue and decided that the Indian Christian church was the one. Never since have I regretted my decision. As a matter of fact I am feeling more and more hopeful about the future of the church and I shall give you my reasons.

The first is that the denationalization of the Indian churches has been arrested. In the early history of the church the missionary had to arrange for all the converts to live together in his compound, away from all other communities, partly because he was afraid of un-Christian influence and partly because the Hindus refused to have anything to do with the converts. The result was that the average Christian community became denationalized. A few only realized that their destinies were bound up with the destinies of the whole of India. There are certain communities in my country, who keep aloof when others agitate and may have to go to jail; but as soon as the British Government makes concessions, they scramble for a share. Only the other day the leaders of the non-Brahman movement of Madras, including the Christians, appeared before the Viceroy. After hearing their various demands, Lord Reading had to remind them that they were asking for their respective communities only and not for India. What other community in India has higher ideals and examples of service than the Christian church? And I am glad to say that more and more Christians are getting into the national movement. They will purify it and strengthen essentially Christian attitudes, like that of Mahatma Gandhi.

At present the national spirit is influencing all activities in India. And I am not ashamed of being a Nationalist even on this platform, where the dominant note has been international. Of course, I know of a narrow nationalism which says, "My country first, right or wrong," but I know also of a "wishy-washy" internationalism. A healthy nationalism is necessary for a real internationalism. If we do not love our brother, how can we love God? If we are not proud of our country, if we are not going to love our country, how are we going to love the world? If the nationalisms of the world could only be built on Christian love! The Church in India has begun to make its contribution to the national life.

The second reason is that the superiority complex with which the Christian Church started is gradually disappearing. There was a time when some devout Christians believed that Christianity was the only religion given by God, and that all others were the handiwork of the Devil. The hymn about India's coral strands that you have just sung, has two lines in it,

> "Though every prospect pleases,
> And only man is vile."

Now what shall I say of America the beautiful? I have certainly found "brotherhood" as I have travelled in thirty-seven States from "sea to shining sea." I have admired her "purple mountain majesties" as I have stood on her "fruited plains" among the "amber waves of grain." But may I tell you confidentially that I have also discovered in your country the particular species of the genus homo described in Heber's great hymn! And I might add that my researches were not confined to the daily papers.

When I was a little boy (I am a Christian of the third generation, my father having been a preacher), I distinctly remember that I felt superior because I was a Christian. The heathen, I thought, bowed before the idols and added to their sins, but I knew the truth and the key to salvation. I pictured in imagination flying around heaven, while my Hindu friends would be suffering in hell! But I have grown. If reverence towards the universe is the beginning of religion, what right have we to look down on the different systems of religion that have flourished in my land? Thousands of years ago the Hindus used to pray, "From the unreal lead me to the real, from darkness lead me to light, from death lead me to immortality." Who can believe that God did not at least partially reveal Himself to them?

The modern missionary presents Christ as the fulfiller of Indian aspirations. Dr. Farquhar calls Jesus the crown of Hinduism. The liberal missionary of today does not dole out charity. Dr. Alden H. Clark speaks of "bringing brotherhood in Bombay," Prof. D. J. Fleming writes about "Building with India." I see a great day coming when the Christians can approach other nationals with due appreciation of the old culture, with sympathy and with genuine Christian love.

The third reason is the opportunity opened out for evangelization on account of the missionary spirit seen in the Hindu religion. We shall now hear less of persecution and more of the triumph of the individual conscience. At the Unity Conference, called by Mahatma Gandhi, in which the Metropolitan Bishop of India and Dr. S. K. Datta represented the Christian church, there was the unequivocal recognition of tolerance for every sincere religious expression and of liberty to convert and be converted, provided it was not done by unworthy means.

My fourth reason is that the spirit of service is not confined to the Christian Church but is gradually permeating the whole fabric of the New India. A large increase of work in education, social service and in other activities is being carried on by the non-Christians. Until recently Christian groups took no part in these non-Christian efforts. But we are learning that "those that are not against us are for us." Soon the Servant of India Society, (Seva-Sadan) and the Social Service League will find Indian Christians offering their services.

As in Europe in the middle ages, so in India at the present time, the Church has to busy itself, not only with the impartation of religious instruction, but with social service, schools, agriculture and hospitals. The time is bound to come when idol-worship will disappear, when the caste system will be crushed, when our agricultural and hygienic conditions will be perfect. And since specialization is the order of the day, even religious education will be handled by the experts in that line. Will there be any further use of the church then? My conviction is that the function of the church will be all the more glorious. Modernize your business and education to their highest efficiency, humanize industries to any degree, rationalize all morality and yet the church will be needed. The church is a dynamo; it will not only explain the whys and the wherefores of all these activities, it will give people power!

It is quite true that the Church in India is poor, pale and dependent. But did not Prof. Rufus M. Jones tell us last night that spiritual energy seeks a medium? My conviction is that the Spirit of God will achieve wonders through this comparatively small church with only about five million souls. All we need to do is to make it worthy of His abode! The Church has already started on its program of introducing indigenous methods of worship and instruction. We may have to eliminate certain Western ways and adapt others. We shall have to add what our religious experience teaches us, as we go on.

I believe in the glorious future of the Indian church. I have been speaking to you of the Church militant. Those of us who believe in the ultimate triumph of the good, those of us who have a faith that our souls have only started on the journey towards being as perfect as our Heavenly Father, need not be told how blessed it is to set other souls along the right path! The hopeful thing is that hundreds of Indian young men are catching a glimpse of this great vision. They are willing to give their entire selves for it!

I have no doubt that this Church of God is going to triumph. This great city of God, this community of loyalty, this great kingdom will surely flourish. The Church in India has been founded on the great sacrifices of thousands of missionaries and Indian workers. And now when it has begun to function so hopefully it is your privilege and mine to strengthen it. It is true that few are now called upon to suffer the inconveniences the earlier missionaries experienced. But India appreciates the sacrifices of today. Every missionary has to leave relatives to go to far-away lands. An even greater sacrifice for Christ is when their children have to leave for their education ten thousand miles away. I know an American mother who could not sleep for nights, when her youngest daughter was about to leave! But missionaries, the noble soldiers of the cross, have been willing to suffer for the founding and nurture of this church. The Indian workers have stood by the missionaries, though receiving a mere pittance. It is our privilege to inherit these responsibilities and to carry on.

THE CHURCH IN THE FAR EAST

BISHOP HENRY ST. GEORGE TUCKER, D.D., FORMERLY OF KYOTO, JAPAN

My theme takes a wide range. I shall, however, limit what I have to say to the church as I know it in Japan, because the principles involved are, I think, the same in all mission fields. It has been said very often in this convention that the first purpose which we put before us in our missionary work is the bringing of the influence of Christianity to bear in a general way upon a non-Christian country, in order to Christianize, if one may call it so, the public opinion of that country, to introduce the practical standards of Christianity, to do away with whatever prejudice may stand in the way of Christian work, and to create a sense of moral obligation which will render the appeal of Christianity intelligible to the people. The second great purpose we have before us in the primary stage of our mission work is the creation of a native church, because if, through our general work we create the opportunity for the evangelization of the nation, it is the native church which alone is fitted to take advantage of this opportunity.

I shall not speak of the first aspect of Christian work except to say that so far as Japan is concerned, its public opinion has been to a very large extent Christianized. That is to say, wherever one goes in Japan, one can assume that the Japanese people from the highest to the lowest will appreciate the moral standards and the social standards of Christianity, and that they will give their support to any program which looks to the realization of those standards. But we are particularly concerned this evening with the church which we have been laboring to create, and the church which we are going to send forth to utilize the opportunity that we have made for its work.

What of the Japanese church? First as to its membership. It is not a particularly large church, and yet, it is one whose membership is peculiarly representative of modern Japan. It includes men and women who represent every class of society. I think, for example, of two churches in Tokyo, in one of which there is on the vestry a man who is a son of one of the old Japanese noble families, an official in the Imperial household. In the other church only a short distance away, two of the vestrymen are reformed criminals. The Japanese church includes in its membership, men and women of all classes of society, and demonstrates that Jesus Christ is able to be the Saviour of every kind of Japanese.

Then again the Japanese church includes among its members just that element in the population of Japan which is fitted by its nature and by its training for the task of leadership. Our Christians have been drawn to a large extent from what are known as the student classes in Japan. This means that the Christians represent the men and women who are leaders in the various departments of life. It would be interesting, if we had time to show to how large an extent Christianity is represented in the governmental classes, among the leading lawyers, the leading doctors, the leading business men of Japan. But it is sufficient to say that the Christian church is made up of men and women who are qualified for the work of leadership.

Then again, if we consider this church from the point of view of the Christian faith, I feel it is not too much to say that our Japanese Christians have demonstrated that both in their practical zeal and in their real appreciation of the teachings of Christianity, they are worthy to be compared with the Christians of any other country or any other time.

And yet, in considering the Japanese church as it exists today with regard to its qualifications for the tasks that lie ahead of it, there are two qualifications we ought particularly to note, because any church which is to be able to carry Christianity to a great nation like the Japanese must at least have these two. It must be a church led by its own people and it must be a church maintained by its own people. I don't think that Japan is ever going to be influenced to any large extent by a Christianity which is under foreign leadership. Therefore, self-government and self-leadership are primary requisites for any widespread evangelistic work in Japan.

No one who knows the results that have been obtained in Japan can fail to recognize that whatever failures may have been made there, at least the Japanese churches are singularly rich in native leaders who have proved by long years of service their practical ability, their thorough understanding of the Christian teaching and their capacity for interpreting Christianity in terms their countrymen can understand. It would be interesting if we had time to give concrete illustrations of the work that has been done by native Christian leaders, and of the type of men who represent Christian leadership in Japan.

Then again, when we come to the question of self-support, self-support has made remarkably rapid progress in Japan. Some of you may have heard Dr. Kagawa say yesterday that last year Japanese Christians gave somewhere in the neighborhood of $2,000,000 for the support of their own work. Here it is sufficient to say that in the larger cities of Japan the Christian churches are already today, for the most part, self-supporting, able to carry on at least the normal work of the church with contributions derived from their own countrymen. This is a matter of great significance, because I feel that Christianity can never have any widespread influence in Japan, until the Japanese feel that it is a Christianity that is supported by themselves.

The question which I wish particularly to consider today is the adequacy of this church for the task that lies ahead of it. Up to the present, we have been engaged in creating an opportunity. Now, we are faced with the need of utilizing that opportunity. How far is the Japanese church by itself qualified for this task? I have mentioned some of its qualifications. Let us for a moment consider what we might call its lack of qualification.

In the first place it must be perfectly evident that in a country of sixty million people, looking at the work extensively, it is impossible for a church so small and so lacking in resources as the Japanese church to meet the opportunities that confront it, unless it has the cooperation of the churches throughout the world.

Financially speaking, the coming to age, as it were, of the Japanese church, the fact that it is capable of supporting its own work does not at all mean that we should cease our financial cooperation with that church. On the contrary, if we are going to enable the Japanese church to use its trained men and women to their full capacity we must give it more financial cooperation in the future than we have given it in the past. The sacrifice which we will be called upon to undergo in order that we may carry our work forward to completion will be greater than that which the work up to the present time has entailed.

Then, again, take the question of missionary cooperation. I do not think that the fact that the time has come, when the leadership of work in Japan should be placed in the hands of the Japanese Church, means that all missionary aid should be withdrawn from Japan. On the contrary, it may be that if the Japanese church has the cooperation of the church at home, it will call for more missionary aid in the future than was needed in the past, because the time has come when perhaps the appeal for Christianity can be made to the Japanese nation as a whole. If that appeal is to be made, it seems certain that the Japanese will need missionaries, not so much to dominate the work, but to stand by and to help Japanese Christians both to extend the work further than their own ability would enable them to do and to act as their counsellors in the very difficult task of interpreting Christianity to the Japanese.

But it seems to me that perhaps the greatest task that lies ahead of the Japanese church in the near future is not so much what you might call the extensive side of the work as it is the domestication, if I may call it so, of Christianity in Japan. We have made wonderful progress in Japan and yet to a large extent Christianity has failed to catch the imagination of the great masses of the Japanese people. Why is this true? Is it not because Christianity up to the present in Japan is largely our American or European Christianity transferred to that country? Christianity has not as yet established points of contact with the ancient modes of thought and the ancient customs of the Japanese people. One cannot but feel that earnest as are our Japanese Christians, much as the Christian faith has meant in the lives of the Japanese, Christianity even today, in Japan, is so expressed that it would be difficult for Christianity to compete with the ancient religions of the country, so far as the great masses of the people are concerned. This is no mere theory. If any one has studied the religious movements which have taken place in Japan during recent years and has seen religions rise up which are crude in their beliefs, which are full of superstitious practices and which yet have spread to an extent that far surpasses anything we have been able to do in our Christian evangelistic work, one will recognize the tremendous importance of placing Christianity before the Japanese people in such a way that all that is true in their old religion, that all that is useful in their old customs and modes of life shall be baptized, as it were, into Christ.

This is a task which Christianity can only accomplish in Japan, when the leadership for Christian work has been transferred to the hands of the Japanese church. So I feel that perhaps the greatest problem that lies ahead of the Japanese church during, say, the next half century is the Orientalizing, if I may call it so, of the Christianity that has been taken there, of its creeds, of its modes of worship, of its customs. Christianity must be expressed in such a way that the Japanese will find in it not only the truth but will recognize in it the fulfilment of all that is true in their own past, that they will be able in Christianity to find in it a satisfaction for those customs, those things that mean so much to the ordinary person which as yet Christianity has failed to imbue with its own spirit.

Yet, while this is a task that calls for Japanese leadership, it is not one which the Japanese church can accomplish by itself. It must have our cooperation. We have made remarkable progress in Japan and yet it seems to me we have only begun the work of the evangelization of the country as a whole.

It may seem to us a matter of course that when a people,

who feel the need of religion so deeply as the Japanese do, have to decide what religion they will accept, they will choose Christianity. But it will not be at all a matter of course. Japan has religions which are older than Christianity. These religions are beginning to show renewed signs of life. Unless Christianity is able to present to the Japanese all that is true in their old religion, unless it is able to come to them in Japanese form, I think it is quite a question as to whether the people, certainly as they are today, would choose Christianity or would choose these old religions with all their defects, if that were the issue that had to be presented to them. We have thus before us the most difficult part of our Christian work, the interpretation of Christianity into forms that will be appreciated by the Japanese, the making of Christianity at home in Japan, without at the same time losing anything that is vital to Christianity itself.

Now, in this work, it seems to me the Japanese church does need the cooperation of the home church. I spoke of the financial cooperation. Take for example one aspect of that cooperation, our educational work. A great part of our success in Japan has been due to the splendid Christian schools and colleges which have been established there, schools and colleges which have enabled us to select from the young men and women of Japan those who can be trained in Christian truth and who can go forth as Christian leaders among their own people.

There never was a time when Christianity in Japan needed leaders trained in Christian schools and colleges so much as at the present, and yet, if these schools and colleges are to be maintained in a way that will enable them to compete on equal terms with the magnificent government schools, it is certain that the Japanese church must have our financial aid. I am sure that we don't realize that our Christian schools and colleges have got to be tremendously strengthened, if Christianity is to continue its progress in Japan, and if it is to be adequate to the great task that lies ahead of it.

Or take again, the question of literature. We have in the past produced some good Christian literature in Japan, but if Christianity is to make its way among the great masses of the people, much more will have to be done in this way. Literature must be produced which will make an appeal to the reading public equal to that of the very interesting and the cleverly written literature that is being produced by the ancient religions of Japan. Here again the Japanese church needs our cooperation.

But then when we speak of the cooperation which the Japanese church needs from us, why, I imagine that the greatest cooperation that is called for at the present time is the demonstration on our part that Christianity is able to produce in human lives the result that it claims to be able to produce. The Japanese church has only a short history behind it. When it goes to the Japanese people to present Christ as the Saviour the Japanese church can only point back to the older churches of the West and say that in our lives they can find a proof that Jesus Christ is able to save men from their own human passions, and to raise them above their own human selfishness in a way that the other religions are failing at the present time to do.

This is the kind of cooperation that is most urgently needed at present. The Christianity that we have developed heretofore has perhaps been adequate to enable us to carry our missionary work through its primary stage. It is not a question today as to whether we should have done better or not. The problem is this; if we are going to carry our missionary work from the primary stage into the next stage; if the opportunity which we have created in Japan and China and the other countries of the Far East is going to be utilized then certainly we have got to offer to the young churches which are acting for us in the East a very much better brand of Christianity than we are offering at present. We are told by a great American bishop that our task is to carry Jesus Christ to Japan and leave Him there. Yet we need to remember that we can only carry Jesus Christ to non-Christian people to the extent to which Jesus Christ is realized in our own lives.

Take some of the difficulties that lie ahead of the Japanese church: Why is it that the 200,000 Christians in Japan are not adequate for the task of carrying forward the Christian campaign in that country? One obvious reason is that those 200,-000 Japanese Christians are divided up into twenty or thirty different denominations. Our forces are divided. We cannot present a common front to the task that lies ahead of us.

There are a good many people who feel that Christian unity will probably be accomplished on the mission field, although it does not seem to be very easy to accomplish here at home. It seems to me that exactly the opposite should be our attitude. We are face to face with a tremendous opportunity to advance the cause of Christ. If Christian unity is the condition on which alone that cause can be successfully carried forward, we should feel our responsibility to an extent that makes us rise above our differences here at home and present to our churches on the field, a Christian church that is one in Christ.

The same thing is true with regard to our Christian conduct and our Christian apprehension of the truth. Our Lord has said that the Spirit will guide us into all truth. What does he say? The Spirit will guide us into all truth. It seems to me that these words indicate that the full Christian truth will be revealed, not to a church which is sitting still and trying to satisfy its own curiosity, but to a church which is earnestly engaged in carrying out our Lord's commission to take his gospel to all nations and preach it to every creature, and that in the accomplishment of that task, in the endeavor to surmount the difficulties which that task presents to us, we shall be led by the Spirit into all truth; and the things which seem to us today to be such problems, even among ourselves, will be resolved for us as we consecrate ourselves more entirely to the task which Christ has left for His church to accomplish.

THE IMPRISONED SPLENDOR OF THE ORIENT

THE REVEREND HARRIS E. KIRK, D.D., BALTIMORE, MARYLAND

I speak to you in a spirit of daring tempered by fear; for even to suggest what may be coming out of the Orient further to illuminate the face of God in Christ is a hazardous adventure; but to do so in the presence of experienced leaders makes one conscious of ignorance and limitation. I am to speak on the imprisoned splendor of the Orient. By Orient I mean China, Japan and India, the great nations that are leading the East. The direction these nations take in the next century will determine not only the character of Oriental development as a whole, but also influence very materially the status of the Western world. For the explosive center of intellectual and political interests is gradually moving towards the East; and soon we shall be looking no longer to Europe or America, but to the Orient to determine the moral and political temperature of the world.

By splendor I mean the indigenous capacity of these peoples to give an original contribution to the comprehension of Christianity. For if Christ be the seed, human nature is the soil in which the seed is to grow; and the soil always makes an original contribution to the life history of the seed. By imprisoned splendor I refer to the discovery and release of this original capacity, through mission work; which when fully expressed shall add lustre to the glowing light of spiritual reality which shines through missionary efforts in these great countries.

At the outset the duty of the Christian church appeared to be very simple. It consisted in giving to these peoples a religion which they needed, and with which in advance of missionary effort they were unacquainted. To give light to those sitting in darkness; to bring good news from a far country, this was the first task of the missionary; and the finest chapter in religious history of the past hundred years is the story of how this work was done.

The seed was well sown, but now that the plant is beginning to mature, a new factor becomes evident, namely the influence of the soil on the seed. For wherever Christ is preached there new and unsuspected capacities are revealed, and as the seed develops it draws into it what is latent in the soil. By giving this unknown element clarity and definiteness it brings to light what was before hidden; so that missionary effort, which began in giving the people what was supposed to be without, gradually comes to be the releasing of what has been imprisoned in the native mind. As I conceive it, to recognize and develop this aspect of human nature is at present the most delicate and important problem of missionary endeavor.

As Browning puts it:

> "To know
> Rather consists in opening out a way,
> Whence the imprisoned splendor may escape,
> Than in effecting entry for a light
> Supposed to be without."

This then is my thought:—the mission movement in the East has now reached a point where it is gradually ceasing to be the impartation of something supposed to be foreign to the native life, and is beginning to call forth and develop what is latent in the Oriental soul. The imprisoned splendor is beginning to escape. That is why there is a justifiable belief among mis sionary leaders that an indigenous church controlled by native peoples, rather than a complex of mission activities under foreign direction, is the logical goal of wise missionary policy. This was the profound conviction of men like Dr. Timothy Richard more than a generation ago; and when we contemplate the intellectual and spiritual ferment in the Orient today; a ferment due in large measure to the active leaven of Christianity, the necessity of a wise transference of control from foreign to native leaders becomes an irresistible conviction. So far then from regarding the demand for an indigenous church as a recent or dangerous innovation, we should recognize it as a clear evidence of Providential direction. For as churches with religious beliefs organized according to indigenous mental aptitudes developed among gentile peoples in apostolic times, quite unlike the type of church functioning at Jerusalem, so shall churches informed and guided by the native spirit of the East rise upon modern mission fields, as the permanent fruitage of foreign endeavor. For it stands to reason to suppose, if we cannot impart Christ to the Orient, and then entrust this great gift to indigenous responsibility, mission work would re-

main an alien influence, attached to the outside of life, instead
of becoming, as it should, an essential and informing part of
the native spirit.

If, then, we are disposed to recognize that there is an imprisoned splendor in the Orient, our problem becomes this:
How shall we release and guide it until it is able to stand on
its own responsibility? This is the most difficult and delicate
of all missionary problems just now, to the solution of which
it is hoped this great convention may contribute some durable
and enlightened policies of missionary adjustment.

If there be such a thing as a philosophy of development to
be drawn from providential leading of the Christian church,
it would appear that while Christianity begins with the lowest,
it must eventually spread to the highest circles of life, if it is
to have a decisive influence upon the racial history of peoples.
At the outset God is interested in the sheep; but eventually the
destiny of the sheep is determined by the character of the
shepherds. And it goes without saying that methods suited
for the interpretation of religion to the highest and most
thoughtful elements of a people must differ from those found
effective among the lowest. A missionary method suited to
coolies, amahs, and children, will not interest highly intelligent
people. Milk for babes, and meat for strong men, is the logical
way of growth. This suggests the most difficult task of the
missionary at the present moment: how to appraise properly
the deeper trends of the Oriental mind, to ascertain what reactions are taking place when such a mentality is confronted
with the gospel of Christ. Simple phrases, unexamined
propositions, and dogmatic deliverances will not do. We have
contributed to the education of the Eastern mind; we have
stimulated its intelligence and awakened its critical powers as
well as arousing its appreciative receptivities. The Oriental
mind of today is dominated by a spirit of intense criticism of all
things Western. The missionary must be able to meet this
spirit with generosity, sympathy, and capacity if it is to be
permanently influenced by missionary endeavor.

One pressing need then, if we are to contribute further
to the awakening of the East, is such a re-examination of our
own conception of Christianity as shall enable us to approach
this critical temper: not with certain provisional concessions
made to a supposedly darkened intelligence, but as an actual
confession on our part that we have not fully understood Christianity, and furthermore that perhaps we have defiled it by
allowing it to be too closely associated with something that is
not essentially Christian at all—Western civilization. The time
has surely come when we should be giving heed to the painful
contrasts that appear between our civilization and that of the

Far East. The time has happily gone, let us hope forever, when we shall be sending out crowds of inexperienced enthusiasts. impregnated with the idea that our civilization is not only the best, but a normal expression of Christianity itself. It is surely a very limited notion that our duty is confined to a proclamation of the gospel to non-Christian nations. This easy understanding of mission work has led to a deal of condescension and impertinent patronage of peoples, the cultural aspects of whose civilization are as high above ours, as was that of the Roman above the Goth, and whose antiquity as compared with ours is as the cedars of Lebanon to a mushroom of a night. We must be prepared to confess that Oriental dislike of our civilization is well founded; that superficially it appears ugly, hurried, without philosophic direction or moral control, and altogether too much of this world; that it has often been menacing and greedy in its demands on other peoples, and that frequently the voice of the missionary cannot be heard because of the strident clamor of the business man, or the rough bellowing of the soldier. And to allow the impression to become fixed that Christianity and Western civilization are not only identical, but that one is the legitimate fruit of the other, is forever to block the way for understanding Christ and the gospel. The Western church has almost forgotten the truth that Christ's Kingdom is not of this world; it is too intimately associated with the dubious and questionable policies of foreign peoples, and we need not wonder that the moral trend of the West is one that is giving the Oriental peoples cause for serious concern. They are fully justified in asking questions, and such questions must be answered, not by the patronizing manner of the mission conventicle, but by hard, straightforward arguments among equals. And, above all, until we can dissociate the mission of Christ's church from a dubious civilization too much indentified with trade expansion and sphere of influence, we have no right to ask the Orient to take our form of religion.

But here we touch an even more difficult question. We have allowed the impression to get about that Christianity is a Western religion. Nothing of course could be more misleading. If we should associate its origin with geographical position we should have to confess that Christianity came from the East. But Christianity has never been a localized religion; it belongs to all mankind. It is true that it moved westward, but has not the time come for us frankly to acknowledge that something happened to it in its westward movement? St. Paul says that God has given us treasure in earthen vessels. The treasure is admittedly the glorious gospel of the blessed God. The justification of missions is the intelligent advocacy of a complete Christ. The Orient will never take a crossless gospel; neither can it become permanently interested in a religion of an ethical life, which, after all is said and done, turns out to be a worn-out and discredited legalism. The East is more familiar with the idea of incarnation and atonement than the West, and that which gives meaning and power to mission work is the stable conviction that the gospel of Christ is the adequate power for the salvation of all mankind. Moreover the gospel is a fluid sort of treasure and must be contained in vessels. I have little sympathy with the impressionistic notion that you can propagate a religion without convictions, creeds and theologies. We cannot do it, first, because we can no more carry the gospel without categories, than we can convey water without vessels. We cannot do it in the second place, because we are so constituted that we cannot believe in anything effectively, unless we can formulate a reasonable philosophy of its meaning and purpose. Let us admit this frankly and then endeavor to remember that while the gospel is treasure, and must be carried in vessels, it must never be identified with the vessels. The gospel is heavenly in origin, and therefore eternal, but the vessels are of the earth, earthy.

Look now at the Western spread of Christianity in Apostolic times. How different is the preaching of Paul in gentile communities from that which prevailed among Jewish peoples in Palestine. Follow this movement into the early church and see how essential it was, if the priceless essence of the gospel was to be imparted, vessels suited to those times be found to contain it. In other words, if Christianity was to move westward, it was necessary that its eternal truths should be caught and contained in those categories of thought which were indigenous to the West. Our thinking is dominated by Greek concepts, and in no other way could we have held on to our priceless heritage. As I have said, while having no sympathy with those who think they can retain the treasure without some kind of containing vessel, I am entirely in sympathy with those who refuse to identify the treasure with the vessel itself; or suppose, if you transfer it from one vessel to another, you lose its precious essence.

One result, a defect of the qualities of the Western mind is that where you have vessels, you are likely to have divisions and denominations; and with this I shall find no fault here; save only to suggest that unless the Eastern mind is used to the same kind of containers, we cannot expect it to accept as a permanent form of Christianity, our Western credal, denominational expression of it, even though in the beginning we are obliged to present it to them in this form. What we should look for and encourage is the formulation of Christianity ac-

cording to the deep structural qualities of the Oriental mind;
see to it that we impart the whole of the precious essence; exercise the greatest skill and patience in transferring it from one
vessel to another; but be willing, nay, even happy to see it
transferred to those forms which are native to the Oriental
mind, and which give the largest possibilities to the development of an indigenous church.

Look again at Christian history; wherever the Lord Jesus
has been preached as the world's Saviour, there the truth of
God has expressed itself in the thought forms indigenous to the
people who received Him. We should never forget that God
Himself is conducting this enterprise. What He has died for
He means to have. The treasure is eternal, but the vessel is
earthen, of this perishable life, and we must never identify the
treasure with the vessel. Let us preach a full gospel of a complete Christ, but let us gladly believe that this tremendous
power can express itself in forms that are indigenous to native
peoples: else why such a difference between Jewish Christian
and Gentile Christian conceptions in Apostolic times? Let us
believe with all our hearts in the precious essence of the gospel,
but also recognize the limitations of the container; and be ready
with a generous hospitality to welcome the original contribution to the comprehension of Christ which the Oriental peoples
are now ready to offer.

And when this spirit of generosity dominates the Western
Christian mind we shall note at least three great contributions
the Orient can make to our apprehension of the Kingdom of
God:

1. Its natural capacity for mystical experience. Have we
of the West, with all our religious thought and activity, ever
appreciated this primary element in religious life? The conversation of our Lord with the woman of Samaria wherein He
told her: "God is a Spirit," slips over our Western mentality,
leaving hardly a trace. We confess our need for mystical experience only as something forever beyond us, or acknowledge
it in some eccentric or superstitious fashion which soon loses
itself in pantheistic delusions. Our life is hurried and fretful,
and while deeply and painful aware of our insecure hold upon
the eternal realities, we cannot keep quiet long enough to listen
to God. For that deep quiet resting upon the Eternal; the ex-
ploration of the grave silences of the higher life; for the experience of the immediacy of God in the processes of the human
spirit we must look to the Orient, and discern beneath its restless changes, its labored social and political ferments, a native
capacity for being still, a sense of living in the hospitable omni-
presence of the eternal God, to which when Christ is revealed,
as one long sought for and loved, the native spirit will respond

with eagerness and joy. Goodness, godliness, is the only currency that circulates at par in all lands. Once Timothy Richard came into a region in China where a brother missionary had recently checked a smallpox epidemic and learned that a Chinese scholar had been led to read the New Testament. On asking him what was the impression made on his mind he received this reply: "The most wonderful truth here is this, that a man may become the temple of the Holy Ghost." It may yet be that the Orient will lead us of the West to lay aside our limitations of outlook and teach us how to discern God face to face, and know that we are spiritual beings, belonging to an eternal order, and not merely creatures of a civilization attached externally to moral reality, indifferent to the deeper movements of the Divine Spirit.

2. The Orient is still the home of the creative joys of life, simply because it is as yet uncursed by a civilization founded upon the machine. In the East, the eye, the hand, and the mind work together in the fabrication of things of necessity and beauty. The most lowly toil imparts something of durable satisfaction beyond the price of material reward. In our Western world we spend much of our time in pulling levers, and pressing buttons, and because there is no necessary connection between the eye, the hand and the mind, while our wealth increases, and with it leisure to enjoy, our discontents grow apace, our demand for sensual indulgence overpowers our feeble moral purposes; and most of us become splendid slaves, richly clad and apparently free, but mentally and spiritually weakened and without vision of that high region from whence cometh the peace of God which passeth understanding. Is not this why our religious interest is too often pitched to the low note of disillusion, instead of being the expression of a glorious communion with the most High God? Is not a perception of this truth; that creative joys dwell only with those whose bodies and minds work together—the reason why Gandhi insists that the people of India forsake the machine of Western civilization, for the hand labor of the native; and who knowing the deep significance of this primitive relation to happiness, can say that he is wrong? A Japanese art critic has recently been telling us that Asia is no longer dazzled with the splendor of our material civilization in some such words as these:

"Asia knows, it is true, nothing of the fierce joys of a time-devouring locomotion, but she has still the far deeper travel culture of the pilgrimage and the wandering monk. For the Indian ascetic, begging his bread of village housewives, or seated at even-fall beneath some tree, chatting and smoking with the peasant of the district is the real traveler. To him a countryside does not consist of its natural features alone. It is a nexus of habits and associations, of human elements and traditions, suffused with the tenderness and friendship of one who has shared, if only for a moment, the joys and sorrows of the personal drama."

This same acute writer says that the difference between East and West is found in this that while the man of the East loves to contemplate the ends of life, the man of the West loses himself in the particular, and in the search for the means of material existence. This may be an exaggeration, but it suffices to remind us of a real distinction. We excel in science, organization, economic efficiency, while they in philosophy, contemplative brooding, and in the high visualization of the fundamental ends of existence, which give rational meaning to labor, and add patient endurance to suffering. We of the West often say, "We do not know where we are going, but we are on the way," identifying life with movement; but the man of the East will humbly confess, "I know where I am going, but I am not yet sure of the way," identifying life with inquiry and the pursuit of a way, and ready to follow anyone who knows. Here at bottom is a real difference between West and East; the man of the East is more tractable, teachable, and susceptible to religious influence. Why then should it be thought an incredible thing that he should yet bring deliverance to the West, by an original expression of the gospel of Christ.

3. The Oriental intuition of a durable bond of human societies. We of the West, in spite of the spirit of Christ, have become obsessed with the idea that the only durable bond of human societies is organized force, so that war becomes a periodic and lawful expression of our civilization. The Great War was not an accident, but the perfect flower of our philosophies of life. As Jeremiah would say, "It was the fruit of our own thoughts." The Orient, in spite of grave exceptions, is at heart deeply persuaded that war is wrong, and still thinks of the durable bond of human societies in other terms entirely. While we with our advancing scientific notions beat our plowshares into swords, and our pruning-hooks into spears, the Orient is striving to reverse the process and attain unto true progress. The Orient has reason to believe in a higher principle, for is it not true that the Emperor of China was the only great ruler who never wore a sword, that in China the scholar has ever been first and the soldier last in the scale of importance, and that China has never in the long centuries of her history been fully organized for war, and on that account is the only ancient nation that has survived until the present day? It is in such high terms of racial relations that young Christian China is seeking to express its thinking. Last summer after a long conference in Peking with some of the leaders of the

indigenous church I seemed to hear the voice of the Orient saying unto me: "Go back, O man of the West, and tell your people, that while the East has every apparent reason for organizing itself for war and strife, the purpose of the Orient in response to its racial spirit is to win its place in the sun by the power of a peaceful ideal." To me this came as a new vision of Macedonian opportunity. Here then is the chance to express our firm faith in providential leading; to consider wisely and well how and by what means we shall release the imprisoned splendor through wise missionary endeavor; and by throwing these great people upon their spiritual resources may we not hope that there may yet break out on these our industrial ages that splendor of God of which Carlyle used to speak; which shall not only be the justification of mission work in the East, but shall enable us of the West to possess ourselves of those durable blessings of the gospel of Christ which shall enable us to realize the brotherhood of man and the Kingdom of God, when the kingdoms of this world shall become the Kingdom of God and His Christ.

It may at first dishearten us to look back over the slow and painful way we have reached our present perplexities, for the westward path of Christianity is not always an encouraging spectacle; but there is another vision if we turn our eyes westward, as the gospel is going home again to the Orient. Look upon this and rejoice!

> "Not by eastern windows only,
>   When daylight comes, comes the light;
> In front the sun climbs slowly,
>   But westward look, the land is bright."

THE FOREIGN MISSIONARY MOVEMENT IN RELATION TO PEACE AND GOOD WILL AMONG NATIONS

"OF ONE BLOOD"

BISHOP MICHAEL BOLTON FURSE, D.D., ST. ALBANS, ENGLAND

Why do we want peace and good will among nations? Because we have seen war, its cruelty, lust, barbarity, futility, its blood and tears? If we desire peace and good will, because we do not want war, the motive behind our wish is fear. There is a whole crowd of people today who don't want war because they are afraid of it. But fear never stopped war. Fear is a thing that produces war. It is the main cause for war. We, as Christians, have got to face this question squarely. We want peace and good will among the nations of the world, because we believe that is God's will and purpose.

It is of no use to talk glibly about "no more war," unless we are prepared to get right down to business and uproot the causes which produce war.

What are the causes of war? As a man "thinketh in his heart, so is he." That, I believe, is as true of nations as it is of individuals. The World War, as I see it, was the logical result of wrong thinking and wrong ideas. It was the logical outcome of the principles upon which we had been building, and are still building, our so-called civilization. These are the principles of the jungle—get, grab, and keep, if you can. These principles are based upon the idea that a man's life and a nation's life consist in the number of things they possess. I know we camouflage this idea; I know that in this great war, which is going on today, this industrial and commercial war, we have appointed our ambulance brigades to pick up the dead and dying and to make our actions look all right; but, if we are honest, the principles on which we have built up our industry and commerce are on the idea of getting what you can.

We said hard things about the profiteer in the war, but, after all, he was only doing what he was brought up to do, to make what he could when he could; and, as peoples, we have been doing it since. We were at war before 1914, potentially. We are at war today, potentially. We shall continue to be so, so long as those principles dominate men and nations.

If you go into the jungle, as I have been myself, both in India and in Africa, you will find that what gets hold of you right away is the feeling of fear. It is all around you. Fear is the dominant factor in the jungle; and fear today is the dominant factor in the world. I believe fear is the devil. If we could eliminate fear we would get more than halfway to where we want to get. There is only one power that can cast out fear, and that is "perfect love." In the Christian interpretation what does "perfect love" mean? It does not mean a wishy-washy sentiment; it means something real and severe; it always means giving. If you are out to give somebody something and to serve him, you are never afraid of him.

What is needed, as far as I can see today, if we really want peace and good will among the nations, is a new idea of life, a new idea of industry, of commerce, of patriotism and of international relationships and a new spirit.

What are these new ideas and new ideals, and above all this new spirit? Our answer is, "Christ, the Prince of Peace." What are Christ's conceptions of life and of the world? Quite shortly, life in Christ's mind is giving, not getting; it is personal and national service, not personal and national success; it is cooperation, not competition; it is sacrifice, not selfishness.

What is Christ's idea of the world and the human race? "Of one blood made he all the nations of the world," one family. He summed up God's idea of the world as a home and a family in the first two words of the Lord's Prayer, "Our Father"; one blood, one Father, one common stuff running through the whole of the human race. And so it was that when God chose to make Himself fully known to men, He used the one language which is common to the whole world, the language of a human life. God became incarnate.

If you go into the heart of Africa tomorrow, you will probable not understand a single word that the native says; nor will they understand a word you say, but they will size you up very soon. They will know all about you. You will take longer to size them up, because, as you know, children size up grown-ups very much quicker than grown-ups size them up. You can fool most people, but you can't fool children; they see through you, as parents well know. So it is with child races. In spite of all the differences of color, language and custom, there is in all races that common stuff of humanity. Every nation understands the language of a human life.

Now, there is little value in generalities; so for a moment or two, let us consider what this Christian conception of the world as a home and a family really entails.

First of all, a family is made up of various members all of whom differ from one another. There are a certain number of people who appear to think that the world would be a much better place, if everybody was exactly like themselves! It might be better but it would certainly be much duller, if at every corner one turned he ran up against himself. I was a member of a large family, and fortunately for me, I came more or less at the end of it. It is the best education one can get. The Christian conception of the human race as a family is that every nation has its own special contribution to make to the richness and the glory of the home.

Secondly, in the home there is law and order. You can't get away from this. Otherwise the home becomes a bear-garden. But that law and order are not enforced at the business end of a big stick. Occasionally one may have to use something of the kind in order to make an impression for a time on some member of the family. I had impressions made upon me which lasted for quite a time, but they were not the basis of the law and order in the home; it was good will, persuasion, reason and common sense, not force. It may be needful to use the big stick when one member of the family of the human race runs amuck, just as one has to do with some children, but what we Christians have got to stand for is that ultimately there can be no peace in the home, unless it be through good will, persuasion, reason and common sense. People must be treated as reasonable beings.

In the third place, every member counts in a family. There is no question of counting the eldest son only, we younger ones see to that. And there is no question of one member of the family being superior to the other. Nor is there such a question in the family of the human race. For two things you and I are not responsible, our parents and the color of our skins. If one happens to be white, why should he stride about for the rest of his natural existence thinking that he is such a superior person to those of another color? People say, "Yes, this idea is all very well; but it is "a wishy-washy cosmopolitanism"! Nonsense. I believe in race and nationality, because I believe God made mountains and rivers and oceans and continents.

And that brings me to the fourth characteristic of the family: in the family every single member has to work making his contribution to the welfare of the whole group. So in the family of the nations of the world I hope to see every nation making the best of itself and developing its resources to the utmost, not for self-aggrandizement, but in order to make the biggest contribution to the welfare of the whole human race.

But some will declare that this cuts out all competition, which is the very life and soul of industry and progress. Was there any competition in the war? Of course there was. I saw it in France and in East Africa; in England, and in South Africa. But what was the competition? It was not the competition of "getting," but it was the competition of "giving"; it was to see how much one could give and not how much he could get. Men and women of all kinds rose to that great appeal; never again must you or I allow people to say that human nature cannot be stirred to its finest and best, except by some sort of mean, material reward. Such a declaration is simply untrue: the facts are against it.

We human beings, made in the image of God, can rise to the highest appeal. And what is the next characteristic of the family? It is this: the weakest in the home does not go to the wall, but is the first concern of all the other members of the family. You hear no talk about "charity"—when one is looking after the sick or lame or blind member of his own family! He does it, because it is the right thing to do. And so, in the family of the nations of the world, the young and little and weak, perhaps sickly nations have a right to exist, and it is up to the big and prosperous and strong nations to help them, not in a condescending way, but declaring, "as a member of our family you have a right to exist and to develop to the fullest possible extent."

And lastly, what is it that keeps the family together as one in the one home? It is the spirit of love and good will and brotherhood. And this spirit is caught by the children from the mother and father. It is their spirit of love for their children which is passed into them day by day, and from them goes back to their parents and so to one another.

Just so, we Christians believe, must it be in the family of nations. The only thing which can keep that family together is the right spirit, the Spirit of God, mediated to man through His Son Jesus Christ in the living power of the Holy Spirit. If there is to be peace and good will among the nations of the world, we believe that it can only be through the unifying spirit of love, mutual service and brotherhood; that is, by every member of the family of nations catching that spirit from God through the mediation of our Lord Jesus Christ in the living power of the Holy Spirit. That as I understand it is the Christian faith.

As I conceive the enterprise of Christian missions, it is to disseminate the right ideas and to demonstrate the right spirit. We have heard a good deal during this splendid convention of how we must not go to other nations in the East, or in Africa, or wherever it may be, with the message of Jesus in a superior way. Well, why? I quite agree, but what is the sound reason behind the suggestion? As I see it, the reason is this: superiority of that kind is really devilish. That is to say, it is not of God. How does God treat us? As a superior person? Never. He made us and took us into partnership with Him. He made us free men and said, "Come along and develop this undeveloped world. And among other things your undeveloped character."

When we rejected that partnership, when sin entered the world, what happened? God in his infinite love and patience did

not turn away, but sent His Only Begotten Son to humble Himself
and take our nature upon Him. And what did our Lord do? He
did not tell people in a superior way that they were not good:
He did not appeal to people to save their own souls. He said,
"Come and give me a hand in the biggest job in the whole world,
which is to make the world what God really means it to be, because
I need you."

Now, when somebody comes and begins to tell me that I am
not as good as I ought to be, I know that is quite true, but I do
not like to have him say it. There is in me an instinct of self-
preservation. When I am attacked physically, I am a little apt
to get my hands up. When I am attacked morally, I put out my
defenses, a sort of primal instinct asserting itself. But when
somebody comes along and says, "You are exactly the man I want
and I can't do without you," I pull myself together, stand up to
my full height and say, "Yes, that is all right," and I come along!
That is the way God treats us. That is why we must go to other
nations, not as superior people conferring a benefit, but as ordinary
human beings, as brothers, and say, "Now, look here. We are in
an awful mess in the world, and we simply cannot get on without
you. Will you come and give us a hand?"

How did our Lord deal with men. He "drew them with cords
of a man by the bands of love." It is only that spirit of Christ, not
the wit of man, not even great statesmanship, not wealth, not
power, not greatness in one's own esteem,—the spirit of Christ,
and that alone will ever persuade the nations of the world that this
is God's plan for them.

I come to my last word. We must preach these ideals, and
proclaim these truths. There is real danger of too much talking
and too little prayer. Why do I say that? Because prayer is the
means, Christ's ordained means, of making our own those great
spiritual resources which are put at our disposal by God. Prayer
is cooperation with God. Prayer is switching on to the power
station. Prayer is getting into line with Him so that the "living
waters" may flow freely into us.

Such prayer we must learn how to offer. There is a science,
an art of prayer, and one must give time, study, thought and devotion to it, as to the pursuit of any other science or art. One must
set aside a portion of the day, of every day, in which to fill up
with the spirit of Christ. Otherwise our work may look very fine,
very big, and very efficient but it will be quite useless and futile
in the long run. My one regret over this glorious convention has
been that sufficient time has not been given to sit in silence, each
one of us getting into touch with our Lord that we may spread
throughout this great continent and throughout the whole world
His spirit of love and wisdom and power and life! We want less

preaching and more teaching; less talking and more silence. It
is only in the power of that spirit that we shall ever be able to
see visions and dream dreams. Where there is no vision the people
perish. Only by that spirit are men's hearts touched and their
consciences quickened and themselves turned to the living God.
We know it can be done. If God could turn my heart to Him, I
know He could turn other hearts. One need never despair, if
he will give God His chance. That is all He asks. It is not
we who are climbing up to God, it is God who comes down to us
that He may lift us and all humanity up to Him. Dreams! visions!
visionaries! yes, thank God for them, because we know that those
dreams will come true, if we just hold on and do our bit.

> "Dreamer of dreams, we take the taunt with gladness,
>   Knowing that God beyond the years you see
> Has wrought those dreams which count with you for madness
>   Into the substance of the world to be."

EDUCATING FOR PEACE AND GOODWILL

MRS. THOMAS NICHOLSON, DETROIT, MICHIGAN

War, in the life of civilized man, is an anachronism. It is a
"vestigial remainder" of barbarism, a survival of paganism. Man
has conquered many of the foes to which he was heir. He has
conquered the elements, harnessed destructive forces, and compelled them to run his machinery. War, the greatest enemy of the
race, has, so far, withstood him. He must end war, or war will
end him. The fight is on between man and his arch-enemy.

Why has war persisted despite man's evolution from the level
of the brute? Why has it wound its loathsome way through the
stages of his upward struggle, entangling his feet, dragging him
back, limiting his powers, menacing his very existence? Why has
man not vanquished his ancient foe? Because of false ideas,
wrong premises, mental perversions and obsessions. He is not
born with them, but by tradition, precept and example, they are
bred into him. He is taught that war is instinctive, inevitable, in-
separable from the life of the race, inherent in ideals of sacrifice,
loyalty, patriotism. Each generation teaches its children's children
that "men always have fought, they always will"; that, as pagan
Rome taught, " 'Tis sweet to die for country," and that the honored and glorious men and deeds of history have been those associated with war. Thus has war been bred into the race. And
thus it can be bred out!

A noted social scientist said, "It is indisputable that an entire
nation can be completely altered in character, outlook and motive
in a single generation by the education of its youth." Japan, the
Hermit Nation, made literate and Western in a generation affords
a striking example. A generation ago, two people entered the

public schools of their respective countries, Frances Willard, to teach scientific temperance; Nietzsche, to teach the doctrine of the superman. The result in the one case was the Eighteenth Amendment, in the other, the World War. What you would put in the life of a nation you must plant in the heart of its childhood. Here is hope for the world reformer, for

> Every day is the world made new,
> Every day is a new beginning—

in that a new generation comes daily on the world's stage.

The Protocol of Geneva, agreed to by representatives of forty-eight great nations, marks a mile post in the progress of the race, by its declaration that "a war of aggression constitutes . . . an international crime."

At last, war is outlawed, or at least stigmatized as "crime." But epithets and promises do not end war. "Nations rarely fight without a conviction that their cause is just and that those who fight for it are heroes and martyrs." Tribunals and courts to punish the aggressor will act as a deterrent, but the hopes of a war-weary world must rest on something more fundamental. Compacts and courts, tribunals and treaties must find their confirmation in spiritual values, and these cannot be imposed by governments or leagues. There must be the will to peace, the desire to co-operate, a sense of kinship and interdependence, mutual respect. All these are inherent in the teachings of Christ and are corollary to his doctrine of the Fatherhood of God and the brotherhood of man.

The Church of Christ holds its commission and charter to teach these ideals to all the nations of the earth. It is in itself a League of Nations functioning now, through its representatives, in every land. It is a recognized educational agency, training not only the intellect but the will and spirit. The missionary has opened schools where there were none, created written languages where none existed, produced literatures for people who had never seen books. In other lands where learning was restricted to the few he has extended its blessings to outcasts and coolies, to women and unprivileged childhood.

We are in a new day, which we have helped create. Science has knit the ends of the earth together. The opening and acquisitive mind of the East is asking many questions and drawing some conclusions. For instance, it wonders whether yesterday it did not concern the isolationist that "the heathen in his blindness bowed down to wood and stone." Today, it is of supreme moment how the native of Central Africa reacts to the radio report that a misguided negro, in New York has consecrated a negro Virgin Mary and Child. The laborer in Battle Creek, Michigan, who loads a power press addressed to Johannesburg, may well consider what the black man who unloads it will read on the pages it prints. So far, nine-tenths of the education in Africa is in the hands of missionary agencies. Here is a supreme, if a passing opportunity for the Church of Christ to teach not only the three R's but the religion which unites while it liberates. Says Dr. Aggrey, that eloquent African, "We did not know we had any rights in South Africa until the missionaries told us. Now we know it and we want them. This newly awakened passion is a Niagara and will engulf you or it may be made a dynamo to drive the wheels of a new civilization."

During the war it was found that by chemical processes which were identical up to the seventh stage two vastly different things could be produced. If, at the seventh stage the chemist used charcoal there resulted those lovely blue and purple aniline dyes which brightened and beautified life. If, at the seventh stage he employed alcohol he produced instead mustard gas which burned, blistered and blasted. The world is at this seventh stage. It has started something it cannot stop.

Restless, yearning classes and races will never return to their former stage of submission and acquiescence. They will become either Niagaras of destruction or the dynamos of a greater civilization. The seventh stage is critical, pivotal, potential. If by divine alchemy the Christian ethic be applied to this new creative force the race will move forward. If not, it is doomed. Can these riotous, clamant elements, brought into sudden proximity and aware of their possibilities live together in mutual regard and helpfulness? Or must frontiers be fortified and each group work out its destiny behind the barricades of color, class or nation? If so, a warless world cannot be achieved.

Paul said to the Ephesians, "You who sometime were far off are made nigh by the blood of Christ. For He is our peace who hath made both one and hath broken down the middle wall of partition between us."

Only as Christ is our peace will the dividing walls of humanity be broken down without destroying the entities on either side. The citizen of Ephesus was not less an Ephesian because he could look across the debris of his dividing wall into the friendly eyes of a Christian Jew.

In Christ alone may the unity and brotherhood of the human family be attained. But a limited Christ cannot do it. A partial Gospel cannot achieve it. If the church teaches at home and practices abroad a bigoted racialism or narrow patriotism she bows to Mars. If she omits from her teaching the Christianizing of human relationships she foments rather than lessens human strife. If she permits a non-Christian Hindu to accept and apply more fully than she has done her Lord's teachings, she can at least acknowledge her failure to interpret her Lord.

Clearly, the Church of Christ is on trial. Not without some cause have the nations of the East so far misinterpreted it as to call it "militaristic." Let us not argue the point, but whatever our prejudices or predilections, let us vow not to project this misconception of our Lord's teachings into other lands. By dint of prayer, sacrifice, and much effort the combined missionary agencies of the Western World raised forty-four million dollars last year for the purpose of extending the Kingdom of the Prince of Peace. The World War cost nine million dollars an hour. Five hours of that ghastly struggle would have exhausted our combined resources. Such losses may be retrieved in time, and so may even the losses in personnel, but the moral losses, the loss of confidence, of prestige, of power are not so easily regained.

The Church failed to avert the World War. She will do her part to prevent the next war. What more effective means can she employ than "the one outstanding possibility that has never been given a fair and full trial," namely, the processes of Christian education? It was her Master's method, "first the corn, then the blade, then the ear." She has His command, His program and plan. Love is the fulfilling of His law. He set the child in the midst, and declared "of such is the Kingdom of Heaven." Children have no racial bigotries, no national antipathies nor inherited hatreds. Let us not pervert them by false teaching, but let us insist that the Church in its educational activities at home and abroad promote friendship, justice and goodwill among the children of all the world. As missionary agencies this is our unique responsibility. We dare not dodge nor shift it. We are making the minds of the children who throng our schools around the world. We can train this contemporaneous generation to think corporately and cooperatively on this theme.

Let us, as Board officers and members and missionaries forever be done with a patronizing attitude. Let us be done with the glorification of war, or even with condoning it in our day. Let us insist that in our educational activities at home and abroad there be selected or prepared not such ideals as "my country right or wrong" but such as; first: Develop national pride in its praiseworthy acts and attitudes, and patriotism that will glory in service to the race; and second: give accurate and unbiased information regarding facts of history as related to other peoples; third: inculcate ideals of justice and fair dealing, and fourth: recognize the gifts, inheritances and potentialities of other peoples and foster comradeship, confidence, mutual understanding and respect.

Let us seek to understand the deep-seated causes of war; economic, political, psychological, social, and to bring to play upon them the full gospel of Christ whatsoever it may cost us.

Let us determine that our mission schools shall produce thinkers instead of fighters,"

> Not popular passion to arise and crush,
>> But popular conscience which may covenant
>> For what it knows.
>
> In hearts too young for enmity
>> There lies the way to make men free
>> When children's friendships are world-wide
>> New ages will be glorified.
>
> Let child love child and strife will cease,
>> Disarm the hearts, for that is peace.

Let us wage peace under the white flag of the Prince of Peace.

THE WILL FOR PEACE

PROFESSOR WILLIAM I. HULL, PH.D., SWARTHMORE, PENNSYLVANIA

Eight centuries ago, all of Western Christendom was moved to war by the cry, "God wills it." The Pope, the ecumenical councils of the church, the regular and secular clergy, wrought upon the minds of the people and led them forth against the Mohammedans who held the Holy Land. Hermits, saints and sages, abbots, monks and missionaries, appealed by all the arts of rhetoric to all the fears and loves and lusts of men to rescue the Holy Sepulchre from the hands of the infidel. And all sorts and conditions of men, from emperor and king to villain and serf,—men, women and children, old and young—responded en masse to the appeal, and set forth on that series of wild and weird expeditions by land and sea which continued generation after generation for two hundred years. Hundreds of thousands of peasants left their whitening bones along the route of half a thousand miles; tens of thousands of Jews were sacrificed to the crusading zeal; terrible excesses were committed upon fellow-Christians in Hungary, Bulgaria and the Eastern Empire. Jerusalem, captured after one month's siege, was made the scene of a frightful slaughter, the blood of the Moslem slain filling the streets and splashing with the crimson hue the Christian warriors as they rode or strode "with sobs of excessive joy" to the Church of the Holy Sepulchre. In such fashion did the men of that age try to find their way to Christ and to make God's will prevail on earth. Most fortunately for man, then as now, God can and does make good come from evil; but sounding through the ages is forever the eternal doom, "Woe unto him through whom evil comes."

A thousand years before the Crusaders, St. Paul and the first Christian missionaries exemplified another method of interpreting God's will. They went forth into the world of unbelievers as lambs among wolves; they feared not those who could kill the body, but could not kill the soul; they rejected the might and the power of earthly hosts, and relied upon the spirit of the Lord. Roman citizens though some of them were, they turned their backs upon the materialism, the imperial autocracy, and the militarism of the mighty Roman Empire which dominated the civilized world, and they set their minds and hearts to the task of establishing the Kingdom of God within the empire of the Cæsars. On gallows, in prison, and in the jaws of beasts, their lives here on earth were snuffed out; but the Kingdom which they established in the minds and hearts of men engulfed the mighty temporal empire of their time and has outlived it by fifteen hundred years.

What a dramatic contrast does history afford! On the one hand, the short sword and shield of the Roman legion, the spear and armor of the crusading knights; on the other hand, the un-armed spirit of the Christian missionary; the mailed fist, and the pierced hand; the flashing eye of hate, the flaming heart of love. Which of these methods, these interpretations of the will of God, was justified—in itself and by its results? What is the verdict of the last two thousand years of history, during which the crusad-ing method and the missionary method have both been tried over and over again and in every century and every land? From Con-stantine to Wilhelm II, the warrior-heads of every people have dared to interpret the symbol of sacrifice of self and love of others as a sign that in *its* shadow they might conquer their fellowmen: while the Christian Church has surrendered the cross of its leader into their blood-stained hands and urged its children to follow in the paths of war. Meanwhile, also, the spirit of Calvary and of Paul of Tarsus has brooded over the earth, and countless mis-sionaries have found and pursued the ways of peace to the sinful hearts of their fellowmen.

Such, through the centuries, have been the two pathways trodden by the feet of men. Such are the two sign-boards before which humanity constantly finds itself pausing in doubt and dread. The war-method, usually urged for some generations now, only for high and holy purposes, and reluctantly sanctioned by the Church of the Prince of Peace; the peace-method, usually scorned by the principalities and powers, the logic and the worldly wisdom of the wise men of earth. The war-method, with its slaughter, its pestilence, its famine, its heaped-up mountains of human misery, its dragon's teeth sown as seeds of endless future war; the peace-method, with its Christian sanity, its brotherhood, its cooperation and its crops of human welfare.

What of our own age? Which road are *we* choosing? On which of these sign-boards do *we* read the will of God? "God wills it, God wills it," is still the cry. What does He will for *us?* In making His will our will, do *we* take the road to war, or the road to peace? Has peace or war become, even now, despite the frightful lessons of the recent war, a fundamental question of morality and Christianity? Does the Christian world as a whole—

not merely individuals scattered here and there—take it with deep and serious and vital earnestness?

A recent incident, doubtless well known to us all, is perhaps significant of the continuation down to this very day of this age-old problem, and of the diverse way in which it is answered. Twenty-five American missionaries in China, repudiating military force and even pecuniary bribes for the safe-guarding of themselves and their families, are said to have been told by the American legation that no exception would be made in their favor and that the same "usual procedure" would be adopted to protect them as is used for other Americans. These "messengers of the gospel of brotherhood and peace" expressed their belief that "the way to establish righteousness and peace is through bringing the spirit of personal good will to bear on all persons under all circumstances, even through suffering wrong without retaliation." That is to say, the Kingdom of God, with its laws, has come at least for them, and they desire to try out, to the uttermost if need be, the law of non-retaliation, the law of love, of not resisting evil with evil, but of overcoming evil with good.

And what of us who live at home in comparative safety? Are we ourselves in need of such missionary service, or have we too become worthy citizens of that Kingdom of God, obedient and loyal so far as in us lies to the letter and the spirit of its laws, inscribed on Sinai's tablets and inspired by the Sermon on the Mount? Have *we* the will to peace? Have our prayers been answered for *us* that God's kingdom come here and now, that His will be done on earth among men and nations as well as in Heaven among cherubim and angels. Quo vadis? is still the insistent question pressing in upon our twentieth-century Christian consciences. Which way are we going? Which way do we will to go?

There is truth as well as encouragement in the old adage that "wherever there's a will there's always a way." This is true in the peace movement of our time, and it is most encouraging, perhaps essential, to our half-willing spirits and wholly weak flesh. There are ways to peace among nations as among individuals, and these have succeeded whenever and wherever they have been whole-heartedly tried. Good offices, mediation, conciliation, commissions of inquiry, arbitral tribunals, the Hague Court of Arbitration, the Hague Court of Justice, conferences on disarmament, the Secretariat and Assembly of the League of Nations, and scores of commissions for accomplishing the real, constructive work of the world, for promoting science, for alleviating the woes of humanity, and for giving a fair chance to the children of the race: such are some of the ways which the will to peace has found and used and made eminently successful. For more than a century, they have been resorted to with increasing frequency and success.

But the lamentable state of the world today, in spite of God's marvelous gifts and opportunities lavished upon us, His children of this generation, is all too melancholy proof that these peace ways have been followed with halting will and backward looks. The will to peace is still infirm; it is still vitiated by a hankering for the delights of Sodom, the flesh-pots of Egypt; it is still blunted by a fear of, or reliance upon, the chariots of Pharaoh, the mighty men of war. The reverse of the old adage is equally true: Wherever there are ways to succeed there must be a will. And, blessed be the Christian's faith that where there is a single-hearted will to peace, it is purified by Christ's own spirit, rendered invincible by God's own omnipotence, and made gloriously successful by applying it in the ways which God himself has pointed out to achieve and perpetuate peace.

The will to peace, the ways to peace: they are both within our reach. Have we grasped them fully? Let us not be deceived. The God of Peace is a jealous God. We may have no other gods than Him. We must love Him, and Him alone, with all our heart, our soul, our mind. We cannot serve two masters. We cannot build up and rely upon armaments, and at the same time hope or expect that our professions of peace will prevail. We may call upon the name of the Prince of Peace, "Lord, Lord"; but if our hearts are far from Him, we shall have war, despite all the ways to peace. And even though our hearts are with Him, the full and reasonable loyalty includes our minds and wills as well. We cannot justify the preparation, the use, or even the threat of armaments, on the plea that we are seeking to preserve the peace. The quality of peace is not strained; it cannot be enforced. We may make a desert, a charnelhouse, a land of children's hospitals and cemeteries, and call it peace. By any name, military and economic coercion of nations will still be war.

And let us not be misled by the will-o'-the-wisp fancy that if we simply prepare the will and the ways to peace we can forget or ignore the instruments and the ways of war. War is not to be gotten rid of by indirection. A direct, conscious, wholehearted struggle alone can dethrone the hoary god of war. The old Adam must be destroyed before the Christ-man can be born within us. We must cease to do evil before we learn to be good. Spears must be beaten into pruning-hooks, swords into plowshares, before the nations can learn war no more. National armaments must be discarded, our *will to war* must be destroyed, before our *will to peace* can make our ways to peace succeed. International courts and the promising paraphernalia of international government have been in the past and will be through all the future mere gossamer threads, mere spider webs, in binding Mars as long as the nations continue to bring to his altar the resources of their land, the bodies and minds of their sons.

The will to peace, a negative and positive task, two halves of but a single whole; namely, the utter rejection of the ways of war,—disarmament of body and of mind; the utter acceptance of the ways of peace—the Christianization of mind and heart and will. Is it a large task, a great task, a divine task? Is it worthy of the devotion of the Church and the followers of Jesus Christ?

THE CHRISTIAN SPIRIT IN INTERNATIONAL RELATIONS

THE HONORABLE NEWTON W. ROWELL, LL.D., OF TORONTO

I approach the consideration of this subject from a somewhat different standpoint from that of the speakers who have preceded me. It has been my duty to take part in the administration of public affairs, to share with my colleagues in the Government the responsibility of enlisting, training and sending men to the front to take part in war, to visit them in the trenches, to call upon the wounded in the hospitals, and to bow the head beside the graves of the fallen. It has also been my privilege, after the war was over, to meet with representatives of other nations, to discuss and plan for the preservation of peace. I, therefore, approach the consideration of this great question this morning from what one may be permitted to say is the practical standpoint, and to ask the question: "Is it possible that the Christian spirit has any contribution to make toward the solution of our international problems?" Or, is the international sphere an area of human life and activity which is to the Christian church a foreign field and a foreign field with closed doors into which the church cannot usefully enter?

At the time when the spirit of nationality was in its infancy, and when nationalism, as we know it today, was just commencing to exert its powerful influence on the thinking of men, Machiavelli proclaimed his theory of the state, his theory of international relations. He proclaimed the theory of the unlimited sovereignty of the national state, of its duty to exert its power solely in its own interests, unrestrained and irrespective of all moral considerations. It is said of Machiavelli that he was not proclaiming a theory of his own invention, but was simply interpreting the hard facts of his own time.

A leading statesman of our own day in Europe has openly and publicly proclaimed his adherence to the Machiavellian ideals of statesmanship; and he is endeavoring to put them into actual prac-

tice, both in domestic and in international affairs. Those who
share his views would say that he, too, is but recognizing the hard
facts of this present time, and that, however far statesmen of
other countries may have departed in the domestic government of
their own states from Machiavellian ideas, they still practice those
ideals in international relations, and there may be some justification
for that view. Machiavelli, while he believed that some form of
religion was a good thing for the masses of the people, because it
made them more obedient to governments, openly proclaimed himself a pagan; and undoubtedly he drew inspiration for his conceptions of the state, its place and its functions, from the pagan
ideals of ancient Rome. Machiavelli's conception as applied to
international relations is essentially pagan in its spirit and outlook,
and yet, that essentially pagan conception dominated the spirit of
international relations for between three and four hundred years.

Has the Christian Church any theory of international relations? Is there any Christian conception and ideal of international relations to set over against the Machiavellian and pagan
conception? If it has not, if it has no substitute to provide, then
let it confess its impotence in the face of some of the gravest
problems of our time. But, if the Christian Church has some
theory of international relations, which it can set opposite the
Machiavellian theory, then is it not incumbent upon all Christian
people to seek to put that Christian conception into actual practice?
I believe there is a Christian theory of international relations.
May I venture to suggest to you, as Mrs. Nicholson brought out
so admirably in her address, that the thinking of our peoples will
determine their attitude on these great questions, so that it is of
fundamental importance that we should have a clear conception
of what such a Christian theory involves and solid ground upon
which to stand in considering these problems. What lies at the
very basis of a Christian conception of international relations?
The President of this Republic, speaking at the Commercial Club
of Chicago on December 4th, 1924, is reported to have said:

"I am profoundly impressed with the fact that the structure of modern society
is essentially a unity, destined to stand or fall as such. At the last, those of us who
are partners in the supreme service of building up and bettering our civilization must
go up or down, must succeed or fail, together in our one common enterprise."

That is a statesman's form of stating the essential unity of
our common humanity. The Bishop of St. Albans this morning
gave us the Christian leader's form of statement of that same
great truth, that "God hath made of one blood, all nations." We
start as the very basis of any Christian conception of international
relations with this fundamental proposition, the essential unity
of our common humanity, under the Lordship of Jesus Christ.

And then, what is the next essential element? It grows out
of the first, a logical development from it. It is not the Machiavel-

lian theory that morals have no relation to the state of international affairs, but the Christian theory that we must recognize the supremacy of public right and of moral law in international affairs just as truly as in domestic affairs. We can make no real progress in dealing with the problems of our time unless nations recognize the vital place of the spiritual and moral considerations and of moral forces in the relations of nation to nation. And so we must lay down the supremacy of public right as the second proposition. In the time at my disposal this morning I can offer little more than an outline; you must fill it in yourselves.

Then the next is the recognition that all the nations are members of one great family which we call the Family of Nations. The Bishop of St. Albans has so clearly expressed the thought I intended to endeavor to convey on this point that I shall simply adopt his argument and proceed.

The members of the family of nations must have relations with one another; they are in continuous contact. How are those relations to be governed? What are the principles that should underlie the relation of one nation to the other? The attitude of men's minds to these questions does not depend upon national boundaries; it oversteps all boundaries. You hear in your country, and we hear in ours, that the state is sovereign. We recognize no power or authority above or beyond the state. The state must act in the interest of the people it represents, and in their interests alone. There are those who would add in private, if not in public, "We stand for our country, right or wrong." That is only another way of stating the Machiavellian conception which has left us where we are today.

We acknowledge allegiance to our city, and our duty and responsibility as citizens. We acknowledge allegiance to our state or province, and our duty and responsibility as citizens in the state. We acknowledge our allegiance to our national government, and our duty and responsibility as citizens to that government. We do not find that the one allegiance conflicts with the other. The man who is the best citizen in the community, in the city, is the best citizen of the state and in the nation. We are not required to do away with these allegiances, but, recognizing their full force and power, we need to add to them one other, our allegiance to the cause of humanity under the leadership of our Lord and Saviour, Jesus Christ.

And that carries with it obligations just as binding, just as inescapable for every honest Christian man and woman as the obligation to the city or the state or the national government. We think of our city as a unity, we think of our state as a unity, we think of our nation as a unity. We must broaden our horizon and take in the sweep of all the nations; we must think of our humanity as one great unity, the children of a common Father, bound together by the ties of human brotherhood. This was that great conception which St. Augustine set forth in "The City of God," that great conception of worldwide unity which dominated the thought of Europe for one thousand years. In modern times the spirit of nationalism has led us away from that great Christian ideal. The problem we face today is how to reconcile and harmonize the two—the idea of nationalism with that of worldwide unity—to recognize the facts and forces of today, and yet inspire all men with the Christian spirit and the recognition of the unity of our race. How then are the relations of the members of the family of nations to be governed? I have already pointed out that there must be the recognition of public right, the moral factor in the relation of nation to nation. There must be an earnest and honest effort to understand and appreciate the point of view of other nations. One of the most difficult things for any people is the recognition and the sympathetic appreciation of the point of view of other races and other peoples. We cannot understand each other and work together as different races and different nations, unless we honestly seek to understand and appreciate the point of view of other peoples. That is one of the very first steps on the road to good international relations.

We must endeavor to secure a more Christian method than war for settling the differences which arise between states. One recognizes the great importance of disarmament, and may I not pause to pay a tribute to that distinguished man who is still Secretary of State of the United States, Mr. Hughes, who has conferred such benefits upon humanity by the great service he rendered in connection with the Conference on the Limitation of Armaments in Washington?

But, important and far-reaching as are plans for disarmament, they do not touch, I venture to think, the fundamental issue. Let me illustrate—during the last great war, in all the bombardments of the city of London from the air some twelve and one-half tons of explosives were dropped upon that city. Such has been the improvement in the art of aerial navigation and in the destructive power of explosives that aeroplane bombing machines exist in Europe today which could drop sixty tons of explosives, five times the total amount dropped during the whole war upon the city of London or any other city, in one day! They could keep that up perhaps for a few days, and for a longer period could drop from thirty to sixty tons a day. We may limit armaments today, but such is the progress of modern science and the skill of man, that though the nations might have limited armaments to start the war, before many months had passed they would be thoroughly equipped to carry on the war in the most destructive way. We have got to go deeper than any question of disarmament if we are to find the solution to this problem.

We must try to find a substitute for war as a means of settling disputes between nations. We have an illustration in the life of the United States and Canada. There was a time in the early history of our race, when men settled their disputes by private war, the blood feud and revenge. You may have some illustrations of this in your own country at the present time, if one may judge from the press reports. But it was recognized that if these conditions continued, human progress was almost impossible; and men were compelled to submit their disputes to courts of law. By slow degrees we have built up courts of law and the rule of law and justice, so today disputes are settled by peaceable and lawful means. The progress made in the establishment of courts of justice and of the rule of law has registered the progress and advancement of our Anglo-Saxon civilization. I ask you, has not war become so destructive today, so wide-reaching in its effect and consequences upon innocent people, as well as participators in the struggle, that humanity has the right to say to any nation and every nation: "If you cannot settle your disputes by negotiation with another nation you must choose some method of settlement less destructive than war."

I believe humanity has the right to say that; and just as in the old days we substituted courts of justice and the rule of law for the blood feud and private vengeance, the time has come when in this family of nations, we should substitute courts of justice and processes of conciliation for the settlement of disputes between the members of the family of nations. May I pay a tribute to the part the United States has taken in promoting the establishment of a Permanent Court of International Justice which is now functioning at The Hague, and upon which sits one of the distinguished jurists of the United States, Mr. John Bassett Moore?

We need more than a permanent court of international justice; we need some common order through which the nations can meet together for conference and cooperation. You cannot have cooperation—effective and continuous cooperation—between the members of the family of nations widely separated as they are, unless you have some organ through which that cooperation can be expressed. I am not now concerned with any particular form of organization. I am only pleading that some form is necessary if our Christian conception is not to evaporate into thin air, but is to assume concrete form and actually influence the life and conduct of nations in international affairs.

Now I come to the last question. Is such a plan practicable? Is it possible that international affairs can be regulated by the application of a Christian theory? I believe they can. I venture to submit to you that the culmination of the materialistic and pagan Machiavellian theory of international relations was found in the last great war; and the last great war, I hope, was the final condemnation of any such conception of international relations. Against that conception and what resulted from it, humanity revolted in the latter years of war, and the heart of humanity cried out for some new and some better order. That voice of humanity was expressed with incomparable clearness and force by the President of this Republic at that time.

The War came to an end on the basis of an agreement negotiated by the Government of the United States, which set forth fourteen points which were to be embodied in the Treaty of ,Peace. Let no one misunderstand. I was a member of a government at the time to which was submitted the terms of peace. As a member of the government, I had to give my assent or dissent. The war came to an end on the basis of an agreement proposed by the Government of the United States, accepted by the enemy and allied forces. It may have been vague, it was vague in certain of those fourteen points. There may have been difficulty; there was difficulty in giving those concrete expression in a Treaty of Peace, but unfortunately, when the war was over, there was a slump in the high idealism that marked many of the aspects in its concluding stages, and the revolt of humanity against its barbarity and atrocity.

We had a treaty of peace which did not fully carry out those fourteen points. It was not because of the attempt to carry them out that we have suffered since; we have suffered, and the world has suffered since because the Treaty of Peace did not adequately express and carry out those fourteen points. But in one respect at least the Treaty did carry them out and that was the stipulation that provision should be made for some form of international organization through which the nations might cooperate for the preservation of peace. I want to pay my tribute to this nation, for unless you had stipulated in the very agreement upon which the war came to an end that such an organization should be established, I doubt if it would have found its place in the Treaty.

What the attitude of any nation should be toward the League of Nations is a matter for that nation alone to determine unaided and uninfluenced by advice from others. But speaking as a Canadian, and the Canadian delegates to this Conference will confirm what I say, we thought when the Covenant of the League was submitted to us, that although we did not like all its provisions, it was a great advance on anything heretofore attempted, and as we had joined in agreeing upon the terms of peace we felt it our duty to join and cooperate in the work of the League of Nations. For that course we have no apologies and no regrets.

But whether one likes that form of organization or not, the problem which faces all the peoples of all the nations is this: How can the members of that one family so order and arrange their affairs and their relations the one with the other that peace and justice may be preserved in the world? And if there be one function of the Christian Church as important—I won't say more important—as any other, surely it must be to endeavor to establish and maintain peace between the nations, to promote harmony and cooperation between the races of mankind, harmony and cooperation in the advancement of civilization, in the promotion of human welfare, and to aid in ushering in the triumph of the Prince of Peace—for He must reign until He hath put all enemies under His feet.

THE PERIOD OF INTERCESSION

JOHN WILSON WOOD, D.C.L., NEW YORK

It has been made abundantly clear in all that has been said this morning that peace must rest upon the practice of Christian conviction. Therefore let us, as we stand, repeat together that common symbol of our belief, recorded in the Apostles' Creed:

I believe in God the Father Almighty, maker of heaven and earth:

And in Jesus Christ, his only Son our Lord; who was conceived by the Holy Ghost, born of the Virgin Mary; suffered under Pontius Pilate, was crucified, dead and buried; he descended into hell. The third day he rose again from the dead; he ascended into heaven, and sitteth on the right hand of God the Father Almighty; from thence he shall come to judge the quick and the dead.

I believe in the Holy Ghost; the holy catholic Church; the communion of saints; the forgiveness of sins; the resurrection of the body; and the life everlasting. Amen.

Let us listen to the voice of God speaking to us through his servants of old:

How beautiful upon the mountains are the feet of him that bringeth good tidings, that publisheth peace, that bringeth good tidings of good, that publisheth salvation, that saith unto Zion, Thy God reigneth.

He shall feed his flock like a shepherd: he shall gather the lambs with his arm and carry them in his bosom, and shall gently lead those that are with young . . .

Other sheep I have, which are not of this fold: them also I must bring, and they shall hear my voice; and there shall be one fold and one shepherd.

The people that walked in darkness have seen a great light: they that dwell in the land of the shadow of death, upon them hath the light shined.

For unto us a child is born, unto us a son is given; and the government shall be upon His shoulder, and His name shall be called Wonderful, Counsellor, The mighty God, The everlasting Father, The Prince of Peace.

Of the increase of his government and peace there shall be no end, upon the throne of David, and upon his kingdom, to order it, and to establish it with judgment and with justice from henceforth even for ever. The zeal of the Lord of hosts will perform this.

The wolf also shall dwell with the lamb, and the leopard shall lie down with the kid; and the calf and the young lion and the fatling together; and a little child shall lead them.

But in the last days it shall come to pass, that the mountain of the house of the Lord shall be established in the top of the mountains, and it shall be exalted above the hills; and the people shall flow unto it.

And many nations shall come and say, Come, and let us go up to the mountain of the Lord, and to the house of the God of Jacob.

And he shall judge among many people, and rebuke strong nations afar off; and they shall beat their swords into plowshares, and their spears into pruninghooks; nation shall not lift up a sword against nation, neither shall they learn war any more.

Glory to God in the Highest and on earth peace, goodwill toward men.

Blessed are the peacemakers: for they shall be called the children of God.

Ye know that the princes of the Gentiles exercise dominion over them, and they that are great exercise authority upon them.

But it shall not be so among you: but whosoever will be great among you, let him be your minister.

He hath made of one blood all nations of men for to dwell on the face of the earth . . . that they should seek the Lord if haply they might feel after him and find him. . . .

And I saw a new heaven and a new earth: for the first heaven and the first earth were passed away . . . I saw the Holy City, New Jerusalem, coming down from God out of heaven, prepared as a bride adorned for her husband.

And the nations of them which are saved shall walk in the light of it: and the kings of the earth do bring their glory and honor into it.

Then said Jesus . . . Put up again thy sword into his place: for all they that take the sword shall perish with the sword.

Ye have heard that it hath been said, Thou shalt love thy neighbor, and hate thine enemy.

But I say unto you, love your enemies, bless them that curse you, do good to them that hate you, and pray for them which despitefully use you and persecute you;

That ye may be the children of your Father which is in heaven.

Be ye therefore perfect even as your Father which is in heaven is perfect.

And Jesus came and spake unto them, saying, All power is given unto me in heaven and in earth.

Go ye therefore, and teach all nations, baptizing them in the name of the Father, and of the Son and of the Holy Ghost:

Teaching them to observe all things whatsoever I have commanded you: and, lo, I am with you alway, even unto the end of the world. Amen.

Let us pray. Let us pray that God will pour His love into our hearts, that we may love others as ourselves.

O God, our Father, we dedicate ourselves anew to Thee and to Thy service. Put into the heart of each one of us such a love for Thee that we may truly love our neighbor as ourselves,—a love that leaps the boundaries of race or color, or creed or kind.

Fill our lives with the single motive of service, and of love, and use us for Thine own purposes just as Thou wilt, and when, and where.

Let us pray for that higher patriotism of which the Bishop of St. Albans spoke this morning.

O God, whose Kingdom is an everlasting Kingdom, and whose dominion endureth from generation to generation, abase our pride and shatter our complacency. Open our eyes to see the vanity of this world's riches and renown. Make us to understand that there is no wealth but life, that living men are Thy glory, and that our life is the vision of Thee.

Keep us from being swayed by wealth and influence, or beguiled by pleas of custom and expediency or distracted by the glamour of prosperity and power. Keep us securely in Thy way of righteousness and truth.

Let us pray for justice in all international relations.

Grant, O Lord, that we may approach every question of foreign policy from the point of sight of our creed, that so our thoughts may be purified and strengthened; that we may check in ourselves and in others every temper which makes for war, all ungenerous judgments, all presumptuous claims, all promptings of self-assertion, the noxious growths of arrogance and passion, that we may endeavor to understand the needs, the feelings, the aspirations of other peoples, that we may do gladly and patiently what lies in us to remove suspicion and misunderstanding, that we may honor all men through Jesus Christ.

Let us pray for humility and understanding and pure motives.

Overrule, we pray Thee, O God, passion and designs of men. Let Thy strong hand control the nations and bring forth out of the present discord a harmony more perfect than we can conceive, a new humility, a new understanding, a new purity, and sincerity of love, a new sense of reality, a new hunger and thirst for Thy love to rule the earth.

Let us pray for the reconstruction and the restoration of our sorely wounded world.

O Thou, in whose hands are the hearts of Thy creatures, shed abroad Thy peace upon the world. By the light of Thy Holy Spirit quench the pride, the anger, and greed which cause man to strive against man and people against people. Lead all nations in the way of mutual help and good will and hasten the time when the earth shall confess Thee indeed for its Saviour and its King.

Let us pray for confidence in God's ever-present and over-ruling providence.

O Lord God, in whom we live and move and have our being, open our eyes that we may behold Thy Fatherly presence ever about us. Draw our hearts to Thee with the power of Thy love. Teach us to be anxious for nothing, and when we have done what Thou hast given us to do, help us, O God our Saviour, to leave the issue to Thy wisdom. Take from us all doubt and distrust. Lift our thoughts to Thee and make us to know that all things are possible to us through Thy Son, our Redeemer.

Bless us, O God, with the vision of Thy beauty that in the strength of it we may work without haste, and without rest for the coming of Thy Kingdom of righteousness and peace.

And now let us lift our eyes to the Cross of Christ.

Blessed Saviour, who at this hour didst hang upon the Cross, stretching forth Thy loving arms, grant that all mankind may look unto Thee and be saved through Thy mercies and merits, who livest and reigneth with the Father and the Holy Ghost, ever One God.

THE CONVENTION SERMON

THE UNSEARCHABLE RICHES OF CHRIST

THE REVEREND CANON H. J. CODY, D.D., LL.D., TORONTO

"Unto me who am less than the least of all saints, is this grace given, that I should preach unto the Gentiles the unsearchable riches of Christ" (Eph. 3:8).

During the sessions of this Convention we have been listening to tales of missionary accomplishment. Our hearts have burned within us, as we have heard what great things God hath done among the nations. We have realized afresh the sense of the urgency of the need. We have heard the call for Christian statesmanship and service coming from various lands in the world. The opportunity is as great and as challenging as ever. At no distant date issues of vast moment to the whole human race, such as those which concern the clash of color, must inevitably be decided. And unless these issues are decided in the light of Christ's own truth and according to Christ's own principles, the results will be regrettable if not disastrous.

This gathering has been informed and thrilled and challenged by the message from the high places in the field. And yet outside this group of interested folk there is a whole world of indifference to these conditions and to the call that comes from the missionary leaders. Why this indifference among the "men in the street" and the average Christian? May I suggest some reasons as they have arisen in my own experience?

First, the ordinary Christian is inclined to distrust assured diagnoses of vast conditions such as those that obtain in India and China and Japan. He is not profoundly impressed, when we assert that something will follow inevitably, if something else is not immediately done. He has a latent consciousness that ultimately all things are in the hands of God, and that it is a mistake to suppose that vast world movements so absolutely depend upon us. Let us indeed always remember that while God works normally in us and through us, he may also by His Spirit, work beyond us and above us.

Again there is some reaction against the almost hyperorganization of plans to do the spiritual task of evangelizing a world and against the military metaphors that we use. There is a recollection of Christ's words about the Kingdom of God coming secretly and working among men as leaven.

There is further a common sense of proportion in the human mind. That sense of proportion rebels when even a good cause seems at times to be presented out of focus. There are many ordinary church members whose hands and whose minds are fully occupied with the legitimate duties and cares of life. Their families and their business, their debts and their taxes, their political problems and their religious duties to their immediate society seem to them real and urgent. They may grow impatient when we, pleading the missionary cause, seem to disparage or minimize these regular and rightful responsibilities. There is perhaps in these mental attitudes something that may give us missionary enthusiasts cause for thought. Let us prune our words, and keep our appeal always within the bounds of reality.

And yet does it not remain utterly unassailable that expansion is of the very essence of the Christian Church; that the Church is really a mission, a sending by Christ; that Christianity is a missionary religion or it is not a worthy religion at all? This expansive enterprise is a fundamental, vital, urgent element in the history of world civilization today. Foreign missions are not merely a realm of sentiment; they have passed out into the region of world statesmanship. It is of the very essence of the church's world-task to send into all parts of the world in need men and women who are spiritually wise enough and spiritually humble enough to help in the building of the world of the future. Christians are in the world to transform it in accordance with the purpose of Christ. Furthermore, is it not unassailably true that always the primary call to the individual Christian is the call to more intimate personal contact with Christ? We were, indeed, immediately after the cataclysm of the world war, prepared to reconstruct politics, to reconstruct educational systems, to reconstruct industry, to reconstruct social life. But the one realm in which, speaking generally, we were not ready and willing to pursue the policy of reconstruction was in personal life. The most vital reconstruction is personal reconstruction through Christ.

It has been aptly said that some people do not believe in missions, because they have little right to believe in missions; they do not believe enough in Christ. Perhaps my task this morning should be this, to emphasize that what we most of all need in our churches at present is not only interest in missions as a movement, but also interest in Christ and His evangel. Unless there is deeper, wider and fresher interest in the everlasting gospel, faith in Christ as our Savior and our Lord, we shall in vain await a response to missionary appeals. But in the gospel itself there is something that forthwith creates missionary interest, because the gospel has no fitting correlative except the whole world.

What, therefore, we need (may I repeat it), is not so much new interest in the non-Christian world as new interest in the gospel of Christ; not so much men and women who wish to preach the gospel in the heathen sphere, as men and women who cannot but preach and teach and live Christ wherever they are. Lives that are redeemed by the precious blood of Christ and indwelt by His glorious spirit will solve our problems at home and broad. Nothing else can really touch them.

Our subject, therefore, this morning, is the fundamental Christian motive and message. A great Scottish teacher, Professor A. B. Bruce, once said to a group of his students in class, as they were discussing some approaching convention, "Gentlemen, go to this conference or that convention if you will; but do not forget to go to Bethlehem,"—*i. e.*, remember Christ incarnate, dying, rising, living.

In this circular letter which we call the "Epistle to the Ephesians," St. Paul's great themes may be broadly summed up as follows: (1) Humanity in its whole range is the subject of the redemption by a universal Saviour. The only barriers henceforth that may exist are moral barriers. (2) Christ is the head of the church. (3) All Christians are one in Christ, whether they recognize that unity or not. (4) There are unexplored possibilities of spiritual fellowship with Jesus, our living Saviour. St. Paul briefly presents his own conception of himself as an ambassador, and of the message he was to carry, in these great words of our text; "Unto me, who am less than the least of all saints, was this grace given, that I should preach unto the nations the unsearchable riches"—the unexplorable wealth—"of Christ."

1. First, then, you have the *man* who speaks, "Unto me, less than the least of all the saints." St. Paul's personal insignificance and unworthiness are compared with the vastness of the field and the glory of the message. St. Paul is constantly bowed or exalted, I know not which, with amazement, that he should be chosen to possess this wealth, and then proclaim it to others. How profound is the humility of the greatest Christian since the days of Christ! As he realizes that he is but an instrument in the hands of his Master, he coins a word to describe himself "less than the least"; it is the comparative of a superlative; it is as though he said, "more least." "Unto me, who am less than the least of all saints," that sentiment is no wild flight of rhetoric, but the strong and true result of a profound view of the mercy and the glory of Christ.

As St. Paul grew in holiness, he grew in humility. He called himself when he wrote to the Corinthians, "the least of the apostles, that am not meet to be called an apostle, because I persecuted the church of Christ." How often, I ask you to remember, as St. Paul looked back in the days when he was scorning the riches of his Master's kingdom, and was persecuting his Master's church, does he suffer the most poignant regret. He thinks of those days that were lost, those days when he lived a rebel to Jesus. Writing to the Romans, he sends his greeting to those *"who were in Christ before me"*— in Christ, serving, teaching, while he was the implacable foe of Christ.

As he grew in grace he called himself in these words to the Ephesians, "less than the least of all saints." Then, drawing toward the end of his mighty missionary march, he described himself in his letter to Timothy, as "the chief of sinners." The man or the woman who feels unworthy or not self-sufficient will always be kept receptive towards the grace of God. "Who are we that we should have been chosen to be ambassadors for Christ, messengers of His eternal grace?"

I remember reading that the famous preacher at the City Temple in London, Joseph Parker, was once greeted by an inquiry after the sermon, "Why did Jesus choose Judas to be a disciple?" His answer was, "It is a mystery, but I know of a greater mystery still. I do not know why Jesus chose me."

What was the real place of St. Paul? That old Puritan father, greatest of Cromwell's preachers, Thomas Goodwin, wrote these words; "In his own opinion St. Paul was the least of all saints, but in my opinion he is the highest saint in heaven and sits nearest the glorified God-Man Himself." What a man he was! He was the great theologian of the Christian Church who set himself to expound the meaning of the person of Christ and of the work of Christ on the Cross and of the continued work of the risen Christ and of the mystery of the body of Christ, His church. What a great Christian he was! He is the living example to all time of what the grace of God can do with a mighty intellect and a great heart. What a many-sided man he was! He did not say, "This one thing I do." That is only a rough paraphrase. He did many things and he did them supremely well; but one mark of consecration was upon them all.

To us he appears as the great master-builder of the Christian Church, the missionary statesman of all the ages. He sought to achieve in the spiritual sphere what the Roman Empire had achieved in the sphere of government. Was not the church (this was the thought that came into the mind of St. Paul), a vaster empire even than Rome? The church, the Kingdom of Christ, has a citizenship open to all, not merely to a privileged minority. Its King is Christ, and He wields and will wield a wider sovereignty than any Cæsar. Its unity was closer than that in the Roman Empire, because it was based on love and brotherhood.

St. Paul had one supreme aim—to lay the firm foundations of this heavenly Kingdom, to plant it in the Roman empire, and to take the gospel to the city of the seven hills itself and claim all for his Master, Christ. In that aim how marvelously he succeeded—for breadth of vision, for Christian statesmanship, for all the practical gifts that make an ideal missionary he stands without a rival.

Still God chooses prepared men for the place for which He needs them. Still He bids us make glorious the place of our service wherever it is. Our faithfulness alone will define its ultimate importance. St. Paul was a titanic man; but let us never forget that God can choose men and women of very ordinary ability and lift them up to such a level of divine vitality that they can do spiritually that which will resound through the high heavens. Even yet the vision of Jesus Christ and the exhibition of the world's needs which have been presented to us in this convention may awaken a wonderful response from generous youth, so that young men and maidens will fling away moderation and worldly discretion and material ambitions and give themselves without reserve to the cause of God and those for whom in Christ He died. Reconstructed and consecrated personality like that of St. Paul and of the humblest, are still the greatest forces in the world.

II. Secondly, after the man, you have *the mission.* "This grace was given to preach," to tell the glad tidings. With profound humility St. Paul mingled an absolute confidence. However shrinking and timid he might be about himself, when he thought that God had chosen him and endowed him with His grace, he was radiantly and triumphantly confident. You may recall Cromwell's pungent remark upon George Fox in his own generation, "He has an enormous sacred self-confidence." St. Paul had that in effect; but St. Paul called it, in essence, an enormous "God-confidence." "This grace was given me." The condescending love of God bestowed upon me this commission and this inspiration, that I should preach Christ. Men and women, let us at this time remember afresh how great, how glorious is the privilege of being an ambassador for Christ. It is a grace, it is a gift, it is something unspeakably good and gracious, something beyond all the dreams or deserts of a man, that he should be commissioned, that he should be endowed with power, to preach the unsearchable riches of Christ. Let us, wherever we are, awake to a renewed sense of the apostolic estimation of the function of the messenger. It is a grace, it is a marvelous privilege. That which is a gift immediately to the missionary or the messenger is a gift to the whole church, because through the missionary the whole church may, in some measure, express her own heart and her own sense of ambassadorship.

Let us emphasize this consciousness of the grandeur of the missionary function. We who come from churches in the home land, have been in company with God's great ones from the high places of the field; and we are dignified by the association. The ambassador is one who is in perfect understanding with the power that sends him forth, one whose supreme quality is that he should be faithful to the mission entrusted to him. He is called upon, not to invent his message, but to deliver it and to say that this is the message. What gives the message its unspeakable value? It is that it is the unsearchable riches of Christ.

St. Paul felt himself, as every one of us may feel himself, to be the representative of Christ. The heart of Christ was beating in his own bosom towards his converts. The mind of Christ was thinking on the high themes of salvation and world redemption through his brain. He was continuing the work of Christ, filling up whatever was lacking, even in the sufferings of Christ. The wounds of Christ were reproduced in the very scars upon his body. Thus was deepest humility blended with boldest expression, for to him to live was Christ—and so it was to preach, or to suffer, or to write, or to comfort a friend in trouble, or to organize a church, or to collect gifts for the poor or to help save the crew of a wrecked ship.

To die—to die was gain because dying was not death; that also was Christ. From the hour on the Damascus road when Paul saw that the crucified Jesus whom he had persecuted was not a heretic Jew, but the true living Christ of God, his many-sided life was organized around a single purpose—to make this Christ known by every means in every relation to every man on the face of the earth. Jesus truly made Paul—made his thought and work and letters and gospel—verily he still can make us. The urgency of St. Paul's message was like a fire; it burned in his bones. This urge has been marvelously expressed by Mr. F. W. H. Myers, in his great poem: "St. Paul."

> "Then with a rush, the intolerable craving
> Shivers throughout me like a trumpet-call.
> Oh to save these! to perish for their saving,
> Die for their life, be offered for them all."

Without this grace there is no herald and no evangel. What the world needs still is individuals possessed by spiritual purpose, receptive of the grace to love Christ, to live Christ, to give Christ.

III. Thirdly, we have growing out of the grace, the *motive*. Upon that I need speak but briefly, because you have heard from this place the masterly presentation of the "why" of missions from the lips of Dr. Brown. We may analyze the missionary motive and find in it the stewardship of grace and truth, human compassion, and loyalty to divine commands. I wish, however, to take two great phrases of St. Paul, and bind them together, as constituting for all ages the inspired missionary motive.

The first is "The love of Christ constraineth us." (2 Cor. 5:14.) The words mean not our love to Him, but His love to us. That was always the motive of St. Paul's preaching—"the love of Christ to me." That is a safer basis than any merely personal emotion. This constraining power of Christian ministration is more effective and stable, when it is based on the love of Christ to us, than it would be if it were based upon our variable affections. The love that is in Christ Himself constraineth me. The love that constrains is the love that went to all lengths, the love that died; and that love always craves in turn to be loved and evokes a responsive love.

The other great motive is found in St. Paul's phrase, "I am a debtor, both to the Greek and to the barbarian, to the wise and to the unwise." (Rom. 1:14.) Suffer a word of exposition here. The secret of St. Paul's missionary enthusiasm gives us a revealing glimpse into the very heart of the man. In form this is a paradox. St. Paul represents himself as lying under some deep, personal obligation to the whole world, to all the nations, Jew and Greek alike, and to every grade of culture, wise and unwise. What had they done for him that he should spend his life in the effort to discharge this overmastering debt? The debt explains his tireless energy, his unbounded devotion, his unquenchable ardor that urged him from city to city, from land to land, from continent to continent, preaching to all the unsearchable riches. These words in principle reveal the key to the life of St. Paul, the missionary. Here is the one master motive of his missionary efforts and of all missionary effort in every age.

St. Paul lived always under the sense of undeserved goodness received from God; salvation was a gift; nothing in him deserved it; his need evoked it. How could he ever show his gratitude to God for his emancipation and for his illumination? Would he try by personal penance, would he endeavor by untold material offerings, would he seek to pay the debt by glorious and gorgeous ceremonial? No. The only way in which he could pay this debt in the realm of the spiritual was to pass on to others the benefits of the spiritual grace he had himself received from Christ. The gift thus became a debt, a debt of service and a debt of helpfulness. Henceforth St. Paul gave his life to spread the gospel among Greeks and barbarians, wise and unwise, believing that only so could he prove his gratitude to God and pay back something of the debt to Christ for His unspeakable gift. That is still the abiding missionary motive. You know how the spiritual law works. In the realm of the material you can pay a debt directly to the person to whom you owe it; the law of the land compels you to do so. But in the realm of the intellectual and spiritual you seldom can pay back your debt to the person to whom you owe it. How shall we ever pay back our debt to the prophets and the psalmists and the poets and the martyrs and the human servants of the past? They are dead; they have gone to the higher service. How can you pay your debt to them? Only by passing on to the present and to the future the inspiration, the illumination they have given you.

How can you pay your debt to your own father and mother? Perhaps they have gone beyond before you have realized your unspeakable gift from them. You can pay your debt only by passing on to your children and your children's children the inspiration and the godliness and the illumination you have gained from your parents. How shall you pay your debt to Christ? By passing on the gift to others.

St. Paul thus felt himself a debtor to the nations, because of what he owed to Christ. But as he witnessed the transforming power of the Gospel when accepted by the nations, his own faith in that gospel was strengthened. He felt indebted to them because of their witness to the power of Christ. The apologetic value of Christian missions adds to our obligation to evangelize.

IV. Fourthly, as to the *multitude*—the nations—I need not now speak. The field has been described again and again. The world is one; the world is a neighborhood. We must think in continents.

V. Fifthly, so I close with the mighty *message,* the substance of the apostolic preaching, "the unsearchable wealth of Christ."

The word "unsearchable" is suggestive and vivid. It is a picture in a word; it means "that which cannot be traced out by foot prints." It is as though you were in the northern regions of our broad Dominion of Canada, where under the pre-Cambrian shield is hidden away untold mineral wealth. You cannot fully explore it. You go on, lode beyond lode, mine beyond mine, and never can you exhaust that wealth. Or it may suggest to you a mighty continent like America. Columbus discovered it, but we are still exploring its almost limitless natural resources. So the unexplorable wealth of Christ is beyond all limit. At its end we never arrive. How better can I express it than the great apostle himself has expressed it in that one phrase, "The love of Christ which passeth knowledge?"

How *broad* is it? As broad as humanity. How *long* is it? As long as the age-long purpose of God, as long as to outreach all human sin, as long as to go the uttermost lengths of sacrifice upon the cross. How *deep* is it? Far down under human sin and sorrow and need. How *high* is it? It can lift us up to the throne where in heavenly places we may dwell with Christ. The facts of redemption are on a scale so vast that they can never be confined to one locality or to one race. If true at all, they are true for all.

But one missionary application, specifically, I would like to make. We shall never begin to interpret or understand the unsearchable riches of Christ, until men and women of every race, of every color, from every land, shall have made their own contribution to that interpretation and shall have found in the unexplorable wealth that section of it, shall I say, that especially expresses their genius. In Christ the Greek found truth and beauty. In Christ the Hebrew found holiness and tender mercies. In Christ the Roman found the embodiment of righteousness and a law that was loved and that created a flexible organization. The Teuton found the fresh consecration of individuality.

Bishop Westcott, one of the greatest interpreters of St. John's writings, said that we shall never have the ultimate interpretation of the writings of St. John until some Indian with all the Indian's and the Oriental's mysticism shall have heard the message, assimilated and reproduced it. Will not the Chinese and the Japanese and those from Africa and the islands of the sea find in the unsearchable riches of Christ something that evokes the answering thrill, something that will express the highest genius of their race?

Men and brethren, surely if this wealth is so unexplorable, the highest and most ennobling task of any human being must be to share it with men and women the whole world over. Cromwell said, on the day before the battle of Dunbar, "We are upon an engagement very difficult." So we are in this spiritual enterprise, but we go not on our own charges. The treasury of the unsearchable riches of Christ is ours; the abiding presence of the glorified Christ is ever with us; and faintly steal from the distance the glorious notes of triumphant song.

Mr. Gandhi was once returning from one of his earlier trips in the interests of India in other parts of the wrold. When he came back to Calcutta a vast meeting of fifteen thousand Bengali had been convened to hear his message. The headmaster of Eton College in England tells this story as he heard it from one of his friends, who was the only white man present at the meeting. The orators who had been called on spoke for hours in praise of Gandhi and of their own local heroes. At last Mr. Gandhi arose and made a speech of one sentence. This is it: "The man to whom I owe most, the man to whom India owes most, is a man who never set his foot in India, and that was Christ." That was his speech. To proclaim that Christ is our task. God grant that this convention may mean the beginning, as my fellow citizen of the British Commonwealth, Prof. Cornelius expressed it, of a new movement to Christ in America.

INTERCESSION: SPIRITUAL QUALIFICATIONS FOR MISSIONARY SERVICE AT HOME AND ABROAD

MR. ROBERT P. WILDER, NEW YORK

To men who had been three years in intimate fellowship with Jesus Christ, of whom he said, "Already ye are clean, because of the word which I have spoken unto you," who had seen His miracles, who had themselves wrought miracles, who had been taught by the Master to pray, who had been sent out by the Master to preach, He said, "Tarry ye in the city, until ye be clothed with power from on high." "Ye shall receive power, when the Holy Ghost is come upon you, and ye shall be my witnesses both in Jerusalem, and in all Judea and in Samaria, and unto the uttermost part of the earth."

First, the world within their hearts was to be filled by the power of His Spirit and then the outer world was to hear of His unsearchable riches. First the intensive, then the extensive; for, "It is expedient for you," the Master said, "that I go away: for if I go not away, the Paraclete will not come unto you; but if I go, I will send Him unto you. And He, when He is come, will convict the world in respect of sin, and of righteousness, and of judgment. . . . "He shall guide you into all the truth . . . He shall glorify me: for He shall take of mine, and shall declare it unto you."

In the words of Pastor Tophel, "The work of Christ is, in fact, the cause and indispensable condition of the work of the Spirit; on the other hand, it is the Holy Spirit who glorifies Christ in the heart of believers, and causes the Person of Christ to dwell in them. It is therefore the life of Christ, the nature of Christ, the sentiments of Christ, the virtues of Christ which the Spirit communicates to believers; it is after the likeness of Christ that He fashions them."

The late Dr. Jowett said that there are many Christians who are pre-Pentecostal as far as their experience is concerned. "We are living," he said, "too much as men lived before the Holy Ghost was given. We have not occupied the new and far-stretching land of Christian privilege . . . Therefore, many of the gifts and graces and perfumes of the Apostolic age are absent from our modern religious life." So that man of God, McCheyne, said, "Whatever you fail of, do not fail of the influences of the Holy Spirit, for only in this way can you move the hearts of men."

But should not the leaders of the missionary enterprise at home have the same spiritual qualifications, as those abroad? Have we the right to expect the missionary stream abroad to reach a higher spiritual level than that reached by the church, which is the source of supply at home? One other thought. There are 14,000 foreign students in the universities of Canada and the United States. If the church at home is at a high spiritual level, many of these foreign students will find the unsearchable riches of Christ, while they are in our midst, and the Christian foreign students will be strengthened in their devotion to Jesus Christ; but on the other hand, if the church at home is at a low level spiritually, some of these Christian foreign students may lose their faith while they are with us, and the non-Christian foreign students will return to their countries confirmed in unbelief.

Last August, at the meeting of the World's Student Christian Federation in England I heard the representative from India say, "When Christianity first came to India, the non-Christians said, 'Christianity is not true.' They have had to abandon that position because of the evidences of the Christian faith. "Then," he said, "the second line of attack was, 'Christianity is not new,' and they tried to parallel from their own sacred books what is found in the Bible; but, he added, "that position has been in the main abandoned, because there is no one like Christ in the Hindu sacred scriptures," "Now, however," he added, "the line of attack is this: 'Christianity is not *you,* Christianity is not *you.'* " Sometime ago there appeared in Japan a book with this strange title, "Why I Am Still a Christian, Though I Have Studied in the West."

What then are some of the spiritual qualifications necessary for missionary work at home and abroad? The first I wish to mention is what our Lord mentioned, "Except a grain of wheat fall into the ground and die, it abideth by itself alone; but if it die, it beareth much fruit." I die daily," said the great missionary, Paul. "If any man would come after me, let him deny himself, and take up his cross daily and follow me," said Jesus. When Scott was preparing for his Antarctic expedition, enough men offered their services, each bringing one thousand pounds, to man and to finance that entire expedition; but not one of those men was accepted, for Scott did not look upon them as fit for that difficult and dangerous task. At the height of His popularity when our Lord had dined in the home of a ruler and the multitudes were thronging and pressing upon Him, He turned to them and said,

"Whosoever he be of you that renounceth not all that he hath, he cannot be my disciple." Can we not imagine the disappointment on the part of Peter on hearing these words? Can we not hear him saying to John, "Why did the Master speak thus? The Kingdom was about to be restored to Israel. Everyone is favoring our cause; why did he not show a little more tact?" Jesus knew the hearts of men. He wanted disciples who would go all the way with him, even to Gethsemane and Golgotha. "We must bleed to bless," said that great leader Baron Nikolai, who brought a new religious epoch to the students of Russia.

A second qualification needed is *humility,* which Andrew Murray of South Africa characterized as the root of all the virtues; the gentleness that gives no offense, the meekness that receives no offense. I have seen a proud Brahman in India so amazed at the humility of a learned missionary that he was willing to study about the man's Master, "who, being in the form of God, counted it not a prize to be on an equality with God, but emptied himself, taking the form of a servant . . . He humbled himself, becoming obedient even unto death, yea, the death of the cross." A learned Hindu said to students in Calcutta, "What India needs for her regeneration is not simply sermons and addresses and Bible texts, but the presentation of a truly Christian life, the gentleness and meekness and forgiveness, such as your Christ exhibited in His life and death." This will not be a weak humility, for "faithful are the wounds of a friend."

A third qualification is *faith.* "This is the victory that overcomes the world," wrote John, "even your faith." "That we might receive the promise of the Spirit through faith," wrote Paul to the Galatians. "Said I not unto thee," were the words of Jesus, "that if thou believedst thou shouldest see the glory of God?" Faith is not sight, but faith is the road to sight. How thankful we should be that in our day there are missionaries of whom we can say, "Who through faith subdued kingdoms, wrought righteousness, obtained promises, from weakness were made strong, waxed mighty in war."

Another qualification is *love,* the first grace mentioned in that cluster of the fruit of the Spirit found in Galatians. No amount of eloquence or earnestness, no ability to organize or skill in administration can make up for the lack of love. "If I speak with the tongues of men and of angels, but have not love, I am become sounding brass, or a clanging cymbal. And if I have the gift of prophecy, and know all mysteries and all knowledge; and if I have all faith so as to remove mountains, but have not love, I am nothing. And if I bestow all my goods to feed the poor, and if I give my body to be burned, but have not love, it profiteth me nothing." When a missionary in India, through his love for Christ and the people, was winning converts, there appeared in one of the vernacular papers an article warning parents and guardians to keep away their sons and wards from the influence of that man, and the article closed as follows: "The love of the Christian is more dangerous than the sword of Mohammed."

A fifth qualification is *patience*. When I went out to India to begin my missionary work, an earnest Christian said, "Remember, the sign of an apostle is patience." You recall how the great missionary apostle wrote, "strengthened with all might according to His glorious power unto all patience and long suffering with joyfulness." Sir Henry M. Stanley, the explorer, once said, "Travelers in Africa suffer far more from mosquitoes than they do from lions." It is these little mosquito troubles that often tempt a missionary to be impatient. My sister, who was a missionary in India, once said that she sometimes found a girl who had been willing to leave America to go to India, was willing to learn a difficult language, was quite resigned to living in a trying climate, but who was not willing to have a curtain hung a little differently from what she liked in the zenana mission house. Three years ago, when I was in an inland province in China, I was told of some devoted missionaries who had a misunderstanding as to which of two stoves should be used during the winter months! I am sure these mosquito troubles are not limited to the mission field. They sometimes get into our Board rooms, do they not, and into the homes of the leaders of the missionary enterprise in this country also?

A sixth spiritual qualification is a *deep and effective prayer life*. Seventeen months ago a few Student Volunteers in a New England university were burdened because of the spiritual deadness of the campus. A prayer group was started. By the end of the year it grew into two prayer groups. Last year, a devotional meeting once a week was added to corporate prayer. Two months ago the overflow started, through the mission of friendship. One Volunteer led fourteen fellow students to accept Jesus Christ as their personal Saviour; another Volunteer led twenty-one fellow students to Christ—there were eighty-five decisions for Christ that week. Of the ten men who engaged in this work eight were Student Volunteers. What better spiritual preparation for work abroad could these Volunteers have than the winning of fellow students to Christ in the homeland? And, abroad, the same spirit of prayer will produce similar results in souls won to Christ. This has been illustrated over and over again in the lives of missionaries like Hyde and Forman of India, like Mary Slessor and Donald Fraser of Africa, like Nevius of China, also in the lives of indigenous Christians like Pandita Ramabai of India, Neesima of Japan and Ding Li-mei of China.

The final qualification I mention is *fellowship with Christ*. Does this not sum up all the qualifications necessary for missionary service at home and abroad? Moses endured as seeing Him who is invisible; the great missionary leaders have thus endured. They have set the Lord always before them. They have walked with God. They have practiced the presence of God. They know that if they are to walk with God they must give time daily to put aside those things that displease God, for two cannot walk together except they be agreed.

Hence these missionary leaders take time, most of them, early in the morning, in order that they may deal rigorously with self in all its moods and tenses, in order that they might do what Gordon described in a letter to his sister when he said, "I have spent half an hour alone hewing Agag in pieces," that is, dealing firmly with self. Dr. Haas, a medical missionary in Turkey, told me that his rule was to give at least one full hour every morning to doing two things: the first was going through a system of auto-massage and making himself physically fit; but most of the hour was given to prayer and Bible reading. When he began the day thus he found himself fit for anything.

Paul in the last verse of the first chapter to the Colossians writes (I am translating freely from the original), "Whereunto I also am spent with toil, agonizing like the athlete in the public games, according to His energy that energizes in me in power." Here we see the great missionary stripped for the race, using every bit of physical and mental energy he possesses in the cause to which he has devoted his life, not according to his own weak energy, but according to the divine energy that energizes in him in power. Shall we then turn to prayer, and as I mention different requests, shall we pray in silence?

Let us, first of all, praise God for the unsearchable riches of Christ. Let us thank Him because the book in which we read of these unsearchable riches has been already translated, in whole or in part, into 800 different languages, and made available for many millions of people. Let us thank God for the indigenous churches in mission lands.

Shall we turn now to confession of sin? Let us confess our own sin that we have not appropriated more of these unsearchable riches of Christ, that we have not experienced in our own lives more of the exceeding greatness of the power which raised Him from the dead, that we have not spent more time in prayer for ourselves and for others.

How often has it been the case, as James writes, that we have not because we ask not, and that we ask and receive not because we ask amiss? "If we confess our sins He is faithful and righteous to forgive us our sins and to cleanse us from all unrighteousness."

And now shall we bring our petitions before him? Let us pray for the church in the mission field that its members may have so much of this spiritual power that the church will grow in grace, winning many to Christ and may soon become self-supporting, self-governing, self-propagating. Let us pray for the foreign missionaries that they may be willing to decrease while the indigenous church leaders increase. Let us pray that the leaders, foreign and indigenous, in these countries may be examples to believers in word, in manner of life, in love, in faith, in purity.

Let us pray for the home base that the home church may bring into the storehouse the whole tithe of prayer, money, lives, for foreign work, so that God may be able to open the windows of heaven and pour out a blessing at home and abroad that there shall not be room enough to receive it.

Let us pray for the missionary candidates who cannot at present be sent to the needy mission fields because the boards are in financial difficulties. Let us pray that the church at home and abroad may be so quickened spiritually that the whole world will be evangelized in this generation. Let us pray for every delegate to this convention, that the love of Christ may so constrain each one of us that we shall gladly do or suffer according to His holy will. Father, we gather up our unspoken petitions in the cry of our hearts that we may have more of these spiritual qualifications in our own lives and that we may be faithful in the ministry of prayer and faithful in serving our fellowmen.

> "Take us, Lord, O, take us truly,
>   Mind and soul and heart and will.
> Empty us and cleanse us throughly,
>   Then with all Thy fulness fill.
>
> "Make us in Thy royal palace
>   Vessels worthy of our king;
> From Thy fulness fill our chalice,
>   From Thy never-failing spring.
>
> "Father, by this blessed filling,
>   Dwell Thyself in us, we pray,
> We are waiting, Thou art willing,
>   Fill us with Thyself today."

NEW FORCES RELEASED BY COOPERATION

JOHN R. MOTT, LL.D., NEW YORK

Chairman, The International Missionary Council

Christian Missions have led the way to the most beneficent and fruitful cooperation between Christian communions, between nations, and between races. This Convention in itself has constituted a convincing demonstration of the practicability and incalculable value of all of these aspects of cooperation. It has also presented one continuous summons, to the Christian forces of all the denominations, nationalities, and racial groups represented here, to devise and to enter into more adequate plans of cooperation and unity. The Christian church needs today, as never before, to employ what the French in the War termed "grand strategy." By this they meant the strategy that took in all fronts, in fact, the whole map. They also meant united action on the part of all the widely extended and scattered forces on land and sea.

Before we indicate new forces which will be released through cooperation, let us remind ourselves of the reasons why larger and more efficient cooperation is today absolutely essential in the world-wide missionary enterprise. It is necessary in order to counteract the marked growth of the divisive forces among men. The world is still filled with misunderstanding, suspicion, fear, friction, and strife. All the arguments in favor of cooperation used in 1910 at the World Missionary Conference in Edinburgh are now accentuated tenfold. Christian missions are indeed the great and the true internationalism. Our 29,000 missionaries are ambassadors, interpreters, and mediators in the most vital aspects of international and inter-racial relationships. The 300 and more mission Boards and societies, and the hundreds of other auxiliary agencies abound in activities the indirect as well as the direct results of which make powerfully for right relationships among the various peoples of the world. If we give ourselves unitedly, in well conceived cooperative plans and efforts, to promoting just, courteous, and kindly relations between our respective denominations and between national groups, we can do more than all other factors combined to relieve the present impossible international and inter-racial strain.

Such cooperation is essential to enable the Christian church to give her true testimony. What is her true testimony or witness? We answer, the absolute and unique ability of Jesus Christ and His church to meet the deepest needs presented by the international and inter-racial situation. Unless the principles and spirit of Jesus Christ can be applied successfully to such relations, the witness of the Church is inevitably impaired. Our different Christian communions preach, "Love your enemies," and yet today how much we see on every hand of racial superiority and un-Christian nationalism. If we cannot have successful cooperation among the Christian forces, where else can we look for this desired and necessary relationship. Moreover, if we have other kinds of international cooperation, without being able to achieve missionary cooperation, what other conclusion can the outside or unbelieving world form than that the Christian church has lost her way and vacated her spiritual leadership.

International cooperation, as well as interdenominational cooperation, is essential, as never before, to emphasize the truly catholic and ecumenical nature of the Christian church. The early Christians made it clear that the church brought men into a fellowship which included all nations, races and social groups. In fact, they looked upon themselves as in a sense a new nation, a people of God united in a bond before which all earthly distinctions faded. In reality, the church of Christ consists of all those of all nations united by the gift of a common faith, loyalty, and experience; but genuine cooperation only can best demonstrate this as a fact.

The magnitude, complexity and great cost of the world-wide missionary enterprise on the one hand, and, on the other, the relatively meager resources in available funds and highly qualified workers, absolutely necessitate and demand cooperation on the part of the Christian forces. Ours is literally a world-wide undertaking, more so than any other. It involves the whole range of the life of every man. It concerns every human relationship. What hope is there to spread adequately the network of Christ's ministry over this vast and complex area of human need, apart from concerted planning and effort on the part of the hundreds of separate missionary agencies?

The baffling difficulties and grave dangers today confronting the Christian movement at home and abroad are such as to make the task impossible, if we seek to accomplish it with divided ranks. In all my thirty-five and more years of work among the nations, never has the missionary undertaking seemed to me to be so difficult. Never have our forces seemed to be so inadequate. At a meeting of Christian workers the other day I stated that in my judgment the next fifteen years will be the most difficult in the history of the Christian religion. Why? Not chiefly because of the forces which oppose us; not because we are called upon to deal with so many great issues simultaneously; not because of the stern challenges that are sounding in the ears of the churches of all lands; but also and principally for the very encouraging reason that never before have so many Christians awakened to the awful implications of the Christian gospel. Thank God, we

have come to a time when large numbers of His followers seem
to think that He meant what He said, believe with depth of conviction that He must be Lord of all or not at all, and are dominated
by the vision of the kingdoms of this world becoming the kingdoms of our Lord and of His Christ. At such a time, only the
united and mobilized wisdom and experience and the sacrificial
devotion of Christians of every name and clime will suffice.

Need it be added that the extreme urgency of the present
world situation summons us irresistibly to present a united front
through constructive cooperative effort? Every field represented
here today, which means nearly all the battlefields of Christianity,
is wide open to the unselfish ministry of our faith. The nations
just now are in a plastic state. There are unmistakable signs of
the breakup or disintegration of non-Christian systems, including
Mohammedanism. On the other hand, the forces of irreligion
are manifesting fresh vigor and activity. Most important of all,
however, are the rising tides of spiritual interest, and the fact that
the Christward movement in so many fields is growing in volume
and momentum. It is a startling fact that in the face of such a
situation, it is entirely possible that in this critical and fateful hour,
the Christian forces may fall short, simply through failure to combine in time. May God help us not only to see, but likewise to
seize the present unprecedented opportunity. Through all these
considerations do we not hear the imperative summons to draw
together in order that there may be liberated fresh and greatly
augmented energies?

In the first place, what are some of the new or added forces
which will be released for the missionary movement through interdenominational, international, and inter-racial cooperation?
Without shadow of doubt, such cooperation will augment the financial resources placed at the disposal of the missionary movement.
Today almost every church and missionary organization is hampered through lack of sufficient available funds. In not a few
bodies represented here the financial situation is truly alarming.
What is the difficulty? The situation is surely not because adequate financial resources do not exist. Within a few days, the
New York "Times" has called attention to two documents recently
issued by the government,—one by the Bureau of the Census,
based on information available up to 1922, and the other by the
Bureau of Internal Revenue, also based on data in hand in 1922.
These two publications estimate that the wealth of the United
States, that year, was not less than $320,000,000,000. This rep-
resents a ten-fold increase within fifty years. The striking fact
about this colossal figure is that, even without including the wealth
of Canada, it is more than the equivalent of the estimated combined
wealth for the same year of Great Britain, Ireland, France, Ger-

many, Holland, Norway, Sweden, Denmark, Finland, Switzerland, Italy, Australia, New Zealand, and South Africa. You will recognize that this catalog of countries includes virtually all of the other home base countries, that is, the countries which send missionaries.

Nor is the financial embarrassment of the missionary cause due to the fact that people in this country are not disposed to devote their money to unselfish causes. Recently, the Boston "Transcript" stated that, in 1924, Americans gave $2,500,000,000 to altruistic causes, apart from all they gave toward religious objects, and apart from all that was given toward welfare enterprises by municipalities and state governments. No other countries in the world have a record at all comparable to this. Nor is the present cramped financial position of our missionary Boards due to the fact that there are not abundantly sufficient resources in the hands of the Christians of our country. Recent studies of lists of donors to various unselfish causes, including not only those making gifts toward religious objects, but also toward general philanthropy and education, show that between seventy and eighty per cent. of the persons on these lists have ecclesiastical connections, that is, are members of churches. These studies also show that the gifts come from only about ten per cent. of the people, and that they are by no means confined to the rich.

Why, then, are not the financial energies of our constituencies more largely liberated for the missionary cause? There are different answers to this question, but one of the most important is that our policies and plans do not impress those who should give as representing the wisest, most economical, and most productive use of funds. They are not at all staggered by the magnitude of the sums required for world-wide missions; many of them are familiar with the requirements of large business enterprises. On the contrary, they cannot but wonder at the smallness of our plans and demands. They do not object to large expenditures, but they do object to any waste due to unnecessary duplication of expenditure and of effort caused by the failure of different groups of Christians to cooperate.

Time after time you and I have heard donors commend what we might call the zoning plan, followed in Korea and Mexico, by which each of certain denominations assumes financial responsibility for the work in a given part of the country; or the economical and effective method employed by the Boards that unite in the support of union colleges and other educational and philanthropic institutions in different parts of the mission field; or the highly multiplying value of the work accomplished by the National Christian Councils of China, India, and Japan, or by the Committee on Cooperation in Latin America, or, above all, by the International

Missionary Council, all of which agencies have united in study, in planning, and in action, the various Churches and missions responsible for work in certain great areas. Without doubt, well conceived plans of cooperation will result in relating new tides of power to the missionary enterprise.

You may be interested in a recent incident which illustrates this point. A certain American citizen, whose name, I fancy, you would not be able to guess, was impressed with the un-Christian differences manifested among the Christians in Jerusalem and in other parts of the Holy Land. On the other hand, he learned of the cooperative plan by which the Young Men's Christian Association in Jerusalem, representing and serving all our churches, has united to such a remarkable degree in membership, in spirit, and in practical effort, the Christians of so many names, and even others in sympathy with the Christian program. He went to one of the banks in New York shortly after Christmas, and deposited $400,000 toward a modern Young Men's Christian Association building for Jerusalem, and did so on two conditions: one, that his name should never be made known; and the other, that when the building is completed there should be placed in it a tablet indicating that the building has been established for the glory of God, and in memory of His Only Begotten Son. You will agree with me that that is what we should call unselfish giving. When the fact was mentioned, a few days later, in the hearing of another Christian layman, he said, on the same condition that his name should not be mentioned, "I would like to give as much as $25,000 toward installing in that building a pipe organ to further the expression of praise to the Redeemer." Another man on Wall Street, learning of this action, has promised as much as $12,000 toward placing chimes on the building, when it is erected, desiring, as he said, "that the praises of Christ may sound out over the hills where He taught and prayed and gave His life for the sin of the world." When my friend, Dr. A. C. Harte, mentioned these gifts to one of the leading Jewish lawyers, this man promised that either he alone, or he in company with his fellow religionists, would provide $50,000 toward the undertaking, because of its unifying influence, not only among Christians, but in establishing fraternal relations between Christians and Jews.

In the second place, a policy of cooperation entered into heartily by our various Christian denominations and by the Christians of different nationalities will inevitably result in strengthening the intellectual leadership of the missionary enterprise. Here our need is admittedly great. It reminds one of an article that appeared in the London "Spectator" entitled, "First-Rate Events; Second-Rate Men." In the world today, events of the first magnitude and significance are transpiring, but is it not true that we have far too few leaders of the highest ability and furnishing to cope with these great and pressing issues? We need on every hand in the Christian missionary movement more thinkers and fewer mechanical workers. We must discover more of the leading minds in the Churches, and relate their constructive abilities to the missionary tasks. There are all too few creative minds. There is need, as has been already pointed out in this convention, of something new to be born, as the foreign missionary movement itself was generated. Great indeed is the need of men and women who can re-think, re-state, re-interpret the missionary message, and, where necessary, revise the missionary methods. I repeat that there are never, in any sphere, too many leading minds. There are seldom enough of them in any given denomination or country.

It is maintained that sound policies of cooperation, widely extended, will result in releasing the desired new intellectual forces. How can this be? In the first place, cooperation among denominations, as among different nationalities, will result in stimulating one another to good and better intellectual works. Every number of the "International Review of Missions" is a demonstration of this fact. Take for example, the article by Professor Hogg of Madras Christian College, in the January number entitled, "To the Rescue of Civilization." This article is based on a penetrating and sympathetic study of the writings of Dr. Schweitzer, the famous German medical missionary working in the heart of Africa. This quarterly magazine, going as it does to thousands of the most thoughtful persons in all parts of the world, makes possible the bringing of the fruitful work of these two stimulating German and Scotch minds to bear on the thinking of missionary administrators and scholars the world over. If it had not been for the cooperative plan which called this periodical into existence and maintains it, it would not be possible for the leading minds of the various countries to make their contribution to one another, and thus to enrich all.

Cooperation, again, augments the intellectual resources of every cooperating body through pooling the intellectual abilities and contributions of all. It would be difficult to overstate the benefits which have come to all the Churches at work in China, and to every missionary society interested in that field, from the work of the Educational Commission composed of President Burton of the University of Chicago, Professor Roxby of Liverpool, President Butterfield, President Woolley, Bishop McConnell, and Dr. Russell, together with their able Chinese collaborators. International cooperative plans have made available to all agencies interested in the uplift of Africa, both missionary and governmental agencies, the results of the discerning and constructive studies of Dr. Thomas Jesse Jones. Mr. W. J. McKee, a Presbyterian industrial missionary in India, has accomplished an educational work of great originality and of the utmost practical value. His experiences and conclusions should be made available to a score of other mission Boards, and some cooperative plan should be devised to ensure that this be done.

It is expensive business for each mission to have to acquire in its own way a rare experience like this, which, through cooperation, can be shared with all. In these days we hear a great deal about group thinking. Emphasis placed on this process is emphasis wisely and productively placed. It is the very essence of cooperation, thus to make possible the thinking of one complementing or supplementing that of others. The need for the enrichment of mind and comprehensiveness of view which comes from such united study and thought is more imperative just now than ever before. Why should certain denominations, missions, and national groups continue longer to suffer intellectual impoverishment, and fall short of the intellectual mastery of their problem, and fail to afford a real intellectual leadership, through intellectual isolation, due in turn to the failure to cooperate?

Thirdly, cooperation on the part of the Churches, as well as of the different nations which are engaged in missionary undertakings, will develop a larger and truer statesmanship for the Kingdom of God. Senator Elihu Root one day remarked to me that we may judge of the stage of advancement of the statesmanship of a nation by its ability to cooperate with other nations. I sometimes think we might reverse his statement, and say that only through cooperation do we have supplied the conditions which make possible the development of the most advanced type of statesmanship. True it is that some of the finest exhibitions of Christian statescraft are those which have come through the concerted thinking and planning of the Christians of different communions and nationalities in great worthwhile common undertakings.

The manner of life of far too many administrators, Board members, and church leaders is not conducive to the development of Christian statesmanship. One has in mind the fact that such a disproportionately large amount of their time and attention is today given to promotive activities. We need to be drawn out of the meshes of our ordinary financial and administrative routine into fellowship with kindred minds of other bodies. Every genuinely cooperative, unselfish enterprise brings us out into a land of larger dimensions. The greatest contribution of the World Missionary Conference of Edinburgh, and of its eight related international and interdenominational Commissions, was that it yielded a few missionary statesmen, such as Oldham, Watson, Allegret, Richter, and Cheng Ching Yi. Great is the need right now of augmenting such leadership of the missionary forces of the world. God grant that the processes again set at work here at Washington may likewise result in giving us another and larger group of men and women who will exhibit in the coming years the true marks of Christian statesmanship—vision, comprehension, foresight, reverential regard for the past, unselfishness, power to cooperate, and unselfish ability.

Again, the missionary message will be wonderfully enriched through the most intimate cooperation of all true believers. In fact, is not genuine cooperation and unity absolutely essential to ensure the giving of full orbed expression to the message of the Church of Christ? Christ has not revealed himself solely or fully through any one nation, race, or communion. No part of mankind has a monopoly of His unsearchable riches. Every national and denominational tradition has a contribution to make which can enrich the whole Body of Christ. The help of all who bear His name and who have had experience of Him is necessary adequately to reveal His excellencies and to communicate His power. For as in Christ who is the Head, there is "neither Jew nor Greek, neither male nor female, barbarian, Scythian, bond nor free"—not because He is none of these, but because He is all of them—so the Church—which is His Body—cannot be perfected until "they shall bring the glory and the honor of the nations into it," that is to say, until the spiritual characteristics of every race and Christian name have been, not submerged, but brought to their individual perfection in a perfect whole.

The reason why you and I, as Americans or Canadians or Europeans, or as Methodists or Baptists, value that which is most distinctive to us, is not because it is ours, but because we honestly believe it is the truth. Should we not, therefore, wish to come into such relations to all other Christians, of whatever name or sign, that we may share our priceless possession with them? Every race, every land—small as well as great,—every denomination, not only has the right, but should also have the opportunity, thus to express itself and thus to make its contribution. How shall this be accomplished, save through cooperation or Christian unity? What deep and inspiring spiritual significance this lends to every such cooperative enterprise as the International Missionary Council, the Foreign Missions Conference of North America, and similar bodies in different parts of the world.

How much the rising national Churches, to which so many references have been made in the sessions of this Convention, will be profited from entering into such cooperative relations as will keep them in touch with organized Christianity of other lands. Surely every Church will profit from preserving intelligent contacts with historical Christianity. Name the century in the life of the Christian religion which does not have its rich contribution to make to every living Church of today. The same is true of credal

Christianity. Name the creed of Christendom which does not embody and state truths in terms which will help to buttress and strengthen every Christian communion. Moreover, what cannot each rising and struggling, as well as each strong and expanding Church, gain from the most intimate relation to vital and applied Christianity wherever it is found the world over.

In the fifth place, such cooperative relations will not only enrich our message but also, therefore, enrich our lives, enrich our spiritual experience, and wondrously enrich our spiritual fellowship. This leads us into one of the most profound mysteries and most transforming truths and processes of the Christian revelation. Well may we ponder, and ever and again ponder, the enriching and unfathomable ideas contained in the words, "Until we all come in the unity of the faith, and (as well as) the knowledge of the Son of God unto the perfect man, unto the measure of the stature of the fullness of Christ." Thus, through the knowledge of one another in the pathway of sacrificial service for one another in the great cooperative and unifying activities of the Kingdom, as well as through the knowledge of the Son of God, we are indeed perfected.

How little have we entered into the marvelous power of genuine Christian fellowship, we of different Christian names. What an incalculable reinforcement of power will come to each one of us, if we enter into such fellowship. Was it not such a fellowship that Christ created, and has forever made possible? It was such a fellowship that conquered the Roman Empire. It has been such a fellowship which has furnished the spring of power of the Moravians, who have so beautifully and triumphantly illustrated the power of international and inter-racial cooperation. In a measure, Edinburgh yielded such a fellowship. One wonders what might have resulted from that fellowship had it not been for the war. Zinzendorf prayed that he might be baptized into a sense of all conditions, that so he might enter into fellowship with all. May we not reverently, the five thousand of us here from so many Christian bodies, and representing so many lands and races, make the same intercession, and, as we go forth from this place, ever lend ourselves to those attitudes, spiritual exercises, and cooperative policies which will result in our entering into an abundant answer to our united prayers?

Again, the apologetic power or influence of the Christian religion will be enormously increased through genuine cooperation and unity. The unity or oneness among His followers down the generations, for which Christ prayed, was not to be regarded as an end in itself, but rather as a means to ensure the great central end of Christian missions, namely, "that the world may believe." Thus, this is the great, the triumphant apologetic. Wherever and whenever we find the Christian faith failing to sweep the field in triumph, we do well to examine ourselves as to whether one of the chief causes, if not the chief one, may not lie right here. Divisions among the Christians—denominational, national, racial—have ever been a stumbling block; but with the recent rapid shrinkage of the world, these divisions have become more serious and intolerable than ever.

In my recent visits to different parts of the Moslem world, I was solemnized and humbled to find that the principal argument the Mohammedans were using against us is that of our divisions. The same is true, when we get to the bottom of it, with reference to the attitude of unbelievers everywhere. To preach the brotherhood of man, and then to stand aloof from one another on the mission field, or at home, or to fail to fraternize or to cooperate, belies our teachings, and creates the impression that Christianity, like other religions, has lofty ideals, but that the practice of its followers or promoters shows that it is impracticable. We must do away with this stumbling block. To this God is unquestionably calling us. If we can forget that we are Americans, Canadians, British, Chinese, Dutch, French, Germans, Indians, Japanese, Scandinavians, or that we are Baptists, Congregationalists, Disciples, Episcopalians, Friends, Methodists, Presbyterians, Lutherans;—in the work of making Christ known to peoples in Asia, Africa, Latin America, or Europe, or of North America, we have gone a great way toward proving to unbelievers who are moved by facts, that the religion of Jesus Christ is the great solvent of the racial and national alienations of the world, and, therefore, is the mightiest force operating among men. The present is the time of times to present this apologetic.

In the seventh place, well considered policies and measures and rich experiences in the realm of cooperation will give the missionary cause a fresh power of appeal to men and women of large affairs, of large capacity, and of large influence. We stand in need of just such a power of appeal. We have lost something which in the pre-war days we had in the interdenominational and international Laymen's Missionary Movement. I am reminded that the man to whom God first gave the vision of this movement, and who gave himself with undiscourageable enthusiasm to its realization, was John B. Sleman, one of the most useful laymen of Washington. He told me that the vision came to him when he was attending a great convention of the Student Volunteer Movement in Nashville. Shortly after that he came to discuss the matter with me in my office in New York. I am ashamed to say that I was not more responsive to his vision and plan. I had acquired the habit of discouraging, on general principles, the launching of new organizations. Time soon convinced me, however, that his vision was God-implanted, and I ever afterward counted it a privilege to collaborate with him.

What was it which enabled the Laymen's Missionary Movement to make such a powerful appeal to the imagination and the will of countless leading laymen on both sides of the Atlantic? In the first place, it was the largeness of the task presented. It took the combined programs of all our Churches to make possible such a presentation. In the second place, these men of large vision and large affairs were appealed to by the wholeness of the task. Above all, in the third place, they were impressed by the presentation of the oneness of the task; in other words, it was presented as a colossal, cooperative undertaking which could not be accomplished apart from the united planning and effort of all the Christian forces. This was, and still is, the language which the modern mind, especially of men and women of large views could understand, and it never failed in any land to call forth from them a great response. Such persons are accustomed to see and to deal in large dimensions.

I think just now of one of the three men of largest affairs in America, if not in the world, a most efficient and helpful layman of one of our principal communions. He is admittedly one of the busiest men in the nation. If we had gone to him for one hour of his time, we probably would have failed to get it. We went to him, however, and asked for three full days of his time, in order to think through with us a large plan for constructive cooperation on the part of all of our Christian bodies. That idea and possibility gripped him, and he gave us, without begrudging, the three days. He became so interested by that time, that when we asked him to join us in a five-day gathering for exposing a large body of laymen and clergymen from all over the country to the cooperative plan, he not only came, but likewise brought his wife, and was an invaluable factor in developing the vital constructive program. Still later, he gave large blocks of his time to advocating the principles underlying the proposed cooperative effort. This is not an isolated case. It could be readily enforced by like striking examples in different countries. To ensure even arresting the attention, still more enlisting the collaboration, of such men we must present to them something really worth while. They do not want to deal with fractions. No sectional appeal will call forth from them a truly great response. But the vastness of the true unity of the sublime undertaking of world-wide missions will draw them like a magnet. As we think of enlisting, as we must enlist if we mean to win out, a large number of the busiest, most important, and most influential laymen of our day, we may well seek to illustrate again the creed of Saint Augustine, "A whole Christ for my salvation, a whole Bible for my staff, a whole church for my fellowship, a whole world for my parish."

Again, the great powers of the new generation will be enlisted through large programs and plans of cooperation, federation, and unity, whereas a failure at this vital point may lose this generation to our cause. We do well to remind ourselves that we have a new generation to win to the missionary program. They have by no means been won, as I can testify from first-hand contacts at home and abroad. At present, our plans do not powerfully appeal to the young men and young women of from twenty to thirty years of age. I have in mind the new generation, not only as we find it in North America, Europe, and Australasia, but also throughout Asia, Latin America, and parts of Africa. We must present to them a challenge vast enough to appeal to their imagination, difficult and exacting enough to call out their latent energies, absorbing enough to save them from themselves, tragic enough to counteract and overcome the growing habits of luxury, love of ease, pleasure, and softness, and overwhelming enough to drive them to God. Moreover, to win their whole-hearted allegiance, we must be able to show them that ours is a united task. Their minds are made up that they will not stand for divisive policies and plans. Never has the indispensability and victorious power of united planning and action been so burned into the consciousness and so anchored in the convictions of a generation, as in the case of the young men and young women whom we have in view when we speak of the new generation. Their intimate collaboration with us, and their increasing acceptance of the burden of responsibility for initiative and leadership, are indispensable to us.

They have powers to bring to us which we simply must have. I refer to their abounding hopefulness, which alone can adequately counteract the pessimism which still so largely obtains even among Christians. They will bring to us a flood of idealism, for, thank God, many of them are still living on the mountains, and have refused to come down into the mists of the valleys in these days of reaction. They will bring to us that priceless power, the power of vision, for this is a distinguishing characteristic of youth. While some old people have the power of vision, is it not true that in nearly every instance the visions which command them were imparted to them in the days of their youth? This new generation will enormously augment the spirit of adventure in the Christian Church, and this is supremely desirable, for we are entering upon a period of unexampled warfare. As I have already pointed out, the next half generation bids fair to constitute the most difficult period in the life of the Christian religion. This means warfare. You and I of an older generation stand ready to die fighting in our tracks for the same ideals and the same vision which command so largely the most discerning and unselfish of the new generation; but we will not live long enough to fill in the vision. Our years will not be sufficiently numerous to effect those extensive, and still more, those profoundly intensive changes which are essential to the establishment of the new order, wherein righteousness, unselfishness and world-wide brotherhood are to dwell. The new generation, however, have at their disposal the necessary unspent years to fill with living content of reality this vision.

And, finally, effective, fruitful, triumphant cooperation is ever accompanied with fresh accessions of spiritual power. The reason is a simple one, but one that we are so prone to forget, namely, that the cooperation we so much desire can never be realized apart from the help which comes from superhuman wisdom, superhuman love, and superhuman power. Therefore, wherever it is achieved, it is found to be in line with the tides of Divine power. No other great desirable process and result is beset with such difficulties. There are the difficulties of isolation—geographical, linguistic, mental; difficulties resulting from narrowness and prejudice—denominational, national, racial; difficulties due to pride and selfishness—personal, ecclesiastical, as well as that of nationality or race; difficulties due to conservatism—inertia, fear, and lack of vision.

Moreover, there are unquestioned dangers which attend the development of cooperation between churches and between nations. Wherever new and great energies are liberated, very real dangers are to be found. Chief among these dangers are those due to ignorance, to neglect of sound guiding principles, to lack of clear thinking, to want of forethought or to failure to count the cost, to lack of sufficiently close collaboration, or of continuous vigilance on the part of all concerned. These difficulties and dangers, however, are in a very real sense our salvation. They will inevitably drive us to God, and serve to deepen our acquaintance with Him, and thus lead to the discovery of His ways, His resources, and, therefore, His abundant adequacy. If we who cherish the vision of a coming better day of cooperation and unity, were not confronted with situations which we honestly know are too hard for us to cope with, not only singly, but also collectively, we would by no means be so likely to seek His face, and to come to know His wondrous power. Some churches, nations, and races are more in danger than others of relying on their strong human organization, their money power, their brilliant intellectual leadership, rather than on the limitless power of God. Cooperation has invariably failed to realize its highest values when it has not rested on the solid ground of a deep spiritual unity.

Jesus Christ was familiar with the problem of disunion, lack of concerted effort, and want of love and spiritual solidarity among His professed followers. His solution was strikingly unique. He summoned them to love one another, to serve one another, and thus actually to unite with one another. By His own example and teaching He made it forever clear that this wonder work of vital union among those who bear His Name, is the work of God. He took them to an upper room. He washed their feet, and then said, "If I being your Master wash your feet, ye also ought to wash one another's feet." He thus revealed the irresistible unifying power of mutual, humble service. He took some of them to the Garden. While they failed to watch with him one hour, their memory did not fail them, and later they pondered the depth of the meaning of His agonizing intercession, and of His sacrificial obedience even unto death, which broke down forever the middle wall of partition, and thus made possible the unity of all believers. He sent His disciples later to another room with instructions to tarry until they entered into a corporate experience—an experience where, as a result of having their differences submerged or gathered up into an unselfish comprehension, the conditions were realized which made possible the outpouring of the Holy Ghost sent down from Heaven, and the triumphant progress of the early Christian Church. That through all time there might be no doubt among Christians, and that we might not miss the way, with reference to the deepest secret of achieving not only triumphant cooperation but genuine spiritual unity, He Himself set the example by praying that His followers through all time might be one. Only as we enter into the mind and heart of Christ, by simple reliance upon a Presence and a Power infinitely greater than our own, will we gain the spiritual dynamic essential for the realization of genuine cooperation and unity.

There are a sufficient number of Christians in this convention, if they would but form the undiscourageable resolution to understand each other, to continue and extend the atmosphere of belief, the vision, the fellowship of these never-to-be-forgotten days, and to unite in planning, action, and intercession,—to advance by unbelievable leaps and bounds the world-wide missionary enterprise. Let each delegate dedicate himself afresh to the Lord Jesus Christ, and resolve so to act with reference to his fellow Christians of other communions, nations, and races, that if his colleagues here would under his influence do likewise, a great many scattered all through this great assembly might not taste death until they see the Kingdom of God come in power.

THE PLACE OF FOREIGN MISSIONS IN THE CHURCH AT HOME

WHY FOREIGN MISSIONS?

THE REVEREND ARTHUR J. BROWN, D.D., LL.D., NEW YORK

The reasons for promoting the foreign mission enterprise must be strong, else why have several thousand delegates come to this convention? Else why have 28,000 foreign missionaries, the best types of Christian character and culture, left their homes and native lands to go to the distant parts of the earth? Else why did the Christian people of Europe and America last year give $44,448,000 to maintain the missionaries and their work? Such effects must have an adequate cause. But since I have been asked to discuss it, I enumerate a few considerations. This audience, of course, requires no argument on this question.

First, because Christ commanded his disciples to preach his Gospel in all the world. I spend no time upon this. For all who count Jesus Christ as Lord, his word is final. "Should we try to convert India?" asked a young clergyman of the Duke of Wellington. "What are your marching orders, sir?" was the stern reply. However, there are other reasons which would be decisive in themselves, even if Christ had not spoken thus. So I add:

Second, because a true Christian experience prompts us to seek all men. Christianity is a world faith. Ruskin quotes Southey as declaring that no man was ever yet convinced of any momentous truth without feeling in himself the power as well as the desire of communicating it. Bishop Wilberforce said: "If my faith be false, I ought to change it; whereas, if it be true, I am bound to propagate it." We believe our faith to be true. That conviction prompts us to give it to all who do not possess it; and by one of the paradoxes of the Christian life the more religion we give away, the more we have left at home. Propagation is a law of the spiritual life. The genius of Christianity is expansive. A living organism must grow or die. The church that is not missionary will become atrophied. All virile faith prompts its possessor to seek others. Christ commanded us to go, but we should have had to go, anyway. Our Lord did not add a new duty. He simply voiced the most inspiring and imperative conviction of the regenerated human heart in that categorical imperative: "Go ye into all the world and preach the Gospel to every creature." Obedience is not a grudging duty, but a natural expression of Christian experience.

223

Third, because all men need the Gospel which we possess. It was not given for us alone. God is not a national deity, but the Sovereign and Father of the race. Jesus Christ is "the propitiation for our sins, and not for ours only, but also for the sins of the whole world." We are told that non-Christian peoples have religions of their own; but if Confucianism and Buddhism are not good enough for us, they are not good enough for the Chinese and the Siamese. Judaism is the best non-Christian faith that the world has seen, but the Son of God came to reveal something better. What right have we to regard as a white man's preserve a faith which was announced for all mankind? If we need Jesus Christ, we may be sure that Asiatics and Africans need Him, for they are our brother men, made in the image of God like ourselves.

He who has knowledge that is essential to the welfare of his fellow men is under solemn obligation to convey that knowledge to them. It makes no difference who those men are, or where they live, or whether they are conscious of their need, or how much inconvenience or expense he may incur in reaching them. The fact that he can help them is sufficient reason why he should do so. We have the revelation of God which is potential of a civilization that benefits man, an education that fits him for higher usefulness, a scientific knowledge that enlarges his powers, a medical skill that alleviates his sufferings, and, above all, a relation to Jesus Christ that not only lends new dignity to this earthly life, but prepares one for eternal companionship with God. "Neither is there salvation in any other." Therefore, we must convey this Gospel to the world. There is no worthy reason for being concerned about the salvation of the man next to us which is not equally applicable to the man far away. Our "neighbor" is man everywhere. The only race is the human race. It was Cain the murderer who said that he was not his brother's keeper. I am sometimes asked: "What becomes of those who die without having heard of Christ?" I can only reply that God will decide that, but that the practical question for us to consider is: "What will become of us if, knowing Christ, we fail to tell the world about Him. Does the world need the Saviour? The lurid glare of its need is writ large upon the earth. Shall we not enter with new intensity of passion into the agony of spirit which led St. Paul, when he looked out upon the world of his day, to cry: "I am debtor!"

Fourth, because Christ can do for all men what He has done for us. Missionary experience of a hundred years has shown that additional chapters in the book of Acts might be written. Transformed lives and great social reforms testify to the continued power of the Gospel. A Chinese merchant was converted. How do we know that he was converted? Well, he went home and destroyed his scales and bought new ones. Conversion to him meant sixteen ounces to the pound. There are some merchants not so far away as China who need that sort of Gospel. A Siamese chief was converted. How do we know that he was converted? He had the reputation of being a hard man. Well, he called his neighbors and friends together and told them his decision. He put away all his wives and concubines, except his first wife, making provision for their support so that they would not suffer. He paid his debts, surprising his creditors who had never expected to get anything out of him. He asked the pardon of all persons whom he had wronged and his desire to make restitution. Then, kneeling down before the assembled company, he solemnly dedicated himself and all that he had to the service of Jesus Christ.

It has been demonstrated that many non-Christian peoples needed only the regenerating touch of the spirit of God to awaken to new life. The peoples of China, India and Japan are higher in the scale of civilization than our ancestors were when the first foreign missionary found them. Why should we doubt that Christ can accomplish in them what He has accomplished in us? There is a phrase that was formerly common in missionary circles which I trust that we have abandoned—"poor heathen." Good taste forbids such phariseeism in talking about peoples whom we wish to win.

Benjamin Kidd declares that there is no scientific ground for regarding one race as inherently superior to others, that the qualities which have given preeminence to the white race have been wrought into it by centuries of Christian teaching. Let the same Christian teaching operate upon the non-Christian world and even more remarkable results may be witnessed. We are not sending missionaries to these people because they are our inferiors, but because they are our brethren, bearing the same burdens, meeting the same temptations, weeping under the same bereavements, and needing the same God as ourselves. We know that Christ can help them, because He has helped us. I have seen something of the meaning of the Gospel to them. There rises to my vision a never-to-be-forgotten scene in Chairyung, Korea. We had arrived at a late hour, hot and tired and dusty. We wanted to go to bed. But we were told that the Christians had assembled in the little church and were expecting us. So we went over. Being too weary to speak, I asked them to tell me what Christ had brought to them. One by one they eagerly jumped up all over the room. "Forgiveness," said one. "Joy," said another. "Strength to meet temptation," "peace," "guidance," "eternal life," "comfort in sorrow," added others. Deeply thrilled, I said, "Let us pray." And lo, the whole company bent prostrate with faces to the floor, and all began to pray at once in audible voice, until my heart was stirred, and I felt that the windows of heaven were opened, and that again angels were chanting as they did over the hills of Judea, "Glory to God in the highest, and on earth peace."

Fifth, because we have passed the age of provincialism and entered the age of cosmopolitanism. Thirty-five years ago my predecessor said that foreign missionary effort was for the peoples who did not touch our lives at any point. He could not say that today. Steam and electricity have brought together the most distant nations. China is nearer to New York than California once was. The inter-relations of Asia and America have become so close that we can no longer be independent of Asiatics, nor can they be independent of us. We must make them better or they will make us worse. Today, as never before since Christ spoke, the field is the world, and we cannot leave any part of it out of our thought. How swiftly, portentously, the non-Christian nations are changing! There is something fascinating and yet something appalling in the spectacle. Asia, where the race was born and where the greater part of it still lives; where art and science, literature and philosophy first appeared; where all the great religions arose; where Hebrew sage and prophet spoke; where the Son of Man walked visibly before men; and where stood the great altar of the world on which the Lamb of God laid down his life for men—Asia is awakening from the torpor of ages!

> "The rudiments of empire here
> Are plastic yet and warm,
> The chaos of a mighty world
> Is rounding into form."

Sixth, because we must Christianize racial relationships. My time is passing and I cannot enlarge upon this. May I simply say that we must have done with the heresy that men can be Christians as individuals and pagans as nations. The time has come for us to say that the law of the jungle shall not determine the policies of governments in their relations with one another; that Christ is for all life and for all the relations of life, and that no man becomes exempt from the law of Christ, when he is elected to a political office.

Seventh, because we want to face the whole problem of the Church. No Christian program today is adequate which ignores the major part of the world. No narrow provincial or sectarian undertaking will stir the modern layman. He is planning big things in other spheres of action, and he is ready to plan big things in religion. It is a vast undertaking which confronts us; nothing less than winning the world for Christ. We like it the better because it is vast, because it summons all the strongest and noblest within us to dare and to do for Christ and the world. Foreign missions is the world program of the Church of God, the international mind upon the highest level, the emancipation of the church from the parochial and provincial into the wide spaces of the Kingdom of God. Such work calls for breadth of mind to comprehend, for statesmanship to plan, for volunteers to go, for money to equip, and for large-hearted men and women at home to sustain the majestic enterprise by sympathies and prayers, as well as by gifts.

Eighth, finally and as supplying the power for these mighty tasks, because "He is able." These three words of Scripture should fire the soul of every missionary worker. We are not dealing with an impotent Christ, but with the Lord and King of the whole race of men. We do not undertake the task in our own strength. We are too weak for it; but "He is able," "able to save to the uttermost," "able to subdue all things unto Himself," "able to do exceeding abundantly above all that we ask or think." We face this stupendous undertaking in His name and in His might. Remember that Paul defined the Gospel in terms of power. "The Gospel," he said, "is the power of God," stupendous, magnificent power. Advancing science, wider knowledge of the universe and its laws, have given us a more and more overwhelming conviction of the mighty power of God. And we are co-workers together with God in giving the Gospel of His Son to every tribe and nation. This is our splendid task; this our inspiring privilege. Therefore, not with doubt, but with confident faith we say in the words of the familiar hymn:

> "March we forth in the strength of God
>   With the banner of Christ unfurled;
> That the light of the glorious gospel of truth
>   May shine throughout the world.
> Fight we the fight with sorrow and sin
>   To set their captives free,
> That the earth may be filled with the glory of God
>   As the waters cover the sea."

THE ADEQUATE FOREIGN MISSIONARY PROGRAM OF A DENOMINATION

THE REVEREND RALPH E. DIFFENDORFER, D.D., NEW YORK

It is becoming increasingly clear that any program adopted by any foreign mission Board or any group of Boards in America at the present time must be acceptable, at least in its method, to the great majority of our churches and the people in our churches. The day has passed, when we can adopt resolutions or frame a program in our Boards and expect that mere adoption to mean acceptability in our churches. Those of us who are concerned with the so-called cultivation of the home base are confronted today by what may be called "the rising consciousness of the churches in America." In order that any program of foreign mission effort for a denomination in the future may become an expression of the normal Christian life of our people and our churches, it must be promoted, I think, throughout our denominations, not so much in a series of speeches, as through a series of round-table conferences for the interchange of opinion and for the reaction of mind upon mind, until it has been accepted.

What I have to say this morning looks toward that method of procedure, and that only. There is time here merely to outline what is in my own mind with reference to the foreign mission situation in the decade ahead of us.

First, the foreign mission Boards must lead off in a new study and a continual study of the foreign mission motive. This is fundamental. Our methods of work throughout the world, our approach to our home constituencies, our relationship to our national Christians, in fact, our whole program will depend upon the motive of our foreign mission effort. There was a time when people said that the Gospel must be preached to the whole world, because it was commanded that it should be done, and many people today are moved by this worthy motive. Once, compassion and pity, especially to save people from the wrath to come, was a very compelling motive for the preaching of the gospel to the non-Christian world. There may be some people still who are moved by that motive. There was a time when the desire to be of help or of service to the world was a very compelling motive to many people, and this is true even in our own day. I am sorry to say, however, that, in the words of one of our nationals yesterday, the service motive is sometimes tinged with what he called "an offensive superiority complex," that makes it difficult for us to proceed in these days with just that kind of motive.

Today we must raise for discussion, and have accepted by our people, a motive that rests squarely upon love. Christian love recognizes the worthwhileness, the inherent value of every man throughout the world in his own right and in his own name, not because of any country or any race or of any color, but because through his nostrils there is breathed the breath of the living God. In our preaching Jesus Christ to every creature and to all creation we are releasing forces hitherto unrecognized by the world, forces that can cooperate with us in establishing the world-wide brotherhood of righteousness and love.

This is the only motive, too, that will satisfy the leaders who are now arising in the new churches of the non-Christian world, who themselves desire in their own way to help in the work of bringing in a Christian world.

Now the chief responsibility for studying these motives, for discussing them with our people and for proclaiming them to our churches rests upon the foreign mission Boards. This duty cannot be left to others, and we must proceed in all of our educational and programizing processes with this very fundamental responsibility defnitely in mind.

In the next place (and answering many people who think that our foreign mission task is finished), the facts as they come to us from the world field show that there are still many unoccupied regions and many millions of people, who have not yet a single witness of Jesus. And as in former days so now, any adequate foreign mission program must take into account these untouched groups. However, in times past, we have programized these untouched groups almost entirely in terms of geography as "unoccupied territory." While I do not desire to minimize this conception, keeping in mind especially the hinterlands of South America and of the continents of Asia and Africa, yet we should realize that when the geographical frontiers are broken down, it amounts to little if we have agents of Christ in territories throughout the world, where the minds of the people are closed against us, and where whole groups in these so-called open countries have not yet been touched by the gospel message. In other words, our "unoccupied territory" has become more than territory. It is untouched groups and non-Christian phases of social living that must be won for Jesus Christ. In the future we will choose our noblest young men and women and send them forth to preach the gospel, and they will go with a conception of the gospel that can be proclaimed to all groups of men and will touch all phases of human living.

A third factor, in an adequate foreign mission program for a denomination is very akin to the second. The first two points have been commonly accepted by us; the third one may not be so clear. The time has now come when the foreign mission Boards of North America must make it an avowed part of their program to see to it that our contacts with the non-Christian world are all Christian. By this, I mean that it is the concern of foreign mission Boards that our race relations shall be Christian, and that every vestige of race prejudice in America and throughout the world is eliminated. It is of concern to us to know whether the governments are proceeding in their mandates to exploit the weaker peoples of the world. It is of prime concern to us that in our industrial and political contacts throughout the world the gospel of Jesus shall be predominant and preeminent, and that these contacts shall be Christian in every sense of the word. We will not be justified in the future in sending our messengers into the world only to have their messages neutralized by these un-Christian contacts. Therefore, I plead that we shall, from now on, take it as a legitimate, normal part of our foreign mission program in America to insist with all of our power and with all of the strength of our massed forces that the agents of so-called Christian nations throughout the world shall be Christian indeed.

Furthermore, in the fourth place, we must have the cooperation of all the agencies concerned. This note has been sounded
many a time in this gathering and I am only mentioning it in
passing. We certainly cannot make any plans for the unevangelized
groups of the world, and face the last problem which I have just
mentioned, that of making all our contacts Christian, unless we
approach them in a united way. Just as in all the sessions of this
convention, there has been so little of that denominational consciousness to mar our unity, so from its close let us go to our
various Boards united on every phase of this work, until we
make an impact upon the world that is really felt. These cooperative relationships will extend beyond our foreign mission
groups. The more I study the task, the more I feel that the program of foreign missions is interrelated to our home missionary
problem. It is certainly intricately related to the work of our
educational institutions and to our whole system of religious education in America.

For instance, what a challenge of Christian opportunity there
is in our educational institutions today with the presence of hundreds, yes, thousands of foreign students? What type of friendliness do they find? We can handle this problem of friendship,
however, if we will only go about it in the right way through
the introduction of these students into Christian homes. We
ought to be concerned, though, with the teaching they are receiving, the philosophy of life they are getting, and the examples of
Christian living with which they are surrounded, for while we
are sending our tens and tens as missionaries throughout the
world, there go from our American institutions every year, hundreds of these well-trained students from Oriental lands, who
are in a real sense missionaries of what America has to teach and
to say.

If, today, I desired to place my finger upon one matter important for the future of foreign missions, I would like to say
to the presidents and the deans and the professors of every educational institution in America, that the days for the minimizing
of religion and the days for the ridicule of the spiritual life in
the class room and on the campus are gone and gone forever!
There is no justification at all for our thinking that foreign missions is an unrelated problem that stands off to one side in our
denominational life. There is no hope of our making an impact
upon the complex and the closely-knit social world of this day,
unless it is a definite part of our program that all Christian agencies
are linked together in certain, common tasks.

The fifth factor in an adequate foreign mission program of
a denomination arises out of our relations with the national
churches. Some plan must be developed in our basic ecclesiastical

policies, as well as in our normal foreign mission and social contacts, for cooperation with these national churches. There is a chance now for us to swing too far to the left with reference to this matter. It has been an avowed purpose of foreign missions that we should go to the mission fields and help to establish the church as a Christian agency. Now we are coming to realize (and may it increase too!) that we must gradually withdraw ourselves, especially from all administrative positions.

The kind of cooperation to which I refer is not the cooperation of supervision, nor is it the cooperation of withdrawal. There is as much danger in the latter, as there is in the former. But, a new problem is arising for us to work out in the basic organization of our church and ecclesiastical life; that is, a plan by which we may cooperate with these rising churches, and link their forces, newly released, with ours, in order that we may bring in the Kingdom of God.

This is one of our most difficult program factors, as we think of the organization of what is technically called the "Mission" on the field, and its relation to the groups of national churches. Such a plan of cooperation goes to the very heart of our ecclesiastical life in North America. It is just as important also that the churches upon the mission field should understand this point of view. It is one of the great opportunities of foreign mission agencies, in a world knit together as ours is today, to promote plans for cooperation between the Japanese churches and the Chinese churches and between the Chinese churches and the Indian churches, and between the Indian churches and the African churches and between the African and the European churches and the Latin-American churches. It is a problem which nothing else than a great united movement like an International Christian Council can possibly undertake and solve for us.

Those who are studying the great currents of life around the world and especially the great migrations of peoples, are feeling acutely that there are points of contact which only the churches of the non-Christian lands can possibly make. Think of East Africa and the Indian migration; of the problems in Argentina and Uruguay and Chile and other Latin-American countries with reference to Europe, and those of the islands of the South Seas in relation to the Chinese churches and elsewhere. This was brought very forcibly to our attention yesterday when a group talked about using Christian negroes from the West Indies to evangelize the Indian population of Central America. In a sort of maze these relationships rise up before us and demand the greatest statesmanship and the most far-sighted policies on our part, as we present to our candidates, our missionaries and our ecclesiastical officers throughout the world this great big world-family conception of the Christian churches of the world united in a common task.

The last point, which it seems to me is the most important of all for this day, is the need of a very greatly enlarged program of missionary education and of a very greatly enlarged conception of missionary education. Some of us who have been studying these problems for many years feel that our missionary education has come to a crisis in its development and must be seen in perspective once more, in order that it may be related to these new needs that are now arising in the programizing policies of the Boards.

There was a time when missionary education consisted pretty largely in telling people about the land, the people, the government, the history, the early missionaries and the present policies and the outlook for Christian work. Each book had just seven or eight chapters, written uniformly about all the countries. Many of these facts are now the common talk of our leaders and our people, the information being available through many other agencies than our own. We have come now to a place where our great missionary enterprises, especially foreign missions, should be related to these great currents of religious thought that are now running through the world, and those great vital religious interests that are stirring the multitudes of people everywhere and out of which there is a deep longing that a new world will be born. There is a relation between war and foreign missions, and it is for us, the leaders of the foreign missionary enterprise, to interpret that relationship to our people in the biggest missionary education movement that we have ever undertaken. Race relations have a relation to our foreign mission enterprise and it is for us, the most vitally interested group in all this country, to interpret race relations of a Christian sort to the people of America.

It is for us to study the problems of economic imperialism, and not to confine the study to some one curtained in some far away office, but bring them out in the open, so that the great mass of public opinion can be brought to bear upon them, in order that we may not have our messages neutralized anywhere in the world by these problems and policies of government. When economic imperialism becomes a policy of any free government, it is the right and duty of such peoples to urge that the policy be so administered as to yield justice and righteousness in these relationships. In the same manner our educational program will relate foreign missions to the exploitation of natural resources of weak peoples for private or corporate gain, and to the spread of modern industry.

Miss Burton, last night, proposed that we secure a certain well-trained type of missionaries to deal with these problems, but I cannot see that in a world of international and industrial relationships, we can depend on a small group of missionaries and of weak churches upon the field to grapple with this question. There may come a day when you and I will have to be discriminating about the things we buy, using a sort of union label of international significance, in order that we may get right industrial relations throughout the world. Our missionary education must reach out into these new fields, and our immediate problem is to integrate these great living vital issues before the world, with our foreign mission policies and programs.

In closing, I think we must go one point further. The foreign mission agencies have the opportunity to interpret the life of God to the world and especially to our people at home, so that He will be to them a missionary God. The God that many of our people worship does not lift them beyond their own confines. The fatherhood of God and the brotherhood of man are not vitally related to race problems and industrial conflicts, and to world-wide international relations. Our God is a comfortable God. To many He is a God of enlightened self-interest. There is no group in America upon whom the responsibility rests, as upon this group of foreign mission students and leaders, to interpret the universality of God and of the provisions of His gospel, and to extend our vision and enlarge our sympathies.

It may easily be seen that from my point of view the foreign mission task is far from finished. It will not be finished in the coming decade or quarter of a century. I see in it an enlarging, and ever enlarging program, until the churches of Christ all over the world are united in one common endeavor for the establishing and maintenance of justice, peace and good-will among all the races and nations of men.

THE ADEQUATE FOREIGN MISSIONARY PROGRAM IN A CONGREGATION

THE REVEREND S. W. HERMAN, D.D., HARRISBURG, PENNSYLVANIA

Since I began to think upon this theme, phrased as it is, one word has haunted me day and night. I speak truthfully. That word has been "adequate." Most of us have some sort of a program in our congregations along missionary lines, but when tested by this word "adequate," we do not feel satisfied with any program which we have been using.

An adequate program of foreign missions in the local congregation is a theme to challenge our thought and mind today. However we may have evaded the direct issues and thrusts of some of the previous addresses, here there is no chance to dodge. Every last delegate here belongs to some congregation, and we may advisedly ask ourselves at this moment, in relation to this great question, the striking question:

"What kind of a congregation would my congregation be,
If every member were just like me?"

The heart-searching quest for each one of us in this hour ought to be in relation to the congregation with which we are identified. Thousands of congregations are represented here in this great convention. They are the units upon which the denominational Boards depend for the carrying on of their work. What would be the significance of all that preceding speakers have said and said so marvelously and challengingly, if what they said cannot be referred directly to the congregations involved and received sympathetically by them.

Some one in a heart-searching moment decided to make some sort of an analysis of conditions in his congregation. He tried for one year to determine certain percentages. He discovered that about fifty per cent of his congregation attended services; that about eighty per cent of his congregation came to the communion at least once a year; that about eighteen per cent or less were regular contributors to the budget of current expenses and benevolences of the church.

I should like to have this question considered honestly and sincerely and truthfully answered. "What is the percentage of efficiency in my congregation in relation to an adequate program for foreign missions?" Am I wrong when I say that I believe not ten per cent of the congregations represented by the Boards here have any adequate program for foreign missions? If it still is true that the most imperative command of our Lord Jesus Christ was to go and teach every creature and baptize them in the Name of the Father and of the Son and of the Holy Ghost—if that is true, then what must be the measurement of our efficiency when this can be safely said?

I pause just long enough for each of you to think over your congregation in the light of the knowledge which has fairly deluged us in these days of this great convention. The past ought not to hold us; the future demands our most careful consideration and attention now. For my remaining period, I desire to state certain things that I believe ought to be in every adequate program adopted by any congregation of any denomination.

In the first place, there must be perfect sympathy and cooperation on the part of a congregation with the great program announced by the denominational boards. We have heard denominational Board secretaries declare that the great difficulty has been that congregations, as such, seem to have no interest in studying the whole question from the standpoint of the Board; that the congregations were only too willing, without making any very great effort to enter into an understanding of the principles and methods of the Board, to criticize most bitterly and destructively its efforts to carry on their great work. You have noted the tremendous sweep which was presented in the viewpoint and from the viewpoint of the Boards of this great question. Was there a heart here unthrilled by such a demanding call to an understanding and an undertaking surpassing all understandings and undertakings of any other department of human activity?

The second thing I should like to emphasize is the necessity of making a most constructive effort in every congregation to develop a thorough educational program that will cover the whole field of the foreign missionary enterprise. It would be a very easy thing for any of us to go into an average congregation of any denomination and submit that congregation to an examination upon their fields of activity, the types of work carried on in the fields, the personnel in the fields, the finished product, if you will, of the fields. You could safely predict that in the replies to such an examination ten per cent correct answers would be a liberal estimate. The time has come when the church needs to approach this whole question from a constructive educational standpoint. Into every department of the church's activity must come this educational process along foreign mission lines.

There came back to our shores sometime since a young missionary upon his first furlough, his face aglow, his heart eager to tell his story. Six months after he had returned I happened to meet him. The change was pathetic. His eyes seemed dull; his heart seemed broken. This was his explanation: "I can't believe it, I can't believe it. The home church seems so utterly indifferent, so utterly unmindful of the great work of foreign missions, there is no adequate response, no adequate appreciation of the great privilege of carrying on this, the greatest work that God has given."

I wonder how many of our missionaries on furlough would echo those tragical words of that young missionary who, as he went back to his field, said he hoped to go back and stay and die and be buried among the people that he loved and that Jesus loved.

There is a partial explanation. The explanation comes through the lack of information. We do not rebuke unduly or criticize too severely that vast number of men and women who have not entered into an appreciation of the values in the great literature of our centuries, seeing that they can't read, never having been instructed. Why should we be unduly severe upon great masses of our Christian folk who have never been taught concerning these great fundamental matters pertaining to the advancing of the Kingdom of God in the hearts of men everywhere throughout the world?

I should like to suggest that the only adequate program in my congregation must take into consideration the education of the little children, and the boys and the girls, and the men and women in every department and organization of the church's activity. Let us, for a little while, forget this eternal struggle to have the best preachers or the best choir or the best church building or to be most successful in promoting social activities, or this or that or the other thing, and get down to the business of the church of the Lord Jesus Christ at home.

Now, to the third point; I do not believe that there can be any adequate missionary program in any local congregation until there has been an adequate stress of the great fundamental principles which have to do with the conservation of spiritual resources. It seems to me that there must be established in the congregation a real effort to have folks appreciate their Christian resources, a new appreciation of faith, faith that will lead men, as we heard last night, to die, a new appreciation of the power of prayer, that great lever that will lift the whole world up to God and marvelously lift us out of ourselves to meet the great requirements that God has put upon us—a new appreciation of the values of prayer, a new appreciation of the values of life service.

Twenty-eight thousand foreign missionaries are at work, but in one segment of my denomination, in 1917, more than that number of young people responded to the call of their country, willing to lay down their lives at once, if need be, for the sake of what they believed to be great principles. In the whole denomination ten times the number of the whole group of missionaries representing the Christian Church on the foreign lands responded to that call. What is each church doing to challenge our young manhood and young womanhood to give themselves in full-time service to the cause of the Kingdom?

I attended a church meeting some time since, at which there was a tendency to boast of their one hundred years of congregational history. I said, "Tell me how many men and women have you sent into the Christian ministry and into the service of Christ in your one hundred years?" They said, "Not one." What a chance there is for a program in that congregation. There needs to be an adequate stress upon the resources of substance that are commanded by the Christian forces of this land. How our hearts thrilled when we learned of that great railroad down through Africa, three hundred million dollars expended, two millions of men giving their services for years, mountains lowered, rivers drained, bridges built, to get at three billion dollars' worth of raw materials in Africa. In Africa one soul is worth more than all material resources.

Just one more fact. Each congregation to have an adequate foreign missionary program ought to support a missionary or missionaries, an evangelist or evangelists, a catechist or catechists, a teacher or teachers, a protege or proteges, thus linking up in a living way with this great enterprise in the foreign field. What a dignity and sanctity will be given to the work of the congregation when it realizes that it is working at an adequate program and that this program is going on to larger things.

Originally the request was made to me, "Will you tell of the experience and ideals of a pastor?" Let the experience go, but the ideal is this: that the congregation that we are privileged to serve shall always be proclaiming the gospel of the Lord Jesus Christ, every hour of every day in some part of the world.

May I use in closing, the figure of speech somewhat transformed as used by Professor Jones last night? I am thinking of the great Son of God, symbolized in this great sun, that Sun of righteousness who shines so magnificently and so gloriously and so savingly everywhere. I am thinking of the moon, that great body that shines with reflected light and lifts with its tremendous power great plateaus of water. I am thinking of that great body of foreign missions that shines by the reflected light of the Lord Jesus Christ. I am thinking of this great body of foreign missions, lifting up all of these congregations represented here, and all of these Boards, lifting them up out of their narrowness, out of their selfishness, out of their miserliness, out of all the things that bind and constrict, and churning them into a great passion of love that will send them dashing everywhere throughout the world, until every coast shall be touched, every valley, and every hill shall be inundated with this great passion of love for Jesus Christ and for our fellowmen.

I challenge you, members of congregations, to take this living gospel of the living Christ to dying souls by means of all the agencies and instrumentalities in your power lying respondent and potential.

THE LAYMAN'S RESPONSIBILITY FOR THE FOREIGN MISSIONARY MOVEMENT

MR. ROBERT A. DOAN, COLUMBUS, OHIO

As laymen we dare not consider the introduction of Christianity into foreign countries as a mere business proposition. Vastly more of a selling proposition is involved in foreign missions than in the sale of Sun Maid raisins, Camel cigarettes or Westinghouse electric bulbs. The salesmanship methods used in disposing of these commodities in the crowded areas of the world could be studied with profit by those engaged in foreign missions. But when one is asked to discuss the layman's responsibility for the foreign missionary movement one is compelled to go far deeper than the consideration of advertising methods or the spending of money for propagation purposes.

For more than a year I have lived among peoples of various races and nationalities whose only estimate of Christianity is that which they form by observing those who call themselves Christians. Most of these peoples I have visited repeatedly in the past ten years. Their countries are being asked to accept a new religion. They see no reason for accepting a purely foreign doctrine. They will never be induced to embrace Christianity until, if ever, they observe that it is a life and not a mere dogma. I was startled at a banquet of Christian men in India, when one of them remarked in an after-dinner speech in which he was sending a message to Christians in America, "Tell them that what they are, we want to become." Involuntarily my heart cried, "No, no, not what we are." Quite in contrast to the complimentary message that earnest Christian would send to you are the words of an Indian quoted at the Glasgow Student Conference in January, 1921. "What bewilders the alien observer is not the occasional aberrations of the Christian nations, but their habitual conduct and organization; not their failures, but their standard of success; not their omission to live up to right principles, but their insistence that wrong principles are right. Your creed is exalted, but your civilization is a nightmare of envy, hate and uncharitableness. I would forego the former in order to escape the latter." Honesty compels an approach to this theme from the standpoint of the genuineness or the falsity of our own Christianity.

1. *Practicing Christianity at home is more essential than preaching it abroad.*—Sending missionaries to other lands is a crazy proposition, unless we admit that the teachings of Christ which they carry have never been literally lived by any nation. We would do well, then, to consider the Christian layman's duty today as a citizen of his own nation and of the world.

Our world today is suffering from too much national sensitiveness. Every nation is "touchy." All of us seem obsessed with the determination to stand on our rights. Nations of power are full of self-conceit. I was in China recently when that nation observed the annual holiday known as "humiliation day." It was for the purpose of reminding the Chinese of the injustice done them by a nation which thought only of itself. I have just spent three months in India, where many claim that the ruling power considers only its own welfare. A month in the Philippines reveals very clearly the intensity with which some of the citizens claim unjust restraint on the part of the United States. In like manner we might call the roll of nations around the world and discover similar conditions. In the light of the sensitive temper and strain in which we find the world today, I ask you in shame what influence we may expect to exert as laymen in the foreign mission program of our church, when our own Congress passes an immigration law made possible by our false assumption that we have a right to do as we please in our own country without due consideration of others? I was in Japan when that act was passed. It was impossible to explain to the Japanese why an ideal religion of love which had entered the United States with its first settlers had so failed. The program of foreign missions in your church and mine is useless, until Christian laymen rid themselves of a race prejudice which often amounts to hatred. I am not speaking abstractly. I have encountered multiplied instances among men in the United States and abroad who are called Christians who deny all Christ's teaching about love by their attitude toward foreign people.

I do not attempt to discuss the merits of the claims and counterclaims of the various nations. But the spirit back of them all—both on the part of those who claim injustice and on the part of those who may be furnishing the occasion for such a claim— is essentially selfish. The spectacle of the contending nations of today has never been duplicated in history outside of actual war. Our travels in the past year not only reveal this supersensitive condition between nations, but also make clear the intensely selfish attitude between groups within each nation itself. Perhaps the most notable example of this is the failure of the non-cooperation movement in India to see in advance that there are certain irreconcilable elements in the population which will prevent any united movement as long as those differences exist. The world is drunk with a desire for selfish power. There is an almost entire forgetfulness of the rights of others. I tremble and search my own heart again, when Tagore in his arraignment of Western civilization says, "The bartering of your higher aspirations of life for profit and power has been of your own free choice, and I leave you there, at the wreck of your own soul, contemplating your protuberant prosperity . . . The West has been systematically petrifying her moral nature in order to lay a solid foundation for her gigantic abstractions of efficiency."

What is our duty? As citizens of the world we must be on the alert that loyalty to our own country does not obscure our belief as Christians that we belong to a common brotherhood. We hear the expression "family of nations" frequently these days, but what a quarrelsome family it is. Every true Christian layman must dedicate his life to the purpose, not of *proclaiming* that all in the world are brothers, but by *living* in his own nation as though he believes it. In order to do this we must oppose powerful influences. Some time ago, one of the big newspapers in this country said, "The churches have wisely, we think, interpreted the sayings of

Christ as ideals for the inspiration and comfort of man, as ideals toward which we strive and hope the race will some day attain. . . . But the altruism of Christ would have destroyed those who adopted it literally, and its very survival has been conditioned upon its limitation in practice."

Such a statement is a menace and it is untrue. Literal adherence to the ideals of Christ may cost life. It has done so in the past, beginning with Jesus Himself. But it did not destroy Christianity. The statement that the survival of Christianity has depended upon the limitation of the practice of its ideals is as dangerous a doctrine as the devil could devise. Our adherence to Christ compels us to accept a world brotherhood regardless of race; otherwise we are not Christians.

We must believe that it is possible for such love as Christ taught to prevail in the world today, or we must admit that our Christianity is but another religion of fine phrases which mean nothing in this practical day. Let us not be misguided into believing that in these days of abominable world politics, Christianity is too ideal. Let us prove it is not, or die in the attempt.

Our participation as laymen in the missionary program of the church is in vain, unless upon every possible occasion we encourage and commend those who stand boldly and courageously against anything of an un-Christian character that would offend another nation. We need, what Dr. Hodgkin calls in his "Christian Revolution" a converted nationalism. There is a great encouragement in the increasing boldness of those who believe in the redemption of the world from war by the adoption of ideals that are essentially Christian. Our program in the church for foreign missions compels the acceptance of some such position as outlined by Dr. Fosdick in the introduction to Kirby Page's book on war. He says: "But this I do see clearly: that war is the most colossal and ruinous social sin that afflicts mankind today; that it is utterly and irremediably un-Christian; that the war system means everything which Jesus did not mean; and means nothing that He did mean; that it is a more blatant denial of every Christian doctrine about God and man than all the theoretical atheists on earth could ever devise. What I do see is that quarrels between fundamentalists and liberals, high churchmen and low churchmen, are tithing mint, anise and cummin, if the church does not deal with this supreme moral issue of our time: Christ against War."

Above all else, then, let us as laymen understand that our part in any foreign missionary program of the church is a farcical performance, if we deny the ideals of Jesus by our denial in practice of a world brotherhood. We must quickly prove we believe in that idealism, or we shall prove on the other hand, to the non-Christian world at least, that H. L. Mencken was right in his indictment of

Christianity in the "American Mercury" for November. His concluding sentences were these: "Christianity is sick all over this pious land. The Christians have poisoned it. One blast upon a bugle horn and the mob will be ready for the wake."

2. *If our Christianity is worth carrying to China or Japan or India it must be inclusive.* The day is rapidly passing, when laymen may be stirred to any sacrificial depths upon a plea for denominational supremacy or rivalry. In the past I have heard secretaries or missionaries plead for the establishment of work in certain centers with the argument that, if it were not done quickly, some other denomination might enter. Not alone in America, but in other lands have I listened to the arrogant assumption of superiority on the part of some denominationalist for his own sect.

We laymen will be moved as little by that kind of an appeal as we are by the statement of some partisan that every county seat in America must have a church of our denomination. Such appeals no longer grip. I favor denominational loyalty only when it considers itself a part of the whole of Christianity. I could as easily be loyal to Ohio and disloyal to the United States, as I could be a partisan for my own denomination to the exclusion of the greater movement of Christianity. Last summer in Japan I heard a Japanese speaking of the work of his own denomination. One reason he gave for its lack of success was that they had too readily given way to other denominations in the observance of Christian comity. So easily does our narrowness spread!

I want to be clearly understood at this point. I believe in working through existing organizations, because I have seen the folly of individual or unorganized effort. But I believe laymen as spiritual stockholders in these organizations should have a voice in shaping the way in which our Boards should work. When you make your investment in time or money or influence, you do wrong, if you do not see to it that what you invest goes to enlarge the spirit of Christ in the hearts of men, and not to build a denomination.

Where was the influence of the Christian laymen of Canada and the United States, when it became apparent that neither the Boards in those countries nor the Christians in Japan intended to make a united move for the cooperative planning of all Christian work in Tokyo and Yokohama following the earthquake? I witnessed that disheartening spectacle in Japan, when those with a vision of unity out of the disaster waited with eagerness, but in vain, for encouragement from the Boards which would make it possible for them to get together. I cannot believe, I do not want to believe, that our theological differences obscured our vision of an expectant Christ, as He waited amid the ruins of those great cities for the beginning of the fulfillment of His prayer that we might all be one.

So far as I know, not a single union Christian enterprise has emerged from the earthquake. I am pleading for more than organic union, though I believe that must come. I am pleading with every atom of strength I possess that a common faith in Christ be our test of fellowship everywhere in the world. As long as there is a divided church, Christianity must linger on the edges of the distracted, restless masses of the races of the earth. There can be no peace, no surcease of spiritual sorrow and pain, no social deliverance, no redemption of a people for Christ, so long as Christianity hugs to itself the delusion that a house divided against itself can stand.

As laymen, we must study for ourselves and impart to others the new situation in lands where religions other than Christianity prevail. For the first time in any serious way, those whom their own religions have failed to satisfy are making comparisons with Christianity. No delusions about so-called Christian countries any longer exist. All religions, including Christianity, are under scrutiny. Along with this investigative study comes the demand from other peoples to be allowed to try each religion in their own way. That reasonable request must be heeded by Christianity. Christ must be set free in the lives of Christians in these lands, to whom He is speaking with a startling clearness. Sectarianism must give way to Him. This new situation is saving the faith of many of us in Christian missions. It is the light of a new day which cannot be hidden. We are recognizing as belonging to the nationals many of the prerogatives we have too long egotistically held as our own. Let us form a great world comradeship with the lovers of our Lord everywhere, but let us cease to be dictators.

3. *A daring but not a blind faith will be the motivation for the layman's participation in foreign missions in the days ahead.* Just above the horizon of the dawning of a new day in Christian experience, I can see the beginning of an intelligent interest in foreign missions on the part of the laymen of our churches. It is an interest born of a fuller conception of the commission to "go." Perhaps it has for its basis a gradual realization that they have borne the name of Christ, while they have fed upon the husks of unworthy ambitions. Not a large group of Christ's men are seeing clearly as yet, but the awakening has begun. There are certain things which must be heeded by those now interested in the foreign missions enterprise if they would see this mighty dynamic of a layman's revival properly directed. The foreign missions program must be conducted along broad lines. These laymen will not be interested merely in saving souls from hell. They will insist that the example of Jesus who healed and fed and comforted people on the spot, regardless of their religion or race, be followed. Theirs will be a faith which will be so deeply spiritual that they will dare

anything, but its foundation will be practicality. They will be interested in bringing men into comradeship with Christ in a real, personal relationship, rather than in securing them as subscribers to a particular interpretation of what Jesus or His Apostles may have said. (I have spent ten years in closely studying foreign missions first-hand and can hardly be accused of speaking hastily or thoughtlessly.)

This breaking of a new day already reveals much for which many hearts are praising God. It is eliminating our conception of all those of other religions as ignorant "heathen." It is helping us to recognize that they have some light from God which need not be destroyed, in order that the master light may shine in. It is even discovering to us that they are able to reveal to us some spiritual depths which in our religious arrogance we had not seen. I think the laymen will demand that any interpretation of God which is taken to other lands by Christians shall be in line with that expressed years ago by that prophetic missionary to Japan, John H. DeForrest, when he said: "We are learning that the word of God is of no use until it is interpreted, first into the thought of the age, and, second, into the living experience of those who teach it. Any revelation of God is powerless until it is the discovery of man. . . . Whatever in the Bible helps me . . . to see God in the lives of others in all churches—Catholic, Greek, Protestant—in all nations, whatever the color of the people, makes my message great, deepens my sympathies with these peoples of the East, because they are God's dear children, is to me inspired. Inspiration is intensely personal."

This great brotherhood which the Christian men of the West desire to bring to humanity in all the world is beginning to manifest itself in its wider implications. My heart leaped with a spiritual joy, such as I have not often felt, when I read in the newspapers a few days ago of the gift of $1,600,000 by a Christian layman for the re-establishment of the library of the Imperial University of Tokyo. I thanked God that a man who professes to follow Christ should contribute of his wealth to enable the youth of Japan to have access to the books of the world. Well does he know that Christianity must bear the investigation of all published knowledge, if it is to endure. He was not deterred from this kindly act by the challenge sent to the missionaries many years ago by the President of this same University in which he said, "If you want to capture Japan for Christ, you must capture this University."

What an example of unprejudiced love that gift was! It was given without restrictions to be administered by intelligent Japanese. No less abandon should be manifest in giving to Christian institutions. The laymen of our churches are bound to be moved by plans that look to the establishment of Christian enterprises that shall be controlled and managed and inspired by the nationals. With a daring faith they will follow Christ as He reveals Himself to these peoples without the hindering confusion of creeds. Foreign missions is experiencing a re-birth; and we may confidently expect an eager, intelligent participation of the laymen with a zeal not manifested when the plan was only that the heathen be saved. What a day it will be when business men will realize that the representatives they send abroad must be of such high character as to disprove the present conception held of us as selfish, brutal money-grabbers!

What a rejoicing there will be in heaven and on earth when, in the Name of Jesus, every humanitarian enterprise in the world will be supported without regard to denominational preferment! Thank God that time is approaching! Universal brotherhood can become a fact only when an international conscience fully recognizes the rights of all. And that day can come only when we have daringly demonstrated Christ's love by actually loving all mankind as He did.

Mahatma Gandhi, a Hindu, says, "My religion has no geographical limits. I have a living faith in it which will transcend even my love for India herself." Viscount Shibusawa, a Confucianist, said to me last summer, "My religion does not permit me to retaliate against the United States by a boycott." Jesus says, "Thou shalt love thy neighbor as thyself." All of these are mere declarations. We are witnessing before our very eyes the attempt of men of various religions to demonstrate their practicality in a world of hate. We must welcome the comparison, though we tremble.

I believe I represent here this morning a vast number of Christian laymen whose hearts are burning within them to show their faith by their works. They do believe Christ was sent by God as no other through the ages. They do believe He declared and lived a universal gospel. They do believe He is the world's only hope and that He must be lived, not taught. "For me to live is Christ." But, oh, my friends, the daring of their faith demands that the winning of the world shall be attempted only with the winsome personality and love of Jesus of Nazareth. They are not concerned with mere theology. They are deeply anxious because the people of the lands which are called Christian have absolutely failed to prove the genuineness of their claim, because of the way in which they have treated others. The laymen will accept the challenge. They believe Christ is supreme. The world constitutes an open court. The deeds of no land may be hidden. The day of trial is here in a world which is desperately, distractingly, feverishly seeking a Saviour. Shall it turn to Confucius, or Buddha, or Mohammed, or Christ? Let those who constitute the rank and file of Christendom answer. May that answer not be a denial of our Lord.

THE RESPONSIBILITY OF WOMAN IN THE FOREIGN MISSIONARY WORK

MRS. CHARLES KIRKLAND ROYS, FORMERLY OF CHINA

In considering woman's place in the missionary enterprise our thought may profitably center around four aspects of the subject. First: Is there for woman a peculiar driving power in the missionary movement? Secondly: What has been woman's achievement in missionary effort in the past? Thirdly: Are there elements of success in the past which should be conserved in future effort? Lastly: In the adequate foreign program of the church, what place shall be assigned to women?

That the missionary enterprise has from the beginning held a compelling interest for women needs no argument. Who should throw themselves wholeheartedly into missions, if not those who owe to Christ their very ability to espouse any cause? The peculiar driving power for women in the missionary effort lies in the determination to open up for others the life of freedom, service and endless possibility which Christ has given to them.

Consider also certain characteristics with which woman is endowed by nature; her protective, tender instincts which are aroused by accounts of suffering womanhood and unprivileged childhood—needs which only woman in her work for woman could meet; her adventuresome faith which is undaunted by distance or difficulty. Columbus would have had a poor time with his proposed voyage of discovery, had he dealt solely with men. It was a woman who believed it could be done. I ask you to think of woman's achievement in that far greater adventure of the discovery for other women of the fair land of fulness of life and freedom.

A brief historic perspective on the emergence of woman into missionary activity reveals certain significant facts: Two months before Carey baptized his first convert in India, the "Boston Female Society For Missionary Purposes" was organized, uniting Congregational and Baptist women. Twenty-five years before Perry's fleet entered the harbor of Yeddo, and thirty years before the Protestant Episcopal Church sent its first pioneer missionary to Japan, a group of women in Brookline, Massachusetts, organized and met regularly to pray for Japan and to contribute to its evangelization. In New England the early societies rejoiced in the name "Female Cent Societies," and of these not a few have existed to celebrate their jubilee.

With what consternation the men of the churches watched these doings of the women is an old story. Turning in desperaiton to his elders, one Michigan pastor implored them to see to it that an elder be designated to attend each meeting, lest the women be indiscreet enough to offer voluntary prayer. There was no telling what women might pray for, if left to themselves! A Board secretary is on record as having said to his associates, "I can not recommend bringing the women into this work." Of all these men one courageous soul stands out who staunchly maintained in the face of the other men "the help of pious females must not be spurned."

The economic condition of our country in the early part of the nineteenth century was such that money was difficult to obtain. Outside the spheres of domestic service and dressmaking there were no opportunities for women to earn money. The contributions to the missionary society, therefore, came in small amounts, and represented chiefly the profits from selling eggs or butter or rags. No more illuminating illustration of the value of small gifts from many sources can be found than is revealed in the activity of those indefatigable women who went from door to door gathering small sums for the cause.

How eloquent are the records found in the treasurers' books of that day! Consider that first legacy received by the American Board, which was given by one Sally Thomas, a domestic whose wages never went beyond half a dollar a week, but who left to that Board three hundred and forty-five dollars and eighty-three cents!

Or listen to this letter written to the Treasurer of the American Board in 1813:

> "Bath, New Hampshire
> August 17, 1813
>
> Dear Sir:
>   Mr. ——————— will deliver $177. into your hands. The items are as follows:
>
> From an obscure female who kept the money for many years for a proper opportunity to bestow it upon a religious object..... $100.
> From an aged woman in Barnet, Vermont, being the avails of a small dairy the past year................................ 50.
> From the same being the avails of two superfluous garments.... 10.
> From the Cent Society in this place, being half their annual subscription .... 11.
> From a woman in extreme indigence .... 1.
> My own donation, being the sum expended hitherto in ardent spirits in my family, but now totally discontinued........ 5.
>
> Total............ $177."

In recording the gifts of women in these early days it is only fair to make note of the fact that much of the earnings of one at least of the Cent Societies was gained from making false bosoms for the shirts of the theological students in Princeton Seminary. The only pattern the good women of the society had was for a man weighing some two hundred and fifty pounds. In the record of missionary self-sacrifice full credit should go to the poor young theologians who bought the false bosoms from the women of the missionary society and suffered the inconvenience of ill-fitting collar bands.

You will find, if you look through the record of gifts in those early days, that the name of the woman donor is often suppressed, while the name of the transmitting pastor or elder is recorded in full, as for example, "From a female friend of missions per the Rev. John Thomas Green."

There is, therefore, revealed in woman's early missionary activity a remarkable, far-seeing faith, prevailing prayer, and conspicuous self-denial. Missions held a tremendous appeal for women. Of zeal and devotion there was no lack, but there was sore need of organization and revision of methods. The Civil War called forth from the women of our land a service in hospital and barracks and home which developed as no other experience could, an organizing ability hitherto unknown. At the close of the Civil War women carried this newly-acquired ability in cooperation and in systematized effort to the unorganized missionary endeavor. Women who formerly had been content to sit at one end of the family pew and watch their husbands at the other end putting into the collection box the family contribution to the work of the church, had experienced during war years the exhilaration of handling money by themselves. They now gave themselves to organizing the finances of their own missionary societies and Boards. Those men who viewed with misgiving the activity of women in the beginning were not so stupid after all. Something had indeed been started!

The women of the churches were prepared by thirty years of prayer and effort for missions to respond at once to the appeal made in 1834 by an American missionary from China who urged them to organize and undertake the work in non-Christian lands which only women could carry. The denominational Boards stoutly resisted this dangerous innovation, and for thirty years or more prevented the organization of women's Boards. The urge to organize these Boards could not, however, permanently be held in check. Timid women who in small societies had been almost prostrated by the thought of reading aloud a portion of a missionary letter, were so inspired by the necessity of an organization of women to conduct work for women, that a perfect epidemic of woman's organizations soon occurred. In 1861 the Woman's Union Missionary Society in New York, an interdenominational organization, came into being. Other organizations soon followed, and by 1900 nearly every leading denomination had a Woman's Board. Today there are over forty Woman's Boards with a combined annual income of over six million dollars. There are an equal number of Woman's Boards of Home Missions with an annual income almost as great. The work of these Boards and the perfection of their organization is well known. The same genius which characterized woman's efforts in the realm of temperance and suffrage has organized in volunteer service a mighty host of eager, intelligent, purposeful women in community, county, state and nation. No phase of missionary activity is so justly appraised at its full value. Men and women alike are sound in their clear appreciation of it.

Consider for a moment the tremendous range of achievement of the woman's missionary societies in practically all the non-Christian lands of the earth: they hold property; rent buildings; recruit and educate thousands of evangelists, Sunday School specialists, teachers, editors, doctors and nurses; provide an educational system from kindergarten through college; maintain hospitals; staff nurses' training schools and medical colleges. In many languages they edit women's and children's magazines and publish books. The culmination of the efforts of women is found in the establishment of seven women's colleges, founded by the Woman's Boards of Scotland, England, Canada and the United States. Eighteen Woman's Boards brought to this united effort many diverse methods of organization, but one great aim inspired them all—namely the purpose to train a Christian leadership for the women of the Orient. Three million dollars was recently raised in the United States for these colleges under the able leadership of Mrs. Henry W. Peabody. The colleges are growing, enlarging their equipment and capacity; but they are holding absolutely to their Christian purpose for existence. They are Christian to the backbone.

Add to this achievement on the foreign field the conspicuous success of woman's work; first, through long years of missionary education in the home churches which now touches even the most remote corner of every State in the Union; and who can contemplate this accomplishment without asking, how is it done? Surely we can with profit ask, as we review the achievement of women, what has been the secret of the effectiveness of women in the past? I am confident that the men of the Church wish above all things to conserve the rich heritage of woman's service for missions. I am equally sure that no adequate missionary program can be carried on, unless certain features of woman's service in the past be counted among the dynamics of our missionary endeavor.

Let me be very explicit. Two facts underlie the conspicuous success of woman's work; first, through long years of indefatigable effort the women of the churches have built up a system of communication from national Board headquarters down to the most remote individual church. This unbroken continuity of function has been accomplished in a brief half century. It is so effective in its working that, like Lincoln's rat-hole, it will bear looking into! Ruthlessly to disrupt by any form of reorganization a system established by such incalculable effort and proved to be of such undeniable efficiency would be little short of madness.

The second secret of woman's success in the past is psychological. Women respond to a definite financial responsibility. They like to raise their own budgets. They enjoy a dual relationship to missions as church members and as members of the woman's organization. Any missionary program for a church which casts aside this wonder-working system of distinctive financial responsibility of women is doomed to failure. I speak for the immediate future. Personally, I am not at all convinced that the remote future may not hold a better plan. For the coming decade, however, I am confident that no adequate missionary program can be built up by the churches which disregards these two aspects of the achievements of the past. The logical masculine mind may not follow this form of argument, but it will be a sad day for missions, if the women of the Church come to feel that any form of reorganization has taken from them their distinctive responsibility, and that their task as women is done.

In most denominations a new phase of the missionary program has been reached. In several communions an entire reorganization of the Church Boards has been effected which unites men and women on equal terms in Board membership and on the staff of administrative officers. Women who in the past have shown an invincible spirit of entire consecration, and have done for the churches a monumental service without proper equipment, with inadequate salaries, and devoid of technical training, are now entering a new phase of activity, facing a wider opportunity in the work of missions. At this transitional stage, the church may well give its best thought to the subject of the partnership of men and women in this work.

There are certain attitudes in the church at large and in Boards in particular, which will ensure success in our common effort; certain others spell unmistakable failure. I am no suffragist, but I can not refrain from emphasizing certain perfectly clear elements in the situation in our churches today. Have we the courage to face all the far-reaching implications, and to make all the necessary readjustments which are involved in this partnership of men and women of which we so glibly speak? A sense of *mission* inspired the women whose past achievements we today laud. Is the church prepared to present to this generation of alert, capable young women a challenging, compelling task whose pull will be felt as much as the appeal from other fields of activity? The church must reckon with other avenues which are open to this generation of women. She must make it very clear that she has work of such vital importance and of such far-reaching influence as to call for the fullest measure of service. She must show unmistakably that to do this work young women of the highest degree of training are needed who will in turn receive the same considerations in living conditions and salary which other occupations offer. Is the opportunity for missionary work in the church today, both as administrative officers of the church Boards and as volunteer workers in the capacity of Board members and in the local Church, to be *actual* or merely *potential?*

This is no theoretic matter. The church at home and abroad must reckon with the awakened womanhood of the world. At one time we were perplexed by the modern movement among women. Now its direction and impulse are perfectly clear. The state thus far has been in advance of the church in recognizing the changed situation. Is it not curious that this should be so, when from the church came the first releasing force to womanhood? Whatever you may think of the modern movement among women, you must admit that the church fostered it. Born of my knowledge of young women and my experience in working with them, I come to you with the deep conviction that the Kingdom of God is more nearly within the reach of the church today that it ever was before, if only, *if only,* we can harness up to this missionary enterprise the boundless capacities, the trained energies, the fearlessness, the courage and the sincere desire to have a part in the big business of this generation, which characterize the young women of today. If thus far the church has failed to enlist them it is not wholly the fault of the young women; it is largely because the church has not adequately presented its task.

In the East and in Europe young women are demanding freedom to live their highest life; to develop to the utmost the powers God has given them; to make their full contribution to the life of the world. The intelligent women of the church have already turned to politics, business and international affairs. At the Institute of International Politics at Williamstown last summer, one-third of the personnel was women. Are we offering young women an adequate opportunity to do a constructive work in the church which will give scope for all their trained capabilities? Will the church awaken *in time* to the fact that this new spirit of womanhood may become an instrument for the advancement of the Kingdom of Him who chose women for his friends and shared with them his most profound spiritual truths?

Again let us be very explicit. We have talked in vague terms quite long enough. Printed reports and addresses without number theorize on this subject. We have come to the place today where we must face the fact that in working out an adequate missionary program for the church, whatever share is assigned to woman must be given her *on the satisfactory and logical basis of ability and capacity, and not on that of sex.* I plead that woman be allowed to enter that natural relationship to which Jesus called her and which the early church assigned her. If the future missionary program is to be carried through successfully, it must be done by men and women in a level partnership. We do not want a union which means merely diverting one of the separate streams into the channel of another. We want a union made necessary by the great task confronting the church today which calls for something far greater than our past achievements if the non-Christian world is to be brought to Christ. Let us speak of union as though— to pursue the figure—the two separate streams had broken their banks and must now be guided into a broader, deeper channel of life-giving water.

In the home, in professions, in church and in state, men and women are needing each other if the complete whole is to be attained. The work of neither alone is or can be wholly complete. Surely the task we are facing today is great enough to capture the imagination of men and women together. We need each other if our sympathies are to become broad enough, our courage high enough, our faith strong enough, our love deep and full enough to meet the requirement of the task in this day. We need as men and women a fresh discovery of the eternal and supreme obligation to give Christ to the world, which shall send us forth determined to stand together, each contributing his own best to the accomplishment of the enormous task to which God is calling our generation.

May He give us in this partnership a more inclusive view and a saner, broader judgment than either men or women could have working separately; and may He crown our united work with achievements and victories which could otherwise never come!

THE PASTOR'S RESPONSIBILITY FOR THE FOREIGN MISSIONARY MOVEMENT

THE REVEREND HUGH T. KERR, D.D., PITTSBURGH, PENNSYLVANIA

When William Carey went forward on his great mission he said to his supporters, "There is a gold mine in India. I will go down, but you must hold the ropes." William Carey and his little band of loyal supporters were comrades in a common crusade. He was the adventurer; they were the admiring administrators. He was the hero; they were the heralds in the home land of the new missionary program. He was the pathfinder; they were the pioneers of progress. He was the miner; they were his ministers, ministering to him in his necessity.

It can be confidently asserted that the pastor is the key to the foreign missionary program. If the light which he holds in his hand burns clear, his whole church is full of light. If it is smoking flax, his people can hardly escape being spiritually asphyxiated. I immediately hear someone say, "Of course this means just one more burden placed on the now overburdened conscience of the modern minister." It means no such thing. It means the simplification of his burden, the right adjustment of his perplexing duties. God knows there is great need for simplifying the burdens of the modern minister. "If theological seminaries," says one of our Divinity deans, "were to teach all the courses which their critics suggest, a theological student would not go out into his parish younger than Moses when he escaped from Egypt. And even thus, he would be so weakened by the cuisine of his educational house of Pharaoh, its table d'hote of political economy, political science, hypnotism, basket ball, religious pedagogy, philosophy, biology, higher criticism, practical athletics, advertising, management of moving pictures and the practice of psycho-therapeutics as to need another forty years of retirement to recover his balance of mind and a practical-minded father-in-law to assist him in leading his chosen people out of bondage."

The first thing an Indian guide does for a tenderfoot is to adjust and simplify his kit; and the first thing the missionary passion will do for the pastor is to unify his ministry. The Christian church has only one task, one program, one gospel, one great commission; and as David Livingstone said long ago, "Christianity requires perpetual propagation to attest its genuineness."

The pastor's responsibility to the missionary movement is twofold. In the first place it is the duty of the pastor to educate himself. This is a present and pressing and primary necessity. A superficial and traditional acquaintance with world problems will awaken no enthusiasm, and ignorance is not apt to be an instrument in the hands of Almighty God. In our town we are told that when college students have a night off, they toss a coin. If it turns heads they go to a dance; if it turns tails they go to the theatre; if it stands on edge they study. Sometimes it would seem with our complex church organization that the modern minister is tempted to leave the most vital thing in his ministry to precarious chance. Nothing can take the place of courageous and persistent intellectual inquiry, for the beating out of old straw is not a means of grace to him or to his people. The intellectual Renaissance which has brought in the stirring of new life to the Orient and has come in like a flood upon our own civilization has made necessary an entirely new intellectual approach to the missionary enterprise. The books of yesterday are today obsolete. The only permanent volumes on our missionary shelves are the great biographies. In the new wonderland of missions we must run and run to stay even where we once were. If a way could be devised by which the rank and file of the ministry could be supplied with the best living literature on missions, and if we could devise some way by which the ministry would study that literature, our problem would be more easily solved.

If some way could be devised by which the spirit of this convention and the report of this convention could be gotten into the hands of the pastors who are not here and who are not interested in being here, our missionary problem would be nearer solution. It is not possible for many of us to travel and see with our own eyes the miracles of modern missions. It is not always possible for hard-pressed ministers to secure the latest literature. When it is a question of a new book or a pair of new boots for John, the book has little chance. It ought to be possible for the latest literature that speaks of those currents that are sweeping around the world, to be put into the hands of our pastors. It ought to be possible for our theological seminaries to do something. It ought to be possible for our mission libraries and our Boards to do more, but in the last analysis the responsibility lies with the pastor. Denominational literature is easily available and it ought to be possible for any pastor to keep in touch with the challenging program of his church. However, it is done, it must be done, for the church will only listen to and follow the man who knows.

In the second place it is the duty of the pastor to educate his people, and this cannot be done without an educational program. This adequate program involves a fourfold challenge.

First; It challenges the pastor to a program of missionary preaching. Archbishop Temple told his students to preach twenty missionary sermons a year. That is not too many, if one is keeping in touch with the far-flung line of battle. Twenty missionary sermons a year are not too many for the pastor who is in touch with world movements today; and, above all, if he is in touch with the scriptural authority which is his only ministerial guide.

I have been following through this present year a course of study in the Acts of the Apostles, discovering under the guidance of a modern scholar that the Acts of the Apostles has a movement within it of ever-widening cycles of interest, ever-expanding, until Paul stood in the very center of imperial Rome. Each one of those cycles ended in a refrain something like this, "And so the word of the Lord grew and was magnified and many were added unto the church." Twenty will not be too many missionary sermons, if a minister is in touch with world currents. The occasion is always arising for the missionary appeal. It may be America's way with Japan, or Europe's way with opium, or the Senate's way with the International Court, or the ebb and flow of military movements in China, or the attempt of daring English adventurers to scale Mount Everest saying, "There it is, and we must catch its secret." Such knowledge challenges to a program of missionary teaching. There is nothing like teaching missions to force a minister to study. It has been my pleasure to teach three, sometimes four mission study groups each year; two of them being made up of University and College students; and I bear glad testimony to the fact that there is no task so enlarging, so broadening, so able to lift up the head and the heart of both pastor and people.

Thomas Hardy has a poem about Sir Walter Scott's monument in Edinburgh which represents the great romancer with his back turned to the old castle on the crag. He says:

> O Scotland! was it well and meetly done
> For see: he sits with head turned on the past;
> He whose imperial edict bade its last,
> While yon grey ramparts kindle to the sun.

There is nothing that will turn a pastor's face toward the East, and put both heart and hope into a congregation like being compelled to face the radiance of the sun rising in the twilight lands of the world. It is fine to have the secretaries of one's Board come with their far-reaching understanding of modern missionary problems to enlighten and instruct the people. It is always a thrill to have a missionary, direct from the field, speak with authority. It is helpful to have the specialist come with his suggestions for improving missionary methods and increasing missionary money, but I would not sell my birthright of missionary educational opportunity for any excellence of imported talent.

Second; This adequate program challenges the pastor to financial oversight. There is no question that good business sense and consecrated Christian judgment calls for the introduction of the budget system in the local church. It unifies and systematizes the benevolence of the congregation and substitutes order for opportunism. As in the days of his flesh Jesus still sits over against the treasury, and I would often take the judgment of my trustees as to a man's loyalty to Christ, rather than the judgment of my session. I speak as a Presbyterian. I am convinced, however, that the pastor who contents himself with a budget to the exclusion of the occasional challenge of a great soul-stirring appeal fails of an adequate financial program. It is the heart that presides over a man's generosities. I had in my church a Scotchman of large means who had shut out of his giving the foreign missionary quota. Scotchmen are, of course, the most generous and lavish of givers, when they do give; but the budget could not reach him. One Sunday in my sermon I called the roll of the great Scotch missionaries. Did you ever do that? It gives one a thrill to name them. Robert and Mary Moffat, David Livingstone, Alexander McKay, Robert Laws, Mary Slessor. You can hardly get out of Africa. Alexander Duff of India, Robert Morrison and William Burns of China, John G. Paton and James Chalmers and an almost endless host, and when it was over the silver cords were loosed and the golden bowl oer-flowed.

Do not, however, shut out of your congregation the missionary who has come home with a passion in his heart to tell his story. Do not shut out of your pulpits the secretaries who come with an authoritative word about the program of our world, for some heart may be touched and your budget will be more than expanded. The resources of the Christian Church have hardly been touched by any budget yet devised. The wealth of the United States in 1900 was estimated at 88,000 millions. Today it is 321,000 millions, and a pastor must have undoubted courage to claim for the Kingdom the crown rights of his Lord.

Thirdly; This adequate program of education challenges the pastor to prayer. In the days of his flesh, the Lord Jesus fed the great multitude with five barley cakes and a couple of fish. He did it. That is the only miracle recorded by all four evangelists and it is significant. It made a deep impression on the disciples. The resources of the early churches were terribly and tragically inadequate, but in all their problems they heard the mandate of Jesus "Bring them hither to me." In His hands meagre resources are magnified. Everything depends on keeping Jesus Christ in the center of our programs; because for love of Him our people will do and dare anything.

The missionary motive through the years has had a changing emphasis. Once it was pity for the great multitude that plunged hourly over the dark precipice into eternity. Today it is fear, and it presses upon us from all sides, racial fear, fear of the possible rising tide of color, economical and industrial fear, fear lest the great surplus of raw material in Asia and Africa and the unlimited supply of cheap labor may in time slow down the wheels of our own industrial life, political and military fear, fear of the arming millions of the East who can count hundreds to our units. How terribly and tragically inadequate are all such motives! A time limit might be set to every one of them. One does not need to know intimately non-Christian lands to be fired with missionary zeal. One needs to know Christ and to hold the deathless conviction that He is able to save unto the uttermost. It was this motive that was sufficient for the great path finders of our challenging enterprise.

Sometime ago I came on a news item in the daily press stating that the British War Commission had finished its task, and in reporting to Parliament had stated that almost the whole world was bound by an iron band of British soldier graves. Starting from the homeland, that line of patriot graves passed over the channel to Flanders and France, across Italy, touching Greece at Saloniki and Asia Minor at Gallipoli, passing through Syria and the Holy Land and Egypt, passing down through Turkey and the Mesopotamia Valley to India, across to China, Australia, Samoa, across the wide Pacific to Canada, and passing across Canada out into the stormy Atlantic, beneath whose waves sleep the brave who for love of country considered their lives not dear unto themselves. When I read that story, I began to visualize another world-encircling chain of graves; the graves of the heroes who loved Christ and gave themselves for Him. Beginning with our own land we think of the graves of John Eliot and David Brainerd and of the nameless Jesuit missionaries of the great interior. One recalls Neesima with his wooden cross in Japan, and Morrison in China and Chalmers in New Guinea and Carey in India and Henry Martyn and Ian Keith Falconer in Arabia and Shedd in Persia and Hannington in Africa. You can stand in the silence of Westminster where sleeps the dust of the immortal Livingstone and then pass out into the great deep under the waves of which rests the body of Judson and think of his lonely wife standing on the shore of Burma saying, "All this I do for my Lord." Concerning them all it can be said, "For the love of their Lord they did it." The devotion to Jesus Christ that sends men and women to the ends of the earth and keeps them there is the only adequate motive to inspire the churches to send them and to keep them there. It is that burning and shining light held aloft in the pulpit that alone can light the path to triumph, and when that light burns true, missionary education, missionary recruiting, missionary budgets will all be adequate for the business of the Kingdom.

NORTH AMERICAN CHRISTIANS AND WORLD MISSIONS

THE REVEREND WILLIAM P. SCHELL, D.D., NEW YORK

There are four things that we North American Christians— Canadians and Americans have to give to the world, the world about which we have been hearing, for which we all are praying and in which many who hear me are working.

The first I would name is *peace and good will toward men*. There are no two countries in the world, joined together by an imaginary boundary as we are, in which there is more peace and goodwill toward men than in Canada and the United States at the present hour.   From New Brunswick to British Columbia, Canada has peace and goodwill within her own borders.   From Maine to California we have.   When we speak of the boundary between the two countries, we are speaking of an imaginary boundary, for in the spiritual service world of Jesus Christ there is no boundary between the United States and Canada and there never will be.

Peace and goodwill toward men was the first note of the gospel, announcing the coming of our Lord into the world.   It is the basis of the foreign missionary enterprise, and without it I do not see how we can ever hope to Christianize the world. It has been said to me several times during this Convention that it seemed to the person who made the remark a little out of place that there should have been any reference to war. For my part I think that if there had not been any reference to war this Convention would have met in vain.   If there is any place where we ought to speak of war it is at a foreign missions Convention.   I am going to refer to it just briefly from one angle.   I have a little girl not yet four years old; she has never heard of the World War. There are some blessings, my friends, not vouchsafed to you and me in this world.   If I should try to tell her of that war she would not have the slightest idea what I was talking about, for on the slate of her infant mind no one has ever written with any chalk the words, "war," "slaughter," "bombs," "trenches," "bayonets" or "poison gas," and I hope and pray that those words will never be written on her heart or mine.   We must admit today that whether we are to have a warless world or not, we have a warless generation coming on the scene of action, and I thank God for that.   The more of that we can have, the more certain is the victory through Jesus Christ, our Lord, that this world war for Him will be won.

Our second gift to the world is life.   I should say, lives— man power, woman power—never so many in the history of the world.   There are about 9,000,000 people in the Dominion of Canada, and about 110,000,000 in the United States of America.

If you eliminate half of them as being outside the realm of
the Christian church and wholly indifferent to it, you have a
stupendous force of 50,000,000 or more in the Christian church.
We talk about the gold mines, the copper mines, the coal mines,
the timber forests—why all of those resources combined cannot
compare to the undeveloped resources in the Christian churches
of North America in the lives of the young people and of the
older people who are already enrolled in those churches. Isn't
it amazing that in the face of a world that is dying we should
not make more use of our lives? If one-tenth of us woke up
and began to live, we could overturn the world before tomorrow
morning. There are approximately 300,000 students in the state
universities of the United States today. There are about 500
college students in this Convention, or young men and women
of college age, and I can see many of them right now before me.
We have the gift of life to give to the world.

Our third North American gift to the world is spiritual dynamite. Dean MacRae in his address on "Christian Education and
Christian Leadership," on Friday morning said that what China
needs is dynamic personalities under the influence of the Holy
Spirit. Exactly. That is what all the world needs. That is
what the Christian church in North America needs more than
anything else, and we have it undeveloped. But it is there.
Did you ever stop to think what would happen to the world
if half of the Christians in North America began to pray, not to
say prayers, not to count the number of times they prayed, not
to read prayers or to have them by habit, but to pray in the
sense of longing for the salvation of the world? I think the
next great revival is going to be a revival of prayer. We have
this spiritual dynamite, this longing for the world in our hearts
and it must find expression. There is no part of the world that
longs for the rest of the world's salvation more than North
America longs for all the world outside of North America.

In the fourth place, we North Americans have to give to
the world *gold,* rivers flowing with it, mountains of it piled
up to the sky. I read an article the other day in which the
statement was made that the wealth of the United States of
America today is three hundred billion dollars. Why, it is a
perfectly enormous sum just to read about! Whenever I hear
people say that we cannot give, because we are so poor, I
think of the fact that it costs those who see football games in
this country from $800,000 to $1,000,000 for one afternoon's
amusement. I am skeptical, when I hear people say, "we have
no money to give to missions." I think of the statements in
the papers that every cruising steamship for the Mediterranean
and for the West Indies and for trips around the world is
crowded, with all staterooms sold. We have money for every-

thing in which we are interested. This last year, the Protestant Christians of North America gave $45,000,000 for the evangelization of the non-Christian world. The United States and Canada together gave 65 per cent of all the money given to evangelize the non-Christian world. We are carrying today two-thirds of the entire load of giving, because I suppose we possess two-thirds of the entire gold to give. At any rate, we North Americans are pouring forth our gold, because we possess it.

May I drive this thing home? May I take each one of these gifts and speak briefly about them as related to you Canadians and you citizens of the United States and myself?

I said that the first possession that we had was peace and good-will toward men. Do you as individuals have that? Is that your attitude toward the world this afternoon? You say, "Why, yes, certainly." Well, *is* it? Don't you hate anybody? Don't you suspect anybody? How do you feel toward the Negro? Toward the Japanese? Toward the German? Toward the Chinese? Toward the Turk? Is your attitude today, as an individual, an attitude of peace and good-will toward all men? If it is not, ought it not to be? Ought we not, as American Christians, to search our hearts to see what is the matter with us in our outlook on all mankind outside ourselves? Is peace our attitude? All right, if it *is,* how far are we willing to go to prevent another world war? What are we willing to do? How much are we willing to pray? How much are we willing to study and work to promote those causes which alone are likely to prevent another world war? That is distinctly a missionary and Christian problem which I lay on the hearts of all of you, just as I lay it upon my own heart.

Secondly, life. Three weeks ago a life that was dearer to me than my own life was called by our Heavenly Father into the life eternal. In all these days I have been thinking, not about death—It is strange that I have not thought about death, but about life, about her life, about the miracles that our Lord Jesus Christ worked through her, especially for the mission fields of the world, and I have asked myself, how does my life square with hers? How does it square with the life of her Lord? I want to ask that question of you. What is your life? What is it? Is it getting up in the morning and going to bed at night and eating three meals a day? Is it merely existing, or is it living? If it is living, what are you living for? If you are not living for anything in particular, why aren't you?

I believe the Lord is addressing those questions to us in this convention. You five hundred college students, you young people, do you believe as Horace Bushnell did that a man's life is a plan of God? Well, if you do, do you know what his plan is for your life? If you do not, are you willing to try to find out? We looked at those slides a minute ago, picturing the terrible need for doctors! Some of you young men in this audience are going to be doctors, and you are going to struggle for a living, competing with other doctors. You can go to the Far East and have a million people for your patients. You won't earn any $100,000 a year or $150,000, but you will earn your everlasting reward. Some of you are going to be teachers. Well, our schools are crowded with teachers, but any of us who have been to the mission fields can tell you that there are hundreds of thousands of children who will never be taught unless some of you go.

Are you willing to place your life against the life of the rest of the world this afternoon, and at least ask yourselves the question, "What am I going to do with my life?" It will be very strange if this convention should adjourn without a number of persons here dedicating their lives, either in the foreign field to this evangelization of the world, or in their home churches by a totally new conception of their duty and opportunity as Christians.

In the third place, prayer. I am tired of hearing people talk about prayer as merely a subjective influence. It is nothing of the kind. Why, Matthew Arnold said that religion is a power, not ourselves, that makes for righteousness. Well, if he could say that, we can. If Christianity is a power not ourselves that makes for righteousness, what is prayer? Prayer is linking up your life and your soul with that power not yours that makes for righteousness for the salvation of all mankind. Prayer works miracles. Prayer overturns continents. People say, "Isn't it too bad there isn't more prayer for missions?" Yes, it is, but the reason we have as much mission work as we have is because it has been upheld by prayer. Missionaries cannot work among non-Christian people, if they are not sustained by prayer. No modern miracle is carried out in the world today except by this almighty supernatural power of prayer that giveth us the victory. We need not worry so much about the money if we only have the prayer.

Now, lastly, the gold. You say, "I have none." Well, what did you do with what you had last year? When the earthquake in Japan came the shirt and collar factories in Troy, New York, sent large quantities of shirts and collars to Japan. People said, "What a foolish gift to give the Japanese, who need rice and blankets and food and clothing and shelter." Well, I don't know. The only things that shirt and collar companies have to give are shirts and collars, and they gave them. What did you give? What did I give? What did we do with the gold we had? I will tell you what we have done with some of it. We have built church edifices costing five hundred thousand dollars and refuse to support a foreign missionary. That is what we do.

May I say something to you pastors who are here. If you are planning to build a great church building, because you think it will serve the Kingdom of God by your having it, go ahead and build it. If you are planning to build it, because you want a better one than the denominational church on the next corner, do not build it. If you plan to build it to cost one hundred thousand or two hundred thousand or five hundred thousand dollars, before you start to lay one stone or one brick, ask yourself this question, "What effect is the building of this church going to have on the congregation's attitude toward the evangelization of the non-Christian world?" You may change the plans of your church before you go very far. I wrote a letter last year to a pastor of a church not one thousand miles from here and told him that the annual pledge of three thousand dollars that that church had made for foreign missions had not been paid and that it did not appear that the church was likely to pay it, judging from the rate the contributions were coming in. What do you think he wrote? "You do not understand our situation here. We have just taken pledges to build a parish house costing four hundred thousand dollars and we are very sorry that we cannot send you the money for the work of your Board."

What did you do, my friends, with the gold you had last year? Far be it from me to say that people ought not to go to football games. I have been to too many of them and I hope to go to many more; but when a man spends ten dollars in an afternoon at a football game for flowers and candy and tickets and then drops a half a dollar into the missionary offering the following Sunday, he is not a Christian, he is a football enthusiast. That is the difference. We may just as well make up our minds to that. Along with the call for prayer is coming the call to restudy our possessions in the light of the world needs. If you want to make your money go a long distance give it to foreign missions. There is no investment in the world that can compare to it. In the denomination that I represent, for every dollar given by American Presbyterians last year the native Christians on the foreign field gave enough more so that one dollar and thirty-nine cents was actually spent at the work. Whenever we tell that to a Presbyterian business man, he gasps. We can say to him, "If you will give us a dollar bill, we will stretch it to one dollar and thirty-nine cents within a month." Where do you get an investment like that? The greatest privilege laid upon our hearts this afternoon is to pour out our good will, our life, our prayer and our gold.

This is the appeal as given in the words of a man who may not call himself a Christian, George Bernard Shaw, the last man in the world, one might think, to quote in a missionary address: "There are more people living in the world today who believe that in Jesus Christ is the only hope of the world than there ever were before in the lifetime of men now living." There probably are more people who believe that in Jesus Christ is the only hope of the world than there ever were before in the lifetime of men now living. What are you going to do with a statement like that, you North-American Christians who are now living?

THE APPEAL OF FOREIGN MISSIONS TO THE INDIVIDUAL CHRISTIAN

THE REVEREND JAMES ENDICOTT, D.D., TORONTO

Instead of telling you what your responsibility is for this great cause (and mark you there is a responsibility, for if this conference breaks down anywhere it will break down in the personal realm), I shall tell you how the movement has affected me. Surely, the most captious critic can have no fault to find with the convention as a whole. The presentations have been large-minded, have been thoroughly Christian, have gripped our consciences, have enlightened our minds. The program is all right, and as a body of people we are all right. If this enterprise fails anywhere at any time, it will fail in that personal region. Therefore, it is a very serious matter for each of us.

However, I would like to show you, if I may, what are the things about the foreign missionary enterprise which most influenced me and captured my life.

I have had three unexpected experiences in life. The first was when I became a Christian. I was not a candidate. I was taken unawares, but I was really brought to my Lord Christ. Christianity from that day has always been a real, an amazing, a beautiful and gracious factor in my life. It has never become commonplace. Again, I did not expect to be a Christian minister and even less did I expect to be a foreign missionary.

What, then, was it about this missionary movement that most deeply moved me and led me to its support in thought and life?

In the first place, it actually brought to me an enrichment of the very conception of Christianity itself. That is an advantage well worth gaining.

I have had conceptions of a different kind presented to me, and I have lived under the dominion of them for many years of my life, for example, a conception something like this: Christianity, as an unearthly thing, so unrelated to the life of the world, so precarious and so narrow, so aloof that the best way to suggest it by picture would be as a little ditch or as a narrow channel, in which is a canoe in which a man sits bolt upright for fear that it will capsize. That is Christianity, as it has been often presented.

Now, what the foreign missionary enterprise did for me in this realm was to suggest another picture of a sailing ship out on the broad ocean with all its sails unfurled, and bounding over to the ends of the earth, looking for new cargo, wholly unafraid and in no sense restricted.

It makes a tremendous difference which conception is to prevail in the minds of the people. I have ceased to wonder that some folks shrink from the Christian religion, that they see no attractiveness in it, that it makes no large appeal to them; but I have found in the foreign missionary movement, to which I have dedicated my life, something which makes the Christian religion spacious, ennobling, divinely generous, really giving us a God who is big enough to worship, and a human race worthy of being redeemed, and worthy of commanding my service.

This matter of foreign missions has not only enlarged my own personal conception of the Christian religion, but it has shed light upon the Bible. I am almost afraid in a Christian congregation to talk about the Bible. That is the fighting ground for thousands of people nowadays. You can get into a row more easily talking about the Bible than you can by talking about almost anything else. I don't want to suggest a new league being formed, but if we did have to form another, I would suggest we form a league against the defending of the Bible. In twenty-five years we would not need to defend it. The Bible itself becomes another book, when viewed in the light of a great enterprise.

There are two ways of finding out about a country. One is to study a map, and connected with that is the study of a book of geography. Another way is to travel along the road and go to the country. There are illuminations and expansions of mind, and enrichments of life, which do come to us through enterprise, which do not come by any other way.

In other words, because the Church has launched out on an enterprise so large and Christian and divine as this is, we have got a light upon the whole Bible that had never been discovered before. It is a larger application, if you will, of the thought of Jesus who declared that if any man willed to know the doctrine he was to do it, by doing the will of God. By doing, we come to knowing. I know that there are many passages of the Word of God, whole regions of it, which have been lit up as the result of our committal, the church's committal to a great enterprise, which were dark heretofore. Even the book of Jonah becomes a new book. Now, I wish no controversy here. I am tremendously orthodox; but, mark you, I shall never forget what a wonderful light came to me upon that marvelous book, that great missionary classic of the Old Testament, when I viewed it from the missionary standpoint. The miracle of the Book of Jonah is not that the whale swallowed a man; the miracle of Jonah is Jonah himself. If Ingersoll or any such man had told that story we would say, "It is a caricature of any possible religion that is in the Bible." Ah, but there it is—a prophet unwilling to go to a great multitude of people who needed God—unwilling! Why? Because he was afraid they would stone him or refuse to listen to him? Nay, but he was afraid they would believe him. Afraid that they wouldn't repent? No, he was afraid they would repent. Afraid that God would not have mercy upon them? Nay, afraid that God would have mercy; and his grievance lay there written for all time as a rebuke to narrow nationalism; a rebuke to our putting limits upon the everlasting mercy of the Eternal God.

I could not get a better illustration of what the Bible may mean than what we had in that rare presentation by Dr. Ross Stevenson at the intercession period. I could not but wish that the statement he gave—I am not talking of the mastery of the Scriptures and the gracious and beautiful sensitiveness of his soul that enabled him to bring out those passages and give them with such power—might be given in every college on this continent, in every high school, in every common school in this country. And what would happen? There are millions of people, your children many of them, who would have a totally new conception of the Christian religion itself. We had a series of passages which not only reveal special truths, but light up the whole Book and give us a picture of the living God, of the river that widened and wherever it went, life sprang up; of the multitudes beyond and the preparation of the Church for its service; of the descent in power of the Holy Spirit, of the great climax of history when all peoples and kindreds and tongues shall be brought into the fold of God.

Some of the finest passages in the Scriptures have had small meanings attached to them. We have taken the great word, "For God so loved the world, that He gave His only begotten Son that whosoever believeth on Him should not perish," and we have proceeded to say "whosoever means *you*." I have no objection to that, but it would be just as true to say "whosoever means *him*"—that African yonder, that Chinese and that Indian. It is a *world text* and it is robbed of its content unless it is given a world application.

Take the great statement, "And I, if I be lifted up from the earth, will draw all men unto me." Give it a merely personal, parochial or national application, and in the process the great depths and richness of its meaning disappear.

These illustrations show what I mean when I say that the missionary enterprise has made the Bible as a whole and also in particular passages so luminous and full of meaning to me.

What shall I say of the church? It means a lot to a minister what he thinks of the Christian church; a lot to a young Christian man. I sometimes wonder at the courage required to call a young man and ask him to join such a church as some of us have. A friend told me that at the close of a speech he made in Chicago once a lady came up to him and said, "I don't believe in sending our religion to a foreign country." "No, madam," he said, "nor would I if I didn't have a better religion to send than you appear to have."

Why should you ask your son or anybody else's son to join your church? What are they joining for? What does it mean? Well, sometimes I think it means to learn a little catechism, to keep the Sabbath day, to come to prayer meeting. Woe to us, if we expect much of a response to that from the young men of today and the young women of today. When I think of what narrow things the church has sometimes set before its people, I am amazed that the Christian church has survived.

Once when Henry Ward Beecher was in England, he was to preach in a church which had a narrow, curling stairway up to a high pulpit. They asked him to go up there, but he wouldn't go. He said he could not preach up in a pulpit like that. At last they yielded. He began his address by saying: "One of the greatest proofs of the divinity of the Christian religion is that it survived the pulpit." It has survived and will survive the church. But, think now, after such an address as we have heard from Mrs. Roys, think of the world into which she introduced us, and then think back into the days when a body of godly women would be gathered together to consult seriously whether the chancel needed a new carpet or not, or whether forsooth, the cemetery needed a new fence, or whether the manse should have a new set of storm windows, exhausting practically the enterprises to which they were committed. Then think of the liberated womanhood of today, founding schools and colleges, preaching the gospel, healing the sick all around the world and leading the womanhood of all the world to larger conceptions of womanhood itself as well as of religion and of the world and of God.

Why do I support Foreign Missions? Because also of the quality of the men and women who have been produced by the movement. I will always prefer that test to any other. No matter what one says that he believes, no matter what he writes in his reports about convictions and ideals, the searching test of any movement is the kind of men it produces. I think of Africa. We have sent there the ablest men of our British Empire—great consuls, travelers, world dreamers, and schemers; but if we were to select one man to represent the best in our empire and the best in our religion, the most representative soul we have produced for Africa, there will be one name mentioned throughout the world. It would be the name of Livingstone.

I think of India where we have sent for generations our most gifted men by the hundreds and thousands and yet, if we were obliged to single out one man to represent us, our Empire, our religion, our church, there is only one man to select, a Baptist cobbler, the immortal Carey.

If we think of China, the name of Morrison rises.

If you of the United States should speak of Burma, the name of Judson would leap to the lips of us all; of Japan, the names of Verbeck and others.

Again, every one who has spent any time in the mission field has seen evidence that the thing works. On this account, I believe in missions. I make it a personal matter of obligation to sustain them, because I know the work.

I am going to tell you of an experience of mine, traveling in the wilds of West China. Millions of the people there are not Chinese; they are pagans. Once on a journey of several months, I reached a mountain top where lived a people of whom two years before every man seen would have been a drunkard, and every woman unchaste. Their huts were miserable. The only public building in the place was the house of shame. If ever a people were demoralized, without literature, without any organized religion, without any thing to elevate life, that was this people. Within two years of the beginning of an effort to reach them with the gospel of Christ I spent a Sunday there and I worshipped in a huge building where hundreds upon hundreds of them were sitting in heavenly places in Christ. The gospel works. It reaches people who are at the bottom and lifts them up.

Again, I believe in the movement because it can reproduce itself. It is raising up the same type of characters in the mission field that it has produced here. Japan has its Christian heroes and saints. India has its Christian heroes and saints; China and other lands also Every proof that a Christian people can give of their loyalty to Christ and their steadfastness in the gospel has been given.

Let me give one illustration from the social area. I speak to you about moral questions and social questions because just now these seem to be in our minds.

I think of prohibition. I simply give it by way of illustration. I want to say this to you, friends, as an outsider—don't be alarmed because queer people from across the ocean say queer things about prohibition. Don't be alarmed if some duke out of work with his gaze fixed upon a wealthy heiress, comes over here and says that prohibition doesn't work. Don't pay any attention to the criticisms that have been offered all around the world. We from Canada want to tell you that it is one of the things for which we love you and believe in you. It is one of the conspicuous contributions you are making to the life of the world. Having put your hand to that furrow don't turn back. I tell you if you want to give up other luxuries, give up your Sunday newspapers and your divorce courts, but hold on tight to prohibition.

But let me take my illustration from China. I saw something more conspicuous there and in some respects more heroic than what you have done here. I saw in a province in China where opium was grown, where the farmers had the best soil planted in opium, where they made vast sums of money out of it, where the traders depended upon it, and the officials depended upon it, where millions in money from opium went up to the imperial treasury at Peking—I saw them blot it out. This is true, even if the soldiers have put it back again for a while. I traveled for two months in all sorts of out-of-the-way places and I failed to see a blade of the poppy. I did not smell one whiff of opium. I did not see a man or hear a man who had any other word to say than that the thing was done. When I came back to the great capital city of Yunnan Fu I saw the big archway of the city gate lined with opium pipes. They had been sent in by the old smokers pledging their support of this movement. This is what I saw. It was not only a fact but a prophesy of another day that is to be when these nations shall come with fresh resources, moral, intellectual and spiritual, to enrich the city of God and to cooperate with us in making the kingdom of God a reality on the earth.

———————

INTERCESSION

PRESIDENT J. ROSS STEVENSON, D.D., PRINCETON, N. J.

Shall we hear the call of God to His church to pray? "Ask of Me, and I will give thee the nations for thine inheritance, and the uttermost parts of the earth for thy possession." "Whatsoever ye shall ask in prayer, believing, ye shall receive." "Hitherto, ye have asked nothing in My name; ask, and ye shall receive, that your joy may be made full."

Let us bow in real prayer, conscious as we are of the presence of our God. And as we pray, do we not all need to join in this one petition—"Lord, teach us to pray"—as we have never expressed it before? May our minds and hearts be united in such a sense of need and desire, and entreaty as will mean for us here and now a new Pentecost.

Blessed Master, when we think of the preëminent place of prayer in Thy program, when we recall Thine explicit commands to ask of Thee, and the great and precious promises Thou has joined thereto, when we bring to mind the example of apostles and missionaries in every age, we realize that we have not taken into account nor availed ourselves of the limitless possibilities of prayer.

Thou has taught us that if two of Thy disciples shall agree on earth as touching anything that they shall ask, it shall be done for them by Thy Father who is in Heaven. Here we are a great throng of Thy believing children with common needs and petitions, and we come into Thy presence humbly, penitently of one accord; and our trust is in Him who only doeth wondrous things, and who has pledged Himself to do exceedingly abundantly above all that we ask or think to the glory of Him who is our crucified and risen Redeemer. In His Name we pray. Amen.

In preparation for our service of intercession, let us in silence before God wait upon Him, while He speaks to us from His own Word regarding our responsibility for the furtherance of the gospel and regarding those expectations which we may cherish as to the triumph of His Kingdom.

Jesus said to His disciples, "Henceforth I call you not servants, for the servant knoweth not what his lord doeth; but I have called you friends; for all things that I have heard of my Father, I have made known unto you. Ye have not chosen me, but I have chosen you, and ordained you, that ye should go and bring forth fruit, and that your fruit should remain; that whatsoever ye shall ask of the Father in My Name, He may give it you. These things I command you that ye love one another." "Ye are my friends, if ye do whatsoever I command you."

"All authority hath been given to me in heaven and on earth. Go ye therefore, and make disciples of all the nations, baptizing them into the name of the Father and of the Son and of the Holy Spirit; teaching them to observe all things whatsoever I commanded you: and lo, I am with you always, even unto the end of the world."

"Wait for the promise of the Father, which, *said he,* ye heard from Me." "Ye shall receive power when the Holy Spirit is come upon you."

"And when they had prayed, the place was shaken wherein they were gathered together; and they were all filled with the Holy Spirit, and they spake the word of God with boldness." "And the Twelve called the multitude of the disciples unto them, and said, It is not fit that we should forsake the Word of God, and serve tables." "We will continue stedfastly in prayer and in the ministry of the word." "And the Word of God increased and the number of the disciples multiplied in Jerusalem exceedingly."

"The weapons of our warfare are not of the flesh, but are mighty through God, to the casting down of strongholds." "For our wrestling is not against flesh and blood, but against the principalities, against the powers, against the world rulers of this darkness, against the spiritual hosts of wickedness in the heavenly places. Wherefore take up the whole armor of God." "Praying at all seasons in the Spirit, and watching thereunto in all perseverance and supplication for all the saints, and on my behalf (a missionary), that utterance may be given unto me in opening my mouth, to make known with boldness the mystery of the gospel, for which I am an ambassador in chains, that in it I may speak boldly, as I ought to speak."

"For this cause I bow my knees unto the Father, from whom every family in heaven and on earth is named, that He would grant you, according to the riches of His glory, that ye may be strengthened with power through his Spirit in the inward man; that Christ may dwell in your hearts through faith; to the end that ye, being rooted and grounded in love, may be strong to apprehend with all the saints what is the breadth and length and height and depth, and to know the love of Christ which passeth knowledge; that ye may be filled unto all the fulness of God.

"Now unto Him that is able to do exceeding abundantly above all that we ask or think, according to the power that worketh in us, unto Him be the glory in the church and in Christ Jesus unto all generations for ever and ever. Amen."

"After these things I saw, and behold, a great multitude, which no man could number, out of every nation and of all tribes and peoples and tongues, standing before the throne and before the Lamb, arrayed in white robes, and palms in their hands; and they cry with a great voice, saying, 'Salvation unto our God who sitteth on the throne, and unto the Lamb.' And all the angels were standing round about the throne, and about the elders and the four living creatures; and they fell before the throne on their faces, and worshipped God, saying, Amen: Blessing, and glory, and wisdom, and thanksgiving, and honor, and power, and might, be unto our God for ever and ever. Amen."

"And the seventh angel sounded; and there followed great voices in heaven, and they said, 'the kingdom of the world is become the kingdom of our Lord, and of His Christ; and He shall reign for ever and ever.'

"And I heard as it were the voice of a great multitude, and as the voice of many waters, and as the voice of mighty thunders, saying, Hallelujah: for the Lord our God, the Almighty, reigneth. Let us rejoice, and be exceeding glad and let us give the glory unto Him."

With this vision of an apostolic precedent, and of an assured triumph, in our minds let us now give ourselves to united intercession. Let us pray.

Shall we not first of all, in our praying, thank God for the victories of the Cross? And for the great company of the redeemed throughout the world with whom we are joined in the body of Christ, and for the self-sacrificing propagators of the faith who have abounded in the work of the Lord? "In everything, give thanks. For this is the will of God in Christ Jesus concerning you."

As we think of the crowd of witnesses who obtained a good report through faith, shall we not confess for ourselves and our churches, great lack of faith, much coldness of heart, weak endeavors, indifferent achievements; and, as we pray, let us pray for pardon, and for cleansing.

> "My faith looks up to Thee,
> Thou Lamb of Calvary,
> Saviour Divine!
> Now hear me while I pray,
> Take all my guilt away,
> O let me from this day,
> Be wholly Thine."

Let us pray that Christ's vision of fields white unto harvest may inspire our imagination and be exceedingly vivid and real to us; and that we may have the discerning mind and outreaching compassion of the Lord of the harvest, as we pray for more laborers. May we pray that our own labor may be charged with redemptive passion and inspired by a holier devotion to Him,

"More love to Thee, O Christ!
More love to Thee;
Hear Thou the prayer I make,
On bended knee;
This is my earnest plea,
More love, O Christ, to Thee,
More love to Thee!"

Let us pray for all ministers and Christian leaders in the Church at home that they may have a full and sympathetic and responsible knowledge of Christian enterprises among the nations; that they may heed their call to missionary leadership and be filled with apostolic boldness and zeal, and the spirit of sacrifice. Let us pray for the colleges and seminaries in which the future ministry is being trained, that these may be baptized with the spirit of loyalty to Christ and of love for all those for whom Jesus Christ died.

Let us pray for the entire membership of our churches, and the organized activities for children, for young people, for men and for women, that these may be controlled by the mind of Christ, may be marked by His disposition, and may contribute directly to His sovereign purpose to redeem mankind!

Let us pray for the Christian church of America, that she may be indeed the church of the living God, the God of all the nations, a church made beautiful, and glorious, and triumphant through the conscious life and power of the ever-present Redeemer.

Let us pray most earnestly that the church may be wholly apostolic, enabled by divine grace to answer the prayer of our Lord for those who believe on him that they may be one as He and the Father are one, that the world may believe that Christ has been sent by the Father for the redemption of His needy children.

O, Thou, who art the hearer of prayer, give ear to our united entreaties. Thou alone canst give the increase, but Thou hast called us to be laborers together with Thee. May we have a clearer comprehension of the work there is for us to do in our day and generation, and may we realize that the time is short, and that the night is coming on.

Enable us, O our Father, to invest aright the spiritual blessings of this conference; forbid that the messages which Thou art giving us through Thine ambassadors should return unto Thee void. May we go back to our appointed tasks with clearer understanding of what Thou dost expect of us in our time, and with courageous resolves not to fail thee, the Captain of our salvation. Out from the convention hall of our capital city may there issue a stream of spiritual blessings, health and joy which shall be like the river of prophetic vision, growing deeper and broader in its onward sweep, and whithersoever the river **cometh, there is life.**"

This is a great thing to ask, but we plead in a Name which is above every name, the Name which every tongue shall one day confess as every knee shall bow to him, the Name of Jesus Christ, our Saviour and our Lord. Amen.

THE EDUCATION OF A CONGREGATION IN MISSIONS

WHAT ONE CONGREGATION DID IN MISSIONARY EDUCATION

PROFESSOR JOHN CLARK ARCHER, NEW HAVEN, CONNECTICUT

The reference is to a program undertaken and put through during the spring of 1924. The general plan followed was that which the director of this program had used on many previous occasions in various churches. The special field of study in this instance was China. The full details of the undertaking may be found in a booklet entitled "China in the Local Parish," published by the Missionary Education Movement and obtainable from any mission board headquarters. The booklet sets forth the general plan applicable to the study of any field or topic and gives detailed directions for the study of China at any time.

There were two main phases of the program put on in the church referred to: (1) Chinese materials correlated with the regular lessons used weekly in the Church School; and (2) various projects culminating in a Grand Project at the close of the whole program.

A small reference library was assembled from which the teachers and pupils could draw the materials desired from week to week. Books were often read as units. More often, however, selections were made from them in accordance with instructions issued in bulletin form, and these selected materials were used for illustration and comparison in connection with the regular lessons. In this way some gradual accumulation of information about China was insured. The lessons were taught with the aid of illustrations from Chinese history, literature, character, etc. The lesson materials thus related time and again to the situation in China, especially to the conduct of the Christian enterprise in China. The detailed references may be found in the book above referred to.

At the same time in various classes projects were undertaken. The Junior folks, for example, set about the construction of a Chinese village, according to directions furnished in various books. This work was done during the sessions of the week-day Bible School. Other classes undertook other things, such as a Chinese tea party as an introduction to the study of Chinese etiquette. Chinese games were learned and played by some of the children as an introduction to the study of Chinese play-time customs. These few items represent the many which

273

were included in the five months' program, and which I have designated "projects." There was the obvious attempt to get "expression" into the program as well as mere study.

During the time of the program various occasions were offered for special features against the background of the general plan; for example, stereopticon lectures, brief addresses on aspects of Chinese life, Chinese story-materials, text-book courses on China, etc. These miscellaneous phases of the program fell into place as units of the whole. The general plan gave coherence to all.

Special attention was paid to the Grand Project. This furnished a strong motive throughout the whole period of activity and study. It was this main feature which contributed most to the church's consciousness of China and things Chinese. It was not a thing apart, but the climax of the entire previous work. Its underlying principle was educational and not spectacular. It could not have stood alone as an educational venture. It would have lacked meaning for real education. It was not a combination of stunts. It was a serious attempt to exercise one's way into an understanding and appreciation of China. The book referred to above gives full details regarding this also.

Putting much in little, I might say this. About one hundred members of the parish (all the work of the program proceeded on the basis of local initiative and capacity), fifty men and fifty women, were enlisted in this part of the program. They included architects, actors, carpenters, story-tellers, shopkeepers, etc. Speaking from the point of view of the roles undertaken they were householders, priests, merchants, school children, street venders, restaurateurs, actors, etc., etc.

A complete Chinese setting was arranged, including shrines of Confucianism, Taoism, and Buddhism, a Chinese garden, several shops, a tea house, memorial arch (pailow),—all, of course, full size. Hundreds of Chinese articles—we have been in the habit of calling them "curios"—were assembled from private homes and mission headquarters. Chinese foods and sweets were stocked in the shops. In the rest room were books and pictures instructive in things Chinese. Chinese food was served to those attending the exercises. In charge of the shrines were men especially trained for the purpose, whose knowledge of Chinese religions and religious practice was greatly enlarged by means of the preparation necessary for their tasks. And they were charged with the responsibility of instructing their audiences in Chinese religion. You will all see by this time how serious was the educational aspect of the program. The Taoist priest, for example, gave daily—the Grand Project ran through three days—illustration of exorcism and worship.

Children were drilled for a village school scene. The persons involved in the wedding and wedding procession were carefully trained. A Chinese play was produced and went far toward creating the necessary Chinese atmosphere. The children were gathered from time to time into graded groups to listen to story-tellers primed with Chinese story materials. There were other features, as well, but there is no time to speak of them.

The whole performance was most informal. Only in the evening at the time of the play were seats provided on the main floor. At other times the visitors might wander at will, looking where they would and listening where they chose. The daily schedule of events was adhered to with some flexibility, and so provided something most of the time in "the main tent." Maybe that was an unfortunate term to use—there were no side shows. Everything had its important place and all together made the harmony and completeness demanded by the undertaking.

If I have "sold" the idea to you, that is all I can expect in this brief space. You must look elsewhere for further particulars. It is true that the church which put on this particular program is an unusually well-appointed plant into whose program of religious education this missionary educational program could be fitted without strain. Other churches, however, have done as well, and several smaller churches have done well at lesser projects. The plan will work in any parish. It is built on the personnel at hand, and aims to use home talent and develop local initiative. The program just sketched has already been used as a community venture in Bennington, Vt., where four churches joined in the attempt, each assuming certain units of the whole, doing parts of the program separately and uniting at the end in the Grand Project. Wesleyan University and the First Methodist Episcopal Church of Middletown, Conn., are now engaged in producing certain phases of the program, especially the projects. Many churches here and there are doing more or less at it. It seems to offer a practically new method—I say *practically* new, for that is the way it works out. In reality all the features are old, if considered separately.

May I say last of all that consideration of the missionary enterprise needs to take some new turns. The average local parish is appallingly ignorant of the work of the Church throughout the world. Too much dependence is placed still upon stock materials of an older day. Or, rather, the materials, fine as they are which are furnished us, fall into old moulds, are made to fit into a more or less stereotyped frame of mind. We must change the minds of the folk of our parishes, renew their outlook, develop a proper assimilative mass. This can be done only by wholesale project work, which stirs up new centers of activity and thought. With new materials and a new method, therefore, we may succeed where we have failed before, and still convince the churches that the greatest task is obedience to the Great Commission. Let our aims be: understanding, appreciation, cooperation, and Christianization. By this we recognize the need of—in this case—knowing who the Chinese really are, what they are worth, how we may work with them toward common ends, and how we may save ourselves while offering them the terms of salvation.

THE OBJECTIVES OF THE MISSIONARY EDUCATION OF A CONGREGATION

PROFESSOR T. H. P. SAILER, PH.D., NEW YORK

The principal direct objective of missionary education is the accomplishment of the missionary enterprise in the right way. This last involves much greater problems than most of us realize. Doing the will of God in accomplishing this enterprise brings many by-products, but these are not our direct objectives. We secure the best personal development, not by cultivating virtues or going through pious motions, but by doing the will of God. If we seek first the Kingdom of God and what it needs for its realization in this world and pursue it with our whole heart, all other things we need shall be added unto us.

Therefore, the more immediate aim of missionary education is to get the Church to give itself whole-heartedly to the needs of the world. This leads us to ask:

(a) What are the needs of the world? We cannot separate those of other countries from those in this land, either individual or social. We cannot uplift the individual and social institutions of other countries without uplifting those at home. This, of course, does not mean that we shall wait until home needs are all met, but that we shall recognize the relationship between those at home and abroad. In order to analyze the needs of the world it will probably be necessary to arrange them in separate classes. Many different divisions have been proposed, such as physical, social, vocational, cultural, spiritual, etc.

(b) We next must ask: What activities of individuals are demanded to meet these needs? And we must analyze these in some detail in order to furnish more specific objectives.

(c) What personal qualities are demanded in order to perform these activities adequately? These may be divided into knowledge and insight, sympathy and devotion, efficient habits. Knowledge and sympathy are preparatory to action. This will give us a large list of very detailed objectives as the aims of missionary education. Such a list should be drafted with great care by a large number of workers.

Meanwhile Dr. Fleming has suggested eight particular objectives of missionary education:

1. Determining what Christianity is. Can it be shown that it is essentially a missionary religion?

2. Leading people to see what there is of good in other religions.

3. Along with this, cultivating discrimination with reference to the uniqueness of Christianity.

4. Attaining the idea of degrees in the possession of the spirit of Christ; recognizing that some who are not called by His name may have more of His spirit than others who are so called.

5. Encouraging the idea of mutuality in world relationships as opposed to the older idea that when the foreign missionary task concerning a nation was performed intercourse would cease.

6. Emphasizing the fact that our nominal Christianity is holding back the Kingdom of God.

7. Ceasing to convey our denominationalism across the sea.

8. Making Christ known, not only geographically in the whole world, but psychologically in all areas of thought.

In closing I may suggest some of the by-products that will be realized from a strong program of missionary education:

1. Adequate missionary education will make Christianity a world rather than a national or racial religion. It will tend to correct the national, racial and denominational limitations of Christianity. It will enlarge parochial imagination.

2. It will make Christianity a religion of service and sharing of privileges, a religion of obligation.

3. It will challenge to sacrifice at a time when Christianity is easy going. It will tend to check luxury by furnishing standards of perspective.

4. It will emphasize the present power of God working in the world.

5. It will help us to realize how Western Christianity and Christendom appear to others.

6. It will ultimately bring us face to face with selfishness and inconsistency.

7. It will make all phases of the Christian life functional and challenge the Church to become more efficient.

THE PLACE OF MISSIONS IN THE CHURCH SCHOOL
THE REVEREND HERBERT W. GATES, BOSTON, MASSACHUSETTS

Before we can determine the appropriateness of any element in the curriculum of the church school, we must have clearly in mind what is the object of the school and of the course of religious education.

We are seeking, I take it, to educate boys and girls, young people, and men and women, in a Christian manner. That is we want them to acquire those attitudes of thought and feeling, and those habits of conduct that shall lead them to respond to all the varied situations of life in accordance with the example and teachings of Jesus Christ.

The type of education that will accomplish this purpose must include several factors. Most important of all, it must actually bring the pupil face to face with real situations, make him aware of the problems which they set, and give him opportunity, under wise and friendly guidance, to think and work his way through to satisfactory solutions.

The element of guidance is important and a part of this is to give the pupil knowledge of the experience of others as they faced the same kind of problems, so that he may learn by their successes and no less by their failures.

To a very large degree we have been in the habit of thinking that most, and practically all of the knowledge required for our purpose is to be found in the Bible. At least we have limited our subject matter in religious education to the Biblical material.

I am convinced that this is a mistake that does injustice both to the Bible and to the pupil. It has resulted in setting the Bible so strictly apart that we have pretty nearly convinced a good many people that it is apart from life and is not expected to be taken seriously in every day affairs. How often have we heard young people, and even older ones say, when reminding them of some precept of Jesus or of the prophets, "Oh, well, that's in the Bible!"

In the field of general education we have fairly well learned that the point of contact which is most effective is the immediate experience of the pupil. It is the present problem, real to him, that interests him most. Facing this, he begins to see the reason for studying the experience of others, that he may learn what they did under similar conditions, what the results were, and guide his own actions accordingly.

It is at just this point that missionary education has a great contribution to make to the program of religious education. The annals of the world-wide enterprise of the Christian Church are the Book of Acts brought down to date. I have often wished that, when our Bibles had been printed, some one had been thoughtful enough to put at the end of Acts, "To be continued." We owe it to our young people that they shall understand the continuity of God's purposes and that they shall never be allowed to imagine that the Divine Spirit has ceased or altered his program since the canon of Scripture was closed.

Another factor in the development of modern education is the project principle of approach. This is not a new thing, nor is it a patent method to take the place of other methods of study and work. It is rather a principle, by the application of which we succeed in getting study and work and learning better done than we can without it. So, in religious education, it is not a substitute for Bible study. It is a means of making Bible study more purposeful and effective.

It means that we shall seek to make the educational activities of the pupil center about worth-while enterprises, which the pupil recognizes and accepts as worth-while to him, and as suggesting an end which he wants to reach. This accomplished, all of the experience of the race which bears upon the problem is gladly studied as a help in accomplishing the thing he wants to do.

Young people are usually energetic and, despite all our ideas to the contrary, ready and willing to be of service when confronted by worthy tasks. Here they are confronting the church with its claims upon their lives. The thing that will make them respond in loyalty and even in a spirit of sacrifice is to show them the greatness of the Christian enterprise in concrete terms.

Take for example the Every Member Canvass of the church. Here is a part of the church life that touches them. They are asked to participate through gifts of money. But what does it mean? How much do they actually know of what becomes of that money, Too often we begin at the other end and appeal in the name of a board that wants support. But suppose we take them where they are, members of, or affiliated with a church with a job to do. In several churches of which I know this has been made a project of study and service.

The aim has been to find out what is actually done with the money they give. More than this they are led to see that they may have a voice in its distribution and use. The budget of the church is studied, the various items therein are translated into the terms of human need and service, they are encouraged to make posters, prepare programs through which they may pass on their knowledge to others and thus actually contribute far more than their modest gifts can do, to the success of the enterprise.

The enterprise of missions, the going work of the church in the community, the nation, and the world, is the finest source of project material imaginable for religious education.

When we look at missionary education from this point of view, we get a standard of judgment which enables us to estimate aright the comparative value of some practices which have gone under the name of missionary education.

For one thing we shall see that it is not a mere scheme of money raising. Many a device has been put over in this name that has exploited spiritual interests in behalf of financial returns. Such is any plan that induces children, or anyone else to part with their money without intelligent knowledge of the cause for which it is asked.

Again, we shall deprecate plans that substitute a lower and unworthy motive for the true one of service. I have known of contests in money raising that have set class against class, or department against department in most unholy fashion. I have seen campaigns in which large sums of money have been raised by appealing to un-Christian motives, such as the love of praise and the esteem of men.

We shall certainly deprecate methods of presenting the missionary appeal which emphasize the inferiorities of others rather than their good points. I am convinced that no little part of our racial problem is due to the habit of leading children to think of all other peoples as queer. The other side of this evil is the attitude of superiority which is one of America's besetting sins today.

We shall wish to do away with the separation and even the competition between home and foreign missions which has often made unfriendly partisans of individuals and groups in our churches. The field is the *world,* said the Master, and he counted as the only valid proof of the Spirit's presence that witnessing and service should begin at home and reach out to the uttermost parts of the earth.

There is an even greater contribution which missionary education has to make to the program of the church school, namely, that it shall make the grandeur and worth of the Christian enterprise so real as to lead the youth to ask himself: "And what shall I do?"

One of the unfortunate effects of a certain type of religious education has been that of leading many young people to think of Christianity as a system of beliefs which one must accept to make himself secure against future disaster. It is the glory of missionary education, rightly conceived and rightly administered, that it leads the youth, not merely to study religion as it was centuries ago, but as a living enterprise which invites him to high spiritual adventure here and now. It helps him to see the Christ, not back in the past, but just ahead, still beckoning and saying, "Follow Me!"

THE HOME AS AN AGENCY FOR MISSIONARY EDUCATION

MRS. E. C. CRONK, PHILADELPHIA, PENNSYLVANIA

Judges, jurors, editors, leaders in every sphere of the world's work are asserting with increasing frequency that "there is no substitute for the home." Institutionally trained childhood is robbed of some things that are childhood's rightful heritage. No amount of institutional missionary training can really take the place of the home as a missionary agency in its relationship to the new generation. When right attitudes in missionary thought and practise are a part of home training they become a very part of the life of a boy or girl. Our churches are full of men and women who regard missionary interest as an elective of Christianity—a sort of optional attachment to be screwed on or left off according to the inclination of the individual.

Let us consider some of the practical methods for missionary education in the home.

I. Boys and girls are influenced by what they see every day with their own eyes. (1) Of supreme importance is the exemplification of the missionary spirit in the home. Parents whose attitudes are truly missionary, and who are Christian internationalists in their relationships to the people of every race, make a deeper impression than can be made by mere word teaching in a Sunday School or missionary society. On the other hand it is next to impossible for any outside influence to counteract a scornful "nigger," "dago," "hunkie" attitude of a home, or the callous indifference of "Charity begins at home. I don't believe in foreign missions. There's plenty to do at home."

(2) Pictures and maps offer large possibility. Boys and girls, especially those of the junior age, have a strong collecting interest. Many of them are intensely interested in making albums of various kinds. The daily papers and the Sunday supplements are generous in supplying movie heroes and matinee idols. If parents will go to the trouble of getting the picture sheets of the Missionary Education Movement, the collecting interest will express itself in albums of China, India, Japan, Africa, people of all nations in America, and children of all lands. The daily papers and the magazines will be searched for contributions. The fostering of stamp and flag collecting will also help to develop international minds and hearts.

One well-known missionary leader hung on the wall of his boys' room a map of the world. At night and in the morning two little fellows travelled around the world pointing out places of which they had read or heard during the day, visiting mission stations in which they were interested. Globes may be used in the same way. Pictures of various missionaries may be placed on the wall or in small frames. Sometimes a missionary guest may be invited for a week's stay by placing his picture in a frame in the living room or bed room. The children become very enthusiastic—"Let's have David Livingstone next week," or "When will we have Ann Hasseltine Judson?"

(3) A missionary treasure chest with objects of interest from various lands, carefully opened on Sunday evenings or on rare occasions is sure to foster interest. Alexander Duff used to say that the idols and other objects from non-Christian lands which his father used to show him when he was only three years old made a deep impression on him, never to be forgotten.

II. Boys and girls are very susceptible to what they hear in their homes. Anna B. Scott says, "The center of American civilization is the dining room table." (1) It is certain that the dining room table is a more valuable vantage ground for forming right missionary attitudes than is a mission study class room. Not the forced sanctimonious table talk that children immediately recognize as veneer, but the frank interested discussion of world relationships on a Christian basis and of individual relationships within the experience of the children. The mother who is enthusiastic over the poor benighted African away over across the sea, but un-Christian in her attitudes to the African in her own kitchen is not a missionary conversationalist of influence with her little son.

(2) The mother who makes a spectacular, melodramatic consecration of her son to foreign missions, and speaks of it repeatedly in his presence and at various public functions is apt to be rewarded by a squirming resentment on the boy's part. Jacob Chamberlain was under the strongest missionary influence in his home, but his mother never told him until he was ready to sail for India that the first thing she did after his birth was to carry her new-born son to her favorite place of prayer there to consecrate him again to the service of God. She had not forced her consecration upon him during the years of his boyhood. She had kept it and pondered it in her heart, yet constantly her life as well as her conversation had led him.

The earnest winning words of Bishop Selwyn when he was a guest in the home of Lady Patteson had large influence in leading Coleridge Patteson into missionary service.

Guests for a home should be more carefully selected than furniture. The international mind should be fostered by international hospitality. Your Chinese laundryman may be a more desirable and courteous guest than the leading citizen who refers to him as "that old Chink.'

III. What boys and girls do in the home is not only a result of their training, but a most valuable part of it. We remember nine-tenths of what we do.

(1) Missionary giving is largely a matter of home training. "How did you happen to make such large gifts to missions?" someone asked a man who had given millions. "No happening about it." he replied. "When I was a boy at home my mother trained me to give at least ten cents out of every dollar. The only thing that has happened is that I have more dollars than I did then."

(2) Missionary service in the community is also largely a matter of home training.

(3) The practise of missionary intercession is best learned in the home.

A program of missionary reading in the home combines the three—seeing, hearing, doing.

Before the gift of Cyrus Hamlin's gingerbread money for missions came the reading of the two missionary magazines which always had place on his mother's table. Before William Carey went to India came the reading of "Captain Cook's Voyages."

Boys and girls are reading constantly yet few homes are giving them missionary reading. Mothers are reading aloud bedtime stories, yet few mothers are reading aloud the stories of missions. The church should cooperate with the home in furnishing and circulating missionary books and periodicals. Every boy and girl in America should have "Everyland," our one magazine of world friendships and world peace. The hope of the future is not in our halls of congress and legislature. The hope of the world is in the boys and girls in our homes. There is no substitute for the home in missionary education.

REASONS FOR BECOMING FOREIGN MISSIONARIES

TESTIMONIES OF STUDENT VOLUNTEERS

MR. E. WARNER LENTZ, URSINUS COLLEGE

Going to the foreign field is not an unusual thing. It is something that is natural, and in my own case it is just another example of the influence of a Christian home in which the life of the youngest member was so guided that it is impossible for that member to do anything else than to just go out into the world and tell people about the things that he learned. Another important factor makes my going to the foreign field a very natural process. There is a certain girl who, with all her heart and soul has backed me up and is going out there too!

Some experiences have come into my life, these last few years, that have made my going out to the field rather difficult. Similar experiences have come into the life of other students throughout the country which have made their going out rather difficult. The first of these is what we call on the campus, the "lagging spirit of the church," the spirit which has been so busy with the mechanics and so lagging with the real dynamics of Christ, the spirit that has caused us to build mammoth buildings, equipped completely from the very top to the very bottom, but seemingly without a vision of the real work of the church.

Students throughout this country are staying home, because there are no more funds to send them. It seems so often a catastrophe to see a great church grow up, equipped completely from chimes to gymnasium, and having no vision bigger than itself. It is like a lighthouse which shows no light. We fail to realize, I believe, and this is the students' message, that the light that is brightest shines farthest. It is just as if my heart would say to my head that day after tomorrow there will be no more blood flowing from my heart into my head, that all that blood is going to be used to build up the walls of my heart. You know what would happen; I would die. There are a great many colleges and churches that are building up their own interest and forgetting the dying souls across the sea. They make a sentiment hard to avoid. Another reason why it is difficult for me to go, and has been difficult has been that the campuses of our Christian colleges have offered a great missionary challenge to me. During these last few months it has been my privilege to visit about thirty colleges in the United States. What has been impressed upon me has been the lack of Christian spirit and Christian interest, and much less the lack of interest in missions. You ask why. From this audience I hear the reply come back, it is because of the student. It is, to a degree, and yet, on the other hand, it is because of the professors, because of the leaders that we people of the church have allowed to go into those colleges and head them up.

Just one more reason why it has been so very hard for some of us to offer for missionary service. This is the way in which we have treated foreign students right here in the United States—the way we have treated those boys and girls who have been entrusted to us. Do you know it is reported that in a single year there are more Chinese students in the United States, who revert from Christianity to atheism, than there are Chinese students who while here are converted to Christianity? There are three thousand Chinese students in the United States today. One quarter of them are baptized Christians. I know a Chinese boy who for eight years lived in a denominational college in the State of Pennsylvania, before ever a mention was made of Jesus Christ as His Saviour.

You say, "Why go?" People all over the country have asked me why I am going. I am going in the spirit of true humility, recognizing that we have partially failed at certain points and recognizing, too, that we have absolutely failed at certain other points, but I am going out there to help in every way I can those people of Bagdad, and primarily to preach Christ to them.

I have honestly studied the things that we people of the United States have that those people of Mesopotamia do not have. I have come to this thought, that there is just one fundamental thing that we have which they do not have, and that is Jesus Christ the Saviour—a Saviour who one day pulled me out of the way I was going toward making good with myself at the center and placed me over here on another road, where I was going to make good too, and I am going to but I am going to have Christ as a Saviour. It is that Christ who is driving us to the foreign field. It is for Him that we are going, to give Him to them, and tonight we are asking your help and your prayers.

MISS LYNDA IRENE GOODSELL, WELLESLEY COLLEGE

When I returned from Turkey a few years ago to enter college here in the United States I fully expected to go back as a foreign missionary. There was nothing else I could do. It was the logical thing. For four years I had been studying in Constantinople College for girls with its seventeen different nationalities. My acquaintances were Greek, Turkish, Armenian, Russian, Hebrew girls. These girls were my friends. I had to return to them. Furthermore, I had a very real chance to see the need and opportunity in Turkey for intelligent and sympathetic cooperation. My heart went out to the little boys, who had no chance for schooling, no chance for physical education or playgrounds. I longed to be a nurse or a doctor, and yet again I wanted to be able to teach physics, history, economics, sociology, psychology and all those subjects that they are eager to learn. Agricultural work is developing. Industrial schools are needed. There is an opportunity for every type of life investment in Turkey, provided that investment shows the love of Christ.

But perhaps the most potent figure in drawing me back home was the fact that I would be returning to my own home circle. That is very near to each one of us. May I digress a moment here to say a word about being a missionary's daughter. I think sometimes people look at us with a little bit of pity. We have been deprived of a few things which matter, perhaps, of some educational advantages, of a few social privileges, but I am proud to be a missionary's daughter. I am thankful for the background that it gives me in college.

But I realize that, if I were going to the foreign field with only this idea of going back to my friends, or because of the great need that I have seen there, or because of my own home ties, I would merit in no way the word "missionary." My intention to go back to Turkey involves no exaggerated idea of sacrifice. I hope I have no superiority complex, because that is wrong and fatal to one's usefulness; but I intend to be a missionary, God bless the word, because I have found in Jesus Christ a friend and a master who is dearer than my life to me and I must share him with others. My duty to Christ is not a debt, but a privilege. I value his friendship so highly, that I must share it with others and introduce others to him, but to introduce others one must know both parties well. Through my medicine I hope to be able to know the Turkish people well and through my own devotional life I hope to be able to appropriate for the inspiration of others in a small measure the unsearchable riches of Christ.

Then I hope that I can help Turkey to find Christ as a Master and a Friend who can guide her in her new era.

I hear Jesus calling me to the people of Turkey, "Follow me" and for his sake I follow. In the words of that stirring hymn, "Young, strong and free, Lord of my life, I come."

WALTER JUDD, M. D., UNIVERSITY OF NEBRASKA

It is quite obvious that I could not give a learned dissertation on the why's and wherefore's of foreign missions. Indeed, after these sessions of this convention it would be idle to attempt to do so. However, I do know why I believe in foreign missions enough to give my own life to that work. There are four reasons. Nine years ago I went to an Older Boys' Conference of the Y. M. C. A. in Lincoln, Nebraska. I met there Jesus Christ. Since that day I have known that there could be but one single dominating motive in my life. That was to do the best I could to mould men after the fashion of Jesus Christ.

I spent the next few months studying as hard as I could on two questions—what shall I do with my life, and where shall I spend it? The second question was answered first. Within a month after reading the life of David Livingstone and all the other church papers and literature I could get hold of, I decided it would have to be in the foreign mission field, unless God prevented it. About six months later, after studying myself and the need I thought that I ought to go to medical work. Medicine to be my profession but not my life work; Christian missions to be my life work.

Here are the reasons that led me to this decision: The first was simply a sense of fairness, a square deal to the non-Christian peoples of the world. I had happened to be born out there in a little town in the state of Nebraska, given a public school education, a high school education, a university education and a medical education. Was I responsible for the fact that I was born in a home, where I was surrounded all my life with Christian influences? No, I had nothing to do with that. In other countries there are men and women without a chance to go to public school, high school, state university or medical school, men and women born without a fraction even of the helpful surroundings under Christian auspices that I had had. Were they responsible for that? No, it was a mere accident, as far as they were concerned.

Did I have a right to appropriate that which came to me through mere accident of my birth and allow other people to go all their lives without any of those opportunities? If we had been neglecting those folks all these years, it would not be quite so bad; but when I thought of it, I realized that I ought to be willing to give my life to try to set right the wrongs that have been done those people by men of my own color and my kind of religion. That was my first reason.

The second is just because of the overwhelming need there, the need from the standpoint of existence, from an educational standpoint, from the standpoint of womanhood and childhood, the need from the standpoint of medicine. That, of course, interested me. I read of a fellow one time who had indigestion. A native doctor gave him fifty pounds of ground stone of some kind during his treatment of him. He came to a well trained missionary doctor and under good treatment he got well. If the people of China had constitutions to stand that kind of treatment, I felt that was the place for me to practice. The statistics showed that there is about one doctor in the foreign field for anywhere from one to five million people. In this country there is one to every 725. What does that mean. It would mean that there would be only one doctor to my home state, which is 400 miles long and 200 miles wide. I didn't care as long as Chinese people had no doctor; but if my mother had been sick and there was no doctor closer than 400 miles away, it would have made a difference. That was enough.

I have been working since I finished my interneship, till I got my debts paid off, with a doctor in Omaha. When I left there the first of September there were applications from twenty-one fellows for my humble position—doctors just as good or better than I am. I could not help but think, if I don't go back to Omaha, I am sure there is nobody out there who is going to suffer for lack of a first rate physician. Next summer, I go to China, to an area about the same size as the state of Connecticut. Back in Omaha there are twenty-one fellows offering for my position. Out there is an opportunity which nobody fills if I do not go. Now what should I do?

The third reason is because the need is so great here at home. That sounds funny, I suppose. A few years ago, when I began to waken up to the terrible iniquity in our own civilization, I was disheartened. I said, "After all, maybe I ought to change my purpose to become a foreign missionary." When I saw our colleges with all the evil and the superficial living and the lack of any serious thought about life or about Christian service, it seemed to me there was a challenge to stay here and work in this country. I seemed to think there was no right to go over there until in America we could set up a demonstration of Christian civilization from which they could learn. I had the idea that to attempt to take our Western medicine and our Western education methods was about the same as taking Christianity. I don't believe that any more.

The need is so great here at home, it seemed to me that I didn't feel it could be remedied without foreign missions of the right sort. As I became more and more conscious of the great evils in our country it seemed to me that we could not begin to solve our inter-racial and international problems, and our own labor problems without the right kind of foreign missions. So the great need at home constituted no reason against foreign missions but rather a fresh challenge to foreign missions of the right sort.

I go to the foreign field because my hope for our own country lies in the Orient. The need is so great here at home it compels me to go there to help meet America's need as well as China's need. Napoleon said 125 years ago, "There lies China, a great giant. Don't awaken her." Well, she is awakening, we can't put her back to sleep. My question is which way will she change the face of the world? Toward Christ or against Christ? The answer does not depend upon China; it depends upon you and upon me. It is our job as Christians to take Christianity to China.

The fourth reason why I believe in foreign missions is because it is Christ's command. It is not my plan for the world. I didn't want to be a missionary any more than anybody else. He asked to have it done by his disciples. I called myself one of his disciples. It has not been done through all these 1,900 years.

What choice did I have except to get busy at it, unless I had some special reason for not being at work at that particular thing? I couldn't get away from that. It was up to me. It seemed to me it was up to me to convince myself that I ought not to become one. I could find no adequate reason for not becoming one.

The biggest obstacle, when it comes to deciding to go to the foreign field is the obstacle of Christian parents at home. Oftentimes leaders of missionary societies, I have found, when it comes to their own sons and daughters, are not willing to have them go. I have thanked God that my mother, even though she had lost three sons, I being the fourth, when I came and told her I was going to be a foreign missionary, she was glad.

Here was the call, where the need was the greatest and the workers the fewest. If I honestly wanted to put my life in where it would count for the most, where else would I go, except where the need was the greatest and the workers the fewest? We pray glibly, "Thy kingdom come." I question if I have a right to pray that, to let it roll off my lips, unless it represents the dominating passion of my every waking hour year in and year out. Not fifteen per cent of my life or ninety-nine and one-half per cent of my life but all my life, all for Him.

I looked for reasons for not going. I could find none. I was physically fit, no dependents, no honest reason except my own selfish ambition. They could not stand alongside of Him. Hence I go.

ASPECTS OF THE MOHAMMEDAN PROBLEM

INTELLECTUAL MOVEMENTS AMONG MOSLEMS

DEAN ROBERT S. MC CLENAHAN, LL.D., CAIRO

It would certainly not be correct to say that there exists any large and striking intellectual movement throughout the Moslem world today, any manifest and far-reaching renaissance at all comparable to what has appeared at times elsewhere. Passing right across eastward from Morocco and North Africa to the East Indies, or from Russia southward to Zanzibar, one cannot find any outstanding center or centers where any more than the most minor intellectual awakening is evident. Here and there, notably at Constantinople, Beirut, Cairo, Bagdad, in the Punjab, at Ali-garh, Madras, and a few other centers, there appear what might be interpreted as the beginnings of something new, something which shows signs of placing the straight-edge of truth and scientific and historical knowledge to test one's intellectual heritage or traditional thinking. Each of these centers stands alone; there is apparently no bond to unite them, no quickening mutually enjoyed or extending beyond, in any sensible way, to others. The inertia of centuries has not been overcome to any such extent that one might speak of the existence of a genuinely intellectual movement in the Moslem world today.

Yet there does exist a breaking away from what the Moslem world has been satisfied with heretofore, that centuries-old seclusion, that contentment with an out-of-date thinking, and a worn-out traditionalism. That isolation, that unwillingness to use or approve what was not cast in the Arabic mould, musty with age, that insulation from the rest of the world's thinking, is breaking down; for it has been proven, is being proven, unprofitable and sterile. There is a sense of recognition that there is, or seems to be, something better somewhere, there is *some* conscious or unconscious looking about for some one who shall be guide, counselor and friend. Gradually, almost imperceptibly, that sense of bankruptcy, of emptiness, of unreliability on the part of what Islam has had to offer, its limitations, the anachronism of its civilization when face to face with a progressive world, has been increasing and extending. In still limited numbers, there are those who look on while international contacts, the give and take of modern life, are showing resources with which the Moslem peoples without a change cannot compete. It does not require much penetration for a citizen of any of those Moslem lands to discover that the good things are coming from yonder lands which are neither

Moslem nor pagan. He may resent it; he may gather his robes about him and exert himself to have nothing to do with yon progressiveness. He may snuggle down into the comfortable and easy heritage of orthodox Islam. Or he may struggle to prove to himself and others that once given a chance, Islam as a religion, as a system, as a state, in every way, can justify itself. Yet after all, he looks about for some things profitable for mankind, in politics, in science, in literature, in social advancement, in industrial life, in economics, in invention, in the application of these to the physical, moral and spiritual welfare of humanity, within the domain of Islam, and is disappointed. He finds that either those things are conspicuous for their absence, or that they have been borrowed, often taken right over wholesale, from outside.

It sets him thinking. He may be but a small boy in the geography class; he may be a more advanced student whose study of history brings before him the comparative values manifest in the rise and extension of Islam, its founder, its propagation, and its characteristic contributions to the nations to which it came. He may be still further on, engaged in reading something of the controversial literature of the day, or the destructive polemics of modern infidels and agnostics. Or his reading and educational processes may bring him face to face with the highest and best things, and to wonder whence they really do spring.

Probably no factor has been more active in the production and extension of this incipient intellectual movement than the almost universal use of the words "independence" and "liberty," among the millions of those we are now considering, during the past two decades, and notably since the beginning of the war. In Turkey, Egypt, Arabia, India, Palestine, Mesopotamia, and now more recently in North Africa, these words have become a slogan, have awakened an ambition which never had a hearing before. It is true that they have had a political meaning, augmented, emphasized and idealized by declarations of the rights of homogeneous peoples to self-determination. Those words *independence* and *liberty* have been on the lips of millions, have set millions to thinking and talking, first in matters political, and from that to other things. Out of discussions in little groups in villages, and gatherings of hundreds in cities, and in the multitude of discussions in the vernacular press, there has been evolved the consciousness, more or less definite, that more was comprehended in those two words than mere political freedom and self-government. Picking the words to pieces, comparing ideas, measuring by other nations, there has dawned upon many that there does exist a very righteous and possible liberty and independence within the realm of one's own thinking; that traditional dogma and authority may or may not be right and true, and that in any case, one has the right and duty of investigation, of inquiry, and of decision. To me, it seems that what there is of intellectual movement in the world of Islam today, has grown out of this more than anything else. It is a contagious awakening, very real, very vital, in its character. When once it has begun to claim its own, whether within its original circle of politics and nationalism, or beyond the boundaries of that, it is irresistible. And it is just this awakening, this appetite for inquiry and investigation, which we call an intellectual movement, and which the spirit of Christian missions welcomes; indeed, without which, the conviction and conversion of individuals and communities can expect to make but little progress. It is at least the destructive element—destructive of self-satisfaction, the inertia of centuries of falsehood and traditional error.

And how does it work? Generally speaking, it produces two quite opposite communities in the Moslem world. First, those who would save Islam at any cost; who cannot entertain any thought of surrender to Christianity or paganism, or lowering of the standards of the Crescent. They would save the face of Islam, its name and prestige, with the conviction that the great system which has been built up around Mohammed and the Koran and the prolific literature behind which it is entrenched, must be right, and that to surrender it means humiliation, means surrendering everything, and puts a man's feet in strange places where he dare not trust himself. It would imperil him as an individual, and the whole civilization which has been created out of Islam, rights, privileges, distinctions, and perquisites. To him it seems too perilous a thing even to think of the possibility of intellectual advancement disturbing the equilibrium of Islam and Islamic civilization. It may be that it calls for some apology, some adjustments, some strained interpretations and applications. But better stay by it than to abandon the ship; it will get one somewhere, others will not, and certainly the repudiation of Islam will have too grave consequences, so he reasons.

The second community which is growing up within this intellectual renaissance, even though it be in its earliest stages, is that of those who incline, as a result of it, to break away from Islam and everything else religious; who transgress its laws flagrantly and frequently; who would jettison the whole cargo, and take nothing in its place. If they go afield into reading or thinking, they incline to repudiate everything religious, ridicule, license, indifference, or open and bitter attack upon any attributing of the best things to spiritual and religious sources.

Between these two camps, that of the intellectually orthodox, if such a term may be used, and the intellectually agnostic, there are, of course, many less pronounced communities. Some are raising the question of retaining or discarding Arabic or the other languages or vernaculars of Moslem peoples. The pendulum of the intellectual movement swings at one time away over in favor of retaining especially the sacred language of the Koran, or Islamic literature and spoken language of millions today. Again it swings far away from Arabic, or other vernacular, with the declaration that to be shut up to them, to be without the field of literature which other languages provide and which they do not, costs too high a price, in one's preparation for profession and general culture. The charge has been made at times in recent years against European governments ruling Moslem peoples, that they were facilitating the use of foreign languages and the literature of conquerors, and that the end would be the annihilation of Arabic and other vernaculars. Again the cry has been raised against the foreign control because it was providing the minimum of knowledge and use of the world's best literature, languages of non-Moslems, simply to prevent the growth and development of peoples, and their enlightenment and culture through popularizing the native languages, whose literature and sources for research are extremely limited.

Within these two camps also, one finds a very considerable variety of types of individuals, differing so widely in their attitudes intellectually, as to offer call for much discretion and wisdom on the part of those who approach them with missionary purpose. For some of these individuals and those in their group, facilities have been provided for a considerable reading, companionship and a comparison of claims and values. Others are, of course, entirely without any such facilities for intellectual stimulus, which provides an intellectualism of its kind. Here are some of the types.

1. One meets in these groups the individual who has come to value the contributions of historical and scientific investigation, in its bearing on one's faith. He is, to a considerable extent, a sincere and honest investigator. He does try to think, and to think soberly. He will certainly have every right to carry his investigations to their conclusions; any limitation of his inquiry would be fatal to the very truth itself. A fair field and no favor, with this man, will ultimately bring him to appreciation of the soundness of some things, and the unsoundness of others.

2. A second type consists of those who are being introduced these days to deistic, rationalistic and destructive literature, much of it entirely out of date, but bearing the names of men who have attained some prominence, especially in Europe. This group are usually filled with the spirit of license, inclining to the sensational, and including large numbers of those who pride themselves that they are students. They enjoy controversy, and in their eagerness for it place themselves frequently on very slippery

ground, and their tendency is quite toward the destructive rather than toward anything constructive. In the presentation of the Gospel message to them, one will do well to remember that "some seed fell among the thorns."

3. The third group would be represented by the thousands of what are known in the Moslem world as the "sheikhs" or "maulvis." Their habits of life, their physical, social, intellectual and spiritual environment has been such as to preclude their making any real study, and yet they themselves would be the first to claim that they are the *intelligentia,* and their communities would at once confirm it. They regard the intellectual movements outside the traditional orbits of Islam as impossible, often absurd and preposterous. Frequently they are very positive against outside thinking, simply because of the lack of it in what they have seen of a gross misrepresentation of simple Christianity, though what they regard as an ecclesiastical idolatry. They reason that the race and color prejudices, the social customs, and what they see of intolerance, and the political greed of non-Moslems are enough to condemn the self-assumed intellectual superiority of others. No doubt if we were placed in the same environment, and had the same outlook, as they have, we would prefer to discard any proffered intellectual values from outside.

4. Probably the most difficult group for the approach of Christian Missions is composed of those who are utterly indifferent to spiritual values; to whom all religions are the same, who brush away considerations of more serious matters, who do not desire to break with any one, and who would have no unpleasant circumstances arise. They will appreciate intellectual awakenings, will be glad to have periodicals, new books, and more or less cultured organizations discuss matters of ethics and the welfare of the state and society, will talk much about the necessity of increasing educational facilities and uplifting womankind, etc., etc. It is an intellectual movement, of a kind. It certainly did not exist a decade or two ago. It is manifested in the very great increase in the circulation of daily, weekly and monthly periodicals, in the multitudes who now follow, even in the villages, the political and social and economic questions of the day; in the appeals which public leaders make to the masses through the press, pamphlets and even more weighty literature. For there is no questioning the fact that there is a reading public, very much larger than ever before, a reading public which does not take things very seriously, after all, but which desires to be fed on this new form of intellectual pabulum, printed matter.

5. We find also that pitiful group who are hopeless; who have found so much in the ordinary processes of thinking, of education, and of conscious or unconscious comparisons and measurements of human life, that they are quite without any definable

guidance. If they are not out and out agnostics, they are close to it. How often we have found them saying that, their former ideals having gone, their former structure having been undermined, they do not propose to take on any thing more, or to erect a second edifice of faith or religion, for it might go the same way of loss and prove unworthy, as truly as did the first. They fear that nothing can ring true any more. They do not talk much, but do think much. If there is a pitiful type among those of the recent intellectual movement, it is this group in the Moslem world.

These all suggest to us that there is on today a transition and intellectual struggle which might be defined as neo-Islamic, as truly as there was one called neo-Platonic in the second and third centuries A. D. It is eclectic, attempting to discard what is found unpalatable in both the traditional and hereditary faith and system, and the more progressive faith and civilization, which is extending all over the world, Christian. It tends to approve of what is best, at least what seems to be profitable, while at the same time retaining the name and credit of the faith of one's ancestors and the fellowship of one's co-religionists.

It is a time of intellectual and religious adolescence, the two combined. One has to meet it in individuals, but we must remember that the same process is going on with communities, peoples, nations. It is a time for patience, grace, human kindness and sympathy, while this difficult period of analysis and synthesis, of disintegration and construction, is going on, and after which the tide of intellectual movements will set in inevitably in the direction of truth. How broad and how deep is that gulf which separates the Moslem thinking from our own, across which a thinking, a careful, sober, honest inquirer, an intellectual pioneer, has to pass, we probably never realize. All the contributions which Christian enlightenment can offer, both direct and indirect, even with the greatest variety of method and application, will be called for during this time of intellectual awakening and the creation of a spiritual appetite for the fruits of Christ's gospel.

MOSLEM AGGRESSION IN AFRICA

PROFESSOR DR. JULIUS RICHTER, UNIVERSITY OF BERLIN

The African continent is one of the great fields of missionary endeavor; unitedly in the second half of the nineteenth century it has been, besides India and China, by far the greatest foreign field of the missionary societies. One-third of the continent, a country as great as Europe or as the United States, with, alas, fifty-nine millions of Mohammedans, is already Islamized whilst among its 185 million inhabitants there are hardly more than ten or eleven million Christians, white and colored, Protestant, Roman Catholic, and Oriental churches taken altogether. The whole northern half from Egypt to Morocco and from the Senegal, French Equatorial and Upper Nigeria to the Somaliland and Zanzibar are overwhelmingly Moslem though in many parts isolated and scattered native tribes have retained their prehistoric animism and tribalism. The situation is the more tragic if we remember that the Christian churches had dominated the whole series of coast lands of the southern Mediterranean, and that Egypt, Tripoli, and North Africa or Mauritania were among the most flourishing provinces of the ancient church. From Egypt Christianity has advanced far up into Nubia and Abyssinia; in all other parts of the hinterland of Northern and Equatorial Africa there are only very slight remains of early Christian missions. And under the rush and turmoil of the rising tide of Moslem advance from the seventh century on the Christian churches disintegrated, crumbled and disappeared and Islam advanced victoriously. And what Christianity had shamefully neglected during the four centuries of its dominance, Islam did slowly yet effectively occupy; it pushed down through the deserts of the Sahara and the swamps of the Nile and its tributaries and advanced victoriously from the north and from the east so that at present doubtless it has a commanding position in North Africa. Is it possible at all to make up for this irreparable loss?

The propaganda of Islam as it was in the nineteenth century had some drawbacks yet many advantages. An outstanding drawback in the nineteenth century was the close connection of Islam with slavery, slave raids, slave wars and all those terrible ravages connected with the slave trade. There was a very strong antipathy of the raided and pillaged, scattered and suffering tribes against the haughty Mohammedan slave chiefs and their hordes. Yet since the abolition of slavery in Equatorial Africa by the joint efforts of the Christian powers of Europe, under the leadership of Great Britain, this obstacle and offense has been to a great extent removed. And since then, the attractive features of Islam on the African mind have become all the more powerful. Islam leaves to the African his primitive social order, it strengthens polygamy and slavery, it does not counteract superstition. It just adds to native life a varnish of a somewhat higher civilization, an attractive dress, new charms which, inscribed in Arabic letters on amulets, are regarded as particularly powerful, a simple sort of rote-school in which parts of the Koran are learned by heart in a language which is not understood, definite prohibitions in the regular order of life like the fasting in the month Ramadan or the prohibitions to eat pork. It gives a sort of respectability to the negro, particularly to the chief and his headmen which is only too readily acknowledged by the white merchants whilst they deny the same acknowledgment to the Christian negroes. Besides, the Moslem propaganda is advancing slowly and imperceptibly. There are no mission stations, no big foreign institutions, no foreigners settling in the midst of the negroes yet living on an altogether different plane. There is the simple brown peddler or merchant settling down in their remote villages, marrying their daughters, mingling with their simple village life yet maintaining scrupulously the five daily prayers and other rites of his religion. And after him come the religious orders—the Senussi, the Kadisiya, the Chadeleyi and others gradually and perhaps only in the course of generations leavening the native life by Moslem convictions and customs. And last but not least, Islam usually appeals most strongly to the powerful tribes advancing victoriously and subjugating mercilessly the weakened and less consolidated tribes. So Islam usually is paramount with the conquering tribes like the Filani, the Mandingo, the Yaos, etc. And there can be no question that in connection with the superiority of the tribes which have accepted Islam and have for generations intermarried with Moslems a remarkable degree of civilization has been propagated in connection with the Moslem propaganda. Powerful states have been established and in some cases maintained through centuries; big cities and rich commercial centers have been created.

There can be no doubt that for great parts of Equatorial Africa Islam indeed meant a great advance in general civilization and the colonial powers in the Moslem territories of Africa almost everywhere formerly preferred to govern by native rule; so they cultivated the Moslem rulers, they scrupulously abstained from interfering with Moslem customs and prejudices; they created the general impression that Islam is a favored religion; they even built mosques and started Moslem schools, whilst putting many hindrances into the way of the Christian propaganda.

Happily, during the last decade they have begun to give up that disastrous policy. By far the greater part of Moslem Africa is under French colonial rule, and without criticizing the colonial policy of France in Africa, it is a well-known fact that Protestant missions in their sphere of influence had for a long time to grapple with many hindrances, most of which could only be overcome if the French Evangelical Missionary Society of Paris could undertake the work which, unhappily, in view of its many engagements in other fields and its limited means, seems to be out of the question. Here, too, a change of French Colonial policy may improve the situation.

What then shall be the attitude of the Protestant missions? Of course, they cannot and will not give up the campaign to conquer the Dark Continent for the Kingdom of God. At first, of course, there is the great other half of pagan Africa with the almost Christianized South Africa. If only the Christianization of the pagan southern half of Africa would be completed within the next generation, and that seems not to be quite out of the range of possibility and practicability, a Christian South and a Moslem North would confront each other, and that alone would mean a decided advance. This strategic view is particularly important in the borderlands where perhaps in the past the Moslem advance has been scarcely felt, yet has become an imminent menace since the beginning of this century, as along the Guinea coast of West Africa, the Uganda Protectorate, and the countries around Lake Nyasa. Wherever in such regions strong Protestant Missions of long standing exist, it is evidently of special importance to strengthen them and to make them pillars of resistance and of advance.

Then there are some important changes in the general situation which appear to alter the outlook helpfully. The Moslem states have all of them crumbled and are disappearing rapidly, making room for an enlightened colonial administration. So the Moslems no longer dominate the situation; their influence is narrowed into definite spheres. However scrupulously the colonial policy of Great Britain or France will take regard of Moslem prejudices they will scarcely promote the Islamization of the many pagan tribes remaining side by side with the Moslem nations. These heathen tribes or clans, often scattered like islands surrounded by an active Moslem propaganda, are the appropriate starting point of the Christian propaganda; and it is an almost general experience that these tribes welcome the Christian missionaries with open arms.

Then there is the great and general fact of the rising tide of European civilization all over the African continent. Roads and railways are built. Commercial and political centers are started. The European with his auto or aeroplane, even with his radio and broadcaster begins to become ubiquitous in Moslem as well as in pagan Africa. And then there can of course be no difference of opinion as to the superiority of the European above the Moslem civilization. This superiority is so impressive and imposing to the African that it can be counteracted so far as we see by one factor which always must be kept carefully in view—that the Moslems become the champions and protagonists of the negro races in the growing antagonisms and race feelings of Ethiopians. The Moslem African might like to pose himself as the leader of the brown race in its attempt to assert itself against white rule.

With the European civilization comes modern education. It is an astounding fact to what extent the colored people develop a real hunger and thirst for knowledge. They will no longer remain the raw heathen of the primeval forest. They crowd the schools wherever such are started. Islam is not able to provide modern schools. The educational problem perhaps is the most burning question of Africa today. Yet more than nine-tenths of the schools are in the hands of the missionary societies. It is their privilege and their chance to command the almost inexhaustible possibilities of the situation.

Yet what shall we do in view of these facts? At first, strengthen the missionary strongholds in the centers of advance and along the border line. It is a wonderful providence that just at the crucial points such flourishing and richly blessed missions as those in Uganda, British Nyasaland, Southern Nigeria, the Gold Coast and Kameroun are maintaining commanding positions.

Secondly, it is highly desirable that the American missionary societies shall have a more active part in Equatorial African missions. Of course, their interest is rightly concentrated on the Far East. We are extremely grateful that during the last decade one American missionary society after the other has entered the African field. There might perhaps be more concentration of effort and a more comprehensive missionary strategy in view of the formidable adversary we have to face.

In the first half of the nineteenth century Australasia was the continent the evangelization of which was the accomplished fact of concentrated missionary efforts. In the first half of the twentieth century, in spite of all overwhelming claims of the Asiatic field, Africa (pagan Africa), puts before the Christian church the great task which can and should be accomplished to stop Moslem advance and to secure Africa for Christ.

GOD'S LOVE FOR THE MOHAMMEDANS
THE REVEREND SAMUEL M. ZWEMER, D.D., CAIRO

The one thing needed by the Mohammedan world of today is a great missionary outpouring of love for the prodigal children of God in all Mohammedan lands. Yet this outpouring of love for the lost is the one thing that the church has always needed most and found last. Abraham sent away from his tent Hagar and Ishmael with a leathern bottle of water and a few loaves of bread. She wandered in the wilderness until the water was gone and then she cast her child under a shrub to die but, "God heard the voice of the lad," and God saved Ishmael.

I love to think of Jesus at Nazareth hearing that story for the first time from the lips of his mother, Mary, and treasuring up in his subconscious mind that great love of God for prodigals. And then when the Pharisees and Sadducees found fault with him because he loved sinners and ate with them, he said, "A certain man had two sons . . . When the prodigal was yet a great way off his father saw him and had compassion and ran and fell on his neck and kissed him."

The Mohammedan religion in a real sense is the prodigal son among all the non-Christian religions, and yet the Church of Jesus Christ for many centuries has had the spirit of the Crusades rather than the spirit of the Cross. We need to read once more the conversion of Paul to a deeper love for Israel. In his First Epistle to the Thessalonians you will remember what he had undergone and how he expressed himself. He said, "The Jews, who killed the Lord Jesus and all their prophets, who are contrary to all men, who forbid us to preach the gospel, upon whom has come the wrath of God to the uttermost," and then those Jews laid on his bare back the stripes forty times, save one, and turned him out of their synagogue and left him a wandering preacher among the Gentiles. Then, after four years, Paul takes up his pen again and the tears fall fast on the page as he writes his Roman Epistle, "I am telling the truth in Christ,—it is no lie, my conscience bears me out in the Holy Spirit, when I say that I am in sore pain, I suffer endless anguish of heart. I could have wished myself accursed and banished from Christ for the sake of my brothers, my natural kinsmen; for they are Israelites, theirs is the sonship, the glory, the covenants, the divine legislation, the worship and the promises." (Moffatt.)

Between that malediction in Thessalonians and the benediction in Romans, there must have been a love kindled in Paul's heart that would not let them go.

Thirty-three years ago my colleague, James Cantine, and I began work in Arabia. In Cantine's home in the Catskills before we sailed, Dr. J. G. Lansing wrote for us the Arabian missionary hymn which we sang when our mission was organized. How often those words have been a challenge to love that will not let go.

> There is a land, long since neglected,
> There is a people still rejected,
> But of truth and grace elected,
> In God's love for them.

> To the host of Islam leading,
> To the slave in bondage bleeding,
> To the desert dweller pleading,
> Bring His love to them.

And the last stanza,

> Till Arabia's raptured millions,
> Sing His love for them.

Years later in Arabia reports came to us, even in those days, of the exceeding great multitude that climbed the steep ascent to heaven, through peril, toil and pain, and of whom the remnants came to us, some blind, helpless, poor, and became teachers, the remnant of the massacred Armenian Church. "They were tortured, not accepting deliverance. They were subject to mockings and scourgings and bonds and imprisonments. They were stoned, they were torn asunder, they were tempted, they were slain with the sword. They wandered about, day and night; some of them wandered about in sheep skins and goat skins, destitute, afflicted, of whom the world was not worthy."

When I thought of the Chinese church and the Indian church represented here in this Convention, I could see that exceeding great multitude of the Oriental churches, Nestorians, Armenians and Greeks, whom Dr. Johannes Lepsius estimated at over one million two hundred thousand martyrs, killed by their Mohammedan neighbors. When we think of all that, there come to us the words of Robert Louis Stevenson:

> I have felt Thy wind in my face,
> Spit sorrow and disgrace;
> I have seen Thine evil doom,
> At Golgotha and Khartoum;
> And, I have seen the brutes,
> The work of Thy hands,
> Fill with injustice the lands,
> And stain with blood the sea. . . .

You know the rest of those verses. They portray the great tragedy of the Near East. But on the other hand, there comes to us that parable of Jesus Christ, "And when he was yet a great way off his father saw him."

One of our missionaries in Bagdad, Dr. Staudt, had two boys in his school a few months ago. One was called Theophilus, the other Mohammed. One was the son of a Nestorian priest and the other was one of a leading Mohammedan of Bagdad. They sat side by side and had to share a book between them. At first, they were unwilling but finally in the lesson there came the Arabic word for "forgiveness" and Dr. Staudt, the teacher, said to Mohammed, "What does 'forgiveness' mean?" Immediately the priest's son spoke up with a sneer and said, "He can't know what that means." Mark the boy's language, not "he does not know" but, "he can't know." Today those two boys are beginning to love the Saviour, our Lord, and they have knitted their lives together in a new friendship through their love of Jesus Christ.

Now, what is there that makes us believe in our deepest heart that God loves this great Mohammedan world and these millions of Mohammedans? First of all we believe that God loves them *because of their vast numbers and their long neglect.*

One-seventh of the human race, 234,000,000 people. The lands where they live have scarcely been mentioned on this platform, Nigeria, Morocco, Algeria, Tunisia, Tripoli, Syria, Palestine, Turkey, the great expanses of Central Asia, 69,000,000 in India, 35,000,000 on the single Island of Java, and in Africa alone nearly 60,000,000 Mohammedans. Surely God's plan of mercy and love does not exclude these millions. Surely He who said, "Suffer little children to come unto me," has compassion on 80,000,000

Mohammedan children under fourteen years of age. "Jesus saw a great multitude," the Bible tells us, and "was moved with compassion toward them."

And they are neglected. In every one of the great mission fields, according to the surveys made and the testimony of your missionaries, the Mohammedans are the most neglected class. At the Jerusalem Conference this finding was recorded: That in India the 69,000,000 Mohammedans may be looked upon as "largely an unoccupied field."

Second, God loves them, *because they are a great way off*. It is not for us to measure that distance, because the chasm between a Holy God and a helpless sinner is equidistant at the Antipodes and here. We who have lived among these people are moved with compassion, when we think of their ignorance, their illiteracy, their groveling superstitions. I speak of ninety-four per cent. of the people who are illiterate, not of the five or six per cent. who have been somewhat freed by education from the trammels that bind them. We think of the degradation of the home and of womanhood and of childhood and of literature, because of the character of this religion.

We think of fanaticism and pride and intolerance which are the fruit of this religion. We think of such moral and social bankruptcy as has arrested the attention of every thinking Mohammedan in Calcutta or Madras, Bombay or Cairo. Listen to one man among them, a university graduate, a splendid example of the educated Mohammedans of India. In his book, "Essays, Indian and Islamic," published a few years ago, he uses these words: "Should we not combat with all our might these social evils which are sapping the very life and spirituality of our Mohammedan community? Are these not problems calling for meditation and solution? I know I am drawing a severe indictment against my own religion, my own community, but we have need of no delicacy any longer if we are to proceed onwards. We want no palliatives, but the surgeon's knife, to cut out the social canker that is corrupting our Mohammedan youth and our Mohammedan homes." But there *is* balm in Gilead and there is a Physician who loves the Mohammedan people long before the missionary arrives.

Third, we believe God loves them, *because they have always and everywhere kept His first and great commandment*, "Hear, O Israel, the Lord our God *is* one Lord."

Islam is a theistic religion, and none of the non-Christian religions, save Judaism has a more glorious, and full and powerful theism than Mohammedanism. I stood in Benares, and after going through the temples of Hinduism, and seeing popular Hinduism, as it blossoms out in the lives of the people, I turned with disgust and looked at those two splendid minarets that crown the city and heard the call to prayer. When the man came down from the minaret I put out my hand and said, "My brother, truly God is greater than all the idols of the non-Christian world." The God of Mohammed, the God of Al Ghazali, the God of Jalal-ud-Din, the God of the Sufis and the mystics, has the attributes and has the personality of the God of Job and Isaiah. God loves them because they have kept this commandment and have not made unto them any graven image but have bowed their heads and hearts before God Almighty. "I perish with hunger," they have said, "in this desert of ritualism, and phariseeism, and outer religion, and I go home to God by the pathway of the mystic, by the pathway of personal communion." They tell us that three-fourths of all the adult Mohammedans in the world belong to these mystic orders.

Fourth, we believe God loves them *because He has not left Himself without a witness.* In no religion is there a stronger and clearer abiding witness to Christ and Christianity than in the Mohammedan religion. Christ and Christianity are mentioned frequently in Mohammed's Bible, the Koran. There are many references to Jesus the Prophet; there are many expressions in regard to the friendliness of the Christian. Again and again the Mohammedan stands face to face with the great outstanding facts of our religion; even when they are perverted or denied.

No wonder that some students of comparative religion have classified Mohammedanism as a Christian heresy. Perhaps that is going too far, but I heard Professor Mohammed Ismail of Lahore say at Jerusalem at a conference (and his testimony is corroborated in Persia and in Arabia and in India), that he learned three things when he was still a Mohammedan, from the Koran. First, that all men were sinners and required forgiveness; second, that Jesus had no sin; and third, that if He wanted to know more about Jesus Christ, he would have to secure a book called the Gospel. By means of that three-fold testimony we missionaries believe that the Koran is indeed in many cases a schoolmaster to lead men to Jesus Christ.

Fifth, we *believe that God loves the world of Islam because He runs out to meet them.* The history of missions to the Mohammedan world is the running out of the love of Jesus Christ, to win these prodigals. You remember what Paul said in one of his epistles, when he talked about the body of Christ and Christ as the Head. His heart leaped with joy when he wrote these words:

"The head cannot say to the feet, 'I have no need of thee.'" Paul felt delight in being the feet of Jesus to go out all the way after His prodigals.

As we think of the Mohammedan world, we may truly say:

"And what are these blood drops all the way
  That mark out the mountain track?"
"They were shed for those who had gone astray,
  Ere the shepherd could bring them back."
"Lord, why are Thy hands so rent and torn?
  They are pierced tonight by many a thorn."

No one has read the life of Raymond Lull or of Henry Martyn, or of Bishop French, or Dr. Pennell of Afghanistan, no one has ever read the story of Miss Holliday in Persia, or Miss de Meyer in Russia, without recognizing in these saints the outgoing love of Jesus Christ for lost Mohammedanism. Seeing we are compassed about by this great cloud of witnesses, let us lay aside every weight and the sin of prejudice and misunderstanding and neglect of centuries which doth so easily beset us, and let us run out to meet these prodigals with a message of forgiveness.

Lastly, we *believe that God loves Mohammedans because they are coming back home.* We have already heard that story from many a missionary in the simultaneous conferences and tonight on this platform have heard of the great changes that God has wrought in Turkey. It is a simple fact that Mohammedans everywhere today are more accessible, more responsive, than they ever were before in thirteen centuries. The gates of brass and the doors of iron have yielded to let the King of Glory pass and the Cross is in the field.

Did not Donaldson unfurl the banner of the Cross in Afghanistan? Did not Dr. Harrison penetrate to the very heart of Arabia? Is not Dr. Lambie building a hospital in the capital of Abyssinia? Have not the missionaries penetrated Morocco and Tripoli and Baluchistan and the borderlands of India? And do they not everywhere find open doors and willing hearts, where formerly the doors were barred and bolted?

The fall of the Caliphate has given a death blow to Pan-Islamism, and has provoked and created a new nationalism, a passion for democracy in which there is a latent desire not only for political but also for social and moral and spiritual freedom. The morning light is breaking—the darkness is disappearing in the old lands of the Near East.

Educational revivals are found everywhere. The enormous activity of the Mohammedan press is a sign of promise. In India alone there are two hundred and twenty Mohammedan newspapers, where fifty years ago there was scarcely a single Mohammedan periodical. In Persia, in Turkey, in Central Asia, in North Africa, the Moslem press is often the ally of the forces of Christianity in moral reform, in advocating popular education, in speaking a word for the emancipation of womanhood and the rights of childhood.

And, finally, I thank God that there have recently been public baptisms in those old Mohammedan countries, where the law of apostasy made public baptism an impossibility. In Egypt I have seen public marriages of Mohammedan converts in the presence of Sheikhs from the Moslem University and public baptisms both in the British and the American missions. In Arabia and Persia the missionaries state that public baptism is now the rule and not the exception.

When we think of Bengal and the Punjab, and Java and Abyssinia, we may truly believe that there are the beginnings of mass movements toward Christ even in Mohammedan lands. In Java and Sumatra there are nearly 45,000 living converts. In Bengal they told me that in one single province, 16,000 Mohammedans had been won from Islam to Christianity. In Abyssinia, under the movement of a converted Sheikh called Zakaria, some 6,000 Mohammedans have turned their backs on their old religion and are studying the Bible and embracing the teaching of Jesus Christ.

It is a new day. The Mohammedan world of yesterday is past, and with this new world, and a new hope, there is not only a new opportunity, but a new and a great and abiding responsibility upon the churches of Christendom. There are churches repsented in this great convention that have never yet touched the awful needs of the Mohammedan world, nay, not so much as the hem of that need in their missionary prayer life and program. There are vast countries and provinces utterly *unoccupied*. There are sections of India and China where the Mohammedans are absolutely neglected, and every one of the *occupied* fields calls to Heaven for reinforcement, not only of men and women but of that prevailing prayer which brought revival to Madagascar in the darkest days, which transformed it from a land of martyrs to a land with a living church; that power of prayer which lays hold of God with a love that will not let Him go. We need to pray with the oldest missionary collect of the ages: "Oh that Ishmael might live before thee." Oh, that God would pour out into our hearts a love for his prodigals and for the prodigal son among the non-Christian religions, Islam!

THE PROGRESS OF MISSIONS IN THE DUTCH INDIES

A BRIEF SURVEY OF DUTCH MISSIONS

BARON VAN BOETZELAER VAN DUBBELDAM, UTRECHT, HOLLAND

It is not an easy task to give a short and at the same time helpful survey of the Dutch Missions in the Dutch Indies. If Dr. Schlunk had not told us about the work of the German Missions in the Dutch Indies, I would have spent some time telling you about the wonderful work which the German Societies* have been doing and I would have spoken in strong appreciation of their wonderful work.

During the years I resided in Netherlands Indies, I sometimes heard Dutch government officials and others say that, although they saw the great value of the work of these German Missions, they would like it better if we could have had Dutch missionaries in their places. However, when the war came, and with it the inability of the German Boards to finance their work, there was only *one* opinion in the Dutch Indies: viz., that a work of such a high cultural value should not be stopped. The Colonial Government of Holland put aside all its principles of neutrality and paid for the support of this German mission work and is still paying yearly about $100,000 to carry on these Missions. This is very strong proof of the great appreciation in which these Missions are held.

It was my great privilege to visit three times the field of the Rhenish Missions in Sumatra. Twice I was in the isle of Nias: once before and once during that most remarkable spiritual awakening of which we have heard this afternoon. I will always regard it as one of the great privileges of my life to have met several times many of the German missionaries in the Dutch Indies.

To understand the general missionary situation in the Dutch East Indies we must keep in view that there is a population of nearly fifty million, while we in Holland count only about seven million inhabitants. Of these fifty million natives about thirty-five million are to be found on the relatively small island of Java, which is four times the size of Holland. Very remarkable is the enormous increase of the population of Java. In 1825 there were about six million; one century later, thirty-five million. We have here evidence that a native population under

*Dr. Schlunk's statement concerning German Missions in the Dutch Indies never reached the editors.

Western rule often flourishes better than under its own rulers and management. The intellectual natives generally must acknowledge that the rule of Holland has been a blessing for the population of Java and the other isles. They see that they could not yet govern themselves and that they must be thankful for what Holland has been doing for them. If Holland withdrew the countries would return to a most deplorable state of anarchy and confusion.

In order to understand the general situation of our Missions, I shall call your attention to these important facts:

1. All the missionary energy of Holland is concentrated in this part of the world. The field is much too great for the forces of Holland, so that we heartily welcome the help of other nations, not only that of the German Missions but also, for a number of years, that of the American Methodists. We would like them to send us many more missionaries and we are glad to find that the cooperation between them and our Dutch Missions, that was perhaps not as good as we would have liked it in the beginning, is getting better every year. The Methodists have opened schools for girls which find general appreciation in Netherlands Indies. This concentration of all the missionary energy of Holland in one field certainly has great advantages but it also brings the danger of isolating us too much from other fields. It is, therefore, very necessary for us to come in touch with the problems on other fields.

2. When the Dutch came into the East Indies in the beginning of the seventeenth century, they found there a few hundred native Christians won by the work of the Portuguese Jesuits. This was for them a very strong reason for sending a few men to convert these people into Protestant Christians. In those times they thought Roman Catholic native Christians much worse than heathens or Mohammedans. We, therefore, have had some missionary work going on in these islands as long as our nation has had any relations with these parts of the world. We find there now strong Christian communities that have existed for centuries where the Protestant Christian religion has become a very important part of the national life and that have rendered invaluable services in providing teachers and helpers for mission work in other parts.

The prevailing religion in these islands is the animistic heathenism that we know in Africa and other parts of the world. It sometimes has been represented as a sort of ideal state of infancy in religious life. Those who know something about it have a very different judgment. They know that these animists lead a life of fear and anxiety of the worst kind. It is remarkable how this animism seems to be able to exist for centuries when untouched by other civilizations. As soon as a country, where it exists, is thrown open for Western civilization and comes in touch with the great world movements, then animism in its simplest form cannot exist any longer. It would have yielded to the Christian religion in many more places, if Islam had not come to these people and given them what they wanted—the privilege of going on with their heathen habits, and also strengthening their position in the world by being taken in a world religion with special Oriental attractions, in which form Islam came to them.

The present situation is, that we have about 250 missionaries working in the Dutch Indies and that the number of native Christians is approaching one million. Remembering that there are fifty million natives in these parts, it will be clear that there is still a great work to be done. The situation, however, is not altogether discouraging. It is remarkable how much more hopeful the outlook is in the work among the Mohammedans. We find there a number of hidden disciples of Jesus Christ and many openly confess that Islam does not satisfy their deeper religious needs.

There is not enough time to take you around to the different mission fields. I will, therefore, mention only the work in New Guinea. Here our Dutch Missions were working fifty years without seeing hardly any result and without being able to establish any contact with the tribes living in the interior. Then, suddenly, a great change came, the doors opened and the missionaries found out that where they had not been able to get in touch with the people living in the interior, these people very well knew whereupon the missionaries at the coast had been waiting all these years, and that they had been discussing the matter among themselves. When the doors were thrown open the demand for teachers and the schools came from so many sides that it proved impossible to meet it. At the present moment we ought to send many more missionaries there than we are able to do.

The cooperation between our Protestant Missions is excellent. Also, the Dutch Colonial Government shows a very clear understanding of the great value and importance of the missionary work. As a general principle the Government has adopted a strict neutrality in religious matters but the Government is ready to support Mission work on educational and social lines. This has established a great area of relations between the Government and the Missions. In view of the great variety of Protestant Missions it proved necessary to appoint a central representative of these Missions to the Government. The Missions appointed one man to deal with the Government in all matters regarding their interests. This official received the title of Missions-Consul. He is appointed and paid by the Missions but accredited by the Government. This Missions-Consulate has proved during the nearly twenty years of its existence an invaluable factor in the missionary administration. It has been my privilege to serve as the first Missions-Consul during twelve years at Batavia.

THE REVIVAL IN NIAS

THE REVEREND A. BETTIN, OF THE RHENISH MISSION SOCIETY

Beside the work in Sumatra and Borneo, the Rhenish Mission has a Mission in some other islands, in Mentawei, Engano, and Nias. Let me tell you of the Mission in Nias, a much smaller island than Sumatra. This work was commenced in 1861. The pioneers met many difficulties and discouragements at the beginning, especially the hostility of the daring head-hunting and murderous chiefs and the unhealthful conditions in the country. Seeing the fast growth of the work and the encouraging success of their fellow-workers in Sumatra, the missionaries in Nias had need to pray to God for patience and for hope that God's blessing would come for their miserable and idolatrous island. And it did come. After twenty-five years of work there were not more than 500 converts in four stations.

So great were the changes for the better in Nias during the next twenty-five years that there was much reason to rejoice at the fiftieth anniversary that the Lord had given over 18,000 converts in the western, the eastern and even the southern part of the country where the independent chiefs had expelled the missionaries many years before. Most of these chiefs had now turned to be friends of the Mission, many had become baptized members of the church and some were even doing evangelistic work. That was indeed a wonderful and notable change. Some wise men would have said: You have done a good work, be satisfied. Your Christian people in Nias have a higher standard of Christian knowledge and morals than could be expected by the common rules of evolution in religious matters in general. They have a knowledge of the teaching of the Old and New Testaments. The second and third generation after this will surely develop into a fine Christian life and spirit.

But most of our missionaries in Nias were neither contented nor satisfied with the spiritual and moral result of their work. They longed for a baptism of the Holy Spirit for their converts and they prayed for it. Two spiritual men, college mates, joined in private prayer-meetings, beseeching God to reveal to them everything displeasing to Him in their own lives that could be a barrier to the revival work of the Holy Spirit. They were whole-hearted and serious about the matter and confessed their sins and shortcomings. Both were blessed with a deeper realization of God's presence and a fuller enjoyment of His grace and love. Before they separated for their respective stations, they agreed to continue in private these meetings, avoiding public invitations to prevent any from taking part who were not serious.

One of the missionaries began these meetings in his parsonage with only two native Christians taking part. But the number increased until in a short time there was not enough room in his house for those who came. After this the meetings were held in the church. In a short time, more than 800 attended each meeting. The fear of the Lord had fallen upon them. The conviction of sin was deep and sincere, the whole body of believers being convulsively shaken. All were anxious to confess sins hidden as a secret for many years which constituted hindrances to the development of their lives as Christians. Depths of darkness, trespasses against God, husband, wife, children, parents, neighbors, business men and others were revealed by confession and forgiveness prayed for. Those who truly repented could trust in the mercy of God and take the Cross of Jesus on Calvary as an atonement of their sin and transgression. In consequence their hearts were filled with peace, joy, and thankfulness. Justification by faith was not only a doctrine but a real personal experience to them.

This religious movement did not begin in a congregation having a highly gifted minister with a noted spiritual standard or winning eloquence—no, he was only a plain but faithful servant of God. But the congregations with better equipped and gifted men were also affected before long, even such with members who opposed at first were compelled by their own consciences to repent and seek God's grace and pray for the gift of His spirit. There were also a few congregations which were not blessed by this revival, although to some of these congregations the blessing came in later years.

Now as to the results which came out of this special blessing of God for the whole Christian Church in Nias, I can make the following statement: The churches are crowded in the 164 congregations for the regular services on Sundays and mid-week days. Bible classes and prayer-meetings are largely attended by both sexes. The Bible is freely bought and anxiously read and studied. Family worship is common. Faithfulness in the marriage relation is the rule among our church members. Stolen articles, money included, have been returned to the owners and God is praised as the just and holy One, who manifested Himself in righteousness and mercy. The number of converts has increased from 18,000 to 58,000 in eight years; 26,000 candidates for baptism are attending the adult classes for religious instruction. The work is growing so rapidly that the fourteen male and fifteen female missionaries with 383 native helpers are overburdened. Before this revival there was always a shortage of native preachers willing to go as evangelists to other counties, but since this spiritual rising they are glad to go where they are needed. The Chinese businessmen in Nias have been influenced. Seeing such strange things as stolen goods returned to them and lies confessed without any public reason and civil force, they became convinced of the reality of the living God. They have established a congregation of Chinese Christians. God still works in wondrous, mysterious, pentecostal ways to fulfil the promises for His church. Whole-hearted conversions which change mind and heart, body and soul, and purify the private and public life are the best and most successful means for the propagation of the Gospel and the extension of the Kingdom of God.

SOME LATIN-AMERICAN PROBLEMS

SPECIAL FIELDS OF SERVICE IN WHICH LATIN-AMERICANS NEED AND WELCOME THE HELP OF THE CHRISTIAN FORCES OF OTHER COUNTRIES

MR. JAY CARLETON FIELD, LIMA, PERU

There are certain basic principles which should be observed in every case, if we are to meet Latin-American needs in a manner that will be welcome to those whom we serve, and with whom we cooperate.

1. The form of service or the institution which we offer must be something of a model which will stimulate the best local elements to emulation and to greater efforts for their people, rather than something only just as good as they already have, which may make us appear to be mere competitors. We must always aim to set an ideal to be reached. This is very clear when we think how inadequately we could meet even the most restricted need of any nation by concentrating the efforts of all the available foreign forces on that one task in that one nation.

2. Whatever organized form our service contribution may take, we should frankly aim to make it indigenous as soon as practicable. To that end, a large part of our task will be the discovering and training of nationals who bid fair to become leaders among their people. This will mean that larger and larger responsibility will be delegated to them as fast as this can be done without lowering the grade of service rendered or jeopardizing its future.

3. It will naturally follow that we will conform to local ideas, except where basic principles are involved. Very great care will be taken, not to wound the pride or susceptibilities of those whom we desire to serve, and we will recognize and use their finest qualities for the good of their fellowmen. Keeping ourselves wisely in the background as much as possible, we will work shoulder to shoulder with them in a cooperative effort to make Christ king in their community.

If these principles are observed there can be no question of the need for the best we can give, and the welcome on the part of the best elements will be almost as sure as soon as our contribution is understood.

While recognizing the danger of too much generalization when speaking of the needs of no less than twenty countries, all at different stages of human progress, let us consider a few of the fields of service where a crying need constitutes a call and an opportunity.

In the field of Christian education alone all the available forces might be mustered in order to provide the kind of models of which we have spoken, without the least danger of becoming mere competitors. In Peru, for example, the Girls' High School of Lima is setting a high standard in a country where as yet the government provides no educational training for girls, beyond the fifth grade. Such schools, while serving as models which need speedy duplication, are producers of Christian leadership for the home, school or office. From what source could there come opposition rather than welcome to such an institution? Surely not from those who understand its work and are interested in the real needs of their people! Yet there is organized opposition from others and this must always be expected.

The problem of the care of orphans, in most of these countries, constitutes so big a task that a model orphanage is welcomed and may set high standards of Christian ethics for dealing with this problem. But this will not be enough unless a great contribution is also made in the study of the social conditions which make the numbers of orphans mount to so high a figure, as well as in cooperative efforts to change these conditions.

Agriculture affords great opportunities for Christian character building and the knowledge of this science has in most of these countries advanced only to a limited degree, leaving a large field of service for those who, in the spirit of Jesus, would lead the way. A model farm-school, such as the one being conducted in Chile, can make a most welcome contribution to the life of a country, dignifying manual labor and releasing great resources, both human and economic.

In some of these twenty countries the outstanding problem is that of the liberation of the Indian population. The Indian must be freed from ignorance, from those who continually exploit him, and from age-long lethargy and vices. We have just listened to a description of present-day conditions among these Indians and have the need clearly before us. Here again, the task is so great that Christian forces of the United States and Canada can only hope, in the spirit of Christ, to help find the solution to this great problem which seems overwhelming to Bolivia, Peru, and many other countries. The results being secured by those working at Puno, Peru, and several other points are such as to give heart to those who study this work.

When we consider that in all the countries of South America, and possibly in all Latin America, there is but one hospital being conducted under evangelical auspices, we are aware of the fact that here is virgin soil, a field of service in which the spirit of Christ can be demonstrated to a high degree. Each hospital will become a center out from which go numerous trained nurses to points not reached by hospitals of any sort. The organized medical profession in these countries will rarely if ever welcome the raising of their standards of efficiency, but the thinking and influential elements of every country will cordially receive Christian cooperation in so vital a problem.

The Young Men's Christian Association is making a most welcome contribution in seven of these countries, carrying on its work in accord with the principles we have been considering. Nationals are everywhere taking an important part in the work and national secretarial leadership is being developed. One Argentine youth of Italian parentage, having received thorough training in the Y. M. C. A. of Buenos Aires, is now rendering great service in one of the new Young Men's Christian Associations in the fatherland of his parents. A Continental Federation of the South American Associations places large responsibility and direction in the hands of numerous representatives of these countries.

One of the most outstanding examples of service rendered to a country is that of the playground system which has developed in Uruguay. A physical director of the Y. M. C. A. had the vision and found his opportunity for large service and had sufficient technical knowledge, diplomacy and unselfish spirit to bring about nation-wide results. The leadership for these playgrounds is largely trained under Christian auspices. Another outstanding contribution of the Y. M. C. A. is the promotion of international and inter-American friendship and understanding. University students, representing their various countries, come together each summer in a beautiful spot in Uruguay, to face together the challenge of the social, moral and spiritual problems of their republics. They find that they have so much in common that life-long ties of friendship are formed among these who will soon fill the most influential positions in their governments.

What we might call the lecture-sermon is another form of service which thinking men everywhere not only need but cordially welcome. Thousands upon thousands of men today are groping for spiritual reality. Men of their own tongue, versed in their history, philosophy and religion, men of exceptional intellectual ability who have a vital message which comes from a personal experience of Christ in their lives, such men will have a hearing everywhere. They will be listened to by men who have lost faith in all religion in its organized forms.

There are a limited few of these leaders and they should be given their full time for delivering their messages, by voice and by pen. The unexpected success of the Dr. Navarro Monzo lectures, given in Lima, Peru, last year shows the importance of this form of service.

The supply of wholesome and purposeful literature, in either book or magazine form, is so limited in Latin America, that he who adds to it will be called blessed. A volume could be written on this need. The value of original Spanish or Portuguese literature as compared with translations, is great. The monthly magazine, "La Nueva Democracia," goes into many a home where similar messages in other forms rarely reach, and it is helping to unite the best elements of the Latin-American countries in their thinking on social, moral and even spiritual matters.

Needless to say there is a crying need for the development of unselfish leadership in every walk of life. Most of these countries are facing rapidly developing problems of society and of state which will overwhelm them unless such leadership can be prepared. An excellent and capable man may become the president of a country in the midst of social and political turmoil, but unless there are numerous such men from among whom he may select his cabinet, but mediocre or even disastrous results may be expected. Whoever inculcates in the youth of a land the idea of unselfish service, renders a Christian service to that nation.

Advanced thinkers in moral and spiritual things are to be found here and there, but they are nearly always isolated from men of similar mind. He who can relate these men to each other in some form of practical service, helps both them and the cause they serve. A Christian leader may often be the unseen, but staying power, a sort of dependable continuation committee, in an important organization which otherwise might fail. Such opportunities are many in social welfare organizations in lands where the nationals are likely to place greater emphasis on the date and opening ceremony of an organization than on its continued program of service.

There seems to be an almost universal tendency on the part of Latin-American leaders to become pessimistic regarding the moral or spiritual future of their countries. This increases as they themselves get clearer vision of Christ's program for mankind. The Christian leader from the United States or Canada is an optimist, or at least should be, and he can be of great service in helping to cure the pessimism of Latin-American leaders, helping them to see farther into the future and deeper into the resources of their Master.

The Americas do not yet understand each other very well. Intellectual interchange, of students and of professors, will greatly help toward mutual understanding and lasting friendship. This will take time and must receive greater' emphasis.

That the needs of Latin-America are great and that he who devotes his life to her interests will find abundant opportunity and a cordial welcome is shown by the message delivered recently in this city to President Coolidge and other representatives of our government, by Gabriela Mistral, the greatly loved Chilean poetess. She said:

"The faith of our America is Catholic—yours is Protestant; but there are already signs of an approach of one church to the other, which would be done for the good of all Christianity to defend the world from the opprobrious materialism of this moment.

"To imprint the Christian norm on all the relations between North and South; to put conscience above all interests— that would be the task. The merely political activity of today would transcend to a spiritual movement and the cooperation of the strong would no longer be seen as domination, but as the vast human help of a prosperous and well-formed nation toward those who are painfully being formed.

"I speak humbly, then, this desire—

"If economic approach has been superseded by intellectual, let this in turn be superseded by a Christian approach to us. The inferior means with which union among men is sought, such as material interests, for example, have a relative fecundity: only the Spirit melts obstacles to great enterprises and the true transformation of the earth. Only flight, free and joyous as the albatross of the sea, far above all terrestrial limitations.

"May God make the United States to carry out, on a Christian standard, its program of help to the suffering world, sick from injustice and hatred, and may the women and the educators who are forming the coming generation be as the very hands of God."

RECENT OUTSTANDING SOCIAL DEVELOPMENTS IN LATIN-AMERICA AND THEIR SIGNIFICANCE AND APPEAL

THE REVEREND J. H. MC LEAN, D.D., CHILE

The Latin-American ancestral strain is a fusion of Indian and European bloods. Wherever the former is found there is proverbial inertia in the presence of reform forces. Spain, Portugal, France and Italy, the neo-Latin nations have experienced political upheavals which have brought attendant changes in the life of these nations. We have only to think of Robespierre, Blanco, Primo de Rivera and Mussolini to account for advanced measures adopted under the scourge of a military dictator. But in Latin-America we have a matriarchal civilization—men and women clinging tenaciously to their customs, which are much stronger than their laws. The mothers are conservative and would rather bear submissively the ills that afflict them than brave the shock and inconvenience of change. In the new world Iberian daughters and grand-daughters have shaped and colored the social order. They are the arbiters of correct form, controllers of social aims and observances, the mainstay of society's institutions with the home as their throne of influence. Latin-American men, enjoying a larger degree of freedom, have developed a greater measure of progressiveness. In the words of Professor Warshaw, "The wealthier educated classes have the European Latin culture and charm and the working people that quietness of bearing and that naturally simple and equable philosophy which mark the Latin working people of Europe." We might well inquire what factors usually combine in producing social development and proceed to search for such forces operative in Latin-American society. They are in general: (a) Peace, freedom and political stability; (b) Growth of a national conscience and emergence of public opinion; (c) Increase of wealth and leisure; (d) Progress of education and religion; (e) Stimulating contacts with social groups in other lands.

For almost three centuries society kept a dead level in Latin-America. The advance of the last half century has been more marked than in the previous two hundred years and the last two decades have witnessed changes which, within limited circles, have amounted to veritable social revolutions. This has been due to a combination of pressures but mainly to the factors labelled (d) and (e).

First of all, *Poverty*. The aristocracy, who have descended from a race of conquerors, enjoyed a monopoly of land and commercial power, whereas the subjugated peoples have been condemned in large numbers to a serfdom in which "chill penury repressed their noble rage and froze the genial current of the soul." One of the leading reformers in South America has stated that the main problem and the most refractory one in his experience has been that of securing adequate pay and healthful living conditions for the toiling masses. An industrial crusade, which has reached all the workers of the world, has already produced a clamor for fairer standards of living. Assuredly every true missionary, every servant of Jesus Christ, will make all possible endeavor to emphasize the dignity of labor and to develop self-respect and a consciousness of the inestimable worth of personality as a direct contribution to human welfare. If an ancient pagan contended that because he was a man, nothing of human interest could be a matter of indifference to him, much more ought we as partakers of the Divine Life to show sympathy, alertness, and sagacity in promoting the well-being of the sons of toil.

Second, *Social Aspects of Education.* It is keeping well within the truth to state that at least half of the Latin-American population are deprived of the chance to obtain sheer defensive training—to master the rudiments of useful elementary knowledge—and as a result much rare talent which we know must exist in humble families, remains untrained and unused by the nation. This traditional neglect of popular education is due to the sophistry of a determinism that balks at all change or evolution. "The son of a shoemaker is destined to be a shoemaker," so spake the fathers of Spain and Portugal. Surprisingly enough, the select sons and daughters of Latin-America are treated to the highest privileges of culture and travel.

Secondary schools may be rated as good, although the curriculum is very theoretical and superficial. The crying need all over Latin-America is for the instruction of her masses, for vocational training, for some reliable person to focus instruction on the well-being of the public and for educators who may be real pilots of youth and guides to the promising children. While a pilot may be entirely ignorant of mechanical engineering or of fine seamanship, he appreciates the preciousness of the life and cargo committed to his care and knows the channel past the shoals and through the cross-currents that lead to the haven of safe delivery. The missionary must put continual and well-directed emphasis on the importance of an educated citizenry. The missionary organizations have unique opportunity to establish specimen institutions in which they may give an objective demonstration of the animating genius that pervades the best type of school. With all who are engaged in public instruction it is the missionary's duty to cooperate and to display sympathy as well as to set the example. Latin-Americans pay glad homage to Christian character and unselfish devotion to others when these traits are conspicuous in a missionary educator.

Third, *Temperance Propaganda and Social Hygiene.* The ravages of vice have awakened the public conscience to the need of some practical measures for their protection. In lands where the basic stock is Indian and where means of destruction and corruption are easily procured, intemperance works with devastating effect. The presence of a body of missionaries and the consistent living of evangelical laymen are a source of blessing and encouragement for Chile. Intemperance is not merely a baffling problem but the nation's perpetual tragedy. We would be recreant to our trust as residents in these lands, if we did not promote the cause of temperance both by precept and practice, in sane, well-balanced, happy lives in the minds of our Latin-American neighbors.

Social relationships afford a field for example rather than for denunciation. Harmful convivial habits have to be displaced by helpful ones and social usages have to be established by courageous social units in the face of stubborn opposition. The argument on topics of personal habit is well nigh irresistible if only we can embody the freedom, vigor, and radiant joy of Christ's standards of living. Years ago Mrs. Waterhouse Wilson, a Methodist teacher, was able to impress upon one of her preparatory boys the transcendent lesson that his body might be a temple of the Holy Spirit. That boy is Dr. Carlos Fernandez Pena, the apostle of temperance in Chile, the advocate of education in that land and the confidential advisor of its progressive president, Alessandri.

Fourth. *The Elevation of Woman to a Wider Sphere of Usefulness.* The heritage of the shackles of Salic law has subordinated woman to her husband in Latin-America, denied her legal rights and confined her self-expression within the channels kept open to the world by male citizens. Hers has been a restricted lot. She has been forced into the seclusion of the home and her instruction has been largely conventional. A generation ago, what vocation was open to the Latin-American daughter? That of wife, teacher, midwife or housekeeper—unless she entered one of the despised occupations with the seamstress and the domestic servants. But brave pioneers have demonstrated the intellectual superiority of women by their articles in the press. Women have dared to display their executive ability in clubs and federations of their sex and have addressed themselves to two main tasks, namely, the mitigation of the ills which men had been impotent to remove and the gradual emancipation of their sisterhood. They have attacked infant mortality and have promoted public health through such organizations as the Red Cross and the Creches. They have sought out underprivileged children and furnished the elements denied them in their homes. They have given young women liberty of action in the world of business and manufacture, thereby establishing financial independence for their sex. They have labored for civic betterment through an uplifted public opinion. They have successfully banished prejudice and restraint and all the time they have been dignified, self-respecting women, cherishing their high ideals with the noble sacrificial devotion of their sex. What missionary would dare to confess his Christian discipleship and fail to align his life with these new and promising forces?

Fifth, *The Passion for Wise Life-Investment*. Multitudes of eager, idealistic American youths are asking, "What is the best use to make of this one life which I possess?" They are actuated by motives of ambition, by the friendly goads of the home circle, but their aspirations require encouragement and guidance. Here lies what, in my opnion, is the greatest missionary opportunity. Aimless, misdirected effort soon becomes perverted and undermined but the missionary may be a sagacious counselor and a true brotherly companion. He need not enter politics—no well-intentioned amateur can contribute much to the Latin-American political game—but he can commend new realms of service and a Christ-centered career. The missionaries ought to throw themselves unreservedly into the youth movement. No missionary ever had his trust in youth betrayed. Again, if the missionaries make no effort to Christianize commerce and industry, who is going to undertake this colossal task which, in the opinion of so many religious leaders, is the most imperative and urgent in the world today? Education for character and efficiency must become ingrafted in the evangelical circle, but always and above all, it is the supreme vocation of the missionary to furnish and cultivate a Christ-engendered motive in life service. Latin-American enthusiasm for humanity must be focussed through widespread loyalty to the Son of God. To make Jesus Christ known and loved is equivalent to making Latin-Americans truly serve their fellow-men after the fashion of Jesus Himself.

THE INDIANS IN LATIN AMERICA: THE APPEAL THEY MAKE AND THE OBLIGATION WE FACE

THE REVEREND H. C. TUCKER, D.D., BRAZIL

At the Congress on Christian Work in Latin-America held at Panama in 1916, a special report considered the Indians in the field, the obligations resting upon the churches in North America and Europe to give them the Gospel and the best methods of approach and for carrying on efficient work among them. A somewhat detailed survey of the whole situation was made and discussed at the Congress. Another Congress on Christian Work in South America is soon to assemble in the city of Montevideo. Further study and investigation has been made during the intervening nine years, and a full report will be made on the Indian problem of the Continent.

At the Panama Congress it was reported that there were at that time an estimated Indian population of unmixed blood of about 17,000,000 in the great region reaching from Mexico to

Chile and from Peru to Brazil. The report to be given at Monte-video will indicate that there are perhaps 10,000,000 Indians in South America, practically untouched by a Christian civilization. Some think the estimate too large, and that a definite census, were such a thing possible, might show that there are about 7,000,000 of them. It is stated that 55 per cent of the population of Peru is Indian, 50 per cent of the population of Bolivia is Indian and another 27 per cent of mixed blood, Indian and Spanish; 75 per cent of the population of Ecuador is Indian and 40 per cent in Colombia. In these four countries alone we would then have 7,700,000 pure-blood Indians.

It will be seen then in the first place that the appeal of numbers is in itself considerable. Seventeen or eighteen millions of souls is no small number to be won for Christ.

The very conditions under which these millions of red men of the forest live, the geography, topographies, climates and nature of the soils, add force to the appeal of need. They have been driven by the white man into the rugged mountains of the great Andean and other ranges, or into the inhospitable jungles of the almost uninhabitable river valleys and barren plains. They many times inhabit regions most difficult of access, shut in by unconquerable mountains that stand as mighty barriers in the way of approach. Tribes of them are in the jungles of the lowlands and in the forests along the river where fevers abound and poisonous and pestiferous insects are innumerable.

The Araucanians, who claim they have never been conquered by the white man, have been driven to the extreme southern portion of Chile and inhabit a cold, bleak region of inlets and low islands.

Colonel Rondon, who planned and successfully carried out the Roosevelt expedition, is the best authority on the numbers and the state of Indians in Brazil. He says there are 1,500,000 of them in the wild regions of the highlands and in the almost impenetrable jungles of the great Amazon River and a number of its tributaries.

The Gran Chaco in the Republics of Argentina, Paraguay and Bolivia, is a wild and little-known region where thousands of Indians are to be found.

Multitudes in Mexico are living in places and conditions that make access most difficult.

In the second place, these red children of the forest in Latin-America make to their more highly favored white brethren the appeal of appalling need. What language can describe the real condition, the darkness, the backwardness, in which they are to be found everywhere? The awful destitution, physical, mental, spiritual as compared with our rich and abundant life, presents a remarkably striking contrast. Many of them live in the mountain fastnesses and jungles as naked as the wild animals that dispute with them the right to the forests. Some of them, as in Ecuador, are living in crude savagery and cannibalism. Their bodies are exposed to fevers, the bites of poisonous insects, to heat and cold, rains and snows and biting winds. They know not how to protect themselves against these ills, and how to cultivate the soil on which they live.

What shall we say of the appalling spiritual darkness in which we find these our brothers? They have not the slightest knowledge of revealed truth concerning God the Father and the way of redemption through the love of Jesus the Saviour. They know nothing of the life He came to give; the life abundant, physical, mental and spiritual. They live enveloped in a cloud of pagan superstitions and are filled with fear. They only know how to worship the sun and moon instead of the Creator and Father of all. If we would realize fully the situation we face and all that is implied in a survey of this field of need we are forced to take into account millions more of mixed bloods, of a semi-civilized life, who, devitalized physically, live in backwardness and ignorance, having received only in a very limited degree a little of the light and blessing of Christian civilization. Hundreds of thousands of these are the offspring of the white man's vices and illegitimate intercourse. They have inherited his vices and diseases without his virtues and the laws of hygiene and health. Illiteracy prevails to as high a degree as 90 per cent or more of the population.

This great missionary convention seeks to clarify for the Church of Christ in the United States and Canada the vision of obligation that rests upon the children of God in these lands to make Christ known to all men everywhere even in the remotest parts of the earth and in the deepest depths of degradation.

These millions of Indians form no insignificant part of the obligation. I need not repeat to an audience like this the grounds upon which this obligation rests. We face the situation I have tried to briefly describe in the light of our well-defined and clearly-comprehended responsibility to go into all the world and make of all men disciples of Jesus Christ. There is upon us the impelling obligation of redeeming love.

There are in this situation we are considering a few things that should add urgency to the obligation. We owe to these red men of the forest a debt of compensation, of just retribution. They have been robbed of their lands, driven from their happy hunting-grounds, exploited, enslaved and ill-treated in many ways. It is not too late yet for the Christian Church of Anglo-Saxon America to at least join hands with the rising young church in Latin-America and make amends for the sins and injustices of our forefathers.

The real picture sets forth the obstacles and difficulties with which the problem abounds. This is an age of heroic faith and service in missionary endeavor. We Anglo-Saxons boast of our ability to accomplish the difficult and almost impossible. There rests upon us the obligation to undertake one of the most difficult tasks the Church of Christ has yet faced. Here is then a great opportunity for heroic endeavor and enterprise.

We face this situation in the light of abundant resources. The very physical and economical conditions of the problem will require the expenditure of large sums of money. There have been marked out for us, or are being marked out for us, judicious methods of procedure and of expenditure that will be involved. There are among the volunteers of North America and the young native workers of South America those who are ready to undertake the task. The churches face the obligation to supply the funds needed to send them forth and to sustain their work. It is not merely to pay salaries of men and women, but to equip and support the industrial, medical and educational enterprises needed.

Something has already been accomplished in an endeavor to evangelize the Indians of Latin America, in Mexico, Central American countries, Bolivia, Peru, Chile, Argentina, Paraguay, Brazil and elsewhere. The very success of these efforts adds force to the obligation and urgency to the appeal. A few have been won to Christ, have come to the knowledge and experience of saving grace, to the enjoyment of a fuller life, and some of them have become evangelists to their own people.

There are in these red men possibilities we know not of. Every race should be given a chance to make its contribution to the building up and enrichment of the Kingdom of Christ on the earth.

We are interested for the progress of Latin-American countries. These millions stand as a menace to the development and extension of agriculture and industry, to stable and enlightened government. Latin-American statesmen recognize this fact and governments are endeavoring to deal with the problem. They are meeting with some success. One of the most efficient directors of this work said recently that they are not accomplishing better results simply for lack of men actuated by the right motive, love of the Indian.

In this great missionary convention we hear reports of the marvelous uplifting power of the Gospel to reach and save even the lowest and most backward. This grace is sufficient for the task we face.

CHRISTIAN LITERATURE IN THE MISSION FIELD

COOPERATION IN THE DEVELOPMENT OF CHRISTIAN LITERATURE

THE REVEREND A. L. WARNSHUIS, D.D., NEW YORK

Secretary, International Missionary Council

There are four reasons that seem to me to make imperative cooperation in the development of Christian literature in the mission field:

1. Most of the books and tracts that are needed—probably ninety-five per cent of them—should be the common possession of all the Christian forces. They will serve the needs of all. They can be used by all. All should share in producing this literature. Such denominational literature as may be needed— which will not exceed five per cent of the total—may need to be prepared and issued by denominational forces separately. But a book like "Pilgrim's Progress" does not need to be translated by more than one person in each language. This is true also of school books, of histories and biographies, of Biblical expositions, and of all other good books. How much of the literature read by our American church members is published by denominational agencies? There is no good reason why a different practice should be adopted in Asia or Africa. Just as the Christian forces unite in publishing the Bible, and as the four great Bible Societies have working agreements for the translation and distribution of the Bible in the various countries of the world, so we should plan unitedly for the development of Christian Literature in the mission field.

2. It is only by such cooperation that the Christian forces may share in the creative literary power discovered in any part of the field. Authors are born, not made. In the mission field, as elsewhere, there seems to be a very limited number of good writers. When such writers are found, it should be possible for them to serve the largest possible number of readers. They should be supported by the united forces whom they can serve.

3. The printed page should be used in these days to the utmost degree of effectiveness. The forces that oppose Christianity are making large use of the printing-press. Political and social revolutions are resulting from the reading of new books and of the newspapers that have increased in number very rapidly in the Orient in these past few years. Just as no great newspaper in America could be issued without the work of the Associated

Press and other news organizations, so, without cooperation, no large measure of effective literary work can be done on the mission field.

4. The need for more and better Christian literature of all kinds for all classes of people is so great that without cooperation it cannot be satisfied. Our failure to make an advance in this department of missionary work during recent years is appalling and scandalous. It is reported that 300,000 are being added annually to the illiterate population of India, and it also appears from official statements that thirty-nine per cent of the children educated in village schools in that country relapse into illiteracy within five years after leaving school, simply because they have nothing to read. The situation in Africa is tragic. The people are thirsting for education, and are crowding into schools that they may learn to read. But, for example, in Swahili, one of the most widely known languages of Africa, used by ten million people, in addition to the Bible, hymn books and catechisms, there are available three commentaries, sixteen school books and twenty-six other books. That is the complete library in the Swahili language. There are few languages in Africa that have so much as that. In most of them, the library could be wrapped in a handkerchief. Ninety per cent of the schools in Africa are supported by the Missions. Any Mission that assumes the responsibility of educational work, and is teaching the people to read, is responsible for producing somehow a healthy Christian literature for those readers. It cannot do this effectively and adequately so long as it does its literary work separately from that of other missions using the same language.

It is impossible to describe in a few words the needs in such countries as China and Japan, where there is a "tide of new thought." A Chinese writer in a recent magazine article said, "Western writers like Tolstoi, Kropatkin, Lenin, Ibsen, Eucken, Einstein, Marx, Bergson, Wells, Russell, Wilde, Elwood, Dewey, Kant, Darwin, Spencer, Huxley, James, Tagore, etc., have all been translated into Chinese." One printing house in Peking issued fourteen editions of Dewey's lectures. There was no trouble about circulation or distribution. There is no corresponding list of books issued by the Christian forces. If we examine our failure in more detail by noting the entire lack of books for children or for women in this day of rapid and great changes in their status, or for young men and young women in this time of youth movements throughout the world, or the provision for any other special class of readers, it only serves to increase the chagrin and dismay which we ought to feel because of our grievous failure to supply these clamant needs.

Surely the needs of genuine cooperation on a large scale

in producing and publishing Christian literature in all parts of the world is exceedingly great. How can we get it?

1. We need not discuss mere theories of cooperation, for plans have been made and are already in effect. For example, in India, the National Christian Council has established what is called the "Indian Literature Fund." The secretaries of the Council serve as its executive officers, and the overhead expenses are less than one-half of one per cent. With the support of this Fund, seventy-eight new books, all of them urgently needed and all of them approved by the Christian forces using them, have been published in the past two years. Some six or eight expert writers have been aided in different language areas. For Africa, committees in Europe and America are working in close cooperation in exploring this field in literature, and they have begun the preparation of what are called "basic texts," which can be easily adapted and translated into any number of African languages. One of the first of these, a Primer of Hygiene, prepared in English and French, has already been translated into half a dozen languages. For the Moslem world, plans have been made for a literature Bureau, with headquarters in Cairo, to serve as a clearing-house for the preparation of Christian books for all Moslem lands. In Japan, the missions unite in the support of a Christian Literature Society.

For the work in China, suggestions of similar plans have been made, and we are waiting for the Christian forces in China to agree upon them.

2. Funds are needed. The sad fact must be recorded that so far these cooperative plans have made comparatively little progress, because only very small sums of money have been given for their support. Only a very few Mission Boards have contributed to this cause. It is not that they disapprove of these plans, but their resources are distributed first to all their own churches, schools, and colleges, and there is nothing left for literature.

There will be no real progress until the churches and missions recognize this literary work as an essential part of their responsibility, and deliberately set apart a certain percentage of their funds for this purpose and then carefully plan how to use such funds most effectively. For such action by the Boards, we would plead most earnestly. If now, as a beginning, the Boards would designate say one per cent of their receipts for the development of Christian literature, and instruct their missions on the various fields to consult with neighboring missions regarding its wisest use, these plans for cooperation in literary work would become more effective, and a long forward step in the most neglected department of missionary work would immediately be taken. Upon this development of Christian literature will very largely depend the growth and vitality of the Christian Church in other lands.

TRAINING AND DEVELOPING GOOD WRITERS

THE REVEREND FRANK RAWLINSON, D.D., SHANGHAI, CHINA

Editor, *"Chinese Recorder"*

In preparation for this short statement I re-read the report prepared by the China Christian Literature Council and presented to the National Council in 1922. Most of what I have to say can be found in that comprehensive report. As a result of re-reading this report and thinking over the situation, a number of important facts bearing on the problem emerged: First, the demand for existing Christian literature is decreasing. Second, there is noticeably a paucity of Chinese Christian literary talent. Third, there is great difficulty in securing from Christian leaders of experience, actually at work, contributions for existing Christian periodicals. Fourth, there is what amounts to a forced silence of the Christian forces in the face of the growing volume of critical scrutiny of Christianity that is now in evidence in China. These facts, taken together demonstrate the existence of a tremendous need for indigenous writers.

At once arises the question, "What are the essentials of a 'good writer'?" It is, of course, self-evident that he must have literary ability. In addition, he must have access to an enlarging field of ideas. No book that was worthwhile, as far as I know, ever came out of the mind of a person who had not previously read many other books and literary products. But in addition to literary capacity and access to literature, there must be an inward urge to utterance. We are forced to ask, "Why, generally speaking, do the Chinese Christian forces have so little to say in response to modern criticisms of Christianity?" Is their silence due to the lack of something to say or the lack of the urge to say it? In addition to the above requisites of a "good writer," there has to be freedom of self-expression. In China at least, the attempt to produce literature of a more modern type on the part of some Chinese writers has been the cause of controversy. One Chinese writer became a center of uncertainty by reason of a book he was planning to write, the title of which, coupled with the attitude of the man, giving some ground for believing it would be different from other books on the subject. Hence, in the minds of some people there was cause for hesitancy as to whether or not they could approve such a book. It is safe to say, however, that good writers must be given freedom of utterance. It may be the feeling of a lack of freedom is one reason why good Christian writers in China do not develop more quickly. Do we, therefore, have to face the fact that, taken as a whole, Chinese Christians have not yet found freedom of expression in existing Christian relationships? If so, steps should be taken to correct this inhibiting condition.

Now we will assume for the sake of further argument that there are some potential writers; that we know of some Chinese Christians who give promise of being able to write. The question then is, "What can we do to help develop and train them?"

As a matter of fact, however, there are only two sources from which Chinese Christian writers can come. First, from the workers already on the field. Second, from the students in the higher institutions of learning. The workers on the field number only about 25,000. Perhaps we cannot expect a great number of able writers from such a comparatively small group of workers. It may be that the greater activity of non-Christian Chinese writers is due to the fact that their source of supply is numerically much greater. As to the second group, there are probably 2,500 students in colleges, of whom only part are Christian. Here again the source of supply is not numerically great.

I. First, how may we help develop the potential Chinese writer already on the field?

In answer to this question, three things may be suggested. Such potential writers need first to be encouraged. This encouragement might well take the form of arrangements that will give them time to write. One thing that has been suggested in this regard is to relieve a worker with literary gifts from his ordinary responsibility that he might have some time in which to write. Clerical help might be provided both to assist in the clerical work involved in writing and in the carrying on of his ordinary duties. This, of course, calls for the existence of funds that may be called on for this purpose. Again such potential writers must have access to good books. One is a little discouraged at the fact that Chinese workers on the field do not read much, generally speaking. A pertinent question in this connection might be asked. Thompson's outlines of science have been translated and published by the Commercial Press of Shanghai, China. "How many of these potential writers will have a chance to read these stimulating volumes?" Perhaps a reading course is needed to help meet this need as well as funds to supply the books. The last thing to be suggested is one that is not new. It is a correspondence course. Correspondence on the problem of writing is possible through the Christian Literature Society and through other people in charge of Christian literature problems. But in order to be efficiently given, a correspondence course calls for better organization than now exists.

II. How may we help develop and train those potential Chinese Christian writers who have shown that they need special educational preparation?

It seems to me that what is needed first is a graduate course or better a special course in some Christian institution that might be taken by promising students and by workers on the field together. Such a course should offer work along the following lines at least: First, the technique of writing. Second, research work in Chinese culture and thought—for no Christian writer can hope to get a reading from the modern reader of China who is not able to put this Christian thought in terms of comparison with Chinese thought. Third, there should be special emphasis laid in this course on the essential message and philosophy of Christianity. Christianity, as a matter of fact, is not as divided in its essential principles of philosophy and activities as the numerous denominational groups suggest. Fourth, there should be a good course given in the history of Christian thought and the spread of the Christian world movement as it exists today. For with all its faults Christianity is a world movement, and its real significance can be brought out when that fact is understood.

III. In the first place, there should be scholarships offered for those who show ability to occupy editorial or other special literary positions. The total number qualified for such a scholarship would not necessarily be very large. It should not, therefore, be very difficult to finance this group.

IV. Provision should be made whereby Chinese writers of note might be given a sabbatical year in which they might travel and study—not necessarily abroad—for the purpose of re-stimulating their mind.

In closing, I wish to point out what is obvious to us all, that only the Chinese can prepare literature that will win the attention of their contemporaries. In addition, I wish to emphasize the fact that the problem of discovering and developing Chinese writers is essentially a Chinese problem. For that reason, the organization of the Chinese Christian Literature Association is encouraging. This organization is controlled entirely by the Chinese. A group of Western Christians have been invited into the organization as honorary members. All the things that I have suggested and many others this new Literature Association has on its program. But it needs financial help, and one, at least, of the difficulties it meets in securing this help is that the ramifications of the various Christian organizations at the home base, national or denominational, are such that it is not yet clear as to what channels are the ones through which help should be given to such an independent literature organization. There seems to be here a Gordian knot that requires to be promptly cut. The home base needs to guard against letting such a promising movement as this get lost in the maze of relationships of the various denominations, national and international, and other missionary organizations.

THE WORK OF THE LITERATURE COMMITTEE OF THE NATIONAL CHRISTIAN COUNCIL OF INDIA

THE REVEREND JOHN ABERLY, D.D., MAYWOOD, CHICAGO

The Literature Committee of the India National Council is interested in both English and vernacular literature. One might ask why English is needed, since the churches can draw on the immense supplies of the West. However, the Literature Committee, noting the signs of the times, has wisely set apart a man, Mr. A. J. Appasamey, to direct the very necessary work of producing an Indian Christian Literature that shall interpret Christianity against the Indian background. A series of books is projected to cover four lines of thought:

(1) The interpretation of Christ to India: The inclusion in it of a book on immanence shows how Christianity has to be interpreted on the background of a Pantheistic philosophy. There are those who believe that this is a needed correction to the one-sided setting forth of Christianity under Greek influences. (2) The *bhaktas*: The *bhaktas* are persons devoted to God. Augustine, Luther, Wesley and others will be treated, but their personal devotion to God will be central in these biographies and this will make them appealing to Indian minds. (3) Books for the times. (4) Books for women: We have not yet reached the time in India when the books for men can be the same as those for women. For this work the Literature Committee has appropriated one-third of its available funds or about Rs 7,000 for the last year.

The bulk of the work, is, however, in the vernacular. Here men are needed to direct the work of producing literature. The Committee assists in the support of such men but only in four of the many vernaculars of India. There ought to be large extension of this work, when we recall that India has over 300 languages and at least twenty that are spoken by very large groups of men. Another one-third of the Committee's funds goes to the support of these vernacular literature production secretaries or committees.

After literature is prepared a subsidy is needed to publish each book. Books do not pay their own way in India as yet.

They have to be made very cheaply if they are to do so. We have an illustration of this in our vernacular papers. There was a time when in Kanarese and Telegu in South India we had the only vernacular newspapers. But they had to pay their own way. The result was that, when reading began—and it did spread in war times—Hindu papers went ahead and we stood still. We lost our lead and it is doubtful whether we can ever regain it. Literature must be subsidized and another one-third of Committee funds goes to this. In looking over the Report of the last Christian Council, I was struck by the fact that only about three American Societies contributed anything to literature work in India. My appeal is that you inquire whether your Society is doing anything for it and if not that you urge it to take its part in this most needed part of Indian mission work.

THE BIBLE IN THE MISSION FIELD

ITS PLACE AND POWER

THE REVEREND ROBERT FORGAN, D.D., EDINBURGH, SCOTLAND

In the well known legend of "King Arthur and his Knights of the Round Table" we are told how the noble King Arthur was equipped for his wars against the pagans. Above the surface of the mystic lake a miraculous arm appeared, brandishing the goodly sword, Excalibur. Instantly King Arthur put off in a boat across the lake and seized the mighty sword thus provided for him. Our Bible societies constitute that projecting arm which holds up to our missionaries a sword far more wonderful than King Arthur's goodly blade. Today they march forth, eighteen thousand of them, from this land, on their spiritual quest, every one of them armed with "the sword of the Spirit, which is the Word of God." And as David said of the sword of Goliath, so every missionary is ready to say of this spiritual weapon, "There is none like it; give it to me that I may wield it as a good soldier of Jesus Christ in conquering the world for Him."

The Word of God is a wonderful weapon. It is quick and powerful and sharper than a two-edged sword, yet it smites only that it may heal. It wounds the guilty conscience and then tenderly upbinds the wounds it has made. In thus describing the Bible I do not forget that the supreme aim of Christian missions is not the mere distribution of a book, however precious, but the presentation to the world of a living person, Jesus Christ, who is himself infinitely more precious to the hearts and consciences of men than any book could ever be. He is the living Word of God, the Word made flesh. That which gives to the Bible its preciousness and its power is the testimony it bears to Him. But between Jesus Christ and the Bible there is no rivalry. There can be no rivalry, for it is equally true to say that it is Christ who gives us our Bible and that it is the Bible which gives us our Christ. The story of the life and death and rising again of Jesus Christ had in it transforming power for many years before any part of that story was committed to writing.

The first apostles, by the story they told with the living voice, won converts wherever they went. Not for long years did they formulate doctrines either of the person or of the work of Christ, or even make a record of his words and deeds. They were content to tell the story as they knew it, and that story sufficed. It presented Jesus Christ to men and that presenta-

332

tion drew men to Him, as He foretold it would—"And I, if I be lifted up from the earth, will draw all men unto me."

But this story telling in course of time came to be put into writing; and letters of explanation and exhortation were also required. And thus within two generations after the Crucifixion, our New Testament was produced. Moreover, in the telling of the Christ-story "to the Jew first," it was natural that the apostles and other speakers and writers should base themselves upon the Old Testament Scriptures, and show that all they had to tell represented the fulfillment, flower and fruit of God's dealings with his chosen people as recorded in the Old Testament. Centuries later, Augustine recognized this, when he said that the New Testament is latent in the Old, and the Old Testament is patent in the New. That is why to this day we search the Scriptures, Old Testament and New Testament together. It is because they both testify of Christ that the peoples of every land and every tongue find in them eternal life.

Now, just here it seems to me we discover the secret of the place and power of the Bible in the mission field. In a very profound sense, we owe both Old Testament and New Testament to Jesus Christ; the one foretells, and the other forthtells the coming of Christ for the redemption of all the peoples of the earth. "We know that the Son of God is come." That is the message our ministers and our missionaries alike are commissioned to proclaim. For the historic content of that message, we are now absolutely dependent upon the Holy Scriptures, and upon them alone. To me it is fundamental to insist upon this truth. There is only one Christ, and we can know him now only as the prophetic and historic facts set forth in the Bible reveal him to us. Apart from the Scriptures many christs have gone forth into the world, but at best these are only fancy figures, creatures of the more or less devout imaginings of men. When it is said to us, "Lo here, or lo there is Christ," the acid test of every such claim is harmony with the facts given us in the Scriptures. There is indeed a Christ of experience, a mystic Christ, revealed to the individual soul, but such a Christ is a mere invention, and a dangerous delusion, unless he conforms strictly and absolutely to the historic Christ depicted in the New Testament.

I shall never forget as long as I live, the impression made upon my mind and upon my spiritual sense by what is now regarded as an old-fashioned book called, "Christ's Presence in the Gospel History," by Dr. Hugh Martin, a Scottish divine, known and honored in the middle of the nineteenth century, but now for the most part forgotten. With incomparable cogency and clearness Dr. Martin showed in that book that it is Christ, the living Christ, Christ still living in the Gospel records, which explains their power.

It is this spiritual fact that the risen Christ lives, and lives again in the pages of those sacred records, which accounts for the extraordinary effects our missionaries have produced simply by first translating and then teaching the contents of the Scriptures to the peoples of every country under Heaven, of every race, of every color, and at every stage of civilization and social development. And in these days, when the Bible is handled by so many people in so many different ways and for so many different purposes, it is well worth reminding ourselves that the use our missionaries are making of the Bible is its highest use.

It is quite legitimate to study these ancient scriptures for literary, historical, antiquarian and other critical purposes, but the supreme purpose for which the Bible exists is to bring home to men's hearts and consciences the reality of the forgiving mercy and fatherly love of God, as prepared for in the Old Testament, and finally and fully revealed in the person and work of Jesus, as these are set forth in the New Testament.

In my home land of Scotland the foremost of all our Old Testament professors, who by his spiritual insight and historic knowledge made the Bible a new book to us who were privileged to be his students (I refer to Professor A. B. Davidson), never failed to remind us amid all our laborious linguistic studies that the highest use of the Bible was its practical use, not the use made of it by scholars and critics, but the use to which we see it put in the homes of the common people, by fathers and mothers with their sons and daughters gathered around them at the family altar, as in Robert Burns' immortal picture of the "Cotter's Saturday Night," by the feeble old man in the chimney corner and the devout old grandmother with her large print Bible on her knee, and John Bunyan's "Pilgrim's Progress" also within her reach.

In view of what I have just said, it is not surprising that our missionaries from every land bear testimony to the value of the Bible societies. It is one of the deep joys of a missionary's life, compensating for many trials and privations, that he is privileged so often to witness with his own eyes the operation of the divine power which the Old Book still wields. Let me give you a single instance and let it be by way of contrast.

Two or three generations ago, some missionaries went to labor in a remote part of Africa. The method they followed in trying to introduce Christianity was defective. They made no translation of the Scriptures, but used only symbols and sacraments in their endeavors to win the people. These symbols and sacraments were impressive, and good results followed; but the time came when tribal war broke out and the missionaries were swept out of the land.

Many years afterwards, other missionaries visited that country, and to their surprise they found the people bowing in terror before a strange fetish, which on examination proved to be a crucifix. That symbol, so sacred to those who understood its meaning, was of itself powerless to express the faith or to preserve the faith for which it stood. It had become a mere thing of fear and ignorant superstition.

Now, contrast with that what occurred not very long ago in China. A Chinese patient in a Christian missionary hospital, after being healed of his disease, was presented with a copy of the Gospel of John in his own language. At first he attached no special value to the gift, but he took it to his home in a far-off part of China which no Christian missionary had ever visited. Out of curiosity he started one day to read the little book. His attention was arrested by its contents, and he felt himself strangely moved. Soon he gathered his relatives and friends and acquaintances and read the little book to them. They also became deeply interested. At regular intervals they came together to have the book read and re-read in their hearing. After three years one Christian missionary, visiting that remote Chinese town, found several hundred Chinese men and women filled with the spirit of Christ and ready to be baptized in His name, so wonderfully had that single copy of the Gospel of John done its divine work in their hearts.

Now, so long as the Bible or any portion of it, produces spiritual results like that, it will continue to prove itself to be indeed "the Word of the living God which is able to save men's souls." And if it be asked under what conditions we are entitled to expect the distribution of the Bible in non-Christian lands to bear such practical fruit, the answer is, "He that hath ears to hear, let him hear." "Faith cometh by hearing, and hearing by the Word of God." All that is required is the hearing ear and the understanding heart. There is that in the Bible story which finds men, which comes home to them, which makes its appeal to all that is best and deepest in their natures. The one test of all true revelation from God is that it is thus heard with the inward ear. The Hindus, who have a fine spiritual sense, call their sacred books, not holy scriptures, but "holy hearings." To every land, and in every language, let the word of God be proclaimed, and the divine voice will be heard, and will call forth a glad response from every prepared heart, and to the end of time it will be true, "Blessed is he that heareth and keepeth the sayings of this book."

There is a story told of an Oriental king who, in celebration of a happy event in his kingdom, issued invitations to all the poor and needy folk in his capital to come together into a great hall, there to receive each one of them a gift from his own hand. Many came and passed, one by one, in front of the king and received his gift. At last when it appeared as if all had been supplied, the door opened at the far end of the hall and a blind man stumbled forward, stretching out his hands and groping his way. Immediately one of the king's attendants hastened toward the blind man, took him kindly by the hand, and guided him up the hall to where the king was still standing with a gift in his hand ready to bestow. Thus the groping hand was led by the guiding hand to the giving hand. That story is a picture and a parable. The groping hand of the blind man represents the world's need today, while the guiding hand shows us the duty of the church of Jesus Christ, of its ministers, its missionaries and its members, to lead all men to Jesus Christ that they may receive through him from the giving hand of the Father, the word of life, the highest and best of all his gifts. "Search the Scriptures, for in them ye think (and think rightly) ye have eternal life," and Jesus declared also, "They are they which testify of Me."

THE BIBLE AND WOMEN

MRS. HENRY W. PEABODY, BEVERLY, MASSACHUSETTS

The Bible carries in itself the proofs that it is no mere human document or mass of traditions. It is the only authoritative record of the direct revelation of God to man and of man to himself. It is our one source of knowledge of God's plan as revealed in His Son, Jesus Christ. Without this record our light becomes darkness. Those of us who are not scholars, but belong to the rank and file of humanity which Jesus touched in his earthly ministry, accept the Bible without question. We may be incapable of comprehending its critical interpretation, but a woman requires less faith to accept the Bible than to harmonize the varying theories of its critics.

Then, too, the critics are apt to eliminate the very parts which are especially dear to the heart of woman. For instance, we cannot give up those first two inspired chapters of Luke, written by a beloved physician, not of our modern scientific school, but the best of his day, and close to the issues of life and death. The luminous detail of that story of Mary, even the hastening over the hills to her older, more experienced woman friend, with the mystery and wonder that had come to her, convinces us. We cannot lose the last of John. The women, "while it was yet dark," with breaking hearts came to the place where they had laid Him. Women then and always, "while it is yet dark" are rising to go where love calls and needs them.

> "Since it is the Easter-time, and little bells are ringing,
>   Let us walk in still pride, with lifting of the head,
> For when He had risen from the grave, as all the world knows,
>   'Mary' was the first name that God ever said."

We cannot lose the Epistles, for again and again we find ourselves in them; and as we are, so are all the women who have lived in all the world. Humble or great, unlettered or learned, tempted, suffering, they find in the Bible their hope; special promises for them, and teachings which all can understand and teach and live. It is the universal book of womanhood. There is little difference in the hearts of women; some have wider opportunities, but the same types have persisted from the beginning. Eve has not passed off the stage, she is the familiar type of woman who today reaches out for forbidden things, often losing Paradise thereby.

Mothers of America and Scotland, India and China, recognize Hannah, the mother, who could even let her little lad go away from her that he might have his religious education which she could not give. And we know Miriam, one of the great protective army of older sisters who have become the women teachers of the world, second not even to mothers in the great gift they are making to childhood and youth in every land.

Read the daily papers in Washington, New York and London. Note the women of power and influence and wealth of almost royal prerogative, and find too seldom a queenly Esther not carried away by gaiety and glamor, but true to God and to her needy people and race. We still meet ambitious mothers who ask for their sons' preferment, though it may separate them from righteousness. And back in the old Scriptures, stands out with startling clearness the figure of the most advanced type of woman of the present day, the woman elected by the people to be judge over Israel. The brave and brilliant Christian woman in the office of the Attorney General of the United States, in the Department of Justice nearby, need not fear the debate as to whether a woman can be qualified for the Federal bench. She has her precedent in the Book of God, and precedent is what lawyers and politicians demand.

Between the old and the new, we hear an interlude of song, the clear voice of a young girl singing to God and to all generations who call her blessed. Women of every nation thrill to that song. And when the Christ came, born of this woman, he understood all women, as no other teacher ever understood.

"Christ praised another Mary whom the saints rebuked for wastefulness;
  For he understood them well, all Marys of His day,
Yes, and of today too, Mary staid and caring,
  Marys wild and home-loving—it was His way.

Martha and Lazarus talked with Christ at supper-time,
  Martha and Lazarus, of crops and folk and wars;
But while the food was cleared away, low by the door-step
  It was Mary spoke to Him, when there were stars.
Not of crops and gossip, not of work and neighbors,
  Christ and Mary talked about the wishing to be good
And of easy falling, and the new beginnings,
  And the way the moon looked, low above the wood."

We need our friend, St. Paul, we women of the world. Some
have interpreted him as critic and hinderer of womankind. He
says modestly that he spoke sometimes without inspiration. He
invariably spoke with good sense. Women were making rapid
progress in that first century when life in Rome and Greece had
become unspeakably corrupt, and women with new liberty and
without a restraining faith were sunk to depths of immorality.
The new faith of Jesus was liberating spiritual forces, the only
hope for the survival of the human race. Women who are the
conservators of this race must now as then hold within themselves this power of the grace of God, protective and constructive. They must commend themselves and the gospel by their
conduct.

A progressive woman in Boston told me that she had become a Buddhist, as she did not find freedom for woman in the
Christian faith. Further conversation disclosed little knowledge
of the Christian faith and none at all of Buddhism, except in
the denatured form imported for American women. The Bible
never limited women. Read that lovely appreciation of Paul's
in the sixteenth chapter of the Epistle to the Romans, where
Paul especially remembers those women who were his friends.
It might have been written by any modern missionary to any
little group in any part of the world, India, Africa, Kansas, New
England, Georgia, Scotland, Germany or France.

"I commend unto you Phoebe, our sister (deaconness), that
ye receive her in the Lord, worthily of the saints, and that ye
assist her in whatsoever matter she may have need of you; for
she hath been a helper of many and of mine own self. Salute
Prisca and Aquila, my fellow-workers in Christ Jesus, who for
my life laid down their own necks, unto whom not only I give
thanks, but also all the churches of the Gentiles: And salute
the church that is in their house. Salute Mary, who bestowed
much labor on you. Salute Andronicus and Junias, my kinsmen, and my fellow-prisoners, who are of note among the apostles, who also have been in Christ before me. Salute Tryphena
and Tryphosa, who labor in the Lord. Salute Rufus, the chosen
in the Lord." And this is exquisite, "and his mother and
mine."

These types are not obsolete. These women walk with us day by day. They are doing the work of the world. Show us any wider field of service, any greater opportunity for the exercise of talents and powers than God provided for women in his plan. There are women who have not measured up to his teaching, women who are capable of wonderful things, but have lost their way looking for a wider sphere, when all the time the opportunities included in the plan of God were within their grasp to be developed and used to the fullest extent.

The divinely appointed main lines of service for women are laid out in the Book of God. There are many avenues leading out from them, and in following these woman need not walk in narrow paths. As a mother she holds the balance of power for the Kingdom of God. As caretaker and teacher she moulds plastic minds and shapes the thoughts and ideals of the nation. As nurse and doctor she may exert an influence far beyond family and community service, for she may bring healing to a world of women and children who suffer and die without care. She may be a sanitary specialist, laboratory worker, maker of doctors and nurses like herself. As writer and speaker, woman may lead in reforms or may offer quiet comfort and guidance to those who lead. As religious worker, missionary or missionary executive she may help to organize the spiritual forces of the church and she may do all these things as her legitimate part of the assigned program of Christianity. She will find admirable precedents recorded in the Old and New Testaments.

We women love the portrait of the aged prophetess Anna, the dainty pastel of the young girl Rhoda, the etching of practical saint Dorcas with her needle, who died and had to be brought back to life, because the church could not live without her. Priscilla was keen as any Scotch woman pictured by Ian MacLaren in teaching homiletics to that young minister Appollos. Lydia, progressive, efficient business-woman, gathered a group to pray, the woman of Macedonia, opened doors of opportunity for the Apostle. All these types today, wherever the Bible has gone, claim their inheritance and enter the service. Women are alike, differing from men, but with as great a work to do, which will not be done by men if they fail. There are wider opportunities for training today, but the same general lines were laid down in the Book of God, which is the book of woman.

Some have lost their way, because they have lost the Book. Isaiah would be more depressed than he was over the dress of women, if he could see our followers of fashion, or if he could watch women of education and talent, power and leisure, playing endless games and seeking excitement and demoralizing pleasures, while the world needs them. Men are helped by the

very rush and business of life and are less liable in this day to
go to extremes than the idle women in Europe and America.
But millions of women are reaching out for better things.

We are told that no woman has ever written a successful
book about men. Certainly men have failed, from Thackeray
down, to portray women. They know chiefly our foibles and
loyalties. But women are startled to find their very selves in
the mirror of God's Universal Book, the revealer of woman to
herself. If woman fails, the world fails. She will not fail, if
she takes the simple teaching of the great Emancipator of
woman. The greatest danger is in our own civilization. The
women of the Orient and the islands are beginning with fewer
temptations. Perhaps they will understand, if we fail. Let us
not lead them astray.

Women dare not let the Bible go, nor any part of it. It
makes the world safe for women and children. They see Him
with the child in His arms, their child. They see the tiny gift
which was "all her living" changed by his appreciation into a
memorial. That contribution was not "in the budget" and was
over and above the apportionment.

Women stood on the edge of the throng and listened to
Him with that thrill we feel when the sermon touches us. He
spoke of the woman in the kitchen like the one He knew in
Nazareth, putting in the leaven and thinking of the Kingdom
of God; or the woman who had lost her piece of silver, and the
woman who lost something finer and in her shame found mercy
and forgiveness. We think of the little daughter raised from
the dead, of the restoration of the demoniac boy, of the fear and
faith of one who touched the hem of His garment, and women
in every part of the world are lifted up and transformed and
find abiding joy in the vision and satisfying activity in the
work He has left to be done. Women do not need a new religion nor a new philosophy. It is all in their Word from God.
They only need to accept and practice it.

I knew a woman, long ago, in the hill country of India. As
I walked one morning she offered me an apple from her tree,
a wonderful sight to an American woman who had not seen an
apple for four years. Her husband was a fruit-contractor who
had come from the plains. She was far from home. We sat on
the doorstep of the little mud house and talked. I knew her
language and no one else in that strange country could talk with
her. She was so happy to talk with a woman. She invited me
into her home, but one glimpse of the interior decorations made
me feel I was safer outside. I told her the story of Mary and
Martha and Jesus, and explained that Martha was a particularly
good housekeeper. She took the hint, as I gave it in some detail. I was only there for a vacation of a few weeks, but as we

met daily she eagerly listened to the stories of Oriental women who live in the Bible and of their Friend. She had little mind and no training, but was able to learn a hymn with constant repetition, "Come to Jesus, Come to Jesus, He will save you, He will save you just now," in her own tongue. She learned with some effort a prayer such as you might teach to a child of five, a prayer for herself and her people, and then we separated, never to meet again. Some six years later, I received a letter from a woman missionary who was taking her vacation in the same place. She wrote as follows: "This morning, as I sat by the window in this lovely spot, a woman passed with her water pot on her head, singing in Telugu, 'Come to Jesus, Come to Jesus, just now.' I sprang to the door and greeted her. She set down the water jar. I asked her, if she was a Christian, and she said, 'No.' I said to her, 'Where did you learn to sing the hymn?' 'Oh,' she said, 'I know something more,' and bending her head she reverently said the prayer; and then lifting her radiant face she told her story of your visit. I said 'I will write her that I have seen you. Have you any word to send?' And she said eagerly, 'Yes. Tell her I have sung the hymn every day, and I pray the prayer, and tell her I am trying to keep the house clean.'"

That is the applied gospel. We rejoice in a universal Saviour and in a universal Book for the universal woman.

CIRCULATION OF THE SCRIPTURES IN THE NEAR EAST

THE REVEREND ARTHUR C. RYAN, D.D., FORMERLY OF CONSTANTINOPLE

In at least two respects the work of circulating the Scriptures in the Near East has a unique interest. First of all the lands of the Near East are the regions from which we received our Bible. There are the places where the authors of the Bible lived and did their work. In these Near East lands we have the only territory made sacred by the earthly life of our Lord Jesus. One can scarcely go anywhere in Palestine, Syria, Mesopotamia, Southern Asia Minor, Macedonia and Greece without finding places of special interest to all Bible students.

In the second place the work of circulating the Scriptures in the Near East is interesting because of the fact that after nearly 2,000 years missionaries from the West must carry back to the Near East and open for the people the Bible which we received from those very lands. In many ways the people of Palestine, Syria, Mesopotamia, Asia Minor and Greece are as ignorant of the sacred writings as are the people living in the Far East thousands of miles away from the land of their origin. As I have traveled up and down these lands I have often asked myself, "Why is it that the church of the West after all these years must send missionaries to these lands to preach and teach from the gospels which these lands originally gave us?" The answer seems to be as follows:

After the early church had collected and canonized the sacred writings of the Bible, it became "weary in well doing." It failed to heed the basic teachings of the Scriptures, namely, that if one would save his life, he must lose it; that only by losing one's life shall he save it. Instead of opening the Scriptures by translating them into the languages of the people and spreading them broadcast, the church shut up the sacred message of the Scriptures in fancy bound books. Instead of setting the light of the gospel on the hill it hid it under a bushel. The result was inevitable. The light that was in them became darkness. The life that was for some centuries vigorous was weakened. Moreover, these Oriental churches after about four or five centuries of vigorous offensive in the spiritual warfare against ignorance, superstitions and false religions, settled down to enjoy what they had gained and to rest complacently behind the strongholds which they had built about them. They became uninterested in carrying the message of Jesus Christ beyond the circumference of its occupied territory. The result was that in the seventh and eighth centuries it lost its ability to maintain even a defensive warfare. Out of Arabia came Mohammed and with Mohammed came Mohammedanism and with Mohammedanism came defeat for the churches of the East. How great has been that defeat we are only now beginning to realize. If we look to Asia Minor we find that within the last decade the Oriental churches have been forced to leave this land of their origin. Only a few days ago the Turkish Government expelled from Constantinople the Greek Patriarch. Scores of church buildings have been razed to the ground in Asia Minor during the last few years and hundreds of thousands of people have been put to death or forced into exile. And the end is not yet!

If we turn to Russia we may see another terrible result of an Eastern church which for centuries was content to remain on the defensive. For generations the Russian Church withheld from the mass of the people the Scriptures in any language which these masses could understand. According to the Russian ecclesiastics the Scriptures were too precious to be translated and too sacred to be entrusted in the vernacular to the rank and file of their people. Only captains, majors, colonels and generals in the army of the Russian Church were privileged to be supplied with one of the greatest of all spiritual weapons against ignorance, superstitions and the growth of atheistic doctrines. The result for the Russian Church is that its defences have fallen one after another and today it is almost destroyed by forces which that church should have prevented from arising.

The lesson which the churches of the West must surely learn from the present situation in the Near East is, that they will be able to live only by maintaining a vigorous offensive both at home and abroad against all the strongholds of our spiritual enemy. Victory will never come to any forces that are content to fight merely a defensive warfare. This lesson is as true for the individual, the local church, the national church, as it is for the church universal. Only as the churches of the West take the spiritual weapons which are mighty through God and launch forth in an attempt to go over the top to destroy the strongholds of the enemy, will it be certain of its own future.

During the past 100 years five great missionary gains for the church have been made by our forces at work in the Near East.

1. Most of the peoples in the Near East now have opportunity to secure the Scriptures in whole or in part in their own vernacular. Only a few dialects remain to be translated. This is a great gain.

2. There exists in the Near East a fair-sized evangelical church which is thoroughly imbued with the idea of using the Scriptures in the language of the people as the basis of their work and teaching. This group has been greatly impoverished and weakened by the recent dozen years of war and turmoil. But it is still a valuable asset and may become a mighty force in evangelizing the rest of the peoples in the Near East.

3. The weakened condition of the Oriental churches themselves has made many of their people—clergy and laity alike—more susceptible to the appeal for the open Bible and more ready to cooperate with the missionary. The sufferings of Oriental Christians have softened their hearts and opened their minds to their failure and caused them to be willing to make use of the Scriptures as they have not done for centuries. In many places Bible classes are being conducted within these Oriental churches. This is a hopeful gain for the cause of Christ.

4. There now exists in the Near East a fairly large missionary force, well organized with valuable experience and preparation for future work. This force ought to be increased, but its presence in the lands of the Near East is a promise of greater victory for the future.

5. The cumulative, even if partly hidden, effects of more than 100 years of faithful missionary work by Mission Boards and Bible Societies in the Near East, is an incalculable gain. In the economy of God this faithful service cannot be lost. Seeds have been sown and the ground cultivated and the harvest will

surely come. Despite the unfavorable conditions in certain regions at the present time, there are many signs that the next century of missionary success in the Near East will be multiplied many-fold. In spite of the apparent strength of Moslems in Turkey, there is a real weakening of the power of Islam as a whole. Islam is now on the defensive as it has never been before. By adequately equipping the Christian forces now at work in the Near East, there is every reason to believe that decades ahead we shall see great gains in the conversion of Moslems to Christianity.

So far as the present work of circulating the Scriptures in the Near East is concerned, outside of the city of Constantinople, nothing can be done in Turkey, in Russia and in the Caucasus republics. While Turkey has not issued any order prohibiting the circulating of the Scriptures it is practically impossible to do any work at the present time. The Bolshevik government in Russia prohibits the importation of the Scriptures in any language into its territories.

When we turn to the other countries of the Near East the present opportunities are unlimited. In Greece the Scriptures in modern Greek may now be imported and circulated freely. This is a great gain in view of the fact that until 1922 the existence of a clause in the Constitution prohibited the importation or circulation of the Scriptures in any language except that of the ancient Greek. As only a few of the people can understand the ancient Greek, this meant that the populations as a whole were deprived of the benefit of the Scriptures in their own languages. Since this prohibition has been lifted, the increase in the circulation of the Scriptures in modern Greek has been phenomenal.

The other Balkan countries are now open for the work of distributing the Scriptures freely and the circulations are increasing year by year. The changes which have come about in all of the Arabic-speaking lands have been favorable to our work. Colporteurs are reporting increasing sales and the Word of God is being largely used in these Arabic regions.

By looking back over the past 100 years with a view to forecasting the future, it seems that in all of the Near East, God has been using the folly of men and nations to plow deeply the soil for a great planting and an abundant spiritual harvest. Minds are open as to the basic principles of the Bible as they have never been before. The past century of missionary activity has laid the foundation for the great work of the present century. If the churches of America will heed well the lesson which we may learn from the churches of the East and if they will take up a vigorous offensive in the spiritual warfare which we are waging, victory is assured.

In closing may I call your attention to the fact that the American Bible Society is the organization for furnishing the Christian forces of America in their world-wide work with one of the mightiest weapons at their command. The printed Word of the gospel in the languages of the people is mighty through God to the pulling down of the strongholds of ignorance, superstition, false ideas of God and to the setting up of the strongholds of good will, love and unselfish service.

THE BIBLE IN LATIN AMERICA
THE REVEREND H. C. TUCKER, D.D., BRAZIL

For three centuries, dating from the discovery of America, the Bible was not in use and was practically unknown among the inhabitants of Latin America. It was not to be found in the lists of books which by royal permission and papal sanction might be admitted into those countries for the use by the Spanish and Portuguese colonists and early settlers.

About a century ago the Bible first began to find its way into Latin American countries. The American and the British and Foreign Bible Societies consigned small grants of Scriptures to Christian merchants from the United States and Great Britain residing in port towns along the coast. These books were distributed among the people as opportunity arose, and many times awakened interest and inquiry.

A little more than a half century ago the Bible Societies through their regularly established agencies, systems of colportage and American missionaries began organized and wisely directed efforts to place in the hands of the people the written Word of God. From the small beginning of a few thousand copies distributed annually the numbers have increased until in recent years the circulation has reached 150,000 and more per annum. There is more interest in Bible reading today than ever throughout Latin America.

The story of these attempts to give the Bible to the people is a chapter of thrilling and illuminating interest in modern missionary annals. It is a record of heroic service and of faith. The opposition faced, the hardships endured and the difficulties overcome have been recounted in the printed reports of the work. The Bible has been denounced as a false and dangerous book and the people have been warned not to read it, and many times have been persuaded to give up, destroy and even burn copies they had bought. The Bible agents and colporteurs have been denounced, persecuted, stoned, arrested and imprisoned. Striking incidents are Francisco Penzotti in Peru, who suffered imprisonment for eight months, and Jose Tonelli in Brazil, who was beaten and his body thrown in the bush by the road-side for dead. Similar instances are on record in the reports from other countries of South America. Bible burnings, some times carried out with great display in public places, have been frequently reported.

Translations of the Scriptures have been made during these years into the Spanish and Portuguese languages and into a few of the dialects of Indian tribes. These endeavors furnish an interesting chapter in the story of Bible translation.

From the very earliest days of the enterprise there were a few persons who received the Bible and read it to advantage. Individual minds and hearts have been enlightened and awakened and men have found Christ the Saviour. These have led others to hear and read the Word. Many of the Protestant churches that have sprung up and are now growing into strong bodies in these countries had their origin from the reading of the Bible by an individual, or a small number of persons.

Interest in the Bible and its influence over the minds and hearts of men is becoming widespread in Latin America. Men of all classes, learned and ignorant, rich and poor, high and low are being influenced by its blessed contents. The circulation and reading of the Bible and the preaching of its truths is having a stimulating effect on the intellectual life of the people. Illiteracy ranges from forty to ninety per cent throughout Latin America. It is not an uncommon thing for adults of thirty, fifty and even seventy years of age to be awakened to learn to read in order that they may be able to examine this wonderful new book and learn for themselves its beautiful stories.

The Bible is influencing the language of the people. A new religious phraseology is noticeable. Likewise a great body of new ideals and ideas are being released among the people, creating new currents of thought and new purposes in life. Its increasing circulation has provoked priests of the long dominant ecclesiastical order to make attempts to give the people the gospel with the notes and comments of the fathers. The question of the source of authority for Christian truth and doctrine is being forced upon a high intellectual and Scriptural plane.

Accumulated testimony shows that the Bible has an important, indeed indispensable, function in the missionary enterprise of the world.

Emphasis should be placed upon the fact that the Bible Societies are not only engaged in this wider distribution of the Scriptures among the people who know it not, but they are supplying them to all missionaries, native pastors, churches and Sunday Schools. There should be increased financial support of the work by the churches in the United States and Canada. The

Societies are doing a work in this regard that the Boards of Missions could not well do for their own work.

In addition to this increased financial support for Scripture distribution and supply this great missionary Convention might well recommend in its findings that the Christian men of the United States and Canada seriously consider the advisability and need of building Bible Houses in Mexico City, in some important city on the Pacific coast, in Buenos Aires and in Rio de Janeiro. Such buildings would greatly add to the economy and efficiency of the work and give stability and importance to the cause.

THE PROBLEMS OF BIBLE TRANSLATION

PROFESSOR OSWALD T. ALLIS, PH.D., PRINCETON, NEW JERSEY

When we think of the great progress which has been made in the task of Bible translation, it would almost seem as if there could be no serious problems connected with this work, or that they had already been solved, and the question were merely one of historical interest. The facts as we know them are surprising. According to recent statistics the entire Bible has been translated into 158 languages or dialects, the New Testament into 142 more (a total of 300), one book or more of the Scriptures into 422, some chapters or verses into 48, a grand total of 770. In 1804 when the British and Foreign Bible Society was founded, "some portion of Scripture had been printed in over 60 languages." One hundred and seventeen years later the number of tongues in which the Society had promoted the translation, printing or distribution of the Bible had grown to 543; and in a little volume *The Gospel in Many Tongues* (1921), the British and Foreign Bible Society gives a verse of Scripture, usually John iii. 16, in each one of these 543 languages or dialects. In 1923 the American Bible Society issued Bibles or portions in 116 languages and dialects. The circulation in China in 1923 by the three great Bible Societies—the British and Foreign, the American, and the National Society of Scotland— was 58,000 Bibles, 85,000 Testaments and nearly seven and one-half million portions, of which total one third and more represents the work of the American Bible Society.

These statistics would seem to indicate, as I have said, that the work of Bible translation has not been a difficult one or that its problems have been largely, if not wholly solved. But such is not the case. The difficulties which have been overcome in the accomplishment of the great feat, which has been just outlined, have been tremendous. Adoniram Judson of Burma, who completed the translation of the Bible in 1834 after seventeen years of much interrupted labor, wrote, "I consider it the work of a man's whole life to procure a really good translation of even the New Testament in an untried language." Robert Morrison of China, the centenary of the completion of whose version in the Chinese (Wen-li) was celebrated a year ago, worked seventeen years on his translation. The splendid Arabic version—the "Van Dyck" as it is usually called—is a monument to the memory of Eli Smith and Cornelius Van Dyck. On its completion in 1865 it had cost nearly twenty years of labor. In fact Dr. Hoskins, of the Beirut Mission, counting from 1837, when the plans for this version were made, to 1895 when Dr. Van Dyck died, speaks of the version as the result of "nearly sixty years" of effort.

It would be possible to speak of many difficulties which are involved in the translation of the Scriptures, but I must confine myself in the few moments at my disposal to a brief discussion of three. The first of these is the *disadvantageous conditions* under which this work of translation has often, perhaps usually, been carried on. We think with pleasure and satisfaction of the enthusiasm with which many native converts have received the gospel and assisted in the translation of the Holy Scriptures by their missionaries. The Aneityumese labored fifteen years in the cultivation of arrow root that they might have the whole Bible printed in their language; $6,000 was the amount raised, and when the first Bibles were printed they came to them fully paid for. This is a bright picture in missionary history. But on the other hand when we think of the version of Acts into Erromangan, we are reminded that before it was completed by Robertson it had cost the lives of the two martyred Gordons, George and James, the one brother murdered in 1861, the other stricken down ten years later while striving to finish the work his brother had begun. Strange as it may seem, it was while revising the translation of Stephen's speech, that the life blood of James Gordon stained the manuscript written by his martyr brother. These two incidents taken from neighboring islands in the New Hebrides illustrate the bright side and the dark side of Bible translation as it concerns the natives. How large a factor by way of incentive and by way of hindrance they have been in this great work of translation only those who have made the translations can tell us. But these are not the only difficulties. We think also of the adverse natural conditions under which many of these translations were made, the intense heat of the tropics, malaria, disease, primitive conditions of all kinds, the pressure of other duties, etc. Those who have worked upon the making or revising of a version in the homeland with the aid of concordances and lexicons and all the helps which the student gathers about him can in no wise appreciate the difficulties which have been overcome by a pioneer missionary in the making of a pioneer translation.

In the second place let us think of the *peculiarities of language* and the problem which they present in the translation of the Bible into many different tongues. On the one hand we have Chinese, a monosyllabic language with few vocables, no grammar to speak of, and a syntax the rules of which, we are told, are frequently more honored in the breach than the observance; yet a language with an ancient literature and a most complicated script. On the other hand we have the agglutinative languages of the American Indians with their extremely long words, so long that Cotton Mather in speaking of the Massachusetts dialect said, "One would think that these words had been growing ever since Babel unto the dimensions to which they are now extended," so long that in Eskimo, we are told, an English sentence with as many as seventeen words can be represented by a single word. Again we have in the Macasser of the Malayo-Javanese group, a language which is singularly weak in the ability to express generalizations. The difficulty of finding equivalent words or expressions in these many foreign languages has given rise to the phrase "term question." Thus, from the very start the missionaries to China had difficulty in deciding upon the exact equivalent for the words "God" and "Spirit." In the Delegates' Version of 1850, blank spaces were left for these words and these were filled in by a special conference at Shanghai. But even today we have in China two kinds of Bibles, *Shangti* and *Shen*. *Shangti* means "supreme power," *Shen*, "spirit." The dispute as to which is the proper rendering of "God" is still unsettled. The difficulty of translation some times presents itself in amusing form. Thus, in the Arabic of Van Dyck's version, the phrase in John ix. 23, "He is of age; ask him" is rendered thus: "He is complete of teeth" (*hua kanil ussinni*). And many other equally strange and amusing renderings might easily be cited.

But the third and in some respects the most important of all the problems of translation is due to the fact that the languages of non-Christian peoples are *unregenerate*. We are accustomed to speak of individuals and peoples as unregenerate, but it is not as natural to us to apply this term to languages. But there is a sense in which it is most appropriate. John Eliot, the missionary to the Indians, wrote in 1653 (ten years before the completion of his translation of the Bible into the Massachusetts dialect), "I have had a great longing desire, if it were the will of God, that our Indian language might be sanctified by the translation of the Holy Scriptures into it." How striking and arresting is that phrase, that our "Indian language *might* be *sanctified* by the translation of the Holy Scriptures into it." Yet every missionary who has been face to face with paganism realizes what this means. George Grenfell of the Congo, has this to say, " I find it very difficult to translate many of the ideas which are really of great importance. For instance, I can find no word for 'forgiveness,' and it has to be rendered by 'cleansing.' 'Sanctification' I have not ventured to grapple with yet. Of course, at the best, in these early days, a translation is only an approximation to what it ought to be, but if I can only manage to give the people an idea of the truth, I shall be very glad." Think of a language which has no word for "forgiveness," and in which "sanctification" represents an unheard-of idea! Yet such languages are to be found where the leaven of the gospel has not yet penetrated. Dr. F. E. Hoskins of the Beirut Mission, who labored for years in the preparation of the First Font Arabic Reference Bible has spoken of the attempt through the Arabic version to elevate and purify the Arabic language. That language is not a crude and undeveloped tongue. It has an immense vocabulary and is capable of great niceties of expression. Yet it has been so corrupted and defiled by the sins of those who use it that scarce a page of its dictionary could be read aloud to a mixed audience. And this redemption of words of which we have been speaking is found even in the Scriptures themselves. We have but to think, for example, of the word "love" (*agape*) of which a well known scholar has recently written that the redemption of the word was "the work of those who had learned of what love is from the divine revelation." "The love of God which passeth knowledge,"—that is a love which only the Christian can understand. Likewise the word "peace" (*eirene*), to the pagan Greek, this meant simply "absence of war and hostility." The Hebrew gave it its positive content of "well-being." But in the New Testament conception of the "peace of God that passeth all understanding" the word is fully sanctified and blessed.

It is, as we have seen, a fact that the Bible can be translated into languages the most diverse and the most widely distributed. We need not argue for the fact, we need not stress the difficulties, the fact has been abundantly demonstrated. And the reason for the fact is perfectly clear. Yet it is one which we need to keep ever in mind. The Bible is the "Word of God"; and "God has made of one flesh all nations of men for to dwell in all the earth." God's Word is meant for all, for all nations and kindreds and peoples, and tongues. It is able by the power of His Spirit to redeem and sanctify them; and it is, therefore, able to redeem and sanctify their several languages. We have no such promise for the wisdom of men, not even for the great works of literature. We might hesitate to attempt to translate Shakespeare into Eskimo, or Kant into Bantu. But we need not hesitate to undertake to translate the Bible into any language, for the Bible has proved its power to sanctify all the languages of mankind. It is our duty, therefore, to give it to all as quickly, as fully, as accurately as possible. It is to this task that the great Bible Societies have devoted themselves. It is in this work that they have been richly blessed. And that they may devote themselves to it without let or hindrance, without dissipation of their energies or division of their forces, they make it their rule to do this "without note or comment," that the peoples of the earth may have this Bible in its simplicity and its purity.

In closing let us think of the concluding words of that prayer with which Adoniram Judson dedicated the Burmese Bible on its completion in 1834: "May He make His own inspired Word, now complete in the Burmese tongue, the grand instrument of filling all Burma with songs of praise to our great God and Saviour Jesus Christ. Amen." The aim of the Bible societies, the aim of the Christian missionaries, is to make this prayer all inclusive. When we can pray the prayer of Judson as he would have gladly prayed it, "May He make His own inspired Word, now complete in all languages and tongues, the grand instrument of filling all the world with songs of praise to our great God and Saviour Jesus Christ. Amen."—the problems of Bible translation will have been solved and the work of translator and missionary will have been accomplished.

TRANSLATING IN THE MISKITO LANGUAGE OF CENTRAL AMERICA

THE REVEREND GEORGE R. HEATH, NICARAGUA

The Lamb who was slain for us has redeemed with His blood men of every tribe and tongue and people and nation; and there is no form of human speech which is not capable of becoming the vehicle of the glorious message of salvation. It is true that some languages are crude, and even debased, because for centuries they have been used for little less than earthly and sensual ideas: but, like those who speak them, they are capable of redemption. Very willingly would we missionaries share with our people the priceless heritage of noble psalmody and wholesome literature enshrined in our own language. But it is far more important to bring Christ as close to the people as possible, so that they may see that He is theirs as much as He is ours: that He will take their lives and purify and ennoble them without demanding the acquirement of any veneer of exotic culture. Until we do so, the Indian especially is liable to lead a double life, placing in one compartment the hopes and ideals of the new message, but reserving room in the other for much of the superstition and impurity familiar from childhood. In Eastern Nicaragua and Honduras this is seen especially in what is known as the "spirit teaching," a compromise which preserves many heathen usages under Christian names. A woman of Saupuka treasured two papers which she said had been given her by the angels, and could only be read by those whose eyes she opened by striking them with a little switch. The visiting missionary found that the papers were merely advertisements of sewing machines and cough medicine; but the woman insisted that he had read them wrong, because she had not opened his eyes. We find that the only way to break the "spirit teaching" is to train the young folks to read the Scriptures in their own tongue.

Many years ago the Miskito Indians were politically independent, and allied with Great Britain. Their chief town and seaport was English-speaking; and in the villages the Indians were encouraged to learn English by their government. English primers were used in the schools, and in church the lessons were read from the English Bible and followed by a free translation. But after many weary years the attempt had to be given up. One of our former leaders, Wilhelm Sieboerger, has told us that in his first years he taught continually in the village school, and saw no result. He prayed to the Lord that he might be enabled to teach at least one Indian to read enough English to understand the Gospels. But not even that was granted to him. Then he saw the need for translating, and brought out a clear, idiomatic version of the Gospels and Acts. At first the Indians did not want it. Had not their colored Creole neighbors always told them that their Miskito language was nothing but a jargon, and that only English was worthy of being written or printed? Prejudice was overcome, especially after a Miskito Liturgy and Hymn Book was also printed and put into common use; and the change has been remarkable. Twenty-five years ago the native Christians seemed completely dependent on the missionary for everything; if he were absent from the station, church services ceased; even prayer-meetings were not held. But from 1911 onwards the village of Karata, for example, was without a resident missionary for twelve years. Yet not only were the church services kept up, but the congregation has evidently grown in grace, and has sent out three active, faithful evangelists to the frontiers of heathenism, and given two teachers to other congregations.

Furthermore, the reading of the Scriptures has seemed to awaken the dormant brains of the people, and many are now ready for further study, and are beginning to acquire a knowledge of Spanish, the present dominant language of the country.

And what shall we say of homes transformed by family worship, where the Miskito New Testament is read and the Miskito hymns are sung day by day? These and many other proofs of God's blessing convince us that the right method of missionary work is that sanctioned from the first by the Holy Spirit, to give the Word of God to every man in his own tongue.

And the marvelous way in which the Spirit uses and blesses the translated message strengthens us more than ever in the conviction that, as our Moravian Synods have repeatedly declared, "the entire Holy Scriptures are the Word of God." Thus our work in the mission field will remain incomplete until we have implanted in our people the same familiarity with those living oracles as we ourselves possess.

TRANSLATING IN PORTUGUESE EAST AFRICA
THE REVEREND E. H. RICHARDS, D.D., FORMERLY OF AFRICA

In 1880, I landed in Portuguese East Africa, a country 1,600 miles long, 300 miles wide, with an estimated population of 3,000,000 people who had never seen a letter of the alphabet, who had never seen a written sign of any kind. While I was busy tumbling boxes about under the tarpaulin, on the day of our arrival my wife took a strip of ceiling board and scraped away the earth—and marked A, B, C's and 1, 2, 3, in the mother earth, and a hundred children round about her learned the A, B, C's and 1, 2, 3 before we had a tent over our head; and three of those children who forty-five years ago learned their A, B, C off the sand are today preachers and teachers in our Mission.

In the evening of the first day there was a mass of people sitting on the ground. It occurred to me that we ought to have evening prayers before we broke up. But how was I to conduct prayers without knowing a word of the language? Previously I had spent some time in Natal where I had learned the Zulu language, which I had spoken for some four years. Although these people did not know Zulu, I conducted prayers in that language—hoping there might be some one who had some knowledge of that language. At the close of the meeting, a young man came to me and spoke in broken Zulu, which I managed to understand. I asked him in Zulu, "How do you say in Tonga, "Our Father who art in heaven?" The Zulu is *'Baba wetu o sezulwini.'*" He immediately replied, *"Babe watu a ku mo njajini."* And we had translated the first part of the Lord's prayer. Then I went on, in Zulu: *"Ma li hlonitywe igama lako.* How do you say that?" He said: *"Li na rungujwe lina lago."* In an hour's time we had the entire Lord's Prayer translated into the Tonga language for the first time. That translation was so well done that in the forty-one years since we wrote it that night only one single word has ever been changed, and that is the word which we ourselves cannot recite together today—the word "debts." Now that prayer which was translated on that evening has been going over the country for four decades and the people are still reciting it and teaching it to their children.

On that same evening we translated the shortest hymn in the English language, "Come to Jesus," into the Tonga. Next morning we conducted prayers with a hymn in the major scale, a scale which the non-Christian world has never known. Then later we taught them to sing "Jesus Lover of my Soul" and "Nearer My God to Thee" and these hymns and these tunes are now being used over tremendous areas today.

In our work of translation one of the first things we did was to whittle out the type with our jackknife, and with printers' ink which we got from the steamship we could print on cloth charts. But you must have something to print, and after the A, B, C's, what are you going to print? It occurred to us that we might just as well give them Bible stories as anything else and we began with the Gospel of Luke, which we translated as best we could, setting up the letters one at a time in the wooden type. In a short time we had a few chapters of Luke printed. Then came the printing-press with which with great effort we could print one page at a time, for neither the natives nor ourselves had ever seen type until it came to us with the press. Now we found out that by putting these proofs in the schools the children committed them to memory, and they made splendid proof-readers too; they could soon tell whether a letter was wrong or misplaced. They committed the Gospel to memory as fast as we could print it.

I never intended to translate, I had a very sacred respect for a person who was so learned that he could translate the Bible. I thought some one else would come along and do that work right. But the point is, it did not take a learned man to do what I did. Having done the Gospel of Luke, we tried the Gospel of Matthew. The children committed that also by the time we had printed it. And in that way we went through the entire New Testament and that is the way we happened to be the translators of the New Testament into the Tonga language.

A little later the Batswa people sent their children to us. We did not intend to learn their language; we thought one language was enough for us, but by hearing it day after day came to us until we could speak it as well as the Tonga, and then they said, "We, too, must have the Bible"; and we gave them the schools and gave them the proof sheets and they committed the Gospel in the same manner as the Tonga people.

That is the way the translation occurred. I take no credit whatever for having translated the Bible. It was natural. It had to be done and we gave them the best we could do, and both of those translations have run on into these decades without revision. We do not say they do not need revision, but our translation is sufficiently perfect that these peoples are getting into the Kingdom of Heaven by the scores of thousands.

Now in the matter of translation certain difficulties should be noted. There are no words for such words as "home" or "love" or "virgin" or the "Holy Spirit." Take the word "God." There is no word for "God" in the Tonga. We call God *"Nkulu Nkulu"* (the Great Great). That is a description, but not a translation, and that is the name we are using today.

Then take the term "Holy Spirit." "Holy" is pure, clean, no dirt in it. And "spirit" is breath, and breath is air. You can find no other term. And when you say "Holy Spirit" as sacredly as ever you can, the native hears nothing but "pure air." You ask him, "Do you want the Holy Spirit?" and he will breathe hard, throwing out his chest, and say "Yes, white man, I have it. See," and by breathing hard he demonstrates that he has pure air. The religious idea is not in him and ink cannot reveal it.

Now another example, "Hallowed be Thy name." The thought in the word "hallowed" is so sacred that words cannot convey the idea. You can feel what it means, but you cannot see it and you cannot translate it. I call attention to this particularly as an example of the difficulties of our task.

There are other words which present obstacles in translation. For instance, "Go tell that fox." Well, we have no foxes in our country. We cannot translate the word. In a case like this the missionaries agree to use the word for some other animal and thus convey the idea, for the word is only the sign of an idea. We use the original word if we can, but if we cannot we use some other word that conveys the idea. Now in our country we have the jackal. He is not at all like the fox and he is not a fox. He is not as cunning as the fox, but he is twice as mean, and the meanness expressed in the idea goes over. So our translation reads: "Go tell that jackal." That puts the idea across and the native understands exactly what is meant.

Now the word for "home" is very indefinite. You ask where a man is and they will reply, *"Hongode kaya"* meaning, literally, he has gone to his *"goto,"* the place where he always goes. There is no word for "home." This is all the term there is.

There is no hint of the human being there, the family group, happiness. The word *"goto"* reveals nothing; but simply, like an animal, he has gone to his *"goto."* So we use that word for "home" in our translation. And in the beginning the idea of home is not there; we know it is not; but later, when he has become a Christian and love has come into his language, then "home" begins to appear, until finally that *"goto"* has become home in his mind. Christianity will do that for a language. It will change words from the utmost poverty into the greatest riches and utmost happiness, and it will do it in any language. In the beginning that *"goto"* was full of polygamy. It was full of microbes. It was full of misery. It was full of everything but happiness. He has scarcely begun to say "Our Father who art in heaven" when that *"goto"* begins to change. Polygamy disappears. They cannot be mean to women; must not sell girls; must not pound them around; got to be decent when the Bible comes into the house! And so that *"goto"* has developed into a "home."

Another word which to me is a very delicate term and a very precious one is "virgin." In our part of Africa a woman is a piece of property. She always belongs to some one. She must be owned. There is no such thing as an unowned woman, and from the time they are born they are married; age has nothing to do with it; and under conditions like that the meaning of the term "virgin" cannot occur. It is a blank in their language. Now how are you going to put that over? I had translated the New Testament into one language and was half way through it in the second language before I found a term for virgin that seemed at all satisfactory. It occurred in this wise: I was going through the country with a boy for a companion when at a certain place we stopped for rest and a cup of tea in the middle of the day, and just as we started to resume our journey the boy stopped suddenly and I heard him exclaim, *"Nbulwa."* It was a new term; I asked him what it meant. He said, "Come and see." I looked and there was a tree. The name of the tree is *"machanjava."* It was a pear-shaped tree, some twenty feet high, and covered with great clusters of a fruit akin to the grape. These fruit were an inch long and a half-inch in diameter and of a ripe royal purple color, and they were so prolific that they covered that tree until one could scarcely see any green foliage. It was one of the most luxuriant, fruitful, beautiful productions I had ever gazed upon, and I said to the boy, "Why did you call it that? What was the idea?" and he said to me, "Here is a tree; it is beautifully perfect, as perfect as any tree can be; it has never been touched." I failed to perceive it at all at the moment, but later it occurred to me that the word for that tree carried the idea that I wanted for "virgin." That tree was perfect. Absolutely perfect on every side. The Almighty could not have made it any more so. Why not use that term for 'virgin?' And we have used that term in our translations from that day to this and it has certainly put the perfection of that idea across.

Now in regard to these translations of religious terms and new ideas, the Holy Spirit enters into the soul of that human being and he is made new and he has experiences which he never had before and these terms take on meanings which they never had before, and in time Christianity puts into the words a meaning which ink and language alone never could have done.

THE TRANSLATION OF THE MALAY BIBLE

PROFESSOR W. G. SHELLABEAR, D.D., MADISON, NEW JERSEY

The word "Malay" is used to describe a race as well as a language. All the people of the brown race inhabiting the Philippine Islands and the Dutch East Indies—Java, Sumatra and Borneo, and thousands of smaller islands—are of the Malay race, and speak nearly 180 different languages, all of which are very similar in formation and somewhat alike in vocabulary. Of all these many Malayan languages the most widespread, the simplest in construction, and the easiest to acquire, is called "The Malay language," and is spoken along the coasts of the Malay Peninsula, and of the islands of Sumatra, Java, Borneo, Celebes and of many other islands further East, not only by the seafaring people who originally brought this language from Sumatra, but even by millions of people who are permanently settled there. Official correspondence addressed by Malay rajahs to Queen Elizabeth and King James I of England prove that the Malay language has remained unchanged in that period.

In the year 1595 the Dutch East India Company began making trading voyages to the Malay islands, and finding that the Portuguese were propagating their faith among the natives, the Directors of the Company decided to send out clergymen to teach the reformed faith. The Malay language was adopted as the official language in the East Indies, and the clergy began to translate the Scriptures into Malay, and the Gospel of Matthew in Malay was printed as early as 1629, and the entire New Testament was published in the Malay language at Amsterdam in 1668 at the expense of the Dutch East India Company. It was not until the year 1733 that the entire Bible was printed in the Malay language; and this version is known as Leydekker's, and was the work of two of the clergy employed by the Company—Revs. Melchior Leydekker and Petrus van der Vorm, assisted by a committee of clergymen and some native teachers; it was reprinted in Holland in 1824, and also by Carey at Serampore, India, at about the same time. When Milne, who assisted Morrison in the first translation of the Chinese Bible, arrived at Malacca, he gave a copy of one of the Leydekker Gospels to the famous Malay Munshi, Abdullah, who describes the book in his "Autobiography." Abdullah says of it, "The words were Malay, and their meanings were Malay, but the idiom of the language of that book was not Malay idiom." When Milne asked if he had read the book, he replied, " I do not understand it, sir; whoever made the book knows what language it is."

When the missionaries of the London Missionary Society and of the American Board came to Malaysia, they at once began the revision of the New Testament. Keasberry, of the London Mission, produced his version at Singapore, and it was used by the British and Foreign Bible Society until my own version was printed in 1910. Dr. Medhurst of the same Mission, with the assistance of a Dutch clergyman named Lenting published the Sourabaya version in Java in the year 1831. A Dutch missionary named Klinkert published his first edition of the New Testament in 1870, and subsequently translated the whole Bible; many editions of both the Old and New Testament have since been printed by the Netherlands Bible Society. The Leydekker version is now only used by the Christians of Amboina, in the extreme East of the Archipelago; elsewhere in the Dutch East Indies Klinkert's version is used by the Christians in Romanized Malay, but it was not found to be suitable for the use of the Mohammedan Malays on the Malay Peninsula and in the island of Sumatra. In 1896 the British and Foreign Bible Society appointed a committee of three to revise the Malay New Testament, a year or two later I was appointed chief reviser, and from 1900 to 1909 I gave my whole time to the work of revision, the other members of the committee gradually dropping off by death or retirement. Two Mohammedan Malays worked with me constantly, one of them for six hours a day until the last proofs had been read in 1912. One of these Malays had a good knowledge of Arabic, and compared the whole of my version with Van Dyke's Arabic Bible. My version of both the Old and the New Testament was printed in the Arabic character for distribution among the Mohammedan Malays of the Peninsula and the island of Sumatra, but it has also been sold to the Malays in Java and Borneo. In order to avoid unnecessary competition with the Netherlands Bible Society, my version has never been printed in the Roman character, and it is therefore almost unknown to the Malay-speaking Christians in the Dutch East Indies, who are still using Klinkert's version.

When I was in Holland in the summer of 1923, I found that there was a demand on the part of some Dutch missionaries for a revision of the version of Klinkert, who died several years ago. As the result of interviews with the President and Secretary of the Netherlands Bible Society, and a long correspondence with their representatives on the Mission field, Drs. Adriani, van der Veen and Kraemer, the whole question of the possibility of producing a union version of the Malay Bible for the use of the Malay-speaking Christians as well as the Malay Mohammedans is now being thoroughly discussed, and I am informed that the British and Dutch Bible Societies are consulting together at the present time with a view to the settlement of this very important question. Even if it is eventually decided that it is necessary to have distinct versions for the Christians and Mohammedans, it is probable that the versions of the two Bible Societies can be brought very much closer together than they are at present, and that will be a great gain.

WILLIAM TYNDALE

THE REVEREND W. B. COOPER, M.A., D.D., TORONTO

I have had the opportunity these last eighteen months or two years of spending a good deal of time in the company of William Tyndale. He was accessible in his works. It was my wish to get on intimate terms with him; to learn the secret of his amazing energy and endurance; and especially to get to know the secret of the very intense spiritual experience he so diffidently hides, but whose emotional surge beats on every page of the Scriptures he translated. The impression this intercourse made on me has been that of a striking moral stature, a real greatness of soul, a prescient intelligence—deep-seeing and far-seeing—which puts the hallmark of greatness or genius upon the man's work, and becomes a fountain of inspiration for those who come after.

Some analysis of that greatness might be made. But I am met by the strange, perplexing scantiness of justice—not to say substantial injustice that his memory suffers in history. We give him a place in our annals rather than the glowing reëchoing tribute of history. Even where history of the period is just to him, its tribute does not ring down the centuries as that of others is made to do. Do you recall the opening words of Charles Reade in his "Cloister and the Hearth," where he speaks of the cold, curt notice in annals being like historic hailstones hitting and glancing off the breast of the reader instead of being human stories appealing to and moving the reader?

I cherish the hope that the occasion of the Four Hundredth Anniversary of the printing of his superb translation may be taken by the New World to redress the scant justice of the Old World.

I have no time in these few minutes to recall the life story except to indicate his being forced into exile—the one man who could ill be spared in England then—the perils of his exile, his flying from place to place, his untiring industry, his betrayal and apparent defeat, but enduring victory.

Nor have I time as I should have liked in a few vivid sentences to suggest the background and environment in which he prepared himself for the high service which he rendered his country, and the limited materials with which he executed so brilliantly the task he undertook.

About this latter I must say one word or two. The manuscripts, codices, palimpsests, texts, business records, in short the multiplicity of documents that are bewildering to all except experts today, had no existence in Tyndale's time. All he had was the Vulgate; the Septuagint; the Hebrew Bible (recently printed for the first time); the Greek Testament of 1516; European versions, various, and Wycliffe's secondary translation: and with these meager materials he has given us "the most majestical thing in our literature, the most spiritual living thing in our tradition."

RELIGIOUS EDUCATION IN THE MISSION FIELD

NOTES OF A CONFERENCE

Mr. J. H. Oldham, Secretary, International Missionary Council:—Looked at from the Boards' point of view religious education covers the whole range of missionary activities. I should like to define it as including all the conscious and deliberate processes by which we seek to lead others into a living relationship with God, who has made his character, purpose and grace known to us in Christ, and to enable them in the light of that experience to grow up into full, mature Christian manhood and womanhood, and worthily to play their part in bringing in the Kingdom of God.

What gives rise to the special problem, however, that brings us together here today is that within the past generation or two there have occurred two very important developments in the general life of mankind. In the first place there has taken place a great growth in the deliberate effort of human society to mould the mind of the rising generation by the establishment of national systems of education. Secondly, there has been a great advance in the study of educational method, and in particular we are witnessing today an increasing determination to apply to the study of the mind, and of human nature generally, these processes of scientific investigation the application of which in the physical world have in the past century or two given to man such an astonishing command over the forces of nature. The bearing of these new conditions and new knowledge on our primary task of education constitutes a very real and vital problem.

The approach to the problem of religious education varies in different countries in consequence of the difference of background due to national conditions. In America the problem is determined by the fact that religion has for the most part no place in the national system of schools. In Europe this is not the case to the same extent. In the mission field we have Christian schools and colleges in which religion can have its place in the curriculum of the day school, and there thus exists a larger opportunity than that provided by the Sunday School.

Within our subject therefore there are included the problems of the Sunday School, to which perhaps most thought has been given. The work of vacation daily Bible schools, religious education in day schools and boarding schools of all grades, from the elementary school to the college, the training of teachers and religious workers to give religious education, the making available of modern knowledge of psychology and of educational method for those engaged in evangelistic and pastoral work, and finally the relating of all these varied activities in a combined policy of religious education.

In considering the subject it is perhaps well to remind ourselves that most of our mistakes come from ignoring the fundamental truth that religious education addresses itself to the whole man. Religious education is something much wider than religious instruction. The latter is addressed primarily to the mind. We shall fall short in our task if we limit our thinking to Bible instruction, and forget what modern psychology is teaching us about the central place in our nature of the emotional and conative elements. We shall fail equally if we limit our efforts to emotional appeals for conversion, and neglect the task of instruction. An uneducated church must always remain a weak and ineffective church. We shall just as certainly fall short of our aim if we are content with appeals that stir the heart and the giving of information to be stored in the mind, and forget that religion, if it is to become vital, has to be worked into the life by habits slowly formed and duties faithfully done day by day. Whether we think of school work or of evangelistic and pastoral work we shall realize the immensity of the problem most adequately if we keep in mind the truth that religion is concerned with and meant to possess the whole man.

Just because the subject is so vast and can be approached from so many angles it has been thought that the best use that we can make of the two hours available for its consideration is to allow as many as possible to contribute from his or her own point of view and experience, in the expectation that out of the variety and wealth of experience represented here each of us may glean suggestions that will enrich our own thought and work.

Dr. W. G. Landes, General Secretary of the World's Sunday School Association, emphasized the very great importance of work with children and young people in the strategy of our mission work, illustrating this by pointing out that it had been stated at the recent conference of workers among Moslems held at Jerusalem that although the adult Moslem was extremely difficult from a missionary point of view, the opportunities for Christian influence upon the child before it had acquired the Moslem impenetrability were very great.

Dr. Eric M. North called attention to the trend of development of religious education at the home base from the seven-year cycle of the Uniform Lessons through the Improved Uniform and Graded Lessons, the rise of week-day religious education and the Daily Vacation Bible School movement, toward a new study being undertaken by the International Council of Religious Education looking to a comprehensive curriculum of Religious Education for the church school. He indicated that a parallel development was going on in the foreign field and as indications of the increased attention being given to the subject referred to the action of the International Missionary Council in asking Mr. Oldham to initiate an inquiry into religious education, as to the work of the Religious Education Commission of the Congress on Christian Work in South America to meet at Montevideo this spring, and to the organization of the Joint Advisory Committee on Methods and Materials of Religious Education on the Foreign Field which is seeking in a coordinated way to make available to other lands the religious education experiences of the United States and Canada.

Mr. W. J. McKee, missionary from India, pointed out that in our rural education on the mission field there are some of the weaknesses appearing in the United States, namely, the tendency for the teaching to become stereotyped, and pointed out that where the mission schools have added courses on the Bible to the subjects required by the educational code no compulsory examination for meeting government requirements could be given and that therefore the pupils felt that the Bible study could be neglected and that too often the teaching was not efficient and not related to the life of the pupil. Little opposition arises to this instruction when it is well taught, the trouble lies in too narrow a conception of religious education and too great an emphasis laid upon instruction and not enough upon the expression of religion through worship and service. The way out Mr. McKee illustrated from one of the schools which had been under his direction, where they place their reliance upon a Christian atmosphere in the class room rather than on formal instruction. In this school they have sought to divide the pupils into groups that would be harmonious, social units and at the same time suitable for developing Christian activity. The method is the one sometimes referred to in Western education as the project method. For example, classes of very little children play at home-making with home activities through which the school seeks to build up in the group as a unit the Christian ideals of family life. Not only is the Bible story used to raise ideals but the ideals are actually put to work. Again, instead of confining the Bible study to a specific period and hour, it is brought in anywhere in the school where a situation arises which needs it. For example, when the rules of the group are violated by some pupil there is an opportunity for development of the ideal of forgiveness, and in this situation the use of a story from the Bible has a value that no formal lesson can have.   The school strives to furnish opportunities by which the Christian ideals of life can be worked out in the group itself.

On a request of a delegate for amplification of points he had made, *Mr. W. J. McKee* stated that what they were seeking in his school was the inspirational effect of the Bible stories and the working of them out in life; that the Bible was used not only as a book to learn about but in part also for its emotional appeal; that they used it also to get the pupils to think about their religion and about character and that the pupils were led to analyze the characteristics of a Bible hero and to name the characteristics that most appealed to them.   Cooperation and the service of one another were learned in a house building project.   Work of this kind was done from the first grade up. The school sought not only to set up ideals but to develop activity and to lead the interest of the pupil out into the community and the world, as is illustrated by the contribution made by the pupils to the Japanese Earthquake Fund and by the pupils going out in bands to help in nearby communities.

Dr. Martin Schlunk, of Germany, spoke of the experience of the German missions in emphasizing the use of the vernacular in religious education as the most intimate expression of the religious life of the people.   The use of translations, however, they had found unsatisfactory and even the common illustrations were not found always to be suitable for the conditions in which they were used.   The development of Christian ideas in the playing, thinking, singing, and living of our peoples on the mission field was a greater task than had been realized. He emphasized the importance of the family as the center of religious education, which he regarded as the most urgent task in our missionary work today.

Professor Lewis Hodous, of Hartford (formerly in China), said that he felt that we had operated too much on the theory of replacing another religion with Christianity but that such replacement was impossible.   For example, the memorization of Christian precepts was not effective because there was not carried into it the whole emotional background such as was already presented in their expressions of their own religions and that we must somehow tap this broad expression by symbolism.   He spoke of the contrast between the temples and the places of worship provided by the Oriental faiths and the bare, uninviting halls used as churches by most Protestant missions.   Even the newly developed Chinese sects were erecting attractive halls of worship.   The churches should be so constructed and furnished as to develop the broader emotions of worship.   This is needed in order to produce the religious educational effect.

A query as to the relation of what *Mr. McKee* had described to the educational recommendations of the government was answered by Mr. McKee that no objections of any kind to the type of work his school was doing had been made.

Dr. Frank Mason North urged that all who are related to religious education be mindful that from the earliest dawn of childhood the spirit of God is present with the child whatever be his nationality, or religion, or parentage and that the presumption of all our education ought to be that the great educator is the spirit of God in the heart of the child. Mechanical construction as of a house we can make, but in the plant and in life there is a power which we do not have, and methods and materials are useless unless through them we can use our powers to let the spirit of God become active in the life of the child. The contact of the child with God must be real, the process of making Christian character is one of cooperation with God.

The Rev. F. A. Brown, of China, expressed the opinion that the conflict which sometimes appears between religious education and evangelism is not a real one and that sometimes what is really needed is to have the evangelist and educator exchange tasks for a little while.

Pastor Daniel Couve, of France, emphasized the great importance of the personality of the people who teach and expressed the conviction that the power of the contagion of personality was more significant than the methods that were used.

Dr. Eric M. North answered a question as to how religious education was effectively carried on in Sunday Schools attended both by pupils who were receiving religious instruction in day schools and those who were not. He pointed out that the recommendations of the China Educational Commission and the Commission on Religious Education of the Montevideo Congress were that effective religious education could not be carried on unless these two groups were separated. He added that it was important that both missionaries on the field and Boards at home cooperate in developing effective policies for promoting religious education and for training effective personnel.

AGRICULTURAL AND INDUSTRIAL MISSIONS

Why the Missionary Forces must in many fields deal with Agriculture and the Simple Industries. Dr. Thomas Jesse Jones, of the African Education Commission, Phelps-Stokes Fund.

Loyalty to the ideals of Him who "came to give life and to give it more abundantly" requires a sincere regard for agriculture and simple industries. Fullness of life includes every opportunity for the full development of human society. Certainly the contribution of agriculture and industry must be involved within the scope of life necessary to the masses of people. While some social groups do not have direct relationship to the cultivation of the soil or the simple mechanical processes, no one is free from direct or indirect dependence upon these human activities. In mission fields the dependence is both intimate and real.

Throughout society at least eighty-five per cent of the people are engaged in one or both of these processes, tillers of the soil or laborers in some form of industry. Under the more primitive conditions of most mission fields the number engaged in agriculture is practically the whole of the working population, both men and women. The development of mind and character is directly related to these activities, not only through the necessity of food to maintain life but through the interaction of these activities on the mind and character. In many mission fields the ravages of disease as well as the temptations to immorality are very directly traceable to the lack of food or improper housing or other physical necessities which could be corrected by a knowledge of even the simplest forms of industry.

The first step towards agricultural instruction as an educational aim is the development of a real appreciation of its importance. One of the unfortunate results of the education so far given has been the depreciation of agriculture. However unintentional and incidental this result has been, it is nevertheless real. The school program has been so exclusively devoted to literary and other conventional elements as to cause people to think that agriculture was not really important. The responsibility for this cannot be placed upon the school alone. Modern civilization and the Christian Church must share it. The decennial census enumerations of Europe and America have given new confirmation of the tendency to desert rural communities for urban areas. There is probably no more vital problem of education than that of helping society the world over to understand the primary importance of agriculture to human welfare.

Mission communities are relatively far more dependent on agriculture than others. Agricultural education should correspondingly receive large consideration in the school plans. While these people have learned much through centuries of experience, there is much more to be learned through scientific study of the possibilities of the soil. However extensive the experience and knowledge of soil cultivation may be and however limited the agricultural knowledge of the school staff, it should be possible to give a new sense of the vital importance of agriculture as an element in education. It is imperative that schools shall cease to give the impression that knowledge of the three Rs and of the usual curriculum subjects is of more importance than agricultural knowledge, even if it is limited to a fresh appreciation of what the people already know.

Industrial education is the response to the demand that education shall be adapted to the daily activities of the masses, to the large commercial and industrial operations of the nineteenth and twentieth centuries and to the requirements of the notable developments of science. So intimately is industrial training related to the daily responsibilities of mechanics and other handworkers that they have at times doubted its value. Education has been so long associated only with books and the art of expression as to seem strange when presented in the form of "learning by doing" or of the creative arts. It is little wonder that workers have been slow to recognize an education so different from the conventional forms even though it is so vital to their own welfare.

With the increasing consciousness of social needs, civilized communities are insisting that education shall provide training for all the activities essential to human welfare. Labor unions and industrial organizations are agreed in their demand for those elements of education that prepare the youth for the responsibilities into which they are entering. Industrial and technical schools are increasing in number every year in both Europe and America. Nor is the movement due to a narrow and selfish economic interest in machinery and construction. It is inspired by a broad conception of the intimate relation of industrial activities to the mental, moral, and social progress of humanity. Comparison of the last two centuries with those preceding reveals the tremendous contribution of machinery not only to the prosperity but much more to the comfort and safety and happiness of humanity. The extension of privileges to the masses is directly related to improved facilities of transportation and communication. The benefits of sanitation are now enjoyed by millions who, but for railways and roads and steamships, would still be subjected to the ravages of disease. So real and intimate is the relation of mechanical devices such as the telegraph, the telephone, the wireless, electric and steam appliances to all the social and altruistic organization of today as to give color to the belief that the one could scarcely exist without the other.

The study of psychological processes is also revealing the value of industrial training. School activities seemed formerly to be based almost exclusively on the approach to the mind through the eye and ear. Practical experience and psychology are demonstrating that the mind may be approached through the hand. Mental development through the innumerable hand processes of modern building and manufacturing has been real and effective. The elimination of these processes in recent years by machinery has been a loss which education now endeavors to correct by introducing hand activities in the schools. Educators are convinced that concrete industrial and scientific education is necessary to supplement education through the printed page and oral instruction.

The value attaching to industrial education in Europe and America will be even greater in mission areas. Educational approach to a people different in language and customs will be more certain through definite processes of industrial training than through reading and writing. Pupils may misunderstand words without being discovered by their teachers or realizing the mistake themselves. Error or neglect in the crookedness of a supposedly straight line, an incomplete circle, a table with unequal legs, or a suit that does not fit, is obvious. A pupil in tailoring remarked that the spoiling of a yard of cloth was a real loss, but the misunderstanding of a page of history could easily be corrected another day. He shares this attitude with many intelligent people in all parts of the world. Recognition of the need for what is concrete in education is stimulating the introduction of laboratories into the schools and, what is even more important and generally possible, giving practice in meeting fundamental needs of the community under school and home conditions.

The inspirational and social value of industrial education has never been more vividly stated than in the following words by General Armstrong:

"In all men, education is conditioned not alone on an enlightened head and a changed heart, but very largely on a routine of industrious habits, which is to character what the foundation is to the pyramid. The summit should glow with a divine light, interfusing and qualifying the whole mass, but it should never be forgotten that it is only upon a foundation of regular daily activities that there can be any fine and permanent upbuilding. Morality and industry usually go together."

Subtract hard work from life, and in a few months all will have gone to pieces. Labor, next to the grace of God in the heart, is the greatest promoter of morality, the greatest power for civilization.

Didactic and dogmatic work has little to do with the formation of character, which is our point. This is done by making the school a little world in itself; mingling hard days' work in field or shop with social pleasures, making success depend on behaviour rather than on study work. School life should be like real life.

Relation of Agriculture to Village Work in India. Mr. W. J. McKee, American Presbyterian Mission, Moga, Punjab. Until recently most of the agricultural education in India has been of high school or college grade. This necessitated considerable preliminary education and large expenditure for land, buildings and equipment. Such schools have turned out men trained for administrative positions, but few of them have returned to the villages to work on the land, or have materially assisted the farmers. From the long preparation and consequent separation from village life, a lack of sympathy with village conditions has often resulted. Because of this the conviction has grown that we need in India another type of agricultural education that should follow certain requirements.

(1) It must be related to economic conditions, simple enough to be given in the village without expensive buildings or equipment, and must deal with the actual problems of the village farmer.

(2) The education should be built up on the farmer's own experience. Even in the Primary Department of the Moga Training School, the work is all organized about vital elements of the village social and economic life. In the later stages, the project idea in agriculture is used. Pupils have their own garden and farm plots and work out the things they are interested in and the problems that face them. They also learn simple home industries related to farm life. Cooperation is emphasized in working, buying and selling.

(3) The school should not only teach a better agriculture, but should build those traits of character which will help the individual to battle successfully against his handicaps. In the class room and out on the field our work is planned to develop self-reliance, initiative, cooperation, and a sense of responsibility. This is supplemented by Scripture lessons and character training efforts.

(4) The education should inspire to service so that the knowledge gained may be used not only for self-betterment, but for the welfare of the community. Practice in this is given in the life of the school. Inspiration comes through Scripture examples and teaching, and leadership is developed by actual working with and leading other students in tasks that are worth while.

The work divides itself into two lines; for those who are able to attend school, and for those who cannot attend school. In the beginning it was impossible to obtain government aid for the Rural Training School at Moga, but after a year of successful work, it was recognized and given a government grant in aid. The school has a garden of eight acres in which each student is given a plot 13 yards square. After paying for seeds and fertilizer, they are entitled to what they produce, and from their earnings pay part of their school expenses.

There are twenty-seven acres in the school farm, all worked by students except for two paid laborers. Eleven acres of this farm are devoted to dry farming. The attempt is made to adapt various agricultural implements to village conditions.

Present Types of Successful Agricultural Work on Foreign Fields.

(a) *Agricultural Education in Colleges. Mr. W. Henry Grant, Secretary, Trustees of the Canton Christian College.* There are only a few colleges under Christian auspices in the mission field dealing to any extent with agricultural education. These are laying the foundation for scientific agriculture in the modern sense, based upon the pre-agricultural college courses in science. In China, the Christian colleges which have the most advanced courses in agriculture are the Canton Christian College and University of Nanking.

Canton Christian College has more than one hundred acres of its campus devoted to a college farm upon which are many kinds of experiments and demonstrations in scientific agriculture. It has especially developed experiments in rice, sericulture, fruits, garden products, dairy and animal husbandry, and there has been considerable study of the soil and introduction of commercial fertilizers.

At Nanking, special experiments and demonstrations have been made in forestry, garden produce, cotton, sericulture, and seed selection. The extension work of this institution is developing. It is estimated that through the bulletins and extension work of the university, 60,000 people outside of the immediate work at Nanking are reached each month.

Peking University has had the cooperation of the Governor of Shansi Province and has been assisting in work there as well as at Peking. To Peking and Nanking Universities has been entrusted the interest on the China Famine Relief Fund for a period of years for the purpose of studying and developing practical measures for famine prevention.

The Agricultural Institute at Allahabad, India, which Mr. Higginbottom has founded, is a farm conducted in connection with the villages, largely as a demonstration and training for the village people.

At Smyrna, in Turkey, the International College is doing some agricultural work.

Mr. B. H. Hunnicutt is in charge of the Agricultural College of the Instituto Evangelico at Lavras, Brazil. A farm of 500 acres gives ample space for experiment, and the government has co-operated with financial aid. A unique feature has been the holding of the annual District Fair on the college grounds, attended by about six thousand visitors. Recently Mr. Hunnicutt has been able to start extension work among the farmers, and more than 60,000 copies of pamphlets written for the government have been distributed.

The agricultural departments in our missionary colleges, while designed especially to instruct students in scientific agriculture, are also demonstration and experiment stations for the states or provinces in which they are located.

The United States Department of Agriculture at Washington has opened its doors to us in every way and aided by cooperation and advice. We should endeavor to realize what the Department is in its relation to the agricultural world, and what facilities it has for furthering the study of the world field. A "List of Workers in Subjects Pertaining to Agriculture" is published annually; first the scientific staff directly employed by the government, of which approximately 1,700 names are given; and second, those employed in State Agricultural Colleges and Experiment Stations, of which about 2,000 are given. At Canton Christian College we have had repeated visits from the explorers of our Department of Agriculture, especially from the Bureau of Plant Industry, and have been greatly benefitted by their work and advice.

(b) *Central Training Schools. Rev. Thomas S. Donohugh, Associate Secretary, Board of Foreign Missions of the Methodist Episcopal Church.* At the meeting of the International Association of Agricultural Missions held at Amherst some four or five years ago, Mr. Reisner of the University of Nanking stated that he had found reports of agricultural work being done in 235 foreign mission stations. One hundred and thirty-five of these were in Africa. It is natural that agricultural training should be developed in Africa where native people, both men and women, take to the cultivation of the soil.

Typical examples of the Central Training School are found at Dunda in Angola, and Mount Silinda in Rhodesia, under the American Board; Old Umtali, Rhodesia, under the Methodist Board; and Luevo in the Belgian Congo, under the Southern Presbyterian Church. In the Central Training School the teaching of agriculture and simple industry is combined with the usual literary education and the special preparation of preachers and teachers. Medical work is often conducted at the same station and training given in the treatment of simple diseases, sanitation and hygiene. Many of these institutions are modeled upon Hampton and Tuskegee and seek to adapt education to present and changing social and industrial conditions.

Some of these schools have sent out scores and hundreds of well trained preachers and teachers. Others have been unusually successful in fitting the African for self-supporting work as a farmer or gardener. In one village near Old Umtali, over forty plows are now owned by the natives, where not one would have been found twenty years ago. In this section natives are raising vegetables and selling them in the towns and even to large farmers. Agricultural exhibits are held and great interest is manifested, not only in products of the soil but also in animal husbandry.

The recent visits of Dr. Jones and his Commissions have resulted in most helpful suggestions as to ways in which this type of school, which seems specially adapted to conditions in Africa, can be made most effective.

(c) *Farm Settlements in India. Mr. Leroy Stockman, Salvation Army.* The Salvation Army is a firm believer in agricultural missions. The work is divided into two classes; for our own converts, and for the criminal tribes. Through government aid we secured a tract of land in the Khanewal district on the border of the Sind Desert, and we were allowed thirty years in which to pay for it. In the village of Shantinagar on this tract we have about 2,000 men, women and children. Each settler is given a lease by which at the end of thirty years he will own the freehold of his land. This has been a great encouragement to thrift and careful cultivation. The settlers support their own officers, three school teachers, have built their own hospital, and contribute generously to Army funds.

I consider our success is due to five facts: (1) the work is God-recognizing and God-honoring; (2) the land is of the best; (3) the water supply is adequate; (4) the settlers are carefully chosen; and (5) they are granted ultimate ownership of the land.

The main crops are American cotton, wheat and sugar-cane. which are sold for cash. The last year I was there the crops yielded rupees 185,000.

How the United States Department of Agriculture May Cooperate With Agricultural Missionaries. Dr. William A. Taylor, Chief Bureau of Plant Industry, Department of Agriculture. The Department of Agriculture came into existence as a separate administrative agency in 1862. Its work relates to the citizen as such, whether at home or abroad, and to our foreign neighbors. The Department employs about 20,000 workers, 16,000 of whom are outside of Washington. There are about twenty major bureaus, boards, etc., in the Department, covering research, extension and regulatory work.

Research in foreign countries especially connects with missionaries. A partial list of missionaries, Protestant and Roman

Catholic, with whom the Bureau of Plant Industry has had correspondence during the past two years shows some 175 individuals, and some of the correspondence was quite voluminous. Contacts are usually made through written inquiries, though frequently through personal visits in the field. During five years 465 lots of seeds and plants have reached the Department from missionaries.

The Washington navel orange now extensively grown in California, was sent to the Department by Rev. Mr. Schneider, a missionary in Bahia, Brazil. More than eleven million boxes of these oranges are now produced annually in California.

The soy bean has been introduced from the Orient in hundreds of varieties. It is a soil-improving crop and good for forage. The seed is imported by millions of pounds for crushing for oil. Several varieties of this crop have been received from missionaries in the last fifteen years. One new variety is the Dixie, brought in ten to fifteen years ago, and now being introduced by the Department, which produced thirty-five bushels to the acre last year at Arlington Farm, and has a high oil content.

The Korean lespendeza is a promising new crop plant for forage. It was received from a missionary in Korea.

We are often asked how missionaries can most effectively get in touch with the Department. A letter received from Dr. John L. Nevius, of Chefoo, in 1893, written ten days before his death, was quoted from as indicating how to present questions effectively to the Department. He was active in trying out American fruits on the Shantung Peninsula. The Chinese were conversant with grafting, budding, etc., and he had put the following questions to the Department: (1) "Is there any way to stop bees and beetles from puncturing pears? (2) How can the occurrence of worms in apples be prevented? By spraying? (3) How can aphis or plant lice be controlled? (4) Is the bagging of pears and grapes to protect them against pests practicable?" This was almost a model letter from a missionary desiring practical results free from formalities, and direct. Such correspondence is suggested as frequently the best way to get into practical cooperative relation with the Department.

Special Problems of Agricultural and Industrial Missions. Dr. Homer Leroy Shantz, Bureau of Plant Industry, U. S. Department of Agriculture. Among the native tribes of East Africa, agriculture is practically the only industry. Some of the tribes are pastoral and others are crop producers. Those who produce crops usually produce only enough for their own support, and a comparatively small amount is exported. Produce varies greatly in different sections. In the drier sections, with marked seasonal changes, cereals are grown and stored against famines. In the more humid sections a great variety of crops is grown, the land producing each day the food required by the family.

New land is generally prepared for cultivation by the men. When once prepared, it is the women's work to put in the crops, care for them and harvest them. After from two to five seasons the land does not produce as well as at first and new land is taken. By this means the natives avoid many troubles with plant diseases, and are also insured a good, rich soil for their crops. Quite generally men regard it as disgraceful to cultivate the food crops, but almost without exception can be induced to grow new or "money crops." This may offer an easy method of leading the men of the tribe to assume greater responsibility in native agriculture.

In order to improve native agriculture it is necessary that the natives understand some of the natural forces which control their crop production. At the present time this is largely attributed to good and bad spirits. This involves a simple type of nature study, for if only religious teaching is given it may merely change the names of the gods which they worship, without introducing new ideas as to their methods of affecting human welfare. In agriculture quite generally there is a tendency to destroy or only to replace the native methods with those with which the teachers are familiar and this is a very dangerous process. In industrial training care should be exercised not to make the conditions so artificial that the trained student, on his return to his village, will not find it possible to carry out and put into practical application the training he has received in the mission.

Recently the Kenya government has established a school among the Masai. These people have hitherto been almost beyond the reach of the missions or government educational system. They are a wild, nomadic tribe, and it was necessary to force attendance in order to start a school. Instead of starting with any preconceived plan, the man in charge began by slowly building on the mental background of the people, took advantage of their interest in cattle to develop a transport train, and from this led to the simple industrial work necessary to maintain the equipment. This led naturally to plowing and wheat growing, wheat being a crop with which the Masai were entirely unfamiliar. From these simple beginnings the school has gradually developed, and this practical work is supplemented with literary, religious and athletic training.

STEWARDSHIP AND FOREIGN MISSIONS

Stewardship as Relating to Our Foreign Mission Obligation, by Harry S. Myers: Stewardship is such an acceptance of the Lordship of Jesus Christ as will lead a person to acknowledge that Lordship in every act of life—time, ability, personality, character, money—as shown in relationship both to God and man.

The United Stewardship Council, composed of the Stewardship officers of about twenty-five of the communions in the United States and Canada, unanimously adopted the following Stewardship Principles which form the basis of such discussions as this today:

1. *Stewardship Fundamental.* The recognition of our responsibility to God as Stewards of everything we are and have—life, time, talents, possessions and spiritual resources—is fundamental to a wholesome Christian faith and experience. Stewardship is primarily spiritual. Its great objective is character. It is the principle on which daily life must be organized in order to be fully Christian.

2. *Not Optional.* Stewardship grows out of our obligation to God as Creator, Owner, and Giver of all things material and spiritual, and is indispensable to a life of obedience, love and gratitude.

3. *Solves Problems.* Stewardship, in its full New Testament meaning, involves responsibility to man and provides a solution for the social, racial, industrial, and economic problems which confront the modern world.

4. *How Acknowledged.* Suitable acknowledgment of our Stewardship can be made only as we set aside for God's service such measure of time, possessions, and vital energies, as a Scripturally enlightened judgment demands.

5. *Relation to Money.* Stewardship involves both the beneficent use of money and the spirit and method of its acquisition, investment and expenditure. The Christian's total attitude toward material things is of great importance to himself, the Church, and the world, in this time of social reconstruction.

6. *Proportionate Beneficence.* Stable provision can be made for the support of Kingdom enterprises only through the systematic, proportionate and adequate contributions of Christian people. System should be adjusted to the needs involved, proportion should be relative to personal income and agreeable to the Scriptures. The dedication of the tenth of income offers a basic principle of beneficence supported by centuries of religious custom, Biblical teaching, and joyful experience. While emphatically recommended to the people of our Churches, it must not be regarded as exhausting the meaning of Stewardship, but rather as the beginning of our service to the Kingdom.

7. *Education in Stewardship.* Stewardship instruction should be included in the program of religious education of both home and Church. It is of primary importance in building the type of Christian character most urgently needed at this hour. Religious leaders and heads of families should be diligent to understand and practice Christian Stewardship, and to instruct in its principles all who come under their care. That the acceptance of Stewardship may speedily become universal, every Steward should be encouraged to bear witness to his faith and to unite in such Stewardship movement as his Communion provides.

The promotion of Stewardship in the life of a church always results in four missionary contributions:

1. The production of missionaries. As the proper uses of life and ability are taught to the young people, it results in the offering of life for missionary service.

2. A more adequate support of the missionary enterprise.

3. Stewardship and Missionary Education properly related in the program of a local church will produce a whole-hearted, intelligent support through attitude, study and prayer.

4. The production of more money. A study of the Christian grace of giving as taught in the Bible will cause all Christians to set aside specific and definite amounts at regular intervals for missionary work and it will train them to adequate habits of Christian finance.

Stewardship as Practiced on the Mission Fields, by the Rev. Harry Bruen of Korea: In this discussion I must confine myself to Stewardship as practised in Korea where as an evangelistic missionary I have had a part in its cultivation and joy in seeing it practiced. Stewardship is the resultant of the realization of God's ownership. It is cultivated by prayer and Bible study. Two Bible classes, one for the women and one for the men of not less than four days of consecutive study once during the year is a regular program for each church, and the first session begins at 5:30 A. M. in the form of an early morning prayer meeting. Recently as I was visiting one of my country churches the evangelist was being paid some back salary by the local church treasurer. Taking out a pocket book he suddenly caught himself with the words, "Oh! no! that is not my pocket book," and then proceeded to take out another. I said smilingly, "That looks rather bad for a Presbyterian elder to be carrying around someone's else pocket book." He replied, "But there is a reason." I asked, "Is that the Lord's pocketbook then?" "Yes," he replied, "Though my pocketbook is frequently empty there is always some in the Lord's."

At another time I had invited our new medical missionary to accompany me on one of my trips to the country. As we neared a little church far up a winding mountain valley we were met by several of the officers, as is their polite custom. After greeting me the leader inquired, "Who is the foreign gentleman with you?" I replied, "He is our new doctor at the Taiku Mission Hospital." "How strange," he said, "surely the word of the Lord is true—'Seek ye first the Kingdom of God and all these things shall be added unto you.'" Upon inquiring what he meant he told me the following story. He said, "We have just completed our new church building but we had no stove. My wife said to me, 'You know that $4 I earned by raising silk worms which I have been saving to go to the Taiku Hospital for treatment, well you take it and see if you can buy a stove with it, for the Bible says "Seek ye first the Kingdom of God." We will have to put off going to the hospital.'" "That was two weeks ago," said her husband, "and here comes the Taiku doctor walking right into my home, so now we have the stove and the doctor too. Verily God's promises are sure."

In a recent letter from a Korean pastor I received a printed form that had been prepared by the native presbytery and sent to every church to enlist them in a campaign of personal evangelism. Among others, occurred this question, "How many are giving more than a tenth?"

One winter's morning I stepped from the train at the city of Pyeng Yang. It was still dark and no lights as yet were to be seen in the homes of the missionaries. As I passed the Union Seminary building I noticed it was lit up and as it is always left unlocked I went in thinking to spend a short time in private devotions. Stepping into one room I found each corner was occupied by a theological student praying out loud. I withdrew to another room only to find the same thing repeated and still a third. What were they praying about? They were stewards of souls. For nine months they were doing pastoral work among a group of churches and now while at the Seminary they were pouring out their hearts each morning in behalf of their flocks. Thus are they seeking to fulfill their stewardship.

How We Can Help the Churches on the Foreign Field to Adopt Stewardship, by Rev. David McConaughy, New York: When assigned this subject (for the wording of which I was not at all responsible) my first impulse was to turn it right around, and talk of how the churches on the Foreign Mission Field are helping the church at home to adopt Stewardship. For we could present a sheaf of testimonies of sacrificial giving along scriptural lines of Stewardship from practically every field the world around. Indeed, I have such a sheaf of testimonies in my hand at this moment, but I pass that by to offer several simple suggestions.

I. Let us pass on to the churches abroad a true conception of Christ's own idea of Stewardship, unreduced and undiluted. No more searching definition of Stewardship can be conceived of than that which He taught, when He said, "Whosoever he be of you that renounceth not all that he hath, he cannot be my disciple." (Luke 14:33.) Paul translated this definition into his own terms when he said (Romans 12:1): "I beseech you, therefore, brethren, by the mercies of God, to present your bodies a living sacrifice, holy, acceptable to God, which is your spiritual service." This definition involves three factors: (1) That Stewardship is an *absolute* transaction, for a "present" necessarily involves the resigning of control over what is presented. (2) It is *unreserved*, for the whole includes the parts: "body" includes both mind and soul. The entire life, all that we are and all that we have. (3) It is *irrevocable*, for it is to become a "sacrifice," a burnt offering to be consumed, and yet it is not a dead sacrifice, but "living"; renewed constantly as consumed, a perpetual miracle.

The Scope of Stewardship includes not only possessions, but the whole of life. Stewardship should not be presented as optional with the disciple. We may choose or refuse to make Christ our Lord; but, having once accepted his lordship, it is incumbent upon us to do what he bids.

II. We should share with the churches abroad a line of Stewardship materials of real and permanent value. Until within a very few years past there was really no material of this sort available; now there is a considerable range of text books for various ages and classes.

III. We must give to the churches abroad an actual demonstration of Stewardship applied. We have been talking for some time a great deal about Stewardship principles, but as yet the actual demonstrations of Stewardship applied in a corporate way by churches are comparatively scarce. We have no desire to multiply machinery, or unnecessarily increase organization. The "Fellowship of Stewardship" is not another organization, but a platform of principles. Upon these four corner-stones: God's sovereignty, man's accountability, offering in worship and service to mankind, rests the superstructure of Stewardship.

On a recent trip I was the guest of a "Fellowship of Stewardship," where admission to its supper conference was conditional upon the dedication of a definite proportion of income for giving. On a stormy night, there were present some sixty people of all ages from seven years to old age, including among those in attendance the mayor, a pastor, an assistant pastor, an editor, a mill worker, a brick mason, a bank clerk, a seamstress, two manufacturers, seven mothers, a school teacher, nine grade school pupils and five high school pupils. All were united upon the common ground of Stewardship. The church to which they belong has no financial problem, but better far than this, it is instinct with the spirit of service. Already about one hundred of its members are dedicating at least one-tenth of income for the extending of the kingdom that shall have no frontier. Such a "Fellowship" may be developed in any church, and when such demonstrations of Stewardship are given the churches on the Foreign Mission Field will need no labored argument for doing likewise.

Stewardship Materials and Their Use, by *Dr. W. H. Denison, Dayton, Ohio:* Only recently have there been many materials available to help emphasize the Stewardship message. Some of such materials are:

1. Study Books—The United Stewardship Council plans a series for adults, young people, and children annually. Some of the splendid books now available .are: "Stewardship for All of Life," by Lovejoy; "Money the Acid Test," by McConaughy; "Life as a Stewardship," by Morrill; "The Message of Stewardship," by Cushman; "Woman and Stewardship," by Pearce; "A Man and His Money," by Calkins; "You and Yours," by Morrill; "The Larger Stewardship," by Cook; "The Christian and His Money

Problems," by Wilson; "Money Talks," by McGarrah, and many others.

2. Stewardship Mottoes—The United Stewardship Council has issued a set of eight select stewardship mottoes available for pastors and churches. 3. Stereopticon slides and lectures. 4. Leaflet literature of excellent character. 5. Pageants, playlets, dialogues, readings. 6. Diary and Budget Account Books, Giving Banks. Information concerning any of these helps may be secured from the denominational Stewardship departments.

The Promotion of Stewardship in the Local Church, by the Rev. M. E. Melvin, D.D., Chattanooga, Tenn.: First, in promoting Stewardship in a local church we must be very clear and certain as to the content of the message. It would manifestly be impossible to promote a study of chemistry in a church. This does not belong to the realm of church activities. Judging by the attitude of the average man in the church, it is very clear that when we speak of Stewardship we are understood to mean something that has to do only with money. In fact, the entire discussion here this afternoon reflects that attitude of mind. It seems to be very difficult to bring the average man to believe that Stewardship means a great deal more than money. Because of this attitude of mind it comes about that the average pastor is not inclined to present or promote Stewardship in his church. He is willing to do this once or twice a year when the time comes to put over his church budget. Believing that Stewardship has to do only with the relation of a Christian to his property, very little is said about it. Therefore, the first thing to be done is to interpret Stewardship in the light of the Scripture and in terms of present day problems and not in terms of property questions alone. This is clear from two passages of Scripture as follows: I Peter 4:10-11, "As every man hath received the gift, even so minister the same one to another, as good stewards of the manifold grace of God. If any man speak, let him speak as the oracles of God; if any man minister, let him do it as of the ability which God giveth; that God in all things may be glorified through Jesus Christ, to whom be praise and dominion for ever and ever, Amen." Nothing whatever is said in this passage that would warrant the interpretation that Stewardship covers only the relation of a man to his property. The second passage is: Romans I:14, "I am debtor both to the Greeks, and to the barbarians; both to the wise, and to the unwise." Let it be noted in this passage that the Apostle Paul had no property at all and yet he uttered one of the greatest Stewardship Formulas of Scripture.

If we interpret Stewardship in terms of personal responsibility we are within the Scriptural meaning of the term and moreover we have a great Scriptural truth of immense practical importance in dealing with the social, political, economic and religious problems of the day. A man can understand what we mean by "American Stewardship," if we explain that we mean America's responsibility for world leadership. The Stewardship of prayer, the responsibility for using the prayer power. The Stewardship of possessions as the responsibility for the accumulation and distribution of wealth. In other words if we insist in broadening the scope of Stewardship, we will give to the ministry of the church a theme that not only covers the economic issues, but one that has a very practical bearing upon every attitude of the Christian's life. It will then become a theme that the pastor will delight in presenting.

This broadening of the scope of Stewardship is very much needed at this time. We must not permit the church any longer to confine this great Scriptural truth to the application of money and wealth alone. Someone has said, "Each new generation makes some transforming discovery out of God's book. What is Stewardship but the discovery for this age?" Stewardship will be promoted therefore in the local church when the leadership of the church comes to realize the broad and deep content of the Stewardship idea in Scripture.

Second, the next important factor is the personal element in the local church. Some man or woman in each church, preferably the pastor, should be the point of contact in developing the sense of Stewardship in the congregation. What is everybody's business is nobody's business. In our denomination, we have adopted the plan of having someone appointed in each church by the pastor and officers who is known as the Congregational Secretary of Stewardship. This man becomes the point of contact in organizing study classes, distributing literature and otherwise helps to bring this great truth of Scripture, which is just emerging, before the church, before his people. The plan is successful and is capable of further improvement.

Third, the third factor necessary is that of tools to work with. By this I mean, study books, literature on Reading Contests, pageants, books of helps for pastors, and any attractive literature for the men, women, Sunday school, or the young people of the church. A few years ago very little of this existed, but today nearly every denomination has developed by mutual cooperation a splendid line of helps. This phase of the matter has been fairly well covered in the previous addresses and nothing more needs to be said at this time.

In conclusion it might be added that in 1928 we have the assurance from the International Lesson Committee that as many as three lessons on Stewardship will be included in the regular Sunday school lessons. The movement is growing in a wonderful way and promises to lift the church and carry it farther than any movement of our day.

GREETINGS TO THE CONVENTION

MESSAGES BY CABLE

READ BY THE REVEREND FRANK MASON NORTH, D.D., CHAIRMAN

Foreign Missions Conference of North America

FROM JAPAN: "To the Foreign Missions Convention, Washington:

"Send hearty greetings. We greatly appreciate your efforts on behalf of friendly relations between United States and Japan.

"Peace on Pacific depends on Christian forces. We earnestly pray for the success of the Washington Conference.

"On behalf of the national Christian Council of Japan."

REV. K. MIYAZAKI,
REV. R. C. ARMSTRONG, PH.D.,
Secretaries.

FROM CHINA: "The National Christian Council of China sends fraternal greetings to the Convention at Washington. Changing conditions make the present time important, even critical. The Christian forces at work in China urge an increasing transfer of responsibility to national churches, the careful appointment of missionaries qualified to meet present needs and the continuing expression of sympathetic cooperation and support."

DR. C. Y. CHENG,
BISHOP LOGAN H. ROOTS,
HENRY T. HODGKIN,
REV. EDWARD C. LOBENSTINE,
Secretaries.

FROM INDIA: "The India National Council sends best wishes to the Washington Convention. India needs your cooperation in prayer for our work, in the comprehension of it, in the consecration to it and in a desire for a spirit of power. 'The deep saith: It is not in me; and the sea saith: It is not with me.'"

REV. WILLIAM PATON,
Secretary.

FROM THE NEAR EAST: "Profound political, economic and intellectual changes have upheaved Western Asia and Northern Africa. Barriers hitherto regarded insuperable now breaking down. Hour manifestly has come for a fresh, adequate, unremitting exhibition to the Moslem World of the life, truth and love of the living Christ. Who will adventure upon this new and living way for the accomplishment of the Church's most difficult and most neglected task?"

381

On behalf of the Preliminary Committee of the Christian Council of North Africa and Western Asia:

BISHOP R. MACINNES,
    Jerusalem.
REV. JAMES H. NICHOL,
    Presbyterian Mission in Syria.
REV. CHARLES R. WATSON, *President,*
    American University at Cairo.
REV. E. S. FREASE,
    Methodist Episcopal Mission of North Africa.

GREETINGS FROM THE PARIS EVANGELICAL MISSIONARY SOCIETY

PRESENTED BY ASSOCIATE DIRECTOR DANIEL COUVE, PARIS

I thank you for your welcome, but let me speak the truth. Although I stand on the platform as a foreign delegate, I have much difficulty in realizing that I am a stranger among you. I feel here quite at home. It is a three-fold message, a real family message, that I bring to you this afternoon.

First of all, I bring to you the message of my country; France is not only a sister country to your two countries; she has been also in the past a mother country to others. Wherever I go among you people, I meet with men and women who tell me, "I had a French grandmother, or a French grandfather. My name in the old days was a French name. It has been a little American-ized, perhaps, but it was a good old French name." We are really one family. Is it not a characteristic of your two nations to have builded with the best precious stones that we have been able to take from the other side? France is always sacred soil, for thou-sands and thousands of your sons and brothers are sleeping their last earthly sleep, one in our memory with our own sons and brothers. We cannot forget; and when we pay our debts—we shall pay them—there will still remain other debts that can only be paid with an unlimited love that will come always to you from France's faithful heart.

I bring to you the message of my church, the Reformed Church of France, the Huguenot. This church is not only a sister church to your churches, it is also a mother church. You all know, even those among you who are neither Presbyterians nor Reformed, that your great democracy owes a good deal to the Church of John Calvin. Our churches are very close, one to another, and our prayer is that God may help all to remain more and more united for the sake of spiritual and moral liberty throughout the whole world.

In the third place, I bring a message from my own Board, the Board of Foreign Missions of our Protestant Churches in France. We have only one missionary society, known as the Paris Evangelical Missionary Society. It has 220 missionaries. Some are Presbyterians, others are Lutherans, still others Wesleyans, some are Baptists. But they are all united in one body, and it has been a privilege for our Society to be a pioneer in the direction of international and inter-denominational cooperation.

Since the beginning of the history of our Society we have united with many of the Swiss churches and also with our brothers from the church in Italy, so that one-third of our missionary staff is Swiss or Italian.

We have been also international in our cooperation. We have been working in the South Seas in the Pacific lands in connection with the London Missionary Society. We are working in West Africa along with the British Wesleyans and the American Presbyterians. We are working in Madagascar side by side with the Society for the Propagation of the Gospel, with the London Missionary Society, with the Norwegian Lutherans, with the American Lutherans and with the Quakers; and we feel it is very easy, when one has the inter-denominational and international spirit, to work thus with the other churches. That is the reason why we believe in the future of this great missionary enterprise more than anything else. It also explains why with the authority of our experience, with the authority also of the inspiration that we have received from you, wherever we have come in touch with you, that I ask you Canadian and American friends to come along to the rescue of all international enterprises. There are others than the missionary enterprise. Never keep aside. The whole world needs your presence and your cooperation. My prayer is that the power and strength that you own in this country, you might turn more and more to work in cooperation with our European nations.

Let me add one word. When any of you come to Paris—and I know that thousands and thousands of you American people will come this very year to Paris—try to remember that we can show you something other than theaters and concerts and beautiful museums and magnificent Roman Catholic cathedrals. Come and see us, and we shall show you the real French life, the life of the people who have struggled with love and perseverance in order to play a part in the advancement of the Kingdom of our Lord.

GREETINGS FROM THE SWEDISH MISSIONARY COUNCIL

PRESENTED BY SECRETARY JAKOB E. LUNDAHL, STOCKHOLM

I want to express my gratitude to God and to you for this conference. I am here as a representative of Sweden, the land of Gustavus Adolphus, the great defender of the evangelical faith.

The Swedish people have always had a deep interest in religion, and their missionary zeal is known over all the world. Swedish missionaries preach the Gospel of Christ in every part of the world. The Christian people in Sweden have begun to understand that the solution of the great and pressing world problems of the present time depends upon two things: First, the disciples of Christ must learn to think and act on the international lines of their Master. Second, the disciples of Christ must learn to understand the meaning and the power of their unity in Him, and the value of mutual cooperation in his work. Christ did everything internationally. In his death He loved all the world and He rose from the dead as the Saviour for the whole world, for every human being, and He has given these words to us, his disciples: "As Thou, Father, hath sent Me into the world, even so have I also sent them into the world." The missionary task is an international task, since we are true followers of our Lord and Master.

Then Christ prayed to his Father that his disciples might be one, "that the world may believe that Thou hast sent Me." When the time comes that all the different Christian churches and the Christian individuals will understand the deep meaning of the Master's unity prayer, and understand the real value of missionary cooperation in spirit and truth, then there will come a new day for Christian missions, a day of eternal blessing to all the world, to every human being.

I bring an especial greeting to you from Sweden and from the Northern countries. From the twenty-third to the twenty-seventh of September of this year there will be held a great missionary conference in Stockholm, the General Northern Missionary Conference of 1925, in which the four Scandinavian countries, Sweden, Norway, Denmark and Finland, will take part.

It will be the greatest and the most important missionary convention that has ever been held in that part of the world. We hope that the blessing of God will rest upon that conference from the beginning to the end. In the name of the Northern Missionary Council I invite you to come to Sweden to attend this convention. I assure you that you will have a hearty welcome from all the missionary friends in my country, a welcome to Sweden.

GREETINGS FROM THE GERMAN EVANGELICAL MISSIONARY UNION

PRESENTED BY MISSIONSINSPEKTOR M. SCHLUNK, HAMBURG

Is it possible to convey fraternal greetings sincerely and cordially from Germany when nearly one thousand missionaries, repatriated in past years, are still waiting after eight years to be allowed to go back to their fields and to the Christians who desire them and need them? Can one bring fraternal greetings from the German missionary societies, if it is a fact that your year's budget has arisen to more than forty million dollars, while our financial power cannot carry a budget of one hundred thousand dollars? Yet I am thankful and proud to bring you the most cordial fraternal greetings, not only for myself and my colleagues here, but also on behalf of all the missionary agencies in my country and of the great constituencies behind them. We can, and must, and will greet you, because we have to thank you. By the generous help of our beloved brethren here in America, it became possible to give food to our children and to our aged, to save a starving people from death. Throughout all the cities of Germany, and the villages, and I may say particularly in many, many parsonages, the gratitude toward our friends here will abide unto eternity. I am sure that you can and will accept these greetings with joy and satisfaction. You gave us more than a cup of cold water. May God bless you for all your kindness and generosity.

But you did more. When we were isolated and without any connection with our fields, your men came and your offerings came and your prayers came to help to maintain our mission work in many fields, in China, in India, in Africa; and you, friends, showed such a fraternal unselfishness, such a wise and Christian attitude toward our Christians there, towards our missionaries, toward our methods of working, that again I am authorized by the German Missions Union to assure you that our gratitude and thankfulness will never cease. You have really been brethren, and that in a time of hatred among nations; therefore, again I thank you.

And again you did more. Here in your country the International Missionary Council, as the most competent authority, declared at Lake Mohonk in 1921, that they could not find any disloyalty by German missionaries during war-time and that you would be glad to open the doors for German mission work, so you stretched out your hands to invite us to work as fellow-workers with you, and you extended your invitation to the German Missions Union to send representatives to your great and brilliant convention.

Here we have been received as brethren, as fellows in the same faith, received with kindness and love, and, therefore, we are free to thank you again and again, and to convey to you officially and personally fraternal greetings. You will understand that our greeting is particularly for those beloved friends who in the past years always stood for the fine and sound principles, so often expressed in our conventions, who gave their hearts and their lives to fight for the freedom and right also of German missions. God knows their names and He will bestow His benedictions upon them.

What is the message Germany has for this convention? What have we learned in the School of God in the past ten years?

First, to be quiet and to wait, to stand aside, without any other chance of sharing in mission work than through prayer. I assure you it has not been easy to learn that, but never have we felt the blessings of our Saviour so vividly as in these sorest years of German missionary history. Not one of our fine old fields has been destroyed. On the contrary, the church in the field arose to such a grade of self-support, self-government, self-propagation, that we can see God's Kingdom coming with power.

We learned the second lesson that times of isolation are times of deepening faith and that times of trouble are full of God's blessings. We learned where the living forces of the Gospel are, and that they are not on the right path, who do mission work through political motives. God's Kingdom is greater than the nations and will take its citizens from all nations and in all nations, notwithstanding the governments of the world.

The third lesson we have had to learn was this: Every nation has within the Kingdom of God its own rights, its own limits, its own responsibilities. In mission work we have become one of the poorest and smallest of nations; but, nevertheless, we know that we have a message and that we have our rights, and we are very, very thankful to see the doors opening and the first German missionaries being greeted in their fields with a really royal reception. May we be able to support them and to send others to share with you this blessed work of God. Power and wealth have come to you in the brilliant development of your country. You have splendid gifts. You are masters of organization. You have missionaries in every part of the world, so you bear greater responsibility for the Kingdom of God than any other peoples of the world. May God be with all your messengers and bless them with His Holy Spirit in order that they may bring nothing else but the old Gospel message of salvation, and that they may win mankind not for the ideal of democracy, but for the Kingdom of God.

Those are the prayers and fraternal greetings of Germany which I have the honor to convey to you, and I beg that you will accept them in the cordial spirit in which they are given.

GREETINGS FROM THE COMMITTEE OF ADVICE—
THE NETHERLANDS

PRESENTED BY BARON VAN BOETZELAER VAN DUBBELDAM, UTRECHT

It surely is a very attractive and inspiring task to convey to you this afternoon the hearty greetings of only a very small country, but a country that has always had a great sympathy for America and for the Americans, a country that has always extended a most hearty welcome to all American visitors. When one of its citizens endeavors to cross the Atlantic and comes over here to the United States he is so overwhelmed by cordiality and friendship that he cannot find words to express his appreciation. Perhaps he might try to do it in his own language but surely he could not in a foreign language.

When you come to Holland we cannot show you as many marvelous and extraordinary things as you like to show us here in this New World, but we could show you, and you would like to see, our old historical places. It is to one of these places I should like to invite you all this afternoon. It is where stands the old castle of Loevenstein. I regret that it would not be possible to take you thoroughly around the castle, through its narrow corridors and staircases, in the short time given to me.

But let me recall to your memory one single name of a man who was imprisoned there and escaped in such a wonderful way, the name of Hugo de Groot (Grotius), a man who dedicated his life to the cause of international justice in a century when there was hardly any idea of what this word meant.

While we are at this old castle may I call your attention to another fact. Just at that same place where this castle is standing two of our great rivers meet. One river we have foolishly given another name, but it is really no other than the old Father Rhine, originating in Switzerland, but going all through Germany, conveying to us memories of what that great German culture had to bring us in poetry, in music, in thought.

The other river we call the Maas. You would, perhaps, pronounce its name in another way. It is a smaller river, that comes out of Belgium and the north of France. That comes to us from that great Latin world and speaks to us of the brilliancy of the spirit of the beautiful language of that Latin world that we have loved and liked for so long a time in Holland.

At that spot the two rivers unite. Perhaps, if you watched them very closely, you might see a slight difference in the color of the water, but very soon it is one big stream going forth to the ocean to meet the other waters coming over to us from that big Anglo-Saxon world. Is it not a touching idea that even in these years of bitter hatred and war, these waters of the great German world and of the Latin world, have been uniting the same as ever at that place. Perhaps these waters would have liked to separate in these times, and if we had allowed them to separate, they would have destroyed a great part of our country, but we placed there at that place strong Dutch dykes and these have kept these waters together, so we have forced them to unite, and they have kept on uniting every day, every hour, every minute.

Well, my friends, is this not an illustration of what the small country of Holland has been trying to do during the centuries? We see coming to us the intellectual and spiritual waters of the great German civilization. We see coming to us the waters—somewhat lighter and brighter of that great Latin civilization, and we are looking over the ocean to a big Anglo-Saxon civilization. We try to take the best of it to unite it with the other streams. Therefore, I think that Holland has always been ready for international cooperation, and, so far as we believe in Jesus Christ and in the coming of His Kingdom, we heartily welcome all international cooperation.

Has He not Himself been telling us that if we believed, we would see rivers of living water flowing through this world? When I stand here and face this big audience, I cannot help thinking that *if we believe,* we would see fountains of living water, sufficient living water to turn all the deserts of this world, all the deserts in these old Oriental civilizations, all the deserts among these nations who have hardly known civilization, and also all the deserts in our Western civilizations—let us acknowledge that we have an appalling number of deserts still there—to turn all these deserts into a Garden of Eden. If we will achieve this task, we shall have to do it—this is the message that I have to bring you from that small country of Holland this afternoon—we shall have to do it through international cooperation to the glory of God.

GREETINGS FROM THE ARCHBISHOP OF CANTERBURY

PRESENTED BY THE RIGHT REVEREND MICHAEL BOLTON FURSE, D.D.
Bishop of the Diocese of St. Albans

Just before I came away from England I received this letter from the Archbishop of Canterbury:

"I hope you will convey to the Missionary Convention in Washington the assurance of the deep interest which we in the Church of England take in the gathering. And above all, will you tell them for myself that I am remembering it in my prayers and am looking forward keenly to the stimulus which it is sure to give to us all? God grant that in 1925 our mission work may go from strength to strength. There are many ways in which those in the United States and Canada set us a good example in the mission field, and

I think that there are some ways in which those whose missionary training has been in England may make a characteristic contribution to the effort which under God's blessing is common to us all.

"(Signed) RANDAL CANTUAR."

I wish to express a word of most grateful personal thanks to those who organized this convention, and to everybody in the United States and Canada, for their extraordinary, overwhelming hospitality. I have never met anything like it in my life. If you on this side of the Atlantic can see this sort of a gathering through with a smile, you can endure anything on God's earth. The English-speaking peoples have had their difficulties; we have had our "scraps," but with all the assurance and confidence and conviction in the world, I can say that if we fail to hold together, it will be a bad thing for us and for the world. We must all hang together or hang separately.

I wish, in any way practicable, to cement the ties between my country and this great country of America. I made a beginning, nearly twenty-two years ago, by coming and getting a wife from this country. I am perfectly certain that from a Christian point of view the responsibility which God is laying upon our shoulders today is tremendously big; and that if we can rise to it now, we shall be able to render to the world in its present broken and shattered condition a, contribution which I believe no man can gauge.

One other word. I spent seventeen years in Africa. I visited England three times during the seventeen years. I love my country and I love my people; but I did not love the way they looked after their over-seas missions, and again and again I was glad, when I got on the boat to sail away back to Africa. I came back nearly five years ago to find an entirely different spirit and outlook on the whole great missionary question. We have not yet reached our ideal nor have you, but the contrast is heartening. I wish to bring the message to you, today, that the trend is in the right direction for Christ and His gospel. The most cheering words in some ways that can be found in the whole of the Bible are those words of our Lord: "He that shall endure unto the end shall be saved." He does not ask of us success, He asks of us service, He asks us to stick to our program and never give up. If we do that, He will see us through.

GREETINGS FROM THE CONFERENCE OF MISSIONARY SOCIETIES IN GREAT BRITAIN AND IRELAND

PRESENTED BY THE REVEREND ROBERT FORGAN, D.D., EDINBURGH

I thank you most heartily for your kind and generous words. Mr. Maclennan, as the Secretary of the Conference of the Missionary Societies of Great Britain and Ireland could have spoken with greater authority and fuller knowledge than I can claim, but his hairs are not so white as mine, he tells me, and I must take precedence of him until he grows somewhat older. And therefore, I humbly submit and obey the Secretary's instructions. In our country the Secretaries rule the Boards! And even the conveners!

But I can assure you that our British Conference of Missionary Societies is a very happy family. The conference meets annually at Swanwick, and its various committees meet more frequently. Practically all the churches are represented; and it is true to say that our missionary cooperation at home and in the mission field is doing much to promote a closer interest and intimacy and a finer spiritual unity among the churches in our home land. It is one of the glories of the missionary enterprise everywhere that it is thus acting as a pioneer of church unity.

On behalf of all the British Missionary Societies, I bring you warmest Christian greetings, and perhaps I may be permitted to add that the Foreign Missions Committee of the United Free Church of Scotland, of which I have the honor to be convener, at their last meeting before I left Scotland, gave me a general commission as their representative, charging me to convey their most cordial greetings to this great convention.

For myself, I have found here in Washington and elsewhere throughout the United States and in Canada, that America appears to have a tender place in her heart for any one who hails from "Bonnie" Scotland. That little country is trying to do its share of the work of world evangelization. There we have good prospects of a coming union between the two largest Presbyterian Churches. Already in different mission fields we have anticipated that home union. Not only do our respective missionaries work together, but they are rapidly uniting the indigenous churches which they have set up.

But we cannot boast. We realize fully how inadequate in men and means are even our best efforts, and it is our prayer that this great convention, so educative, so inspiring and so practically helpful, will result in the diffusion of information and the deepening of interest regarding all that pertains to Christian missions, whether they be carried on from America and Canada or from the Old World. I believe that something like three-fourths of the missionary work of Protestant Christendom is now carried on by your American missions. Perhaps some of you in your modesty may not be aware that you are entitled to all the credit! May God ever more and more fully bless the labors of all your missions and ours, and hasten the glad coming of His Kingdom! The one hope for this distracted world is the gospel of Jesus Christ in all its power to purify and uplift alike the individual men and women of every land and the social and moral life of all the nations of the earth.

It was said in my hearing some months ago by the Archbishop of Upsala that what the world needs today is a new soul, and he added, "If the Christian Church fails to provide for the world that new soul, there is a danger that this world will get a devil for a soul, and the last state of it will be worse than the first." Amid the clash of selfish interests and recurrent storms among the nations, the ship of humanity is being tossed on the angry waves. What hand is strong enough to hold the helm? Is there a statesman living today, or a philosopher or an inventor, who can stretch forth his finger and touch the spring which will set in motion the impulses and aims and aspirations needed to raise mankind to a higher level of living than has yet been reached?

There is only one Master who can rise above the storm and still the angry waves, and speak the word of universal peace. There is only one name which is above every name; when will men be wise enough, simple enough, humble enough, penitent enough to bow the knee at the name of Jesus Christ, and confess that their one hope lies in the receiving of His Spirit, the Spirit of His Cross? The gospel of Jesus is a big thing for the nations, if only they would recognize it, for it alone can change the hearts of men, establish peace and concord and true brotherhood, dispel the darkness of selfishness and shed a radiant and enduring sunshine over all the world.

THE RESPONSE ON BEHALF OF THE FOREIGN MISSIONS CONFERENCE OF NORTH AMERICA

THE REVEREND WILLIAM I. CHAMBERLAIN, PH.D., NEW YORK

Chairman, Committee of Reference and Counsel

We of Canada and the United States should be strangely lacking in intellectual apprehension or, indeed, in emotional response with respect to a singularly unique circumstance if we did not at once make confession of the very real and deep pleasure, and the grateful appreciation that we cherish, because of the presence among us of these representatives of the historic nations and the historic churches of Europe, and of their very gracious messages.

We are not unaware of the contribution of time which they have made in accepting our invitation, involving separation from immediate and very responsible tasks in their several countries. We are not unmindful of the very large contributions which they have made to this convention, and to other gatherings where they have been present since they have been among us in this country, and we are very far from being insensible of the profound significance of the circumstance that their fraternal messages have been presented to us at one time and in one place.

We welcome the representative from Holland for the reason that by his presence we are reminded that, had it not been for the missionary zeal of the historic Classis of Amsterdam in the early years of the seventeenth century, at least two of the Reformed churches in America might not now be in existence. We welcome him because by his presence he also reminds us of the missionary work so characteristically carried on in loyalty and in persistence by the Protestant people of the Netherlands in one of the most difficult fields of the world—among Moslems.

We welcome the representative from Scandinavia for the reason that by his presence he reminds us of the missions carried on by Norway and Sweden and Denmark in various parts of the non-Christian world, all of them illustrating a devotion and a loyalty which we might well follow.

We welcome the representative from France for the reason that by his presence we are reminded that notwithstanding the grave losses of life and treasure in these recent years, the Reformed church of France is today maintaining a missionary work enriched by life and by treasure, quite equal to that of the two churches in this country who still retain the title Reformed in their official designation.

We welcome the representatives from Germany for the reason that by their presence we are reminded of the great missions maintained in the past by the Protestant people of Germany, and the variety and the efficiency of the work carried on by them in Asia and Africa, and we welcome them further, because by their presence they give reality to our expectation and our confidence that not long hence they will be bearing their full share in the missionary responsibilities of the world.

We welcome the representatives from Great Britain, for the reason that by their presence they remind us of that of which we have already been reminded this afternoon, and of which possibly we need no reminder—the closeness of kinship in race and language that exists between us. The earliest missionary Societies were organized in Great Britain. The first missionaries went out from England and from Scotland and from Ireland. Great has been the contribution towards the establishment of the Kingdom of God in the world by Great Britain. Some of us who have shared in the missionary work of the world in those areas where the British influence has been dominant are deeply conscious of that very favoring circumstance in the work that was ours.

On this side of the Atlantic cooperative organizations have been developed after two types. The first and the older has been illustrated by those organizations whose governing bodies have been constituted by members of various denominations, but not officially appointed by those denominations to represent them in those organizations. The illustrations of that earlier type are the Evangelical Alliance, the American Bible Society, the Young Men's and the Young Women's Christian Associations.

The second and later and a rapidly growing type has been that illustrated by organizations whose governing bodies have been composed of representatives of denominations, officially designated to those governing boards in the names of the denominations of which they are members. The organizations that illustrate this type are the Federal Council of the Churches of Christ in America, the Councils of Home and Foreign Missions and the Educational Boards.

First among these councils is the Foreign Missions Conference of North America, embracing the societies of the United States and of Canada. This organization was formed in 1892. Its first meeting was held in 1893. This week we shall hold the thirty-second annual meeting of this Foreign Missions Conference of North America. It represents not less than ninety-five societies of these two countries, cooperating with them in various ways.

It is interesting to note something of the progress of the work of the missionary societies in the United States and Canada. In 1844 when the first report was made regarding our work, the United States was credited with nine hundred missionaries and an income from the societies cooperating of $500,000. In 1900, at the time of the assembly of the Ecumenical Conference in New York, the societies of the United States and Canada were credited with 5,000 missionaries, and an income of approximately $7,000,000. In 1910, at the assembling of the World Missionary Conference in Edinburgh these North American societies that are welcoming the representatives from Europe today were credited at that time with missionaries numbering about 7,000, and an income of approximately $12,000,000. Today there is placed upon our tables a report which shows that the societies of the United States and Canada are maintaining approximately 19,000 missionaries in the mission fields of the world with an income at their disposal of more than $40,000,000.

These are large resources of life and of treasure that are placed at the disposal of the societies of the United States and Canada, and great is the task to which we have set our hand. The obligation resting upon the Christian Church to convey the message of its Founder to the men and women of all nations is inherent in the very nature of the gospel itself, as we were so impressively reminded in the convention sermon this morning. The gift of love and mercy by God through Jesus Christ cannot be fully understood or accepted by the individual, unless it be a universal love and a mercy offered to all men.

Today, as witness this Convention, this Church in all the main seats of evangelical Christendom is being aroused afresh to the immeasurable scope of its mighty task. Our churches have set for themselves the endeavor to do nothing less than this—the establishment of the Kingdom of God effectively over and in the life of all races. In the fulfilment of this great task appointed by the Almighty Himself, we humbly and gratefully join hands with the representatives of the churches of Europe, and with the rising churches in Asia and in Africa, so that Orient and Occident, joining hands together around the globe, shall lift it so close to the bosom of God that the sound of the beating of His heart shall be the marching song of all the ages.

THE CALL OF OUR UNFINISHED MISSIONARY TASK

DR. ROBERT E. SPEER, NEW YORK

If we think and speak carefully and truthfully as we ought, we will recognize that our missionary task is not our entire Christian task, and we will discern that the missionary task itself requires for its accomplishment instrumentalities and agencies in addition to those which we include in the missionary enterprise strictly conceived. We are all of us members of families, and citizens of communities, and members of churches and citizens of nations. In each one of these four capacities, as well as because of our connection with a foreign missionary enterprise, strictly conceived, we have missionary duties and responsibilities.

It is easy, it is inevitable, it is not wholly evil that these various activities should be oftentimes confused. There are two things that make it easy to confuse them. One of them is the comprehensiveness of the Christian principle of life which calls us to do all the good we can as we go along our way. It is easy for us to think that the doing of any and all good is a legitimate and integral part of our distinctive foreign missionary responsibility.

This confusion arises also from the simple fact that we ourselves are not divisible. We function in many different relationships, but each of us is still just his single self, and we are always tempted to express our whole selves, in whatever may be the easiest way, and again and again we attempt to utter our whole self in some channel of human action that may, in the end, not turn out to be the wisest or most effective way of achieving the end.

I say again, it is easy and inevitable, and not wholly evil that this confusion of thinking and acting should exist among us. But for the sake of the very interests which produce it, it is necessary for us as far as possible to clear it away. It is conceivable that in the desire to do good we may do less good than would be possible if we saw the whole process clear and complete. Our Lord might have lavished all of those great powers of His in healing a mere fraction of the sickness of the day in which He lived. He might have done more good to the contemporary population of the world, measured in terms of the relief of human hunger and human pain than in His short and intense life He did, but how much less good would He have wrought across the centuries? We might take the entire missionary income of all the churches of the United States and Canada today. It would be inadequate to cope with the problem of poverty in the United Provinces of India alone. It is often better, hard as it may be to say it, to let a great deal of possible present good go undone in the interest of far greater good reaching across the years.

Even in the interest of the instrumentalities that we use, it is better for us to keep as far as we can the lines of distinction clear. Again and again we have seen men tempted to seize some instrument of action that lay nearest to their hand for the accomplishment of an end because that was the easiest form of procedure for the moment, when at the last they discovered that that was not the right instrument to use, and that they had marred that instrument for its right use in thus using it. We are lifting today from the Christian home and transferring to the Christian Church and to the state functions that belong in the home. And again and again across the line of proper functional division between church and state, one agency or the other strays across to the other side. There is no small danger in our world today that in the interest of the great ends that we seek we should relieve the state of religious obligations because we have not patience to wait until the state shall assume them, only to discover at the last that we have incapacitated the state for ever taking them over.

I say again that while it may be inevitable and not altogether evil it would be most desirable this last night before we go that we shall try to gather our thoughts in as earnest, corporate meditation as we can, and focus them upon our agreement as to what the great task is to which from these gatherings we pass out when this hour is gone by.

There is the one other obvious reason why we must do this. I am to speak this evening on the call of our unfinished missionary task. How shall we know what that call is? How can we measure how much of the task remains undone if we do not clearly see and are not substantially agreed as to the task itself?

We have said again and again in these days that we need the entire body of humanity in order that we may apprehend the fullness of God's revelation in Christ. We have had in our gathering here in miniature the justification and illustration of that conviction. How richly in our corporate assembly has each one of us been led on to fuller and ampler points of view and judgments than by ourselves we could have attained! As one after another has spoken out of what was most real in his own or her own life, though it represented a different experience from our own, we said, "Yes, there is an aspect of truth that had eluded me. Thank God that I am here to have my heart enlarged, my apprehension of God's wealth in Christ increased and my own understanding of the glory of this great task amplified beyond the comprehensions of my own single life!"

And how richly as we have gathered here have we felt ourselves entering into the great corporate inheritance of the church that lies behind us! It is not only that here we have come from all the corners of the earth, each to contribute what God has given him; we are surrounded by an innumerable host of invisible witnesses. We feel here pouring through our own hearts tonight the life-blood of the long and glorious past.

How far we have been led even within our memory who are gathered here this evening! I have watched the development of this missionary enterprise since I heard the report of the delegates who came back from the first great conference in London in 1888. There are a few of us here also who sat in that first gathering in 1892, a generation ago when a little company of a few score came together representing the missionary boards of the United States and Canada in their first annual convention. Very richly has God led us across these years. Even as compared with twenty-five years ago—many of you can recall those days when we assembled in New York—how much surer is the step of this missionary enterprise, and thank God how clear and steadfast and unmoved across the years has been its central loyalty to the things that can never change.

We rejoice tonight in this last hour to gather all our hearts together in one common prayer and one common effort, to see so far as we can come home to the heart of our undertaking, and to ask ourselves as we go out now, "How much of this task still remains to be done? For what does this unfinished task call?"

Well, we are all agreed here that primarily the missionary task is to release the Gospel of Jesus Christ throughout the world, and to start such a propagation of that Gospel as shall carry it to every man and woman and child in the world. It is not the business of foreign missionaries from any country to complete this task for any other land, but it is their business to make the beginning, to see that the work is started, and then to let the living power flow out and on. I like the phrase that Mr. Edward S. Martin used some years ago in an essay in the "Atlantic Monthly" entitled, "Much Ado About Women," in which he was commenting upon the views of Mr. W. L. George. "Mr. George," Mr. Martin said in substance, "seems to be entirely unaware of the fact that the religion of Jesus Christ is loose in the world."

I do not know whether Mr. Martin meant by that phrase "the religion of Christ" all that we would mean, but I think he does and I like his way of speaking about the Gospel of Jesus Christ as loose in the world. Our primary business is to set that Gospel loose in every land, to make sure that it has been set loose in as much of its purity and its power as we are able to bear, and then to let it pour on and on across the world.

We are agreed in the second place that our task is not alone to carry to all men the glad tidings of something that happened 1,900 years ago, the story of some great facts that faith did not create, and that unbelief cannot dissolve, but that stand there sure and immovable forever at the beginnings of Christian history. We agree that we are to bear that message, the glad tidings of something that occurred long ago, when a great delivering deed was done and the Saviour came among men. But we are agreed also that there is something more than a story of what took place 1,900 years ago that it is our missionary task to bear to the world.

I call your own hearts to witness what response we made on Thursday morning to the lovable words that Mr. McLaurin and Dr. Jones spoke to us about the thing that is first and central, about bearing our living Lord, Jesus Christ, who was and still is the one Person who can satisfy, the living, personal power, bearing Him in all His grace and living beauty across the world. We are agreed that our missionary task is unaccomplished until, with that Gospel of what happened we carry the Gospel also of something that is, of a living Person who stands among men, the greatest of all realities.

But my friends, we are agreed too (surely we are agreed), that this language has not exhausted all that is involved in our missionary task. For what is Christ? Christ is not a word; Christ is not a statement of incidents in history; Christ is not a statement with regard to a person who was or a person who appeared to be or a person who is. We speak of Christ as we have spoken of Him again and again during these days as the Life, but what is a life? How is a life known? In what does a life result? We know nothing about life except as we see it in relationships. It is revealed in relationships. It must result in relationships. There is no way of spreading it except in relationships. And this, said our Lord, is eternal life that they may know Thee, that they may be related to Thee, the only true God, and Jesus Christ whom Thou hast sent.

One sometimes wishes we were not driven on to difficulties and perplexities such as these, but you cannot carry Christ to the world save as you carry Him in all that he involves and implies, in all the implications that are essential to His understanding, in all the reproducible institutions that make His power permanent and accessible in human life. To be sure, we can only bear Him in the vessels we have got, and they are earthen vessels; but they are all we have, and what we know about the Christian Church, however far it may fall short of Christ's ideal for it, whatever we have learned about hospital and school, however inadequate they will seem to be to the wiser generations that will come after us, whatever we know of Christ's place in human relationships or what Christian faith and Christian character must be, we are bound to carry the best we have got of all this, or we cannot carry what I have spoken of before, to the world as an essential part of our missionary task.

Once more, to round out briefly, before we press on, what

we are agreed is the task that is set for us: We believe it is part of our missionary responsibility to lay the great ideals of Christ upon all that makes up human life, to claim for Christ His Lordship over everything that there is in His world. Our friend, Mr. Rowell, was speaking this morning of a new conception of foreign fields. A foreign field, he suggested, is any area in human life where Christ is a stranger. We who are going out into the foreign missionary enterprise must bear Him into all the areas of life, into all the relationships and personalities, into all the forces and energies where Christ is still a stranger. We must hold up the Christian ideal and lay down the Christian law as obligatory for every activity and agency and organization and relationship of men.

Now there is nothing from which we need to shrink in this; it is all unequivocally explicit in the terms of the great commission itself. Read it over again; say it in your memory now. "Go ye into all the world and preach the Gospel"—to whom?—"to every creature," we read. Turn back to the Greek Testament and see what it says. We are to preach this Gospel according to the great commission as recorded there in the last chapter of St. Mark, "to all creation," to every creation. The most powerful creatures in the world today are not little human individuals like you and me. They are great impersonal forces, aggregations of individuals, huge economic and political and industrial and commercial and educational groupings of power, creations of man. The great commission from Christ's own lips lays down upon every one of them the same Gospel that falls on our personal hearts. And this exegesis is not forced, for we turn back to the great commission in the last chapter of St. Matthew's Gospel and does it not read with equal explicitness, "Go ye into all the world and make disciples"— of what, of whom?—of men and women, yes, to be sure, but that is not the language. "Go ye into all the world and make disciples of all the nations, teaching the nations to observe all things whatsoever I have commanded you."

And if we turn to St. Paul we find him realizing the great task with which he was grappling, as a task that launched him not against individual men and women alone but against all the powers of the world in which he lived, which were meant to be subdued to the mastery of Christ. "For we wrestle not." Now, he did not mean he did not wrestle with flesh and blood, but only that that was a small part of his wrestling. "We wrestle not with flesh and blood but with principalities and powers, with the rulers of the darkness of this world, with spiritual wickedness in high places." He flung himself and the Gospel that he was given to bear into the world against all the world that Jesus Christ came to save, for the Father sent the Son—let us say it over again and again—to be not the loser but the Saviour of the world.

Here tonight we are agreed that these are the elements of our common, our comprehensive missionary task. As individuals we will find our several places in different parts of the great undertaking. One of us may see this aspect and another that aspect. Thank God we go out tonight realizing better than we have ever realized before how rich and glorious and varied an undertaking it is, claiming each of us his own place and rejoicing that side by side with us there are other men and women supplementing us in our narrowness of vision and partiality of view, and making up, all of us together, that one great body of Christ through which He will adequately function to complete in His day His task for man.

Now of this great task that we have been surveying in the days of our gathering here—how much must we recognize tonight as still unfinished and incomplete?

Have we evangelized our world? One looks out over the generation of which we are a part and there are probably more people in the world today who do not know of Christ than there were when the modern missionary enterprise began. There are great areas of the earth as untouched and uninfluenced today as when William Carey first went down into that mine of India. There are many here in this house tonight who could bear testimony of them, the great regions, hundreds and hundreds of miles, where no Christian messenger has ever gone, the thousands and thousands of villages where the Christian message has never been spoken. Even in great centers where you would think the missionary forces were adequately massed, there are great bodies of folk to whom Christ is stranger still. I suppose in Tokyo alone today there are more people who do not know the Gospel than there were people in the city of Tokyo when Christian missionaries first went to Japan.

Even where we thought we had evangelized the world, are we content with the adequacy of the work that has been done? Even here, in our own land, where we think of the Gospel as known, there are people by the millions who have no true idea of what the Gospel is, to whom the word Gospel signifies only a travesty of what Christ brought and what He is. If that be true here, how much more true is it of that other world where the fringe of our task has barely been touched as yet? Let no young man or young woman here this evening think that our work has been so far done that it brings no call to his or her life today, to follow in the footsteps of those who first went out to evangelize the unevangelized world.

Have we released Christ across the world today in the fulness of His grace and His power and His beauty? Well, yes, in a sense we have. All over the world there are men and women who have lived the life of Christ, who have lived the life of Christ as well as men or women can ever live it, for the people to whom they have given their lives. I remember the word of a poor old blind woman in the city of Hamadan years ago, on whose cataract-covered eyes Dr. Holmes had operated and given her back her sight. In speaking of it to a friend, she said, "Do you know, when I felt Dr. Holmes' hands on my face, they seemed to me to be the very hands of Christ."

I once asked an Englishman, who lived in India, if he had ever heard of George Bowen, and he said, "Yes, George Bowen was the lamb of India." I saw the other day Dr. Jack's essay on "The Lost Radiancy of the Christian Religion." I do not know where he has been looking for it, but I can see the radiancy of the Christian religion here tonight. I have seen it shining all across the world. Jesus Christ has been truly given in His beauty and His power, and His strength to these other nations.

It is no ground of misgiving, with regard to the realities of that gift to have it said to us, as sometimes it has been, that if only we would let Christ shine forth in the fulness of His glory, men would inevitably and irresistibly be drawn to Him. There was a day when Christ shone forth in the fulness of grace and truth, and men crucified Him. Some would crucify Him today if He were to come back into our modern world. It is no proof that Christ is not present in the world today that men turn from Him now just as they turned from Him in the days of His flesh when He came to His own and His own received Him not.

We have released Christ to the world, only, my friends, how inadequately have we released Him! How dissatisfied are they who have released Him most purely with the form in which they have been able to communicate Him. How far short we have fallen of doing what Christ would have us do! I received not long ago a letter from an Indian friend who had been studying here in America. He had served Christ before he came here. He was going back to serve Christ again when he returned. Friends of his were a little uncertain as to what effect his stay in America might have upon him. I think he would not mind my reading a paragraph or two from his letter:

"I have been able to rethink for myself the fundamentals of our faith, resulting in a more genuine assurance of all that my Master has meant to me. It has enabled me to get the people of this land interested in my country, and the work of the Kingdom. I think I have done all that I could in this respect. I have had opportunities of exchanging views with some of the best men from other Oriental countries. I have been able to learn the history of my own country, covering the last two centuries, as I could never have done in India.

"The result of all these things has been an awakening experience, with the formation of certain convictions. I have begun to love my country as I never loved before. India does not need new religions. It has too many already, and religion instead of being a unifying force in India, has proved to be divisive. It does need Christ in His purity and love. Christ will enter into all the problems of India and solve them for it. We, his representatives and co-workers, have to see that we do not hinder Christ from entering into the life problems of India. Christ is the Lord of not only the life to come as a substitute for transmigration, but He is the Lord of our present life.

"Let us crown Him as such and let Him enter and purify all that is covered under the term of life. I am afraid we are liable to hinder Christ's work in the life of the people of India, as long as we stand back passively from it and preach a Gospel of other-worldliness.

"I do not very much like the narrow, self-satisfied patronizingly spiritual atmosphere in which I lived in India, and I wonder if it can be changed on account of innumerable handicaps."

Well, perhaps he sees things only partially as we all do, but is there one of us tonight who does not wish that in some purer and fuller and richer way we could pass Christ on to the world?

There are great ranges of unfulfilled duty, of possibilities of human service in making Christ known that constitute areas yet inadequately touched of our unfinished task. Can we say that we have pressed with Christ into all these foreign fields where Christ is not yet recognized as Master and Lord? In the field of religious freedom have we claimed for Christ and His brethren their rights in the world. For my part, I believe that the right of absolute religious liberty is an inalienable human right that ought not to be denied a single child of God. There are great areas of the world tonight where that fundamental right is denied. It is abridged in Turkey, to Mohammedan and Christian alike. It is denied in Afghanistan, to Christian and Mohammedan alike. Mohammedans stoned to death in the streets of Cabul a few weeks ago a fellow Mohammedan of another sect because they counted him a heretic. And outside of these Moslem lands there are other great areas of the world where the inalienable right of every human soul to religious liberty is denied or abridged.

I believe it is the missionary task of government to assert this universal right, and I can cite at least three times in our own American history when our Government conceived it to be its right and duty to deal with other governments not in the interest of religious liberty for American citizens in those lands but in the interest of religious liberty for the subjects of those nations themselves. But whether governments recognize their missionary duty or not, our enterprise has its duty here, and I imagine that if we were willing enough to die for religious freedom in every land where it was necessary we might win it for all the world and perhaps there is no other way than that by which we may win it.

Have we in the field of education around the world, here at home with our own students and over 14,000 foreign students, much less out in these other lands, done our missionary duty? The foundations were laid by Christian men, by William Carey and Alexander Duff in India, by Guido Verbeck in Japan, by William A. P. Martin in China, by missionary after missionary across the non-Christian world, and little by little there, as so largely here at home, education has slipped out from under the control of Christ. We do not believe that education is an area of human life that has any right to repudiate the lordship of Christ. I believe it to be part of our missionary task to claim His mastery there.

In the field of human industry and the rights of little children, have we won Christ's place or even claimed it for Him? We have heard the tales here again and again in this Convention of the way in which the exploiters of child labor across the world are playing havoc with the little children of God. The line of one of their hymns has been coming back to me. I don't know any of the hymn but this line but when Miss Burton was speaking the other evening it kept running through my mind, "Like lambs they shall still to their shambles be borne,"—these little children of the Orient, victims, defenseless victims of the ever-invading, all-crushing impact of our Western economic industry.

Nor these children only. I was reading some facts about child mortality today. Dr. Neve wrote regarding Kashmir that fifty per cent. of the little children died under five years of age. Dr. Lichtwardt wrote about eastern Persia that seventy-one per cent of the children died under the age of five. And Dr. Howard Cook had written from Uganda that seventy-five per cent of the children in Uganda died before they were one week old.

This is good news for the Malthusians but not to us who hear across the world the wails of the little children. Has Jesus Christ had His place claimed for Him adequately in the protection of the life of little children in the midst of these great, unfortunate masses of mankind? Can we say we have begun here our missionary task?

There are said to be 100,000 blind in the United Provinces of India alone, and not one blind institution for them except a few broken-down barracks in the City of Allahabad, where 20 or 30 of the 100,000 are miserably housed. I have seen it stated, although it is hard to credit it, that there are 2,000,000 lepers in the world. One thanks God for all that Christian missions have done for them, but one thinks of the hundreds of thousands of lepers whom, if Christ were in the world today, He would touch, to whom we have never gone as yet with any mention of His love and His power.

I think of the field of trade that ought to be one of the greatest areas of mutual human helpfulness, of the fields of human thought which we have surrendered to other influences and allowed Christ to be driven off. Our missionary task, so far from being done, is now at the end of the first century just in the way of being really begun.

We ask ourselves with regard to the degree in which we have been able to pass on to these other peoples satisfactory and reproducible models of the Christian church and the Christian school. We have heard in these days things said to give us joy, but there is not an educational missionary in this convention who would say that what he has been able to do in his institution was anything but a fraction of what the missionary enterprise ought to be doing today in establishing in the non-Christian world the kind of institutions that Christ should have as the power houses with which to work in these lands. Not one. Nowhere across the world have we today a single educational institution that is what it ought to be, that is what the men who are in control of it would like to make it.

And while we thank God for these churches that have arisen, where is there one that is what we would want it to be, that is what it itself is longing to be?

Once again if we go beyond these things to ask how far we have been able to lay Christ's controlling hand on all the other agencies of human life that are as vitally affecting mankind, perhaps, as this enterprise that commands all our devotion, can we be satisfied with what has been achieved? Well, thank God we have come a long way. Turn back sometime and read our treaty with Tripoli in the earlier years of the last century, in which our government explicitly disavowed any Christian character, and compare that with the decision of the Supreme Court in the matter of the Contract Alien Labor Law twenty years or so ago; or, with the words that the President spoke here on our opening afternoon. We have come a long way in the recognition by the governments of the West of their own primary missionary obligation. Or, read the early history of our great trading corporations, the East India Company, the Netherlands Trading Company, and the rest, and measure all those over against the terms of the mandates by which the League of Nations has passed over the colonial administration into the hands of trustee governments, and one will see what a long way we have come.

Thank God we have come some distance, too, in the matter of relationship of race to race, but not far. A man sent to me the other day a book entitled, "My Wonderful Dream." It was a book which held the thesis that mankind started with two great races, one human, the "ivory whites," as the author described them, and the other animal, the "ebony blacks," the patricians and the plebians, the masters and the servants. The whites were made to enjoy pleasure, and the blacks were made to do their menial tasks. All the other races were the degraded and illegitimate production of the mixture of these two great aboriginal groups.

Well, one passes this by as insane anthropology, but the idea has been taken right over and is being preached as moral doctrine for racial relationships to our generation in a devilish book (I choose the word with careful moderation), by Professor Josey, entitled "Race and National Solidarity," in which the doctrine is unblushingly set forth that now is our chance if indeed it is not too late, with the power we have got in our hands to choke into subordination all the other races of the world, and make them do our work for us, that we may enjoy in the affluence and the ease and the leisure which their labor will buy for us, the fullest possible self-expression of our race. We have got a long, long way, to go on this road that stretches before us still.

These are aspects of our unfinished task, and this whole night were too short for us to confront the great responsibilities that, undischarged, now stand before Christ's Church in our generation. What is their call to us in these last moments before we go? They are making their call to us as Christian citizens, a call to tasks that we are to discharge, not in the Church nor in this missionary enterprise, but in the great nations to which we belong.

But we pass those by tonight that before we go out we may think quietly together of the distinctively religious missionary call that comes from this unfinished task to us Christian men and women here tonight committed with all that we are and have to this enterprise of foreign missions.

It is a call, first of all, to see and to keep our Lord Jesus Christ in his rightful place. Our gathering here would not have been complete if we had not joined this morning, when Dr. Wood called us to it, in that great reaffirmation of our deepest convictions and that central word with regard to our Lord, of Jesus Christ in whom we believe, God's only Son, our Lord, conceived by the Holy Ghost, born of the Virgin Mary, suffered under Pontius Pilate, crucified, dead, and buried, and risen again from the dead to live forevermore. If there is any language that could give Christ a larger place than we have given Him, let us learn that tongue. There is nothing that can be said about Him that we are not prepared to say about Him if only we may learn the speech by which to say it.

The first of all calls is to see and to keep Jesus Christ in his central and primary place in this enterprise and in our lives, where St. Paul kept Him. "I am crucified with Christ. Nevertheless I live yet, not I, but Christ liveth in me, and the life that I now live in the flesh I live by the faith of the Son of God Who loved me and gave Himself for me." Do not think that that is the outworn form of an old and bygone experience. All that those words meant for St. Paul they are meant to mean for us men and women today. They meant it all to David Livingstone. Turn, when you go home, to his diaries, and read the entries made on his birthdays. With the picture before your eyes of the lonely, weary figure, trudging through Africa's night by himself, save for the little company of black men who were as his brethren and who bore his poor, worn and wasted body home, read those words of David Livingstone's and find the place that Jesus Christ must have in the missionary enterprise throughout all the days, and let Christ have that place now and forevermore.

It is a call to a fearless and unhesitating and joyfully avowed faith in the accessibility and the present supernatural power of God. I believe that Jesus Christ walked upon the sea. I believe that Jesus Christ fed, with a few loaves and fishes, the five thousand hungry folk who sat before Him. I believe that Jesus Christ raised the dead. And I believe as much as God did through Jesus Christ nineteen hundred years ago God waits to do again through men. As our Lord said: "And he that believeth on Me, the works that I do shall he do also, and greater works than these shall he do, because I go unto my Father." True words have been spoken here about prayer. Prayer is a power by which we can achieve the impossible. Prayer is a power by which we can over-ride all that men say psychologically cannot be. Prayer is a power by which we can effect in the world today what Christ wrought in the world when He was here. We need this bold, sure faith in the supernatural and yet I do not like this way of putting it; I do not think that prayer is supernatural. I think that prayerlessness is infranatural. We would not concede that nature is the world with God eliminated from it and then speak of God as supernature. Nature is God and the world and the man who does not believe in God is holding an infra-natural view of the real world in which we live. God is the greatest of all realities in this world. The most natural thing of all is God. All else is only garment and habiliment of Him.

We have access to a living God, a heart of love, beating at the very soul of all things, a will unhampered in its freedom to work through us, to build here on earth today the Kingdom of God. Our unfinished task calls us to a new and a fearless faith in a living God, able to do anything in this modern world.

It calls us in the third place to bring all our resources to His feet and to draw with fresh courage and faith upon the resources that are hidden in Him. It has not been amiss that we have been reminded here of the immeasurable resources of these two sister lands that are gathered in this Convention. I can remember myself when the population of the United States was only 35,000,000. It has grown now to over 100,000,000. I can remember when its wealth was $30,000,000,000; it has grown now, as we have been told once or twice to over $320,000,000,000. These are great resources that we are to bring and lay at Christ's feet for his use.

But I tell you, my friends, there are greater resources than these. What is $320,000,000,000 to God? What are all the men of power and strength and influence in the world to God? It was a little boy who was born in a manger and grew up in a carpenter's home and of whom men spoke slightingly as one who had never learned, who was the Saviour of the world. It was a poor German miner's wife who brought forth in a public place, in the bustle of a market day, her first born little son and sent Martin Luther out to put those sturdy shoulders of his under human history and by God's grace heave it into new grooves. It is not how great we are or how much money we have got but how ready we are to hand ourselves over to the uses of God. It is not how much we give but whether we give everything. If all we have got of life and power we give, there are resources enough there for God to do whatever needs to be done in the world. The call of this unfinished task is for us to lay these paltry resources of ours down for God's use, and to draw on God for our use in the world upon the unlimited resources that are hidden in Him.

In the fourth place, it is a call,—perhaps we are not the right group to understand all of this,—it is a call not so much to us but to these churches whose representatives we have among us here, whom God gave us the joy of founding around the world. The great burden of the unfinished missionary task is their burden. All we can do is to offer them our help, but the work will never be done until they take it over and carry it through. There should be some clearer thinking done here and some more direct speaking than we have indulged in in the past. It is not a matter of our giving these churches their independence. If I am dependent upon another man for my independence, where is my independence? No man can give another man his true freedom. A man is free or he is not free. No other man can make him free.

Let there be no misunderstanding here. We have been asked again and again in this Convention whether we are willing to give these churches their liberty. Willing? Why, we wait eagerly for the day when they will take it. Passing over to them the administration of forty or fifty millions of dollars, that is a trifling thing. What we want is to see them take the responsibility for evangelizing one thousand millions of human souls. Let them rise to that responsibility and the friend of the bridegroom, hearing the bridegroom's voice will rejoice. For that hour we wait. We long for them to increase that we may decrease.

What a call this unfinished task is speaking to these little flocks scattered across the world! Let those who go back to them from this gathering tell them that they heard here only one note, that they met here with only one purpose, that we do not conceive this task to be ours but theirs, and that we want everyone to help them. We were only called in God's providence to pass on a torch that centuries ago was passed to our fathers before us out of Asia. It is for them to take this torch up now and with it to light the world.

Yet once more this call, my friends, is a call for our lives. It is a call for not part of our lives, not for some area or period of them, not for a fraction of their possessions; it is a call for our lives. Let me put it straight to the young men and young women here, these students who have been a part of this gathering. Let them not go away thinking that this task is done and that it does not open to them today the same field that was open to the fathers who went before.

All that Carey, and Duff, and Livingstone and Moffat, and the long line that laid the foundations, found to their hand, this generation will find to its hand, too, with a challenge of difficulty far greater even than tested the men and women who went before.

They will be welcomed as there was no one to welcome those who went before. Going in the spirit of Christ, they will find in every land to which they go arms open to receive them in that spirit. It is a new world of fellowship and unity and common possibilities of service that is open to us, not the lonely world into which the missionary pioneers went out a century and a quarter ago.

It is a call for life, not only to finish the task, but to complete the lives laid down. "These all died in faith," we read, "not having received the promise, God having reserved some better thing for us, that they without us might not be made perfect."

I wish I could some day go to that tree in Eastern Equatorial Africa, the big mvula tree, at whose roots the little company of black men buried David Livingstone's heart. I should like to kneel down where that heart is buried and see if I could hear it beat there beneath the soil of Africa, and know what it was that Livingstone's heart was thinking of and longing for. But one does not need to go to that lonely spot in Eastern Africa. He can read it on the great slab there in the nave of the abbey, "I pray for a blessing on any man, Englishman, American, or Turk, who will put forth one effort to heal the world's open sore."

More than David Livingstone are calling. I heard that call more vividly than ever before or since in life three years ago as the shadows of a November evening fell on the banks of one of the sacred rivers of India, and I went with my hat in my hand into the quiet shadows of the little cemetery where the dead of the Mutiny lay buried beside the old English Church in Fatehgarh. There, on the face of the square monument, confronting us were the names, Indian, American, English, I think, of the men and women and little children, who had fallen, and underneath a startled thrill ran through one as he read the solitary word, "Forsaken." I thought, "Yes, one had not expected to find it, but that is the truth. Forsaken. We have forsaken and forgotten these dead." I walked to the left to read the other face of the monument, and there I think were more names, Indian, English, American, and the preceding word from St. Paul's letter to the Corinthians, "But not forsaken." Thank God. They may not be forsaken.

Out of this great past that lies back of us one hears the whispering voices tonight, "Will they come, will they ever come?" The unfinished task is calling, and the uncompleted lives, they are calling.

Last of all, we would not wish to go out tonight with any other thought upon our hearts than this: they are calling us to a new and joyful and sure and deathless hope. All around us today the despairing voices speak. "It is a world of war, and hate, and failure," they are saying to us. But we are of those who far off hear angels singing on a wintry night, a song of peace, goodwill for all mankind. And we know that in a day to come there will be no more war. We are of those who across the racial gulfs have clasped the hands of brothers. We know that for us the racial barriers are gone forever, and that as the old Chinese sage and St. Paul alike said, "There is under Heaven only one family." We are of those who know that what Jesus Christ began, He will complete, who see afar off the long gray streamers that speak of dawn, for the night is far spent, and the day is at hand. And out of this place we go steadfast, immovable, always abounding in the work of our Lord, for as much as we know that our labor is not in vain in the Lord, and that out of that labor there will arise at last,— though we shall not see it so, it will not seem to us to be rising out of that toil, we shall see it coming down from God out of Heaven,—the City of God that is to be built in the pleasant meadows of England, on the torn fields of France, in the city streets, and the little villages of Germany; in India, China, Africa; here, in spite of all selfishness and sin, in our own dear lands, the City of God with the nations bringing their glory and the kings of earth their honor into it, and war, and hate, and failure, the long dark night gone, thank God, gone, forever! Christ came for this and for this He sends us into the world.

STATISTICS

Number of delegates registered........................... 3,419
Representatives of National Missionary Organizations....   9
Officers of International Missionary Council.............   4
Visitors 181
Speakers not included in the above....................... 27

                                                         ———
                                                        3,640
Number of Washington people registered............... 1,150

              Total Registered Attendance 4,790

                    ——————

Meetings held in the Auditorium 16
Simultaneous Conferences 27
Denominational Conferences 34
Boards and Societies represented........................ 85
Missionary and Training Schools represented............. 11

                    ——————

It is estimated that over 8,000 different people from Washington attended one or more sessions.

CONVENTION PROGRAM

WEDNESDAY, JANUARY 28, 1925

AFTERNOON. 3.00-5.00 o'clock. In the Auditorium.

The Rev. James L. Barton, D.D., Chairman, Committee of Arrangements, called the Convention to order.

PRAYER—The Rev. W. S. Abernethy, D.D., Washington.

ADDRESS OF WELCOME—President Calvin Coolidge.

ADDRESSES—"The Gospel for the Whole World."

    (a) "The Compulsion"—Bishop Edwin D. Mouzon, D.D., Nashville, Tenn.

    (b) "The Promise"—Miss Jean Kenyon Mackenzie, formerly of Africa.

BENEDICTION—The Rev. J. R. Sizoo, D.D., Washington.

EVENING. 8.00-10.00 o'clock. In the Auditorium.

PRESIDING OFFICER—The Rev. William I. Chamberlain, Ph.D., New York.

PRAYER—The Rev. Charles Wood, D.D., Washington.

ADDRESSES—"The Present World Situation."

    Bishop Herbert Welch, D.D, Korea.

    Bishop Charles H. Brent, D.D., Buffalo, New York.

BENEDICTION—The Rev. Samuel H. Chester, D.D., Nashville, Tenn.

THURSDAY, JANUARY 29, 1925

FORENOON. 9.30-12.00 o'clock. In the Auditorium.

PRESIDING OFFICER—Miss Margaret E. Hodge, New York.

PRAYER—The Rev. L. B. Wolf, D.D., Baltimore, Md.

THEME—"Christ: The Solution of the Problems of the World."

    (a) "His Message to the Individual"—The Rev. John McLaurin, India.

    (b) "His Message to Society"—Miss Mabel K. Howell, Nashville, Tenn.

    (c) "His Message to Nations and Races"—Mr. J. H. Oldham, M.A., London.

    (d) "The Aim and Motive of Foreign Missions"—The Rev. E. Stanley Jones, D.D., India.

INTERCESSION—President W. Douglas Mackenzie, D.D., Hartford, Connecticut.

BENEDICTION—The Rev. W. A. Lambeth, D.D., Washington.

AFTERNOON. 2.30-4.30 o'clock. Simultaneous Conferences. See pages 415-418.

AFTERNOON. 4.45-5.45 o'clock. In the Auditorium.

Pictures were shown, beginning at 4.35.

PRESIDING OFFICER—The Rev. J. C. Robbins, D.D., New York.

PRAYER—The Rev. W. L. Darby, D.D., Washington.

ADDRESSES—The Rev. Robert Forgan, D.D., Scotland.

    Mrs. Henry W. Peabody, Beverly, Mass.

BENEDICTION—The Rev. Earle Wilfley, D.D., Washington.

EVENING. 8.00-10.00 o'clock. In the Auditorium.

PRESIDING OFFICER—Bishop David Williams, D.D., London, Ontario.
PRAYER—The Rev. J. E. East, D.D., formerly of Africa.
ADDRESSES—
    (a) "The Gospel in a Great Oriental City"—The Rev. William Axling, D.D, Japan.
    (b) "Winning a Province"—The Rev. Watts O. Pye, China.
    (c) "Movements Towards Christ in India"—Prof. John Jesudason Cornelius, India.
    (d) "The Gospel Among Primitive Peoples"—The Rev. H. C. McDowell, D.D., Africa; The Rev. C. E. Hurlburt, D.D., Africa.
BENEDICTION—Bishop W. B. Beauchamp, D.D., Brussells, Belgium.

FRIDAY, JANUARY 30, 1925

FORENOON. 9.30-12.00 o'clock. In the Auditorium.

PRESIDING OFFICER—President George W. Richards, D.D., Lancaster, Pa.
PRAYER—The Rev. John E. Kuizenga, D.D., Holland, Mich.
THEME—"Christian Education in the Mission Field"
    (a) "The School as an Agency in the Building of Character"— Miss Ida Belle Lewis, Ph.D., China.
    (b) "Christian Education and Christian Leadership"—Dean J. D. MacRae, Shantung University, China.
    (c) "Christian Education and Christian Womanhood"—Miss Helen K. Hunt, Dean of Women in Judson College, Burma.
    (d) "The Significance of Christian Education in the Evangelizing Process"—President James M. Henry, Canton Christian College, China.
INTERCESSION—The Rev. Robert Forgan, D.D., Scotland.
BENEDICTION—The Rev. J. H. Taylor, D.D., Washington.

AFTERNOON. 2.30-4.30 o'clock. Simultaneous Conferences. See pages 418-422.

AFTERNOON. 4.45-5.45 o'clock. In the Auditorium.

    Pictures were shown, beginning at 4.35.
PRESIDING OFFICER—Bishop A. R. Clippinger, D.D., Dayton, Ohio.
PRAYER—The Rev. William B. Olmstead, Chicago.
ADDRESSES—The Rev. Arthur Judson Brown, D.D., New York.
    President Mary E. Woolley, Ph.D., South Hadley, Mass.
BENEDICTION—The Rev. Henry Beets, LL.D., Grand Rapids, Mich.

EVENING. 8.00-10.00 o'clock. In the Auditorium.

PRESIDING OFFICER—Mrs. Thomas Nicholson, Detroit, Mich.
PRAYER—The Rev. Charles E. Creitz, D.D., Reading, Pa.
ADDRESSES—
    (a) "Medical Missions"—Prof. T. Dwight Sloan, M.D., Peking Union Medical College, Peking.
    (b) "Women and Children in Industry in the Far East"—Miss Margaret E. Burton, New York.
    (c) "Sixteen Years of Campaigning for Chirst"—Dr. T. Kagawa, Japan.
    (d) "The Power of Christ Revealed in Personal Life"—Prof. Rufus M. Jones, Ph.D., Haverford, Pa.
BENEDICTION—The Rev. George Drach, D.D., Baltimore, Md.

SATURDAY, JANUARY 31, 1925

FORENOON. 9.30-12.00 o'clock. In the Auditorium.

PRESIDING OFFICER—Mrs. E. H. Silverthorn, New York.
PRAYER—The Rev. William B. Anderson, D.D., Philadelphia, Pa.
THEME—"The Place of Foreign Missions in the Church at Home."
  (a) "The Adequate Foreign Missionary Program of a Denomination"—The Rev. Ralph E. Diffendorfer, D.D., New York.
  (b) "The Adequate Foreign Missionary Program in a Congregation"—The Rev. S. W. Herman, D.D., Harrisburg, Pa.
  (c) "The Layman's Responsibility for the Foreign Missionary Movement"—Mr. R. A. Doan, Columbus, Ohio.
  (d) "The Responsibility of Women in the Foreign Missionary Work"—Mrs. Charles K. Roys, New York.
  (e) "The Pastor's Responsibility for the Foreign Missionary Movement"—The Rev. Hugh T. Kerr, D.D., Pittsburgh, Pa.
INTERCESSION—President J. Ross Stevenson, D.D., Princeton, N. J.
BENEDICTION—The Rev. G. M. Diffenderfer, D.D., Washington.

AFTERNOON. 2.30-4.30 o'clock. Simultaneous Conferences. See pages 422-423.

AFTERNOON. 4.45-5.45 o'clock. In the Auditorium.

Pictures were shown, beginning at 4.35.
PRESIDING OFFICER—Bishop S. C. Breyfogel, D.D., Reading, Pa.
PRAYER—The Rev. Charles D. Bonsack, Elgin, Ill.
ADDRESSES—The Rev. William P. Schell, D.D., New York.
       The Rev James Endicott, D.D., Toronto.
BENEDICTION—The Rev. A. R. Bird, Washington.

EVENING. 8.00-10.00 o'clock. In the Auditorium.

PRESIDING OFFICER—The Rev. F. H. Knubel, D.D., New York.
PRAYER—The Rev. Jason N. Pierce, D.D., Washington.
THEME—"The Church in the Mission Field."
  (a) "In Latin America"—The Rev. J. H. McLean, D.D., Chile.
  (b) "The Church in India"—The Rev. Bhaskar P. Hivale, Bombay.
  (c) "In the Far East"—Bishop H. St. George Tucker, D.D., recently of Japan.
  (d) "The Imprisoned Splendor of the Orient"—The Rev. Harris E. Kirk, D.D., Baltimore.
BENEDICTION—The Rev. G. F. Dudley, D.D., Washington.

SUNDAY, FEBRUARY 1, 1925

FORENOON. 9.00 o'clock. In the Auditorium.

(Hour of session at nine o'clock to avoid conflict with regular morning church services.)
PRESIDING OFFICER—The Rev. Paul de Schweinitz D.D., Bethlehem, Pa.
PRAYER—The Rev. William I. Haven, D.D., New York.
THE CONVENTION SERMON—"The Unsearchable Riches of Christ"—The Rev. Canon H. J. Cody, D.D., Toronto.
INTERCESSION—"Spiritual Qualifications for Missionary Service at Home and Abroad"—Mr. Robert P. Wilder, M. A., New York.
BENEDICTION—The Rev. Allen E. Armstrong, Toronto.

AFTERNOON. 3.00-5.00 o'clock. In the Auditorium.

PRESIDING OFFICER—The Rev. Frank Mason North, D.D., New York.
PRAYER—Bishop Ethelbert Talbot, Bethlehem, Pa.
(a) Cabled Messages from China, India, Japan, and the Near East.
(b) Fraternal messages from representatives of Holland, Scandinavia,
    France, Germany and Great Britain.
  Response on behalf of the Foreign Missions Conference of North
      America by The Rev. William I. Chamberlain, Ph. D., Chair-
      man, Committee of Reference and Counsel.
(c) ADDRESS—"New Forces Released Through Co-operation"—Dr. John
    R. Mott, New York.
PRAYER—Prof. Dr. Julius Richter, Berlin.

EVENING. 8.00-10.00 o'clock. In the Auditorium.

PRESIDING OFFICER—The Rev. Stephen J. Corey, LL.D., St. Louis,
    Missouri.
PRAYER—Prof. R. S. McClenahan, LL.D., Cairo.
Testimonies—"Reasons Why We Go as Foreign Missionaries."—E. War-
    ner Lentz, Lynda Irene Goodsell, Walter Judd, M.D.
ADDRESS—The Rev. F. F. Goodsell, D.D., Constantinople.
ADDRESS—The Rev. Samuel M. Zwemer, D.D., Cairo.
BENEDICTION—The Rev. Prof. Harlan P. Beach, D.D., New Haven,
    Connecticut.

MONDAY, FEBRUARY 2, 1925

FORENOON. 9.30-12.00 o'clock In the Auditorium.

PRESIDING OFFICER—Mr. James M. Speers, New York.
PRAYER—Bishop James E. Freeman, D.D., Washington.
THEME—"The Foreign Missionary Movement in Relation to Peace and
    Goodwill Among Nations."
  (a) "Of One Blood"—Bishop Michael Bolton Furse, St. Albans,
      England.
  (b) "Educating for Peace and Goodwill"—Mrs. Thomas Nichol-
      son, Detroit, Michigan.
  (c) "The Will for Peace"—Prof. William I. Hull, Swarthmore,
      Pennsylvania.
  (d) "The Christian Spirit in International Relations"—The Hon.
      Newton W. Rowell, Toronto.
INTERCESSION—Dr. John W. Wood, New York.
BENEDICTION—The Rev. H. E. Stillwell, Canada.

AFTERNOON. 2.30-5.00 o'clock. Simultaneous Conferences by Boards
and Societies. See pages 424-427.

EVENING. 8.00-10.00 o'clock. In the Auditorium.

PRESIDING OFFICER—The Rev. James L. Barton, D.D.
PRAYER—Bishop William F. McDowell, D.D., Washington.
ADDRESS—"The Call of Our Unfinished Missionary Task"—Dr. Robert
    E. Speer, New York.
PRAYER—The Rev. James H. Franklin, D.D., New York.
BENEDICTION—The Rev. James L. Barton, D.D.

SIMULTANEOUS CONFERENCES
THURSDAY AFTERNOON, JANUARY 29
2.30 to 4.30 o'clock

1. EVANGELISTIC WORK (DIRECT):

Place of Meeting—Mt. Vernon Methodist Church, 9th and K Sts., N.W.
Chairman REV. A. E. ARMSTRONG.
Secretary—REV. A. B. PARSON.

SYLLABUS:

1. The Evangelistic Missionary at Work"—Dr. Jonathan Goforth and Miss Jean Kenyon Mackenzie.

2. "The Place of Direct Evangelistic Work in the Missionary Enterprise of Today."
   (a) "What Is Its Relation to Other Phases of the Work?"
   (b) "To What Extent, If Any, Is Its Primary Place Impaired by the Complex Character of the Missionary Activities of Today?"
   (c) "What Is the General Attitude of non-Christians in Mission Lands Toward Direct Evangelistic Work?"
       Discussion opened by Dr. John Aberly.

3. "Evangelism in the Native Church."
   (a) "To What Extent Are the Native Churches Carrying on the Work of Evangelism?"
   (b)"How Far May the Leadership in This Work Be Left With the Native Church?"
       Discussion opened by Bishop B. T. Badley, D.D.

4. "Present Day Demands."
   (a) "What Are the Most Urgent Demands of Evangelistic Work at the Present Time?"
   (b) "Does the Present Situation Call for a Material Increase in the Number of Evangelistic Missionaries?"
       Discussion opened by Dr. A. F. Groesbeck.

2. MEDICAL WORK:

Place of Meeting—Calvary Baptist Church, 8th and H Sts., N.W.
Chairman—P. H. J. LERRIGO, M. D.
Secretary—E. M. DODD, M. D.

SYLLABUS:

1. "How Are Medical Missions Contributing to the Advance of Christian Civilization in Mission Lands?"
       Discussion opened by W. J. Wanless, M. D.

2. "The Present Trend in the Policy of Medical Missions and Their Significance—To What Extent, If Any, Does the Creation or Development of the Medical Profession in Mission Lands Modify the Need for Medical Missions?"
       Introduced by O. R. Avison, M. D.

3. "What Are the Most Urgent Needs Today in Connection With Medical Missionary Work?"
       Discussion opened by J. G. Vaughan, M. D.

3. EDUCATIONAL WORK:

Place of Meeting—Church of the Epiphany, G St. near 13th St., N. W.
Chairman—REV. ANSON PHELPS STOKES, D.D.
Secretary—REV. H. E. STILLWELL.

SYLLABUS:

1. "The Contribution and Special Problems of Elementary Education."
   Discussion opened by Dr. Ida B. Lewis.
2. "Mission Education in Relation to the Development of Government Education."
   Discussion opened by J. H. Oldham.
3. "The Adaptation of Mission Education to the Needs of the People."
   Discussion opened by Dr. Thomas Jesse Jones.
4. "Union and Co-operation in Educational Work."
   (a) In India—Rev. J. Roy Strock.
   (b) In China—Dean J. D. MacRae.

4. AGRICULTURAL AND INDUSTRIAL:

Place of Meeting—Concordia Church, G and 20th Sts,. N.W.
Chairman—REV. THOMAS S. DONOHUGH.

SYLLABUS:

1. "Why the Missionary Forces Must in Many Fields Deal With Agriculture and Simple Industries."
   Discussion opened by Dr. Thomas Jesse Jones.
2. "Relation of Agriculture to Village Work in India."
   Discussion opened by Principal W. J. McKee.
3. "Present Types of Successful Agricultural Work on Foreign Fields."
   (a) "Agricultural Education in Colleges."
   (b) "Central Training Schools."
   (c) "Farm Settlements."
   (d) "Agricultural Extension Work."
   Discussion.
4. "How the United States Department of Agriculture May Co-operate With Agricultural Missionaries."
   Introduced by Dr. W. A. Taylor, Chief of the United States Bureau of Plant Industry.
5. "Special Problems of Agricultural and Industrial Missions."
   Introduced by Dr. Homer LeRoy Shantz.
   Discussion.

5. SOCIAL SERVICE:

Place of Meeting—Metroplitan Methodist Church, John Marshal Place and C Street, N.W.
Chairman—PROF. D. J. FLEMING.

SYLLABUS:

Co-operative credit societies, agricultural setlements and other forms of economic betterment—famine, earthquake, and flood relief, welfare directors of factories, social surveys, schools as community centers, criminal reclamation, adult education, institutional churches, social settlements.

1. "What is the Range and Importance of the Social and Community Service Actually Being Carried on By Missions?"—Rev. T. Kagawa.
2. "Why Should Such Work Be Carried on by Mission Boards?"—Rev. Alden H. Clark.
3. "What Emphasis Should Be Placed on This Work in the Education of the Home Churches?"—Dr. William P. Schell.
4. "What New Kinds of Social and Community Service (if any) Should Be Taken Up By Missionary Agencies?"

6. CHRISTIAN LITERATURE:

Place of Meeting—First Congregational Church, 10th and G Sts., N.W.
Chairman—DR. CORNELIUS H. PATTON.
Secretary—DR. A. L. WARNSHUIS.

SYLLABUS:

1. The Present Situation and the Urgent Needs—How Far These Are
   Being Met in—
   (a) Moslem Lands—Dr. Samuel M. Zwemer.
   (b) China—Dr. Donald MacGillivray.
   (c) India—Dr. John Aberly.
   (d) Africa—Miss Jean Kenyon Mackenzie.
   Questions.

2. "The Training and Development of Good Writers."
   Discussion introduced by Dr. Frank Rawlinson.

3. "The Urgent Necessity of Co-operation."
   Discussion opened by Dr. A. L. Warnshuis.

7. WORK AMONG MOHAMMEDANS:

Place of Meeting—Church of the Covenant, 18th and M Sts., N.W.
Chairman—DR. WILLIAM B. ANDERSON.
Secretary—FRANK V. SLACK.

SYLLABUS:

GENERAL THEME—"The New World of Islam."

1. "The Intellectual Movement Among Moslems."
   Discussion opened by Dr. R. S. McClenahan.

2. "Moslem Aggression in Africa."
   Discussion opened by Prof. Dr. Julius Richter.

3. "The Moslem Situation in India."
   Discussion opened by Dr. Samuel M. Zwemer.

8. EDUCATING THE CHURCH IN FOREIGN MISSIONS:

Place of Meeting—New York Avenue Presbyterian Church, New York
   Ave. between 13th and 15th Sts.
Chairman—MISS GERTRUDE SCHULTZ.
Secretary—F. D. COGSWELL.

SYLLABUS:

1. "To What Extent Is the Church Being Reached Today By Missionary
   Education?"

2. "What Some Churches Are Doing."

3. "Adequate Objectives and Means for Their Realization."

4. "The Church School of Missions."

5. "Educating Through Mission Study."
   (a) "Types of Groups and Relative Values."
   (b) "Present Status and Future Possibilities."

6. "Training Our Leaders."
   (a) "What Type of Leadership Is Required?"
   (b) "Are the Facilities for Training Leaders Adequate?"

9. RECRUITING AND TRAINING FOR MISSIONARY SERVICE:

Place of Meeting—Luther Place Memorial Church, 14th and N Sts., N.W.
Chairman—PRESIDENT DOUGLAS MACKENZIE.
Secretary—DR. FRANK K. SANDERS.

SYLLABUS:

1. Opening Address by the Chairman—President Mackenzie.

2. "Suggestions from German Experience in the Training of Missionaries"—Prof. Dr. Julius Richter.

3. "What Are the Essential Questions to be Considered in Determining the Fitness of a Candidate for Appointment?"
Introduced by Rev. William N. Wysham.

4. "Is It Vitally Necessary That the Board Shall Determine in Advance the Region and Character of a Candidate's Future Service and Make Direct Arrangements for His Special Training?"
Introduced by Prof. E. D. Soper.

5. "What Are the Essential Elements in a Program of Special Training at Home?"
   (a) "For Theological Students?"—Prof. Homer C. Wark.
   (b) "For Other Forms of Professional Service?"—Dean Edward W. Capen, Ph.D.
   (c) "For College-bred Women Without Previous Theological Training?"—Mrs. Hume R. Steele.

FRIDAY AFTERNOON, JANUARY 30
2.30 to 4.30 o'clock

1. JAPAN:

Place of Meeting—Mt. Vernon Methodist Church, 9th and K Sts., N.W.
Chairman—DR. E. H. RAWLINGS.
Secretary—DR. S. G. ZIEGLER.

SYLLABUS:

1. "The Strength and Weakness of the Christian Church in Japan Today."
   (a) "As Seen by a Japanese Leader"—Rev. T. Kagawa.
   (b) "As Seen by a Missionary"—Dr. William Axling.

2. "Forces in Japan Helping and Hindering the Progress of the Christian Movement."
   (a) "In the Field of Religion, Literature, and International Relations"—Bishop H. St. George Tucker, D.D.
   (b) "In the Field of Industry, Government, Family Life, Education and Social Conditions"—Miss Isabelle McCausland.

3. "What Are the Chief Contributions Needed From the Christians of North America?"
   (a) "The Missionary Force—Kind, Number, Relationships."
   (b) "Special Lectures and Deputations."
   (c) "Money—For What Objects and on What Terms."
   (d) "Race Relations—Christianizing Legislation and Social Contacts."
   Discussion opened by Rev. A. K. Reischauer.

2. KOREA:

Place of Meeting—Grace Reformed Church, 15th Street, N.W., between Rhode Island Avenue and P Street.
Chairman—DR. CHARLES R. ERDMAN.
Secretary—MRS. G. ERNEST FORBES.

SYLLABUS:

1. "Present Conditions in Korea in Relation to the Missionary Enterprise."
   > Discussion opened by Bishop Welch and Mrs. Welling T. Cook.
2. "The Development of the Korean Church.
   (a) "In Self-support."
   (b) "In Self-government."
   (c) "In Spiritual Power."
   (d) "In Foreign Missions."
   > Introduced by O. R. Avison, M.D.
3. "The Challenge of Korea to the Home Churches."
   (a) "The Challenge of Opportunity."
   (b) "The Challenge of Achievement."
   > Introduced by Rev. C. N. Weems.

3 CHINA:

Place of Meeting—Metroplitan Methodist Church, John Marshal Place and C Street, N.W.
Chairman—DR. JAMES H. FRANKLIN.
Secretary—DR. GEORGE T. SCOTT.

SYLLABUS:

1. "Outstanding Instances of Recent Missionary Advance."
2. "The Christian Church in China."
   (a) "What is the Present Status of the Chinese Church (1) in the National Life of the People, (2) in Its Leadership, (3) as an Agency in China's Evangelization?"
   (b) "How Far Has the Christian Church in China Advanced in Self-government, Self-support and Spiritual Power?"
   (c) "In the Light of Present Development, What Hope Does It Carry?"
   (d) "What Are Its Special Problems?"
   (e) "What is the Relation of the Chinese Church to Our Home Churches?"
   > Discussion opened by Dr. Frank Rawlinson.
3. "Features of the Present-day Situation in China With Which the Home Churches Should be Challenged."
   (a) "How Far is the Country 'occupied' by Christian Missions?"
   (b) "Are There Areas or Special Groups Upon Which An Immediate Emphasis Should be Laid?"
   (c) "What Features of the So-called Renaissance Movement in China Carry Particular Significance for Christianity?"
   (d) What Challenge Does the Industrial Development in China Present to the Christian Church?"
   (e) "What Has Been the Effect of the Present Intellectual Awakening Upon the Womanhood of China?"
   (f) "How Far Is the Present Missionary Force Adequate?"
   > Discussion introduced by Rev. Milton T. Stauffer.

4. INDIA:

Place of Meeting—Calvary Baptist Church, 8th and H Sts., N.W.
Chairman—Dr. WILLIAM I. CHAMBERLAIN.
Secretary—WILLIAM B. LIPPHARD.

SYLLABUS:
1. "India's Present Need and How That Need is Being Met by the Christian Message."
   Discussion opened by Dr. E. Stanley Jones and Mr. R. B. Manikam.
2. "The Native Church in India."
   (a) "What is Its Present Status?"
   (b) "How Far Has It Advanced in Self-government, Self-support and Spiritual Power?"
   (c) "What Are Its Special Problems?"
   (d) "In the Light of Present Developments, What Hope Does It Carry?"
   (e) "What is Its Relation to Our Home Churches?"
      Discussion introduced by Rev. J. H. Warnshuis and Mr. B. P. Hivale.
3. "Features of the Present-day Situation in India With Which the Home Church Should be Challenged."
   (a) "How Far is the Country 'occupied'?"
   (b) "Upon What Areas or Social Groups Should An Immediate Emphasis be Laid?"
   (c) "How Far is the Present Missionary Force Adequate?"
   (d) "To What Extent and in What Departments Can Union or Co-operative Work be Effectively Carried on?"
   (e) "What Are the Outstanding Weaknesses and What Are the Main Features of Strength in Missionary Work as Carried on in India Today?"
      Discussion opened by Dr. Alden Clark and Prof. J. J. Cornelius.

5. SIAM AND MALAYSIA:

Place of Meeting—Church of the Covenant, 18th and M Sts., N.W.
Chairman—Dr. JOHN R. EDWARDS.

SYLLABUS:
1. "German Missions in Malaysia"—Dr. Schlunk and Dr. Bettin.
2. "Missions in the Dutch Indies"—Baron Van Boetzelaer.
3. "Missions in Siam"—Miss Bertha A. Blount.
4. "Mohammedanism in Malaysia"—Dr. Samuel M. Zwemer.

6. PHILIPPINES:

Place of Meeting—Church of the Epiphany, G St. near 13th St., N.W.
Chairman—Dr. JOHN W. WOOD.

SYLLABUS:
1. "Features of the Present-day Situation in the Philippines With Which the Home Churches Should Be Challenged."
   Introduced by Dr. J. C. Robbins.
2. "Progress and Promise.
   (a) "In Industrial Work"—H. F. Stuart.
   (b) "In Medical Work"—Miss Eliza R. Davis.
   (c) "In Educational Work."
   (d) "In Evangelization of Primitive Tribes"—Rev. E. A. Sibley.
3. "The Native Church in the Philippines."
   (a) "What is Its Present Status?"
   (b) "How Far Has It Advanced in Self-government, Self-support and Spiritual Power?"
   (c) "What Are Its Special Problems?"
   (d) "In the Light of Present Developments, What Hope Does It Carry?"
      Introduced by Dr. George W. Wright.

7. NEAR EAST:

Place of Meeting—First Congregational Church, 10th and G Sts., N.W.
Chairman—CANON S. GOULD.

SYLLABUS:
1. "In Turkey"—Dr. Fred F. Goodsell.
2. "In Syria"—Miss Margaret B. Doolittle.
3. "In Palestine"—Mr. Kenneth Maclennan.
4. "In Egypt"—Dr. R. S. McClenahan.

8. AFRICA:

Place of Meeting—Vermont Avenue Christian Church, Vermont Avenue
    above N Street, N.W.
Chairman—DR. STEPHEN J. COREY.
Secretary—REV. MORRIS H. EHNES.

SYLLABUS:
1. "The Present Situation in Africa and the Significance to Missions of
    Recent Developments."
        Discussion introduced by J. H. Oldham.
2. "Our Educational Opportunity in Africa."
        Discussion opened by Dr. Thomas Jesse Jones.
3. "The Development of the Native Church in Africa."
    (a) "In French Africa"—M. Daniel Couve.
    (b) "In East Africa"—Rev. Charles E. Hurlburt.
    (c) "In the Congo"—Rev. Herbert Smith.
    (d) "In West Africa"—Rev. H. C. McDowell.
        Discussion.

9. LATIN AMERICA:

Place of Meeting—Foundry Methodist Church, 16th St., near P St., N.W.
Chairman—BISHOP FRANCIS J. McCONNELL.
Secretary—DR. SAMUEL G. INMAN.

SYLLABUS:
1. "Recent Outstanding Social Developments in Latin America and Their
    Missionary Significance."
        Discussion opened by Dr. J. H. McLean.
2. "The Indians of Latin America—the Appeal They Present and the
    Obligations We Face."
        Introduced by Dr. H. C. Tucker.
3. "Special Fields of Service in Which Latin Americans Need and Wel-
    come the Help of the Christian Forces of Other Countries."
        Discussion opened by J. C. Field.

10. RECRUITING AND TRAINING FOR MISSIONARY SERVICE:

Place of Meeting—Luther Place Memorial Church, 14th and N Sts., N.W.
Chairman—PRESIDENT W. DOUGLAS MACKENZIE.
Secretary—DR. FRANK K. SANDERS.

SYLLABUS:
1. "How Can a Candidate in Professional Training for Service in Medi-
    cine, Education, Agriculture, etc., Best Be Enabled to Secure the
    Religious Background and Knowledge Necessary for His Mission-
    ary Service?"
        Discussion opened by Dr. J. Lovell Murray.
2. "How Shall We Best Promote the Development of the Spiritual Life
    of the Candidate in Training?"
        Discussion opened by Dr. W. B. Anderson.
3. "How Can the Biblical Instruction of Missionary Candidates Be Used
    to Fit Them to Become Efficient Bible Teachers?"
        Introduced by Prof. Caroline L. Palmer.
4. "Some Observations on Missionary Training"—Mr. J. H. Oldham.

11. FOREIGN MISSIONS IN THE CHURCH SCHOOL:

Place of Meeting—New York Avenue Presbyterian Church, New York Avenue between 13th and 14th Streets.
Chairman—DR. J. C. ROBERTSON.
Secretary—FRANKLIN D. COGSWELL.
SYLLABUS:
   1. "The Place of Foreign Missions in the Program of the Church School."
   2. "The Missionary Opportunity Presented and the Objective to Be Sought in—
      (a) "The Sunday Session."
      (b) "The Week-day Session."
      (c) "The Daily Vacation Bible School."
   3. "Some Best Methods Now in Use."
   4. "Material Now Available and Material Required."

SATURDAY AFTERNOON, JANUARY 31
2.30 to 4.30 o'clock

1. FOREIGN MISSIONS IN THE DENOMINATIONAL PROGRAM:

Place of Meeting—Calvary Baptist Church, 8th and H Sts., N.W.
Chairman—DR. RALPH E. DIFFENDORFER.
   A discussion of the very highest importance on the place of Foreign Missions in the life and work of the Denomination.

2. FOREIGN MISSIONS IN THE CONGREGATION OR PARISH:

Place of Meeting—First Congregational Church, 10th and G Sts., N. W.
Chairman—DR. HUGH T. KERR.
Secretary—REV. RAYMOND L. EDIE.
SYLLABUS:
   1. "An Adequate Foreign Mission Program for the Congregation"— Presented by Prof. J. C. Archer.
      Discussion.
   2. "What Some Churches Are Doing."
   3. "Men and the Missionary Enterprise."
      Discussion introduced by Dr. Ernest Hall.
   4. "Cultivating the Missionary Prayer Life of the Congregation."
      Discussion introduced by Mrs. Hume R. Steele.

3. FOREIGN MISSIONS AND THE NEW GENERATION:

Place of Meeting—New York Avenue Presbyterian Church, New York Avenue between 13th and 14th Streets.
Chairman—MISS RUTH I. SEABURY.
Secretary—FRANKLIN D. COGSWELL.
SYLLABUS:
   1. "Our Educational Responsibility to the New Generation in View of the Development of the Foreign Missionary Enterprise."
   2. "The Home as a Missionary Agency in Its Relationship to the New Generation."
   3. "The Responsibility of Young People's Organizations to the Missionary Undertaking."
   4. "Foreign Missions in—
      (a) "High Schools."
      (b) "Denominational Colleges."
      (c) "Universities."
      (d) "Theological Seminaries."
   5. "The Content Required in the Missionary Education for the New Generation."

4. STEWARDSHIP AND FOREIGN MISSIONS:

Place of Meeting—Metropolitan Methodist Church, John Marshal Place and C Street, N.W.
Chairman—DR. WILLIAM E. LAMPE.
Secretary—DR. HARRY S. MYERS.

SYLLABUS:
1. "Stewardship as Related to Our Foreign Mission Obligation."
    Discussion opened by Dr. Harry S. Myers.
2. "Stewardship as Practiced on the Mission Fields."
    Discussion introduced by O. R. Avison, M.D.
3. "How We Can Help the Churches on the Foreign Field in Their Development of Stewardship."
    Discussion opened by David McConaughy.
4. "Stewardship Materials and Their Use."
    Introduced by Dr. Luther E. Lovejoy.
5. "The Promotion of Stewardship in a Local Church."
    Discussion opened by Rev. M. E. Melvin.

5. RECRUITING AND TRAINING FOR MISSIONARY SERVICE:
   Place of Meeting—Luther Place Memorial Church, 14th and N Sts., N.W.
   Chairman—PRESIDENT W. DOUGLAS MACKENZIE.
   Secretary—DR. FRANK K. SANDERS.
   SYLLABUS:
   1. "What Measures at Home or on the Field Can Be Taken to Secure the Wisest Guidance in the Language Study of Every New Missionary?"
       Introduced by Prof. Harlan P. Beach.
   2. "What Steps Ought to Be Taken to Insure That the First Furlough Shall Be Used for the Further Training Which the First Term on the Field Has Shown to Be Necessary?"
       Introduced by Miss Helen B. Calder.
   3. "Should a Fresh Emphasis Be Laid on the Selection and Training of Oriental Christians for Missionary Work Among Their Own People."
       (a) "In Their Own Country?"—Dr. Frank Rawlinson.
       (b) "From Among Oriental Students in America?"—Mr. Chas. D. Hurrey.

6. TRANSLATION AND DISSEMINATION OF THE BIBLE:
   Place of Meeting—Church of the Covenant, 18th and M Sts., N.W.
   Chairman—DR. WILLIAM I. HAVEN.
   Secretary—DR. W. B. COOPER.
   SYLLABUS:
   1. "The Bible for All Peoples"—Mr. James Wood.
   2. "The Bible in Their Own Tongue."
       Introduced by Dr. Henry A. Stimson, with George R. Heath, Paul Burgess and E. H. Richards participating.
   3. "The Bible in the Mission Field."
       (a) "In the Far East"—Rev. Donald MacGillivray, D.D.
       (b) "In the Near East"—Rev. Arthur C. Ryan, D.D.
       (c) "In Latin America"—Rev. H. C. Tucker, D.D.
   4. "The Tyndale Celebration—Four Hundred Years and Their Challenge."
       Introduced by Dr. W. B. Cooper.

7. RELIGIOUS EDUCATION IN THE MISSION FIELD:
   Place of Meeting—Church of the Epiphany, G St. near 13th St., N.W.
   Chairman—Mr. J. H. OLDHAM.
   Secretary—DR. ERIC M. NORTH.
   SYLLABUS:
   This Conference reviewed from as many different angles as possible this vitally important subject with a view to discovering how all forms of missionary activity might be most effectively directed toward building up Christian character.

CONFERENCES OF FOREIGN MISSION BOARDS AND SOCIETIES

MONDAY AFTERNOON—2:30 to 5:30

CANADA

BAPTIST:

Canadian Baptist Foreign Mission Board.
Women's Baptist Foreign Missionary Society of Ontario (West).
Women's Baptist Foreign Missionary Society of Eastern Ontario and Quebec.
United Baptist Woman's Missionary Union of the Maritime Provinces.
Leader—REV. H. E. STILLWELL.
Place of Meeting—Foundry Methodist Church.

CHURCH OF ENGLAND

Missionary Society of the Church of England in Canada.
Woman's Auxiliary to the Missionary Society of the Church of England in Canada.
Leader—REV. CANON S. GOULD, M.D., D.C.L.
Place of Meeting—Foundry Methodist Church.

METHODIST:

Missionary Society of the Methodist Church, Canada.
Woman's Missionary Society of the Methodist Church, Canada.
Leader—REV. JAMES ENDICOTT, D.D.
Place of Meeting—Foundry Methodist Church.

PRESBYTERIAN:

Board of Foreign Missions, Presbyterian Church in Canada.
Woman's Missionary Society, Presbyterian Church in Canada, Eastern Section and Western Section.
Leader—PRINCIPAL ALFRED GANDIER, LL.D.
Place of Meeting—Foundry Methodist Church.

UNITED STATES

BAPTIST, NORTHERN CONVENTION:

American Baptist Foreign Mission Society.
Woman's American Baptist Foreign Mission Society.
Leader—REV. W. H. BOWLER, D.D.
Place of Meeting—Calvary Baptist Church, 8th and H Sts.

BRETHREN, CHURCH OF (DUNKERS):

General Mission Board of the Church of the Brethren.
Leader—REV. OTHO WINGER, D.D.
Place of Meeting—North Carolina Avenue Church of the Brethren, North Carolina Ave. and 4th St., S.E.

CHRISTIAN CHURCH:

Mission Board of the Christian Church, Foreign Department.
Woman's Mission Board of the Christian Church, Foreign Department
Leader—Rev. W. H. Denison, D.D.
Place of Meeting—New Ebbitt Hotel, 14th and F Sts., N.W.

DISCIPLES OF CHRIST (CHRISTIAN):

United Christian Missionary Society.
Leader—Rev. Stephen J. Corey, LL.D.
Place of Meeting—Vermont Avenue Christian Church, Vermont Ave.
near N Street.

CONGREGATIONAL:

American Board of Commissioners for Foreign Missions.
Woman's Board of Missions.
Woman's Board of Missions of the Interior.
Woman's Board of Missions for the Pacific.
Leader—Rev. Oscar E. Maurer, D.D.
Place of Meeting—First Congregational Church, 10th and G Sts., N.W.

CHURCH OF GOD:

Missionary Board of the Church of God.
Leader—Rev. J. W. Phelps.
Place of Meeting—Church of God, 15th and D Sts., S.E.

CHURCHES OF GOD:

Board of Missions of the Churches of God in N. A.
Leader—Rev. J. L. Updegraph.
Place of Meeting—New Ebbitt Hotel, 14th and F Sts., N.W.

EPISCOPAL:

Domestic and Foreign Missionary Society of the Protestant Episcopal
Church in the United States of America.
Woman's Auxiliary to the Domestic and Foreign Missionary Society of
the Protestant Episcopal Church in the United States.
Leader—John W. Wood, D.C.L.
Place of Meeting—Church of the Epiphany, G St. bet. 13th and 14th Sts.

EVANGELICAL SYNOD:

The Board of Foreign Missions of the Evangelical Synod of North
America.
Leader—Rev. Charles Enders.
Place of Meeting—Concordia Church, 20th and G Sts., N.W.

EVANGELICAL:

Missionary Society of the Evangelical Church.
Woman's Missionary Society of the Evangelical Church.
Leader—Rev. B. R. Wiener.
Place of Meeting—Hotel Hamilton, 14th and K Sts.

FRIENDS:

American Friends Board of Foreign Missions.
Board of Missions of the Friends Church of California.
Mission Board of Philadelphia Yearly Meeting of Friends.
Friends Foreign Missionary Society of Ohio Yearly Meeting.
Leader—Rev. B. Willis Beede.
Place of Meeting—Friends Meeting House, 13th and Irving Sts., N.W.

LUTHERAN:

Board of Foreign Missions of the United Lutheran Church in America.
Board of Foreign Missions, Augustana Synod of the Lutheran Church.
Leader—Rev. L. B. Wolf, D.D.
Place of Meeting—Luther Place Memorial Church, 14th Street and Vermont Avenue, N.W.
Board of Foreign Missions of the Evangelical Lutheran Joint Synod of Ohio and Other States.
Leader—Rev. J. H. Schneider.
Place of Meeting—Grace Lutheran Church, Joppa Hall, 9th and Upshur Sts., N. W.
Lutheran Board of Missions.
Leader—Rev. Johan Mattson.

MENNONITE:

Mennonite Board of Missions and Charities.
Leader—Bishop S. C. Yoder, Litt. B.S.
Place of Meeting—Mennonite Mission Hall.

METHODIST EPISCOPAL:

Board of Foreign Missions of the Methodist Episcopal Church.
Woman's Foreign Missionary Society of the Methodist Episcopal Church.
Leader—Rev. John R. Edwards, D.D.
Place of Meeting—Union Methodist Episcopal Church, 20th St. bet. H St. and Pennsylvania Ave., N.W.

METHODIST EPISCOPAL, SOUTH:

Board of Missions of the Methodist Episcopal Church, South.
Woman's Missionary Council of the Methodist Episcopal Church South.
Leader—Rev. W. W. Pinson, D.D.

METHODIST, FREE:

General Missionary Board of the Free Methodist Church of North America.
Woman's Missionary Society of the Free Methodist Church of North America.
Leader—Rev. William B. Olmstead, M.A.

METHODIST PROTESTANT:

Union Board of Foreign Missions.
Leader—Rev. J. C. Broomfield, D.D.
Place of Meeting—Rhode Island Avenue Methodist Protestant Church, Rhode Island Ave. and 1st St., N.W.

MORAVIAN:

The Society of the United Brethren for Propagating the Gospel Among the Heathen.
Leader—Paul de Schweinitz, D.D.

PRESBYTERIAN, U. S. A. (NORTH)

Board of Foreign Missions of the Presbyterian Church in the United States of America.
Leader—President J. C. R. Ewing, D.D.
Place of Meeting—New York Avenue Presbyterian Church, New York Ave. and 13th St.

PRESBYTERIAN, U. S. (SOUTHERN)

Executive Committee of Foreign Missions of the Presbyterian Church in the United States.
Woman's Auxiliary of the Presbyterian Church in the United States.
Leader—DR. J. P. MCCALLIE.
Place of Meeting—Assembly Room, Powhatan Hotel, 18th St. and Pennsylvania Ave., N.W.

PRESBYTERIAN, REFORMED:

Board of Foreign Missions of the Synod of the Reformed Presbyterian Church in N. A.
Leader—REV. WALTER MCCARROLL, D.D.
Place of Meeting—St. James Hotel, 6th St. and Pennsylvania Ave.

PRESBYTERIAN, UNITED:

Board of Foreign Missions of the United Presbyterian Church of North America.
Women's General Missionary Society of the United Presbyterian Church of N. A.
Leader—REV. W. B. ANDERSON, D.D.
Place of Meeting—Wallace Memorial United Presbyterian Church, New Hampshire Ave. and Randolph St., N.W.

REFORMED IN AMERICA:

Board of Foreign Missions of the Reformed Church in America.
Woman's Board of Foreign Missions of the Reformed Church in America.
Leader—F. M. POTTER.
Place of Meeting—New York Avenue Presbyterian Church, New York Ave. and 13th St.

REFORMED, CHRISTIAN:

Christian Reformed Board of Missions.
Leader—REV. HENRY BEETS, LL.D.

REFORMED IN THE UNITED STATES:

Board of Foreign Missions of the Reformed Church in the United States.
Woman's Missionary Society of the General Synod of the Reformed Church in the United States.
Leader—REV. ALLEN R. BARTHOLOMEW, D.D.
Place of Meeting—Grace Reformed Church, 1405 Fifteenth St., N.W.

SCHWENKFELDER:

Home and Foreign Board of Missions
Met with Congregational group in
First Congregational Church, 10th and G Sts., N.W.

UNITED BRETHREN:

Foreign Missionary Society of the United Brethren in Christ.
Woman's Missionary Association of the United Brethren in Christ.
Leader—REV. S. G. ZIEGLER, D.D.
Place of Meeting—United Brethren Memorial Church, North Capital and R Streets.

UNIVERSALIST:

Board of Foreign Missions.
Leader—REV. ROGER F. ETZ.
Place of Meeting—Church of Our Father, 13th and K Sts.

ORGANIZATION OF THE CONVENTION

COMMITTEE OF ARRANGEMENTS

Dr. James L. Barton...*Chairman*

Dr. Joseph C. Robbins..................................*Vice-Chairman*

Fennell P. Turner...*Secretary*

Alfred E. Marling...*Treasurer*

Miss Helen Calder	Dr. Frank Mason North
Dr. William I. Chamberlain	Dr. E. H. Rawlings
Dr. Stephen J. Corey	Mrs. Charles K. Roys
Dr. George Drach	Dr. William P. Schell
Dr. James Endicott	Dr. Egbert W. Smith
Miss Mabelle Rae McVeigh	Mrs. Hume R. Steele
Mrs. Thomas Nicholson	Dr. John Wilson Wood

Leslie B. Moss.........................*Assistant Secretary and Registrar*

Wm. P. McCulloch..................................*Assistant Secretary*

H. J. Williams ....*Assistant Registrar*

Harry C. Priest ....*Secretary of Simultaneous Conferences*

PRESS COMMITTEE......................Arthur E. Hungerford, *Chairman*

COMMITTEE ON DAILY BULLETIN..........Dr. J. Lovell Murray, *Chairman*
Miss Corilla Brodnax

EXHIBIT COMMITTEE..................Miss Hollis W. Hering, *Chairman*
Dr. Gilbert LeSourd
Clarence C. Dittmer

COMMITTEE ON USHERS.........................E. W. Hearne, *Chairman*

COMMITTEE ON FRATERNAL DELEGATES......Dr. A. L. Warnshuis, *Chairman*

COMMITTEE ON ENTERTAINMENT OF SPEAKERS AND LEADERS,
Wm. G. Schram, *Chairman*

COMMITTEE ON RAILWAY ARRANGEMENTS........Frank E. Binns, *Chairman*

PRECENTOR.....................................Prof. Charles C. Washburn

PIANISTS.......................Miss Blanche Geary; Mrs. H. J. Williams

LOCAL ARRANGEMENTS COMMITTEE—
Dr. W. S. Abernethy, *Chairman;* Harry L. Heinzman, *Secretary;*
Rex Hopper, *Assistant Secretary.*

HOSPITALITY COMMITTEE....................E. H. de Groot, Jr., *Chairman*

COMMITTEE ON PULPIT SUPPLY................Dr. W. L. Darby, *Chairman*

OFFICERS OF THE FOREIGN MISSIONS CONFERENCE OF NORTH AMERICA

Chairman..............................Rev. Frank Mason North, D.D.
First Vice-Chairman..........................Sir Robert A. Falconer
Second Vice-Chairman.........................Mrs. Anna R. Atwater
Secretary...Fennell P. Turner
Treasurer ....Alfred E. Marling
Honorary Secretary...................................W. Henry Grant

Committee of Reference and Counsel
(The Standing Committee of the Conference)

Chairman........................Rev. William I. Chamberlain, Ph.D.
Vice-Chairman..............................Rev. James Endicott, D.D.
Recording Secretary............................Mrs. Hume R. Steele
Assistant Recording Secretary.............Rev. Frank K. Sanders, Ph.D.
Secretaries.......................Fennell P. Turner; Leslie B. Moss
Treasurer...Alfred E. Marling

William B. Anderson	Miss Mabelle R. McVeigh
Allen E. Armstrong	John R. Mott
Mrs. Anna R. Atwater	Mrs. Thomas Nicholson
Allen R. Bartholomew	B. H. Niebel
James L. Barton	Frank Mason North
Charles D. Bonsack	Cornelius H. Patton
Miss Helen B. Calder	E. H. Rawlings
William I. Chamberlain	Joseph C. Robbins
Stephen J. Corey	William P. Schell
Paul de Schweinitz	Egbert W. Smith
Thomas S. Donohugh	Robert E. Speer
George Drach	James M. Speers
James Endicott	Mrs. Hume R. Steele
William I. Haven	J. G. Vaughan
Miss Margaret E. Hodge	George Grafton Wilson
A. T. Howard	John W. Wood
Miss Sarah S. Lyon	

Ex-Officio:

W. Henry Grant   Alfred E. Marling   Fennell P. Turner

CONVENTION COMMITTEES IN WASHINGTON
GENERAL COMMITTEE
Rev. W. S. Abernethy, D.D., *Chairman*

Rev. W. L. Darby, D.D., *Secretary*

Holcombe G. Johnson, *Treasurer*

Rev. B. F. Bryan, D.D.

Rev. G. M. Diffenderfer, D.D.

Rev. G. F. Dudley, D.D.

Rev. C. E. Fultz, D.D.

Rev. J. Phelps Hand, D.D.

Rev. C. E. Hawthorne

Rev. Murray Kenworthy

Rev. W. A. Lambeth, D.D.

Rev. J. N. Pierce, D.D.

Rev. H. H. Ranck, D.D.

Rev. J. H. Straughn, D.D.

Rev. J. H. Taylor, D.D.

Rev. Earle Wilfley, LL.D.

Rev. Charles Wood, D.D.

FINANCE COMMITTEE
Holcombe G. Johnson, *Chairman*

A. G. Bishop

W. Sinclair Bowen, M.D.

Rufus P. Clarke

F. A. Coffin

J. H. Cooper

Charles Easterly

Fred L. Fishback

T. A. Groover, M.D.

Harold Hayden

Paul E. Lesh

H. D. Ormsby

S. J. Richards

W. McK. Stowell

HALLS AND CHURCHES
Rev. W. A. Eisenberger, *Chairman*

Rev. L. C. Clarke, D.D.   Percy F. Foster   Mrs. H. S. Irwin

HOSPITALITY COMMITTEE
E. H. DeGroot, Jr., *Chairman*

Burns C. Downey

L. W. Glazebrook, M.D.

Mrs. J. M. Heagy

Harry L. Hoskinson

Norton M. Little

Rev. C. S. Longacre

Mrs. W. A. Metz

Mrs. John Nelson Mills

Chas. Warden

Robert Zacharias

C. J. Ziegler

PUBLICITY COMMITTEE
Rev. H. E. Dickens, *Chairman*

B. A. Harlan

J. R. Hildebrand

Gardner Johnson

Jas. P. Schick

WHO'S WHO
Among Speakers and Leaders

ABERLY, REV. JOHN, D.D. Missionary of the United Lutheran Church in India (1890-1923); Instructor of Missions in the Lutheran Theological Seminary, Maywood, Illinois (since 1923).

ABERNETHY, REV. WILLIAM S., D.D. Pastor of Calvary Baptist Church, Washington, D. C.; member Board of Managers of the American Baptist Foreign Mission Society and of the Baptist World's Alliance; Chairman, local Committee of Arrangements of the Convention.

ANDERSON, REV. WILLIAM B., D.D. Corresponding Secretary of the Board of Foreign Missions, United Presbyterian Church; missionary in India, 1897-1909; author of "Far North in India" and "A Watered Garden."

ARCHER, REV. JOHN C., Ph.D. Professor of Missions in the Divinity School, Yale University.

ARMSTRONG, REV. A. E., M.A. Secretary of the Foreign Mission Board, Presbyterian Church in Canada.

AVISON, REV. O. R., M.D. President of the Chosen Christian College in Seoul; missionary of the Board of Foreign Missions of the Presbyterian Church in the U. S. A. (since 1893).

AXLING, REV. WILLIAM, D.D. Missionary of the American Baptist Foreign Missionary Society in Japan (since 1901); author of "Japan on the Upward Trail."

BADLEY, BISHOP BRENTON THOBURN, D.D. Missionary in India (since 1900); Bishop of the Methodist Episcopal Church in India (since 1924); author of "New Etchings of Old India," "Hindustan's Horizons."

BARTHOLOMEW, REV. ALLEN R., D.D. General Secretary of the Board of Foreign Missions of the Reformed Church in the United States; Editor *Outlook of Missions*, author "Won by Prayer," "The Martyr of Huping."

BARTON, REV. JAMES L., D.D., LL.D. Foreign Secretary of the American Board; missionary in Turkey, 1885-1894; Moderator of the International Congregational Council; Chairman of the Executive Committee of the Near East Relief; member International Missionary Council; author of "Educational Missions," "The Christian Approach to Islam," etc.; Chairman of Committee of Arrangements for the present Convention.

BEACH, PROF. HARLAN P., D.D. Professor of Theory and Practice of Missions in the Divinity School, Yale University, 1906-1921; formerly missionary in China; Educational Secretary of Student Volunteer Movement, 1895-1906; co-editor of the World Atlas of Christian Missions (1925) and of the World's Living Religions series; author of "India and Christian Opportunity," "Dawn on the Hills of T'ang," "Renaissant Latin America," etc.

BEAUCHAMP, BISHOP WILLIAM B., of Brussels, Belgium, in charge of Missions in Europe for the Methodist Episcopal Church, South.

BEEDE, B. WILLIS. General Secretary of the American Friends Board of Foreign Missions.

BEETS, REV. HENRY, LL.D. Secretary of Missions, Christian Reformed Church (since 1920); author of "The Christian Reformed Church—Its History, Work and Principles."

BETTIN, REV. A. D.D. Representative of the Rhenish Missionary Society, Germany.

BINNS, FRANK E. Chairman of Committee on Railway Arrangements of the Convention.

BLOUNT, MISS BERTHA A. Missionary in Siam under the Board of Foreign Missions of the Presbyterian Church in the United States of America.

BONSACK, REV. CHARLES D. General Secretary of the General Mission Board of the Church of the Brethren (Dunkers).

BOWLER, REV. W. H., D.D. General Secretary of the Board of Missionary Cooperation of the Northern Baptist Convention.

BRENT, BISHOP CHARLES HENRY, D.D., LL.D. Bishop of the Protestant Episcopal Diocese of Western New York; member of the United States delegation to the International Opium Conferences; Chairman Board of Chaplains of the U. S. Expeditionary Forces; Bishop of the Philippine Islands, 1901-1918; author of "The Mind of Christ," etc.

BREYFOGEL, BISHOP S. C., D.D., LL.D. Bishop of the Evangelical Church (since 1891); author of "Great Sermons by Great Preachers."

BRODNAX, MISS CORILLA G. Secretary, Student Volunteer Movement for Foreign Missions; Secretary of the Daily Bulletin Committee of the Convention.

BROOMFIELD, REV. J. C., D.D. President of the Union Board of Missionary Administration of the Methodist Protestant Church.

BROWN, REV. ARTHUR JUDSON, D.D., LL.D. Secretary, Board of Foreign Missions of the Presbyterian Church in the U. S. A. (since 1895); member of International Missionary Council; author of "The Foreign Missionary," "The Mastery of the Far East," "Unity and Missions," etc.

BRYAN, REV. B. F., D.D. Pastor, Washington, D. C.

BURGESS, REV. PAUL, Ph.D. Missionary in Guatemala, under the Board of Foreign Missions of the Presbyterian Church in the U. S. A.

BURTON, REV. CHARLES E., D.D. Secretary of the National Council of Congregational Churches (since 1921).

BURTON, MISS MARGARET E. Executive Secretary of the Division of Education and Research, National Board of the Young Women's Christian Associations (since 1922); author of "The Education of Women in China," "The Education of the Women of Japan," "Women Workers of the Orient," etc.

CALDER, MISS HELEN B. Home Secretary, Women's Board of Missions (Congregational); member of the International Missionary Council.

CAPEN, REV. EDWARD W., Ph.D. Dean of the Kennedy School of Missions, Hartford Seminary Foundation (since 1919); author of "Sociological Progress in Mission Lands."

CHAMBERLAIN, REV. WILLIAM I., Ph.D. Secretary, Board of Foreign Missions of the Reformed Church in America; missionary in India, 1887-1905; author of "Education in India from B. C. to 1900"; member of the International Missionary Council; Chairman, Committee of Reference and Counsel.

CHESTER, REV. SAMUEL H., D.D., LL.D. Secretary for Foreign Correspondence of the Presbyterian Church in the U. S.; author of "Lights and Shadows of Missionary Work in the Far East"; member of the International Missionary Council.

CLARK, REV. ALDEN H. Missionary in Bombay, India, of the American Board of Commissioners for Foreign Missions (since 1904); recently Candidate Secretary of that Board.

CLIPPINGER, BISHOP A. R., D.D. Bishop of the United Brethren in Christ.

COBB, REV. HENRY E., D.D. Pastor of the West End Reformed (Dutch) Collegiate Church of New York City (since 1903); President of the Board of Foreign Missions, Reformed Church in America; author of "The Ships of Tarshish."

CODY, CANON HENRY J., D.D., LL.D. Rector of St. Paul's Anglican Church, Toronto, Canada; formerly Minister of Education of Ontario; Chairman of Board of Governors, University of Toronto; member of Missionary Society of the Church of England in Canada.

COGSWELL, FRANKLIN D. Secretary, Missionary Education Movement of the United States and Canada; formerly missionary in India.

COOK, MRS. WELLING T. Missionary in Korea of the Presbyterian Church in U. S. A. (since 1908).

COOLIDGE, PRESIDENT CALVIN, LL.D. President of the United States.

COOPER, REV. WILLIAM B., D.D. Secretary of the Canadian Bible Society.

COREY, REV. STEPHEN J., LL.D. Secretary and Vice-President, Department of Foreign Missions, United Christian Missionary Society; member of the International Missionary Council.

CORNELIUS, PROF. J. J. Professor of Philosophy at Lucknow University, India; delegate from India to the Methodist General Conference of 1924; now pursuing special studies at Columbia University, New York.

COUVE, M. DANIEL, D.D. Associate Director of the Paris Evangelical Missionary Society; member of International Missionary Council.

CREITZ, REV. CHARLES E., D.D. President of the Board of Foreign Missions, Reformed Church in the U. S.

DARBY, REV. W. L., D.D. Executive Secretary of the Washington Federation of Churches; Chairman, Committee on Pulpit Supply of the Convention.

DAVIS, MISS ELIZA R. Member of the National Council of the Protestant Episcopal Church.

DENISON, REV. W. H., D.D. Stewardship Secretary of the Foreign Mission Board of the Christian Church.

DE SCHWEINITZ, REV. PAUL, D.D. Secretary of Missions of the Moravian Church in America (since 1898); member of the International Missionary Council.

DIFFENDERFER, REV. G. M., D.D. Pastor of Luther Place Memorial Lutheran Church, Washington, D. C.

DIFFENDORFER, REV. RALPH E., D.D. Secretary of the Board of Foreign Missions of the Methodist Episcopal Church; author of "The Church and the Community," "Missionary Education in Church and School," etc.

DITTMER, CLARENCE C. In charge of Literature Department of the Committee of Reference and Counsel; member of Exhibit Committee of the present Convention.

DOAN, ROBERT A. Manufacturer in Columbus, Ohio; layman of the United Christian Missionary Society; recently returned from a tour of mission fields.

DODD, E. M., M.D. Acting Secretary, Medical Department, Board of Foreign Missions of the Presbyterian Church, U. S. A.; formerly missionary in Persia of that Board.

DONOHUGH, REV. THOMAS S. Associate Secretary, Board of Foreign Missions of the Methodist Episcopal Church; Secretary of International Association of Agricultural Missions; formerly missionary in India.

DOOLITTLE, MISS MARGARET B. Missionary in Colombia of the Presbyterian Church, U. S. A.

DRACH, REV. GEORGE, D.D. Secretary of the Board of Foreign Missions of the United Lutheran Church in America; author of "Forces in Foreign Missions."

DUDLEY, REV. GEORGE F., D.D. Rector of St. Stephen's Protestant Episcopal Church, Washington, D. C.

EAST, REV. J. E. Secretary of the Foreign Mission Board of the National Baptist Convention; editor of *The Mission Herald.*

EDDY, REV. D. BREWER, D.D. Associate Secretary of the American Board of Commissioners for Foreign Missions.

EDIE, REV. RAYMOND L. Secretary of United Presbyterian Board of Foreign Missions.

EDWARDS, REV. JOHN R., D.D. Corresponding Secretary of the Board of Foreign Missions, Methodist Episcopal Church.

EHNES, REV. MORRIS W., D.D. Treasurer of the Board of Foreign Missions, Methodist Episcopal Church.

ENDERS, REV. CHARLES. Pastor of the Evangelical Church, Washington, D. C.

ENDICOTT, REV. JAMES, D.D. General Secretary, Foreign Department, Missionary Society of the Methodist Church, Canada; formerly missionary in West China; member of the International Missionary Council.

ERDMAN, REV. CHARLES R., D.D. Professor of Practical Theology in Princeton Theological Seminary (since 1906); member of the Board of Foreign Missions, Presbyterian Church, U. S. A.; author of "Within the Gateways of the Far East."

ETZ, REV. ROGER F. Secretary of the Board of Foreign Missions of the Universalist Church.

EWING, REV. JAMES C. R., D.D. Formerly missionary in India; President of Forman Christian College (1888 to 1918); Vice Chancellor University of the Punjab, 1910-1917; President of the Board of Foreign Missions of the Presbyterian Church in the U. S. A.; lecturer on Missions, Princeton Theological Seminary; from King George V, Knight Commander of Indian Empire, 1923.

FIELD, JAY C. Secretary of the Foreign Division, National Council of Y. M. C. A., in Peru, South America (since 1910).

FLEMING, REV. PROF. D. J., Ph.D. Professor of Missions in Union Theological Seminary, New York (since 1915); missionary in India of the Presbyterian Board of Foreign Missions, U. S. A., 1904-1913; author of "Building With India," "Contacts With Non-Christian Cultures," etc.

FORBES, MRS. G. ERNEST. President of the Presbyterian Woman's Missionary Society of Canada (Eastern Division).

FORGAN, REV. ROBERT, D.D. Cosvener of the Foreign Missions Committee of the United Free Church of Scotland; member of the International Missionary Council.

FRANKLIN, REV. JAMES H., D.D. Foreign Secretary of the American Baptist Foreign Mission Society (since 1912); member of the International Missionary Council; author of "Ministers of Mercy."

FREEMAN, BISHOP JAMES E., D.D. Bishop of the Diocese of Washington, D. C. (since 1923); author of "The Man and the Master."

FURSE, BISHOP MICHAEL BOLTON, D.D. Bishop of the Diocese of St. Albans, England (since 1919); formerly Archdeacon of Johannesburg, 1903-1909, and Bishop of Pretoria, 1909-1919; Dean and Fellow of Trinity College, Oxford, 1895-1903; Chairman of Home Base Committee, Missionary Council of the Church of England.

GAMEWELL, REV. FRANK D., LL.D. Missionary in China under the Methodist Episcopal Board since 1881; General Secretary of the China Christian Educational Association since 1912; editor of the *Educational Review* (China).

GANDIER, REV. ALFRED, D.D., LL.D. Principal of Knox College, Toronto, Canada; Chairman of the Board of Foreign Missions of the Presbyterian Church in Canada; ex-Moderator of the General Assembly of that church; member of the International Missionary Council; author of "The Son of Man Coming in His Kingdom."

GATES, REV. HERBERT W., D.D. Secretary of the Missionary Education Department of the Congregational Educational Society; author "Life of Jesus," (for intermediate pupils), "Heroes of the Faith," "Recreation and the Church."

GEARY, MISS BLANCHE. Formerly Secretary of the National Board of the Young Women's Christian Association; one of the pianists for the Convention.

GOFORTH, REV. JONATHAN, D.D. Missionary in China of the Canadian Presbyterian Board of Foreign Missions for more than thirty years.

GOODSELL, REV. FRED F. Missionary in Turkey of the American Board of Commissioners for Foreign Missions (since 1907); Principal of the School of Religion and of the Language School, Constantinople.

GOULD, CANON S., M.D., D.C.L. General Secretary of the Missionary Society of the Church of England in Canada; formerly missionary in Palestine of that Society; member of the International Missionary Council.

GRANT, W. HENRY. Secretary of the Canton Christian College; Honorary Secretary of the Foreign Missions Conference; for twenty-five years active Secretary of the Conference.

GROESBECK, REV. A. F., D.D. Missionary in China of the American Baptist Foreign Mission Society for twenty-seven years.

DEGROOT, E. H., JR. Director of Signal and Train Controls, Interstate Commerce Commission, Washington, D. C.; President, District Council of Religious Education and Board of Directors, Central Union Missions; Chairman of the Hospitality Committee of the Convention.

HALL, REV. ERNEST F., D.D. Secretary of the Eastern District Home Base Department, Board of Foreign Missions of the Presbyterian Church, U. S. A.; formerly missionary in Korea.

HAVEN, REV. WILLIAM I., D.D., LL.D. General Secretary of the American Bible Society (since 1899).

HEARNE, E. W. State Secretary of the Young Men's Christian Association for Massachusetts and Rhode Island; Chairman of Committee on Ushers for the Convention.

HEATH, REV. GEORGE R. Agent of the American Bible Society in Nicaragua.

HEINZMAN, HARRY L. Religious Work Director of the Young Men's Christian Association, Tulsa, Oklahoma; Secretary, local Arrangements Committee of the Convention.

HENRY, REV. JAMES M., D.D. President of Canton Christian College; missionary in China since 1917.

HERING, MISS HOLLIS W. Librarian, Missionary Research Library of the Foreign Missions Conference of North America, New York City; Chairman of the Exhibit Committee of the Convention.

HERMAN, REV. S. W., D.D. Pastor of the Zion Lutheran Church in Harrisburg, Pa.

HIVALE, REV. BHASKAR PANDURANG. Graduate of Bombay University and Andover Theological Seminary; connected with the Marathi Mission of the American Board and former editor of the "Dnyanodaya," the second oldest Anglo-Vernacular weekly paper in Bombay.

HODGE, MISS MARGARET E. Vice-president of the Board of Foreign Missions of the Presbyterian Church in the U. S. A.; formerly President of the Federation of Women's Boards of Foreign Missions.

HOPPER, REX D. Assistant Secretary of the Local Arrangements Committee of the Convention.

HOWELL, MISS MABEL K. Secretary of the Department of Foreign Missions of the Board of Missions, Methodist Episcopal Church, South.

HULL, PROF. WILLIAM I., Ph.D. Professor of History and International Relations at Swarthmore College; author of various books on International Relations.

HUNGERFORD, ARTHUR E. Chairman of the Press Committee for the Convention.

HUNT, MISS HELEN K. Dean of Women in Judson College, Burma; missionary of the American Baptist Foreign Mission Society (since 1919).

HURLBURT, REV. CHARLES E. General Director of the Home Council for North America of the Africa Inland Mission.

HURREY, CHARLES D. Secretary of the Committee on Friendly Relations of the National Council of Young Men's Christian Associations; one of the Secretaries of the World's Student Christian Federation.

INMAN, REV. SAMUEL G., D.D. Secretary of the Committee on Cooperation in Latin America (since 1915); missionary in Mexico of the United Christian Missionary Society (1906-1915); author of "South America Today," "Problems in Pan-Americanism," etc.

JONES, REV. E. STANLEY, D.D. Missionary in India of the Methodist Episcopal Church (since 1907).

JONES, PROF. RUFUS M., LL.D. Professor of Philosophy at Haverford College (since 1904); author of "The Abundant Life," "Studies in Mystical Religion," "Religious Foundations," etc.

JONES, THOMAS JESSE, Ph.D. Educational Director, Phelps-Stokes Fund (since 1913); Chairman of Educational Commissions to West, South, and Equatorial Africa; author of "Negro Education in the United States" and "Education in Africa."

KAGAWA, REV. T. Graduate of Princeton Theological Seminary; pastor in a slum church of Kobe, Japan; lecturer at the Imperial University in Tokyo; one of the founders of the Japan Labor Federation and of the Peasants' Union; author of "Psychology of Poverty," "Across the Death Line," etc.

KERR, REV. HUGH T., D.D. Pastor of Shadyside Presbyterian Church in Pittsburgh, Pa.; author of "Missionary Sermons for Children" (two series), etc.

KIRK, REV. HARRIS E., D.D. Pastor of the Franklin Street Presbyterian Church in Baltimore, Md. (since 1901); professor in Princeton University; author of "The Religion of Power" and "The Consuming Fire"; recently returned from a tour in the Far East.

KNUBEL, REV. F. H., D.D., LL.D. President of the United Lutheran Church in America (since 1918).

LAMBETH, REV. W. A. Pastor of the Mt. Vernon Place Church, Methodist Episcopal, South, Washington, D. C.

LAMPE, REV. WILLIAM E., Ph.D. Secretary of the United Stewardship and Missionary Committee of the General Synod, Reformed Church in the U. S.

LANDES, WILLIAM G., C.E.D. General Secretary of the World's Sunday School Association.

LERRIGO, P. H. J., M.D. Home Secretary of the American Baptist Foreign Mission Society (since 1921); missionary in the Philippines (1902-1913).

LESOURD, DR. GILBERT Q. Conference and Promotion Secretary of the Missionary Education Movement for the United States and Canada; member of Exhibit Committee of the Convention.

LEWIS, MISS IDA BELLE, Ph.D. Missionary in China of the Women's Foreign Missionary Society of the Methodist Episcopal Church.

LIPPHARD, WILLIAM B. Secretary of the American Baptist Foreign Mission Society.

LOVEJOY, REV. LUTHER E. Secretary for Stewardship of the Board of Foreign Missions, Methodist Episcopal Church.

LUNDAHL, REV. JAKOB E. Secretary of the Svenska Missionsförbundet, and of the Swedish Missionary Council.

MACGILLIVRAY, REV. DONALD, D.D., LL.D. Secretary of the Christian Literature Society for China; missionary in China of the Presbyterian Church in Canada (since 1888).

MACKENZIE, MISS JEAN KENYON. Missionary in Africa of the Presbyterian Church, U. S. A., 1904-1913; author of "Black Sheep," "An African Trail," "The Story of a Fortunate Youth," etc.

MACKENZIE, PRESIDENT WILLIAM DOUGLAS, D.D., LL.D. President of the Hartford Seminary Foundation (since 1904); author of "John Mackenzie, South African Missionary and Statesman," "The Final Faith," "Christian Ethics in the World War"; Chairman, Committee on the Preparation of Missionaries, Foreign Missions Conference of North America.

MACLENNAN, KENNETH. Secretary of the Standing Committee of the Conference of Missionary Societies in Great Britain and Ireland; Secretary of the United Council for Missionary Education in Great Britain; member of the International Missionary Council.

MACRAE, PROF. J. D. Dean of the School of Theology, Shantung Christian University, Tsinan, China; missionary of the Presbyterian Church in Canada (since 1909).

MCCALLIE, JAMES P., Ph.D. Head Master of McCallie School, Chattanooga, Tennessee; member of the Executive Committee of Foreign Missions of the Presbyterian Church in the U. S.

MCCARROLL, REV. WALTER, D.D. Pastor of the Reformed Presbyterian Church in New York City.

MCCAUSLAND, MISS ISABELLE. Missionary in Kobe, Japan, of the Woman's Board of Missions (Congregational).

MCCLENAHAN, ROBERT S., LL.D. Dean, College of Arts and Sciences of the American University at Cairo; missionary in Egypt of the United Presbyterian Church in America (since 1897).

MCCONAUGHY, DAVID. Secretary for Stewardship of the Home Base Division, Board of Foreign Missions, Presbyterian Church, U. S. A.

MCCONNELL, BISHOP FRANCIS J., Ph.D., D.D. Bishop of the Methodist Episcopal Church (since 1912); President of De Pauw University, 1909-1912; author of "Democratic Christianity," "The Preacher and the People," etc.

McCULLOCH, WILLIAM P.   Assistant Treasurer, Princeton Theological Seminary; Business Secretary of the Student Volunteer Movement for Foreign Missions, 1906-1922; Assistant Secretary of the Convention.

McDOWELL, REV. HENRY C.   Missionary in Angola, Africa, of the American Board.

McDOWELL, BISHOP WILLIAM F., D.D., LL.D.   Bishop of the Methodist Episcopal Church (since 1904); author of "A Man's Religion" and "Good Ministers of Jesus Christ."

McKEE, REV. W. J.   Missionary in India of the Presbyterian Board (since 1909).

McLAURIN, REV. JOHN B., B.Th.   Missionary in India of the Canadian Baptist Missionary Society (since 1909); Principal of Canadian Baptist Theological Seminary, Madras Presidency.

McLEAN, REV. J. H., D.D.   Missionary in Chile of the Presbyterian Church, U. S. A. (since 1906); author of "The Living Christ for Latin America."

MANIKAM, R. B.   Student from India, now at the Union Theological Seminary, New York City, preparing for educational work in connection with the United Lutheran Church in India.

MARLING, ALFRED E.   President, Horace Ely & Co., New York City; formerly Chairman International Committee, Young Men's Christian Association; member of Presbyterian Board of Foreign Missions, U. S. A.; Treasurer of the Foreign Missions Conference of North America.

MATHER, ASHER K.   Missionary of the American Baptist Foreign Mission Society in Assam (1914-1920); recorder of Denison University since 1920.

MATTSON, REV. JOHAN.   Secretary of the Lutheran Board of Missions.

MAURER, REV. OSCAR E., D.D.   Pastor of the Center Congregational Church, New Haven, Conn.; author of "The Brotherhood of the Burning Heart."

MELVIN, REV. M. E.   Secretary of the Assembly Stewardship Committee of the Presbyterian Church in the U. S.; member of the Executive Committee of Foreign Missions of that Church.

MOSS, LESLIE B., M.A.   Secretary of the Committee of Reference and Counsel, Foreign Missions Conference of N. A.; missionary in Nanking, China, of the American Baptist Foreign Mission Society, 1915-1920; Assistant Secretary and Registrar of the Convention.

MOTT, JOHN R., LL.D.   General Secretary of the National Council of Young Men's Christian Associations (since 1915); Chairman of the International Missionary Council (since 1920); Chairman of the General Committee, World's Student Christian Federation; author of "The Pastor and Modern Missions," "Confronting Young Men with the Living Christ," etc.

MOUZON, BISHOP EDWIN D., D.D.   Bishop of the Methodist Episcopal Church, South; President of the Board of Education of that Church; author of "Fundamentals of Methodism."

MURRAY, REV. J. LOVELL, D.D.   Director of the Canadian School of Missions, Toronto, Canada; Educational Secretary of the Student Volunteer Movement, 1906-1921; formerly a missionary in India; author of "The Call of a World Task," "World Friendship, Inc.," etc.; Chairman of Daily Bulletin Committee of the Convention.

MYERS, REV. HARRY S.   Recording Secretary of the Missionary Education Movement of the United States and Canada.

NICHOLSON, MRS. THOMAS.   President of the Woman's Foreign Missionary Society of the Methodist Episcopal Church; member of the International Missionary Council; author of "Educating for Peace."

NORTH, REV. ERIC M., Ph.D.   Secretary of China Union Universities.

NORTH, REV. FRANK MASON, D.D., LL.D.   Secretary of the Board of Foreign Missions of the Methodist Episcopal Church (since 1912); Chairman of the Foreign Missions Conference of North America; formerly President of the Federal Council of the Churches of Christ in America; member of the International Missionary Council.

OLDHAM, JOSEPH H., M.A.   Secretary, World Missionary Conference, Edinburgh, 1910; Secretary of the Edinburgh Continuation Committee and, since 1920, of the International Missionary Council; editor of the *International Review of Missions;* author of "The World and the Gospel," "Christianity and the Race Problem," etc.

OLMSTEAD, REV. WILLIAM B.   General Secretary of the General Missionary Board of the Free Methodist Church of North America.

PALMER, MISS CAROLINE L.   Professor of the English Bible and Sociology in the Biblical Seminary of New York (since 1902).

PARSON, REV. ARTLEY B. Educational Secretary of the Domestic and Foreign Missionary Society of the Protestant Episcopal Church; formerly a missionary in the Philippines.

PATTON, REV. CORNELIUS H., D.D. Home Secretary of the American Board of Commissioners for Foreign Missions (since 1904); author of "The Lure of Africa" and "The Business of Missions."

PEABODY, MRS. HENRY W. Chairman of Central Committee for the United Study of Missions; formerly a missionary in India; President of Woman's National Committee for Law Enforcement; founder and editor of *Everyland;* former President, Federation of Women's Boards of Foreign Missions.

PHELPS, REV. J. W. Secretary of the Missionary Board of the Church of God.

PIERCE, REV. JASON N., D.D. Pastor of the First Congregational Church, Washington, D. C. (since 1920); author of "The Masculine Power of Christ" and "Together in the Heavenly Home."

PINSON, REV. W. W., D.D. Secretary of the Board of Missions of the Methodist Episcopal Church, South; author "Life of Walter Russell Lambuth."

POTTER, FRANCIS M. Formerly missionary in India, Home Secretary and Treasurer of the Board of Foreign Missions of the Reformed Church in America.

PRIEST, REV. HARRY C. Secretary of the Canadian Council, Missionary Education Movement (since 1910); Secretary of the Interchurch Advisory Council of Canada; formerly a missionary in India of the Canadian Baptist Foreign Mission Board; Secretary of Simultaneous Conferences of the Convention.

PYE, REV. WATTS O. Missionary in Shansi, China, of the American Board (since 1907).

RAWLINGS, REV. EUGENE H., D.D. Foreign Secretary of the Board of Missions of the Methodist Episcopal Church, South (since 1917).

RAWLINSON, REV. FRANK, D.D. Editor of *The Chinese Recorder* (since 1912); missionary in China (since 1902); author of "The Life of Christ" (in Chinese).

REISCHAUER, REV. AUGUST K., Ph.D. Professor of Theology in Meiji Gakuin, Japan; missionary in that country of the Presbyterian Church, U. S. A. (since 1905); member National Christian Council of Japan; author of "Studies in Japanese Buddhism."

RICHARDS, REV. E. H., D.D. Agent of the American Bible Society.

RICHARDS, REV. GEORGE W., D.D. President of the Theological Seminary of the Reformed Church in the U. S.; President of the General Synod of that church; author of "Historical and Doctrinal Studies on the Heidelberg Catechism."

RICHTER, REV. PROF. JULIUS, D.D. Professor in the Department of Missions in the University of Berlin; author of "History of Missions in India," "A History of Protestant Missions in the Near East," etc.; editor, *Allgemeine Missionszeitschrift.*

ROBBINS, REV. JOSEPH C., D.D. Foreign Secretary of the American Baptist Foreign Mission Society (since 1916); missionary in the Philippines, 1902-1909; formerly Candidate Secretary and later Chairman of the Executive Committee of the Student Volunteer Movement; author of "The Appeal of India," "Following the Pioneers"; Vice-Chairman of Committee of Arrangements of the Convention.

ROBERTSON, REV. J. C., D.D. Secretary of the Board of Sunday Schools and Young People's Work, Presbyterian Church in Canada.

ROWELL, HON. NEWTON W., LL.D. A leading Canadian lawyer; during the war years President of the Canadian War Cabinet; member of the International Missionary Council; member of the Missionary Society of the Methodist Church, Canada.

ROYS, MRS. CHARLES K. Secretary of the Board of Foreign Missions of the Presbyterian Church, U. S. A.; missionary in Shantung, China, 1904-1920; author of "The Missionary Wife."

RYAN, REV. ARTHUR C. Secretary of the American Bible Society in Constantinople.

SANDERS, REV. FRANK K., Ph.D., D.D. Director of Committee on Missionary Preparation of the Foreign Missions Conference of North America; author of "Messages of the Earlier Prophets," "History of the Hebrews" and "The Program of Christianity"; Assistant Recording Secretary of Committee of Reference and Counsel.

SCHELL, REV. WILLIAM P., D.D. Executive Secretary of the Home Base Department, Board of Foreign Missions, Presbyterian Church in the U. S. A.

SCHLUNK, MISSIONSINSPEKTOR M., D.Th. Secretary of the North German Missionary Society (Bremen Mission); Secretary of the Deutscher Evangelischer Missionsbund; member of the International Missionary Council.

SCHNEIDER, REV. J. H. Secretary of the Board of Foreign Missions of the Evangelical Lutheran Joint Synod of Ohio and Other States.

SCHRAM, WILLIAM G. Controller, Foreign Department International Committee, Y. M. C. A.; Assistant Treasurer, Committee of Reference and Council; Secretary of Committee on Entertainment of Speakers and Leaders of the Convention.

SCHULTZ, MISS GERTRUDE. Executive Secretary of the Home Base Department, Board of Foreign Missions, Presbyterian Church in the U. S. A.

SCOTT, REV. GEORGE T., D.D. Secretary of the Board of Foreign Missions, Presbyterian Church in the U. S. A.

SEABURY, MISS RUTH I. Secretary of the Young People's Department, Woman's Board of Missions (Congregational).

SHANTZ, HOMER LEROY, Ph.D. Plant Physiologist of the Bureau of Plant Industry, U. S. Department of Agriculture, Washington, D. C.

SIBLEY, REV. E. A. Member of the National Council of the Protestant Episcopal Church.

SILVERTHORN, MRS. E. H. President of the Federation of Women's Boards of Foreign Missions of North America.

SIZOO, REV. J. R. Pastor of New York Avenue Presbyterian Church, Washington, D. C.

SLACK, FRANK V. Personnel Secretary for Southern Asia at the Home Base, in the Foreign Division, International Committee Y. M. C. A.

SLOAN, T. DWIGHT, M.D. Medical Superintendent of Peking Union Hospital; former missionary of the Presbyterian Board, U. S. A.

SMITH, REV. HERBERT. Missionary in Africa of the United Christian Missionary Society.

SOPER, REV. EDMUND D., D.D. Professor of History of Religion, Northwestern University (since 1919); author of "The Faiths of Mankind" and "The Religions of Mankind."

SPEER, ROBERT E., D.D. Secretary of the Board of Foreign Missions, Presbyterian Church in the U. S. A. (since 1891); Chairman of the Committee on Cooperation in Latin America; ex-President of the Federal Council of the Churches of Christ in America; author of "South American Problems," "Christianity and the Nations," "Of One Blood," etc.; member of the International Missionary Council.

SPEERS, JAMES M. President of James McCutcheon and Company (since 1914); Chairman of International Committee of Young Men's Christian Associations; Vice-president of Presbyterian Board of Foreign Missions, U. S. A.; Treasurer of the International Missionary Council.

STAUFFER, REV. MILTON T., F.R.G.S. Educational Secretary of the Student Volunteer Movement of North America (since 1922); missionary in China, 1916-1922; editor of "The Christian Occupation of China."

STEELE, MRS. HUME R. Woman's Department of the Board of Missions of Methodist Episcopal Church, South; Recording Secretary of the Committee of Reference and Counsel of Foreign Missions Conference of North America.

STEVENSON, REV. J. ROSS, D.D., LL.D. President of Princeton Theological Seminary (since 1914); Chairman of the Department of Church Cooperation and Union of the General Assembly, Presbyterian Church in the U. S. A.; ex-Moderator of that body.

STILLWELL, REV. HARRY E. Secretary of the Canadian Baptist Foreign Mission Board; formerly missionary in India under that Board.

STIMSON, REV. HENRY A., D.D. Pastor emeritus of Manhattan Congregational Church, New York City; author of "The New Things of God" and "While the War Rages."

STOKES, CANON ANSON PHELPS, D.D., LL.D. President of the Phelps-Stokes Foundation; President of the Yale Foreign Missionary Society; Secretary Yale University, 1899-1921; author of "University Schools of Religion" and "What Jesus Christ Thought of Himself."

STRAUGHN, REV. J. H., D.D. Pastor of Rhode Island Avenue Methodist Protestant Church of Washington, D. C.

STROCK, REV. J. ROY. Missionary in India of the United Lutheran Church (since 1908); Principal of Noble College, Masulipatam.

STUART, H. F. Missionary in the Philippines of the American Baptist Foreign Mission Society.

TAYLOR, REV. JAMES HENRY, D.D. Pastor of the Central Presbyterian Church, Washington, D. C.

TAYLOR, W. A., D.Sc. Chief of the Bureau of Plant Industry, Department of Agriculture, Washington, D. C. (since 1913).

TUCKER, REV. HENRY C., D.D. Secretary of the American Bible Society in Brazil.

TUCKER, BISHOP HENRY ST. GEORGE, D.D. Missionary in Japan of the Protestant Episcopal Church for many years; Bishop of the Diocese of Kyoto (1899-1923); author of "Reconciliation Through Christ."

TURNER, FENNELL P. Secretary of the Foreign Missions Conference of North America and the Committee of Reference and Counsel (since 1919); General Secretary, Student Volunteer Movement, 1897-1919; member of the International Missionary Council; Executive Secretary of the Convention.

UPDEGRAPH, REV. J. L. Secretary of the Board of Missions of the Churches of God in North America.

VAN BOETZLAER VAN DUBBELDAM, BARON, C. W. Th., of Utrecht, Holland; formerly Missionary Consul in Batavia, Dutch East Indies; member of the International Missionary Council.

VAUGHAN, J. G., M.D. Medical Director, Board of Foreign Missions, Methodist Episcopal Church; missionary in China under that Board, 1909-1916.

WANLESS, W. J., M.D. Missionary in India of the Board of Foreign Missions of the Presbyterian Church in the U. S. A. (since 1889).

WARK, REV. HOMER C., Ph.D. Professor of Missions in the Boston University School of Theology, Boston, Mass.

WARNSHUIS, REV. A. L., D.D. Secretary of the International Missionary Council (since 1920); missionary in China of the Reformed Church in America, 1900-1920; Secretary of China Continuation Committee, 1915-1920; author of "Manual of the Amoy Language"; Chairman of Committee on Fraternal Delegates of the Convention.

WARNSHUIS, REV. JOHN H., M.A. Missionary in South India, under the Board of Foreign Missions of the Reformed Church in America.

WASHBURN, CHARLES C. Professor in Scarrett College for Christian Workers, Nashville, Tenn.; Leader of Music at present Convention.

WEEMS, REV. C. N. Missionary in Korea of the Methodist Episcopal Church, South (since 1909).

WELCH, BISHOP HERBERT, D.D., LL.D. Bishop of the Methodist Episcopal district of Japan and Korea; President of Ohio Wesleyan University, 1905-1916; editor of "Selections from the Writings of John Wesley."

WIENER, REV. B. R. Field Secretary of the Board of Missions of the Evangelical Church.

WILDER, ROBERT P., M.A. Founder and (since 1919) General Secretary of the Student Volunteer Movement of North America; missionary in India, 1892-1902; member of General Committee, World's Student Christian Federation; author of "Among India's Students" and "The Red Triangle in the Changing Nations."

WILFLEY, REV. EARLE, D.D. Pastor of the Vermont Avenue Christian Church, Washington, D. C.

WILLIAMS, RT. REV. DAVID, D.D., Bishop of Huron; Chairman of the Executive Committee, Missionary Society of the Church of England in Canada.

WILLIAMS, HUGH J. Missionary of the United Christian Missionary Society under appointment to South America; Assistant Registrar of the Convention.

WILLIAMS, MRS. HUGH J. Also under appointment to South America; one of the pianists for the Convention.

WINGER, REV. OTHO, D.D. President of the General Mission Board of the Church of the Brethren.

WOLF, REV. LUTHER B., D.D. General Secretary of the Board of Foreign Missions of the United Lutheran Church in America; missionary in India, 1883-1907; author of "Missionary Heroes of the Lutheran Church"; member of the International Missionary Council.

WOOD, REV. CHARLES, D.D., LL.D. Pastor of the Church of the Covenant (Presbyterian), Washington, D. C.; author of "The Living Christ and Some Problems of Today."

WOOD, JAMES, LL.D. President emeritus of the American Bible Society.

WOOD, JOHN W., D.C.L. General Secretary of the Domestic and Foreign Missionary Society of the Protestant Episcopal Church (since 1900); member of the International Missionary Council.

WOOLLEY, PRESIDENT MARY E., Litt.D., LL.D. President of Mount Holyoke College (since 1900); member of China Educational Commission in 1921-1922; member, Board of Directors, World Alliance for Promoting International Friendship Through the Churches.

WRIGHT, REV. GEORGE W., D.D. Missionary in the Philippines of the Board of Foreign Missions, Presbyterian Church, U. S. A.

WYSHAM, REV. WILLIAM N. Acting Candidate Secretary of the Board of Foreign Missions, Presbyterian Church, U. S. A.; missionary in Persia of that Board.

YODER, BISHOP S. C., Litt. B.S. Secretary of the Mennonite Board of Missions and Charities.

ZIEGLER, REV. S. G., D.D. Secretary of the Foreign Missionary Conference, United Brethren in Christ.

ZWEMER, REV. SAMUEL M., D.D., LL.D. Missionary in Arabia and Egypt of the Reformed Church in America (since 1891); Field Secretary, American Christian Literature Society for Moslems; editor of *The Moslem World;* author of "The Unoccupied Fields of Africa and Asia," "Raymond Lull," "A Moslem Seeker After God," "The Moslem Doctrine of God," etc.

INDEX

INDEX

A

Abdullah, Malay Munshi, quoted, 358.
Abyssinia, 23, 304.
Achimota, work done by Fraser in, 118.
Acts, book of, additional chapters to, 224-225; described, 253; "To be continued," 278-279.
Address by President Calvin Coolidge, 4-7: missionary spirit, 4; missionary movement in early centuries, 4; spread of Christianity in Roman world, 4; promise of immortality brought to Roman world, 4; early Christians charged with trust, 4; need for revival of faith, 4-5; Christianity practical mode of life, 5; Christianity added to complexity of civilization, 5; education encouraged by Christianity, 5; brotherhood of races through Christianity, 5; neighborship true basis of Christianity, 5; problems of Christianity to be solved by neighborship, 5; missionary movements hampered by un-Christian motives, 6; early Christians, 6; service must rest on toleration, 6; spirit of brotherhood, 6; lessons from mission lands, 6.
Aden, Gulf of, 94
"Adequate Foreign Missionary Program in a Congregation," address by S. W. Herman, 233-237: conditions in the average congregation, 234; congregation must be in sympathy with boards, 234; missionary program of average congregation, 234; program of education in the congregation, 235; congregation must appreciate its spiritual resources, 236; each congregation should support its own workers on the mission field, 236-237.
"Adequate Foreign Missionary Program of a Denomination," address by Ralph E. Diffendorfer, 227-233: mission program must be promoted throughout denominations at home, 227-228; methods of cultivating home base for new mission program, 228; continual study of motive necessary, 228; responsibility for study of missions lies on boards, 228, 229; former and present motives, 228; love present motive, 228; still many regions unoccupied by missions, 229; phases of social living yet to be reached, 229; agents of Christian nations must be Christian, 229; problem to make all our contacts Christian, 230; problem of cooperation with national churches, 230-231; challenge of foreign students in America, 230; cooperation with national churches, 230-231; problems for churches of non-Christian lands to solve, 231; need of greatly enlarged program of missionary education, 232; early books on missions, 232; economic imperialism to be studied, 232; narrow conceptions of God, 233.
Adriani, N., translator, 359.
Aegean Sea, gospel preached near, 144.
Afghanistan, 23; liberty denied in, 402.
Africa, interracial relations in, 9; sacrifices in, 13; dancing in, 14; control of white race, 19; address by Henry C. McDowell on "The Gospel Among Primitive Peoples," 88-94; reception of missionary in, 89; method of preaching in, 89; evangelizing through schools in, 89; missionary spirit in, 90; death of convert in, 92; story of brush fire in, 94; address by Charles E. Hurlburt on "The Gospel Among Primitive Peoples," 94-97; story of conversion of tribe in, 95; visit of Theodore Roosevelt in, 95;

lepers in, 96; need in, 96; need of educated missionaries in, 97; East and South, competition of giving in, 173; Central, native of, and radio, 177; nine-tenths of education in, in hands of missionaries, 178; railroad built in, 236; article by Julius Richter on "Moslem Aggression in Africa," 295-299; colonial policies of France and Great Britain in, 296-298, rising tide of European civilization in, 298-299; missionary strongholds in, 299; Mohammedans in, 301; paucity of Christian literature in, 325; work on literature for, 326; address on "Translating in Portuguese East Africa," 353-357; agricultural missions, 371-372; visited by Archbishop of Canterbury, 389; conferences on, 421.
Aggrey, Dr. J. E. K., of Africa, 178.
Agra, royal city of, 37.
"Agricultural and Industrial Missions," notes of a conference on, 366-374.
"Agricultural Education in Colleges," conference notes by W. Henry Grant, 370-371.
Agricultural, education in India, results and requirements of, 369; colleges in China, 370-371; work done in 235 mission stations, 371; work done by Salvation Army, 372; problems and methods in East Africa, 373-374; conferences on, 416.
Agriculture, teaching of, in Latin America, 313; and fulness of life, 366; importance of, 366; depreciation of, 366; mission communities dependent on, 367; scientific study of, 367.
Agriculture, United States Department of, work of, 371; correspondence of, with missionaries, 372-373; seeds furnished by, 373; contributions to, by missionaries, 373; how to get in touch with, 373.
"Aim and Motive of Foreign Missions," address by E. Stanley Jones, 52-60; criticisms of missionaries, 52; Western civilization point of attack, 52; motive of missions, 52-53; solution of missionary problem in India, 53; aims of religions of world, 53-54; Jesus' life itself supreme motive, 54-55; new revelation in India, 56; Western civilization at ebb in India, 56; Mahatma Gandhi quoted, 57; no mild form of Christianity needed, 57; love the central thing, 58; Christ the Inescapable, 59; Christ bidding for heart of world, 60.
Aims, of religions of world epitomized, 53; see Objectives.
Albania, 23.
Albert, Lake, 95.
Albums, suggested for children, 281.
Alessandri, Arturo, President of Chile, mentioned, 319.
Allahabad, India, Agricultural Institute, 370.
Allahabad, India, blind in, 403.
Allegiances, need not conflict, 186.
Allégret, E., missionary statesman, 215.
Allis, Oswald T., address by, on "The Problems of Bible Translation," 347-351.
Amazon River, Indians in jungles of, 321.
Amboina, Dutch East Indies, and Bible version, 358.
American Bible Society, source of supply of printed Word, 345; work of, 347; mentioned, 393.
American Board of Missions, in Malaysia, 358.
American College of Surgeons, 127.
Amsterdam, Classis of, 392.

and societies at convention, listed, 424-427.

Conferences, simultaneous, listed, 415-427.

Conferences, various international, 2.

Confucian, ethics, 101.

Confucianism, aims of, 53; referred to, 224.

Confucius, 111.

Congo, Africa, 95; mission in Belgian, 96; example of training schools found at Luevo in Belgian, 371.

Congregation, address by S. W. Herman on "The Adequate Foreign Missionary Program in a Congregation," 233-237; conditions in the average, 234; must be in sympathy with boards, 234; must appreciate its spiritual resources, 236; each, should support its own workers on the mission field, 236-237; addresses on education of, in missions, 273-283; foreign missions in the, conference at convention on, 422

Congregational Churches, conferences of mission boards and societies at convention on, 425.

Congressmen, influence of letters to, 32.

Consecration, fullness of, required, 407.

Constantine, 181.

Constantinople, 25; Woman's College of, 99; Christian College of, 100; college for girls in, 286; mentioned, 342.

Contents, table of, ix-xii.

"Continuous Promise of Our Lord," address by Miss Jean Kenyon Mackenzie, 12-15: power of God available, 12-13; companionship of Christ, 13; problems of volunteers, 13; pecuniary sacrifices, 13; sacrifices for Christianity, 14; dancing in Africa, story of, 14-15.

Contract Alien Labor Law, and missionary obligation, 404.

Contribution, financial, by native Christians to missions, 261; of each race, 323.

"Contribution of Christianity to the Womanhood of the Orient," address by Miss Mary E. Woolley, 141-144: women aided by education in China, 141-143; physical education in China, 142; training of teachers in China, 142; opportunity for women in social service in China, 143; Christianity a stabilizing force, 143-144.

Contributions, of races to Christianity, 101; of Orient to Christianity, 167-170; every nation has own, 173; early, of women to missions, 245-247; of North America to world, 257-262.

Convention, organization, 428; officials, 428-430; Washington committees of, 430; "Who's Who" of, 431-440.

Convention program, 411-427.

Convention Sermon, the, 194-203.

Convention, significance of, v, vi, viii; kinds of, v; purpose of, inspirational, vi; testimonies concerning, vi; preparation for, vi-vii; statistics, vii-viii, 410; significance of presence of delegates of churches of other lands at, viii; not novel idea, 2; mentioned, 322, 323.

Conversion, of students in Christian schools, 100; of children, statistics of, 102.

Conversions, in China, 76, 78; proof of, 224-225; see Evangelism.

Converts, in India, 16; in Korea, China, 17; in Java, Sumatra, Bengal, Abyssinia, 305.

Cook, Dr. Howard, quoted as to baby mortality in Uganda, Africa, 403.

Coolidge, President Calvin, address by, 4-7; quoted, 185; address of, referred to, 404.

Cooper, W. B., address by, on "William Tyndale" 359-360.

Cooperation, in missions promoted by meetings, v-vi; address by Dr. John R. Mott on "New Forces Released by Cooperation," 209-222; missions have led way to, between communions and races, 209; necessary to cope with divisive forces, 209; international, 209-222; new forces to be released through, 211-222; of all believers will enrich missionary message, 216; will profit rising native churches, 216; basis of appeal to men of large affairs, 218-219; needed to enlist new generation, 220; dangers of, 221; with national churches, 230-231; of missionary societies in South Seas, etc., 383; international, Holland ready for, 388.

"Cooperation in the Development of Christian Literature," address by A. L. Warnshuis, 324-327: Christian books should be common possession, 324; writers in mission fields should be shared, 324; need for more and better Christian literature, 325; need for Christian literature in China and Japan, 325; gains in illiteracy in India, 325; paucity of Christian literature in Africa, 325; lack of books for women and children, 325; methods of supplying Christian literature, 326; responsibility of churches for supplying Christian literature, 326-327.

Copec, meeting of, 35.

Copernicus, 43.

Cornelius, John Jesudason, address by, on "Movements Toward Christ in India," 78-85.

Corona, of God, 64.

Correspondence course, for writers suggested, 328.

Cosmopolitanism, age of, 226

Cotton, key word in East Africa, 47; mill in Shanghai, story of, 131-132.

Couve, Pastor Daniel, quoted as to significance of personality, 365; greetings from Paris Evangelical Missionary Society presented by, 382-383.

Creches, in Latin America, 319.

Cronk, Mrs. E. C., address by, on "The Home as an Agency for Missionary Education," 281-283.

Cross, of Christ, 10; of Christ in India, 10, 62; and the eclipse, 63.

Crusaders, described, 180.

Cushman, Ralph S., book on stewardship by, 378.

D

Dancing, in Africa, story of, 14.

Daring, to be Christians, 9.

Darwin, Charles, mentioned, 43; works of, translated into Chinese, 325.

Datta, S. K., representative of Christian Church in India, 154.

Davidson, A. B., and use of Bible, 334.

Death, of convert in Africa, 92.

DeForrest, John H., missionary to Japan, quoted, 243.

deGroot, Hugo, mentioned, 387.

Delegates, organizations represented by, at convention, 2.

Delegates' Version, of Bible (Chinese), 349.

Deliverance of humanity from sin, 51.

de Meyer, Miss Jennie, missionary in Russia, 304.

Democracy, progress of, in Far East, 20; incomprehensible to masses in East, 112.

Denison, W. H., conference notes on Stewardship Materials and Their Use, 378-379.

Engano, 309.
England, competition of giving in, 173; Church of, conference at convention of foreign mission boards and societies of Canadian bodies of, 424.
English, language and Miskito Indians, 352.
Episcopal Church, first missionary to Japan sent by, 245; conference of mission bodies of, at convention, 425.
Equality, of men, 49.
Erasmus, work of, 98.
Erromangan, translation of Acts into, 348.
Eskimo, language described, 349.
Eton College, England, headmaster of, quoted, 202-203.
Eucken, Rudolf, works of, translated into Chinese, 325.
Evangelical Alliance, 393.
Evangelical Church, conference of foreign mission boards and societies of, at convention, 425.
Evangelical Synod, conference of foreign mission boards and societies of, at convention, 425.
Evangelism, in Japan, 69; by church members in China, 75; danger to, from administrative work, 86; task of, to care for great groups of converts, 88; by Christian schools in China, 104; classes to be reached in Japan, 138; see Converts.
"Evangelism in the Native Church," address by Bishop Badley, 85-88: growth of Christianity in India, 85; danger to evangelism from administrative work, 86; organization over-emphasized, 86; requirements for missionary success in Asia, 86; methods of Mohammedanism to be used, 86; methods of evangelism by converts in India, 86; Singh referred to, 87; methods witnessing rather than sermonizing, 87; entire caste ready for baptism, 87; task of evangelism to care for great groups of converts, 88.
Evangelistic, campaigns in Japan, 68.
"Evangelistic Methods in Honan," address by Jonathan Goforth, 76-78: conversions and evangelists in Honan, 76; evangelists in China, 76; open house in China, 76-77; saving a class, reaching students, dealing with chief men, conversions, in China, 77-78.
Evangelistic work, conferences on, at convention, 415.
Evangelists, in China, 76.
Everest, Mount, scaling, 254.
Every Member Canvass, in church discussed, 279.
Everyland, a magazine of world friendship, 283.
Expenditures, of mission boards represented in convention, 2.
Ewing, Dr. J. C. R., referred to, 14.

F

Fairbank, Samuel, 139.
Faith, need for revival of, 4; a higher sort of, 36; needed, 205; daring, motivation of layman in mission work, 242-243; in supernatural power of God, call to, 406.
Falconer, Ian Keith, of Arabia, 256.
Family, of the world, 172-174; of nations, 186.
Far East, world situation in, 16; address by Bishop Herbert Welch on situation in, 16-23; converts in, 17; Christ coming to own in, 18; opposition to Christianity in, 18; white peril feared in, 18; women and children in industry in,

128-134; address by Bishop Henry St. George Tucker on "The Church in the Far East," 156-162; opportunities for physicians in, 260.
"Farm Settlements in India," conference notes by Leroy Stockman, 372; agricultural work done by Salvation Army, 372.
Farquhar, John Nicol, 154.
Fategarh, India, story of cemetery at, 408-409.
Fear, dominant factor in the world, 171-172.
Federal Council of the Churches of Christ in America, 393.
Fellowship, of Christ, 62; with Christ needed, 206; Christian, enriched by cooperation, 217; of Stewardship, mentioned, 378.
Female cent societies, 245-247.
Feng Yu-hsiang, 106.
Field, Jay Carleton, address by, on "Special Fields of Service in Which Latin Americans Need and Welcome the Help of the Christian Forces of Other Countries," 312-316.
Financial, situation in mission bodies, 211-212.
Fleming, D. J., book by, 154, quoted as to objectives of missionary education, 277.
Force, West obsessed by idea of, 169.
"Foreign Missionary Movement in Relation to Peace and Good Will Among Nations," subject of addresses, 171-190.
Foreign Missions Conference of North America, annual sessions of, v; other bodies similar to, 2; organization and composition of, 393; progress of work of, summarized, 393; list of officers of, 429.
Foreign Missions Convention; see Convention.
Foreword, v-viii: significance of convention, v, vi, viii; kinds of convention, v; purpose of convention inspirational, vi; annual sessions of foreign Missions Conference of North America, v; cooperation in missions promoted by meetings, v-vi; New York Conference referred to, vi; testimonies concerning convention, vi; preparation for convention, vi-vii; committee of arrangements for convention, vii; consultations for convention program, vii; convention statistics, vii-viii; significance of presence of delegates of churches of other lands to convention, viii.
Forgan, Robert, Period of Intercession conducted by, 118-122; address by, on "The Bible's Place and Power, 332-336; greetings from the Conference of Missionary Societies in Great Britain and Ireland presented by, 389-391.
Formalism, in present-day religion, 80.
Forman, John N., of India, 206.
Formosa, missionary from Japan sent to, 137.
"Forsaken, But Not," story of, 408-409.
Fosdick, Harry Emerson, books of, translated into Japanese, 70; quoted, 240.
Fox, George, of England, 146.
France, competition of giving in, 173; colonial policy of, 297,298.
Fraser, Donald, work of, in Achimota, 118; mentioned, 206.
Free Methodist missionary boards and societies of, conference of, at convention, 426.
French, Bishop, Thomas V., 304.
Friends, conference of mission boards and societies of, at convention, 425.
Friendship, between China, Russia, Japan, 21; between white and yellow races, 22.
Fuji Spinning Company, 68.
Fukien, China, Christian University, 104.

J

to China, 214; Christian statesmanship developed through cooperation, 215-216; promotive activities take disproportionate time of administrators, 215-216; Edinburgh Conference's contribution, 215-217; cooperation of all believers will enrich missionary message, 216; Christ not revealed solely to one race, 216; cooperation will profit rising native churches, 216; Christian fellowship enriched by cooperation, 217; divisions among Christians a stumbling block, 218; cooperation basis of appeal to men of large affairs, 218-219; appeal of Laymen's Missionary Movement, 218-219; cooperation needed to enlist new generations, 220; powers of youth needed, 220-221; vision a characteristic of youth, 220-221; accessions of spiritual power through cooperation, 221; difficulties of isolation, narrowness and prejudice, 221; dangers of cooperation, 221; solution of disunion by Christ, 221-222.

New Guinea, Dutch missions in, 308, demand for schools in, 308.

New Hebrides, 348.

"New Leadership of Turkey," address by Fred F. Goodsell, 23-27: new era in Near East, 23; nationalism melting traditions, 24; protest against Western control in East, 24; movements in Turkey, 24; John Dewey quoted re Turkey, 24; Lausanne Conference, 24; temperance, women, and polygamy in Turkey, 25; solution of international questions, 26; religious education in Turkey, 26; why religion considered failure in Turkey, 26; treaty with Turkey, 27; charity not enough—international good will needed for Near East, 27.

New York Missionary Conference, vi, 2, 393.

New York Times, 211.

Newspaper, quoted on action of churches, 239-240.

Newspapers, in Kanarese and Telegu, 331; of Washington, New York, and London, 337.

Nias, visited, 306; address by A. Bettin on "The Revival in Nias," 309-311; regeneration of, 309-311.

Nicaragua, spirit teaching in, 352.

Nicholson, Mrs. Thomas, address by, "Educating for Peace and Goodwill," 176-180; mentioned, 185.

Nicodemus, 149.

Nietzsche, and doctrine of super-man, 177.

Nigeria, Africa, 299.

Nile, 95.

Ningpo, China, English missionary school at, 141.

Noble College, at Masulipatam, 116.

North, Eric M., conference notes by, on uniform lessons, etc., 362-363, and on religious education in day and Sunday schools, 365.

North, Frank Mason, quoted as to presence of God with child, 365.

"North American Christians and World Missions," address by William P. Schell, 257-262: peace and goodwill in North America, 257; war a fit topic for conversation, 257; contributions of North America to world, 257-262; power and wealth in lives of men and women of America, 257-258; students have gift of life to world, 258; revival of prayer, 258; wealth of North America, 258-259; good will toward men, 259; opportunities for doctors and teachers in Far East, 260; prayer not a subjective influence merely, 260; church buildings and missions, 261; financial contribution by native Christians to missions, 261.

Norton, A. H., medical missionary in Korea, 125.

Nyas, see Nias.

O

"Objectives of the Missionary Education of a Congregation," address by T. H. P. Sailer, 276-277: eight objectives of missionary education, 277.

Obligation, to convey gospel to world, 224; of churches in work for American Indians, 323.

"Of One Blood," address by Bishop Michael Bolton Furse, 171-176: fear dominant factor in world, 171-172; Christ's ideal of world, 172; family of the world, 172-174; Christian conception of world as family, 172-176; every nation has own contribution, 173; color no ground of superiority, 173; competition of giving, 173-174; spirit of brotherhood in family of nations, 174; feeling of superiority un-Christian, 174-175; too little prayer, 175-176; more teaching needed, 176.

Officers, of Foreign Missions Conference of North America, 429.

Officials, convention, 428-430.

Old Umtali, Rhodesia, 371-372.

Oldham, Joseph H., address by, "Christ's Message to Nations and Races," 46-52; address by, "Christian Education in Relation to Government Developments," 116-118, 215; quoted as to inclusive needs of religious education, 361, 363.

Omaha, Nebraska, medical work of student volunteer at, 288.

Opening Address, by James L. Barton, 1-3: Committee of Reference and Counsel, 1; mission boards represented, 1, number of missionaries sent out, 1, expenditures of mission boards represented at convention, 2; mission expenditures, 2; organizations represented at convention, 2; other bodies, 2; convention not novel idea, 2; Edinburgh Missionary Conference, Ecumenical, Mildmay Park, London, Liverpool, New York and various other international missionary conferences mentioned, 2-3; way of redemption, 3.

Opium, in China, 108; Europe's way with, 254; in China, 267.

Opportunity, of Christian education, 101, for women in social service in China, 143; new vision of, in East, 170; for young missionary in Latin America, 320; for work among American Indians, 323.

Orange, navel, 373.

Organization, over-emphasized, 86; of convention, 428.

Organizations, represented in convention, 2, Christian, in Japan, 68; woman's beginnings of, 247-248.

Orient, address by Harris E. Kirk on the imprisoned splendor of the, 162-170; home of creative joys of life, 168-169.

Orientalizing, of Christianity, 159-160.

Orphanages, needed in Latin America, 313.

Osaka, Japan, gospel in, 69; labor school in, 137.

Other-wordliness, too much lost, 36.

Outcasts, of India, 55.

Ovimbundu, of Africa, 88.

Ozawa, of Japan, 70.

P

Pacific Islands, 19

Page, Kirby, introduction to book by, quoted, 240.

education for East, 110; to give self-
expression in education to East, 110-111;
of East insoluble without women,, 112;
for churches of non-Christian lands to
solve, 231; see Difficulties, Methods,
Solutions.
"Proclamation of the Gospel," subject of
addresses, 67-98.
Program, address by Ralph E. Diffendorfer,
"The Adequate Foreign Missionary Program of a Denomination," 227-233; of
mission effort must be promoted throughout denominations at home, 227-228;
need of greatly enlarged, of missionary
education, 232; address on "The Adequate Foreign Missionary Program in a
Congregation," by S. W. Herman, 233-
237; missionary, of average congregation,
234; place of prayer in mission, 268;
of missionary education in a congregation, 273-276; of convention, 411-427;
foreign missions in the denominational,
conference on, at convention, 422; see
Methods.
Progress, in stages of mission work, 109.
"Progress of Missions in the Dutch Indies," subject of addresses, 306-311.
Prohibition, movement in Japan, 17; a
contribution of United States to world,
267.
Project method, referred to, 363-364; for
missions, 273-276.
Promise, address "The Continuous Promise
of Our Lord," 12-15.
"Promotion of Stewardship in the Local
Church," conference notes by M. E.
Melvin, 379-380: stewardship means
more than money, 379-380; scriptural
basis for wider conception of steward-
ship, 379-380; stewardship the discovery
of this age, 380; a congregational secre-
tary of stewardship, 380.
Promotive activities, take disproportionate
time of administrators, 215-216.
Propagation, law of spiritual life, 223.
Proportion, sense of, in presenting mis-
sions, 194-195.
Protocol of Geneva, 177.
Punjab, India, baptisms in, 83; converts
in, 305.
Puno, Peru, encouraging work at, 313.
Pye, Watts O., address by, "Winning a
Province" (in China), 72-76.
Pyeng Yang, Korea, 377.

Q

Qualifications, spiritual, for missionary
service, prayer for, 203-204.
Quo vadis?—peace or war, 181-182.

R

Race, consciousness in East, 112; none
inherently superior to others, 225.
Races, complementary, 51; to contribute
to understanding of wealth of Christ,
202.
Racial, differences a barrier, 48; antago-
nism, 50; solidarity, 405.
Railroad, building of, in Africa, 236.
Ramabai, Pandita, of India, 206.
Rangoon, Burma, 111.
Rao, Ananda, story of redemption of, 41.
Rawlinson, Frank, address by, "Training
and Developing Good Writers," 327-330.
Reade, Charles, quoted, 359.
Reading, Lord, 153.
"Reasons for Becoming a Foreign Mis-
sionary," address by E. Warner Lentz,
student volunteer, 284-285: lagging spirit
of the church, 284-285; difficulties of

student volunteers, 284-285; foreign students in America neglected, 285.
"Reasons for Becoming a Foreign Missionary," address by Miss Lynda Irene
Goodsell, student volunteer, 285-286;
opportunity in Turkey, 286; daughter
of a missionary, 286.
"Reasons for Becoming a Foreign Missionary," address by Walter Judd, M.D.,
student volunteer, 287-289: gratitude
motive of mission service, 287-288;
scarcity of physicians in foreign field,
288; need of mission service in America,
288-289; Christ's command motive for
mission service, 289; greatest difficulty
to mission service is obstacle of Christian parents, 289; sacrifice of mother
for mission field, 289.
Reasons, for Turks' considering religion a
failure, 26; for indifference of average
Christian, 194-196; for not giving to missions, 212-213; for missions, address on,
223-227; for supporting missions, 266;
see Motives.
"Recent Outstanding Social Developments
in Latin America and Their Significance
and Appeal," address by J. H. McLean,
316-323: ancestral strain in Latin America, 316; matriarchal civilization of
Latin Amreica, 317; men and women,
and forces operative in Latin-American
society, 317; peace, public opinion,
wealth, education, international contacts
in Latin America, 317-320; social aspects
of education, 318; missionary must emphasize need of educated citizenry, 318;
temperance and social hygiene in Latin
America, 318-319; opportunity for young
missionary in Latin America, 320.
Recruiting and training for missionary
service, conferences on, at convention,
418, 421, 423.
Red Cross, in Latin America, 319.
Redeeming power, of God, 63.
Redemption, way of, 3; of community in
West China, 266; of language by translation of Bible, 351, 356.
Reference and Counsel, Committee of, vi;
committee of arrangements for convention of, vii.
Reformed Church mission boards and societies, conference of, at convention,
427.
"Relation of Agriculture to Village Work
in India," conference notes by W. J.
McKee, 369-370: results and requirements of agricultural education in In-
dia, 369.
Religion, why considered a failure in Turkey, 26; in the home, 30; needs no toning down, 57; and politics, 81-82; in
America, 84; Orient needs reality in
personal, 106-107.
Religions, aims of various, 53; of Japan
infused with new life, 70; broader conception of other, 243.
Religious education, in China, 75; of the
whole man, 362; in the mission field,
conference on, at convention, 423; see
Education.
"Religious Education in the Mission
Field," conference notes on, 361-365:
J. H. Oldham quoted as to inclusiveness
of religious education, religious education in the mission field, religious education for the whole man, 361-362; W.
G. Landes quoted as to importance of
educating children in strategy of missions, 362; Eric M. North as to uniform
lessons, 362-363; W. J. McKee as to
rural education on field and project
method, 363-364; Martin Schlunk on
experience of German missions, 364; W.
J. McKee quoted further on use of Bible

T